Readings in Ancient History

Thought and Experience from Gilgamesh to St. Augustine

SEVENTH EDITION

Edited and with introductions by

NELS M. BAILKEY, EMERITUS
Tulane University

RICHARD LIM
Smith College

 WADSWORTH
CENGAGE Learning™

Australia • Brazil • Japan • Korea • Mexico • Singapore • Spain • United Kingdom • United States

WADSWORTH
CENGAGE Learning™

Readings in Ancient History: Thought and Experience from Gilgamesh to St. Augustine, Seventh Edition
Nels M. Bailkey, Richard Lim

Senior Publisher: Suzanne Jeans

Acquisitions Editor: Nancy Blaine

Development editor: Larry Goldberg

Assistant Editor: Lauren Floyd

Editorial Assistant: Emma Goehring

Senior Media Editor: Lisa Ciccolo

Marketing Manager: Katherine Bates

Marketing Coordinator: Loreen Pelletier

Marketing Communications Manager: Caitlin Green

Content Project Management: PreMediaGlobal

Senior Art Director: Cate Rickard Barr

Print Buyer: Sandra Milewski

Rights Acquisitions Specialist, Image: Jennifer Meyer Dare

Rights Acquisitions Specialist, Text: Shalice Shah-Caldwell

Production Service: PreMediaGlobal

Cover Designer: Susan Shapiro

About the Cover Image: A marble relief detail that shows Dionysus' Indian triumph. An exuberant procession of *sileni*, satyrs, maenads, and exotic beasts precedes the elephant-drawn chariot bearing the Greek god of wine, irrationality, and dramatic performances (not shown). The early third-century A.D. Roman sarcophagus is now in the Museum of Fine Arts, Boston. Photograph © Museum of Fine Arts, Boston

For product information and technology assistance, contact us at **Cengage Learning Customer & Sales Support, 1-800-354-9706**

For permission to use material from this text or product, submit all requests online at **www.cengage.com/permissions**. Further permissions questions can be emailed to **permissionrequest@cengage.com**.

Library of Congress Control Number: 2011926062

ISBN-13: 978-0-495-91303-0

ISBN-10: 0-495-91303-0

Wadsworth
20 Channel Center Street
Boston, MA 02210
USA

Cengage Learning is a leading provider of customized learning solutions with office locations around the globe, including Singapore, the United Kingdom, Australia, Mexico, Brazil and Japan. Locate your local office at **international.cengage.com/region**.

Cengage Learning products are represented in Canada by Nelson Education, Ltd.

For your course and learning solutions, visit **www.cengage.com**.

Purchase any of our products at your local college store or at our preferred online store **www.cengagebrain.com**.

Instructors: Please visit **login.cengage.com** and log in to access instructor-specific resources.

Printed in the United States of America
2 3 4 5 6   23 22 21 20 19

Contents

Preface

Currently in its seventh edition, *Readings in Ancient History* has long enjoyed success as an annotated anthology of historical sources designed for Western Civilization and Ancient History survey courses. This edition, as with its predecessor, contains more than one hundred and thirty primary source readings that are distributed into six book chapters: Near Eastern Civilizations, Greek Civilization: Ancient Greece, Hellenistic Civilization, the Roman Republic, the Roman Empire, and Early Christianity and Late Antiquity. In order to provide a readily easily comprehensible structure within each of these chapters, we have introduced major chapter subheadings to organize the readings into thematic (and mainly also chronological) clusters. This addition, we hope, will make it easier for instructors and students to examine a circumscribed set of key ideas, institutions, and developments within clearly defined historical contexts. Ideas raised in readings within each chapter subheading may then also be instructively related to ones found in similar sections in other chapters for a richer understanding of the complexity and richness of human historical development.

As with the sixth and still earlier editions, we maintain a commitment to offering a set of readings that speak to central historical themes and questions. Yet as the discipline of history changes, so too has its scope and focus. Thus we continue to strengthen readings that address important cultural and social historical issues such as the roles, imagined and real, of women and family; the nature of the ancient institution of slavery; and the ethnic and religious interactions, and indeed conflicts, between different groups especially from the Hellenistic period to the time of Late Antiquity.

The creation of the seventh edition owes much to the insightful labor of many individuals. Professor Nels M. Bailkey, who edited Readings in Ancient History from its inception through to the fifth edition, deserves first mention as still its chief guiding spirit. The present edition remains one that is shaped by his original vision that students can derive much useful instruction from an anthology of selected texts that speak to thought and experience from the age of

Gilgamesh to that of Augustine of Hippo. Nancy Blaine, formerly senior sponsoring editor in history at Cenage Learning, took the lead in initiating the process of revision and manuscript preparation. Larry Goldberg, this edition's developmental editor, helped guide the project through its main stages with patience and skill. Project manager Divya Divakaran and her team helped transform the manuscript into beautifully type-set pages while Cate Barr designed an attractive book cover to house those pages. Cornelia Pearsall, with characteristic cheerfulness and generosity of spirit, provided indispensable editorial help and moral support throughout the process. Finally, the following reviewers provided essential feedback that helped us identify desirable changes to the sixth edition: Patrick Bass, Morningside College; Christopher Bellitto, Kean University; Marc Cooper, Missouri State University; Christine McCann, Norwich University; Andrew Nichols, University of Florida; Nadejda Popov-Reynolds, Florida Gulf Coast University; and Miriam Vivian, California State University, Bakersfield. We are fortunate to have the benefit of this insight and collaboration and have gratefully incorporated many of the excellent suggestions we received in the present volume.

Credits

PHOTO

p. 1, Scala/Art Resource, NY; *p. 7,* © The Trustees of The British Museum/ Art Resource, NY; *p. 27,* Réunion des Musées Nationaux/Art Resource, NY; *p. 39,* Bildarchiv Preussischer Kulturbesitz/Art Resource, NY; *p. 54,* Scala/Art Resource, NY; *p. 46,* Erich Lessing/Art Resource, NY; *p. 99,* The Art Archive/ Museo di Villa Giulia Rome/Dagli Orti; *p. 131,* © The Art Gallery Collection/ Alamy; *p. 163,* © Peter Horree/Alamy; *p. 185,* © Photos 12/Alamy; *p. 199,* The Art Archive/Archaeological Museum Naples/Dagli Orti; *p. 251,* © David Lees/ CORBIS; *p. 310,* Erich Lessing/Art Resource, NY; *p. 313,* Erich Lessing/Art Resource, NY; *p. 386,* Bust of Marcus Tullius Cicero (marble), Roman/Musei Capitolini, Rome, Italy/Alinari/The Bridgeman Art Library International; *p. 398,* © Photos 12/Alamy; *p. 413,* Scala/Art Resource, NY; *p. 422,* Augustus of Prima Porta (marble) (b/w photo), Roman, (1st century AD)/Vatican Museums and Galleries, Vatican City, Italy/Alinari/The Bridgeman Art Library International; *p. 457,* The Arch of Titus, detail of the Temple treasures being carried after the Sack of Jerusalem in 70 AD, 81 AD (stone) (b/w photo), Roman, (1st century AD)/ Forum, Rome, Italy/Alinari/The Bridgeman Art Library International; *p. 472,* Erich Lessing/Art Resource, NY; *p. 505,* Scala/Art Resource, NY; *p. 515,* Scala/ Art Resource, NY; *p. 564,* Alinari/Art Resource, NY.

TEXT

p. 4, From PRITCHARD, JAMES B. (ed.): *ANCIENT NEAR EASTERN TEXTS RELATING TO THE OLD TESTAMENT—THIRD EDITION WITH SUPPLEMENT.* (c) 1950, 1969, renewed 1978 by Princeton University Press. Reprinted by permission of Princeton University Press.

Chicago Press, 1936), pp. 35–39. Courtesy of the Oriental Institute of the University of Chicago.

p. 87, Excepted from *The Annals of Sennacherib*, by Daniel David Luckenbill, Ph.D., pp. 23–35. Copyright © 1924 by The University of Chicago Press.

p. 94, From PRITCHARD, JAMES B. (ed.): *ANCIENT NEAR EASTERN TEXTS RELATING TO THE OLD TESTAMENT—THIRD EDITION WITH SUPPLEMENT.* (c) 1950, 1969, renewed 1978 by Princeton University Press. Reprinted by permission of Princeton University Press.

p. 97, From *The New Oxford Annotated Bible* with the Apocrypha. Revised Standard Version, ed. Herbert G. May and Bruce M. Metzger (New York: Oxford University Press, 1962), pp. 573–574. Used by permission.

p. 101, From the Iliad, based on the translation by Samuel Butler.

p. 113, Reprinted by permission of the publishers and the Trustees of the Loeb Classical Library from Hesiod, Homeric Hymns, Loeb Classical Library Volume L 57, translated by Hugh G. Evelyn-White, Cambridge, Mass.: Harvard University Press, 1914. The Loeb Classical Library® is a registered trademark of the President and Fellows of Harvard College.

p. 120, "Fair Helen, All for Love" is from A. R. Burn, *The Lyric Age of Greece* (London: Edward Arnold, Ltd., 1961), p. 236.

p. 120, "The Fairest Thing on Earth" and "When I See You" are from Werner Jaeger, Paideia: *The Ideals of Greek Culture*, Vol. I, second edition (New York: Oxford University Press, 1945), p. 135. Reprinted by permission of Basil Blackwell, London.

p. 121, From The Works of Hesiod, Callimachus, and Theognis, translated by John Hookham Frere (London: H.G. Bohn, 1856).

p. 123, Reprinted by permission of the publishers and the Trustees of the Loeb Classical Library from The Odes of Pindar, Vol. II, Loeb Classical Library Vol. 485, translated by Sir John Sandys, Cambridge, Mass.: Harvard University Press, 1958. The Loeb Classical Library® is a registered trademark of the President and Fellows of Harvard College.

p. 127, Herodotus, Histories 4.150–51, 153, 156–59; Herodotus. The Persian wars; tr. by George Rawlinson, with an introd. by Francis R. B. Godolphin. New York: Modern Library, [1947, c1942], pp. 350–355. (+ 1.5 pp.)

p. 129, From Plutarch, *Parallel Lives*, "Lycurgus," based on the translation by Aubrey Stewart and George Long.

p. 137, From Plutarch, "*Life of Solon*," based on the translation by John Dryden and A. H. Clough.

p. 144, From Plutarch, "*Life of Solon*," based on the translation by John and William Langhorne (Solon's poetry translated by John Dryden).

p. 147, From Herodotus, *History of the Persian Wars*, Bk. VII, Chs. 8–10, 19–21, 33–37, 44–46, 56, 60, 100–105, 131–33, 138–39, 145–47, 175, 184, 201–205, 207–13, 219–26, 228, based on the translation by George Rawlinson.

p. 162, From Thucydides, *History of the Peloponnesian War*, Book II, 36–46; in The Greek Commonwealth: Politics and Economics in Fifth-Century Athens, translated by Alfred Zimmern, 4th edition (Oxford: the Clarendon Press, 1924), pp. 202–209.

p. 228, From *The Politics of Aristotle*, translated by Benjamin Jowett, edited by H. W. C. Davis (Oxford: Oxford University Press, 1905).

p. 241, From *First Philippic*, Chs. 2–12, 38–45, 48–50, based on the translation by Charles R. Kennedy.

p. 244, From "*The Philippus*," Chs. 8, 9, 12–16, 30, 31, 36–45, 72–75, 89–120, 121, 152–55, based on the translation by J. H. Freese in Orations of Isocrates, Vol. I. By permission of G. Bell & Sons, Ltd.

p. 253, From *The Campaigns of Alexander*, translated by Aubrey de Selincourt, revised with a new introduction and notes by J. R. Hamilton, 112–114, 120–128, 353–367. Copyright © 1971 by Penguin Books. Reproduced by permission of Penguin Books, Ltd.

p. 263, From *The Age of Alexander: Nine Greek Lives* by Plutarch, translated and annotated by Ian Scott-Kilvert, with an introduction by G. T. Griffith, pp. 336–351. Copyright © 1973 by Penguin Books. Reproduced by permission of Penguin Books, Ltd.

p. 267, Reprinted by permission of the publishers and the Trustees of the Loeb Classical Library from Athenaeus: Vol. III The Deipnosophists, Loeb Classical Library Vol. 224, translated by Charles Burton Gulick, Cambridge, Mass.: Harvard University Press, 1929. The Loeb Classical Library® is a registered trademark of the President and Fellows of Harvard College.

p. 268, Reprinted by permission of the publishers and the Trustees of the Loeb Classical Library from Diodorus Siculus, Vol. III, Library of History, Loeb Classical Library Vol. 340, translated by C. H. Oldfather, Cambridge, Mass.: Harvard University Press, 1939. The Loeb Classical Library® is a registered trademark of the President and Fellows of Harvard College.

p. 270, Excerpted from *The Hellenistic World from Alexander to the Roman Conquest*, by M. M. Austin, pp. 57–61. Copyright © 1981 by Cambridge University Press. Reprinted with permission of Cambridge University Press.

p. 273, Reprinted by permission of the publishers and the Trustees of the Loeb Classical Library from Atheanaeus: Vol. II The Deipnosophists, Loeb Classical Library Vol. 208, translated by Charles Burton Gulick, Cambridge, Mass: Harvard University Press, 1928. The Loeb Classical Library® is a registered trademark of the President and Fellows of Harvard College.

p. 280, M. M. Austin, *The Hellenistic World from Alexander to the Roman Conquest: A Selection of Ancient Sources in Translation*. Cambridge: Cambridge University Press, 1981, pp. 374–377.

p. 284, Roger S. Bagnall and Peter Derow, *The Hellenistic Period: Historical Sources in Translation*. Oxford: Blackwell, 2004, pp. 230–233, 278–284.

p. 286, Reprinted by permission of the publishers and the Trustees of Loeb Classical Library from Select Papyri: Volume II, Official Documents, Loeb Classical Library Vol. 282, translated by A. S. Hunt and C. C. Edgar, Cambridge, Mass.: Harvard University Press, 1934. The Loeb Classical Library® is a registered trademark of the President and Fellows of Harvard College.

p. 289, Reprinted by permission of the publishers and the Trustees of the Loeb Classical Library from Lucian, Vol. VIII "The Cynic," Loeb Classical Library Vol. 432, translated by M. D. Macleod, Cambridge, Mass.: Harvard University

pp. 311–317. (c) 1940 The Johns Hopkins University Press. Reprinted with permission of The Johns Hopkins University Press.

p. 550, From *The Ante-Nicene Fathers*, edited by Alexander Roberts and James Donaldson. Copyright © 1982 by Wm. B. Eerdmans Publishing Company. Reprinted by permission.

p. 546, From Lactantius, *On the Deaths of the Persecutors*, ch. 7, based on the translation by William Fletcher.

p. 560, © Averil Cameron and Stuart Hall 1999. Reprinted from Eusebius: *Life of Constantine. Introduction*, translation, and commentary by Averil Cameron and Stuart G. Hall (1999) by permission of Oxford University Press.

p. 567, Athanasius, *Life of Anthony* 1–5, 8–17, 30, 64, 72, 91–94; in Athanasius: Select Works and Letters, Volume IV of *NICENE AND POST-NICENE FATHERS*, Series II, Philip Schaff and Henry Wace, editors, Grand Rapids, Mich.: W.B. Eerdmans, 1980–1983, pp. 195–201, 204, 213, 215, 220–221.

p. 574, John Chrysostom, *On the Priesthood* 3.4–6, 10–17; in *Nicene and post-Nicene fathers of the Christian Church*: [first series] v. 9, edited by Philip Schaff, Grand Rapids, Mich.: Eerdmans, 1980–1983, pp. 46–59.

p. 582, PHARR, Clyde, *THE THEODOSIAN CODE AND NOVELS AND THE SERMONDIAN CONSTITUTIONS*. (c) 1952 in the name of the author, 1980 renewed in name of Roy Pharr, executor. Reprinted by permission of Princeton University Press.

p. 589, From Jerome, Letter 128.4; in *Nicene and Post-Nicene Father of the Christian Church*, series 1, Vol. VI, edited by Philip Schaff and Henry Wace (Grand Rapids, Mich.: Eerdmans, 1980–83, revised edition 1983), p. 260.

p. 590, From St. Augustine, *Concerning the City of God Against the Pagans*, translated by Henry Bettenson, pp. 6–7, 14–20. Copyright © 1972 by Penguin Books. Reproduced by permission of Penguin Books, Ltd.

p. 597, Augustine, Confessions 6.2, 7–8; in *Saint Augustine Confessions*, translated and introduced by Henry Chadwick. Oxford: Oxford University Press, 1991, pp. 91–92, 98, 100–101.

p. 609, From *The Writings of Salvian*, the Presbylter, translated by Jeremiah F. O'Sullivan, Ph.D., pp. 132–141. Copyright © 1962 by The Catholic University of America Press. Reprinted by permission.

CHAPTER I

Near Eastern Civilizations

Is there a thing whereof men say,
"See, this is new"? It
Hath been already, in the ages
Which were before us.

—ECCLESIASTES 1:10

Relief of Scribes, Eighteenth Dynasty

Few aspects of civilization in the ancient Near East hold the attention of modern students for long as they hurry on to the serious study of the Greeks. As pertinent today as it was in the first century A.D. is the observation of the first-century A.D. Jewish historian Josephus of "the current opinion that, in the study of ancient history, the Greeks alone deserve serious attention" (*Against Apion*, 1.2). The achievements of the Greeks were indeed phenomenal, and the broad range of their thought and experience is recognized in such statements as "The Greeks went over the same road before us." The reading selections in this section reveal, however, that the peoples of the ancient Near East produced ideas and institutions that deserve comparison with those of the Greeks and, indeed, merit study in their own right.

Ancient Mesopotamia and Egypt were home to some of the world's earliest and most sophisticated settled communities and states. The evolution of literacy in their midst means that many of these developments are attested to in texts such as cuneiform tablets and Egyptian hieroglyphs. The successful decipherment of these texts in modern times combined with scientific archaeological excavations helped to reveal some of the complex and varied traditions from this region's past.

Selected readings in this chapter offer an opportunity to sample this rich material through the following thematically arranged sections: Foundation Epics; Early Society, Justice, and Moral Order; Social and Work Life; Divine Worship, Kingship, and Nation; War and International Diplomacy; and Persia: The Last Ancient Near Eastern Empire.

Foundation Epics

Religious developments in the ancient Near East are particularly significant not only because they represent a legacy that was handed on to later civilizations but also because they provide a recognizable pattern of development from "lower" to "higher" forms of religious belief and practice. The three phases of this pattern, and the changing values that give meaning to life in each phase, can be summarized as follows.

The earliest period in the history of a civilization is commonly called a "heroic age" because the values that give meaning to life are connected with a life of heroic action on earth. Material success and the prestige that comes from the accomplishment of notable deeds are the paramount goals of life, and a person's success is measured by glory or fame as a hero. The boast of a nobleman of the Old Kingdom of Egypt, "I filled an office which made my reputation in this Upper Egypt. Never before had the like been done in this Upper Egypt," reflects the same heroic outlook on life as the words of the valorous Sumerian hero Gilgamesh, who could not be deterred from combat with a fierce dragon: "Should I fall, I shall have made me a name. 'Gilgamesh'—they will say—'against fierce Huwawa has fallen!'"

When we turn to the religious beliefs of this first, or heroic, age of the Near Eastern civilizations, we find that they shared the same materialistic interest in this earthly life. Death, which cuts short the exciting life of action, was dreaded as the worst of evils. To offset this catastrophe, people sought some means of prolonging their earthly existence and avoiding the final journey to what the Sumerians called the "land of no return." The relationship between mortals and the gods, who were cut from the same heroic pattern as mortals, was purely material and premoral—premoral in the sense that rewards and punishments meted out by the gods had nothing as yet to do with the kind of conduct that was based upon man's love for his fellow man. Religion was on a materialistic *quid pro quo* basis: people believed that the more they gave to the gods in the form of sacrifices, the more they would be rewarded. This close reciprocal relationship was viewed as completely satisfactory to both parties, and this fact is the main theme of the earliest religious literature. "Well tended are men, the cattle of god," states an early Egyptian text, "he made heaven and earth according to their desire."

The values of the heroic age and their accompanying religious beliefs and practices did not continue forever. In each of the civilizations we shall examine, time brought changes that resulted in a collapse of the old order. Largely as a result of what is often called a "time of trouble"—a term for social calamity that was first used by the ancient Hebrews—old practices and beliefs were swept away amid political, economic, and social disintegration. "No sudden change of outward affairs," wrote the philosopher Boethius in the sixth century A.D. as he viewed the collapse of his Roman world, "can ever come without some upheaval in the mind." The ancient Near Eastern civilizations were affected in the same fashion by similar disastrous events. As a result, they turned away from the gods, who no longer seemed to answer the petitions of the sacrifice, and they rejected the pursuits and values of the heroic age. People lamented their sad lot in a new age empty of the old values; and while some sought refuge by immersing themselves in such new and, as it turned out, temporary values as romantic love and other excitements, others turned to the task of constructing a stable and meaningful way of life based on more permanent values.

The values of this new way of life were moral values, for it was discovered that the only way to restore order and stability to society was by laying stress upon right conduct by its members. A life of justice and righteousness, inspired by a love for one's fellows and a golden rule, became the goal for which to strive. Religion reflected this profound change in the values of life, and there arose moral religions in which rewards and punishments from the gods were thought to be based solely upon human conduct. The contrast between the old and the new in religion, the premoral and the moral, was put in one short sentence by an Egyptian sage who witnessed the collapse of the Old Kingdom and reflected upon that disaster: "More acceptable [to the gods] is the virtue of the upright man than the ox of him that does inequity." The prophet Micah proclaimed the same moral view at a similar moment in the development of Hebrew religious beliefs: "What does the Lord require of thee, but to do justly, and love kindness, and to walk humbly with thy God?"

1 The Epic of Gilgamesh

The Sumerian Heroic Age

Folk epics are impersonal accounts of heroic deeds composed in a simple and forceful meter. They were at first unwritten, transmitted by minstrels who chanted them to the accompaniment of a musical instrument. They form the early literature of many civilizations and are of great interest not only for the tales they tell but also for the institutions and ideas they describe.

The Sumerians were among the first peoples to produce epic tales of semi-legendary heroes, the most famous of whom was Gilgamesh, ruler of the Mesopotamian city-state of Uruk (or Erech) about 2700 B.C. About 2000 B.C., or somewhat later, an unknown Babylonian collected some of the Gilgamesh stories, together with other tales, and wove them into a new whole. The following selections are from this *Babylonian Epic of Gilgamesh*.

A. THE QUEST OF GILGAMESH: "WHO IS MOST SPLENDID AMONG THE HEROES?"

The theme that gives unity to the varied heroic adventures described in the *Epic of Gilgamesh* is that of death—the sudden realization that death will cut short the glorious career of the great hero and the frantic but unsuccessful search for some means of living forever. The story opens with an account of the friction between Gilgamesh and the nobles of Uruk, who claim that their ruler is acting tyrannically. (Their complaint that Gilgamesh drafted their sons to serve in his army is described in a separate epic tale; their charge in the tale below that he mistreated their wives and daughters is probably pure propaganda.) The nobles appeal to the gods for aid, with the result that Enkidu is created by Aruru, the mother goddess, to check Gilgamesh's "arrogance." Gilgamesh sends a temple prostitute, "harlot" in the text below, to tame

From James B. Pritchard, ed., *Ancient Near Eastern Texts Relating to the Old Testament*, 3rd rev. ed. with Supplement (Princeton: Princeton University Press, 1969), pp. 73–75, 78–79, 84–85, 87, 89–90, 96. Reprinted by permission of Princeton University Press. Translated by E. A. Speiser.

Enkidu's barbarous nature before he is brought to Uruk, where the two heroes fight to a draw and thereafter become fast friends. Together they set out on dangerous adventures, slaying the terrible monster Huwawa who guards the Cedar Forest for the storm-god Enlil, insulting the goddess Ishtar who falls in love with Gilgamesh—love that here, as elsewhere in the epic, contains no romantic element—and destroying the awesome Bull of Heaven sent by the angered Ishtar to kill Gilgamesh. When next Enkidu dies as the result of Enlil's displeasure over the slaying of Huwawa, Gilgamesh is panic-stricken by the sudden realization of the stark reality of death. His life is henceforth dominated by the one aim of finding everlasting life. This leads him to search out Utnapishtim, the one man to whom the gods have granted immortality, in order to learn from him the secret of eternal life.

The remainder of the epic incorporates the story of the Flood (Selection 1B), which originally existed as an independent tale. Utnapishtim relates how he obtained eternal life as a reward for the deeds he performed at the time of the Flood. But this unique event can no longer be replicated. As a parting gift to the dejected Gilgamesh, Utnapishtim tells him of the Plant of Life that grows on the bottom of the sea and renews the life of him who eats it. But once again Gilgamesh's hopes are ended when the Plant of Life is stolen from him by a snake. The epic ends with Gilgamesh's bitter lament over the failure of his quest; though snakes may hereafter slough off their old skins and eternally renew their youth, the sad lot of man is old age and death.

> He who saw everything to the ends of the land,
> Who all things experienced, considered all!...
> Two-thirds of him is god, one third of him is human....
> The onslaught of his weapons verily has no equal.
> By the drum are aroused his companions.

Gilgamesh's despotic behavior leads to the creation of Enkidu.

> The nobles of Uruk are gloomy in their chambers:
> "Gilgamesh leaves not the son to his father;
> Day and night is unbridled his arrogance.
> Yet this is Gilgamesh, the shepherd of Uruk.
> He should be our shepherd: strong, stately, and wise!
> Gilgamesh leaves not the maid to her mother,
> The warrior's daughter, the noble's spouse!"
> The gods hearkened to their plaint,
> The gods of heaven, Uruk's lords...
> The great Aruru they called:
> "Thou, Aruru, didst create Gilgamesh;
> Create now his double;
> His stormy heart let him match.
> Let them contend, that Uruk may have peace!"...
> Aruru washed her hands,
> Pinched off clay and cast it on the steppe.
> On the steppe she created valiant Enkidu,...
> Shaggy with hair is his whole body,

He is endowed with head hair like a woman....
He knows neither people nor land;...
With the gazelles he feeds on grass,
With the wild beasts he jostles at the watering-place,
With the teeming creatures his heart delights in water....

Having heard of the animal-like Enkidu, Gilgamesh sends a "harlot" to civilize him by means of the unromantic, purely physical love found in heroic-age epic tales. Enkidu performs heroically.

The lass beheld him, the savage-man,
The barbarous fellow from the depths of the steppe:...
The lass freed her breasts, bared her bosom,
And he possessed her ripeness.
She was not bashful as she welcomed his ardor.
She laid aside her cloth and he rested upon her.
She treated him, the savage, to a woman's task,
As his love was drawn unto her.
For six days and seven nights Enkidu comes forth,
Mating with the lass.
After he had had his fill of her charms,
He set his face toward his wild beasts,
On seeing him, Enkidu, the gazelles ran off,
The wild beasts of the steppe drew away from his body.
Startled was Enkidu, as his body became taut,
His knees were motionless—for his wild beasts had gone.
Enkidu had to slacken his pace—it was not as before;
But he now had wisdom, broader understanding.
Returning, he sat at the feet of the harlot.
He looks up at the face of the harlot,
His ears attentive, as the harlot speaks;
The harlot says to him, to Enkidu:
"Thou art wise, Enkidu, art become like a god!
Why with the wild creatures dost thou roam over the
     steppe?
Come, let me lead thee to ramparted Uruk,
To the holy temple, abode of Anu and Ishtar,
Where lives Gilgamesh, accomplished in strength,
And like a wild ox lords it over the folk."
As she speaks to him, her words find favor,
His heart enlightened, he yearns for a friend....
Enkidu says to her, to the harlot:
"Up, lass, escort thou me,
To the pure sacred temple, abode of Anu and Ishtar,
Where lives Gilgamesh, accomplished in strength,
And like a wild ox lords it over the folk.
I will challenge him and will boldly address him,

A detail from the "War Side" of the "Standard of Ur," an inlaid plaque from the Royal Cemetery of Ur. About 2700 B.C. Above the line of helmeted Sumerian soldiers advancing against the enemy is the first known depiction of a war chariot. It is drawn by two asses.

> I will shout in Uruk: 'I am he who is mighty!...'"
> The nobles rejoiced:
> "A hero has appeared
> For the man of proper mien!
> For Gilgamesh, the godlike,
> His equal has come forth."...

Enkidu and Gilgamesh meet and battle to a draw.

> They met in the Market-of-the-Land.
> Enkidu barred the gate with his foot,
> not allowing Gilgamesh to enter.
> They grappled each other, butting like bulls,
> They shattered the doorpost, as the wall shook.
> As Gilgamesh bent the knee—his foot on the ground—
> His fury abated and he turned away....
> They kissed each other
> And formed a friendship....

Enkidu quails at the prospect of fighting the monstrous Huwawa, guardian of the Cedar Forest, and Gilgamesh reassures him with a reminder of the heroic meaning of life.

> Gilgamesh opened his mouth, saying to Enkidu:
> "In the forest resides fierce Huwawa.
> Let us, me and thee, slay him,
> That all evil from the land we may banish! [...]
> Enkidu opened his mouth, saying to Gilgamesh:
> "I found it out, my friend, in the hills,
> As I was roaming with the wild beasts.
> For ten thousand leagues extends the forest.

Who is there that would go down into it?
Huwawa—his roaring is the flood-storm,
His mouth is fire, his breath is death!
Why dost thou desire to do this thing?
An unequal struggle is tangling with Huwawa.".…
Gilgamesh opened his mouth, saying to Enkidu:
"Who, my friend, is superior to death?
Only the gods live forever in the sun.
As for mankind, numbered are their days;
Whatever they achieve is but the wind!
Even here thou art afraid of death.
What of thy heroic might?
Let me go then before thee,
Let thy voice call to me, 'Advance, fear not!'
Should I fall, I shall have made me a name:
'Gilgamesh'—they will say—'against fierce Huwawa
Has fallen!' Long after
My offspring has been born in my house, […]
Thus calling to me, thou hast grieved my heart.
My hand I will poise and will fell the cedars.
A name that endures I will make for me!…"

After slaying Huwawa, Gilgamesh next rejects the goddess Ishtar's request for love ("Come, Gilgamesh, be thou my lover!/Do but grant me of thy fruit."), and she forces the gods to create the Bull of Heaven to punish his insolence.

Ishtar was enraged and mounted to heaven.
Forth went Ishtar before Anu, her father,
To Antum, her mother, she went and said:
"My father, Gilgamesh has heaped insults upon me!…"
Anu opened his mouth to speak,
Saying to glorious Ishtar:
"But surely thou didst invite […]."
Ishtar opened her mouth to speak,
Saying to Anu, her father:
"My father, make me the Bull of Heaven that he smite
    Gilgamesh.…
If thou dost not make me the Bull of Heaven,
I will smash the doors of the nether world,
I will […],
I will raise up the dead eating and alive,
So that the dead shall outnumber the living!"…

The heroes slay the Bull of Heaven and again insult Ishtar.

Up leaped Enkidu, seizing the Bull of Heaven by the horns,
The Bull of Heaven hurled his foam in his face,
Brushed him with the back of his tail.…
Between neck and horns he thrust his sword.

When they had slain the Bull, they tore out his heart,
Placing it before Shamash [See Selection 3].
They drew back and did homage before Shamash.
The two brothers sat down.
Then Ishtar mounted the wall of ramparted Uruk,
Sprang on the battlements, uttering a curse:
"Woe unto Gilgamesh because he insulted me
By slaying the Bull of Heaven!"
When Enkidu heard this speech of Ishtar,
He tore loose the right thigh of the Bull of Heaven
And tossed it in her face:
"Could I but get thee, like unto him
I would do unto thee.
His entrails I would hang at thy side!"...
In the Euphrates they washed their hands,
They embraced each other as they went on,
Riding through the market street of Uruk.
The people of Uruk are gathered to gaze upon them.
Gilgamesh to the lyre maidens of Uruk
Says these words:
"Who is most splendid among the heroes?
Who is most glorious among men?"
"Gilgamesh is most splendid among the heroes,
Gilgamesh is most glorious among men."

By means of a dream, Enkidu learns two things: that the gods have decided he must die as punishment for the insolent behavior of the two heroes, and that the land of the dead is a most dismal place.

Gilgamesh in his palace holds a celebration.
Down lie the heroes on their beds of night.
Also Enkidu lies down, a dream beholding.
Up rose Enkidu to relate his dream,
Saying to his friend:
"My friend, why are the great gods in council?...
My friend, I saw a dream this night:
The heavens moaned, the earth responded;
[...] I stood alone.
[...] his face was darkened....
Looking at me, he leads me to the House of Darkness,
The abode of Irkalla,
To the house which none leave who have entered it,
On the road from which there is no way back,
To the house wherein the dwellers are bereft of light,
Where dust is their fare and clay their food.
They are clothed like birds, with wings for garments,
And see no light, residing in darkness.
In the House of Dust, which I entered,

I looked at rulers, their crowns put away;
I saw princes, those born to the crown,
Who ruled the land from the days of yore...."

Enkidu dies, and the reality of death as the common lot of all humankind—
even fearless heroes—strikes home to Gilgamesh. The remainder of the epic
deals with his attempt to find everlasting life, a quest that all tell him is hopeless. In the following selection, Gilgamesh is talking to a barmaid who gives
him sage advice.

"He who with me underwent all hardships—
Enkidu, whom I loved dearly,
Who with me underwent all hardships—
Has now gone to the fate of mankind!
Day and night I have wept over him.
I would not give him up for burial—
In case my friend should rise at my plaint—
Seven days and seven nights,
Until a worm fell out of his nose.
Since his passing I have not found life,
I have roamed like a hunter in the midst of the steppe.
O ale-wife, now that I have seen thy face,
Let me not see the death which I ever dread."
The ale-wife said to him, to Gilgamesh:
"Gilgamesh, whither rovest thou?
The life thou pursueth, thou shalt not find.
When the gods created mankind,
Death for mankind they set aside,
Life in their own hands retaining.
Thou, Gilgamesh, let full be thy belly,
Make thou merry by day and by night.
Of each day make thou a feast of rejoicing,
Day and night dance thou and play!
Let thy garments be sparkling fresh,
Thy head be washed; bathe thou in water.
Pay heed to the little one that holds on to thy hand,
Let thy spouse delight in thy bosom!
For this is the task of mankind!"...

Gilgamesh next searches out Utnapishtim, the immortal hero of the Flood (Selection 1B), who also cannot help him. The dejected Gilgamesh is about to depart
when he is told of the Plant of Life—his last and most disappointing hope.

His spouse says to him, to Utnapishtim the Faraway:
"Gilgamesh has come hither, toiling and straining.
What wilt thou give him that he may return to his land?"
At that he, Gilgamesh, raised up his pole,
To bring the boat nigh to the shore.

Utnapishtim says to him, to Gilgamesh:
"Gilgamesh, thou hast come hither, toiling and straining.
What shall I give thee that thou mayest return to thy land?
I will disclose, O Gilgamesh, a hidden thing,
And about a plant I will tell thee:
This plant, like the buckthorn is [...].
Its thorns will prick thy hands just as does the rose.
If thy hands obtain the plant, thou wilt attain [eternal] life."
No sooner had Gilgamesh heard this,...
He tied heavy stones to his feet.
They pulled him down into the deep and he saw the plant.
He took the plant, though it pricked his hands.
He cut the heavy stones from his feet.
The sea cast him up upon it shore.
Gilgamesh says to him, to Urshanabi, the boatman:
"Urshanabi, this plant is a plant apart,
Whereby a man may regain his life's breath.
I will take it to ramparted Uruk....
Its name shall be 'Man Becomes Young in Old Age.'
I myself shall eat it
And thus return to the state of my youth."
After twenty leagues they broke off a morsel,
After thirty more leagues they prepared for the night.
Gilgamesh saw a well whose water was cool.
He went down into it to bathe in the water.
A serpent snuffed the fragrance of the plant;
It came up from the water and carried off the plant,
Going back it shed its slough.
Thereupon Gilgamesh sits down and weeps,
His tears running down over his face.
He took the hand of Urshanabi, the boatman:
"For whom, Urshanabi, have my hands toiled?
For whom is being spent the blood of my heart?
I have not obtained a boon for myself.
For the serpent have I effected a boon!"

B. THE EPIC OF THE FLOOD:

THE BABYLONIAN NOAH

Archaeologists have discovered evidence of great floods in the Tigris-Euphrates valley, one of which left a deposit of sediment some eight feet deep. Undoubtedly historical memories of one such disastrous flood became

From "The Epic of Gilgamesh." Tablet XI, based on the translation in Morris Jastrow, *The Civilization of Babylonia and Assyria* (Philadelphia: J. B. Lippincott Company, 1915), pp. 445–52.

the basis for a Sumerian flood epic, fragments of which have survived. It told how a Sumerian Noah, Ziusudra, warned beforehand by the god Ea of the intention of the gods "to destroy the seed of mankind" by a flood, built a ship and embarked upon it with his household, his possessions, and all types of living things. Because Ziusudra had thus "perceived the secret of the gods," they decided to give him "life like a god" and so made him one with themselves.

The later Babylonians incorporated the flood story into their composite version of the *Epic of Gilgamesh*. When the yearning for everlasting life takes hold of Gilgamesh after the death of his friend Enkidu, he searches out Ziusudra, whom the Babylonians called Utnapishtim, to gain from him the secret of eternal life. Utnapishtim tells him his story, and it is this more complete Babylonian version that is given in part below. The striking similarities with the later Hebrew story (Selection 2) are quite evident, but the great gulf between them needs to be emphasized: the Hebrew version has been completely moralized. In the Hebrew account, the Flood is sent because of sin, and the hero is saved because he is righteous. In the Sumero-Babylonian version, the hero is saved out of mere favoritism and the gods send the Flood, as we learn from a separate account, because their sleep has been disturbed: "oppressive has become the clamor of mankind, by their uproar they prevent sleep." Above all, the one supreme righteous God of the Hebrews contrasts with the gang of weak, quarrelsome, greedy gods who "cowered like dogs" in the presence of the Flood and who later "like flies gathered around the sacrificer."

> Gilgamesh speaks to him, to Utnapishtim, the far-removed:
> "I gaze at thee, Utnapishtim!
> Thy appearance is not different. As I am, so art thou....
>
> Tell me how thou didst enter into the assembly of the gods
>   and secure [eternal] life."
> Utnapishtim said to him, to Gilgamesh:
> "I will reveal to thee, Gilgamesh, a secret story,
> And the decision of the gods I will tell thee.
> The city Shuruppak, a city which thou knowest,
> The one that lies on the Euphrates,
> That city was old, as were the gods thereof,
> When the great gods decided to bring a flood over it....

The God Ea Warns Utnapishtim

> "The lord of brilliant vision, Ea, was with them.
> He repeated their decision to the reed-hut.
> 'Reed-hut, reed-hut, wall, wall,
> Reed-hut, hear! Wall, give ear!
> O man of Shuruppak, son of Ubara-Tutu,
> Break up this house, build a ship,
> Abandon your property, seek life!
> Bring into the ship seed of all living things!
> The ship that thou shalt build,

Let its dimension be measured, so that
Its breadth and length be made to correspond.
On a level with the deep, provide it with a covering.'
I understood and spoke to Ea, my lord:
'The command of my lord which thou hast commanded,
As I have understood it, I will carry out.
But what shall I answer the city—the people and the elders?'
Ea opened his mouth and spoke:
'As answer thus speak to them:
Know that Enlil [god who rules all Sumer] has conceived
    hatred towards me,
So that I can no longer dwell in your city.
On Enlil's territory I dare no longer set my face.
Therefore, I go to the Deep to dwell with Ea, my lord.
Over you he will cause blessings to rain down.'...

The Ship Is Built and Loaded

"On the fifth day, I designed its outline.
Its walls were ten *gar* [180 feet] high;
Ten *gar* the measure of its width.
I determined its shape and drew it.
I gave it six decks.
I divided [the superstructure?] into seven parts.
Its interior I divided into nine sections.
Water-plugs I constructed in the interior.
I selected a punting-pole and added accessories.
Six measures of asphalt I poured on the outer wall.
Three measures of pitch I poured on the inner wall....
All that I had I loaded on her.
All that I had of silver I loaded on her.
All that I had of gold I loaded on her.
All that I had of living beings of all kinds I loaded on her.
I brought to the ship all my family and household;
Cattle of the field, beasts of the field, all the workmen
    I brought on board....

The Flood

"As morning dawned,
There arose on the firmament of heaven black clouds;
Adad thundered therein;...
Adad's roar reaches to heaven,
All light is changed to darkness....
For one day the hurricane raged,
Storming furiously,...

Coming like a combat over men.
Brother sees not brother,
And from heaven people cannot be recognized.

"The Gods Are Terrified"

"The Gods are terrified by the deluge,
They flee and mount to the heaven of Anu;
The gods cowered like dogs in an enclosure.
Ishtar cried aloud like one in birth throes,
The mistress of the gods howls aloud:
'The former days are turned to clay....
My people are like fish, they fill the sea.'
All of the Anunnaki gods weep with her;
The gods sit down, depressed and weeping....

The Flood Subsides

"Six days and nights
The storm and flood continued to sweep over the land.
When the seventh day approached, the storm and flood
    ceased the combat,
After having fought like warriors....
I looked at the day and the roar had quieted down,
And all mankind had returned to clay.
The landscape was level as a flat roof.
I opened a window and light fell on my face,
I bowed down and sat and wept,
Tears flowed over my face.
I looked in all directions of the sea.
At a distance of twelve miles an island appeared.
On Mount Nisir the ship stood still.
Mount Nisir held the ship so that it could not move.
One day, two days, Mount Nisir held the ship fast....
When the seventh day arrived,
I sent forth a dove, letting it free.
The dove went hither and thither;
Not finding a resting place, it came back.
I sent forth a swallow, letting it free.
The swallow went hither and thither.
Not finding a resting place, it came back.
I sent forth a raven, letting it free.
The raven went and saw the decrease of the waters.
It ate, croaked, but did not turn back.
Then I let all out to the four regions and brought an
    offering.

I brought a sacrifice on the mountain top.
Seven and seven cult jars I arranged.
Beneath them I strewed reeds, cedarwood and myrtle.
The gods smelled the odor,
The gods smelled the sweet odor.
The gods like flies gathered around the sacrificer.

The Gods Quarrel

"As soon as [Ishtar] the mistress of the gods arrived, … [she
    cried out:]
'Ye gods … I will remember these days—never to forget
    them.
Let the gods come to the sacrifice,
But let not Enlil come to the sacrifice,
Because without reflection he brought on the flood,
And decreed destruction for my people.'
As soon as Enlil arrived,
He saw the ship, and Enlil was enraged,
Filled with anger at the gods.
'Who now has escaped with his life?
No man was to survive the destruction!'
Ninib opened his mouth and spoke,
Spoke to the warrior Enlil,
'Who except Ea can plan any affair?
Ea indeed knows every order.'
Ea opened his mouth and spoke,
Spoke to the warrior Enlil:
'Thou art the leader and warrior of the gods.
But why didst thou, without reflection, bring on the flood?
On the sinner impose his sin,
On the transgressor impose his transgression,
But be merciful not to root out completely, be considerate
    not to destroy altogether!…
I did not reveal the secret of the great gods,
I sent Utnapishtim a dream and he understood the secret of
    the gods.
Now take counsel for him.'

Utnapishtim Is Granted Eternal Life

"Enlil mounted the ship,
Took hold of my hand and led me up,
Led me up and caused my wife to kneel at my side,
Touched our foreheads, stepped between us and blessed us.
'Hitherto Utnapishtim was a man;

> Now Utnapishtim and his wife shall be on a level with the
> gods.
> Utnapishtim shall dwell in the distance, at the mouth of the
> rivers.'
> Then they took me and settled me at the mouth of the
> rivers."

2 Hebrew Bible

Earliest Relations Between Humans and God

The Hebrew Bible, broadly identical to the Old Testament of the Christian Bible, represents a compendious anthology of folktales, historical chronicles, utterances of men possessed of deep religious insight, love lyrics, and skeptical wisdom literature. Tradition has it that final approval of its present form and content was given ca. A.D. 90 by rabbis at the Council of Jamnia (Yavneh) in Roman-ruled Palestine. The Torah (Pentateuch in Greek), or the Five Books of Moses, stands at the beginning of the Bible and contain core traditions associated with the origins and identity of the Hebrew people. These traditions speak to how historical experience, as culturally remembered, crystallized into certain key ideas over a period of nearly two thousand years that began around 1800 B.C., the traditional date for Abraham's entrance into the land of Canaan. Much that the Hebrews experienced and expressed can also be seen in the literature of Mesopotamia and Egypt, but in their views on God and on history the Hebrews broke with the thought of the ancient Near East.

The gods of Mesopotamia and Egypt—sun-gods, earth gods, storm-gods, and so on—were immanent in nature. The Hebrews, however, distinguished completely between God and nature, placing God entirely outside the physical universe. He was the Creator who stood above and apart from what he had created; as the psalmist expressed it, "The heavens declare the glory of God; and the firmament showeth his handiwork" (Psalm 19:1). This view of God as the Creator of all things everywhere inevitably led to monotheism and, equally important, to the view that mortals, because they stood apart from God, had free will and were therefore responsible for their own failures. History was viewed as the story of the clash of God's will with the will of mortals, but since God was righteous and ruled all, he employed these clashes to instruct the Hebrews and, through them, all humankind.

Accordingly, while other ancient peoples viewed history as an endless recurrence of cycles leading nowhere, the Hebrews, with the exception of

From Genesis 11–12, 46–47; the King James Version of the Bible.

the author of the Book of Ecclesiastes, understood history as moving in a straight line from a beginning to an end, in accordance with God's purpose for the good of all humankind. "It is the work of a personal divine will, contending with the foolish, stubborn wills of men, promising and warning, judging and punishing and destroying, yet sifting, saving, and abundantly blessing those found amenable to discipline and instruction."[1] This essentially optimistic view of history as the story of progress to better things was passed on to Christianity and, after being divested of its theological underpinnings, to modern Western civilization.

Many of the selections from the Old Testament that follow are from the King James Version of the Bible, first published in 1611, which the late John Livingston Lowes called "the noblest monument of English prose." "Its phraseology," he wrote, "has become part and parcel of our common tongue.... Its rhythms and cadences, its turns of speech, its familiar imagery, its very words are woven into the texture of our literature.... The English of the Bible... is characterized not merely by a homely vigor and pithiness of phrase but also a singular nobility of diction and by a rhythmic quality which is, I think, unrivalled in its beauty."

***

The earliest extant Hebrew views on the relationship between humans and God are found in the early chapters of Genesis, the first book of the Torah or Pentateuch (or the first five books of the Christian Old Testament), whose earliest strand, according to some modern biblical scholars, was composed by a great Hebrew historian during the reign of Solomon. This tenth-century historian prefaced his account of Hebrew origins, which begins with Abraham, with several early folk tales that have their parallels in the folklore of other peoples. The particular purpose for which these stories were used is clear: they were viewed as incidents in the history of sin and punishment that left early people at odds with their Creator and with others.

The Garden of Eden: Wisdom Gained, Immortality Lost

And the Lord God formed man of the dust of the ground, and breathed into his nostrils the breath of life; and man became a living soul.

And the Lord God planted a garden eastward in Eden; and there he put the man whom he had formed. And out of the ground made the Lord God to grow every tree that is pleasant to the sight, and good for food; the tree of life also in the midst of the garden, and the tree of knowledge of good and evil....

And the Lord God commanded the man, saying, Of every tree of the garden thou mayest freely eat: But of the tree of knowledge of good and evil, thou shalt not eat of it: for in the day that thou eatest thereof thou shalt surely die.

And the Lord God said, It is not good that the man should be alone; I will make him a help meet for him.... And the Lord God caused a deep sleep to fall upon Adam, and he slept; and he took one of his ribs, and closed up the

---

1. Millar Burrows, "Ancient Israel," in *The Idea of History in the Ancient Near East,* edited by Robert C. Dentan (New Haven, Conn.: Yale University Press, 1955), p. 128.

flesh instead thereof. And the rib, which the Lord God had taken from the man, made he a woman, and brought her unto the man.... Therefore shall a man leave his father and mother, and shall cleave unto his wife: and they shall be one flesh. And they were both naked, the man and his wife, and were not ashamed.

Now the serpent was more subtile than any beast of the field which the Lord God had made. And he said unto the woman, Yea, hath God said, Ye shall not eat of every tree of the garden? ... Ye shall not surely die: For God doth know that in the day ye eat thereof, then your eyes shall be opened, and ye shall be as gods, knowing good and evil.

And when the woman saw that the tree was good for food, and that it was pleasant to the eyes, and a tree to be desired to make one wise, she took of the fruit thereof, and did eat, and gave also unto her husband with her; and he did eat. And the eyes of them both were opened, and they knew that they were naked; and they sewed fig leaves together, and made themselves aprons.

And they heard the voice of the Lord God walking in the garden in the cool of the day: and Adam and his wife hid themselves from the presence of the Lord God amongst the trees of the garden. And the Lord God called unto Adam, and said unto him, Where art thou?

And he said, I heard thy voice in the garden, and I was afraid, because I was naked; and I hid myself.

And he said, Who told thee that thou wast naked? Hast thou eaten of the tree, whereof I commanded thee that thou shouldest not eat?

And the man said, The woman whom thou gavest to be with me, she gave me of the tree, and I did eat.

And the Lord God said unto the woman, What is this that thou hast done? And the woman said, The serpent beguiled me, and I did eat.

And the Lord God said unto the serpent, Because thou hast done this, thou art cursed above all cattle, and above every beast of the field; upon thy belly shalt thou go, and dust shalt thou eat all the days of thy life....

Unto the woman he said, I will greatly multiply thy sorrow and thy conception; in sorrow thou shalt bring forth children; and thy desire shall be to thy husband, and he shall rule over thee.

And unto Adam he said, Because thou hast hearkened unto the voice of thy wife, and hast eaten of the tree, ... cursed is the ground for thy sake; in sorrow shalt thou eat of it all the days of thy life; Thorns also and thistles shall it bring forth to thee; and thou shalt eat the herb of the field: In the sweat of thy face shalt thou eat bread, till thou return unto the ground; for out of it wast thou taken; for dust thou art, and unto dust shalt thou return....

And the Lord God said, Behold, the man is become as one of us, to know good and evil: and now, lest he put forth his hand, and take also of the tree of life, and eat, and live for ever: Therefore the Lord God sent him forth from the garden of Eden, to till the ground from whence he was taken. So he drove out the man: and he placed at the east of the garden of Eden cherubim, and a flaming sword which turned every way, to keep the way of the tree of life....

The Marriage of the Sons of God

And it came to pass, when men began to multiply on the face of the earth, and daughters were born unto them, That the sons of God saw the daughters of men that they were fair; and they took them wives of all which they chose. And the Lord said, My Spirit shall not always strive with man, for that he also is flesh: yet his days shall be a hundred and twenty years. There were giants in the earth in those days; and also after that, when the sons of God came in unto the daughters of men, and they bare children to them, the same became mighty men which were old, men of renown.

The Story of the Flood

And God saw that the wickedness of man was great in the earth, and that every imagination of the thoughts of his heart was only evil continually. And it repented the Lord that he had made man on the earth, and it grieved him at his heart. And the Lord said, I will destroy man whom I have created from the face of the earth; both man, and beast, and the creeping thing, and the fowls of the air; for it repenteth me that I have made them. But Noah found grace in the eyes of the Lord....

And God looked upon the earth, and behold, it was corrupt; for all flesh had corrupted his way upon the earth. And God said unto Noah, The end of all flesh is come before me; for the earth is filled with violence through them; and, behold, I will destroy them with the earth. Make thee an ark of gopher wood; rooms shalt thou make in the ark, and shalt pitch it within and without with pitch. And this is the fashion which thou shalt make it of: The length of the ark shall be three hundred cubits, the breadth of it fifty cubits, and the height of it thirty cubits. A window shalt thou make to the ark, and in a cubit shalt thou finish it above; and the door of the ark shalt thou set in the side thereof; with lower, second, and third stories shalt thou make it.

And, behold, I, even I, do bring a flood of waters upon the earth, to destroy all flesh, wherein is the breath of life, from under heaven; and every thing that is in the earth shall die. But with thee will I establish my covenant; and thou shalt come into the ark, thou, and thy sons, and thy wife, and thy sons' wives with thee. And of every living thing of all flesh, two of every sort shalt thou bring into the ark, to keep them alive with thee; they shall be male and female.... And take thou unto thee of all food that is eaten, and thou shalt gather it to thee; and it shall be for food for thee, and for them. Thus did Noah; according to all that God commanded him, so did he.

And the Lord said unto Noah, Come thou and all thy house into the ark; for thee have I seen righteous before me in this generation....

And it came to pass after seven days, that the waters of the flood were upon the earth. In the six hundredth year of Noah's life, in the second month, the seventeenth day of the month, the same day were all the fountains of the great deep broken up, and the windows of heaven were opened. And the rain was upon the earth forty days and forty nights ... and the Lord shut him in. And the flood was forty days upon the earth; and the waters increased, and bare up the ark, and it was lifted up above the earth. And the waters prevailed, and were increased greatly upon the earth; and the ark went upon the face of the waters. And the waters prevailed exceedingly upon the earth; and all the high hills, that were under the whole heaven, were covered. Fifteen cubits [22½ feet] upward did the waters prevail; and the mountains were covered.

And all flesh died that moved upon the earth, both of fowl, and of cattle, and of beast, and of every creeping thing that creepeth upon the earth, and every man: All in whose nostrils was the breath of life, of all that was in the dry land, died.… and Noah only remained alive, and they that were with him in the ark. And the waters prevailed upon the earth a hundred and fifty days.

And God remembered Noah, and every living thing, and all the cattle that was with him in the ark: and God made a wind to pass over the earth, and the waters assuaged. The fountains also of the deep and the windows of heaven were stopped, and the rain from heaven was restrained. And the waters returned from off the earth continually:… And the ark rested … upon the mountains of Ararat.…

And it came to pass at the end of forty days, that Noah opened the window of the ark which he had made: And he sent forth a raven, which went forth to and fro, until the waters were dried up from the earth. Also he sent forth a dove from him, to see if the waters were abated from off the face of the ground. But the dove found no rest for the sole of her foot, and she returned unto him into the ark; for the waters were on the face of the whole earth. Then he put forth his hand, and took her, and pulled her in unto him into the ark.

And he stayed yet other seven days; and again he set forth the dove out of the ark. And the dove came in to him in the evening, and lo, in her mouth was an olive leaf plucked off: so Noah knew that the waters were abated from off the earth. And he stayed yet other seven days, and sent forth the dove, which returned not again unto him any more.

… and Noah removed the covering of the ark, and looked, and behold, the face of the ground was dry.… And God spake unto Noah, saying, Go forth of the ark, thou, and thy wife, and thy sons, and thy sons' wives with thee. Bring forth with thee every living thing that is with thee,… that they may breed abundantly in the earth, and be fruitful, and multiply upon the earth. And Noah went forth, and his sons, and his wife, and his sons' wives with him: Every beast, every creeping thing, and every fowl, and whatsoever creepeth upon the earth, after their kinds, went forth out of the ark.

And Noah builded an altar unto the Lord; and took of every clean beast, and of every clean fowl, and offered burnt offerings on the altar. And the Lord smelled a sweet savor; and the Lord said in his heart, I will not again curse the ground any more for man's sake; for the imagination of man's heart is evil from his youth; neither will I again smite any more every thing living, as I have done. While the earth remaineth, seedtime and harvest, and cold and heat, and summer and winter, and day and night shall not cease.

And God blessed Noah and his sons, and said unto them, Be fruitful, and multiply, and replenish the earth.…

And the sons of Noah, that went forth of the ark, were Shem, and Ham, and Japheth: and Ham is the father of Canaan. These are the three sons of Noah: and of them was the whole earth overspread.…

The Tower of Babel

And the whole earth was of one language, and of one speech. And it came to pass, as they [the descendants of Noah] journeyed from the east, that they found a plain in the land of Shinar [Sumer]; and they dwelt there. And they said one to another, Go to, let us make brick, and burn them thoroughly. And they had brick for stone, and slime had they for mortar. And they said, Go to, let us build us a city, and a tower, whose top may reach unto heaven; and let us make us a name, lest we be scattered abroad upon the face of the whole earth.

And the Lord came down to see the city and the tower, which the children of men builded. And the Lord said, Behold, the people is one, and they have all one language; and this they begin to do: and now nothing will be restrained from them, which they have imagined to do. Go to, let us go down, and there confound their language, that they may not understand one another's speech. So the Lord scattered them abroad from thence upon the face of all the earth: and they left off to build the city. Therefore is the name of it called Babel; because the Lord did there confound the language of all the earth: and from thence did the Lord scatter them abroad upon the face of all the earth.

Early Society, Justice, and Moral Order

While Greek political experience was so rich and varied that it has been said with pardonable exaggeration that the ancient Greeks "invented politics," that of ancient Mesopotamia is commonly said to have been limited to an unvarying despotism that was total and not benevolent, whose subjects knew only "the language of the whip." There is good evidence, however, that not only were many of these despots exceptionally benevolent, but also that ancient Mesopotamia experienced forms of government other than despotism.[1]

The greatest political achievement of the Greeks was democracy, which never developed in Mesopotamia or elsewhere in the ancient Near East. But before the Greeks attained democracy, they had experienced three other major types of government, which they called monarchy, oligarchy, and tyranny. These three constitutional forms did develop in Mesopotamia.

---

1. See Nels Bailkey, "Early Mesopotamian Constitutional Development," *American Historical Review*, 72 (1967), pp. 1211–36.

The Greeks called their earliest form of government monarchy because of the prominent part played by the warleader, as shown in the Homeric epics. But because the power of this early monarch was greatly limited—his actions had to be approved by an aristocratic council of nobles and, in moments of crisis such as war, by a popular assembly of all arms-bearing men—modern scholars prefer the term "primitive monarchy," or even "primitive democracy." Primitive monarchy was followed by oligarchy ("rule of the few") when the council of nobles succeeded in eliminating both the king and the popular assembly. In time, discontent with the oppressive rule of the oligarchs caused the common people, both peasantry and rising middle class, to support the rise of usurping despots called "tyrants," a non—Greek word meaning "boss" or "chief" that was borrowed from the Lydians in Asia Minor.

That "primitive monarchy" was the earliest form of government in Mesopotamia is revealed in a number of epic tales. In the *Epic of the Flood*, for example, Utnapishtim consults his city's assembly and council—"the people and the elders"—before obeying the order of the gods. And in the *Epic of Gilgamesh* the nobles resent Gilgamesh's "arrogance," and they seek to curtail his arbitrary actions by setting up Enkidu as anti-king. Again, Enkidu in a dream sees "the great gods in council," an illustration of the way in which men attribute to the gods in heaven institutions similar to their own on earth. An independent Gilgamesh tale describes how Gilgamesh circumvented the opposition of his council to his proposal for a preventive war against the ruler of Kish. He is described as turning to the "convened assembly of the men of his city," who readily supported him and upbraided the nobles:

> O ye who are raised with the sons of the king,
> O ye who press the donkey's thigh…
> Do not submit to the house of Kish,
> let us smite it with weapons.[2]

There is also evidence that the nobles of Uruk ultimately resorted to the use of force, severely wounded Gilgamesh, and drove him into temporary exile.

Gilgamesh was the last of the early Sumerian primitive monarchs whose exploits were celebrated in epics. Thereafter, for more than a century, priest-dominated aristocratic councils ruled the Sumerian city-states through weak and compliant magistrates called *ensi-gars*, "governors installed (by a superior)"—the chief god of the city acting through his priests. But from roughly 2550 B.C., when true historical sources first became relatively abundant, to about 2350 B.C., when Sargon of Akkad conquered Sumer, dissatisfaction with oligarchic rule led intermittently to the rise of tyrants in the later Greek sense of the term.

---

2. "Gilgamesh and Agga," translated by Samuel N. Kramer in James B. Pritchard, ed., *Ancient Near Eastern Texts Relating to the Old Testament*, 3rd rev. ed. with Supplement (Princeton: Princeton University Press, 1969), pp. 45–46. Reprinted by permission of Princeton University Press.

3 The Shamash Hymn

Moral Religion and Social Justice

By the middle of the third millennium B.C., the fact of human suffering had produced a high level of social consciousness in Sumer. From at least that time onward, ideals of social justice not only motivated the domestic policies of some rulers but were also regarded as the basis for the rewards and punishments that the gods bestowed on humankind. Thus, for example, a hymn to the goddess Nanshe of Lagash honors her as the guarantor of justice who "searches the heart of the people" in order to punish those "walking in transgression," who "knows the oppression of man over man, is the orphan's mother, ... who cares for the widow, who seeks out justice for the poorest, ... brings the refugee to her lap, finds shelter for the weak."[1]

But it was the sun-god Utu, called Shamash by the Babylonians, who emerged from relative obscurity to become the preeminent god of justice. The following lines from the great two-hundred-line Babylonian hymn to Shamash, considered the noblest example of Mesopotamian lyric poetry and worthy of being compared with the best of the Hebrew psalms, reveal Shamash to have achieved such a position of importance that the Igigi and Anunnaki gods (the great gods of the Upperworld and the Underworld) humble themselves before him. He is even seen as a universal god who receives the worship of men in foreign lands. It is also noteworthy that as the guardian of the moral order, Shamash is particularly concerned with the plight of the weak and the oppressed and with the malpractices of businessmen. The evident emphasis placed on commercial activity is a reflection of the known fact that large numbers of enterprising capitalists flourished during the Old Babylonian period (roughly 2000–1600 B.C.). The Babylonian word translated "capital" is this selection is *qaqqadum*, literally "head." The Roman word *caput*, also meaning "head," was used in the same context, and the English word *capital* is borrowed from the Latin.

> Shamash, at your arising mankind bows down, [...] every
>   land.
> Illuminator, dispeller of darkness of the vault of the heavens,
> Who sets aglow the beard of light, the corn field, the life of
>   the land.
> Your splendour covers the vast mountains,
> Your fierce light fills the lands to their limits.

1. Samuel N. Kramer, *The Sumerians: Their History, Culture, and Character* (Chicago, Ill.: University of Chicago Press, 1963), pp. 124–25.

From *Babylonian Wisdom Literature*, translated by W. G. Lambert (Oxford: Clarendon Press, 1960), pp. 127–37. Reprinted by permission of the Clarendon Press.

You climb to the mountains surveying the earth,
You suspend from the heavens the circle of the lands.
You care for all the peoples of the lands,
And everything that Ea [god of wisdom], king of the coun-
sellors, had created is entrusted to you.
Whatever has breath you shepherd without exception,
You are their keeper in upper and lower regions.
Regularly and without cease you traverse the heavens,
Every day you pass over the broad earth....
In the underworld, you care for the counsellors of Kusu, the
Anunnaki,
Above, you direct all the affairs of men,
Shepherd of that beneath, keeper of that above,
You, Shamash, direct, you are the light of everything....
Among all the Igigi there is none who toils but you,
None who is supreme like you in the whole pantheon of gods.
At your rising the gods of the land assemble;
Your fierce glare covers the land.
Of all the lands of varied speech,
You know their plans, you scan their way.
The whole of mankind bows to you,
Shamash, the universe longs for your light....
You stand by the traveller whose road is difficult,
To the seafarer in dread of the waves you give [...]
It is you who patrol the unseen routes,
You constantly tread paths which confront Shamash alone.
You save from the storm the merchant carrying his capital,
The [...] who goes down to the ocean you equip with wings.
You point out settling-places to refugees and fugitives,
To the captive you point out routes that only Shamash
knows....
A man who covets his neighbour's wife
Will [...] before his appointed day.
A nasty snare is prepared for him [...]
Your weapon will strike at him, and there will be none to
save him....
You give the unscrupulous judge experience of fetters,
Him who accepts a present and yet lets justice miscarry you
make bear his punishment.
As for him who declines a present, but nevertheless takes the
part of the weak,
It is pleasing to Shamash, and he will prolong his life....
What is he benefited who invests money in unscrupulous
trading missions?
He is disappointed in the matter of profit and loses his
capital.

As for him who invests money in distant trading missions
and pays one shekel per [...],
It is pleasing to Shamash, and he will prolong his life.
The merchant who practices trickery as he holds the
balances,
Who uses two sets of weights, thus lowering the [...],
He is disappointed in the matter of profit and loses his
capital.
The honest merchant who holds the balances and gives
good weight—
Everything is presented to him in good measure [...]
The merchant who practices trickery as he holds the corn
measure,
Who weighs out loans of corn by the minimum standard,
but requires a large quantity in repayment,
The curse of the people will overtake him before his time,
If he demanded repayment before the agreed date, there will
be guilt upon him....
The honest merchant who weighs out loans of corn by the
maximum standard, thus multiplying kindness,
It is pleasing to Shamash, and he will prolong his life.
He will enlarge his family, gain wealth,
And like the water of a never-failing spring his descendants
will never fail....
The progeny of evildoers will fail.
Those whose mouth says "No"—their case is before you.
In a moment you discern what they say;
You hear and examine them; you determine the lawsuit of
the wronged.
Every single person is entrusted to your hands;
You manage their omens; that which is perplexing you
make plain.
You observe, Shamash, prayer, supplication, and
benediction,
Obeisance, kneeling, ritual murmurs, and prostration.
The feeble man calls you from the hollow of his mouth,
The humble, the weak, the afflicted, the poor,
She whose son is captive constantly and unceasingly con-
fronts you....
Which are the mountains not clothed with your beams?
Which are the regions not warmed by the brightness of your
light?
Brightener of gloom, illuminator of darkness,
Dispeller of darkness, illuminator of the broad earth,...

4 The Laws of Hammurabi

"To further the welfare of the people"

The last major period (roughly 2000–1600 B.C.) in the early history of Mesopotamia is commonly called the Old Babylonian period because of the importance of the First Dynasty of Babylon, and especially of Hammurabi (ca. 1792–1750 B.C.), the outstanding member of that dynasty. Known also as the Era of Warring States, this turbulent period was characterized by political instability, chronic economic depression, and extremes of wealth and poverty. Incessant wars to maintain the balance of power, fought by continually shifting coalitions of city-states, beset the land together with resurgent oligarchy. Temporary respite from the latter evil was at times provided by strong rulers, but, with the exception of Hammurabi, who temporarily united all of Mesopotamia under the sway of Babylon, hardly more than locally.

Of major interest are the social reforms promulgated by these stronger rulers of the Old Babylonian period. In broad reference to their work as social reformers, these rulers commonly employed the phrase first used, as we have seen, by Urukagina, "I have established freedom," meaning the removal of abuses from the oppressed and the restoration and safeguarding of their rights. In part, these reformers viewed social justice as a return to *kittum*, "truth," the fixed and invariable body of law upon which society had been founded, the creation of the gods who had entrusted it to the ruler's care. But greater emphasis was placed on a new, dynamic type of law that had emerged as a supplement to *kittum*. Called *misharum*, literally "rightings" and hence translated "equity," "justice," or "righteousness," this new law was of human origin, the work of a true legislator. Promulgated as "judgments" and "decisions" of the ruler, these misharu-acts sought to alleviate the injustices produced by the economic and social dislocations of the Old Babylonian period for which *kittum* had no specific remedy. The distinction between these two types of law, which are found in all civilizations, was briefly stated by Hammurabi in calling himself "the king of justice (*misharum*), to whom Shamash has committed truth (*kittum*)."

While many misharu-acts only proclaimed the remission of various obligations, including indebtedness, and, at times, the freeing of persons enslaved for debt, others comprised extensive collections of remedial legislation. The best-known and only virtually complete example of the latter "codes" (there are four from the Old Babylonian period and one from the preceding Third Dynasty of Ur) is that of Hammurabi. Its prologue and epilogue set forth the divine commission that Hammurabi received from the gods to secure the general welfare, while the nearly three hundred individual laws, touching on a wide variety of abuses, justify Hammurabi's claim of having acted "like a real father to his people ... [who] has established prosperity ... and given good government to the land."

Based on the translation by Robert F. Harper, *The Code of Hammurabi* (Chicago, Ill.: The University of Chicago Press, 1904).

The stele of Hammurabi, nearly eight feet high, on which his code of laws is inscribed. The relief at the top depicts the king saluting the sun god Shamash, god of justice, who extends to him a rod and a ring, symbols of royal authority.

Prologue

When the lofty Anu, king of the Anunnaki gods, and Enlil, lord of heaven and earth, he who determines the destiny of the land, committed the rule of all mankind to Marduk, the chief son of Ea; when they made him great among the Igigi gods; when they pronounced the lofty name of Babylon; when they made it famous among the quarters of the world and in its midst established an everlasting kingdom whose foundations were firm as heaven and earth—at that time, Anu and Enlil named me, Hammurabi, the exalted prince, the worshiper of the gods, to cause justice to prevail in the land, to destroy the wicked and the evil, to prevent the strong from oppressing the weak, to go forth like the sun over the black-headed people, to enlighten the land and to further the welfare of the people. Hammurabi, the shepherd named by Enlil, am I, who brought about plenty and abundance; ... obedient to the mighty Shamash; ... who rebuilt [the temple] Ebabbar for Shamash, his helper; ... the powerful king, the sun of Babylon, who caused light to go forth over the lands of Sumer and Akkad; the king who caused the four quarters of the world to render obedience; the favorite of Ishtar, am I.

When Marduk sent me to rule the people and to bring help to the country, I established law and justice in the language of the land and promoted the welfare of the people. At that time (I decreed):

The Administration of Justice

1. If a man brings an accusation against another man, charging him with murder, but cannot prove it, the accuser shall be put to death.

3. If a man bears false witness in a case, or does not establish the testimony that he has given, if that case is a case involving life, that man shall be put to death....

4. If he bears (false) witness concerning grain or money, he shall himself bear the penalty imposed in that case.

5. If a judge pronounces a judgment, renders a decision, delivers a verdict duly signed and sealed, and afterward alters his judgment, they shall call that judge to account for the alteration of the judgment which he has pronounced, and he shall pay twelve-fold the penalty in that judgment; and, in the assembly, they shall expel him from his seat of judgment, and with the judges in a case he shall not take his seat....

Property

9. If a man who has lost anything finds that which was lost in the possession of (another) man, and the man in whose possession the lost property is found says, "It was sold to me, I purchased it in the presence of witnesses"; and the owner of the lost property says, "I will bring witnesses to identify my lost property"; if the purchaser produces the seller who has sold it to him and the witnesses in whose presence he purchased it, and the owner of the lost property produces witnesses to identify his lost property, the judges shall consider their evidence. The witnesses in whose presence the purchase was made and the witnesses to identify the lost property shall give their testimony in the presence of god. The seller shall be put to death as a thief; the owner of the lost property shall recover his loss; the purchaser shall recover from the estate of the seller the money which he paid out.

10. If the purchaser does not produce the seller who sold it to him and the witnesses in whose presence he purchased it, and if the owner of the lost property produces witnesses to identify his lost property, the purchaser shall be put to death as a thief. The owner of the lost property shall recover his lost property.

11. If the (alleged) owner of the lost property does not produce witnesses to identify his lost property, he has attempted fraud, he has stirred up strife, he shall be put to death....

22. If a man practices robbery and is captured, that man shall be put to death.

23. If the robber is not captured, the man who has been robbed shall, in the presence of god, make an itemized statement of his loss, and the city and the governor in whose province and jurisdiction the robbery was committed shall compensate him for whatever was lost.

24. If it is a life (that is lost), the city and governor shall pay one mina [about one pound] of silver to his heirs....

Irrigation

53. If a man neglects to maintain his dike and does not strengthen it, and a break is made in his dike and the water carries away the farmland, the man in whose dike the break has been made shall replace the grain which has been damaged.

54. If he is not able to replace the grain, they shall sell him and his goods and the farmers whose grain the water has carried away shall divide (the results of the sale).

55. If a man opens his canal for irrigation and neglects it and the water carries away an adjacent field, he shall pay out grain on the basis of the adjacent field.

56. If a man opens up the water and the water carries away the improvements of an adjacent field, he shall pay out ten *gur* of grain per bur [of damaged land]....

Loans and Interest

88. If a merchant lends grain at interest, for one *gur* [300 *sila*] he shall receive one hundred *sila* as interest [33⅓ per cent], if he lends money at interest, for one shekel of silver, he shall receive one-fifth of a shekel as interest [20 per cent]....

90. If a merchant increases the interest on grain above one hundred *sila* for one *gur*, or the interest on silver above one-fifth of a shekel (per shekel), and takes this interest, he shall forfeit whatever he lent....

94. If a merchant lends grain or silver at interest and when he lends it at interest he gives silver by the small weight and grain by the small measure but when he gets it back he gets silver by the large weight and grain by the large measure, the merchant shall forfeit whatever he lent....

Regulation of Trade

104. If a merchant gives to an agent grain, wool, oil, or goods of any kind with which to trade, the agent shall write down the value and return (the money) to the merchant. The agent shall take a sealed receipt for the money which he gives to the merchant.

105. If the agent is careless and does not take a receipt for the money which he has given to the merchant, the money not receipted for shall not be placed to his account....

108. If a wine seller does not take grain for the price of a drink but takes money by the large weight, or if she makes the measure of drink smaller than the measure of grain, they shall call that wine seller to account and throw her into the water.

109. If bad characters gather in front of the house of a wine seller and she does not arrest those bad characters and bring them to the palace, that wine seller shall be put to death.

110. If a priestess who is not living in a convent opens a wine shop or enters a wine shop for a drink, they shall burn that woman....

Debt Slavery

117. If a man is in debt and sells his wife, son, or daughter, or binds them over to service, for three years they shall work in the house of their purchaser or master; in the fourth year they shall be given their freedom.

118. If he binds over to service a male or female slave and lets the time (of redemption) expire and the merchant transfers or sells such slave, there is no cause for complaint....

Marriage and the Family

128. If a man takes a wife and does not arrange a contract for her, that woman is not a wife.

129. If the wife of a man is caught lying with another man, they shall bind them and throw them into the water. If the husband of the woman wishes to spare his wife, then the king shall spare his servant....

131. If a man has accused his wife but she has not been caught lying with another man, she shall take an oath in the name of god and return to her house....

136. If a man deserts his city and flees and afterwards his wife enters into another house, if that man returns and wishes to take back his wife, the wife of the fugitive shall not return to her husband because he hated his city and fled....

138. If a man wishes to divorce his wife who has not borne him children, he shall give her money to the amount of her marriage price and he shall make good to her the dowry which she brought from her father's house and then he may divorce her....

141. If the wife of a man who is living in his house sets her face to go out and plays the part of a fool, neglecting her house and belittling her husband, they shall call her to account; and if her husband says, "I divorce her," he may let her go. On her departure nothing shall be given to her for her divorce. If her husband says, "I will not divorce her," her husband may marry another woman. The first woman shall dwell in the house of her husband as a maidservant.

142. If a woman hates her husband and says, "You may not possess me," the city council shall inquire into her case; and if she has been careful and without reproach and her husband has been going about and greatly belittling her, that woman has no blame. She may take her dowry and go to her father's house.

143. If she has not been careful but has gadded about, neglecting her house and belittling her husband, they shall throw that woman into the water....

145. If a man takes a wife and she does not present him with children and he sets his face to take a concubine, that man may take a concubine and bring her into his house. That concubine shall not rank with his wife.

146. If a man takes a wife and she gives a maidservant to her husband, and that maidservant bears children and afterwards claims equal rank with her mistress because she has borne children, her mistress may not sell her, but she may reduce her to bondage and count her among the slaves....

148. If a man has married a wife and a disease has seized her, if he is determined to marry a second wife, he shall marry her. He shall not divorce the wife whom the disease has seized. In the home they made together she shall dwell, and he shall maintain her as long as she lives...

150. If a man gives to his wife a field, garden, house, or goods and delivers to her a sealed deed, after (the death of) her husband her children cannot enter a claim against her. The mother may will her estate to her son whom she loves, but to an outsider she may not....

159. If a man, who has brought a gift to the house of his father-in-law and has paid the marriage price, looks with longing upon another woman and says to his father-in-law, "I will not marry your daughter," the father of the daughter shall take to himself whatever was brought to him.

160. If a man has brought a gift to the house of his father-in-law and has paid the marriage price and the father of the daughter says, "I will not give you my daughter," he shall double the amount that was brought to him and return it....

162. If a man takes a wife and she bears him children and that woman dies, her father may not lay claim to her dowry. Her dowry belongs to her children....

165. If a man presents a field, garden, or house to his favorite son and writes for him a sealed deed, after the father dies, when the brothers divide (the estate), he shall take the present which the father gave him, but otherwise they shall divide the goods of the father's estate equally....

168. If a man sets his face to disinherit his son and says to the judges, "I will disinherit my son," the judges shall inquire into his record, and if the son has not committed a crime sufficiently grave to cut him off from sonship, the father may not cut off his son from sonship....

170. If a man's wife bears him children and his maidservant bears him children, and the father during his lifetime says to the children which the maidservant bore him, "My children," and reckons them with the children of his wife, after the father dies the children of the wife and the children of the maidservant shall divide the goods of the father's estate equally. The son of the wife shall have the right of choice at the division....

Personal Injury and Manslaughter

195. If a son strikes his father, they shall cut off his hand.

196. If a man destroys the eye of another man, they shall destroy his eye.

197. If he breaks another man's bone, they shall break his bone.

198. If he destroys the eye of a client or breaks the bone of a client, he shall pay one mina of silver.

199. If he destroys the eye of a man's slave or breaks the bone of a man's slave, he shall pay one-half his price.

200. If a man knocks out a tooth of a man of his own rank, they shall knock out his tooth.

201. If he knocks out a tooth of a client, he shall pay one-third mina of silver....

206. If a man strikes another man in a quarrel and wounds him, he shall swear, "I struck him without intent," and he shall pay for the physician.

207. If he dies as the result of the blow, he shall swear (as above), and if the man was a free man, he shall pay one-half mina of silver.

208. If he was a client, he shall pay one-third mina of silver....

Physician's Fees and Malpractice

215. If a physician operates on a man for a severe wound with a bronze lancet and saves the man's life, or if he opens an abscess (in the eye) of a man with a bronze lancet and saves that man's eye, he shall receive ten shekels of silver.

216. If he is a client, he shall receive five shekels.

217. If he is a man's slave, the owner of the slave shall give two shekels of silver to the physician.

218. If a physician operates on a man for a severe wound with a bronze lancet and causes the man's death, or opens an abscess (in the eye) of a man with a bronze lancet and destroys the man's eye, they shall cut off his hand.

219. If a physician operates on a slave of a client for a severe wound with a bronze lancet and causes his death, he shall restore a slave of equal value....

221. If a physician sets a broken bone for a man or cures a sprained tendon, the patient shall give five shekels of silver to the physician.

222. If he is a client, he shall give three shekels of silver.

223. If he is a man's slave, the owner shall give two shekels of silver to the physician....

Building Regulations

228. If a builder builds a house for a man and completes it, he shall give him two shekels of silver per sar of house as his fee.

229. If a builder builds a house for a man and does not make its construction sound, and the house which he has built collapses and causes the death of the owner of the house, the builder shall be put to death....

233. If a builder builds a house for a man and does not make its construction sound, and a wall cracks, that builder shall strengthen that wall at his own expense....

Wage Regulations

257. If a man hires a field laborer, he shall pay him eight *gur* of grain per year.

258. If a man hires a herdsman, he shall pay him six *gur* of grain per year....

268. If a man hires an ox to thresh, twenty *sila* of grain is its [daily] hire.

269. If a man hires an ass to thresh, ten *sila* of grain is its hire....

271. If a man hires oxen, a wagon, and a driver, he shall pay 180 *sila* of grain per day....

273. If a man hires a laborer, from the beginning of the year until the fifth month he shall pay six *she* of silver per day; from the sixth month till the end of the year he shall pay five *she* of silver per day.

274. If a man hires an artisan, the [daily] wage of a [potter?] is five *she* of silver; the wage of a bricklayer is five *she* of silver; the wage of a tailor is five *she* of silver; the wage of a stonecutter is [...] *she* of silver; the wage of a jeweler is [...] *she* of silver; the wage of a smith is [...] *she* of silver; the wage of a carpenter is four *she* of silver; the wage of a leather worker is [...] *she* of silver; the wage of a basketmaker is [...] *she* of silver; the wage of a builder is [...] *she* of silver.

Epilogue

(These are) the just laws which Hammurabi, the wise king, established and by which he gave the land stable support and good government. Hammurabi, the perfect king, am I. I was not careless, nor was I neglectful of the black-headed people, whose rule Enlil presented and Marduk delivered to me....

The great gods called me, and I am the guardian shepherd whose scepter is just and whose beneficent shadow is spread over my city. In my bosom I carried the people of the land of Sumer and Addad; under my protection they prospered; I governed them in peace; in my wisdom I sheltered them.

In order that the strong might not oppress the weak, that justice be given to the orphan and the widow, in Babylon, the city whose turrets Anu and Enlil raised, in Esagila, the temple whose foundations are firm as heaven and earth, for the pronouncing of judgments in the land, for the rendering of decisions for the land, and to give justice to the oppressed, my weighty words I have written upon my monument, and in the presence of my image as king of justice have I established it.

The king who is preeminent among kings am I. My words are precious, my wisdom is unrivaled. By the command of Shamash, the great judge of heaven and earth, may I make justice to shine forth on the land. By the order of Marduk, my lord, may no one scorn my statutes, may my name be remembered with favor in Esagila forever.

Let any oppressed man, who has a cause, come before my image as king of justice! Let him read the inscription on my monument! Let him give heed to my weighty words! And may my monument enlighten him as to his cause and may he understand his case! May he set his heart at ease! (and he will exclaim): "Hammurabi indeed is a ruler who is like a real father to his people; he has given reverence to the words of Marduk, his lord; he has obtained victory for Marduk in north and south; he has made glad the heart of Marduk, his lord; he has established prosperity for the people for all time and given good government to the land."...

In the days that are yet to come, for all future time, may the king who is in the land observe the words of justice which I have written upon my monument! May he not alter the judgments of the land which I have pronounced, or the decisions of the country which I have rendered! May he not scorn my statutes! If that man have wisdom, if he wish to give his land good government, let him give attention to the words which I have written upon my monument! And may this monument enlighten him as to procedure and administration, the judgments which I have pronounced, and the decisions which I have rendered for the land! And let him rightly rule his black-headed people; let him pronounce judgments for them and render for them decisions! Let him root out the wicked and the evil from his land! Let him promote the welfare of his people!

Hammurabi, the king of justice [*misharum*], to whom Shamash has committed truth [*kittum*], am I. My words are weighty; my deeds are unrivaled; only to the fool are they vain; to the wise they are worthy of every praise.

5 The Instruction of Ptah-hotep

Early Material Values in Egypt

The values pursued in a heroic age are ordinarily found described in epic poetry. Egypt has left us no epics, but the same zest for worldly success and fame can be seen in texts inscribed within the tombs of the kings and nobles of the Old Kingdom (2700–2200 B.C.). The "Instruction of Ptah-hotep," the author of which lived around 2450 B.C. and was the vizier of a Fifth Dynasty pharaoh, is an outstanding example of this early type of literary expression. It consists of precepts addressed to the vizier's son instructing the young man in rules of behavior conducive to worldly success. These early precepts reflect no concern for a life beyond the grave, nor do they emphasize mankind's dependence upon the gods. No moral principles of good and evil are involved; right and wrong are equivalent to what works and makes for success and what does not.[1]

In this text, therefore, the term *maat*, usually translated "justice," should be viewed in the more static sense of "norm," "path," "tradition," "truth," "correctness," referring to that which is customary and accepted because it has always worked. (Compare Babylonian *kittum*, discussed in the introduction to Selection 4.) Ptah-hotep has no doubts about the value and eternity of *maat*, the creation of the gods that can be handed down from father to son like property: "A great thing is *maat*, enduring and surviving; it has not been upset since the time of its creator.... it endureth long, and a man can say, 'It is the property

---

1. "The high achievements of the Old Kingdom were attained by an amoral people, or rather by a people whose morals were pragmatic and materialistic." John A. Wilson. *The Burden of Egypt* (Chicago, Ill.: University of Chicago Press, 1951), p. 110.

Based on the translation by F. L. Griffith in *A Library of the World's Best Literature*, XIII, pp. 5329–40.

of my father.'" But we shall see that this materialistic conception of *maat* did not outlast the Old Kingdom; it was undermined by the total disorder produced by a time of troubles—the "Dark Period" or First Intermediate Period—and men were forced to create a new foundation for conduct in positive moral principles and redefine *maat* to embrace justice and righteousness. (Compare Babylonian *misharum*, discussed in the Introduction to Selection 4.)

Preface: Royal Approval

The mayor and vizier Ptah-hotep said: "O king, my lord, years come on, old age is here, decrepitude arrives, weakness is renewed.... Let it be commanded of your servant to make a staff of old age: let my son be set in my place. Let me tell him the sayings of those who obeyed, the conduct of them of old, of them who listened to the gods...."

Said the majesty of this god [the king]: "Instruct him in the sayings of the past.... Speak to him, for no one is born wise."

Title and Aim

Beginning of the maxims of good words spoken by the ... mayor and vizier, Ptah-hotep, teaching the ignorant to know according to the standard of good words, expounding the profit to him who shall listen to it, and the injury to him who shall transgress it. He said to his son:

Intellectual Snobbery

Be not arrogant because of your knowledge, and be not puffed up because you are a learned man. Take counsel with the ignorant as with the learned, for the limits of art cannot be reached, and no artist is perfect in his skills. Good speech is more hidden than the precious greenstone, and yet it is found among slave girls at the millstones....

Leadership and "Maat"

If you are a leader, commanding the conduct of many, seek out every good aim, so that your policy may be without error. A great thing is truth [*maat*], enduring and surviving; it has not been upset since the time of Osiris. He who departs from its laws is punished. It is the right path for him who knows nothing. Wrongdoing has never brought its venture safe to port. Evil may win riches, but it is the strength of truth that it endures long, and a man can say, "I learned it from my father."...

Conduct as a Guest at Table

If you are a guest at the table of one who is greater than you, take what he offers as it is set before you. Fix your gaze upon what is before you, and pierce not your host with many glances, for it is an abomination to force your attention upon him. Speak not to him until he calls, for no one knows what may be offensive; speak when he addresses you, for then your words will give satisfaction. Laugh when he laughs; that will please him, and then whatever you do will please him....

Patience with Suppliants

If you are a leader be kind in hearing the speech of a suppliant. Treat him not roughly until he has unburdened himself of what he was minded to tell you. The complainant sets greater store by the easing of his mind than by the accomplishments of that for which he came. As for him who deals roughly with a petition, men say, "Why, pray, has he ignored it?" Not all that men plead for ever comes to pass, but to listen kindly soothes the heart.

Relations with Women

If you wish to prolong friendship in a house into which you enter as master, brother or friend, or any place that you enter, beware of approaching the women. No place in which that is done prospers. There is no wisdom in it. A thousand men are turned aside from their own good because of a little moment, like a dream, by tasting which death is reached.... He who ... lusts after women, no plan of his will succeed.

Greed

If you want your conduct to be good, free from every evil, then beware of greed. It is an evil and incurable sickness. No man can live with it; it causes divisions between fathers and mothers, and between brothers of the same mother; it parts wife and husband; it is a gathering of every evil, a bag of everything hateful. A man thrives if his conduct is right. He who follows the right course wins wealth thereby. But the greedy man has no tomb....

Marriage

If you are prosperous you should establish a household and love your wife as is fitting. Fill her belly and clothe her back. Oil is the tonic for her body. Make her heart glad as long as you live. She is a profitable field for her lord....

Conduct in Council

If you are a worthy man sitting in the council of his lord, confine your attention to excellence. Silence is more valuable than chatter. Speak only when you know you can resolve difficulties. He who gives good counsel is an artist, for speech is more difficult than any craft....

Behavior in Changed Circumstances

If you are now great after being humble and rich after being poor in the city that you know, do not boast because of what happened to you in the past. Be not miserly with your wealth, which has come to you by the god's [the king's] gift. You are no different from another to whom the same has happened.

Obedience to a Superior

Bend your back to him who is over you, your superior in the administration; then your house will endure by reason of its property, and your reward will come in due season. Wretched is he who opposes his superior, for one lives only so long as he is gracious....

Exhortation to Listen

If you listen to my sayings, then all your affairs will go forward. They are precious; their memory goes on in the speech of men because of their excellence. If each saying is carried on, they will never perish in this land....

If the son of a man accepts what his father says, no plan of his will fail.... Failure follows him who does not listen. He who hears is established; he who is a fool is crushed....

A son who hears is a follower of Horus: there is good for him who listens. When he reaches old age and attains honor, he tells the like to his children, renewing the teaching of his father. Every man teaches as he has acted. He speaks to his children so that they may speak to their children....

Conclusion

May you succeed me, may your body be sound, may the king be well pleased with all that is done, and may you spend many years of life! It is no small thing that I have done on earth; I have spent one hundred and ten years of life, which the king gave me, and with rewards greater than those of the ancestors, by doing right for the king until death.

Social and Work Life

Ancient monuments, documentary records and literary texts, which constitute a greater portion of our historical evidence, were mostly commissioned by kings, priests, and other members of the elite and reflect their own concerns and points of view. These monuments and texts rarely have cause to speak to the lives and experiences of more ordinary men and women in society. Yet even representations of daily life could at times find their way on to royal funeral art just as the occasional reference to the imagined experience of a commoner might come to be included in a text made by and for the high and mighty. One group at least did break this pattern: the literate scribes of the Ancient Near East had both the means and the cultural habit to inscribe themselves onto the historical record.

6 Work Songs from Ancient Egypt

Voices of Ordinary Men and Women

"Let not your hearts be weary...."

Ancient monuments and texts only occasionally depict the lives of the vast majority of ordinary men and women. Even with its abundant records, ancient Egypt's case is much the same. The rich and powerful Egyptians were concerned about the afterlife, which they essentially saw as a continuation of the life in this world, and thus they sometimes included representations of ordinary life in their tombs.

The following texts are work songs that Egyptian laborers sang as they carried out their tasks and that happened to have been recorded and inscribed onto the walls of tombs (from around the sixteenth to the fourteenth century B.C.). Some accompanied paintings of scenes from daily life. The songs were sung by a leader and a chorus: the leader led off and the chorus gave the answering refrains. While we already know a great deal about the beliefs and ideas of the royal and aristocratic Egyptians from the monuments they left, these songs may convey some of the hopes and dreams of rather ordinary men and women in the Old Egyptian Kingdom as they carried out their daily work.

Songs of the Peasants

Over the Plowmen

A good day—it is cool.
The cattle are pulling,
And the sky does according to our desire—
Let us work for the noble!

Over the Reapers

The answering refrain which they say:
This good day is come forth in the land;
The north wind is come forth,
And the sky does according to our desire—
Let us work as our hearts may be bound!

A Threshing Song

In the same scene, a herdsman is shown driving his cattle around and around to thresh out the grain. He urges them that their monotonous labor is easy and profitable.

From James B. Pritchard, ed., *Ancient Near Eastern Texts Relating to the Old Testament*, 3rd rev. ed. with Supplement (Princeton: Princeton University Press, 1969). Reprinted by permission of Princeton University Press.

A wall painting with scenes of agricultural work from an Egyptian tomb from ca. 1451–1413 B.C. On the bottom right is the image of the deceased watching over his estate's farm workers. On the top right, men with sickles harvest the crops; on the top left, women gather flax for weaving. On the bottom left appear scenes of ploughing and sowing; in the middle stands the abundant harvest that attests to the wealth of the deceased.

Thresh ye for yourselves, thresh ye for yourselves, O cattle!
Thresh ye for yourselves, thresh ye for yourselves!
Straw to eat, and barley for your masters—
Let not your hearts be weary, for it is cool.

A Song of the Herdsman

The herdsman is in the water among the fish:
He talks with the shad
And greets the oxyrhynchus fish.
O west, where is the herdsman (now),
The herdsman of the west?

A Song of the Carriers of a Palanquin

Go down into the palanquin, and it is sound!
Go down into the palanquin, and it is well!
The carrying-poles are on the support of the carriers.
O palanquin of Ipi, be as heavy as I wish—
It is pleasanter full than when it is empty!

Songs at a Feast

An annual feast at Luxor had as its central feature the journey of the god Amon and of the pharaoh by boat between Karnak and Luxor. In scenes of the time of Tut-ankh-Amon (about 1361–1352 B.C.) in the Temple of Luxor, this ceremonial procession is shown, and there are two brief songs about a drinking place set up for the entertainment of the sailors of the god's boat. Each song is credited to the goddess Neith....

> A drinking place has been built for the menials who are in
>   the ship of ships.
> The ways of the earth god have been hacked open for
>   (thee), O Nile, great and high!
> Mayest thou satisfy thy Two Goddesses
> For Horus, the strong of arm,
> When the god is rowed, carrying the beauty of the god.
> Hat-Hor has effected the beauty of good things
> For King (Tut-ankh-Amon), beloved of Amon and favored
>   of the gods.
> So says Neith.

Close by this song there are depicted eight women with sistrum-rattles and eight priests clapping their hands in measure. The text relates them to the songs of the entire scene.

> The chorus which sets the measure while the journey takes
>   place upon the river:
> O Amon, Lord of the Thrones of the Two Lands, thou
>   livest forever!

In the same large scene units of soldiers swing along in gay and vigorous movement ... [and] breaking out in jubilant dance. Over the heads of the soldiers their songs of festivity are written....

> [The leaders of] the army. They rejoice in front of his maj-
>   esty: "How happy is the good ruler when he has con-
>   veyed Amon, for He decreed to him valor against the
>   south and victory against [the north]! Amon [is the god
>   who decreed] the victory to the ruler!"
> [The soldiers] who are following his majesty. The chorus of
>   jubilation which they utter: "King (Tut-ankh-Amon) is
>   conveying Him who begot him! Decreed for him was
>   kingship from the beginning of the lifetime of Re in
>   heaven. He is rewarded with valor and victory over every
>   foreign country that attacks him. Amon decreed the vic-
>   tory to King (Tut-ankh-Amon)! Amon is the god who
>   decreed the victory to the ruler!"

7 School Days in Sumer

"All the fine points of the scribal art"

By the early third millennium B.C., ancient Sumer had already developed into an urbanized and sophisticated civilization. It existed as a number of competing and mutually independent city-states that shared key cultural and institutional features. Among these are temples of the gods that stood at the hearts of the communities and the adoption of kingship as a form of government. Consisting of nobles, commoners, clients, and slaves, Sumerian societies were highly stratified with a commensurate degree of division of labor. The skilled labor of meticulously trained scribes made possible administrative and bureaucratic regimes that depended on literacy as a form of record-keeping. Using styluses to press Semitic Akkadian syllabic letter-forms onto clay tablets, these scribes created texts that, after they were accidentally fired and thereby preserved, later scholars would come upon and eventually decipher. Sumer developed the scribal art to a very high point during the second half of the third millennium B.C. The *edubba*, "house of tablets," was the Sumerian scribal school that imparted the professional skills of reading and writing to individuals who went on to serve in temples, royal courts, and civic institutions. The operations of these schools have come to light with the discovery of cuneiform texts representing exercises or practice writings. "From all these sources we get a picture of the Sumerian school, its aims and goals, its students and faculty, its curriculum and teaching techniques, which is quite unique for so early a period in the history of man" (Kramer p. 230). School children came from the well-to-do families in the city and were almost exclusively male. The curriculum was as traditional in cast as the discipline was harsh; after all, literacy in this mode required the mastery of technical skills that only long-suffering apprenticeship could provide.

The first text (A) reflects a schoolteacher's reminiscences of his earlier years as a young pupil, offering insight into both the harsh realities of school life as well as the sheer irrepressibility of youth. The second (B) is a school essay entitled "A Scribe and His Perverse Son" in which the narrator presents himself as a highly disappointed father who admonishes his wayward son for having failed to do well in school and, moreover, choosing not to continue in his (the father's) footsteps as a scribe. According to its editor and translator Samuel Noah Kramer, this text is "noteworthy as one of the first documents in the history of man in which the word 'humanity' (Sumerian, *namlulu*) is used not only to designate mankind but in the sense of conduct and behavior befitting human beings" (Kramer p. 243).

From Samuel Noah Kramer, *The Sumerians. Their History, Culture and Character* (Chicago, Ill.: University of Chicago Press, 1963), pp. 237–40, 244–46.

A.

I recited my tablet, ate my lunch, prepared my (new) tablet wrote it, finished it; then my model tablets were brought to me; and in the afternoon my exercise tablets were brought to me. When school was dismissed, I went home, entered the house, and found my father sitting there. I explained (?) my exercise-tablets to my father, (?) recited my tablet to him, and he was delighted, (so much so) that I attended him (with joy)....

[the schoolboy turned to the house servants....]

I am thirsty, give me water to drink; I am hungry, give me bread to eat; wash my feet, set up (my) bed, I want to go to sleep. Wake me early in the morning, I must not be late lest my teacher cane me.

When I arose early in the morning, I faced my mother and said to her: "Give me my lunch, I want to go to school!" My mother gave me two rolls, and I set out; my mother gave me two rolls, and I went to school. In school the fellow in charge of punctuality said: "Why are you late?" Afraid and with pounding heart, I entered before my teacher and made a respectful curtsy.

> My headmaster read my tablet, said:
> "There is something missing," caned me.
> *(There follow two unintelligible lines)*
> The fellow in charge of neatness (?) said:
> "You loitered in the street and did not straighten up (?) your
>   clothes (?)," caned me.
> *(There follow five unintelligible lines)*
> The fellow in charge of silence said:
> "Why did you talk without permission," caned me.
> The fellow in charge of the assembly (?) said:
> "Why did you 'stand at ease (?)' without permission," caned
>   me.
> The fellow in charge of good behavior said:
> "Why did you rise without permission," caned me.
> The fellow in charge of the gate said:
> "Why did you go out from (the gate) without permission,"
>   caned me.
> The fellow in charge of the whip said:
> "Why did you take .. without permission," caned me.
> The fellow in charge of Sumerian said:
> "Why didn't you speak Sumerian," caned me.
> My teacher (*ummia*) said:
> "Your hand is unsatisfactory," caned me.
> (And so) I (began to) hate the scribal art, (began to) neglect
>   the scribal art.
> My teacher took no delight in me; (even) [stopped teaching
>   (?)] me his skill in the scribal art; in no way prepared me
>   in the matters (essential) to the art (of being) a "young
>   scribe," (or) the art (of being) a "big brother."...

[he turned to his father and asked him to approach the teacher....]

Give him a bit extra salary, (and) let him become more kindly (?); let him be free (for a time) from arithmetic; (when) he counts up all the school affairs of the students, let him count me (too among them; that is, perhaps, let him not neglect me any longer).

To that which the schoolboy said, his father gave heed. The teacher was brought from school, and after entering in the house, he was seated on the "big chair." The schoolboy attended and served him, and whatever he learned of the scribal art, he unfolded to his father. Then did the father in the joy of his heart say joyfully to the headmaster of the school: "My little fellow has opened (wide) his hand, (and) you made wisdom enter there; you showed him all the fine points of the scribal art; you made him see the solutions of the mathematical and arithmetical (problems), you (taught him how) to make deep (?) the cuneiform script (?)...."

[the father turned to his household servants....]

Pour for him *irda*-oil, bring it to the table for him. Make fragrant oil flow like water on his stomach (and) back; I want to dress him in a garment, give him some extra salary, put a ring on his hand....

[the servants did as told and the teacher spoke to the schoolboy....]

Young fellow, (because) you hated not my words, neglected them not, (may you) complete the scribal art from beginning to end. Because you gave me everything without stint, paid me a salary larger than my efforts (deserve), (and) have honored me, may Nidaba, the queen of guardian angels, be your guardian angel; may your pointed stylus write well for you; may your exercises contain no faults. Of your brothers, may you be their leader; of your friends may you be their chief; may you rank the highest among the school graduates, satisfy (?) all who walk (?) to and from in (?) the palaces. Little fellow, you "know" (your) father, I am second to him; that homage be paid to you, that you be blessed— may the god of your father bring this about with firm hand; he will bring prayer and supplication to Nidaba, your queen, as if it were a matter for your god. Thus, when you put a kindly hand on the ... of the teacher, (and) on the forehead of the "big brother," then (?) your young comrades will show you favor. You have carried out well the school's activities, you are a man of learning. You have exalted Nidaba, the queen of learning; O Nidaba, praise!

B.

"Where did you go?"

"I did not go anywhere."

"If you did not go anywhere, why do you idle about? Go to school, stand before your 'school-father' (professor), recite your assignment open your schoolbag, write your tablet, let your 'big brother' write your new tablet for you. After you have finished your assignment and reported to your monitor, come to me, and do not wander about in the street. Come now, do you know what I said?"

"I know, I'll tell it to you."

"Come, now, repeat it to me."

"I'll repeat it to you."

"Tell it to me."

"I'll tell it to you."

"Come on, tell it to me."

"You told me to go to school, recite my assignment, open my school bag, write my tablet, while my 'big brother' is to write my new tablet. After finishing my assignment, I am to proceed to my work and to come to you after I have reported to my monitor. That's what you told me.

"Come now, be a man. Don't stand about in the public square or wander about the boulevard. When walking in the street, don't look all around. Be humble and show fear before your monitor. When you show terror, the monitor will like you.

(About fifteen lines destroyed)

"You who wander about in the public square, would you achieve success? Then seek out the first generations. Go to school, it will be of benefit to you. My son, seek out the first generations, inquire of them.

"Perverse one over whom I stand watch—I would not be a man did I not stand watch over my son—I spoke to my kin, compared its men, but found none like you among them.

"What I am about to relate to you turns the fool into a wise man, holds the snake as if by charms, and will not let you accept false phrases.

"Because my heart had been sated with weariness of you, I kept away from you and heeded not your fears and grumblings—no, I heeded not your fears and grumblings. Because of your clamorings, yes, because of your clamorings, I was angry with you—yes, I was angry with you. Because you do not look to your humanity, my heart was carried off as if by an evil wind. Your grumblings have put an end to me, you have brought me to the point of death.

"I, never in all my life, did I make you carry reeds to the canebrake. The reed rushes which the young and the little carry, you, never in your life did you carry them. I never said to you 'Follow my caravans.' I never sent you to work, to plow my field. I never sent you to work, to dig up my field. I never sent you to work as a laborer. 'Go, work and support me,' I never in my life said to you.

"Others like you support their parents by working. If you spoke to your kin and appreciated them, you would emulate them. They provide 10 *gur* [about 180 cubic meters] of barley each—even the young ones provided their fathers with 10 *gur* each. They multiplied barley for their father, maintained him in barley, oil, and wool. But you, you're a man when it comes to perverseness, but compared to them you're not a man at all. You certainly don't labor like them—they are the sons of fathers who make their sons labor, but me—I didn't make you work like them.

"I, night and day am I tortured because of you. Night and day you waste in pleasures. You have accumulated much wealth, have expanded far and wide, have become fat, big, broad, powerful, and puffed. But your kin waits expectantly for your misfortune and will rejoice at it because you looked not to your humanity."

(Here follows an obscure passage of forty-one lines… ; the essay then concludes with the father's poetic blessing:)

From him who quarrels with you may Nanna, your god,
   save you,
From him who attacks you may Nanna, your god, save you,
May you find favor before your god,
May your humanity exalt you, neck and breast,
May you be the head of your city's sages,
May your city utter your name in favored places,
May your god call you by a good name,
May you find favor before your god Nanna,
May you be regarded with favor by the goddess Ningal.

Divine Worship, Kingship, and Nation

Kingship emerged as a dominant political and religious institution throughout the ancient Near East and shaped the destinies of major states such as Egypt and more peripheral societies such as ancient Israel, which—by tradition— strongly resisted monarchy as a form of government in its early years. The royal rulers acknowledged that their power stemmed from their close association with the patron gods of their community, and they represented themselves as privileged intermediaries who stood between these divine beings and the rest of society. The sacral form of kingship that became prevalent was deeply tied to rites of divine worship as well as to the communal self-understanding of these early societies.

8 Unas Pyramid Incantations

The Afterlife of a Pharaoh

Unlike the preceding instruction of Ptah-hotep, this text is very much concerned with life after death. Much of official Egyptian religion was connected to the preparation of the dead for passage into the afterlife. The wealthiest

From Miriam Lichtheim, *The Old and Middle Kingdoms*, vol. 1, *Ancient Egyptian Literature: A Book of Readings* (Berkeley and Los Angeles: University of California Press, 1973), pp. 30–39.

and most privileged members of society could and did make the most elaborate arrangements to ensure that this transition to the afterlife was smooth
and successful. In addition to constructing monumental burial complexes, the
most extravagant ones being the great pyramids, and carefully mummifying
the bodies of the deceased, the Egyptians also performed rituals for the
dead. Among such rituals was the use of religious incantations that invoked
the names of the gods, calling on them to aid the recently deceased as they
crossed the boundary between the living and the dead. Many of these pro-
nouncements were carved on the walls inside or very near the burial chamber
in which the sarcophagus containing the mummified body was placed. It is
likely that Egyptian priests recited these incantations as part of the burial ceremonies of the dead.

The oldest collection of such incantations to have survived comes from
the Pyramid of Unas, the pharaoh of the Old Kingdom's Fifth Dynasty, which
ended around 2300 B.C. It served as a model for other similar collections
found in pyramids built by subsequent pharaohs. The following incantations
are chosen from the 288 utterances in the Unas collection. They reveal to us
the official Egyptian views regarding the afterlife and deification of a
deceased ruler. A major element is the story of the king's resurrection and
ascent into the skies, where he would become a member of the pantheon
of the gods.

A wall painting showing the ceremony of the "opening of the mouth," part of the
mummification process thought to give the dead a new body in preparation for passage
into the afterlife. Priests anoint the mouth of the mummy, held by the god Anubis, with
a ritual instrument featuring a ram's head. From the New Kingdom (ca. 1550–1090 B.C.).
Now in the British Museum.

Utterance 217

Sarcophagus Chamber, South Wall

THE KING JOINS THE SUN-GOD

Re-Atum, this Unas comes to you,
A spirit indestructible
Who lays claim to the place of the four pillars!
Your son comes to you, this Unas comes to you,
May you cross the sky united in the dark,
May you rise in lightland, the place in which you shine!
Seth, Nephthys, go proclaim to Upper Egypt's gods
And their spirits:
"This Unas comes, a spirit indestructible,
If he wishes you to die, you will die,
If he wishes you to live, you will live!"
Re-Atum, this Unas comes to you,
A spirit indestructible
Who lays claim to the place of the four pillars!
Your son comes to you, this Unas comes to you,
May you cross the sky united in the dark,
May you rise in lightland, the place in which you shine!
Orisis, Isis, go proclaim to Lower Egypt's gods
And their spirits:
"This Unas comes, a spirit indestructible,
Like the morning star above Hapy,
Whom the water-spirits worship;
Whom he wishes to live will live,
Whom he wishes to die will die!"

Re-Atum, this Unas comes to you,
A spirit indestructible
Who lays claim to the place of the four pillars!
Your son comes to you, this Unas comes to you,
May you cross the sky united in the dark,
May you rise in lightland, the place in which you shine!
Thoth, go proclaim to the gods of the west
And their spirits:
"This Unas comes, a spirit indestructible,
Decked above the neck as Anubis,
Lord of the western height,
He will count hearts, he will claim hearts,
Whom he wishes to live will live,
Whom he wishes to die will die!"

Re-Atum, this Unas comes to you,
A spirit indestructible
Who lays claim to the place of the four pillars!

Your son comes to you, this Unas comes to you,
May you cross the sky united in the dark,
May you rise in lightland, the place in which you shine!
Horus, go proclaim to the powers of the east
And their spirits:
"This Unas comes, a spirit indestructible,
Whom he wishes to live will live,
Whom he wishes to die will die!"
Re-Atum, your son comes to you,
Unas comes to you,
Raise him to you, hold him in your arms,
He is your son, of your body, forever!...

Utterance 245

Passage to the Sarcophagus Chamber, South Wall

THE KING JOINS THE STARS

This Unas comes to you, O Nut,
This Unas comes to you, O Nut,
He has consigned his father to the earth,
He has left Horus behind him.
Grown are his falcon wings,
Plumes of the holy hawk;
His power has brought him,
His magic has equipped him!

THE SKY-GODDESS REPLIES

Make your seat in heaven,
Among the stars of heaven,
For you are the Lone Star, the comrade of Hu!
You shall look down on Osiris,
As he commands the spirits,
While you stand far from him;
You are not among them,
You shall not be among them!

Utterance 253

Antechamber, West Gable

THE KING IS CLEANSED IN THE FIELD OF RUSHES

Cleansed is he who is cleansed in the Field of Rushes:
Cleansed is Re in the Field of Rushes;

Cleansed is he who is cleansed in the Field of Rushes:
Cleansed is this Unas in the Field of Rushes.
Hand of Unas in hand of Re!
O Nut, take his hand!
O Shu, lift him up!
O Shu, lift him up!

In the ensuing incantations, the Pharaoh crosses the Eastern Sky, summons the sky's ferryman, feeds on the power of ancestors and gods, and finally ascends to the heavens.

He has encompassed the two skies,
He has circled the two shores;
Unas is the great power that overpowers the powers,
Unas is the divine hawk, the great hawk of hawks,
Whom he finds on his way he devours whole.
Unas's place is before all the nobles in lightland,
Unas is god, oldest of the old,
Thousands serve him, hundreds offer to him,
Great-Power rank was given him by Orion, father of gods.

Unas has risen again in heaven,
He is crowned as lord of lightland.
He has smashed bones and marrow,
He has seized the hearts of gods,
He has eaten the Red, swallowed the Green.
Unas feeds on the lungs of the wise,
Likes to live on hearts and their magic;
Unas abhors licking the coils of the Red
But delights to have their magic in his belly.

The dignities of Unas will not be taken from him,
For he has swallowed the knowledge of every god;
Unas's lifetime is forever, his limit is eternity
In his dignity of "If-he-likes-he-does if-
    he-hates-he-does-not,"
As he dwells in lightland for all eternity.
Lo, their power is in Unas's belly,
Their spirits are before Unas as broth of the gods,
Cooked for Unas from their bones.
Lo, their power is with Unas,
Their shadows (are taken) from their owners,
For Unas is of those who risen is risen, lasting lasts.
Not can evildoers harm Unas's chosen seat
Among the living in this land for all eternity!

Utterance 304

Antechamber, North Wall

THE KING CLIMBS TO THE SKY ON A LADDER

Hail, daughter of Anubis, above the hatches of heaven,
Comrade of Thoth, above the ladder's rails,
Open Unas's path, let Unas pass!
Hail, Ostrich on the Winding Water's shore,
Open Unas's path, let Unas pass!
Hail, four-horned Bull of Re,
Your horn in the west, your horn in the east,
Your southern horn, your northern horn:
Bend your western horn for Unas, let Unas pass!
"Are you a pure westerner?"
"I come from Hawk City."
Hail, Field of Offerings,
Hail to the herbs within you!
"Welcome is the pure to me!"

Utterance 309

Antechamber, North Wall

THE KING SERVES THE SUN-GOD

Unas is gods' steward, behind the mansion of Re,
Born of Wish-of-the-gods, who is in the bow of Re's bark;
Unas squats before him,
Unas opens his boxes,
Unas unseals his decrees,
Unas seals his dispatches,
Unas sends his messengers who tire not,
Unas does what Unas is told.

9 Hymn to the Aton

Religious Reform and Monotheism

The high moral and ethical content that Egyptian religion acquired during the Middle Kingdom became obscured during the New Kingdom as the various

From James B. Pritchard, ed., *Ancient Near Eastern Texts Relating to the Old Testament*, 3rd rev. ed. with Supplement (Princeton: Princeton University Press, 1969), pp. 370–71. Reprinted by permission of the Princeton University Press. Translated by John A. Wilson.

priesthoods successfully sought after power and wealth. The priests of the supreme god Amun or Amon vied with the god-king pharaoh for power, and those of Osiris venally stressed outward forms and paid only lip service to the moral content of their popular funerary religion. A monument to this latter development is the Book of the Dead, largely composed of formulas, often magical, which were sold by the priests to guarantee to the deceased access to the hereafter without regard for his sins. Even the "Negative Confession" was sold as a magical spell with instructions for use that guaranteed that "for him on whose behalf this book was made, ... He cannot be held back at the door of the West, but he shall be ushered in with the Kings of Upper and Lower Egypt, and he shall be in the retinue of Osiris. Right and true a million times!"

This common development in the history of religion produced in Egypt an equally common reaction—a reformer arose who challenged the power of the priests and taught a more exalted type of religion. This was the pharaoh Amenhotep IV (1369–1353 B.C.) of the Eighteenth Dynasty, who ignored the military and administrative problems of the Egyptian empire to concentrate upon religious reform. He changed his name from Amenhotep, "Amon is satisfied," to Akhenaten, "He who is serviceable to the Aten," and his magnificent hymn to the Aten or Aton, the sun disc, as the source of all life is not only filled with profound religious feeling, but also for the first time in the history of religion expresses a belief in a sole god of the universe.

Akhenaten's reformed religion did not last beyond his own lifetime. A powerful combination of forces compelled his weak successor, the well-known Tutankhamen, to renounce the new teaching. The priests of the old cults bitterly resented the domination they had lost at the hands of the man they called "the criminal"; the army leaders were ever ready to revolt against a king who neglected Egypt's imperial interests in Palestine and Syria; and the great mass of the people longed for the solace of the blessed hereafter, promised them by the Osiris cult and not contained in the intellectualized teaching of the reformer-king.

> Thou appearest beautifully on the horizon of heaven,
> Thou living Aton, the beginning of life!
> When thou art arisen on the eastern horizon,
> Thou hast filled every land with thy beauty.
> Thou art gracious, great, glistening, and high over every
>   land;
> Thy rays encompass the lands to the limit of all that thou
>   hast made:
> As thou art Re, thou reachest to the end of them;
> Thou subduest them for thy beloved son.
> Though thou art far away, thy rays are on earth;
> Though thou art in their faces, no one knows thy going.
>
> When thou settest in the western horizon,
> The land is in darkness, in the manner of death.
> They sleep in a room, with heads wrapped up,
> Nor sees one eye the other.

All their goods which are under their heads might be stolen,
But they would not perceive it.
Every lion is come forth from his den;
All creeping things, they sting.
Darkness is a shroud, and the earth is in stillness,
For he who made them rests in his horizon.

At daybreak, when thou arisest on the horizon,
When thou shinest as the Aton by day,
Thou drivest away the darkness and givest thy rays.
The Two Lands are in festivity every day,
Awake and standing upon their feet,
For thou has raised them up.
Washing their bodies, taking their clothing,
Their arms are raised in praise at thy appearance.
All the world, they do their work....

Creator of seed in women,
Thou who makest fluid into man,
Who maintainest the son in the womb of his mother,
Who soothest him with that which stills his weeping,
Thou nurse even in the womb,
Who givest breath to sustain all that he has made!
When he descends from the womb to breathe
On the day when he is born,
Thou openest his mouth completely,
Thou suppliest his necessities.
When the chick in the egg speaks within the shell,
Thou givest him breath within it to maintain him.
When thou has made him his fulfillment within the egg, to
    break it,
He comes forth from the egg to speak at his completed time;
He walks upon his legs when he comes forth from it....

How manifold it is, what thou hast made!
They are hidden from the face of man.
O sole god, like whom there is no other!
Thou didst create the world according to thy desire,
Whilst thou wert alone:
All men, cattle, and wild beasts,
Whatever is on earth, going upon its feet,
And what is on high, flying with its wings.

The countries of Syria and Nubia, the land of Egypt,
Thou settest every man in his place,
Thou suppliest their necessities:
Everyone has his food, and his time of life is reckoned.

Their tongues are separate in speech,
And their natures as well;
Their skins are distinguished,
As thou distinguishest the foreign peoples.
Thou makest a Nile in the underworld,
Thou bringest it forth as thou desirest
To maintain the people of Egypt
According as thou madest them for thyself,
The lord of all of them, wearying himself with them,
The lord of every land, rising for them,
The Aton of the day, great of majesty.

All distant foreign countries, thou makest their life also,
For thou has set a Nile in heaven,
That it may descend for them and make waves upon the
    mountains,
Like the great green sea,
To water their fields in their towns.
How effective they are, thy plans, O lord of eternity!
The Nile in heaven, it is for the foreign peoples
And for the beasts of every desert that go upon their feet;
While the true Nile comes from the underworld for
    Egypt....

Thou art in my heart,
And there is no other that knows thee
Save thy son [Akhenaten],
For thou hast made him well-versed in thy plans and in thy
    strength.

The world came into being by thy hand,
According as thou hast made them.
When thou hast risen they live,
When thou settest they die.
Thou art lifetime thy own self,
For one lives only through thee.

Eyes are fixed on beauty until thou settest.
All work is laid aside when thou settest in the west.
But when thou risest again,
Everything is made to flourish for the king,...
Since thou didst found the earth
And raise them up for thy son,
Who came forth from thy body:
The king of Upper and Lower Egypt,... Ahk-en-Aton,...
    and the Chief Wife of the King... Nefert-iti, living and
    youthful forever and ever.

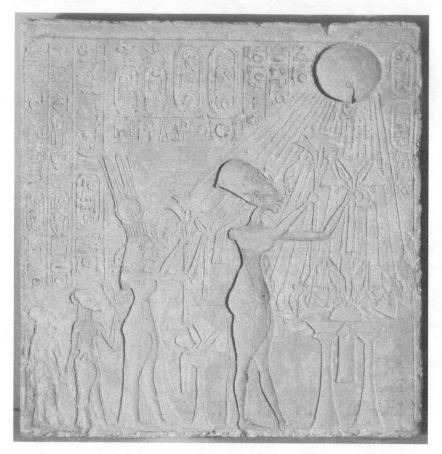

A stone carving from the Temple of Amarna representing Pharaoh Akhentaton (ca. 1380–1312 B.C.) and Queen Nefertiti, probably accompanied by their daughter on the far left, in the act of worshipping the Sun Disc representing the god Aton. The sun's rays terminate in hands, two of which hold the "ankh," the Egyptian hieroglyph and sign for "life."

10 God and the Early Hebrews

In the Hebrew Bible or Old Testament, the name "Hebrew" is first applied to the wandering patriarch Abram ("exalted father"), later called Abraham ("father of a multitude" of nations), a ninth-generation descendant of Shem, one of Noah's three sons who is considered to be the progenitor of the Semites. The nomadic character of the early Hebrews, described in several places in the Old Testament, is confirmed by references made in Mesopotamian documents of the early second millennium B.C. to nomads called "Habiru," a word phonetically identical with "Hebrew" and meaning "wanderer" or "outsider." When the Hebrews finally settled and became a nation, they took the name "Israelites" ("Children of Israel"), just as other Habiru groups became known as Moabites, Ammonites, Edomites, and Midianites.

A. HEBREW ORIGINS: THE PATRIARCHS

The following selections from the Book of Genesis describe the two most important episodes in the patriarchal history of the Hebrews: the wandering of Abraham and his family (about 1800 B.C.) from Ur in Sumer to the promised land of Canaan, and the descent into Egypt (about 1700 B.C.) of a group of Hebrews, fleeing famine, who followed the call of Joseph, son of Jacob (also called Israel) and great-grandson of Abraham. Modern scholars attribute Joseph's rise to power in Egypt, and the hospitable reception of his father's people there, to the presence of the mainly Semitic Hyksos, a multi-ethnc confederation of northern peoples that came to dominate Egypt by the eighteenth century B.C.

Abraham: The First Patriarch

Now these are the generations of Terah: Terah begat Abram, Nahor, and Haran; and Haran begat Lot. And Haran died before his father Terah in the land of his nativity, in Ur of the Chaldees. And Abram and Nahor took them wives; the name of Abram's wife was Sarai; and the name of Nahor's wife, Milcah, the daughter of Haran, the father of Milcah, and the father of Iscah. But Sarai was barren, she had no child.

And Terah took Abram his son, and Lot the son of Haran his son's son, and Sarai his daughter-in-law, his son Abram's wife; and they went forth with them from Ur of the Chaldees, to go unto the land of Canaan; and they came unto Haran, and dwelt there. And the days of Terah were two hundred and five years; and Terah died in Haran.

Now the Lord had said unto Abram, Get thee out of thy country, and from thy kindred, and from thy father's house, and unto a land that I will show thee: And I will make of thee a great nation, and I will bless thee, and make thy name great; and thou shalt be a blessing; And I will bless them that bless thee, and curse him that curseth thee; and in thee shall all families of the earth be blessed.

So Abram departed, as the Lord had spoken unto him; and Lot went with him: and Abram was seventy and five years old when he departed out of Haran. And Abram took Sarai his wife, and Lot his brother's son, and all their substance that they had gathered, and the souls that they had gotten in Haran; and they went forth to go into the land of Canaan; and into the land of Canaan they came. And Abram passed through the land unto the place of Shechem, unto the plain of Moreh. And the Canaanite was then in the land.

From Genesis 11–12, 46–47; the King James Version of the Bible.

And the Lord appeared unto Abram, and said, Unto thy seed will I give this land; and there builded he an altar unto the Lord, who appeared unto him. And he removed from thence unto a mountain on the east of Beth-el and pitched his tent, having Beth-el on the west, and Hai on the east; and there he builded an altar unto the Lord, and called upon the name of the Lord. And Abram journeyed, going on still toward the south....

Joseph: The Migration to Egypt

And Israel took his journey with all that he had, and came to Beer-sheba, and offered sacrifices unto the God of his father Isaac. And God spake unto Israel in the visions of the night, and said, Jacob, Jacob. And he said, Here am I. And he said, I am God, the God of thy father: fear not to go down into Egypt; and I will there make of thee a great nation, I will go down with thee into Egypt; and I will also surely bring thee up again: and Joseph shall put his hand upon thine eyes.

And Jacob rose up from Beer-sheba: and the sons of Israel carried Jacob their father, and their little ones, and their wives, in the wagons which Pharaoh had sent to carry him. And they took their cattle, and their goods, which they had gotten in the land of Canaan, and came into Egypt, Jacob and all his seed with him: His sons, and his sons' sons with him, and his sons' daughters, and all his seed brought he with him into Egypt.... All the souls that came with Jacob into Egypt, which came out of his loins, besides Jacob's sons' wives, all the souls were threescore and six; ...

And he sent Judah before him unto Joseph, to direct his face unto Goshen; and they came into the land of Goshen. And Joseph made ready his chariot, and went up to meet Israel his father, to Goshen, and presented himself unto him; and he fell on his neck, and wept on his neck a good while. And Israel said unto Joseph, Now let me die, since I have seen thy face, because thou art yet alive.

And Joseph said unto his brethren, and unto his father's house, I will go up, and show Pharaoh, and say unto him, My brethren, and my father's house, which were in the land of Canaan, are come unto me; And the men are shepherds, for their trade hath been to feed cattle; and they have brought their flocks, and their herds, and all that they have. And it shall come to pass, when Pharaoh shall call you, and shall say, What is your occupation? That ye shall say, Thy servants' trade hath been about cattle from our youth until now, both we, and also our fathers: that ye may dwell in the land of Goshen; for every shepherd is an abomination unto the Egyptians.

Then Joseph came and told Pharaoh, and said, My father and my brethren, and their flocks, and their herds, and all that they have, are come out of the land of Canaan, and, behold, they are in the land of Goshen. And he took some of his brethren, even five men, and presented them unto Pharaoh. And Pharaoh said unto his brethren, What is your occupation? And they said unto Pharaoh, Thy servants are shepherds, both we, and also our fathers. They said moreover unto Pharaoh, For to sojourn in the land are we come; for thy servants have no pasture for their flocks; for the famine is sore in the land of Canaan; now, therefore, we pray thee, let thy servants dwell in the land of Goshen.

And Pharaoh spake unto Joseph saying, Thy father and thy brethren are come unto thee: The land of Egypt is before thee; in the best of the land make thy father and brethren to dwell; in the land of Goshen let them dwell: and if thou knowest any men of activity among them, then make them rulers over my cattle.

And Joseph brought in Jacob his father, and set him before Pharaoh: and Jacob blessed Pharaoh. And Pharaoh said unto Jacob, How old art thou? And Jacob said unto Pharaoh, The days of the years of my pilgrimage are a hundred and thirty years; few and evil have the days of the years of my life been, and have not attained unto the days of the years of the life of my fathers in the days of their pilgrimage. And Jacob blessed Pharaoh, and went out from before Pharaoh.

And Joseph placed his father and his brethren, and gave them a possession in the land of Egypt, in the best of the land, in the land of Rameses, as Pharaoh had commanded. And Joseph nourished his father, and his brethren, and all his father's household, with bread, according to their families.

B. BONDAGE AND DELIVERANCE

The Hebrews in Egypt experienced a sudden reversal of their fortunes after about 1570 B.C. when the first pharaoh of the Eighteenth Dynasty succeeded in ousting the Hyksos. Under a pharaoh "which knew not Joseph," the Hebrews became state slaves and were forced to build fortress-cities in the Delta. After approximately a century and a half of oppression, God called on Moses to be his instrument in freeing the Hebrews from bondage. In answer to Moses' request, God tells him that his name YHWH, a form of the verb "to be" that is usually written Yahweh or Jehovah (most English translations of the Old Testament follow the practice, begun by Jewish priests who considered the name too sacred to be pronounced, of substituting the word "Lord"). Shortly after 1300 B.C., Moses led the "mixed multitude" in a dramatic escape across the Sea of Reeds (erroneously translated "Red Sea"), a shallow estuary of the Gulf of Suez, and into "the wilderness" of Sinai.

Bondage in Egypt

And Joseph died, and all his brethren, and all that generation. And the children of Israel were fruitful, and increased abundantly, and multiplied, and waxed exceeding mighty, and the land was filled with them.

Now there arose up a new king over Egypt, which knew not Joseph. And he said unto his people, Behold the people of the children of Israel are more and mightier than we: Come on, let us deal wisely with them; lest they multiply, and it come to pass that, when there falleth out any war, they join also unto our enemies, and fight against us, and so get them up out of the land. Therefore

From Exodus 1–3, 6, 12–14; the King James Version of the Bible.

they did set over them taskmasters to afflict them with their burdens. And they built for Pharaoh treasure cities, Pithom and Raamses. But the more they afflicted them, the more they multiplied and grew. And they were grieved because of the children of Israel. And the Egyptians made the children of Israel to serve with rigor; And they made their lives bitter with hard bondage, in mortar, and in brick, and in all manner of service in the field; all their service, wherein they made them serve, was with rigor....

God's Call to Moses

And it came to pass in process of time, that the king of Egypt died: and the children of Egypt sighed by reason of the bondage, and they cried, and their cry came up unto God by reason of the bondage. And God heard their groaning, and God remembered his covenant with Abraham, with Isaac, and with Jacob. And God looked upon the children of Israel, and God had respect unto them.

Now Moses kept the flock of Jethro his father-in-law, the priest of Midian: and he led the flock to the back side of the desert, and came to the mountain of God, even to Horeb.[1] And the Angel of the Lord appeared unto him in a flame of fire out of the midst of a bush: and he looked, and, behold, the bush burned with fire, and the bush was not consumed. And Moses said, I will not turn aside, and see this great sight, why the bush is not burnt.

And when the Lord saw that he turned aside to see, God called unto him out of the midst of the bush, and said, Moses, Moses. And he said, Here am I. And he said, Draw not nigh hither: put off thy shoes from off thy feet; for the place whereon thou standest is holy ground. Moreover he said, I am the God of thy father, the God of Abraham, the God of Isaac, and the God of Jacob. And Moses hid his face, for he was afraid to look upon God.

And the Lord said, I have surely seen the affliction of my people which are in Egypt, and have heard their cry by reason of their taskmasters; for I know their sorrows; and I am come down to deliver them out of the hand of the Egyptians, and to bring them out of that land unto a good land and a large, unto a land flowing with milk and honey; unto the place of the Canaanites, and the Hittites, and the Amorites, and the Perizzites, and the Hivites, and the Jebusites. Now, therefore, behold the cry of the children of Israel is come unto me: and I have also seen the oppressions wherewith the Egyptians oppress them. Come now therefore, and I will send thee unto Pharaoh, that thou mayest bring forth my people the children of Israel out of Egypt.

And Moses said unto God, Who am I, that I should go unto Pharaoh, and that I should bring forth the children of Israel out of Egypt? And he said, Certainly I will be with thee; and this shall be a token unto thee, that I have sent thee: When thou hast brought forth the people out of Egypt, ye shall serve God upon this mountain.

---

1. Named Sinai elsewhere in the Book of Genesis.

And Moses said unto God, Behold when I come unto the children of Israel, and shall say unto them, the God of your fathers hath sent me unto you; and they shall say to me, What is his name? What shall I say unto them?

And God said unto Moses, I AM THAT I AM: Thus shalt thou say unto the children of Israel, I AM hath sent me unto you. And God said moreover unto Moses, Thus shalt thou say unto the children of Israel, The Lord God of your fathers, the God of Abraham, the God of Isaac, and the God of Jacob, hath sent me unto you: this is my name forever, and this is my memorial unto all generations....

And I am sure that the king of Egypt will not let you go, no, not by a mighty hand. And I will stretch out my hand, and smite Egypt with all my wonders which I will do in the midst thereof: and after that he will let you go. And I will give this people favor in the sight of the Egyptians; and it shall come to pass that, when ye go, ye shall not go empty: But every woman shall borrow of her neighbor, and of her that sojourneth in her house, jewels of silver, and jewels of gold, and raiment: and ye shall put them upon your sons and upon your daughters; and ye shall spoil the Egyptians....

And God spake unto Moses, and said unto him, I am the Lord: And I appeared unto Abraham, unto Isaac, and unto Jacob, by the name of God Almighty; but by my name JEHOVAH was I not known to them. And I have also established my covenant with them to give them the land of Canaan, the land of their pilgrimage, wherein they were strangers....

The Escape

Now the sojourning of the children of Israel, who dwelt in Egypt, was four hundred and thirty years. And it came to pass at the end of the four hundred and thirty years, even the selfsame day it came to pass, that all the hosts of the Lord went out from the land of Egypt. It is a night to be much observed unto the Lord for bringing them out from the land of Egypt: this is that night of the Lord to be observed of all the children of Israel in their generations....

And it came to pass, when Pharaoh had let the people go, that God led them not through the way of the land of the Philistines, although that was near; for God said, Lest peradventure the people repent when they see war, and they return to Egypt: But God led the people about, through the way of the wilderness of the Red Sea: and the children of Israel went up harnessed out of the land of Egypt. And Moses took the bones of Joseph with him: for he had straitly sworn the children of Israel, saying, God will surely visit you; and ye shall surely carry up my bones away hence with you. And they took their journey from Succoth, and encamped in Etham, in the edge of the wilderness. And the Lord went before them by day in a pillar of a cloud, to lead them the way; and by night in a pillar of fire, to give them light; to go by day and night....

And it was told the king of Egypt that the people fled: and the heart of Pharaoh and his servants was turned against the people, and they said, Why have we done this, that we have let Israel go from serving us? And he made ready his chariot, and took his people with him: And he took six hundred chosen chariots, and all the chariots of Egypt, and captains over every one of them.

And the Lord hardened the heart of Pharaoh king of Egypt, and he pursued after the children of Israel: and the children of Israel went out with a high hand. But the Egyptians pursued after them, all the horses and chariots of Pharaoh, and his horsemen, and his army, and overtook them encamping by the sea....

And when Pharaoh drew nigh, the children of Israel lifted up their eyes, and behold, the Egyptians marched after them; and they were sore afraid: and the children of Israel cried out unto the Lord. And they said unto Moses, Because there were no graves in Egypt, has thou taken us away to die in the wilderness? Wherefore has thou dealt thus with us, to carry us forth out of Egypt? Is not this the word that we did tell thee in Egypt, saying, Let us alone, that we may serve the Egyptians? For it had been better for us to serve the Egyptians, than that we should die in the wilderness.

And Moses said unto the people, Fear yet not, stand still, and see the salvation of the Lord, which he will show to you today: for the Egyptians whom ye have seen today, yet shall see them no more for ever. The Lord shall fight for you, and ye shall hold your peace....

And the Angel of God, which went before the camp of Israel, removed and went behind them; and the pillar of the cloud went from before their face and stood behind them: And it came between the camp of the Egyptians and the camp of Israel; and it was a cloud and darkness to them, but it gave light by night to these: so that the one came not near the other all the night. And Moses stretched out his hand over the sea; and the Lord caused the sea to go back by a strong east wind all that night, and made the sea dry land, and the waters were divided. And the children of Israel went into the midst of the sea upon the dry ground: and the waters were a wall unto them on their right hand, and on their left. And the Egyptians pursued, and went in after them to the midst of the sea, even all Pharaoh's horses, his chariots, and his horsemen. And it came to pass, that in the morning watch the Lord looked unto the host of the Egyptians through the pillar of fire and of the cloud, and troubled the host of the Egyptians, And took off their chariot wheels, that they drave them heavily: so that the Egyptians said, Let us flee from the face of Israel; for the Lord fighteth for them against the Egyptians.

And the Lord said unto Moses, Stretch out thine hand over the sea, that the waters may come again upon the Egyptians, upon their chariots and upon their horsemen. And Moses stretched forth his hand over the sea, and the sea returned to his strength when the morning appeared; and the Egyptians fled against it; and the Lord overthrew the Egyptians in the midst of the sea. And the waters returned, and covered the chariots, and the horsemen, and all the host of Pharaoh that came into the sea after them; there remained not so much as one of them. But the children of Israel walked upon dry land in the midst of the sea; and the waters were a wall unto them on their right hand, and on their left.

Thus the Lord saved Israel out of the hand of the Egyptians; and Israel saw the Egyptians dead upon the seashore. And Israel saw that great work which the Lord did upon the Egyptians: and the people feared the Lord, and believed the Lord, and his servant Moses.

C. THE SINAI COVENANT

Because it led to the formation of the nation of Israel, the Hebrews looked upon their deliverance from bondage in Egypt as the decisive divine act in their history. The sequel to the Exodus was the Sinai pact or covenant between Yahweh and the nation of Israel, which replaced the older covenants made with individual patriarchs such as Abraham. From this time on, the Israelites considered themselves the chosen people of the Lord, who would protect them in return for obedience to his Law.

Like an eagle bearing its young on its wings, Yahweh brought the people to Mount Sinai for the purpose of announcing, through Moses, the laws of the covenant. These laws are of two types, absolute and conditional. Absolute law is best illustrated by the Decalogue, or Ten Commandments: it expresses unconditional demands and general principles. Conditional law, on the other hand, is case law such as we have seen in the Code of Hammurabi: its object is the detailed regulation of society—if or when a circumstance occurs, then a specific legal consequence will follow. Most of the many laws of the Covenant Code, which follows the Decalogue, are of this conditional type. Because they reflect a settled agricultural rather than a nomadic life, most scholars conclude that they are from a period several centuries later than Moses and the Decalogue. They bear the stamp of the later settled life in Palestine, where Babylonian cultural influences—including law—had long been felt. This is thought to explain certain similarities between the Covenant Code and the Code of Hammurabi.

On the third new moon after the people of Israel had gone forth out of the land of Egypt, on that day they came into the wilderness of Sinai.... and there Israel encamped before the mountain. And Moses went up to God, and the Lord called him out of the mountain, saying, "Thus you shall say to the house of Jacob, and tell the people of Israel: You have seen what I did to the Egyptians, and how I bore you on eagles' wings and brought you to myself. Now therefore, if you will obey my voice and keep my covenant, you shall be my own possession among all peoples; for all the earth is mine, and you shall be to me a kingdom of priests and a holy nation. These are the words which you shall speak to the children of Israel." ...

And the Lord said to Moses, "Go to the people and consecrate them today and tomorrow, and let them wash their garments, and be ready by the third day; for on the third day the Lord will come down upon Mount Sinai in the sight of all the people. And you shall set bounds for the people round about, saying, 'Take heed that you do not go up into the mountain or touch the border of it; whoever touches the mountain shall be put to death; no hand shall touch him, but he shall be stoned or shot; whether beast or man, he shall not live.' When the trumpet sounds a long blast, they shall come up to the mountain." So Moses went down from the mountain to the people, and consecrated the people; and they washed their garments. And he said to the people, "Be ready by the third day; do not go near a woman."

On the morning of the third day there were thunders and lightnings, and a thick cloud upon the mountain, and a very loud trumpet blast, so that all the people who were in the camp trembled. Then Moses brought the people out of the camp to meet God; and they took their stand at the foot of the mountain. And Mount Sinai was wrapped in smoke, because the Lord descended upon it in fire; and the smoke of it went up like the smoke of a kiln, and the whole mountain quaked greatly. And as the sound of the trumpet grew louder and louder, Moses spoke, and God answered him in thunder. And the Lord came down upon Mount Sinai, to the top of the mountain; and the Lord called Moses to the top of the mountain, and Moses went up....

The Ten Commandments

And God spoke all these words, saying,

"I am the Lord your God, who brought you out of the land of Egypt, out of the house of bondage.

"You shall have no other gods before me.[2]

"You shall not make yourself a graven image, or any likeness of anything that is in heaven above, or that is in the earth beneath, or that is in the water under the earth; you shall not bow down to them or serve them; for I the Lord your God am a jealous God, visiting the iniquity of the fathers upon the children of the third and the fourth generation of those who hate me, but showing steadfast love to thousands of those who love me and keep my commandments.

"You shall not take the name of the Lord your God in vain, for the Lord will not hold him guiltless who takes his name in vain.

"Remember the sabbath day, to keep it holy. Six days you shall labor, and do all your work; but the seventh day is a sabbath to the Lord your God; in it you shall not do any work, you, or your son, or your daughter, or your manservant, or your maidservant, or your cattle, or the sojourner who is within your gates; for in six days the Lord made heaven and earth, the sea, and all that is in them, and rested the seventh day; therefore the Lord blessed the sabbath day and hallowed it.

"Honor your father and your mother, that your days may be long in the land which the Lord your God gives you.

"You shall not kill.

"You shall not commit adultery.

"You shall not steal.

"You shall not bear false witness against your neighbor.

"You shall not covet your neighbor's house; you shall not covet your neighbor's wife, or his manservant, or his maidservant, or his ox, or his ass, or anything that is your neighbor's." ...

---

2. The existence of other gods is here not denied.

Various Laws of the Covenant Code

"Now these are the ordinances which you shall set before them. When you buy a Hebrew slave, he shall serve six years, and in the seventh he shall go out free, for nothing. If he comes in single, he shall go out single; if he comes in married, then his wife shall go out with him. If his master gives him a wife and she bears him sons and daughters, the wife and her children shall be her master's and he shall go out alone. But if the slave plainly says, 'I love my master, my wife, and my children; I will not go out free,' then his master shall bring him to God, and he shall bring him to the door or the doorpost; and his master shall bore his ear with an awl; and he shall serve him for life.

"When a man sells his daughter as a slave, she shall not go out as the male slaves do. If she does not please her master, who has designated her for himself, then he shall let her be redeemed; he shall have no right to sell her to a foreign people, since he has dealt faithlessly with her. If he designates her for his son, he shall deal with her as with a daughter. If he takes another wife to himself, he shall not diminish her food, her clothing, or her marital rights. And if he does not do these three things for her, she shall go out for nothing, without payment of money.

"Whoever strikes a man so that he dies shall be put to death. But if he did not lie in wait for him, but God let him fall into his hand, then I will appoint for you a place to which he may flee. But if a man willfully attacks another to kill him treacherously, you shall take him from my altar, that he may die.

"Whoever strikes his father or his mother shall be put to death.

"Whoever steals a man, whether he sells him or is found in possession of him, shall be put to death.

"Whoever curses his father or his mother shall be put to death.

"When men quarrel and one strikes the other with a stone or with his fist and the man does not die but keeps his bed, then if the man rises again and walks abroad with his staff, he that struck him shall be clear; only he shall pay for the loss of his time, and shall have him thoroughly healed.

"When a man strikes his slave, male or female, with a rod and the slave dies under his hand, he shall be punished. But if the slave survives a day or two, he is not to be punished; for the slave is his money.

"When men strive together, and hurt a woman with child, so that there is a miscarriage, and yet no harm follows, the one who hurt her shall be fined, according as the woman's husband shall lay upon him; and he shall pay as the judges determine. If any harm follows, then you shall give life for life, eye for eye, tooth for tooth, hand for hand, foot for foot, burn for burn, wound for wound, stripe for stripe....[3]

---

3. This law, similar to those of Hammurabi (see Selection 4), reflects social progress. It substitutes a stipulated legal punishment appropriate to the injury for the practice of the blood feud common to many archaic societies. Compare, for example, the boastful Song of Lamech in Genesis 4:23–24: "I have slain a man for wounding me, / a young man for striking me. / If Cain is avenged sevenfold, / truly Lamech seventy-sevenfold."

"When a man causes a field or vineyard to be grazed over, or lets his beast loose and it feeds in another man's field, he shall make restitution from the best in his own field and in his own vineyard....

"For every breach of trust, whether it is for ox, for ass, for sheep, for clothing, or for any kind of lost thing, of which one says, 'That is it,' the case of both parties shall come before God; he whom God shall condemn shall pay double to his neighbor....

"If a man seduces a virgin who is not betrothed, and lies with her, he shall give the marriage present for her, and make her his wife. If her father utterly refuses to give her to him, he shall pay money equivalent to the marriage present for virgins.

"You shall not permit a witch to live....

"You shall not wrong a stranger or oppress him, for you were strangers in the land of Egypt. You shall not afflict any widow or orphan. If you do afflict them, and they cry out to me, I will surely hear their cry; and my wrath will burn, and I will kill you with the sword, and your wives shall become widows and your children fatherless.

"If you lend money to any of my people with you who is poor, you shall not be to him as a creditor, and you shall not exact interest from him. If ever you take your neighbor's garment in pledge, you shall restore it to him before the sun goes down; for that is his only covering, it is his mantle for his body; in what else shall he sleep? And if he cries to me, I will hear it, for I am compassionate....

"The first-born of your sons you shall give to me. You shall do likewise with your oxen and with your sheep: seven days it shall be with its dam; on the eighth day you shall give it to me....

"Three times in the year you shall keep a feast to me. You shall keep the feast of unleavened bread; as I commanded you, you shall eat unleavened bread for seven days at the appointed time in the month of Abib, for in it you came out of Egypt. None shall appear before me empty-handed. You shall keep the feast of harvest, of the first fruits of your labor, of what you sow in the field. You shall keep the feast of ingathering at the end of the year, when you gather in from the field the fruit of your labor. Three times in the year shall all your males appear before the Lord God....

"The first of the first fruits of your ground you shall bring into the house of the Lord your God.

"You shall not boil a kid in its mother's milk...."[4]

Moses came and told the people all the words of the Lord and all the ordinances; and all the people answered with one voice, and said, "All the words which the Lord has spoken we will do." And Moses wrote all the words of the Lord.

---

4. Recovered Canaanite literature reveals this peculiar prohibition to be a borrowing from Canaanite religion.

D. THE PEOPLE DEMAND A KING

"To govern us like all the nations"

The ineffectiveness of the loose Israelite tribal confederacy in the face of danger became fully apparent in the eleventh century. By that time the Philistines, who shortly after 1200 B.C. had settled along the coast of what is now called the Gaza Strip, were threatening to conquer all of Palestine. Israel's fortunes reached their lowest ebb around 1050 B.C. when the Philistines destroyed the central sanctuary of the confederacy at Shiloh and carried away the Ark of the Covenant as a trophy of war. The resulting demand of the people for a more effective type of centralized government was reinforced by the prevalence of injustice under the weak rule of judges. "In those days," we read in Judges 17:6, "there was no king in Israel; every man did what was right in his own eyes." This desire to end lawlessness is touched on in the beginning of the following selection, in which the great prophet-judge Samuel, before reluctantly giving in to the demand of the people for a king, presents the conservative argument against strong, centralized government.

When Samuel became old, he made his sons judges over Israel.... Yet his sons did not walk in his ways, but turned aside after gain; they took bribes and perverted justice.

Then all the elders of Israel gathered together and came to Samuel at Ramah, and said to him, "Behold, you are old and your sons do not walk in your ways; now appoint for us a king to govern us like all the nations." But the thing displeased Samuel when they said, "Give us a king to govern us." And Samuel prayed to the Lord. And the Lord said to Samuel, "Hearken to the voice of the people in all that they say to you, for they have not rejected you, but they have rejected me from being king over them. According to all deeds which they have done to me, from the day I brought them up out of Egypt even to this day, forsaking me and serving other gods, so they are also doing to you. Now then, hearken to their voice; only, you shall solemnly warn them, and show them the ways of the king who shall reign over them."

So Samuel told all the words of the Lord to the people who were asking a king from him. He said, "These will be the ways of the king who will reign over you: he will take your sons and appoint them to his chariots and to be his horsemen, and to run before his chariots; and he will appoint for himself commanders of thousands and commanders of fifties, some to plow his ground and to reap his harvest, and to make him implements of war and the equipment of his chariots. He will take your daughters to be perfumers and cooks and bakers. He will take the best of your fields and vineyards and olive orchards and give them to his servants. He will take the tenth of your grain and of your vineyards and give it to his officers and to his servants. He will take your menservants and maidservants, and the best of your cattle and your asses, and put them to his work. He will take the tenth of your flocks, and you shall be his slaves. And in that day you will cry out because of your king, whom you have chosen for yourselves; but the Lord will not answer you in that day."

But the people refused to listen to the voice of Samuel; and they said, "No! but we will have a king over us, that we also may be like all the nations, and that our king may govern us and go out before us and fight our battles." And when Samuel had heard all the words of the people, he repeated them in the ears of the Lord. And the Lord said to Samuel, "Hearken to their voice, and make them a king." Samuel then said to the men of Israel, "Go every man to his city."

E. THE UNITED KINGDOM OF ISRAEL

"A great name, like the name of the great ones of the earth"

The beginning of the Hebrew monarchy under Saul (1020–1000 B.C.) was not auspicious. The prey of his own moody nature, jealous of the fame of the boy-hero David, and plagued by tribal disloyalty and the opposition of Samuel and the conservatives, Saul died tragically in his last unsuccessful battle with the Philistines. During the reign of the popular David (1000–961 B.C.), both the foreign and the domestic problems of Israel were solved. The Philistines were defeated and restricted to a narrow coastal plain, and among Israel's other neighbors, from the Gulf of Aqaba in the south to the Euphrates in the north, only the Phoenicians were not subdued. Tribal independence was greatly weakened when David established a national capital and a centralized administration at Jerusalem, a Canaanite stronghold that he captured despite the boast of its inhabitants that even "the blind and the lame" could defend it. Royal administrators replaced the elders and judges of the confederacy period, and a census of all Israel was taken, to be used as a basis for military service, taxes, and forced labor. David shrewdly provided a religious sanction for the new monarchy by transferring with great pomp and ceremony the recovered Ark of the Covenant to Jerusalem, and by building a royal shrine—the forerunner of Solomon's great Temple—that he placed in the hands of an official priesthood. Thus was established the doctrine of the divine origin of David's monarchy and that of his successors.

David's son Solomon (961–922 B.C.) completed the work of his father in establishing an oriental type of centralized monarchy. Tribal loyalties were further weakened by the division of Israel into twelve administrative districts, which did not always correspond to the old tribal territories. Each district was supervised by a royal official, who was also responsible for provisioning the royal household during one month of the year. The construction of the Temple, together with a palace complex, government buildings, and "store cities," required the frequent levying of taxes and an oppressive program of forced labor. The "chariot cities" served to protect the trade that flowed through Palestine from places such as Egypt, Arabia, Phoenicia, and Cilicia (Kue). In cooperation with the Phoenicians of Tyre, Solomon built a trading fleet to exploit the Red Sea area, and the "hard questions" that the Queen of Sheba travelled a thousand miles from southwest Arabia to put to Solomon are thought to have been connected with Solomon's monopoly of trade in this area.

Yet as Samuel had foretold when he sought to dissuade the people from their desire to have a king, the price of monarchy was high—limitations on freedom and exploitation by a despot. The resentment caused by Solomon's oppressive policies led to a revolution at his death that split the kingdom into two parts: Israel (or Ephraim) in the north and Judah in the south. Threatened by the rise of new great empires, these two weak kingdoms were to have little rest before Israel fell to the Assyrians (722 B.C.) and Judah to the Chaldeans (586 B.C.). Unlike the northern Israelites, the Judeans, or Jews, survived their exile in Babylonia and returned to their homeland after Cyrus the Persian conquered Babylon (539 B.C.) and liberated them. From the turmoil of these years rose the great Hebrew prophets of doom and righteousness, who saw the history of their people as one of stubborn rebellion against "the one eternal, living God [who] is working out his own sovereign purpose for the good of his creatures, first for his chosen people, and through them for the rest of mankind."[5]

"David Reigned Over All Israel"

Then all the tribes of Israel came to David at Hebron, and said, "Behold, we are your bone and flesh. In times past when Saul was king over us, it was you that led out and brought in Israel; and the Lord said to you, 'You shall be shepherd of my people Israel, and you shall be prince over Israel.'" So all the elders of Israel came to the king at Hebron; and King David made a covenant with them at Hebron before the Lord, and they anointed David king over Israel. David was thirty years old when he began to reign, and he reigned forty years....

And the king and his men went to Jerusalem against the Jebusites, the inhabitants of the land, who said to David, "You will not come in here, but the blind and the lame will ward you off"—thinking, "David cannot come in here." Nevertheless David took the stronghold of Zion, that is, the city of David.... And David built the city round about from the Millo inward. And David became greater and greater, for the Lord, the God of hosts, was with him.

And Hiram king of Tyre sent messengers to David, and cedar trees, also carpenters and masons who built David a house. And David perceived that the Lord had established him king over Israel, and that he had exalted his kingdom for the sake of his people Israel....

So David went and brought up the ark of God ... to the city of David with rejoicing; and when those who bore the ark of the Lord had gone six paces, he sacrificed an ox and a fatling. And David danced before the Lord with all his might; and David was girded with a linen ephod. So David and all the house

---

5. Millar Burrows, "Ancient Israel," in *The Idea of History in the Ancient Near East*, edited by Robert C. Dentan (New Haven, Conn.: Yale University Press, 1955), p. 128.

of Israel brought up the ark of the Lord with shouting, and with the sound of the horn....

Now when the king dwelt in his house, and the Lord had given him rest from all his enemies round about, the king said to Nathan the prophet, "See now, I dwell in a house of cedar, but the ark of God dwells in a tent." And Nathan said to the king, "Go, do all that is in your heart; for the Lord is with you."

But that same night the word of the Lord came to Nathan, "Go and tell my servant David, 'Thus says the Lord: Would you build me a house to dwell in? I have not dwelt in a house since the day I brought up the people of Israel from Egypt to this day, but I have been moving about in a tent for my dwelling. In all places where I have moved with all the people of Israel, did I speak a word with any of the judges of Israel, whom I commanded to shepherd my people Israel, saying, "Why have you not built me a house of cedar?"' Now therefore thus you shall say to my servant David, 'Thus says the Lord of hosts, I took you from the pasture, from following the sheep, that you should be prince over my people Israel; and I have been with you wherever you went, and have cut off all your enemies from before you; and I will make you a great name, like the names of the great ones of the earth. And I will appoint a place for my people Israel, and will plant them, that they may dwell in their own place, and be disturbed no more; and violent men shall afflict them no more, as formerly, from the time I appointed judges over my people Israel; and I will give you rest from all your enemies. Moreover the Lord declares to you that the Lord will make you a house. When your days are fulfilled and you lie down with your fathers, I will raise up your son after you, who shall come forth from your body, and I will establish his kingdom. He shall build a house for my name, and I will establish the throne of his kingdom for ever. I will be his father, and he shall be my son. When he commits iniquity, I will chasten him with the rod of men; but I will not take my steadfast love from him, as I took it from Saul, whom I put away from before you. And your house and your kingdom shall be made sure for ever before me; your throne shall be established for ever.'" In accordance with all these words, and in accordance with all this vision, Nathan spoke to David....

After this David defeated the Philistines and subdued them, and David took Methegh-ammah out of the hand of the Philistines.

And he defeated Moab,... And the Moabites became servants to David and brought tribute.

David also defeated Hadadezer the son of Rehob, king of Zobah, as he went to restore his power at the river Euphrates. And David took from him a thousand and seven hundred horsemen, and twenty thousand foot soldiers; and David hamstrung all the chariot horses, but left enough for a hundred chariots. And when the Syrians of Damascus came to help Hadadezer king of Zobah, David slew twenty-two thousand men of the Syrians. Then David put garrisons in Aram of Damascus; and the Syrians become servants to David and brought tribute. And the Lord gave victory to David wherever he went....

When Toi king of Hamath heard that David had defeated the whole army of Hadadezer, Toi sent his son Joram to King David, to greet him, and to congratulate him; for Hadadezer had often been at war with Toi. And Joram brought with him articles of silver, of gold, and of bronze; these also King David dedicated to the Lord, together with the silver and gold which he dedicated from all the nations he subdued, from Edom, Moab, the Ammonites, the Philistines, Amalek, and from the spoil of Hadadezer the son of Rehob, king of Zobah.

And David won a name for himself. When he returned, he slew eighteen thousand Edomites in the valley of Salt. And he put garrisons in Edom; throughout all Edom he put garrisons, and all the Edomites became David's servants. And the Lord gave victory to David wherever he went.

So David reigned over all Israel; and David administered justice and equity to all his people....

"King Solomon: His High Officials"

King Solomon was king over all Israel, and these were his high officials: Azariah the son of Zadok was the priest; Elihoreph and Ahijah the sons of Shisha were secretaries; Jehoshaphat the son of Ahilud was recorder; Benaiah the son of Jehoiada was in command of the army; Zadok and Abiathar were priests; Asariah the son of Nathan was over the officers; Zabud the son of Nathan was priest and king's friend; Ahishar was in charge of the palace; and Adoniram the son of Abda was in charge of the forced labor.

Solomon had twelve officers over all Israel, who provided food for the king and his household; each man had to make provision for one month in the year. These were their names: Ben-hur, in the hill country of Ephraim; Ben-deker, in Makaz....

Solomon's provision for one day was thirty measures of fine flour, and sixty measures of meal, ten fat oxen, and twenty pasture-fed cattle, a hundred sheep, besides harts, gazelles, roebucks, and fatted fowl. For he had dominion over all the region west of the Euphrates from Tiphsah to Gaza, over all the kings west of the Euphrates; and he had peace on all sides round about him. And Judah and Israel dwelt in safety, from Dan even to Beer-sheba, every man under his vine and under his fig tree, all the days of Solomon....

"The House Solomon Built for the Lord"

Now Hiram king of Tyre sent his servants to Solomon, when he heard that they had anointed him king in place of his father; for Hiram always loved David. And Solomon sent word to Hiram, "You know that David my father could not build a house for the name of the Lord his God because of the warfare with which his enemies surrounded him, until the Lord put them under the soles of his feet. But now the Lord my God has given me rest on every side; there is neither adversary nor misfortune. And so I purpose to build a house for the name of the Lord my God, as the Lord said to David my father, 'Your son, whom I will set upon your throne in your place, shall build the house of my name.' Now therefore command that cedars of Lebanon be cut for me; and my servants will join your servants, and I will pay you for your services such wages as you set; for you know that there is no one among us who knows how to cut timber like the Sidonians."

When Hiram heard the words of Solomon, he rejoiced greatly, and said, "Blessed be the Lord this day, who has given to David a wise son to be over this great people.".... So Hiram supplied Solomon with all the timber of cedar and cypress that he desired, while Solomon gave Hiram twenty thousand cors of wheat as food for his household, and twenty thousand cors of beaten oil. Solomon gave this to Hiram year by year. And the Lord gave Solomon wisdom, as he promised him; and there was peace between Hiram and Solomon; and the two of them made a treaty.

King Solomon raised a levy of forced labor out of all Israel; and the levy numbered thirty thousand men. And he sent them to Lebanon, ten thousand a month in relays; they would be a month in Lebanon and two months at home; Adoniram was in charge of the levy. Solomon also had seventy thousand burden-bearers and eighty thousand hewers of stone in the hill country, besides Solomon's three thousand three hundred chief officers who were over the work, who had charge of the people who carried on the work. At the king's command, they quarried out great, costly stones in order to lay the foundation of the house with dressed stones. So Solomon's builders and Hiram's builders and the men of Gebal did the hewing and prepared the timber and the stone to build the house.

In the four hundred and eightieth year after the people of Israel came out of the land of Egypt, in the fourth year of Solomon's reign over Israel, in the month of Ziv, which is the second month, he began to build the house of the Lord. The house which King Solomon built for the Lord was sixty cubits long, twenty cubits wide, and thirty cubits high [90 ∞ 30 ∞ 45 feet].... He was seven years in building it....

"Solomon Excelled All Kings in Riches and Wisdom"

King Solomon built a fleet of ships at Ezion-geber, which is near Eloth on the shore of the Red Sea, in the land of Edom. And Hiram sent with the fleet his servants, seamen who were familiar with the sea, together with the servants of Solomon; and they went to Ophir, and brought from there gold, to the amount of four hundred and twenty talents; and they brought it to King Solomon.

Now when the queen of Sheba heard of the fame of Solomon concerning the name of the Lord, she came to test him with hard questions. She came to Jerusalem with a very great retinue, with camels bearing spices, and very much gold, and precious stones; and when she came to Solomon, she told him all that was on her mind. And Solomon answered all her questions; there was nothing hidden from the king which he could not explain to her. And when the queen of Sheba had seen all the wisdom of Solomon, the house that he had built, the food of his table, the seating of his officials, and the attendance of his servants, their clothing, his cupbearers, and his burnt offerings which he offered at the house of the Lord, there was no more spirit in her.

And she said to the king, "The report was true which I heard in my own land of your affairs and of your wisdom, but I did not believe the reports until I came and my own eyes had seen it; and, behold, the half was not told me; your wisdom and prosperity surpass the report which I heard. Happy are your wives!

Happy are these servants, who continually stand before you and hear your wisdom! Blessed be the Lord your God, who has delighted in you and set you on the throne of Israel! Because the Lord loved Israel for ever, he has made you king, that you may execute justice and righteousness." Then she gave the king a hundred and twenty talents of gold, and a very great quantity of spices, and precious stones; never again came such an abundance of spices as these which the queen of Sheba gave to King Solomon....

And King Solomon gave to the queen of Sheba all that she desired, whatever she asked besides what was given her by the bounty of King Solomon. So she turned and went back to her own land, with her servants.

Now the weight of gold that came to Solomon in one year was six hundred and sixty-six talents of gold, besides that which came from the traders and from the traffic of the merchants, and from all the kings of Arabia and from the governors of the land. King Solomon made two hundred large shields of beaten gold; ... The king also made a great ivory throne, and overlaid it with the finest gold. The throne had six steps, and at the back of the throne was a calf's head, and on each side of the seat were arm rests and two lions standing beside the arm rests, while twelve lions stood there, one on each end of a step on the six steps. The like of it was never made in any kingdom. All King Solomon's drinking vessels were of gold, and all the vessels of the House of the Forest of Lebanon were of pure gold; none were of silver, it was not considered as anything in the days of Solomon. For the king had a fleet of ships of Tarshish at sea with the fleet of Hiram. Once every three years the fleet of ships of Tarshish used to come bringing gold, silver, ivory, apes, and peacocks.

Thus King Solomon excelled all the kings of the earth in riches and in wisdom. And the whole earth sought the presence of Solomon to hear his wisdom, which God had put into his mind. Every one of them brought his present, articles of silver and gold, garments, myrrh, spices, horses, and mules, so much year by year.

And Solomon gathered together chariots and horsemen; he had fourteen hundred chariots and twelve thousand horsemen, whom he stationed in the chariot cities and with the king in Jerusalem. And the king made silver as common in Jerusalem as stone, and he made cedar as plentiful as the sycamore of the Shephelah. And Solomon's import of horses was from Egypt and Kue, and the king's traders received them from Kue at a price. A chariot could be imported from Egypt for six hundred shekels of silver, and a horse for a hundred and fifty; and so through the king's traders they were exported to all the kings of the Hittites and the kings of Syria.

"Solomon Did What Was Evil in the Sight of the Lord"

Now King Solomon loved many foreign women: the daughter of Pharaoh, and Moabite, Ammonite, Edomite, Sidonian, and Hittite women, from the nations concerning which the Lord had said to the people of Israel, "You shall not enter into marriage with them, neither shall they with you, for surely they will turn away your heart after their gods"; Solomon clung to these in love. He had seven hundred wives, princesses, and three hundred concubines; and his wives turned away his heart. For when Solomon was old his wives turned away his heart after other gods; and his heart was not wholly true to the Lord his God, as was the heart of David his father. For Solomon went after Ashtoreth the goddess of the Sidonians, and after Milcom the abomination of the Ammonites. So Solomon did what was evil in the sight of the Lord, and did not wholly follow the Lord, as David his father had done. Then Solomon built a high place for Chemosh the abomination of Moab, and for Molech the abomination of the Ammonites, on the mountain east of Jerusalem. And so he did for all his foreign wives, who burned incense and sacrificed to their gods.

And the Lord was angry with Solomon, because his heart had turned away from the Lord, the God of Israel, who had appeared to him twice, and had commanded him concerning this thing, that he should not go after other gods; but he did not keep what the Lord commanded. Therefore the Lord said to Solomon, "Since this has been your mind and you have not kept my covenant and my statutes which I have commanded you, I will surely tear the kingdom from you and will give it to your servant. Yet for the sake of David your father I will not do it in your days, but I will tear it out of the hand of your son. However I will not tear away all the kingdom; but I will give one tribe to your son, for the sake of David my servant and for the sake of Jerusalem which I have chosen."

F. JEREMIAH: PROPHET OF THE NEW COVENANT

Between roughly 750 and 550 B.C., what is called the "prophetic revolution" raised the religion of the Hebrews to new heights. The great prophets who arose during these two centuries "spoke for" (from the Greek word pro-phetes) Yahweh in condemning social injustice and the general unfaithfulness of the people of Israel and Judah to the covenant with Yahweh. "I am filled with power," proclaimed Micah, "with the Spirit of the Lord, and with justice and might, to declare to Jacob his transgression, and to Israel its sin" (3:8). Amos, the first of these "literary" prophets, was a peasant shepherd of Judah who travelled to the northern kingdom of Israel to denounce the greed, violence, luxury, and idolatry that flourished there and to predict, as a consequence, the destruction of that kingdom by Assyria, called by Isaiah "the rod of Yahweh's anger." Driven back to the south, Amos became the first of the prophets to write down his message of Yahweh's demand for social justice and adherence to his covenant. Amos' successors among the prophets of the eighth century—Hosea, Micah, and Isaiah—elaborated on the same message that Micah summed up in a statement often cited as the essence of all higher religion: "He has showed you, O man, what is good; and what does the Lord require of you but to do justice, and to love kindness, and to walk humbly with your God?" (6:8)

From Jeremiah 7–8, 18, 23, 31; the Revised Standard Version of the Bible, copyright 1946 and 1952. Reprinted by permission of the National Council of the Churches of Christ.

One of the greatest of the prophets—so great that later generations of Jews referred to him as The Prophet—was Jeremiah. His career (626–586 B.C.) coincided with the troubled era that ended with the Babylonian conquest of Jerusalem and the kingdom of Judah in 586 B.C. and the exile of an estimated fifteen thousand leading Jews (Jeremiah escaped to Egypt). As illustrated by the following selections, Jeremiah's teachings in part echo those of the eighth-century prophets in condemning social injustice, "burnt offerings and sacrifices," and going "after other gods." Like Isaiah before him, Jeremiah affirms that Yahweh will save a "remnant" of his dispersed people and will raise up a king of the House of David to "execute justice and righteousness in the land." Such prophecies of the coming of a Messiah, "the Anointed One," were to sustain the hopes of the Jews for centuries and were also to prepare the way for Jesus.

But Jeremiah's most profound expression of hope is his preaching of a "new covenant" between God and his people. God destroys and overthrows but he also builds anew; he is like the potter who reworks the clay of a spoiled vessel into something new and better. The old vessel was the Sinai Covenant announced by Moses, which bound the nation as a whole. It failed because it became overlaid with ritual and ceremony formalized by priests and centered in the Temple. According to Jeremiah, God now demands a new covenant not with the nation but with each individual. External conformity is useless; what is needed is a moral and spiritual renewal on the part of each individual. Religion is now a matter of a person's own heart and conscience. No longer is the Lord to be viewed as he had described himself in the Book of Exodus: "a jealous God, visiting the iniquity of the fathers upon the children of the third and fourth generation of those who hate me" (see the section entitled "The Ten Commandments" in Selection 10C). Such teachings brought Jeremiah into conflict with the priests: "How can you say, 'We are wise, and the law of the Lord is with us'? But, behold, the false pen of the scribes has made it into a lie." Ultimately, however, his teachings made it possible for non-Jews to accept Judaism since they placed no stress on nationality or race. We know that Jesus admired Jeremiah above all other prophets, and his Sermon on the Mount was a profound expression of the new concept that God's law is written upon the individual heart rather than upon tablets of stone.

"Amend Your Ways and Your Doings"

The word that came to Jeremiah from the Lord: "Stand in the gate of the Lord's house, and proclaim there this word, and say, Hear the word of the Lord, all you men of Judah who enter these gates to worship the Lord. Thus says the Lord of hosts, the God of Israel, Amend your ways and your doings, and I will let you dwell in this place. Do not trust in these deceptive words: 'This is the temple of the Lord, the temple of the Lord, the temple of the Lord.'

"For if you truly amend your ways and your doings, if you truly execute justice one with another, if you do not oppress the alien, the fatherless or the widow, or shed innocent blood in this place, and if you do not go after other gods to your own hurt, then I will let you dwell in this place, in the land that I gave of old to your fathers for ever.

"Behold, you trust in deceptive words to no avail. Will you steal, murder, commit adultery, swear falsely, burn incense to Baal, and go after other gods that you have not known, and then come and stand before me in this house, which is called by my name, and say, 'We are delivered!'—only to go on doing all these abominations? Has this house, which is called by my name, become a den of robbers in your eyes? Behold, I myself have seen it, says the Lord. Go now to my place that was in Shiloh, where I made my name dwell at first, and see what I did to it for the wickedness of my people Israel. And now, because you have done all these things, says the Lord, and when I spoke to you persistently you did not listen, and when I called you, you did not answer, therefore I will do to the house which is called by my name, and in which you trust, and to the place which I gave to you and to your fathers, as I did to Shiloh. And I will cast you out of my sight, as I cast out all your kinsmen, all the offspring of Ephraim.[6]

"As for you, do not pray for this people, or lift up cry or prayer for them, and do not intercede with me, for I do not hear you. Do you not see what they are doing in the cities of Judah and in the streets of Jerusalem? The children gather wood, the fathers kindle fire, and the women knead dough, to make cakes for the queen of heaven [Astarte]; and they pour out drink offerings to other gods, to provoke me to anger. Is it I whom they provoke? says the Lord. Is it not themselves, to their own confusion? Therefore thus says the Lord God: Behold, my anger and my wrath will be poured out on this place, upon man and beast, upon the trees of the field and the fruit of the ground; it will burn and not be quenched."

Thus says the Lord of hosts, the God of Israel: "Add your burnt offerings to your sacrifices, and eat the flesh. For in the days that I brought them out of the land of Egypt, I did not speak to your fathers or command them concerning burnt offerings and sacrifices. But this command I gave them, 'Obey my voice, and I will be your God, and you shall be my people; and walk in all the way that I command you, that it may be well with you.' But they did not obey or incline their ear, but walked in their own counsels and the stubbornness of their evil hearts, and went backward and not forward. From the day that your fathers came out of the land of Egypt to this day, I have persistently sent all my servants the prophets to them, day after day; yet they did not listen to me, or incline their ear, but stiffened their neck. They did worse than their fathers.

"So you shall speak all these words to them, but they will not listen to you. You shall call to them, but they will not answer you. And you shall say to them, 'This is the nation that did not obey the voice of the Lord their God, and did not accept discipline; truth has perished; it is cut off from their lips....'

"You shall say to them, Thus says the Lord:
When men fall, do they not rise again?
If one turns away, does he not return?

---

6. The northern Kingdom of Israel, conquered by the Assyrians in 721 B.C. Ephraim was the most important of its ten tribes, each of whose leading people were deported ("the ten lost tribes of Israel"). In tradition, those who remained behind became mixed with alien colonists and were despised as "Samaritans" (from Samaria, capital of the Kingdom of Israel) by the Jews of the Kingdom of Judah.

Why then has this people turned away
    in perpetual backsliding?
They hold fast to deceit,
    they refuse to return.
I have given heed and listened,
    but they have not spoken aright;
no man repents of his wickedness,
    saying, 'What have I done?'
Every one turns to his own course,
    like a horse plunging headlong into battle.
Even the stork in the heavens
    knows her times;
and the turtledove, swallow, and crane
    keep the time of their coming;
But my people know not
    the ordinance of the Lord.

"How can you say, 'We are wise,
    and the law of the Lord is with us'?
But, behold, the false pen of the scribes
    has made it into a lie.
The wise men shall be put to shame,
    they shall be dismayed and taken;
lo, they have rejected the word of the Lord,
    and what wisdom is in them?
Therefore I will give their wives to others
    and their fields to conquerors,
because from the least to the greatest
    every one is greedy for unjust gain;
from prophet to priest
    every one deals falsely...."

"Like the Clay in the Potter's Hand"

The word that came to Jeremiah from the Lord: "Arise, and go down to the potter's house, and there I will let you hear my words." So I went down to the potter's house, and there he was working at his wheel. And the vessel he was making of clay was spoiled in the potter's hand, and he reworked it into another vessel, as it seemed good to the potter to do.

Then the word of the Lord came to me: "O house of Israel, can I not do with you as this potter has done? says the Lord. Behold, like the clay in the potter's hand, so are you in my hand, O house of Israel. If at any time I declare concerning a nation or a kingdom, that I will pluck up and break down and destroy it, and if that nation, concerning which I have spoken, turns from its evil, I will repent of the evil that I intended to do to it. And if at any time I declare concerning a nation or a kingdom that I will build and plant it, and if it does evil in my sight, not listening to my voice, then I will repent of the good which I had intended to do to it. Now, therefore, say to the men of Judah and the inhabitants of Jerusalem: 'Thus says the Lord, Behold I am shaping evil against you and devising a plan against you. Return, every one from his evil way, and amend your ways and your doings.'

But they say, 'That is in vain! We will follow our own plans, and will every one act according to the stubbornness of his evil heart.'" ...

The Remnant and a Righteous King

"Woe to the shepherds who destroy and scatter the sheep of my pasture!" says the Lord. Therefore thus says the Lord, the God of Israel, concerning the shepherds who care for my people: "You have scattered my flock, and have driven them away, and you have not attended to them. Behold, I will attend to you for your evil doings, says the Lord. Then I will gather the remnant of my flock out of all the countries where I have driven them, and I will bring them back to their fold, and they shall be fruitful and multiply. I will set shepherds over them who will care for them, and they shall fear no more, nor be dismayed, neither shall any be missing, says the Lord.

"Behold, the days are coming, says the Lord, when I will raise up for David a righteous Branch, and he shall reign as king and deal wisely, and shall execute justice and righteousness in the land. In his days Judah will be saved, and Israel will dwell securely. And this is the name by which he will be called: 'The Lord is righteousness.'

"Therefore, behold, the days are coming, says the Lord, when men shall no longer say, 'As the Lord lives who brought up the people of Israel out of the land of Egypt,' but 'As the Lord lives who brought up and led the descendants of the house of Israel out of the north country and out of all the countries where he had driven them.' Then they shall dwell in their own land...

The New Covenant

"Behold the days are coming, says the Lord, when I will sow the house of Israel and the house of Judah with the seed of man and the seed of beast. And it shall come to pass that as I have watched over them to pluck up and break down, to overthrow, destroy, and bring evil, so I will watch over them to build and to plant, says the Lord. In those days they shall no longer say:

> The fathers have eaten sour grapes,
> and the children's teeth are set on edge.

But every one shall die for his own sin; each man who eats sour grapes, his teeth shall be set on edge.

"Behold, the days are coming, says the Lord, when I will make a new covenant with the house of Israel and the house of Judah, not like the covenant which I made with their fathers when I took them by the hand to bring them out of the land of Egypt, my covenant which they broke, though I was their husband, says the Lord. But this is the covenant which I will make with the house of Israel after those days, says the Lord: I will put my law within them, and I will write it upon their hearts; and I will be their God, and they shall be my people. And no longer shall each man teach his neighbor and each his brother, saying 'Know the Lord,' for they shall all know me, from the least of them to the greatest, says the Lord; for I will forgive their iniquity, and I will remember their sin no more."

War and International Diplomacy

Societies in the Ancient Near East developed their distinctive identities as a result of local conditions and regional interactions, as well as through the mutual influence that they came to exert over each other. The development of a "global" long-distance network during the early Bronze Age was one of the signal achievements of these early civilizations. For a time, this network created such a high degree of integration that rulers of the different states regarded themselves as comprising a "brotherhood of kings." While this early international system did not long survive the middle of the second millennium B.C., the major Ancient Near Eastern states continued to engage with each other across vast distances through diplomacy, gift-exchange, warfare, and the movement of people and ideas.

11 Amarna Letters

A Brotherhood of Kings

The ancient kingdoms of Egypt, Babylonia, Mittani (northern Syria), and the Hittites were the international superpowers of their time. By the latter part of the fourteenth century B.C., they had developed such a degree of integration through long-distance diplomatic and economic ties that one may speak of an early Ancient Near Eastern world order. The so-called Amarna letters, a collection of some 350 cuneiform tablets found on the site of Pharaoh Akhenaten's new capital El-Amarna (See Selection 9), attest to the diplomatic relationships that the Kingdom of Egypt maintained with the wider world. Mostly written in Semitic Akkadian cuneiform, these letters illustrate how a shared scribal tradition among the Near Eastern courts made possible a meaningful international network. Those letters, addressed to and received from foreign rulers whom

From William L. Moran, *The Amarna Letters* (Baltimore, Maryland: Johns Hopkins University Press, 1992), pp. 1–3, 6–9.

the Egyptian pharaoh treated as peers, draw upon a language of the familial kinship; some historians see this language as evidence that the kingdoms had constituted themselves effectively into an exclusive club of "Great Powers" or a "Brotherhood of Kings." Other letters directed at or received from Egyptian vassals in regions such as Syria and Palestine were cast in a formulaic language with which Egyptian rulers communicated with their subjects. Some of the international letters, a number of which are reproduced below, have to do with the Babylonian king's request for an Egyptian princess as his bride. Dynastic marriages and the exchange of gifts (often in the form of dowries) represented an important aspect of these long-distance diplomatic ties. The tone of intimacy in the letters and their use of language of friendship reflect not only a degree of cultural affinity but also close mutual scrutiny of local conditions and resources at the respective courts. The speakers in the letters make use of subtle forms of persuasion as well as open and specific demands to their royal brethren. Tapping into a language of international royal kinship, they unabashedly lay claims on each other so as to secure the greatest prestige and advantage for themselves. The letters illustrate not only the competition among these kings but also the common concerns and needs that united them. In their negotiations with each other over royal brides, dowries, and presents, these texts reveal not only the virtually familial or domestic relationship that seems to obtain between members of this international family of kings but also to the real and symbolic goods that were necessary for the maintenance of royal prestige and standing within the competitive ancient Near Eastern world system.

THE PHARAOH COMPLAINS TO THE
BABYLONIAN KING

Say [t]o Kadašman-Enlil, the king of Karadun[i]še, my brother: Thus Nibmuarea, Great King, the king of Egypt, your brother. For me all goes well. For you may all go well. For your household, for your wives, for your sons, for your magnates, your horses, your chariots, for your countries, may all go very well. For me all goes well. For my household, for my wives, for my sons, for my magnates, my horses, the numerous troops, all goes well, and in my countries all goes very well. I have just heard what you wrote me about, saying, "Here you are asking for my daughter in marriage, but my sister whom my father gave you was (already) there with you, and no one has seen her (so as to know) if now she is alive or if she is dead." These are your words that you sent me on your tablet. Did you, however, ever send here a dignitary of yours who knows your sister, who could speak with her and identify her? Suppose he spoke with her. The men whom you sent here are nobodies. One was the [...] of Zaqara, *[the ot]her, an assherder [fr]om [...]* There has been no one among the [m *wh]o [knows her, wh]o* was an intimate of your father, and *w[ho could identify her]*. Moreover, the messengers *[who]* ... [...]And as for your writing me,

"You addressed my me[ssen]gers as your wives were standing gathered in your presence, saying, 'Here is your mistress who stands before you.' But my messengers did not know her, (whether) it was my sister who *was at your side*"—*about whom* you yourself have now written me, "My messengers did not know her," and (still) you say, "Who is to identify her?"—Why don't you send me a dignitary of yours who can tell you the truth, the well-being of your sister who is here, and then you can believe the one who enters to *see* her quarters and her relationship with the king? And as for your writing me, "Perhaps the one my messengers saw was the daughter of some poor man, or of some Ka(s)kean, or the daughter of some Hanigalbatean, or perhaps someone from Ugarit. Who can believe them? *The one who was at your side ...,* she did not op[en] her mouth.' One cannot believe them at all." These are your words. But if your [sister] were de[ad], what reason would there be for one's concealing *her de[ath, and]* our presenting someone [else]? *[May]* Aman *[be my witness]... [...]*And as for your writing me, "My daughters who are married to *neigh[bori]ng* kings, if my messengers *[go]* there, they speak with th[em], and they bri]ng me a greeting gift. *The one with you* [... "Th]ese are your words. Undoubtedly *[your neigh]boring* kings are *[ri]ch* (and) mighty. Your daughters can acquire something from them and send (it) to you. But what does she have, your sister who is with me? But should she make some acquisition, I will send (it) to you! It is a fine thing that you give your daughters *in order to acquire a nugget of gold* from your neighbors! As for your writing me the words of my father, never mind! you do not cite his (exact) words. Furthermore, "Establish friendly brotherhood between us"— these are the words that you wrote me. Now, we are brothers, you and I, but I have quarreled because of your messengers, since they report to you saying, "Nothing is given to us who go to Egypt." Those who come to me—has a single one of them ever come *[and not]* received silver, gold, oil, solemn garb, every sort of finery, *[more than i]n* any other country? He does not tell the truth to the one who sends him! The first time the messengers went off to *[y]our f[ather], and their mouths told lies. The next time they went off [and] they told lies to you. So I said to myself, "Whether I [gi]ve them anything or do not give them anything, they are going to go on te(l)ling [l]i[e]s just the same." So I made up my mind in their regard and I did not gi[ve t]o them anymore.* And as for your writing me, "You said to my messengers, 'Has your master no troops? The girl he gave to me is not beautiful.'"—these are your words, (but) it is not so! Your messengers keep telling you what is not true, (saying things) like this. Whether soldiers are on hand or not can be found out for me. What reason is there for asking about whether there are troops on hand belonging to you, whether there are horses on hand also belonging to you? Please, do not listen to *them*! Your messengers, of whom the mouths of both groups are untruthful and whom you sent here, I swear that they have not served you; and so they go on t(el)ling lies in order to escape your punishment. As for your saying to me, "He put my chariots among the chariots of the mayors. You did not *review* them *separately*. You *humiliated* them before the country *where you are*. You did not rev(iew) (them) *separately*." *Whether* the chariots were *here or there, the chariots needed the horses of my [coun]try*—all were my horses. As for your writing me in order to aggrandize yourself (and) to put oil on the *h[ea]d* of a girl, you for your part sent me one *pr[es]ent*. *Are we to laugh?*

PROPOSALS OF MARRIAGE

[Say] to Mimmuwareya, the king of Egypt, [my] brother: Thus [K]a[d]aš [m]a[n-En]lil, the king of Kara[duniyaš]. For me and [m]y country all goes very [well]. For you, for [yo]ur wi[ves], for your sons, fo[r your *magnates]*, your horses, your chariots, and your entire country, may all go very we[ll].

With regard to my brother's writing me ab[out *marriage]*, saying, "[*I desir*]e [*your daughter*]," why should you not marry (her)? [...] ...My daughters are available, *[but their husbands must be a king o]r of* royal blood. *[These are the only ones whom I accept for my daughters. No king has ever gi]ven [his daughters to anyone not of royal blood].*

[Your daughters are available. Why have you not g]iven me (one)? [...]...[...]

Reverse [...] fine horses [...] 20 wooden [...]... *of gold, 120 shekels* [... I send] to you as [your] greeting-[gift]. 60 shekels of lapislazu[li I send as the greeting-gift of] my *[si]s[te]r;* [...] your wife.

MARRIAGE, GRUMBLINGS, A PALACE-OPENING

[S]ay [to Nim]u'wareya, the king of Eg[ypt, m]y [brother]: [Thus Kad]ašman-Enlil, the king of Karaduniyaš, your brother. [For me all indeed goes w]ell. For you, your household, your wives, [and for you]r [sons], your country, your chariots, your horses, your [mag]nates may all go very well.

With regard to the girl, my daughter, about whom you wrote to me in view of marriage, she has become a woman; she is nubile. Just send a delegation to fetch her. Previously, my father would send a messenger to you, and you would not detain him for long. You qui[ck]ly sent him off, and you would also send here to my father a beautiful greeting-gift.

But now when I sent a messenger to you, you have detained him for six years, and you have sent me as my greeting-gift, the only thing in six years, 30 minas of gold that *looked like silver.* That gold was melted down in the presence of Kasi, your messenger, and he was a witness. When you celebrated a great festival, you did not send your messenger to me, saying, "Come t[o eat an]d drink." No[r did you send me] my greeting-gift in connection with the festival. It was just 30 minas of gold that you [sent me]. My [gi]ft *[does not amoun]t to what [I have given you] every yea[r].*

I have built a *[ne]w [house].* I[n my house] I have built a [l]arge [...]. Your [mes]sengers have see[n *the house and the ..., and are pleased. No]w* I am going to hav[e] a house-opening. Come *[yourself]* to [eat an]d drink with me. [*I shall not act a*]s you yourself did. [25 *men* and] 25 women, altogether 50 i[*n my service],* I send [to you *in connection with the house-opening].*

[...] for 10 wooden chariots, [and 10 teams of hor]ses I send to you as your greeting-gift.

ROYAL DECEIT AND THREATS

[Moreove]r, you, my brother, when I wrote [to you] about marrying your daughter, in accordance with your practice of not gi[ving] (a daughter), [wrote to me], saying, "From time immemorial no daughter of the king of Egy[pt] is given to anyone." Why *n[ot]*? You are a king; you d[o] as you please. Were you to give (a daughter), who would s[ay] anything? Since I was told of this message, I wrote as follows *t[o my brother],* saying, "[*Someone's*] grown daughters, beautiful women, must be available. Send me a beautiful woman as if she were [you]r daughter. Who is going to say, 'She is no daughter of the king?'" But holding to your decision, you have not sent me anyone. Did not you yourself seek brotherhood and amity, and so wrote me about marriage that we might come closer to each other, and did (nor) I, for my part, write you about marriage for this very same reason, i.e., brotherhood and amity, that we might come closer to each other? Why, then, did my brother not send me just one woman? Should I, perhaps, since you did not send me a woman, refuse you a woman, just as you did to me, and *n[ot send her]*? But my daughters being available, I will not refuse *[one]* to y[ou].

Perhaps, too, when I [*wrote you*] about marriage, *[and]* when I wrote you about the animals, … […] Now, you *need* not *ac[cept]* the offspring of my daughter whom I shall s[end to you, but] *s[end me] any* animals *requested of you.*

And as to the gold I wrote you about, send me *whatever i[s on hand],* (as) much (as possible), before your messenger *[comes]* to me, right now, in all haste, this summer, either in the month of Tammuz or in the month of Ab, so I can finish the work that I am engaged on. If during this summer, in the months of Tammuz or Ab, you send the gold I wrote you about, I will give you my daughter. So please send me the gold you *[feel prompted t]o.* But if in the months of Tammuz or Ab you do not send me the gold and (with it) I do not finish the work I am engaged on, what would be the point of your being pleased to send me (gold)? Once I have finished the work I am engaged on, what need will I have of gold? Then you could send me 3,000 talents of gold, and I would not accept it. I would send it back to you, and I would not gi[ve] my daughter in marriage.

12 An Egyptian-Hittite Treaty

Imperialism and International Diplomacy

The pharaohs of the Nineteenth Dynasty undertook to save the Egyptian empire from the decline that had resulted from Akhenaten's preoccupation

From S. Langdon and A. H. Gardiner, "The Treaty of Alliance between Hattusilis, King of the Hittites, and the Pharaoh Ramesses II of Egypt," translated by A. H. Gardiner, *Journal of Egyptian Archaeology,* 6 (1920), 186 ff.

with religious reform. Ramses II (1279–1212 B.C.) was successful in restoring Egyptian control in Palestine and southern Syria, but in so doing he came into conflict with the Hittite empire, which was expanding southward from its center in Asia Minor. After a stubborn struggle that ended in a draw, both sides accepted a treaty of peace and alliance, the earliest international treaty in existence. The treaty is a complex one, with provisions for nonaggression, mutual aid against attack, and extradition of political fugitives. Both Hittite and Egyptian versions of the treaty exist, and it is interesting to observe that each of the rival kings, Ramses II and Hattusilis III, sought to save face by claiming to have assented to the appeal of the other for peace. The Egyptian version, selections from which follow, is the more blunt: Hattusilis sent messengers to "beg peace" from Ramses, "who makes his boundary where he will in every land."

Copy of the tablet of silver which the great chief Hatti, Hattusilis, caused to be brought to Pharaoh by the hand of his messenger Tartesub and his messenger Ramose, in order to beg peace from the Majesty of Usi-ma-Re-setpen-Re, son of Re, Ramesse-mi-Amun [Ramses II], bull of rulers, who makes his boundary where he will in every land....

Peace and Brotherhood

Behold, Hattusilis, the great chief of Hatti, has made himself in a treaty with [Ramses], the great ruler of Egypt, beginning with this day, to cause to be made good peace and good brotherhood between us forever; and he is in brotherhood with me and at peace with me, and I am in brotherhood with him and at peace with him forever.

And since Muwattallis, the great chief of Hatti, my brother, hastened after his fate, and Hattusilis took his seat as great chief of Hatti on the throne of his father; behold I have become with Ramesse-mi-Amun, the great ruler of Egypt, we being together in our peace and our brotherhood; and it is better than the peace and the brotherhood of formerly, which was in the land.

Behold, I, being the great chief of Hatti, am with Ramesse-mi-Amun, the great ruler of Egypt, in good peace and good brotherhood.

And the children of the children of the great chief of Hatti shall be in brotherhood and at peace with the children of the children of Ramesse-mi-Amun, the great ruler of Egypt; they being in our policy of brotherhood and our policy of peace.

And the land of Egypt with the land Hatti shall be at peace and in brotherhood like us forever; and hostilities shall not be made between them forever.

Mutual Nonaggression

And the great chief of Hatti shall not trespass into the land of Egypt forever to take aught from it; and [Ramses], the great ruler of Egypt, shall not trespass into the land of Hatti to take aught from it forever....

Mutual Defense

And if another enemy come to the lands of [Ramses], the great ruler of Egypt, and he send to the great chief of Hatti saying, "Come with me as help against him"; the great chief of Hatti shall come to him, the great chief of Hatti shall slay his enemy.

But if it be not the desire of the great chief of Hatti to come, he shall send his troops and his chariotry and shall slay his enemy.

Or if Ramesse-mi-Amun, the great ruler of Egypt, become incensed against servants of his, and they do another offense against him, and he go to slay his enemy; the great chief of Hatti shall act with him to destroy everyone against whom they shall be incensed....

Extradition of Fugitives

If any great man flee from the land of Egypt and he come to the lands of the great chief of Hatti; or a town or a district... belonging to the lands of Ramesse-mi-Amun, the great ruler of Egypt, and they come to the great chief of Hatti: the great chief of Hatti shall not receive them. The great chief of Hatti shall cause them to be brought to [Ramses], the great ruler of Egypt, their lord, on account of it.

Or if one [common] man or two men who are unknown flee... and they come to the land of Hatti, they shall be brought to Ramesse-mi-Amun, the great ruler of Egypt....

Divine Witnesses

As for these words of the treaty made by the great chief of Hatti with Ramesse-mi-Amun, the great ruler of Egypt, in writing upon this tablet of silver; as for these words, a thousand gods, male gods and female gods of those of the land of Hatti, together with a thousand gods, male gods and female gods of those of the land of Egypt—they are with me as witnesses hearing these words....

As to these words which are upon this tablet of silver of the land of Hatti and of the land of Egypt, as to him who shall not keep them, a thousand gods of the land of Hatti and a thousand gods of the land of Egypt shall destroy his house, his land and his servants. But he who shall keep these words which are on this tablet of silver, be they Hatti, or be they Egyptians, and who do not neglect them, a thousand gods of the land of Hatti and a thousand gods of the land of Egypt will cause him to be healthy and to live, together with his houses and his land and his servants.

13 Sea Peoples' Inscriptions

Egypt and Its Neighbors Under Ramses III

The New Kingdom of Egypt was established around 1500 B.C. after a period of political turmoil during which Egypt was for a time ruled by a foreign people, the chariot-riding Hyksos. It was an age characterized by more active

From William F. Edgerton and John A. Wilson, eds., *Historical Records of Ramses III. The Texts in Medinet Habu*, vols. 1 and 2 (Chicago, Ill.: University of Chicago Press, 1936), pp. 35–39. Courtesy of the Oriental Institute of the University of Chicago.

contacts between the Nile-based civilization and other societies in the Mediterranean and Near East than had existed before. Some of these contacts, however, took the form of warfare. Egypt came under attack after about 1200 B.C. by a confederation of foreign tribes referred to as the "Sea Peoples." They comprised many different ethnic groups that sought new lands on which to settle after having been displaced from areas further north. While the Sea Peoples were successful in gaining a foothold in many other places throughout the Mediterranean world, they faced an organized political and military opponent in the New Egyptian Kingdom. A set of impressive carvings showing the wars between the Egyptians and the Sea Peoples was found in Medinet Habu in the western district of Thebes in Upper (southern) Egypt. It was part of the great funerary temple complex built by Ramses III, pharaoh of Upper and Lower Egypt during the Twentieth Dynasty (ca. 1184–1075 B.C.).

Ramses's career was notable for its monumental buildings and military campaigns: both accomplishments were celebrated in these reliefs and inscriptions. Colossal carvings flanked the gates to the Temple of Medinet Habu, whose portals stood nearly one hundred feet tall. Many of the scenes depict the pharaoh mustering his troops in preparation for war; others show him triumphant in battle over various enemies, whose distinctive costumes have allowed scholars to identify them variously as Nubians, Libyans, and Sea Peoples. The latter were identified with the Philistines (a people known from the Hebrew Bible as having inhabited the area that is now Palestine), for both sported plumes of feathers in their headdresses. The following texts represent the "captions" to the great carvings, which show scenes of Ramses's victorious battles. The pharaoh's boastful account underscores official Egyptian attitudes toward hostile outsiders and the image of the pharaoh as the military protector of the land of Egypt. His task was to secure Egypt against all outside threats. Note especially the many titles by which a pharaoh was known to his people.

A. RAMSES III ISSUING EQUIPMENT TO HIS TROOPS FOR THE CAMPAIGN AGAINST THE SEA PEOPLES

Description

Ramses III, standing in a rostrum, supervises the issuing of equipment to his army. Above, a bugler sounds a call, while standard-bearers and officials salute the King. Below, a prince gives his orders, which are taken down by a scribe. Other scribes record the army units and list the equipment issued. We may recognize helmets, spears, bows, sickle-swords, corselets, quivers, and a shield among the arms and armor issued.

Text over the Officials

Words spoken by the officials, the companions, and the leaders of the infantry and chariotry: "Thou art Re, as thou risest over Egypt, for when [thou] appearest the

Two Lands live. Great is thy strength in the heart of the Nine [Bows], and thy battle cry (reaches) to the circuit of the sun. The shadow of thy arm is over thy troops, so that they walk confident in thy strength. Thy heart is stout; thy plans are excellent, so that no land can stand firm when [thou] art seen. Amon-Re leads thy way; he casts down for thee every land beneath thy soles. Glad is the heart of Egypt forever, for she has a heroic protector. The heart of the land of Temeh is removed, the Peleset are in suspense, hidden in their towns, by the strength of thy father Amon, who assigned to thee every [land] as a gift.

Text Before the King

The King himself says to the officials, the companions, and every leader of the infantry and chariotry who is in the presence of his majesty: "Bring forth equipment! Send out troops to destroy the rebellious [countries] which know not Egypt, through the strength of my father Amon!"

Text in a Horizontal Line in the Center of the Scene

———— [Usermare-Meri]amon, the mighty bull, crushing the Asiatics, lord of [————] in the lands, like ———— entering [into] the midst ————.

Text over the Two Scribes in the Center

———— giving equipment to the infantry and chariotry, to the troops, the Sherden, and the Nubians.

Text over Two Officials on the Left

Receiving equipment in the presence of Usermare-Meriamon, rich of strength.

Text over Soldiers on the Left

The infantry and chariotry, who are receiving equipment in the presence of [his] majesty.

Text over a Prince at the Base

The Crown Prince, Great Royal Scribe, and Royal Son ———— he says to the commanders of the army, the captains of the troops, and the officers of the troops. "One speaks thus, namely Pharaoh: 'Every picked man, good ————, every valiant one who is in the knowledge of his majesty, let them pass by in the presence of Pharaoh to receive equipment.'"

Text over the Officials at the Base

That which the officials and the commanders of the troops said. "We will act! We will act! The army is assembled, and they are the bulls of the land: every picked man of all Egypt and the runners, capable of hand. Our lord goes forth in valor, so that we may plunder the plains and the hill-countries. He is like Montu, the strong ————."

Text over Soldiers at the Lower Left

(Unintelligible.)

Text Behind the King

All the gods are the (magical) protection of his body, to give him valor against every country.

Text by the Scene-Divider on the Right

Live the good god, smiting the Nine Bows, making them non-existent, King of Upper and Lower Egypt, Lord of the Two Lands: Usermare-Meriamon: Son of Re, Lord of Diadems: Ramses III, beloved of Amon-Re, King of the Gods.

B. RAMSES III ON THE MARCH TO ZAHI AGAINST THE SEA PEOPLES

Description

Ramses III in his chariot sets out against the Sea Peoples, accompanied by Egyptian and foreign troops....

Text Before the King

The King, rich in strength as he goes forth abroad, great of fear and awe in the heart of the Asiatics; sole lord, whose hand is capable, conscious of his strength, like a valiant lion hidden and prepared for wild cattle, freely going forward, his heart confident, beating myriads into heaps in the space of a moment. His potency in the fray is like a fire, making all those who assail him to become ashes. They have fear of his name, (even) when he is afar off, like the heat of the sun upon the Two Lands; a wall casting a shadow for Egypt, so that they rest under the strength of his arms; King of Upper and Lower Egypt, Lord of the Two Lands: Usermare-Meriamon; Lord of Diadems: Ramses III.

Text Behind the King

His majesty sets out in valor and strength to destroy the rebellious countries.

Text over the Troops at the Base

His majesty sets out for Zahi like unto Montu, to crush every country that violates his frontier. His troops are like bulls ready on the field of battle; his horses are like falcons in the midst of small birds before the Nine Bows, bearing victory. Amon, his august father, is a shield for him; King of Upper and Lower Egypt, Ruler of the Nine Bows, Lord of the Two Lands, ——— ———.

Text by the Scene-Divider on the Right

Live the good god, lord of strength, mighty of arm, charging into hundred-thousands, King of Upper and Lower Egypt, Lord of the Two Lands: Usermare-Meriamon; Son of Re, Lord of Diadems: Ramses III, beloved of Amon-Re.

Over the Span

The great chief span of his majesty, "Amon Gives the Sword."

C. RAMSES III IN BATTLE WITH THE LAND FORCES OF THE SEA PEOPLES

Description

Ramses III in his chariot charges into the thoroughly disorganized Sea Peoples. He is supported by Egyptian infantry and chariotry and by foreign auxiliaries. The Sea Peoples flee on foot and in their chariots, while their women, children, and baggage move away in heavy oxcarts.

Text Before the King

[T]he sight of him, as when Set rages, overthrowing the enemy in front of the sun bark, trampling down the plains and hill-countries, (which are) prostrate, beaten from tail to head before his horses. His heat burns up their bodies like a flame. Hacked up is their flesh to the duration of eternity.

Text by the Scene-Divider on the Right

Horus, mighty of strength, conquering hundred-thousands, overthrowing those who attack him, gathered together beneath his soles; King of Upper and Lower Egypt, Lord of the Two Lands: Usermare Meriamon; Son of Re, Lord of Diadems: Ramses III.

Text over the Span

The great chief span of his majesty, "Beloved of Amon."

14 Prism of Sennacherib

An Assyrian King's Wars

In the middle of the ninth century B.C., a new conquest state, the Assyrian Empire, emerged in the northern Mesopotamia. From that time on, powerful Assyrian armies invaded neighboring countries almost every year so that, a

Excerpted from *The Annals of Sennacherib*, by Daniel David Luckenbill, Ph.D., pp. 23–35. Copyright © 1924 by University of Chicago Press.

century and a half later, the Assyrians laid claim to a large empire that made its presence felt in Asia Minor, Egypt, and Iran. Nineveh, its capital, became one of the most important cities in western Asia during that time. Their impact there was reflected in many books from the Hebrew Bible (the Christian Old Testament), such as II Kings and the Book of Isaiah. After the Assyrian king Sennacherib came to the throne in 705 B.C., he struggled to put down resistance to his and Assyrian rule. The peoples of Syria and Palestine had counted on Egyptian help to throw off the Assyrian yoke, but Sennacherib brought them all under control. In 701 B.C., he laid siege to Jerusalem, seat of the Kingdom of Judah, then ruled by King Hezekiah, who was confined "like a bird in a cage." Although the Assyrians finally left without taking the city, they took large quantities of plunder and numerous captives. The following texts come from a series of inscribed prisms on which the kings of Assyria recorded the warlike deeds by which they wished to be remembered.

Column I

Sennacherib, the great king,
the mighty king, king of the universe, king of Assyria,
king of the four quarters (of the earth); the wise ruler (lit.
    shepherd, "pastor"),
favorite of the great gods, guardian of the right,
lover of justice; who lends support,
who comes to the aid of the needy, who turns (his thoughts)
    to pious deeds;
perfect hero, mighty man;
first among all princes, the powerful one who consumes
the insubmissive, who strikes the wicked with the thunderbolt;
the god Assur, the great mountain, an unrivaled kingship
has entrusted to me, and above all those
who dwell in palaces, has made powerful my weapons;
from the upper sea of the setting sun
to the lower sea of the rising sun,
all humankind (the black-headed race) he has brought in
    submission at my feet
and mighty kings feared my warfare—
leaving their abodes and
flying alone, like the sudinnu, the bird of the cave (? cliffs),
to (some) inaccessible place.
In my first campaign I accomplished the defeat of
    Merodach-baladan,
king of Babylonia, together with the army of Elam,
his ally, in the plain of Kish.
In the midst of that battle he forsook his camp,
and made his escape alone; (so) he saved his life.
The chariots, horses, wagons, mules,
which he left behind at the onset of battle,
my hands seized. Into his palace, which is in

Babylon, joyfully I entered.
I opened his treasure-house:—gold, silver, vessels of gold
    and silver,
precious stones of every kind (name) goods and property
without limit (number), heavy tribute, his harem,
(his) courtiers and officials, singers, male and
female, all of his artisans,
as many as there were, the servants of his palace,
I brought out, I counted as spoil. In the might of Assur
my lord, 75 of his strong walled cities,
of Chaldea, and 420 small cities
of their environs (within their borders), I surrounded, I
    conquered, their spoil I carried off.
The Arabs, Aramaeans, and Chaldeans,
who were in Erech, Nippur, Kish, Harsagkalamma,
Kutha and Sippar, together with the citizens,
the rebels (lit. sinners), I brought out, as booty I counted.
On my return (march) the Tu'muna
Rihihu, Yadakku, Ubudu
Kibrê, Malahu, Gurumu,
Ubulu, Damunu, Gambulu
Hindaru, Ru'ûa, Bukudu,
Hamrânu, Hagarânu, Nabatu,
Li'tâu, Aramaeans (who were) not submissive,
all of them I conquered. 208,000 people, great and small,
male and female, horses, mules, asses,
camels, cattle and sheep, without number,
a heavy booty, I carried off to Assyria.
In the course of my campaign, I received from
    Nabû-bêl-shumâte,
governor of the city of Hararate, gold, silver, great
    musukkani-trees,
asses, camels, cattle and sheep,
as his onerous contribution. The warriors of
Hirimme, wicked enemies, I cut down with the sword.
Not one escaped. Their corpses
I hung on stakes, surrounding the city (with them).
That district (province) I reorganized: One ox,
10 lambs, 10 homers of wine, 20 homers of dates,
its choicest, (as gifts) for the gods of Assyria,
my lords, I established for all time.
In my second campaign, Assur my lord, encouraged me, and
against the land of the Kassites and the land of the
    Yasubigallai,
who from of old had not been submissive to the kings, my
    fathers,

I marched. In the midst of the high mountains
I rode on horseback where the terrain was difficult,
and had my chariot drawn up with ropes:
where it became too steep, I clambered up on foot like the
    wild-ox.
The cities of Bît-Kilamzah, Hardishpi
and Bît-Kubatti, their strong, walled cities,
I besieged, I captured. People, horses,
mules, asses, cattle and sheep,
I brought out from their midst and counted as booty.
And their small cities, which were numberless,
I destroyed, I devastated, I turned into ruins. The houses of
    the steppe, (namely) the tents,
wherein they dwelt, I set on fire and
turned them into (a mass of) flames. I turned round, and
made that Bît-Kilamzah into a fortress,—
I made its walls stronger than they had ever been before,—

Column II

and settled therein people of the lands my hands had
    conquered.
The people of the land of the Kassites and the land of the
    Yasubigallai,
who had fled before my arms,
I brought down out of the mountains and
settled them in Hardishpi and Bît-Kubatti.
Into the hand(s) of my official, the governor of Arrapha,
I placed (lit. counted) them. I had a stela made, and
the might of my conquering hand which I had
established upon them, I had inscribed thereon.
In the midst of the city I set it up. The front of my yoke I
    turned (that is, I turned about) and
took the road to the land of the Elippi.
Before me (my approach) Ispabâra, their king,
forsook his strong cities, his treasure-houses (cities),
and fled to distant (parts).
Over the whole of his wide land I swept like a hurricane.
The cities Marubishti and Akkuddu,
his royal residence-cities, together with 34 small cities
of their environs, I besieged, I captured, I destroyed, I
    devastated,
I burned with fire. The people, great and small, male and
    female,
horses, mules, asses, camels,
cattle and sheep, without number, I carried off.

I brought him to naught, I diminished his land.
Sisirtu and Kummahlum,
strong cities, together with the small cities of their environs,
the district (province) of Bît-Barrû in its totality,
I cut off from his land and added it to the territory (lit.
    border) of Assyria.
Elenzash I turned into the royal city
and stronghold of that district.
I changed its former name,
calling its (new) name Kar-Sennacherib. Peoples of the lands
    my hands had conquered
I settled therein. To my official,
the governor of Harhar, I handed it over (counted it). Thus
    I extended my land.
On my return, I received the heavy tribute
of the distant Medes, whose name no one among the kings,
    my fathers, had (ever) heard.
To the yoke of my rule I made them submit.
In my third campaign I went against the Hittite-land.
Lulê, king of Sidon,—the terrifying splendor (lit. terrors of
    splendors)
of my sovereignty overcame him and far off
into the midst of the sea he fled. (There) he died.
Great Sidon, Little Sidon,
Bît-Zitti, Zaribtu, Mahalliba,
Ushu, Akzib, Akko,
his strong, walled cities, where there were supplies (lit. fodder
    and drinking places),
for his garrisons,—the terrors of the weapon of Assur,
my lord, overpowered them and they bowed in submission
    at my feet.
Tuba'lu I seated on the royal throne
over them, and tribute, gift(s) for my majesty,
I imposed upon him for all time, without ceasing. [...]
The officials, nobles and people of Ekron,
who had thrown Padi, their king, bound by (lit. lord of)
    oath and curse of Assyria,
into fetters of iron and
had given him over to Hezekiah, the Jew,—he kept him in
    confinement like an enemy,—
they (lit. their heart) became afraid,
and called upon the Egyptian kings, the bowmen, chariots
    and horses
of the king of Meluhha (Ethiopia), a countless host, and
these came to their aid.
In the neighborhood of Eltekeh,
their ranks being drawn up before me,

Column III

they offered battle. (Trusting) in the aid of Assur,
my lord, I fought with them and
brought about their defeat. The Egyptian charioteers and
    princes,
together with the charioteers of the Ethiopian king,
my hands took alive in the midst of the battle.
Eltekeh (and) Timnah
I besieged, I captured and took away their spoil.
I drew near to Ekron and slew the governors and nobles
who had committed sin (that is, rebelled), and
hung their bodies on stakes around the city. The citizens
who sinned and treated (Assyria) lightly, I counted as spoil.
The rest of them, who were not guilty (carriers) of sin
and contempt, for whom there was no punishment,—
I spoke their pardon. Padi, their king,
I brought out of Jerusalem,
set him on the royal throne over them and
imposed upon him my kingly tribute.
As for Hezekiah, the Jew,
who did not submit to my yoke, 46 of his strong, walled
    cities, as well as
the small cities in their neighborhood,
which were without number,—by levelling with battering-
    rams (?)
and by bringing up siege-engines (?), by attacking and
    storming on foot,
by mines, tunnels and breaches (?), I besieged and took
    (those cities).
200,150 people, great and small, male and female,
horses, mules, asses, camels,
cattle and sheep, without number, I brought away from them
and counted as spoil. Himself, like a caged bird
I shut up in Jerusalem his royal city.
Earthworks I threw up against him,—
the one coming out of the city-gate, I turned back to his misery.
The cities of his, which I had despoiled, I cut off from his
    land and
to Mitinti, king of Ashdod,
Padi, king of Ekron, and Silli-bêl
king of Gaza, I gave. And (thus) I diminished his land.
I added to the former tribute,
and laid upon him the giving (up) of their land, (as well as)
    imposts—gifts for my majesty.
As for Hezekiah,
the terrifying splendor of my majesty overcame him, and

the Urbi (Arabs) and his mercenary (?) troops which he had
   brought in to strengthen
Jerusalem, his royal city,
deserted him (lit. took leave). In addition to the 30 talents of
   gold and
800 talents of silver, (there were) gems, antimony,
jewels (?), large sandu-stones, couches of ivory,
house-chairs of ivory, elephant hide, ivory (lit. elephant's
   "teeth")
ebony (?), boxwood (?), all kinds of valuable (heavy) treasures,
as well as his daughters, his harem, his male and female
musicians, (which) he had (them) bring after me
to Nineveh, my royal city. To pay tribute
and to accept (lit. do) servitude, he dispatched his messengers.

Persia: The Last Ancient Near Eastern Empire

15 A Conquering Messiah

Cyrus the Great and the Persian Empire

The Persian Empire was the last universal empire that managed to bring to uni-
fied rule much of the Near East prior to the conquest of Alexander the Great of
Macedon and the arrival of the Hellenistic Age. The founder of this empire,
Cyrus the Great (d. 529 B.C.), a Persian or Elamite, was a colorful figure who
was born into a local royal family in Anshan, a region in modern Iran. In time,
through skillful diplomacy and warfare, he managed to unite the Persians and
the Medes, both Indo-European-speaking Iranian peoples. On the basis of this
Iranian solidarity, he proceeded to conquer the Near East, first subduing the
Lydian kingdom in Asia Minor, ruled then by the legendary King Croesus, who
owned vast stores of gold. Then Cyrus turned to the Neo-Babylonian empire
that ruled Mesopotamia, Syria, and Palestine and quickly succeeded in conquering it also. His successor, Cambyses, later added Egypt to the empire.

   During his lifetime, Cyrus ruled this universal empire with singular intelligence and an intuitive understanding of his limits. While the Persians and

Medes formed a ruling group that occupied positions of the highest political authority, local notables were often allowed to administer their own peoples. Cyrus was so concerned about demonstrating support for local traditions and the religious practices of the various ethnic groups within the empire that he granted numerous privileges to native leaders and allowed their peoples to practice their ancestral customs. He did not even impose the use of Persian as the official administrative language: instead, he used Aramaic, the *lingua franca* of the Ancient Near East, for this purpose. Neither did the Persians attempt to make others worship their own gods. Due to this uniquely tolerant policy, Cyrus appeared in many of the subject territories as a liberator rather than a foreign conqueror. In time, Cyrus gained almost legendary status in various lands, being hailed by the people of Israel as a "messiah"—the chosen or anointed of God—and treated as an archetypal ideal king by Greeks such as Xenophon, who wrote a long treatise entitled Cyropaedia, "The Education of Cyrus." Another great ruler, Alexander III of Macedon, became an ardent admirer of Cyrus and paid homage at the latter's tomb during his conquest of the Persian Empire.

The following two texts illustrate Cyrus' characteristic interactions with local peoples and their responses to his policy of tolerance and considerate treatment. The Persians' lack of any desire or effort to impose Iranian values, religious beliefs, and practices on conquered peoples was a distinctive characteristic of their empire. Local peoples could abide by their own religious traditions, laws, and customs, which the Persians supported directly or indirectly. Much of this would begin to change during the subsequent (Hellenistic) period when Greek universalism and Hellenism posed a unique challenge to the traditional cultures of the Ancient Near East.

A. CYRUS' CYLINDER: THE CHOSEN
OF MARDUK

Cyrus brought much of the Near East once again under the rule of a single political entity. The ruling peoples of this empire hailed from Media and Persia, in modern Iran. Through conquest, they assumed control of societies, particularly in Mesopotamia, that claimed far greater sophistication and antiquity than their own. Babylon was the capital of the last great Near Eastern Empire, that of the Neo-Babylonians or Chaldeans. It was a city of great wealth and power, and boasted tremendous cultural prestige in light of its historical significance.

But the Persians did not come to Babylon as foreign conquerors or aggressors. The priests of Marduk, the chief god of Babylon, greeted Cyrus as a savior and a deliverer from the injustices of the last Neo-Babylonian king, Nabonidus (555–539). Nabonidus had intervened decisively in the affairs of the Babylonian temples, installing senior priests of his own choosing in positions of authority and altering the way in which temple sacrifices were made. This reforming king was also alleged to have attempted to introduce the cult of a moon god called Sin to various cities in Mesopotamia, much to the chagrin of the local priests and

From James B. Pritchard, ed., *The Ancient Near East*, vol. 1 (Princeton: Princeton University Press, 1985). Reprinted by permission of Princeton University Press.

other worshippers. As a result, the priests regarded Nabonidus as an enemy of Marduk, who therefore raised up another ruler to take his place. This new ruler was Cyrus the Persian, a former ally of Nabonidus.

When Cyrus sought to conquer Mesopotamia, he first cultivated the friendship of the local priests and promised to restore the divine statues and religious cults of many cities in Babylonia. As a result, he was welcomed as a legitimate ruler and even as the one ordered by Marduk to govern in Babylon. Cyrus' proclamation of religious toleration and support for traditional local religions in Babylonia was publicized in Akkadian, an ancient Mesopotamian language, on a clay cylinder.

Throughout this text, which can properly be read as a product of royal (and priestly) propaganda, Cyrus sought to represent himself as a friend and not an invader, and as the rightful ruler of Babylon. When he received the title of the "Chosen of Marduk," Cyrus assumed a mantle of political legitimacy that hearkened back to very ancient times: the great law-giving king Hammurabi had himself ruled as the "Chosen of Marduk."

(one line destroyed)

... [r]ims (of the world)... a weakling has been installed as the end[1] of his country; [the correct images of the gods he removed from their thrones, imi]tations he ordered to place upon them. A replica of the temple Esagila he has... for Ur and the other sacred cities inappropriate rituals... daily he did blabber [incorrect prayers]. He (furthermore) interrupted in a fiendish way the regular offerings, he did... he established within the sacred cities. The worship of Marduk, the king of the gods, he [chang]ed into abomination, daily he used to do evil against his (i.e., Marduk's) city.... He [tormented] its [inhabitant]s with corvée-work (lit.: a yoke) without relief, he ruined them all.

Upon their complaints the lord of the gods became terribly angry and [he departed from] their region, (also) the (other) gods living among them left their mansions, wroth that he had brought (them) into Babylon. (But) Marduk [who does care for]... on account of (the fact that) the sanctuaries of all their settlements were in ruins and the inhabitants of Sumer and Akkad had become like (living) dead, turned back (his countenance) [his] an[ger] [abated] and he had mercy (upon them). He scanned and looked (through) all the countries, searching for a righteous ruler willing to lead him (i.e., Marduk) (in the annual procession). (Then) he pronounced the name of Cyrus, king of Anshan, declared him (lit.: pronounced [his] name) to be(come) the ruler of all the world. He made the Guti country and all the Manda-hordes bow in submission to his (i.e., Cyrus') feet. And he (Cyrus) did always endeavour to treat according to justice the black-headed whom he (Marduk) has made him conquer. Marduk, the great lord, a protector of his people/worshipers, beheld with pleasure his (i.e., Cyrus') good deeds and his upright mind (lit.: heart) (and therefore) ordered him to march against his city Babylon. He made him set out on the road to Babylon going at his side like a real friend. His widespread troops—their number, like that of the water of a river, could not be established—strolled along, their weapons packed away.

---

1. This old Sumerian title is used here to refer to Nabonidus.

Without any battle, he made him enter his town Babylon, sparing Babylon any calamity. He delivered into his (i.e., Cyrus') hands Nabonidus, the king who did not worship him (i.e., Marduk). All the inhabitants of Babylon as well as of the entire country of Sumer and Akkad, princes and governors (included), bowed to him (Cyrus) and kissed his feet, jubilant that he (had received) the kingship, and with shining faces. Happily they greeted him as a master through whose help they had come (again) to life from death (and) had all been spared damage and disaster, and they worshiped his (very) name.

I am Cyrus, king of the world, great king, legitimate king, king of Babylon, king of Sumer and Akkad, king of the four rims (of the earth), son of Cambyses, great king, king of Anshan, grandson of Cyrus, great king, king of Anshan, descendant of Teispes, great king, king of Anshan, of a family (which) always (exercised) kingship; whose rule Bel and Nebo love, whom they want as king to please their hearts.

When I entered Babylon as a friend and (when) I established the seat of the government in the palace of the ruler under jubilation and rejoicing, Marduk, the great lord, [induced] the magnanimous inhabitants of Babylon [to love me], and I was daily endeavouring to worship him. My numerous troops walked around in Babylon in peace, I did not allow anybody to terrorize (any place) of the [country of Sumer] and Akkad. I strove for peace in Babylon and in all his (other) sacred cities. As to the inhabitants of Babylon, [who] against the will of the gods [had/were... , I abolished] the corvée which was against their (social) standing. I brought relief to their dilapidated housing, putting (thus) an end to their (main) complaints. Marduk, the great lord, was well pleased with my deeds and sent friendly blessings to myself, Cyrus, the king who worships him, to Cambyses, my son, the offspring of [my] loins, as well as to all my troops, and we all [praised] his great [godhead] joyously, standing before him in peace.

All the kings of the entire world from the Upper to the Lower Sea, those who are seated in throne rooms (those who) live in other [types of buildings as well as] all the kings of the West land living in tents brought their heavy tributes and kissed my feet in Babylon. (As to the region) from... as far as Ashur and Susa, Agade, Eshnunna, the towns Zamban, Me-Turnu, Der as well as the region of the Gutians, I returned to (these) sacred cities on the other side of the Tigris, the sanctuaries of which have been ruins for a long time, the images which (used) to live therein and established for them permanent sanctuaries. I (also) gathered all their (former) inhabitants and returned (to them) their habitations. Furthermore, I resettled upon the command of Marduk, the great lord, all the gods of Sumer and Akkad whom Nabonidus has brought into Babylon to the anger of the lord of the gods, unharmed, in their (former) chapels, the places which make them happy.

May all the gods whom I have resettled in their sacred cities ask daily Bel and Nebo for a long life for me and may they recommend me (to him); to Marduk, my lord, they may say this: "Cyrus, the king who worships you, and Cambyses, his son,..."... all of them I settled in a peaceful place... ducks and doves,... I endeavoured to fortify/repair their dwelling places....

(six lines destroyed)

B. CYRUS AS THE MESSIAH: RETURN OF THE JEWS
AND THE REBUILDING OF JERUSALEM

Jerusalem, the capital and most sacred city of the Kingdom of Judah, was besieged, captured, and mostly destroyed in 597 B.C. by King Nebuchadnezzar II, ruler of the Neo-Babylonian or Chaldean Dynasty. Many inhabitants of Jerusalem, including members of the local aristocratic families, were marched into exile in Babylon. The so-called Babylonian captivity witnessed the establishment of a substantial Jewish population in Mesopotamia. These Jewish settlers would later become very influential in the Jewish diaspora—it was in Mesopotamia that one of the two Talmudic collections (the Babylonian Talmud) was assembled. The Book of Ezra, from the Hebrew Bible or Old Testament, begins its story about the Jewish return to Jerusalem after the Babylonian captivity with a reference to Cyrus I, the founder of the great Achaemenid Persian Empire. This return of Jewish exiles from Babylon took place around 538 B.C.

In the first year of Cyrus king of Persia, that the word of the Lord by the mouth of Jeremiah might be accomplished, the Lord stirred up the spirit of Cyrus king of Persia so that he made a proclamation throughout all his kingdom and also put it in writing.

"Thus says Cyrus king of Persia: the Lord, the God of heaven, has given me all the kingdoms of the earth, and he has charged me to build him a house at Jerusalem, which is in Judah. Whoever is among you of all his people, may his God be with him, and let him go up to Jerusalem, which is in Judah, and rebuild the house of the Lord, the God of Israel—he is the God who is in Jerusalem; and let each survivor, in whatever place he sojourns, be assisted by the men of his place with silver and gold, with goods and with beasts, besides freewill offerings for the house of God which is in Jerusalem."

Then rose up the heads of the fathers' houses of Judah and Benjamin, and the priests and the Levites, every one whose spirit God had stirred to go up to rebuild the house of the Lord which is in Jerusalem; and all who were about them aided them with vessels of silver, with gold, with goods, with beasts, and with costly wares, besides all that was freely offered. Cyrus the king also brought out the vessels of the house of the Lord which Nebuchadnezzar had carried away from Jerusalem and placed in the house of his gods. Cyrus king of Persia brought these out in charge of Mithredath the treasurer, who counted them out to Shesh-bazzar the prince of Judah. And this was the number of them: a thousand basins of gold, a thousand basins of silver, twenty-nine censers, thirty bowls of gold, two thousand four hundred and ten bowls of silver, and a thousand other vessels; all the vessels of gold and of silver were five thousand four hundred and sixty-nine. All these did Shesh-bazzar bring up, when the exiles were brought up from Babylonia to Jerusalem....

From *The New Oxford Annotated Bible with the Apocrypha*. Revised Standard Version, edited by Herbert G. May and Bruce M. Metzger (New York. Oxford University Press, 1962), pp. 573–74.

SELECTED BACKGROUND READING

General

Amélie Kuhrt, *The Ancient Near East, C. 3000–330 B.C.* (London: Routledge, 1995).

Amanda H. Podanyi, *Brotherhood of Kings: How International Relations Shaped the Ancient Near East* (Oxford: Oxford University Press, 2010).

William H. Stiebing Jr., *Ancient Near Eastern History and Culture* (New York: Longman, 2003).

Marc Van de Mieroop, *A History of the Ancient Near East, Ca. 3000–323 B.C.* (Malden, Mass.: Blackwell, 2004).

Mesopotamia, Syria, and Anatolia

Trevor Bryce, *The Kingdom of the Hittites* (Oxford: Clarendon Press, 1998).

Samuel Noah Kramer, *The Sumerians: Their History, Culture, and Character* (Chicago: University of Chicago Press, 1963).

A. Leo Oppenheim and Erica Reiner, *Ancient Mesopotamia: Portrait of a Dead Civilization*, rev. ed. (Chicago, Ill.: University of Chicago Press, 1977).

Susan Pollock, *Ancient Mesopotamia: The Eden That Never Was* (Cambridge, U.K.: Cambridge University Press, 1999).

J. N. Postgate, *Early Mesopotamia: Society and Economy at the Dawn of History* (London: Routledge, 1992).

Michael Roaf, *Cultural Atlas of Mesopotamia and the Ancient Near East* (New York: Facts on File, 1990).

H. W. F. Saggs, *Babylonians* (Norman, Okla.: University of Oklahoma Press, 1995).

Egypt

John Baines and Jaromír Málek, *Cultural Atlas of Ancient Egypt* (New York: Facts on file, 2000).

Alan Henderson Gardiner, *Egypt of the Pharaohs: An Introduction* (Oxford: Clarendon Press, 1961).

Nicolas-Christophe Grimal, *A History of Ancient Egypt* (Oxford: Blackwell, 1992).

Erik Hornung, *History of Ancient Egypt An Introduction* (Edinburgh: Edinburgh University Press, 1999).

Michael Rice, *Egypt's Making: The Origins of Ancient Egypt, 5000–2000 BC* (London: Routledge, 2003).

Israel and Palestine

John Bright, *A History of Israel* (Philadelphia: Westminster Press, 1981).

Donald B. Redford, *Egypt, Canaan, and Israel in Ancient Times* (Princeton, New Jersey: Princeton University Press, 1992).

CHAPTER 11

Greek Civilization:
Ancient Greece

King of Lydia, as God has given the Greeks
a moderate proportion of other things,
so likewise has He favored them with
a democratic spirit and a liberal kind of wisdom.

—PLUTARCH, "LIFE OF SOLON"

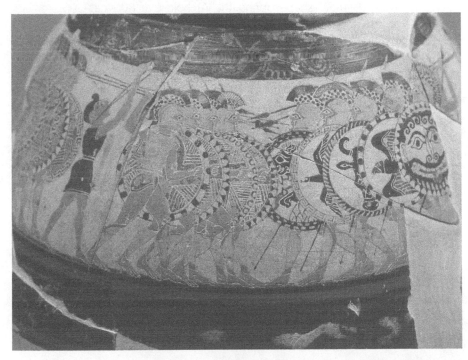

Two phalanxes, or battle lines, of heavily armored hoplite soldiers marching against each other to the sound of flutes. This stylized image of typical Greek warfare comes from a detail on the Protocorinthian "Chigi Vase" found near Veii, Italy, now in the Villa Giulia, Rome.

99

The words on the preceding page were in tradition addressed by Solon, a sixth-century B.C. Athenian statesman, lawgiver, and poet, to Croesus, king of the Lydians in western Asia Minor. They convey what ancient Greeks regarded as the primary distinction between the civilizations of the Ancient Near East and their own. Living in autonomous city-states that were dominated neither by temple priesthoods nor by all-powerful kings, the Greeks came to achieve a freedom of thought and action—the "democratic spirit and a liberal kind of wisdom" of Solon's quotation—that some still maintain never came into being in the Ancient Near East. We can easily understand, therefore, the bewilderment of King Croesus as he listened to the words of his Greek guest, and the author Plutarch adds that Solon "was dismissed, having given Croesus some pain, but no instruction." It would be a mistake to regard the Greek view and practice of life as an expression of qualities uniquely inherent in the Greek people or to understand these qualities as a continuous and permanent possession that others might at best learn or obtain from their original inventors. Such characterizations lead to the dilemma faced by one modern scholar who, having described Homer as a typical manifestation of the Greek genius, was forced to conclude that Plato was, rather unfortunately, non-Greek. Both Homer and Plato appear as "typical" Greeks when each is seen as the product of a different period and context within the course of Greek or Hellenic history. Hellenic civilization was diverse from the start and also underwent many changes through time, achieving its main shape during the Archaic (ca. 800–ca. 500 B.C.) and Classical (ca. 500 B.C.–ca. 330 B.C.) periods; later, during the Hellenistic period, Hellenic culture was disseminated even more widely than before following the conquests of Alexander the Great (d. 323 B.C.).

From around 1200 B.C. to the time of Alexander, the Greeks developed many key ideas and institutions that would long continue to exert a significant influence over the course of human development. These achievements can perhaps be explained as the varied and rich responses of a gifted and competitive people to a fluctuating historical environment. Indeed the Greek experience was by no means unique. Similar ideas and institutions had been created by the people of the Ancient Near East, often in response to comparable historical challenges. Many others have since had the occasion to re-create them in their own historical development, especially (but not only) in the West.

This chapter presents readings that address the following historical themes: Foundation Stories: Gods, Heroes, and the Individual; Archaic Greek City-States, Colonization, and Tyranny; War and Peace in the Classical Age; Society, Culture, and Intellectual Life; and Late Classical Greece.

Foundation Stories: Gods, Heroes, and the Individual

The reemergence of Greek literacy in the eighth century B.C. spurred the composition of epic poems that would go on to occupy a central place in Greek culture. Many of these early works by authors such as Homer and Hesiod tell of the competing relations between gods and men and helped establish the contours of a body of knowledge now familiar to us as Classical Mythology. The actions of humans feature centrally, with the individual hero emerging as an iconic figure in such tales. The celebrated individual is not merely confined to mythology and heroic epics but, with the growth of the Greek athletic tradition associated with festivals of the gods during this same time, came to be associated with the person of the victorious athlete. In general, early Greek poetry gave voice to an appreciation of the value of the individual human being by conferring on his or her achievements a measure of literary immortality.

16 Homer

The Greek Heroic Age

In addition to its well-deserved fame as one of the great classics of world literature, Homer's *Iliad* represents a historical document that helps us understand developments in early Greek history and cultural identity. Homer's epic poem, composed around 750 B.C., drew on an oral tradition about heroic deeds during the Trojan War, an event of the Mycenaean period that preceded the literary compositions by some four hundred years. As a historical document, the *Iliad* incorporates elements that refer variously to the succession of periods: the late Mycenaean period of it dramatic setting, the Greek Dark Age during which underlying traditions circulated orally, and the early Archaic period when it was written. Whereas palace-states ruled by kings or warrior chieftains were a central feature of the Mycenaean world age, many of the detailed descriptions of ideas and institutions refer to social realities that date from Homer's own time when the city-state or *polis* was key. This composite

From the Iliad, based on the translation by Samuel Butler.

"World of Homer" continued to influence Greek cultural memories and sense of self-identity. Aristocratic males in particular looked to the heroes of the epic as both ancestors and models and sought to emulate their conduct and actions. In time, the *Iliad* became the "national epic" of all Greeks. Here, as always, great literature reflects contemporary life. Except for Books I and II, no attempt has been made in the following selections to present the entire plot of the *Iliad*. Rather, our main concern is with the value of Homer's works as historical evidence for the Greek "heroic age": his description of the values of life; the religious beliefs and practices; and the political, economic, and social institutions of his day. As in other "heroic ages," the ideals for which men strive are the products of heroic valor; men seek the prize of imperishable fame through hardship, struggle, and even death. The denial of honor due a preeminent warrior is the greatest of human tragedies, and the wrath of Achilles—the theme of the *Iliad*—is the result of such a denial. The gods possess all the traits of humans, including some that a later age considered immoral (in the sixth century B.C., the poet-philosopher Xenophanes said disapprovingly that "Homer and Hesiod [in his *Theogony*] ascribed to the gods everything that among men is a shame and disgrace: theft, adultery, and deceiving one another"). Zeus asserts his superiority through threats of violence when he is not the undignified victim of the plots of his wife and other deities. Gods mingle freely with mortals and aid their favorites, who have propitiated them with sacrifices and with prayers that are usually childishly selfish petitions for some material reward.

Hades ruled the abode of the dead, a subterranean land of dust and darkness, and Achilles, as Homer tells us in his slightly later work *Odyssey* (ca. 725 B.C.), would rather be "the poor servant of a poor master" on earth than be king in the netherworld. Society is clearly aristocratic, a word coming from *aristoi,* the "best men" or "aristocrats," who alone possess *aretē,* "excellence" or "goodness," and the common man puts in an appearance only to be reviled and beaten when he dares to question his betters. Yet the common man has certain political rights as a member of the popular assembly that is summoned whenever a crisis, such as war, arises that requires his participation. Two other institutions of government described by Homer are the king and his council. The king is hardly more than a chief among his peers, with his fellow nobles who sitting in the council to advise him and to check his every attempt to exercise arbitrary power. Economic conditions are those of a simple and self-sufficient agricultural economy in which private ownership of land is replacing collective group ownership.

The Quarrel

Agamemnon, ruler of Mycenae and leader of the Achaean (also called Danaan and Argive) army besieging Troy [Ilium], is compelled to restore the captive Chryseis to her father, but in retaliation takes from Achilles the lovely Briseis. Achilles, enraged at this slight to his honor, vows he will fight no more for Agamemnon and through his mother, the sea nymph Thetis, secures the aid of Zeus for the Trojans. This provokes the wrath of the goddess Hera, wife of Zeus.

Sing, O goddess, the anger of Achilles, son of Peleus, that brought countless ills upon the Achaeans. Many a brave soul did it send hurrying down to Hades, and many a hero did it yield a prey to dogs and vultures, for so were the counsels of Zeus fulfilled from the day on which the son of Atreus, king of men, and great Achilles first fell out with one another.

And which of the gods was it that set them on to quarrel? It was [Apollo] the son of Zeus and Leto; for he was angry with the king and sent a pestilence upon the host to plague the people, because the son of Atreus had dishonored Chryses, his priest. Now Chryses had come to the ships of the Achaeans to free his daughter and had brought with him a great ransom. Moreover, he bore in his hand the scepter of Apollo wreathed with a suppliant's wreath, and he besought the Achaeans, but most of all, the two sons of Atreus, who were their chiefs.

"Sons of Atreus," he cried, "and all other Achaeans, may the gods who dwell in Olympus grant you to sack the city of Priam and to reach your homes in safety; but free my daughter and accept a ransom for her in reverence to Apollo, son of Zeus."

On this the rest of the Achaeans with one voice were for respecting the priest and taking the ransom that he offered; but not so Agamemnon, who spoke fiercely to him and sent him roughly away. "Old man," said he, "let me not find you tarrying about our ships, nor yet coming hereafter. Your scepter of the god and your wreath shall profit you nothing. I will not free her. She shall grow old in my house at Argos far from her own home, busying herself with her loom and visiting my couch. So go, and do not provoke me or it shall be the worse for you."

The old man feared him and obeyed. Not a word he spoke, but went by the shore of the sounding sea and prayed apart to King Apollo whom lovely Leto had borne. "Hear me," he cried, "O god of the silver bow, that protectest Chryse and holy Cilla and rulest Tenedos with thy might, hear me, O thou of Sminthe! If I have ever decked your temple with garlands or pleased you by burning thighbones of bulls or goats, grant my prayer and let your arrows avenge these my tears upon the Danaans."

Thus did he pray, and Apollo heard his prayer. He came down furious from the summits of Olympus, with his bow and his quiver upon his shoulder, and the arrows rattled on his back with the rage that trembled within him. He sat himself down away from the ships with a face as dark as night, and his silver bow rang death as he shot his arrow in the midst of them. First he smote their mules and their hounds, but presently he aimed his shafts at the people themselves, and all day long the pyres of the dead were burning.

For nine whole days he shot his arrows among the people, but upon the tenth day Achilles called them in assembly—moved thereto by Hera, who saw the Achaeans in their death throes and had compassion upon them. Then, when they were got together, he rose and spoke among them.

"Son of Atreus," said he, "I deem that we should now turn roving home if we would escape destruction, for we are being cut down by war and pestilence at once. Let us ask some priest or prophet, or some reader of dreams (for dreams, too, are of Zeus) who can tell us why Phoebus Apollo is so angry, and say whether it is for some vow that we have broken, or hecatomb [a large-scale animal sacrifice] that we have not offered, and whether he will accept the savor of lambs and goats without blemish, so as to take away the plague from us."

With these words he sat down, and Calchas, son of Thestor, wisest of augurs, who knew things past, present, and to come, rose to speak. He it was who had guided the Achaeans with their fleet to Ilium, through the prophesyings with which Phoebus Apollo had inspired him. With all sincerity and good will he addressed them thus:...

"The god," he said, "is angry neither about vow nor hecatomb, but for his priest's sake, whom Agamemnon has dishonored, in that he would not free his daughter nor take a ransom for her. Therefore has he sent these evils upon us and will yet send others. He will not deliver the Danaans from this pestilence till Agamemnon has restored the girl without fee or ransom to her father and has sent a holy hecatomb to Chryse. Thus we may perhaps appease him."

With these words he sat down, and Agamemnon rose in anger. His heart was black with rage, and his eyes flashed fire as he scowled on Calchas and said: "Seer of evil, you never yet prophesied smooth things concerning me, but have ever loved to foretell that which was evil. You have brought me neither comfort nor performance, and now you come seeing among the Danaans, and saying that Apollo has plagued us because I would not take a ransom for this girl, the daughter of Chryses. I have set my heart on keeping her in my own house, for I lover her better even than my own wife, Clytemnestra, whose peer she is alike in form and feature, in understanding and accomplishments. Still I will give her up if I must, for I would have the people live, not die; but you must find me a prize instead, or I alone among the Argives shall be without one. This is not well; for you behold, all of you, that my prize is to go elsewhither."

And Achilles answered: "Most noble son of Atreus, covetous beyond all mankind, how shall the Achaeans find you another prize? We have no common store from which to take one. Those we took from the cities have been awarded; we cannot disallow the awards that have been made already. Give this girl, therefore, to the god, and if ever Zeus grants us to sack the city of Troy we will requite you three and fourfold."

Then Agamemnon said: "Achilles, valiant though you be, you shall not thus outwit me. You shall not overreach and you shall not persuade me. Are you to keep your own prize, while I sit tamely under my loss and give up the girl at your bidding? Let the Achaeans find me a prize in fair exchange to my liking, or I will come and take your own, or that of Ajax or of Odysseus; and he to whomsoever I may come shall rue my coming. But of this we will take thought hereafter; for the present, let us draw a ship into the sea, and find a crew for her expressly; let us put a hecatomb on board, and let us send Chryseis also. Further, let some chief man among us be in command, either Ajax, or Idomeneus, or yourself, son of Peleus, mighty warrior that you are, that we may offer sacrifice and appease the anger of the god."

Achilles scowled at him and answered: "You are steeped in insolence and lust of gain. With what heart can any of the Achaeans do your bidding, either on foray or in open fighting? I came not warring here for any ill the Trojans had done me. I have no quarrel with them. They have not raided my cattle or my horses, or cut down my harvests on the rich plains of Phthia; for between me and them there is a great space, both mountain and sounding sea. We have followed you, Sir Insolence! for your pleasure, not ours—to gain satisfaction from the Trojans for your shameless self and for Menelaus. You forget this, and threaten to rob me of the prize for which I have toiled, and which the sons of the Achaeans have given me. Never when the Achaeans sack any rich city of the Trojans do I receive so good a prize as you do, though it is my hands that do the better part of the fighting. When the sharing comes, your share is far the largest, and I, forsooth, must go back to my ships, take what I can get and be thankful, when my labor of fighting is done. Now, therefore, I shall go back to Phthia; it will be much better for me to return home with my ships, for I will not stay here dishonored to gather gold and substance for you."

And Agamemnon answered: "Fly if you will, I shall make you no prayers to stay you. I have others here who will do me honor, and above all Zeus, the lord of counsel. There is no king here so hateful to me as you are, for you are ever quarrelsome and ill-affected. What though you be brave? Was it not heaven that made you so? Go home, then, with your ships and comrades to lord it over the Myrmidons. I care neither for you nor for your anger; and thus will I do: since Phoebus Apollo is taking Chryseis from me, I shall send her with my ship and my followers, but I shall come to your tent and take your own prize, Briseis, that you may learn how much stronger I am than you are, and that another may fear to set himself up as equal or comparable with me."

The son of Peleus was furious, and his heart within his shaggy breast was divided whether to draw his sword, push the others aside, and kill the son of Atreus, or to restrain himself and check his anger....

"Wine-bibber," he cried, "with the face of a dog and the heart of a fawn, you never dare to go out with the host in fight, nor yet with our chosen men in ambuscade. You shun this as you do death itself. You had rather go round and rob his prizes from any man who contradicts you. You devour your people, for you are king over a feeble folk; otherwise, son of Atreus, henceforward you would insult no man. Therefore I say, and swear it with a great oath—nay, by this my scepter, which shall sprout neither leaf nor shoot, nor bud anew from the day on which it left its parent stem upon the mountains—for the ax stripped it of leaf and bark, and now the sons of the Achaeans bear it as judges and guardians of the decrees of heaven—so surely and solemnly do I swear that hereafter they shall look fondly for Achilles and shall not find him. In the day of your distress, when your men fall dying by the murderous hand of Hector, you shall not know how to help them and shall rend your heart with rage for the hour when you offered insult to the bravest of the Achaeans."

With this the son of Peleus dashed his gold-bestudded scepter on the ground and took his seat, while the son of Atreus was beginning fiercely from his place upon the other side. Then uprose smooth-tongued Nestor, the facile speaker of the Pylians, and the words fell from his lips sweeter than honey. Two generations of men born and bred in Pylos had passed away under his rule, and he was now reigning over the third. With all sincerity and good will, therefore, he addressed them thus:

"Of a truth," he said, "a great sorrow has befallen the Achaean land. Surely Priam with his sons would rejoice, and the Trojans be glad at heart if they could hear this quarrel between you two, who are so excellent in fight and counsel. I am older than either of you; therefore be guided by me. Moreover, I have been the familiar friend of men even greater than you are, and they did not disregard my counsels.... Therefore, Agamemnon, though you be strong, take not this girl away, for the sons of the Achaeans have already given her to Achilles; and you, Achilles, strive not further with the king, for no man who by the grace of Zeus wields a scepter has like honor with Agamemnon. You are strong and have a goddess for a mother, but Agamemnon is stronger than you, for he has more people under him. Son of Atreus, check your anger, I implore you; end this quarrel with Achilles, who in the day of battle is a tower of strength to the Achaeans."

And Agamemnon answered: "Sir, all that you have said is true, but this fellow must needs become our lord and master: he must be lord of all, king of all, and captain of all, and this shall hardly be. Granted that the gods have made him a great warrior, have they also given him the right to speak with railing?"

Achilles interrupted him. "I should be a mean coward," he cried, "were I to give in to you in all things. Order other people about, not me, for I shall obey no longer. Furthermore I say—and lay my saying to your heart—I shall fight neither you nor any man about this girl, for those that take were those also that gave. But of all else that is at my ship you shall carry away nothing by force. Try, that others may see; if you do, my spear shall be reddened with your blood."

When they had quarreled thus angrily, they rose, and broke up the assembly at the ships of the Achaeans. The son of Peleus went back to his tents and ships with the son of Menoetius and his company, while Agamemnon drew a vessel into the water and chose a crew of twenty oarsmen. He escorted Chryseis on board and sent moreover a hecatomb for the god. And Odysseus went as captain....

But Agamemnon did not forget the threat that he had made Achilles and called his trusty messengers and squires, Talthybius and Eurybates. "Go," said he, "to the tent of Achilles, son of Peleus. Take Briseis by the hand and bring her hither; if he will not give her I shall come with others and take her—which will press him harder."...

Achilles Asks His Goddess Mother for Aid

Then Achilles went all alone by the side of the hoar sea, weeping and looking out upon the boundless waste of waters. He raised his hands in prayer to his immortal mother. "Mother," he cried, "you bore me doomed to live but for a little season. Surely Zeus, who thunders from Olympus, might have made that little glorious. It is not so. Agamemnon, son of Atreus, has done me dishonor, and has robbed me of my prize by force."

As he spoke he wept aloud, and his mother heard him where she was sitting in the depths of the sea hard by the old man, her father. Forthwith she rose as it were a gray mist out of the waves, sat down before him as he stood weeping, caressed him with her hand, and said, "My son, why are you weeping? What is it that grieves you? Keep it not from me, but tell me, that we may know it together."...

Achilles drew a deep sigh and said: "You know it; why tell you what you know well already?... Help your brave son, therefore, if you are able. Go to Olympus, and if you have ever done him service in word or deed, implore the aid of Zeus. Ofttimes in my father's house have I heard you glory in that you alone of the immortals saved the son of Cronus from ruin, when the others, with Hera, Poseidon, and Pallas Athene would have put him in bonds. It was you, goddess, who delivered him by calling to Olympus the hundred-handed monster whom gods call Briareus, but men Aegaeon, for he is stronger even than his father. When, therefore, he took his seat all-glorious beside the son of Cronus, the other gods were afraid, and did not bind him. Go, then, to him, remind him of all this, clasp his knees, and bid him give succor to the Trojans. Let the Achaeans be hemmed in at the sterns of their ships, and perish on the seashore, that they may reap what joy they may of their king, and that Agamemnon may rue his blindness in offering insult to the foremost of the Achaeans."

Thetis wept and answered: "My son, woe is me that I should have borne or suckled you. Would indeed that you had lived your span free from all sorrow at your ships, for it is all too brief; alas, that you should be at once short of life and long of sorrow above your peers. Woe, therefore, was the hour in which I bore you. Nevertheless, I will go to the snowy heights of Olympus, and tell this tale to Zeus, if he will hear our prayer. Meanwhile stay where you are with your ships, nurse your anger against the Achaeans, and hold aloof from fight. For Zeus went yesterday to Oceanus to a feast among the Ethiopians, and the other gods went with him. He will return to Olympus twelve days hence. I will then go to his mansion paved with bronze and will beseech him, nor do I doubt that I shall be able to persuade him."

A Sacrifice

On this she left him, still furious at the loss of her that had been taken from him. Meanwhile Odysseus reached Chryse with the hecatomb.... He gave the girl over to her father, who received her gladly, and they ranged the holy hecatomb all orderly round the altar of the god. They washed their hands and took up the barley meal to sprinkle over the victims, while Chryses lifted up his hands and prayed aloud on their behalf. "Hear me," he cried, "O god of the silver bow, that protectest Chryse and holy Cilla, and rulest Tenedos with thy might! Even as thou didst hear me aforetime when I prayed, and didst press hardly upon the Achaeans, so hear me yet again, and stay this fearful pestilence from the Danaans."

Thus did he pray, and Apollo heard his prayer. When they had done praying and sprinkling the barley meal, they drew back the heads of the victims and killed and flayed them. They cut out the thighbones, wrapped them round in two layers of fat, set some pieces of raw meat on top of them, and then Chryses laid them on the wood fire and poured wine over them, while the young men stood near him with five-pronged spits in their hands. When the thighbones were burned and they had tasted the inward meats, they cut the rest up small, put the pieces upon the spits, roasted them till they were done, and drew them off: then, when they had finished their work and the feast was ready, they ate it, and every man had his full share, so that all were satisfied. As soon as they had had enough to eat and drink, pages filled the mixing bowl with wine and water and handed it round, after giving every man his drink offering. Thus all day long the young men worshipped the god with song, hymning him and chanting the joyous paean, and the god took pleasure in their voices....

But Achilles abode at his ships and nursed his anger. He went not to the honorable assembly, and sallied not forth to fight, but gnawed at his own heart, pining for battle and the war cry.

Life Among the Gods

Now after twelve days the immortal gods came back in a body to Olympus, and Zeus led the way. Thetis was not unmindful of the charge her son had laid upon her, so she rose from under the sea and went through great heaven with early morning to Olympus, where she found the mighty son of Cronus sitting all alone upon its topmost ridges. She sat herself down before him, and with her left hand seized his knees, while with her right she caught him under the chin, and besought him, saying:

"Father Zeus, if I ever did you service in word or deed among the immortals, hear my prayer, and do honor to my son, whose life is to be cut short so early. King Agamemnon has dishonored him by taking his prize and keeping her. Honor him then yourself, Olympian lord of counsel, and grant victory to the Trojans, till the Achaeans give my son his due and load him with riches in requital."

Zeus sat for a while silent, and without a word, but Thetis still kept firm hold of his knees, and besought him a second time. "Incline your head," said she, "and promise me surely, or else deny me—for you have nothing to fear—that I may learn how greatly you disdain me."

At this Zeus was much troubled and answered: "I shall have trouble if you set me quarreling with Hera, for she will provoke me with her taunting speeches; even now she is always railing at me before the other gods and accusing me of giving aid to the Trojans. Go back now, lest she should find out. I will consider the matter, and will bring it about as you wish. See, I incline my head that you may believe me. This is the most solemn token that I can give to any god. I never recall my word, or deceive, or fail to do what I say, when I have nodded my head."

As he spoke, the son of Cronus bowed his dark brows, and the ambrosial locks swayed on his immortal head, till vast Olympus reeled.

When the pair had thus laid their plans, they parted—Zeus to his own house, while the goddess quitted the splendor of Olympus, and plunged into the depths of the sea. The gods rose from their seats, before the coming of their sire. Not one of them dared to remain sitting, but all stood up as he came among them. There, then, he took his seat. But Hera, when she saw him, knew that he and the old merman's daughter, silver-footed Thetis, had been hatching mischief, so she at once began to upbraid him. "Trickster," she cried, "which of the gods have you been taking into your counsels now? You are always settling matters in secret behind my back, and have never yet told me, if you could help it, one word of your intentions."

"Hera," replied the sire of gods and men, "you must not expect to be informed of all my counsels. You are my wife, but you would find it hard to understand them. When it is proper for you to hear, there is no one, god or man, who will be told sooner, but when I mean to keep a matter to myself, you must not pry or ask questions."

"Dread son of Cronus," answered Hera, "what are you talking about? I? Pry and ask questions? Never. I let you have your own way in everything. Still, I have a strong misgiving that the old merman's daughter Thetis has been talking you over, for she was with you and had hold of your knees this selfsame morning. I believe, therefore, that you have been promising her to give glory to Achilles, and to kill much people at the ships of the Achaeans."

"Wife," said Zeus, "I can do nothing but you suspect me and find it out. You will take nothing by it, for I shall only dislike you the more, and it will go harder with you. Granted that it is as you say; I mean to have it so. Sit down and hold your tongue as I bid you, for if I once begin to lay my hands about you, though all heaven were on your side it would profit you nothing."

On this Hera was frightened, so she curbed her stubborn will and sat down in silence. But the heavenly beings were disquieted throughout the house of Zeus, till the cunning workman Hephaestus began to try and pacify his mother Hera. "It will be intolerable," said he, "if you two fall to wrangling and setting heaven in an uproar about a pack of mortals. If such ill counsels are to prevail, we shall have no pleasure at our banquet. Let me than advise my mother—and she must herself know that it will be better—to make friends with my dear father Zeus, lest he again scold her and disturb our feast. If the Olympian Thunderer wants to hurl us all from our seats, he can do so, for he is far the strongest, so give him fair words, and he will then soon be in a good humor with us."

As he spoke, he took a double cup of nectar and placed it in his mother's hand. "Cheer up, my dear mother," said he, "and make the best of it. I love you dearly, and should be very sorry to see you get a thrashing; however grieved I might be, I could not help you, for there is no standing against Zeus. Once before when I was trying to help you, he caught me by the foot and flung me from the heavenly threshold. All day long from morn till eve, was I falling, till at sunset I came to ground in the island of Lemnos, and there I lay, with very little life left in me, till the Sintians came and tended me."

Hera smiled at this, and as she smiled she took the cup from her son's hands. Then Hephaestus drew sweet nectar from the mixing bowl, and served it round among the gods, going from left to right; and the blessed gods laughed out a loud applause as they saw him bustling about the heavenly mansion.

Thus through the livelong day to the going down of the sun they feasted, and everyone had his full share, so that all were satisfied. Apollo struck his lyre, and the Muses lifted up their sweet voices, calling and answering one another.

But when the sun's glorious light had faded, they went home to bed, each in his own abode, which lame Hephaestus with his consummate skill had fashioned for them. So Zeus, the Olympian lord of thunder, hied him to the bed in which he always slept; and when he had got on to it he went to sleep, with Hera of the golden throne by his side.   (From *Book I*)

> Zeus, keeping his promise to Thetis, tricks Agamemnon with a dream into imagining he can capture Troy at once. Agamemnon, however, craftily tests the spirit of his men by telling them that Zeus has bidden him give up the siege. Athene, sent by Hera, inspires Odysseus to oppose the plan, and he incites the Greeks to continue the struggle.

The Lying Dream

Now the other gods and the armed warriors on the plain slept soundly, but Zeus was wakeful, for he was thinking how to do honor to Achilles and destroy much people at the ships of the Achaeans. In the end he deemed it would be best to send a lying dream to King Agamemnon. So he called one to him and said to it: "Lying Dream, go to the ships of the Achaeans, into the tent of Agamemnon, and say to him word for word as I now bid you. Tell him to get the Achaeans instantly under arms, for he shall take Troy. There are no longer divided counsels among the gods. Hera has brought them to her own mind, and woe betides the Trojans."

The dream went when it had heard its message, and soon reached the ships of the Achaeans. It sought Agamemnon, son of Atreus, and found him in his tent wrapped in a profound slumber. It hovered over his head in the likeness of Nestor, son of Neleus, whom Agamemnon honored above all his councilors....

The dream then left him, and he thought of things that were surely not to be accomplished. He thought that on that same day he was to take the city of Priam, but he little knew what was in the mind of Zeus, who had many another hard-fought fight in store alike for Danaans and Trojans. Then presently he woke, with the divine message still ringing in his ears, so he sat upright, and put on his soft shirt so fair and new, and over this his heavy cloak. He bound his sandals on to his comely feet, and slung his silver-studded sword about his shoulders; then he took the imperishable staff of his father and sallied forth to the ships of the Achaeans.

Meeting of the King's Council

The goddess Dawn now wended her way to vast Olympus that she might herald day to Zeus and to the other immortals, and Agamemnon sent the criers round to call the people in assembly; so they called them and the people gathered thereon. But first he summoned a meeting of the elders at the ship of Nestor, king of Pylos, and when they were assembled he laid a cunning counsel before them.

"My friends," said he, "I have had a dream from heaven in the dead of night, and its face and figure resembled none but Nestor's. It stood beside me and addressed me...."

He then sat down, and Nestor, the prince of Pylos, with all sincerity and good will addressed them thus: "My friends," said he, "princes and councilors of the Argives, if any other man of the Achaeans had told us of this dream we should have declared it false, and would have had nothing to do with it. But he who has seen it is the foremost man among us; we must therefore set about getting the people under arms."

Meeting of the Popular Assembly

With this he led the way from the council, and the other sceptered kings rose with him in obedience to the word of Agamemnon; but the people pressed forward to hear. They swarmed like bees that sally from some hollow cave and flit in countless throng among the spring flowers, bunched in knots and clusters; even so did the mighty multitude pour from ships and tents to the assembly, and range themselves upon the wide-watered shore, while among them ran Wildfire Rumor, messenger of Zeus, urging them ever to the fore. Thus they gathered in a pell-mell of mad confusion, and the earth groaned under the tramp of men as the people sought their places. Nine heralds went crying about among them to stay their tumult and bid them listen to the kings, till at last they were got into their several places and ceased their clamor. Then King Agamemnon rose, holding his scepter....

Agamemnon Tests the Greeks' Spirit

"My friends," he said, "heroes, servants of Ares, the hand of heaven has been laid heavily upon me. Cruel Zeus gave me his solemn promise that I should sack the city of Priam before returning, but he has played me false, and is now bidding me go ingloriously back to Argos with the loss of much people. Such is the will of Zeus, who has laid many a proud city in the dust, as he will yet lay others, for his power is above all.... Nine of Zeus' years are gone. The timbers of our ships have rotted; their tacking is sound no longer. Our wives and little ones at home look anxiously for our coming, but the work that we came hither to do has not been done. Now, therefore, let us all do as I say: let us sail back to our own land, for we shall not take Troy."

With these words he moved the hearts of the multitude, so many of them as knew not the cunning counsel of Agamemnon. They surged to and fro like the waves of the Icarian Sea, when the east and south winds break from heaven's clouds to lash them; or as when the west wind sweeps over a field of corn and the ears bow beneath the blast, even so were they swayed as they flew with loud cries towards the ships, and the dust from under their feet rose heavenward. They cheered each other on to draw the ships into the sea; they cleared the channels in front of them; they began taking away the stays from underneath them, and the air rang with their glad cries, so eager were they to return.

Then surely the Argives would have returned after a fashion that was not fated. But Hera said to Athene, "Alas, daughter of aegis-bearing Zeus, unweariable, shall the Argives fly home to their own land over the broad sea, and leave Priam and the Trojans the glory of still keeping Helen, for whose sake so many of the Achaeans have died at Troy, far from their homes? Go about at once among the host, and speak gently to them, man by man, that they draw not their ships into the sea."

Athene was not slack to do her bidding. Down she darted from the topmost summits of Olympus, and in a moment she was at the ships of the Achaeans. There she found Odysseus, peer of Zeus in counsel, standing alone. He had not as yet laid a hand upon his ship, for he was grieved and sorry; so she went close to him and said, "Odysseus, noble son of Laertes, are you going to fling yourselves into your ships, and be off home to your own land in this way? Will you leave Priam and the Trojans the glory of still keeping Helen, for whose sake so many of the Achaeans have died at Troy, far from their homes? Go about at once among the host, and speak gently to them, man by man, that they draw not their ships into the sea."

Odysseus knew the voice as that of the goddess: he flung his cloak from him and set off to run. His servant Eurybates, a man of Ithaca, who waited on him, took charge of the cloak, whereon Odysseus went straight up to Agamemnon and received from him his ancestral, imperishable staff. With this he went about among the ships of the Achaeans.

Whenever he met a king or chieftain, he stood by him and spoke to him courteously, "Sir," said he, "this flight is cowardly and unworthy. Stand to your post, and bid your people also keep their places. You do not yet know the full mind of Agamemnon; he was sounding us, and ere long will visit the Achaeans with his displeasure. We were not all of us at the council to hear what he then said. See to it lest he be angry and do us a mischief; for the pride of kings is great and the hand of Zeus is with them."

The Lot of the Common Man

But when he came across any common man who was making a noise, he struck him with his staff and rebuked him, saying: "Sirrah, hold your peace, and listen to better men than yourself. You are a coward and no soldier; you are nobody either in fight or council; we cannot all be kings; it is not well that there should be many masters; one man must be supreme—one king to whom the son of scheming Cronus has given the scepter and right of judgment over you all."

Thus masterfully did he go about among the host, and the people hurried back to the assembly from their tents and ships with a sound as the thunder of surf when it comes crashing down upon the shore, and all the sea is in an uproar.

The rest now took their seats and kept to their own several places, but Thersites still went on wagging his unbridled tongue—a man of many words, and those unseemly; a monger of sedition, a railer against all who were in authority, who cared not what he said, so that he might set the Achaeans in a laugh. He was the ugliest man of all those that came before Troy—bandy-legged, lame of one foot, with his two shoulders rounded and hunched over his chest. His head ran up to a point, but there was little hair on the top of it. Achilles and Odysseus hated him worst of all, for it was with them that he was most wont to wrangle. Now, however, with a shrill, squeaky voice he began heaping his abuse on Agamemnon. The Achaeans were angry and disgusted, yet nonetheless he kept on brawling at the son of Atreus.

"Agamemnon," he cried, "what ails you now, and what more do you want? Your tents are filled with bronze and with fair women, for whenever we take a town we give you the pick of them. Would you have yet more gold, which some Trojan is to give you as ransom for his son, when I or another Achaean has taken him prisoner? Or is it some young girl to hide away and lie with? It is not well that you, the ruler of the Achaeans, should bring them into such misery. Weakling cowards, women rather than men, let us sail home, and leave this fellow here at Troy to stew in his own meeds of honor, and discover whether we were of any service to him or no. Achilles is a much better man than he is, and see how he has treated him—robbing him of his prize and keeping it himself. Achilles takes it meekly and shows no fight; if he did, son of Atreus, you would never again insult him."

Thus railed Thersites, but Odysseus at once went up to him and rebuked him sternly. "Check your glib tongue, Thersites," said he, "and babble not a word further. Chide not with princes when you have none to back you. There is no viler creature come before Troy with the sons of Atreus. Drop this chatter about kings, and neither revile them nor keep harping about going home. We do not yet know how things are going to be, nor whether the Achaeans are to return with good success or evil. How dare you gibe at Agamemnon because the Danaans have awarded him so many prizes? I tell you, therefore—and it shall surely be—that if I again catch you talking such nonsense, I will either forfeit my own head and be no more called father of Telemachus, or I will take you, strip you stark naked, and whip you out of the assembly till you go blubbering back to the ships."

On this he beat him with his staff about the back and shoulders till he dropped and fell a-weeping. The golden scepter raised a bloody welt on his back, so he sat down frightened and in pain, looking foolish as he wiped the tears from his eyes. The people were sorry for him, yet they laughed heartily, and one would turn to his neighbor, saying: "Odysseus has done many a good thing ere now in fight and council, but he never did the Argives a better turn than when he stopped this fellow's mouth from prating further. He will give the kings no more of his insolence."...   (From *Book II*)

17 Hesiod

Changing Times and the Moral Order

The world of Hesiod as seen in his partly autobiographical *Works and Days*, written around 700 B.C., is far different from that described in the slightly earlier works of Homer. The monarchical society of the *Iliad* in which the

From *Hesiod, Homeric Hymns and Homerica*, Loeb Classical Library Volume 57, translated by Hugh G. Evelyn-White (Cambridge, Mass.: Harvard University Press, 1914). The Loeb Classical Library® is a registered trademark of the President and Fellows of Harvard College. Reprinted by permission of the publishers and the Trustees of the Loeb Classical Library.

common man still exercised some rights as a member of the army and popular assembly has been replaced by an oligarchy made up of nobles that could oppress the lower classes without check. Hesiod was himself a commoner who had suffered from what he saw as the rapacity of the nobility, whom he calls "lords" and "princes." His own brother Perses had connived with the "bribe-swallowing" aristocratic judges to deprive him of much of his rightful share in their father's small estate and was even now threatening him with another lawsuit. To Hesiod, all this was symbolic of the nature of the time of troubles in which he lived, a time in which there was no justice or happiness for men. In his poem, he portrays the history of humankind as one of progressive degeneration through five distinct ages—from an idealized golden age in a faraway past to the present harsh age of "black iron." Hesiod's mythological account of the five ages of man is a good example of his mingling of fable with fact in an effort to give meaning to the realities of his time and explain their origin. Noteworthy also is his personification of justice (*dikē*) as a goddess who once lived among men but who has long since fled to Mt. Olympus. As *Dikē*, Goddess of Justice, she sits there beside her father Zeus, who, following her instructions, rewards the just on earth and punishes the unjust. Hesiod's message seems clear: even though justice has left the earth and exists as an ideal in heaven, it continues to be concerned with human affairs. Thus, despite Hesiod's gloomy concern with present evils, his viewpoint is essentially optimistic because he looks ahead to a new and better future. He is the impassioned prophet of a new moral religious reformation in which Zeus, as an ethical force, demands and rewards only righteous conduct, and in which a new rational ideal of moderation—including work, a form of "strife in moderation" and no longer considered ignoble by gods and men—replaces the aristocratic valor of Homer's day as the chief virtue or "Goodness" [*aretē*] of man. As has been noted in the earlier history of the peoples of the Ancient Near East, so now in Greece an age of confusion and suffering has brought forth a demand for a social conscience and a moral order. In Hesiod's words, "Only when he has suffered does the fool learn."

Invocation in Praise of a Moralized Zeus

Muses of Pieria who give glory through song, come hither, tell of Zeus your father and chant his praise. Through him mortal men are famed or unfamed, sung or unsung alike, as great Zeus wills. For easily he makes strong, and easily he brings the strong man low; easily he humbles the proud and raises the obscure, and easily he straightens the crooked and blasts the proud—Zeus who thunders aloft and has his dwelling most high. Attend thou with eye and ear, and make judgments straight with righteousness. And I, Perses, would tell of true things.

Two Kinds of Strife: The Ideal of Moderation

So, after all, there was not one kind of Strife alone, but all over the earth there are two. As for the one, a man would praise her when he came to understand her; but the other is blameworthy: and they are wholly different in nature. For one fosters evil war and battle, being cruel: her no man loves; but perforce, through the will of the deathless gods, men pay harsh Strife her honor due.

But the other is ... far kinder to men. She stirs up even the shiftless to toil; for a man grows eager to work when he considers his neighbor, a rich man who hastens to plough and plant and put his house in good order; and neighbor vies with his neighbor as he hurries after wealth. This Strife is wholesome for men. And potter is angry with potter, and craftsman with craftsman, and beggar is jealous of beggar and minstrel of minstrel.

Perses, lay up these things in your heart, and do not let that Strife who delights in mischief hold your heart back from work, while you peep and peer and listen to the wrangles of the court-house. Little concern has he with quarrels and courts who has not a year's victuals laid up betimes, even that which the earth bears, Demeter's grain. When you have got plenty of that, you can raise disputes and strive to get another's goods. But you shall have no second chance to deal so again: nay, let us settle our dispute here with true judgment which is of Zeus and is perfect. For we had already divided our inheritance, but you seized the greater share and carried it off, greatly swelling the glory of our bribe-swallowing lords [the Greek word is *basileis*, "kings"] who love to judge such a cause as this. Fools! They know not how much more the half is than the whole, nor what great advantage there is in mallow and asphodel ["cheese and crackers"]....

The Five Ages of Man

Or if you will, I will sum you up another tale well and skillfully—and do you lay it up in your heart—how the gods and mortal men sprang from one source.

First of all the deathless gods who dwell on Olympus made a golden race of mortal men who lived in the time of Cronos when he was reigning in heaven. And they lived like gods without sorrow of heart, remote and free from toil and grief: miserable age rested not on them; but with legs and arms never failing they made merry with feasting beyond the reach of all evils. When they died, it was as though they were overcome with sleep, and they had all good things; for the fruitful earth unforced bare them fruit abundantly and without stint. They dwelt in ease and peace upon their lands with many good things, rich in flocks and loved by the blessed gods.

But after the earth had covered this generation—they are called pure spirits dwelling on the earth, and are kindly, delivering them from harm, and guardians of mortal men; for they roam everywhere over the earth, clothed in mist and keep watch on judgments and cruel deeds, givers of wealth; for this royal right also they received—then they who dwell on Olympus made a second generation which was of silver and less noble by far. It was like the golden race neither in body nor in spirit. A child was brought up at his good mother's side an hundred years, an utter simpleton, playing childishly in his own home. But when they were full grown and were come to the full measure of their prime, they lived only a little time and that in sorrow because of their foolishness, for they could not keep from sinning and from wronging one another, nor would they serve the immortals, nor sacrifice on the holy altars of the blessed ones as it is right for men to do wherever they dwell. Then Zeus the son of Cronos was angry and put them away, because they would not give honor to the blessed gods who live on Olympus.

But when earth had covered this generation also—they are called blessed spirits of the underworld by men, and, though they are of second order, yet honor attends them also—Zeus the Father made a third generation of mortal men, a brazen race, sprung from ash-trees; and it was in no way equal to the silver age, but was terrible and strong. They loved the lamentable works of Ares and deeds of violence; they ate no bread, but were hard of heart like adamant, fearful men. Great was their strength and unconquerable the arms which grew from their shoulders on their strong limbs. Their armor was of bronze, and their houses of bronze, and of bronze were their implements: there was no black iron. These were destroyed by their own hands and passed to the dank house of chill Hades, and left no name: terrible though they were, black Death seized them, and they left the bright light of the sun.

But when earth had covered this generation also, Zeus the son of Cronos made yet another, the fourth, upon the fruitful earth, which was nobler and more righteous, a god-like race of hero-men who are called demi-gods, the race before our own, throughout the boundless earth. Grim war and dread battle destroyed a part of them, some in the land of Cadmus at seven-gated Thebes when they fought for the flocks of Oedipus, and some, when it had brought them in ships over the great sea gulf to Troy for rich-haired Helen's sake: there death's end enshrouded a part of them. But to the others father Zeus the son of Cronos gave a living and an abode apart from men, and made them dwell at the ends of the earth. And they live untouched by sorrow in the Islands of the Blessed along the shore of deep swirling Ocean, happy heroes for whom the grain-giving earth bears honey-sweet fruit flourishing thrice a year, far from the deathless gods, and Cronos rules over them; for the father of men and gods released him from his bonds. And these last equally have honor and glory.

And again far-seeing Zeus made yet another generation, the fifth, of men who are upon the bounteous earth.

Thereafter, would that I were not among the men of the fifth generation, but either had died before or been born afterwards. For now truly is a race of iron, and men never rest from labor and sorrow by day, and from perishing by night; and the gods shall lay sore trouble upon them. But, notwithstanding, even these shall have some good mingled with their evils. And Zeus will destroy this race of mortal men also when they come to have grey hair on the temples at their birth. The father will not agree with his children, nor the children with their father, nor guest with his host, nor comrade with comrade; nor will brother be dear to brother as aforetime. Men will dishonor their parents as they grow quickly old, and will carp at them, chiding them with bitter words, hardhearted they, not knowing the fear of the gods. They will not repay their aged parents the cost of their nurture, for might shall be their right: and one man will sack another's city. There will be no favor for the man who keeps his oath or for the just or for the good; but rather men will praise the evildoer and his violent dealing. Strength will be right and reverence will cease to be; and the wicked will hurt the worthy man, speaking false words against him, and will swear an oath upon them. Envy, foul-mouthed, delighting in evil, with scowling face, will go along with wretched men one and all. And then Aidos [Reverence] and Nemesis [Retribution], with their sweet forms wrapped in white robes, will go from the wide-pathed earth and forsake mankind to join the company of the deathless gods: and bitter sorrow will be left for mortal men, and there will be no help against evil.

The New Moral Order

But you, Perses, listen to right and do not foster violence, for violence is bad for a common man. Even a noble cannot easily bear its burden, but is weighed down under it when he has fallen into delusion. The better path is to go by on the other side towards justice; for [*Dikē*, Goddess of] Justice beats Outrage when she comes at length to the end of the race. But only when he has suffered does the fool learn this. For Oath keeps pace with wrong judgments. There is a noise when Justice is being dragged in the way where those who devour bribes and give sentence with crooked judgments take her. And she, wrapped in mist, follows to the city and haunts of the people, weeping, and bringing mischief to men, even to such as have driven her forth in that they did not deal straightly with her.

But they who give straight judgments to strangers and to the men of the land, and go not aside from what is just, their city flourishes, and the people prosper in it; Peace, the nurse of children, is abroad in their land, and all-seeing Zeus never decrees cruel war against them. Neither famine nor disaster ever haunt men who do true justice; but light-heartedly they tend to fields which are all their care. The earth bears them victuals in plenty, and on the mountains the oak bears acorns upon the top and bees in the midst. Their woolly sheep are laden with fleeces; their women bear children like their parents. They flourish continually with good things, and do not travel on ships, for the grain-giving earth bears them fruit.

But for those who practice violence and cruel deeds far-seeing Zeus, the son of Cronos, ordains a punishment. Often even a whole city suffers for a bad man who sins and devises presumptuous deeds, and the son of Cronos lays great trouble upon the people, famine and plague together, so that the men perish away, and their women do not bear children, and their houses become few, through the contriving of Olympian Zeus. And again, at another time, the son of Cronos either destroys their wide army, or their walls, or else makes an end of their ships on the sea.

You princes, mark well this punishment you also: for the deathless gods are near among men and mark all those who oppress their fellows with crooked judgments, and reck not the anger of the gods. For upon the bounteous earth Zeus has thrice ten thousand spirits, watchers of mortal men, and these keep watch on judgments and deeds of wrong as they roam, clothed in mist, all over the earth. And there is virgin Justice, the daughter of Zeus, who is honored and reverenced among the gods who dwell on Olympus, and whenever anyone hurts her with lying slander, she sits beside her father, Zeus the son of Cronos, and tells him of men's wicked heart, until the people pay for the mad folly of their princes who, evilly minded, pervert judgment and give sentence crookedly. Keep watch against this, you princes, and make straight your judgments, you who devour bribes; put crooked judgments altogether from your thoughts.

He does mischief to himself who does mischief to another, and evil planned harms the plotter most....

But you, Perses, lay up these things within your heart and listen now to right, ceasing altogether to think of violence. For the son of Cronos has ordained this law for men, that fishes and beasts and winged fowls should devour one another, for right is not in them; but to mankind he gave right which proves far the best....

A New Definition of Goodness: Work and Wealth

To you, foolish Perses, I will speak good sense. Badness can be got easily and in shoals: the road to her is smooth, and she lives very near us. But between us and Goodness [arete] the gods have placed the sweat of our brows: long and steep is the path that leads to her, and it is rough at the first; but when a man has reached the top, then indeed she is easy, though otherwise hard to reach.

That man is altogether best who considers all things himself and marks what will be better afterwards and at the end; and he, again, is good who listens to a good adviser; but whoever neither thinks for himself nor keeps in mind what another man tells him, he is an unprofitable man. But do you at any rate, always remembering my charge, work, well-born Perses, that Hunger may hate you, and venerable Demeter, richly crowned, may love you and fill your barn with food; for Hunger is altogether a meet comrade for the sluggard. Both gods and men are angry with a man who lives idle, for in nature he is like the stingless drones who waste the labor of the bees, eating without working; but let it be your care to order your work properly, that in the right season your barns may be full of victual. Through work men grow rich in flocks and substance, and working they are much better loved by the immortals. Work is no disgrace: it is idleness which is a disgrace. But if you work, the idle will soon envy you as you grow rich, for fame and renown attend on wealth. And whatever be your lot, work is best for you, if you turn your misguided mind away from other men's property to your work and attend to your livelihood as I bid you. An evil shame is the needy man's companion, shame which both greatly harms and prospers men: shame is with poverty, but confidence with wealth.

Wealth should not be seized: god-given wealth is much better; for if a man take great wealth violently and perforce, or if he steal it through his tongue, as often happens when gain deceives men's sense and dishonor tramples down honor, the gods soon blot him out and make that man's house low, and wealth attends him only for a little time. Alike with him who does wrong to a suppliant or a guest, or who goes up to his brother's bed and commits unnatural sin in lying with his wife, or why infatuately offends against fatherless children, or who abuses his old father at the cheerless threshold of old age and attacks him with harsh words, truly Zeus himself is angry, and at the last lays on him a heavy requital for his evildoing. But do you turn your foolish heart altogether away from these things, and, as far as you are able, sacrifice to the deathless gods purely and cleanly, and burn rich meats also, and at other times propitiate them with libations and incense, both when you go to bed and when the holy light has come back, that they may be gracious to you in heart and spirit, and so you may buy another's holding and not another yours.

... He who adds to what he has, will keep off bright-eyed hunger; for if you add only a little to a little and do this often, soon that little will become great.

What a man has by him at home does not trouble him: it is better to have your stuff at home, for whatever is abroad may mean loss. It is a good thing to draw on what you have, but it grieves your heart to need something and not to have it, and I bid you mark this. Take your fill when the cask is first opened and when it is nearly spent, but midways be sparing: it is poor saving when you come to the lees.

Let the wage promised to a friend be fixed; even with your brother smile—and get a witness; for trust and mistrust, alike ruin men.

Do not let a flaunting woman coax and cozen and deceive you: she is after your barn. The man who trusts womankind trusts deceivers.

There should be an only son, to feed his father's house, for so wealth will increase in the home; but if you leave a second son you should die old. Yet Zeus can easily give great wealth to a greater number. More hands mean more work and more increase.

If your heart within you desires wealth, do these things and work with work upon work.

18 Early Greek Lyric Poetry

Individualism Emergent

Additional evidence of the course taken by Greek culture after the Dark Age is found in the poetry of the seventh and sixth centuries B.C. The poets of these centuries belonged to a different time, and they responded to different needs. Hesiod in his *Works and Days* had been the first Greek poet to turn from the impersonal narration of great deeds, in the manner of Homer, to the expression of his own individual experience. In the following opening lines from his other long poem, the *Theogony,* which traces the history of the divine government of the universe to the point at which it culminates in the benevolent monarchy of Zeus, Hesiod describes the new role of poetry as the expression of a deep personal reaction to life. His view anticipates the later doctrine of Aristotle's *Poetics* that has ever remained an important element in art criticism—a work of art is the product of a sensitive person's attempt to be purged of, and thereby gain relief from, the intense emotions aroused by significant personal experience.

> Oh, blessed is the man
> Whome'er the Muses love! Sweet is the voice
> That from his lips flows ever. Is there one
> Who hides some grief in his wounded mind
> And mourns with aching heart? ... Straight he feels
> His sorrow stealing in forgetfulness:
> Now of his griefs remembers aught: so soon
> The Muses' gift has turned his woes away.

The Greek poets who followed Hesiod intensify this exploration of purely individual experience. With the old way of life now lost, and living amidst the upheaval caused by political, social, and spiritual change, these poets came to express a corresponding turbulence of beliefs and emotions in a new literary form called the lyric, a short, highly personal poem accompanied by a musical instrument, usually the lyre. They rejected old values, cried out in pain over life's woes, sang of romantic love and flowing wine, and lamented the inevitable coming of old age.

A. SAPPHO

Sappho lived at the end of the seventh century B.C. in Mitylene on the island of Lesbos, where she conducted a school for girls. She is the first and among the greatest of all female poets. Her main theme is love and loveliness, and few have ever explored this theme with deeper passion, more delicate grace and simplicity in the choice of words, richer imagination, or greater beauty. The romantic love that is Sappho's theme is rarely if ever found in Homer or in any heroic-age poetry. In the Homeric epics, Helen had been unwillingly abducted by Paris and taken to Troy, while in Sappho's version, she willingly leaves husband and family "all for love."

Fair Helen, All for Love

She, who the beauty of mankind
Excelled, fair Helen, all for love
The noblest husband left behind;
Afar, to Troy she sailed away,
Her child, her parents, clean forgot;
The Cyprian [Aphrodite] led her far astray
Out of the way, resisting not.

The Fairest Thing on Earth

Some say the fairest thing on earth is a troop of horsemen,
others a band of foot-soldiers,
others a squadron of ships.
But I say the fairest things is the beloved.

When I See You

When I even see you,
my voice stops,
my tongue is broken,
a thin flame runs beneath all my skin,
my eyes are blinded,

"Fair Helen, All for Love" is from A. R. Burn, *The Lyric Age of Greece* (London: Edward Arnold, Ltd., 1961), p. 236. Reprinted by permission of Edward Arnold, Ltd.

"The Fairest Thing on Earth" and "When I See You" are from Werner Jaeger, *Paideia: The Ideals of Greek Culture*, Vol. I, second edition (New York: Oxford University Press, 1945), p. 135. Reprinted by permission of Oxford University Press.

there is thunder in my ears,
the sweat pours from me,
I tremble through and through,
I am paler than grass,
and I seem almost like one dead.

Love Rends Me

Lo, Love once more my soul within me rends
Like wind that on the mountain oak descends.

Translated by John Addington Symonds

The Moon Is Set

The silver moon is set;
   The Pleiades are gone;
Half the long night is spent, and yet
   I lie alone.

Translated by J. H. Merivale

B. THEOGNIS

Theognis of Megara, near Athens, was a mid-sixth-century local aristocrat who filled his verse with outraged bitterness toward the lower classes and their tyrant leaders (see Selection 23) under whom he suffered confiscation of property and exile. Although he claims to be no narrow reactionary "leaguing with the proud and arbitrary few" but a moderate who will "incline to neither side," Theognis expresses the ultraconservative viewpoint on social and political change; to him, the nobles are always "good," and the commoners are always "base." His elegiac poems became greatly favored by Greek aristocrats in subsequent centuries as his verse speaks eloquently to the latter's shared values and outlook in life.

"A Discontented Cry Fills All the Earth"

This is Theognis, the Megarian poet,
So celebrated and renowned in Greece!
Yet some there are, forsooth, I cannot please;
Nor ever could contrive, with all my skill,
To gain the common liking and goodwill
Of these my fellow-citizens.—No wonder!
Not even he, the god that wields the thunder,
The sovereign all-wise, almighty Jove,
Can please them with his government above:
Some call for rainy weather, some for dry.
A discontented and discordant cry
Fills all the earth, and reaches to the sky,...
To rear a child is easy, but to teach

From *The Works of Hesiod, Callimachus, and Theognis,* translated by John Hookham Frere (London: H.G. Bohn, 1856).

Morals and manners is beyond our reach;
To make the foolish wise, the wicked good,
That science never yet was understood.
The sons of Aesculapius, if their art
Could remedy a perverse and wicked heart,
Might earn enormous wages!...

"Our Common People Are No More the Same"

Our Commonwealth preserves its former frame,
Our common people are no more the same:
They that in skins and hides were rudely dressed,
Nor dreamt of law, nor sought to be redressed
By rules of right, but in the days of old
Flocked to the town, like cattle to the fold,
Are now the brave and wise; and we the rest,
Their betters nominally, once the best,
Degenerate, debased, timid, mean!
Who can endure to witness such a scene?...

"I Incline to Neither Side"

I walk by rule and measure, and incline
To neither side, but take an even line;
Fix'd in a single purpose and design.
With learning's happy gifts to celebrate,
To civilize and dignify the state:
Not leaguing with the discontented crew,
Nor with the proud and arbitrary few....
Waste not your efforts, struggle not, my friend,
Idle and old abuses to defend:
Take heed! the very measures that you press
May bring repentance with their own success.

"Zeus, I Marvel at Thy Ways"

Blessed, almighty Zeus! With deep amaze
I view the world—and marvel at thy ways!
All our devices, every subtle plan,
Each secret act, and all the thoughts of man,
Your boundless intellect can comprehend!
On your award our destinies depend.
How can you reconcile it to your sense
Of right and wrong, thus loosely to dispense
Your bounties on the wicked and the good?
How can your laws be known or understood?
When we behold a man faithful and just,
Humbly devout, true to his word and trust,
Dejected and oppressed—whilst the profane,

And wicked and unjust, in glory reign,
Proudly triumphant, flushed with power and gain,
What inference can human reason draw?
How can we guess the secret of the law,
Or choose the path approved by power divine?...
Not to be born—never to see the sun—
No worldly blessing is a greater one!
And the next best is speedily to die,
And lapt beneath a load of earth to lie!

"Longing Again to View This Land of Mine"

You, great Apollo, with its walls and towers
Fenc'd and adorn'd of old this town of ours!...
Yet much I fear the faction and the strife,
Throughout our Grecian cities, raging rife,
And their wild councils. But do thou defend
This town of ours, our founder and our friend!
Wide have I wander'd, far beyond the sea,
Even to the distant shores of Sicily,
To broad Euboea's plentiful domain,
With the rich vineyards in its planted plain;
And to the sunny wave and winding edge
Of fair Eurotas, with its reedy sedge;
Where Sparta stands in simple majesty,
Among her manly rulers, there was I!
Greeted and welcom'd (there and everywhere)
With courteous entertainment, kind and fair;
Yet still my weary spirit would repine,
Longing again to view this land of mine.

Translated by J. H. Frere

19 Pindar's Odes to Athletic Victors

The Heroic Ideal

A lyric poet from the central Greek region of Boeotia, Pindar achieved early fame as the most desirable composer of commissioned poems for the celebration of athletic victories. During this time, Greek youths and men, mainly

From *The Odes of Pindar, Vol. II,* Loeb Classical Library 485, translated by Sir John Sandys (Cambridge, Mass.: Harvard University Press, 1958). The Loeb Classical Library® is a registered trademark of the President and Fellows of Harvard College. Reprinted by permission of the publishers and the Trustees of the Loeb Classical Library.

though not always from aristocratic circles, traveled from Greek city-states throughout the Mediterranean world, including North Africa and Sicily, to the sites of the most prestigious Panhellenic athletic festivals, or the Crown Games, that were held once every four years. The most famous of these were the Games of Zeus at Olympia. The victories that the athletes won at the Panhellenic festivals conferred on them a sort of immortality. Those who came first (the Greeks did not give prizes to runners-up at the Crown Games) at these games were given crowns of vegetation, were granted the right to erect a statue in the sacred precincts, and were fêted as semi-divine heroes upon their return to their cities.

Most competing athletes trained and traveled at their own expense to attend the games. Few athletes were poor. The most costly games were the equestrian events, especially the chariot race, for such events required the contestants to pay for the upkeep of horses, an expensive proposition in ancient Greece. Indeed, the contestants for the chariot races were almost invariably the sponsors who paid for the horse teams and the charioteers rather than the charioteers themselves. Many important Greek leaders, aristo-crats, kings, and tyrants entered horse teams at these games to showcase their wealth and power. They were mostly interested in their own reputation and eagerly sought the services of a poet to secure their own place in people's memories and in history.

The following ode was commissioned by Arcesilas, king of the Greek city of Cyrene in North Africa (modern Libya), to celebrate the victory of his horse teams at the Pythian Games dedicated to the god Apollo in 462 B.C. Pindar was in the habit of relating an athlete's victory to the native history and myth-ological tales of that individual's own community, and this poem makes repeated reference to the original Greek colonization and foundation of Cyrene (see Selection 20), which in tradition took place at the behest of the Oracle of Apollo at Delphi.

Wide is the power of wealth, whene'er it is wedded with stainless honour, wealth that a mortal man receiveth at the hands of Destiny, and taketh to his home as a ministrant that bringeth him many friends.

O blest of Heaven! Arcesilas! From the first steps of thy famous life thou dost indeed seek for that wealth, and fair fame withal, by the help of Castor of the golden chariot, who, after the wintry storm, sheddeth beams of calm upon thy happy hearth.

They that are noble bear with a fairer grace even the power that is given of God; and thou, while thou walkest in the straight path, hast prosperity in abun-dance around thee. First, as thou art a king over mighty cities, the eye of thy ancestry looketh on this as a meed most fit for reverence, when wedded to a soul like thine; and even to-day art thou happy in that thou hast already, with thy coursers, won glory from the famous Pythian festival, and hast given wel-come to this triumph-band of men, in whom Apollo delighteth.

Therefore, when thou art hymned in song in Cyrene's sweet garden of Aphrodite, forget not to give God the glory; do not forget to love, above all thy comrades, Carrhôtus, who, on returning to the palace of them that reign by right, did not bring in his train Excuse, that daughter of After-thought, who is wise too late; but, when welcomed beside the waters of Castalia, flung over thy locks the guerdon of glory in the chariot-race with his reins unsevered in the sacred space of the twelve courses of swift feet. For he brake no part of his strong equipage; nay, he hath dedicated all the dainty handiwork of skilled craftsmen, with which he passed the hill of Crisa on his way to the god's own hollow glen. Wherefore are they all placed in the shrine of cypress-wood, hard by the statue cloven as a single block, that the Cretan bowmen dedicated beneath the roof Parnassian.

Therefore is it fitting to require with ready mind the doer of a good deed. Son of Alexibius! thy name is lit up by the fair-haired Graces. Thou art happy in that, after labour sore, thou hast the noblest praise to keep thy memory green. For, amid forty drivers who were laid low, thou, with thy fearless spirit, didst bring thy chariot through unscathed, and, from the glorious games, hast now returned to the plain of Libya, and to the city of thy sires. But no man is now, or ever shall be, without his share of trouble; yet, in spite of chequered fortune, there is present still the olden prosperity of Battus, that tower of the city of Cyrene, and that light most radiant to strangers from afar.

Even the loudly-roaring lions fled before Battus in terror when he unloosed on them his strange tongue, and Apollo, the founder of the State, doomed the wild beasts to dread fear, that so his oracles might not be unfulfilled for the ruler of Cyrene. 'Tis Apollo that allotteth to men and to women remedies for sore diseases. 'Twas he that gave the cithern, and bestoweth the Muse on whomsoever he will, bringing into the heart the love of law that hateth strife. 'Tis he that ruleth the secret shrine of the oracles; wherefore, even for sake of Lacedaemon, he planteth the valiant descendants of Heracles and Aegimius in Argos, and in hallowed Pylos.

But mine it is to sing of the dear glory that cometh from Sparta, whence sprang the Aegeidae, my own forefathers, who, not without the gods, but led by some providence divine, once went to Thêra, whence it was that we have received the festal sacrifice in which all have part, and, in thy banquet, O Carneian Apollo, we honour the nobly built city of Cyrene, which is held by bronze-armed Trojans from a foreign shore, even by the descendants of Antênôr. For they came with Helen, after they had seen their native city burnt in war, and that chariot-driving race was heartily welcomed with sacrifices by men who greeted them with gifts, men who were brought by Aristoteles, when, with his swift ships, he opened a deep path across the sea. And he made the groves of the gods greater than aforetime, and ordained that, for the festivals of Apollo, which bring health unto mortals, there should be a straight and level road, paved with stone and trodden by the hoofs of horses, where now, in death, he resteth apart, at the further end of the market-place. Blessed was he, while he dwelt among men, and thereafter a hero worshipped by the people; and asunder, before the dwellings, are the other holy kings, whose portion is in Hades, and in their soul, in the world below, they haply hear of lofty prowess besprent with soft dew beneath the outpourings of revel-songs—a happy lot for themselves and a glory shared by their son, Arcesilas, and his rightful claim.

Meet it is that, amid the minstrelsy of youths, he should proclaim the praise of golden-lyred Apollo, now that he receiveth from Pytho the gracious song that is the victor's guerdon for all cost. That hero is praised by the prudent. I shall only say what is said by others. He cherisheth a mind and a tongue that are beyond his years; in courage he is like a broad-winged eagle among birds, while his might in athlete-contests is a very tower of strength; and, even from his mother's lap, he hath soared among the Muses; and he hath proved himself a skilful charioteer; and all the openings for noble exploits around him, hath he boldly essayed. Even now doth God readily bring his powers to perfect issue, and, in the time to come, do ye blessed sons of Cronus grant him a like boon, both in deeds and counsels, lest haply some stormy blast of autumn make havoc of his life. Lo! it is the mighty mind of Zeus that guideth the fate of men that he loveth. I beseech him to grant the race of Battus this new guerdon [gift] at Olympia.

Archaic Greek City-States, Colonization, and Tyranny

The return to trade and prosperity in the early Archaic period created new strains and fissures in many Greek communities in which population growth began to outstripp the local resources to support them. This population growth combined with an unequal distribution of wealth and agricultural land led to risks associated with farming marginal lands that, even in the best conditions, did not provide surpluses that would serve as buffers in hard time, so that crises such as droughts increasingly brought on the threat of famine. The resulting social tensions created critical needs for radical changes to be made. Some cities took to the implementation of tyranny, others to colonization abroad by a portion of their population, while Sparta sought to subjugate its Messenian neighbors and control their lands. Colonization meant the transplanting of Greeks and the re-establishment of their former way of life in a new territory; in the aggregate, this phenomenon resulted in the progressive expansion of Greek city-state communities around the Mediterranean world.

20 Herodotus

The Foundation of Cyrene in Libya

Early Greek colonization was motivated by the search for arable land for resettlement as domestic resources were unable to cope with the demand of a growing population. Cyrene in modern-day Libya was the Greeks' most important new settlement in North Africa. From its foundation to the end of the Roman period, a period of some one thousand years, Cyrene served as a prominent center and outpost of Greek civilization. A literary account of its foundation is to be found in Herodotus' *Histories*, which represents one of the earliest known descriptions of the historical foundations of Greek cities. Drought and famine on the island of Thera created the preconditions that compelled many of its inhabitants to emigrate, and they sought to find a destination by consulting with the Oracle of Apollo at Delphi in Central Greece as well as by interviewing ship captains who traveled in distant parts. In time, they were commanded by the Oracle to seek the shores of Libya (or Africa) and after an abortive attempt to colonize Platea, an island off the coast, managed to establish ca. 631 B.C. an enduring settlement. The Greeks from Thera were joined by other Greeks from the mainland and the islands; together they formed the core of the citizenship body of the new *polis*. Battus, the heroic founder, became the first king, and his descendants formed a dynasty that ruled the city. Herodotus offers the following literary account of the city's founding that contains two separate traditions, one from Thera and the other from Cyrene.

4.150. Grinus (they say), the son of Aesanius, a descendant of Theras, and king of the island of Thera, went to Delphi to offer a hecatomb on behalf of his native city. He was accompanied by a large number of the citizens, and among the rest by Battus, the son of Polymnestus, who belonged to the Minyan family of the Euphemidae. On Grinus consulting the oracle about other matters, the priestess gave him for answer that he should found a city in Libya. Grinus replied to this, "I, O lord, am too far advanced in years, and too inactive, for such a work. Bid one of these youngsters undertake it." As he spoke, he pointed towards Battus; and thus the matter rested for that time. When the embassy returned to Thera, small account was taken of the oracle by the Theraeans, as they were quite ignorant where Libya was, and were not so venturesome as to send out a colony in the dark.

4.151. Seven years passed from the utterance of the oracle, and not a drop of rain fell in Thera: all the trees in the island, except one, were killed with the drought. The Theraeans upon this sent to Delphi, and were reminded reproachfully, that they had never colonised Libya. So, as there was no help for it, they sent

From Herodotus, *Histories* 4, 150–51, 153, 156–59; in *Herodotus. The Persian Wars*, translated by George Rawlinson (New York: Modern Library, 1942, reprinted 1947), pp. 350–51, 352, 354–55.

messengers to Crete, to inquire whether any of the Cretans, or of the strangers sojourning among them, had ever travelled as far as Libya: and these messengers of theirs, in their wanderings about the island, among other places visited Itanus, where they fell in with a man, whose name was Corobius, a dealer in purple. In answer to their inquiries, he told them that contrary winds had once carried him to Libya, where he had gone ashore on a certain island which was named Platea. So they hired this man's services, and took him back with them to Thera. A few persons then sailed from Thera to reconnoitre. Guided by Corobius to the island of Platea, they left him there with provisions for a certain number of months, and returned home with all speed to give their countrymen an account of the island....

4.153. The Theraeans who had left Corobius at Platea, when they reached Thera, told their countrymen that they had colonised an island on the coast of Libya. They of Thera, upon this, resolved that men should be sent to join the colony from each of their seven districts, and that the brothers in every family should draw lots to determine who were to go. Battus was chosen to be king and leader of the colony. So these men departed for Platea on board of two fifty-oared ships....

4.156. After a while, everything began to go wrong both with Battus and with the rest of the Theraeans, whereupon these last, ignorant of the cause of their sufferings, sent to Delphi to inquire for what reason they were afflicted. The priestess in, reply told them that if they and Battus would make a settlement at Cyrene in Libya, things would go better with them. Upon this the Theraeans sent out Battus with two fifty-oared ships, and with these he proceeded to Libya, but within a little time, not knowing what else to do, the men returned and arrived off Thera. The Theraeans, when they saw the vessels approaching, received them with showers of missiles, would not allow them to come near the shore, and ordered the men to sail back from whence they came. Thus compelled to return, they settled on an island near the Libyan coast, which (as I have already said) was called Platea. In size it is reported to have been about: equal to the city of Cyrene, as it now stands.

4.157. In this place they continued two years, but at the end of that time, as their ill luck still followed them, they left the island to the care of one of their number, and went in a body to Delphi, where they made complaint at the shrine, to the effect that, notwithstanding they had colonised Libya, they prospered as poorly as before. Hereon the priestess made them the following answer:

> Knowest thou better than I, fair Libya abounding in fleeces?
> Better the stranger than he who has trod it? O clever Theraeans!

Battus and his friends, when they heard this, sailed back to Platea: it was plain the god would not hold them acquitted of the colony till they were absolutely in Libya. So, taking with them the man whom they had left upon the island, they made a settlement on the mainland directly opposite Platea, fixing themselves at a place called Aziris, which is closed in on both sides by the most beautiful hills, and on one side is washed by a river.

4.158. Here they remained six years, at the end of which time the Libyans induced them to move, promising that they would lead them to a better situation. So the Greeks left Aziris, and were conducted by the Libyans towards the west, their journey being so arranged, by the calculations of their guides, that they passed in the night the most beautiful district of that whole country, which is the region called Irasa. The Libyans brought them to a spring, which goes by the name of Apollo's fountain, and told them, "Here, Grecians, is the proper place for you to settle; for here the sky has a hole in it."

4.159. During the lifetime of Battus, the founder of the colony, who reigned forty years, and during that of his son Arcesilaus, who reigned sixteen, the Cyrenaeans continued at the same level, neither more nor fewer in number than they were at the first. But in the reign of the third king, Battus, surnamed the Happy, the advice of the Pythian priestess brought Greeks from every quarter into Libya, to join the settlement. The Cyrenaeans had offered to all comers a share in their lands; and the oracle had spoken as follows:

> He that is backward to share in the pleasant Libyan acres, Sooner or later, I warn him, will feel regret at his folly.

Thus a great multitude were collected together to Cyrene, and the Libyans of the neighbourhood found themselves stripped of large portions of their lands. So they, and their king Adicran, being robbed and insulted by the Cyrenaeans, sent messengers to Egypt, and put themselves under the rule of Apries, the Egyptian monarch; who, upon this, levied a vast army of Egyptians, and sent them against Cyrene. The inhabitants of that place left their walls and marched out in force to the district of Irasa, where, near the spring called Theste, they engaged the Egyptian host, and defeated it. The Egyptians, who had never before made trial of the prowess of the Greeks, and so thought but meanly of them, were routed with such slaughter that but a very few of them ever got back home. For this reason, the subjects of Apries, who laid the blame of the defeat on him, revolted from his authority....

21 Lycurgus

The Spartan Military Machine

Lycurgus was traditionally represented as the lawgiver who created the unique system that turned his native Sparta (or Lacedaemon) into a successful militaristic society. The so-called Lycurgan system privileged social stability, group values, and devotion to an overarching state, and in turn it marginalized cultural and economic innovations as well as individual family life. For the full Spartan citizens, the Spartiates, training to fight as hoplite soldiers all their lives required them to subordinate everything to the goal of creating the perfect Greek soldier. A state formed of such men, it was thought by the

From Plutarch, "Life of Lycurgus," based on the translation by Aubrey Stewart and George Long.

Spartans, was the most capable of defending its own freedom. Yet this freedom, just as with other Greek notions of freedom, came with definite costs that had to be borne by others. Helots, or agricultural serfs, supplied their Spartiate overlords with the resources with which to attend their common messes and devote all their time to military training.

Until late in the seventh century, Sparta's development had paralleled that of the rest of Greece. Sparta was culturally advanced, being famed as a center for poets, musicians, and painters. But faced with the problems of overpopulation like many other Greek communities of the times, the Spartans began to send colonists abroad and, around 740 B.C., they also sought to take over the fertile plains of neighboring Messenia to the west. They eventually reduced the Messenians to helotage or serfdom, and yet revolts around 650 B.C. took nearly two decades of bitter fighting to crush. Complicating this crisis was the demand of the Spartan commoners for land division and a share of political power. The Spartan aristocrats were fearful lest popular discontent would lead as elsewhere in the Greek world to the rise of a tyrant—ever the greatest dread of the Spartans who were fully aware of the ever-present threat of the helots who outnumbered their masters as much as ten to one. Thus, the Spartan aristocrats moved successfully to deal with both dangers by reshaping Spartan society in radical ways. A popular assembly was created with the right to elect the ephors and approve or veto the proposals of the thirty-member aristocratic Council of Elders, and the land was divided among all citizens. A system of state education, the only one in Greece, was inaugurated; in the words of Plutarch, it "accustomed the citizens to have neither the will nor the ability to lead a private life, but, like bees, to be organic parts of their community, clinging together around their leader, forgetting themselves in their enthusiastic patriotism, and belonging wholly to their country" ("Life of Lycurgus," 25). Some scholars are of the opinion that if Lycurgus "the lawgiver" was a historical person, he probably played the same role in Sparta that Solon played at Athens—a mediator between commoners and aristocrats whose political and economic reforms sought (successfully in the case of Lycurgus) to provide an alternative to tyranny. The social reforms that transformed Sparta into a totalitarian state came somewhat later than Solon's time and were attributed to Lycurgus. The fullest ancient accounts of the Lycurgan system are *The Constitution of the Lacedaemonians* by Xenophon (died ca. 355 B.C.) and the "Life of Lycurgus" by Plutarch. Selections from Plutarch's more vivid and anecdotal treatment are given below.

1. With regard to Lycurgus the lawgiver there is nothing whatever that is undisputed; his birth, his travels, his death, and, above all, his legislation, have all been related in various ways. Even the dates given for his birth are not in agreement.... However, in spite of these discrepancies I shall endeavor, by following the least inconsistent accounts and the best known authorities, to write the history of his life....

Economic Reforms

8. The ... boldest of Lycurgus' reforms was the redistribution of the land. Great inequalities existed in this regard, with the result that many poor and needy people had become a burden to the state while wealth was concentrated

Bronze statuette of a Spartan girl running (520-500 B.C.); now in the British Museum.
Lycurgus "strengthened the bodies of the girls in exercise in running, wrestling, and hurling the discus or the javelin, in order that their children might spring from a healthy source and so grow up strong, and that they themselves might have strength to easily endure the pains of childbirth."

in a very few hands. Lycurgus abolished all pride, envy, crime, and luxury, which flowed from those old and terrible evils of riches and poverty, by inducing all landowners to offer their estates for redistribution and prevailing upon all citizens to live on equal terms with equal incomes. They were to strive only to surpass one another in courage and virtue, there being henceforth no social inequalities among them except as praise or blame can create....

Each man's allotment of land was large enough to produce annually seventy medimni [about 50 liters by volume] of barley for himself and twelve for his wife, with oil and wine in proportion. He thought this would be sufficient because it was enough to maintain them in health, and they needed nothing more. It is said that some years later, as he was returning from a journey through the country at harvest time and saw the sheaves of grain lying in equal parallel rows, he smiled and said to his companions that all Laconia seemed as if it had just been divided among many brothers.

9. He desired to distribute movable property also, in order completely to do away with inequality; but, seeing that actually to take away these things would be a most unpopular measure, he managed to end all avarice by a different method. First, he abolished the use of gold and silver money and made iron money alone legal, and this he made of great size and weight and of so small value that the equivalent for ten minae required a large store-room and a yoke of oxen to transport it. As soon as this happened, many types of crime became unknown in Lacedaemon. For who would steal, or take as a bribe or as plunder, a mass of iron which he could not conceal, which no one envied him for possessing, and which he could not even cut up and make use of? For the hot iron was, it is said, quenched in vinegar so as to make it useless by rendering it brittle and hard to work.

After this he ordered a general expulsion of the workers in unnecessary trades. Indeed, most of them would have left the country anyway when the old currency came to an end, since they could not sell their wares. The iron money had no value and could not be carried elsewhere in Greece, where it was regarded as ridiculous. Nor could it be used for the purchase of foreign trumpery, and so no cargo was shipped to a Laconian port, no sophists came into the country, no vagabond soothsayers, no panderers, no goldsmiths or silversmiths, since there was no money to pay them with. Luxury, thus cut off from all encouragement, gradually became extinct. The rich were on the same footing with other people, as they could not spend their money but were forced to keep it idle at home....

10. Wishing still more to attack luxury and remove the desire for riches, he introduced ... the most admirable of his reforms, that of the common dining-table. Here the men were to meet and dine together on a fixed allowance of food instead of eating in their own homes, lolling on expensive couches at rich tables, fattened like beasts in private by the hands of servants and cooks, and undermining their health by indulgence to excess in every bodily desire, long sleep, warm baths, and much rest, as though they required a sort of daily nursing like sick people.... Men were not even allowed to dine previously at home and then come to the public table; the others would watch him who did not eat or drink with them and reproach him as a weakling, too effeminate to eat the rough common fare....

"Regulating Marriages and the Birth of Children"

13. Lycurgus did not establish any written laws; indeed, this is distinctly forbidden by one of the so-called Rhetras [decrees]. He thought that the principles of most importance for the prosperity and honor of the state would remain most securely fixed if implanted in the citizens by habit and training, as they would then be followed from choice rather than necessity; for the habits that education produced in the youth would answer in each the purpose of a lawgiver. The trifling conventions of everyday life were best left undefined by hard-and-fast laws, so that they might from time to time receive corrections or additions from men educated in the spirit of the Lacedaemonian system. On this education the whole scheme of Lycurgus' laws depended....

14. Considering education to be the most important and the noblest work of a lawgiver, he began at the very beginning by regulating marriages and the birth of children.... He strengthened the bodies of the girls by exercise in running, wrestling, and hurling the discus or the javelin, in order that their children might spring from a healthy source and so grow up strong, and that they themselves might have strength to easily endure the pains of childbirth. He did away with all seclusion and retirement for women, and ordained that girls, no less than boys, should go naked in processions, and dance and sing at festivals in the presence of young men. There the jokes they made about certain youths were sometimes of great value as reproofs of ill-conduct, while, on the other hand, by reciting verses written in praise of the deserving they inspired great ambition and thirst for distinction in the young men. For he who had been praised by

the maidens for his valor went away congratulated by his friends, while the raillery which they used in sport and jest was as sharp as a serious reproof, especially as the kings and elders were present at these festivals along with all the other citizens.

This nakedness of the maidens had in it nothing disgraceful. It was done modestly, not licentiously, and it produced habits of simplicity and taught them to desire good health and beauty of body, and to love honor and courage no less than the men. This it was that made them speak and think as Gorgo, the wife of Leonidas, is said to have done. Some foreign lady, it seems, said to her, "You Spartan women are the only ones who rule men." She answered, "Yes, for we are the only ones who give birth to men."

15. ... Their marriage custom was for the husband to carry off his bride by force. They did not carry off little immature girls, but grown-up women who were ripe for marriage. After the bride had been carried off, the women in charge of the wedding cut her hair close to her head, dressed her in a man's cloak and sandals, and placed her upon a couch in a dark chamber alone. The bridegroom, without any feasting or revelry, but sober as usual after dining at his mess, comes into the room, unties her girdle, and takes her to himself. After spending a short time with her, he returns composedly to his usual quarters to sleep with the other young men. And so he continues afterwards, passing his days with his companions and visiting his wife by stealth, feeling ashamed and afraid that some one in the house might hear him. His bride uses her wit to contrive occasions for meeting unobserved. This went on for a long time, and some even had children born to them before they ever saw their wives by daylight. These meetings not only exercised their powers of self-restraint, but also brought them together with their bodies in full vigor and their passions unblunted by unrestrained intercourse. As a result, their passion and love for each other remained undiminished.

Having thus honored and dignified marriage, Lycurgus destroyed the vain womanish passion of jealousy. While carefully avoiding any disorder or licentiousness, he permitted men to share with worthy persons the task of begetting children. He taught them to ridicule those who insisted on the exclusive possession of their wives and were ready to fight and kill people to maintain that right. For example, an elderly husband with a young wife was permitted to introduce her to some well-born and handsome young man, and then to adopt their offspring as his own.

Furthermore, it was allowable for a respectable man, if he admired a virtuous mother of fine children who was married to someone else, to induce her husband to permit him to have access to her in order, as it were, to sow seed in a fertile field and obtain a fine son from a healthy stock. Lycurgus did not view children as belonging to their parents, but as the property of the state, and therefore he desired his citizens to be born of the best possible parents. Besides, he noticed the inconsistency and folly of the rest of mankind: they are willing to pay money or use their influence with the owners of well-bred stock to obtain a good breed of horses or dogs, but they lock up their women in seclusion and permit them to have children by no one but themselves, even though they be mad, decrepit, or diseased. It is as though the good or bad qualities of children did not depend entirely upon their parents and did not affect the parents more than anyone else.

But although men loaned their wives in order to produce healthy and useful citizens, yet this did not encourage the licentiousness of Spartan women that prevailed in later times. Adultery was regarded among them as an impossible crime. A story is told of a very old Spartan named Geradas, who, when asked by a stranger what was done to adulterers in Sparta, answered, "Stranger, there are no adulterers among us." "And if there were one?" asked the stranger. "Then," said Geradas, "he would have to pay as compensation a bull big enough to stand on Mount Taygetus and drink from the river Eurotas." The stranger, astonished, asked, "Where can you find so big a bull?" "Where can you find an adulterer in Sparta?" answered Geradas. This is the account we have of their marriages.

State Education

16. A father had not the right of bringing up his offspring but had to carry it to a place called Lesche, where the elders of the tribes sat in judgment upon the child. If they thought it well-built and strong, they ordered the father to rear it and they assigned it one of the nine thousand plots of land; but if it was mean-looking or misshapen, they sent it away to the place called Exposure, a glen at the foot of Mount Taygetus, for they considered that a child who did not start out healthy and strong would be handicapped in its own life and of no value to the state....

Nor was each man allowed to bring up and educate his son as he chose, but as soon as the boys were seven years old Lycurgus took them from their parents and enrolled them in companies. Here they lived and ate in common and shared their play and work. One of the noblest and bravest men of the state was appointed superintendent of the boys, and they themselves in each company chose the wisest and bravest as captain. They looked to him for orders, obeyed his commands, and endured his punishments, so that even in childhood they learned to obey. The older men watched them at their play, and by instituting fights and trials of strength, accurately learned which were the bravest and strongest. They learned to read and write, because that is necessary, but all the rest of their education was meant to teach them to obey with cheerfulness, to endure hardship, and to win battles. As they grew older their training became more severe. Their heads were closely shorn and they were taught to walk barefooted and to play naked. They wore no tunic after their twelfth year, but received one garment for all the year round. They were necessarily dirty, as they had no warm baths and ointments, except on certain days as a luxury. They slept together in troops and companies, on beds of rushes which they had picked with their own hands on the banks of the Eurotas, for they were not allowed to use a knife for that purpose. In winter they mixed a thistledown called lycophon with the rushes, as it is thought to possess some warmth.

17. ... [They are taught to steal, bringing to their captain] what they steal from the gardens and from the men's dining-tables, where they creep in very cleverly and cautiously; for if one is caught he is severely whipped for stealing

carelessly and clumsily. They also steal food from those who are asleep or off their guard. Whoever is caught is punished by flogging and starvation. Their meals are purposely scanty in order that they may exercise their ingenuity and daring in obtaining more....

18. The boys steal with such earnestness that there is a story of one who had taken a fox's cub and hidden it under his cloak, and, though his entrails were being torn out by the claws and teeth of the beast, persevered in concealing it until he died....

19. The boys were taught to use a sarcastic yet graceful style of speaking, and to compress much thought into few words. Lycurgus made the iron money have little value for its great size, but on the other hand he made their speech short and compact, yet full of meaning, by teaching the young, after long periods of silent listening, to speak sententiously and to the point. For those who allow themselves much licence in speech seldom say anything memorable. When some Athenian jeered at the small Spartan swords, saying that jugglers on the stage could easily swallow them, King Agis answered, "And yet with these little daggers we can generally reach our enemies."...

20. ... One may also judge their character by their jokes; for they are taught never to talk at random, nor to utter a syllable that does not contain some thought. For example, when one of them was invited to hear a man imitate the nightingale, he answered, "I have heard the original."...

"They Lived as if in a Camp"

24. The training of the Spartan youth continued till their manhood. No one was permitted to live according to his own pleasure, but they lived in the city as if in a camp, with a fixed diet and fixed public duties, thinking themselves to belong not to themselves but to their country. Those who had no other duty either looked after the young and taught them what was useful, or themselves learned such things from the old. For ample leisure was one of the blessings with which Lycurgus provided his countrymen, since they were absolutely forbidden to practice any mechanical craft, and moneymaking and business were unnecessary because wealth was disregarded and despised. The Helots tilled the soil and produced the usual crops for them. Indeed, a Spartan who was at Athens while the courts were sitting and learned that some man had been fined for idleness and was leaving the court in sorrow accompanied by his grieving friends, asked to be shown the man who had been punished for gentlemanly behavior. So slavish did they deem it to labor at a trade and in business....

27. ... In Sparta nothing was left without regulation, but with all the necessary acts of life Lycurgus mingled some ceremony which might enkindle virtue or discourage vice; indeed, he filled his city with examples of this kind, by which the citizens were insensibly molded and impelled towards honorable pursuits. For this reason he would not allow citizens to leave the country at pleasure to wander in foreign lands, where they would contact strange habits and learn to imitate the untrained lives and ill-regulated institutions to be found abroad. Also, he banished from Lacedaemon all strangers who were there for no useful purpose;

not, as Thucydides says, because he feared they might imitate his constitution and learn something serviceable for the improvement of their own countries, but rather for fear that they might teach the people some mischief. Strangers introduce strange ideas, and these could lead to subversive discussions and political views which would jar with the established constitution, like discord in music. Therefore he thought that it was more important to keep bad habits from entering the city than it was to keep out the plague.

The Krypteia and the Helots

28. In all this we cannot find any traces of the injustice and unfairness which some complain of in the laws of Lycurgus, which they say are excellent to produce courage but less so for justice. The secret service, called Krypteia, if indeed it is one of the institutions of Lycurgus as Aristotle says, may have given Plato also this view of the man and his system. The Krypteia operated in this way: The magistrates at intervals sent out the most discreet of the young soldiers into different parts of the country, equipped only with daggers and food. In the daytime they concealed themselves in unfrequented spots and lay quiet, but at night they came down into the roads and killed every Helot they found. And often they would move through the fields and slay the strongest and bravest Helots they could find. Also, as Thucydides mentions in his *History of the Peloponnesian War*, those Helots who were especially honored by the Spartans for their valor were crowned as free men and taken to the temples with rejoicings; but in a short time they all disappeared, more than two thousand of them, in such a way that no man, either then or afterwards, could tell how they perished. Aristotle says that the Ephors, when they first take office, declare war against the Helots in order that it may be lawful to destroy them. And other harsh treatment was inflicted upon them; for example, they were compelled to drink much unmixed wine and then were brought into the public dining-halls to show the young men what drunkenness was....

Lycurgus' Laws Approved by Divine Will

29. When the men of the city were thoroughly imbued with the spirit of his institutions and the newly constituted state was strong enough to operate and preserve itself, then, as Plato says of the Deity, that he was pleased with the world he had created after it first began to live and move, so it was with Lycurgus. He admired the spectacle of his laws in operation and, as far as human wisdom would permit, he desired to leave it eternal and unchangeable. He therefore assembled all the citizens and told them that the city was now well provided with material happiness and virtue, but that he would not bestow upon them the most valuable gift of all until he had consulted with Heaven. It was therefore their duty to abide by the already established laws and to change and alter nothing until he had returned from Delphi, and then he would do whatever the god [Apollo] commanded. They all agreed and bade him depart. After making the kings and elders and then the rest of the citizens swear that they would keep the present constitution until he returned, he set out for Delphi.

Upon reaching the temple he sacrificed to the god and inquired whether his laws were sufficient to provide prosperity and happiness for his country. Receiving answer from the oracle that his laws were excellent and the state would become famous if it kept the constitution of Lycurgus, he wrote down this prophecy and sent it to Sparta. But he himself, after offering a second sacrifice to the god and embracing his friends and his sons, resolved never to release his countrymen from their oath by putting an end to his own life. Though life was still pleasant, he had reached an age when it seemed time to go to his rest after having so excellently arranged all his people's affairs. He departed by starvation, as he thought that even the death of a true statesman ought to be of service to the state, not insignificant but recognized as a virtuous act. His death came in the fullness of time, after he had done an excellent work, and it was left as the guardian of all the good that he had done because the citizens had sworn that they would abide by his constitution until he returned to them. Nor was he deceived in his expectations, for his state was by far the most celebrated in Greece for good government at home and renown abroad during a period of five hundred years....

Conclusion

30. ... I am amazed at those who say that the Lacedaemonians "knew how to obey, but not how to rule," and as proof quote the saying of King Theopompus. When told that the safety of Sparta lay in her kings knowing how to rule, he replied: "No, it lies in her citizens knowing how to obey." But people do not obey unless rulers know how to command....

31. ... Seeing that, in states as in individuals, happiness is derived from virtue and concord, Lycurgus directed all his efforts to implant in his countrymen feelings of honor, self-reliance, and self-control. These were also taken as the basis of their constitutions by Plato, Diogenes, Zeno [Greek philosophers], and all who have written with any success upon this subject. But they have left mere dissertations; Lycurgus produced an inimitable constitution,... showing them the spectacle of an entire city acting like philosophers, and thereby obtained for himself a greater reputation than that of any other Greek legislator at any period.

22 Solon

Economic and Political Reforms at Athens

Later Greeks looked back upon Solon as the greatest of statesmen and the wisest of men. His contemporary reputation for wisdom led him to be called

From Plutarch, "Life of Solon," based on the translation by John Dryden and A. H. Clough.

upon to rescue his native Athens from a long-simmering crisis in 594/593 B.C. Elected as one of the archons, or civic magistrates, of that year, Solon came to power at a time when the tensions between the rich and the poor were reaching a crisis point. An oppressed and much-indebted peasantry felt itself exploited by a rapacious aristocracy, and their conflicts threatened to overturn the existing order. Many peasants progressively lost their meager landholdings and became tenant farmers working for the rich, becoming the so-called "sixth-parters" who had to surrender a sixth of their yield to the rich. The erosion of the power of the monarchy in Athens led to a virtual monopoly of power held by an oligarchy of nobles, many of whom also benefited at the time from the economic expansion and resumption of long-distance trade that effectively made the rich richer and the poor poorer. Without a royal figure who could at least in theory champion the cause of the poor and help dispense a disinterested notion of justice, members of the lower classes came to be oppressed by their social superiors in the manner described earlier by Hesiod, and an increasing number sank further into debt-bondage, a common archaic form of dependency akin to slavery. Around 632 B.C., the Athenian noble Cylon sought unsuccessfully—some of his followers were massacred—to capitalize on the discontent of the lower classes to make himself tyrant in Athens This event appears to have frightened the nobility into compromise by allowing an archon named Draco in 621 B.C. to put into written form the hitherto unwritten customary laws, particularly though not only those associated with cases of homicide. This written code was to prevent aristocratic magistrates from administering the laws unjustly after the manner of the judges who, as described by Hesiod, "devour bribes and give crooked decisions." The lower classes found this concession unsatisfactory, and the struggle between rich and poor continued unabated.

Solon's economic and political reforms aimed to produce a compromise between the rich and the poor in a way that allowed neither to triumph over the other. Rejecting calls from the latter for land redistribution, he instituted a one-time cancellation of existing debts, called the "shaking off of burdens," in an effort to avert the worst plight of those who faced default and enslavement. This measure was not only inadequate, but it was also taken advantage by some of the rich who took out loans just before the appointed time and received "free money," as it were. Other reforms by Solon were more consequential and durable, including the organization of the citizenry into four census classes based on property that reshaped the distribution of political rights in a way that diminished the monopoly over power that nobles had enjoyed. Having laid down his laws, Solon supposedly traveled abroad for some ten years to prevent his measures from being overturned. But Solon's success in averting open civil strife during his own magistracy was both temporary and illusory, as subsequent events show.

It is worth noting that Solon's reforms were linked with the new religious ideal of justice and the new rational ideal of moderation, both expounded a century earlier by Hesiod. "My spirit commands me to teach the Athenians," Solon declared in the poetry he wrote to justify his reforms; this motivating spirit was the product of the new ethical religion of Zeus and *Dikē*, Goddess of Justice. The Athenians must be taught that greed and injustice are pushing their city toward disaster, for "they do not preserve the venerable foundations of *Dikē*, who in her silence knows all the past and all the present, but does not fail to come in time to punish." To avoid the ruin that such punishment brings, the opposing factions must learn that "the hardest thing of all is to recognize the invisible Mean of judgment, which alone contains the limits of all things." They must, in other words, compromise their differences by accepting the middle-of-the-road reforms of Solon.

The following account of Solon's economic and political reforms—the latter started Athens on the road to full democracy—is taken from the "Life of Solon," one of the series of biographies in Plutarch's *Parallel Lives* of famous Greeks and Romans. Plutarch, who died about A.D. 127, was educated at Athens, lectured on philosophy at Rome, held political office in Greece, and finally retired to his birthplace, the small town of Chaeronea in Central Greece, to devote the rest of his life to writing and teaching. His chief interest was in moral philosophy, a fact clearly evident in his *Lives* in which the emphasis is upon the delineation of character. As a moral philosopher, Plutarch believed that the course of history was determined by the actions of great men rather than by economic or other forces.

The Revolutionary Situation at Athens

13. The Athenians, now that Cylon's sedition was over and those polluted by blood-guilt had gone into banishment, fell into their old quarrels about the form of government, there being as many different parties as there were geographical diversities in the country. The Hill quarter favored an extreme democracy, the Plain an extreme oligarchy, and the Shore stood for a mixed form of government and opposed the other two parties, thus preventing either of them from prevailing [See Selection 23]. At that time, too, the disparity between rich and poor had reached its height. The city was on the brink of revolution, and the only way to stop disorder and achieve stability seemed to be by changing to a tyranny. All the common people were in debt to the rich. They either tilled their land for them, paying them a sixth of the produce and were therefore called Hectemorii [or Hektemoroi: "Sixth-parters"] and Thetes [the free poor], or they pledged their bodies to raise money and could be seized by their creditors and either enslaved at home or sold to foreigners. Some (for no law forbade it) were forced to sell their children or go into exile to avoid the harshness of their creditors. The most and the bravest of them, however, began to band together and encourage one another not to submit to injustice but to choose a leader, liberate the enslaved debtors, redivide the land, and change the form of government.

Solon Refuses Absolute Power

14. At this point the wiser among the Athenians began to think of Solon. They knew that he, more than anyone else, was not implicated in the troubles of the time, that he had not joined in the extortions of the rich or been involved in the privations of the poor. Therefore they urged him to come forward and settle the differences. Phanias the Lesbian, however, maintains that in order to save his city, Solon played a trick upon both parties by secretly promising the poor a division of the land and the rich security for their debts. But Solon

himself says that he entered politics reluctantly, being afraid of the greediness of one party and the arrogance of the other. He was chosen archon, however, after Philombrotus, and empowered to act as arbitrator and lawgiver, the rich consenting because he was wealthy and the poor because he was honest. There was a saying of his current before the election to the effect that when things are equal there never can be war, and this pleased both the rich and the poor, the first assuming him to mean an equality based on merit and achievement, the second an equality based on the counting of votes. Consequently, there were great hopes on both sides and their leaders repeatedly pressed Solon to establish a tyranny and manage the city freely according to his pleasure. There were also many citizens, belonging to neither party, who saw that it would be difficult to bring about change by debate and legislation and who therefore were willing to have one wise and just man placed at the head of the state. Some also say that Solon received this oracle from Apollo:

> Take the mid-seat, and be the vessel's guide;
> Many in Athens are upon your side.

But most of all his close friends chided him for rejecting absolute power only because of the name of tyrant, without considering that the virtues of the man who seized such power would at once transform it into a lawful sovereignty. Euboea, they argued, had found this true of Tynnondas, and now Mitylene had made Pittacus its tyrant.

None of these arguments could shake Solon's resolution. He replied to his friends, we are told, that it was true that tyranny was a fine spot, but there was no way out of it, and in one of his poems he writes to Phocus:

> That I spared my land,
> And withheld from usurpation and from violence my hand,
> And forbade to fix a stain and a disgrace on my good name,
> I regret not; I believe that it will be my chiefest fame.

From this it is clear that he was a man of great repute even before he drafted his laws. As for the ridicule that was heaped upon him for refusing to be a tyrant, he has written these words:

> Solon surely was a dreamer, and a man of simple mind;
> When the gods would give him fortune, he of his own will
>   declined;
> When the net was full of fishes, over-heavy thinking it,
> He declined to haul it up, through want of heart and want
>   of wit.
> Had but I that chance of riches and of tyranny, for one day,
> I would give my skin for flaying, and my house to die away.

15. Thus he makes the multitude and the unscrupulous speak of him. Yet, though he refused to be a tyrant, he was not at all mild in his handling of public affairs, and his legislation was not the product of a feeble spirit. He did not make concessions to the powerful or tailor his laws to please the voters. Where things

were well before, he attempted no remedy or change for fear lest by turning every-thing upside down and disorganizing the state he might be too weak to restore it to a workable condition. But what he thought he could effect by persuasion or by the force of his authority, this he did, as he himself says, "With force and justice working in harmony." And so when he was later asked if he had left the Athenians the best laws that could be enacted, he replied, "The best they would accept."

Immediate Economic Reforms

Later writers note that the Athenians have a way of disguising the ugliness of things by giving them endearing and innocent names, calling harlots, for exam-ple, "companions," taxes "contributions," a garrison a "guard," and the jail the "chamber." Solon seems to have been the first to use this device when he called cancelling debts scisachtheia, a "disburdenment." For the first of his enactments decreed that existing debts should be forgiven and that in the future no one could accept the body of a debtor as security. Though writers such as Androtion maintain that Solon relieved the poor not by cancelling debts but by reducing the interest on them, which so pleased the people that they called not only this humanitarian act seisachtheia, but also the enlargement of measures and the rise in the purchasing power of money which took place at this time. For Solon fixed the value of the mina at one hundred drachmas, whereas before it had con-tained only seventy-three. In this way, although the amount of the payment remained the same, its value was less, which proved a considerable benefit to the debtors and no loss to the creditors. But most writers agree that it was the removal of all debt that was called seisachtheia, which is supported by Solon's poems in which he prides himself that

> The mortgage stones that covered her, by me
> Removed—the land that was a slave is free.

He adds that some of those who had been seized for debt were brought back from foreign countries where

> so far their lot to roam,
> They had forgot the language of their home.

And some he says he set free "Who here in shameful servitude were held."

This undertaking is said to have involved him in the greatest trouble of his life. When he had decided to abolish debts and was considering the best arguments and the proper moment for it, he told his closest friends, Conon, Clinias, and Hipponicus, that he would not touch the land but intended only to abolish debts. They promptly took advantage of this confidence and antici-pated Solon's decree by borrowing large sums of money and buying up big estates. Then, when the decree was enacted, they kept their properties but refused to pay their creditors. This affair brought upon Solon great suspicion and dislike, as though he himself had not been the victim of a trick but was a party to the fraud. However, he soon stopped this suspicion by his well-known sacrifice of five talents; for it was discovered that he had lent this amount ... and was the first to comply with his own law and cancel the debt. His friends, on the other hand, were ever after called chreocopidai, or "swindlers."

16. His policy pleased neither party, however. The rich were angry on account of their money, and the poor even more so because Solon had not divided the land or, as Lycurgus had done [at Sparta; Selection 21], reduced all men to equality. But Lycurgus was an eleventh-generation descendant of Heracles and had reigned many years in Sparta.... Solon, on the other hand, could not go to such extremes in his constitution, since he was a man of modest fortune and had been chosen by the people. Yet he made full use of his power, relying on the good will of the citizens and their confidence in him. Nevertheless he offended many who looked for different results, as he declares in these words:

> Formerly they boasted of me vainly; with averted eyes
> Now they look askance upon me; friends no more, but
>   enemies.

And yet had any other man, he adds, received the same power,

> He would not have forborne, nor let alone,
> But made the cream of the milk his own.

Political Reforms

Soon, however, seeing the value of his policy, they laid aside their complaints, offered a public sacrifice—which they called the Seisachtheia—and appointed Solon to reform the constitution and draft a code of laws. They gave him full power over everything—magistracies, assemblies, courts, and councils. He had authority to decide the property qualifications and times of meeting of each of these bodies, and also to preserve or dissolve any existing institution as he saw fit.

17. First, then, he repealed all of Draco's laws, except those concerning homicide, because they were too severe and their penalties too heavy. For death was the penalty for almost all offenses, so that even those convicted of idleness were put to death, and those who stole a cabbage or an apple suffered the same punishment as those who committed sacrilege or murder. This is why Demades, in later times, became famous when he said the Draco's laws were written not in ink but in blood. Draco himself, when asked why he made death the punishment for most offenses, replied that the minor ones deserved it, and no heavier penalty was left for major crimes.

18. Next, Solon wished to continue the magistracies in the hands of the rich, but to give the people a share in the rest of the government, which they had never before enjoyed, and he therefore took a census of every citizen's property. Those who were worth 500 measures of dry and liquid goods he placed in the first class and called them Pentacosiomedimni [literally "men of 500 measures"]. The second class was composed of those who could afford a horse, or were worth 300 measures, and they were called Knights because they paid a horse tax. The third class, whose income was 200 measures, was called Zeugitae. All the rest of the citizens were called Thetes; they were not admitted to any office but could attend the assembly and act as jurors. This last

privilege at first seemed of little worth, but later became very important because almost every dispute came before them as jurors. Even in the cases which Solon assigned to the jurisdiction of a magistrate, he also allowed the right of appeal to a popular court. In addition, it is said that he purposely was obscure and ambiguous in the wording of his laws in order to increase the power of the popular courts; for since the parties to a dispute could not settle it according to the letter of the law, they had to place it before the jurors, who thus became in a sense masters of the laws. Solon himself mentions this equality in the following lines:

> Such power I gave the people as might do,
> Abridged not what they had, nor lavished new,
> Those that were great in wealth and high in place
> My counsel likewise kept from all disgrace.
> Before them both I held my shield of might,
> And let not either touch the other's right.

Desiring to further protect the common people, Solon gave every citizen the right of bringing suit on behalf of anyone who had suffered injury. If a man was assaulted and suffered violence or injury, any who wished and was able to do so could prosecute the offender. He intended by this to accustom the citizens, as members of the same body, to feel and sympathize with one another's injuries. We are told of a saying of Solon's relating to this law. Being asked what city was best governed, he replied, "That city where those who have not been wronged try to punish the offender as much as those who have been wronged."

19. He reorganized the Council of the Areopagus to be composed only of those who had held the annual office of archon, which meant that he was also a member. He then observed that the people, now free from debt, were becoming uneasy and bold, and he therefore formed another Council of Four Hundred, composed of a hundred men from each of the four tribes. This council was to inspect all matters before they were presented to the people, and was not to allow any matter to be brought before the popular assembly without its approval. He made the upper council, or Areopagus, the supervisor and guardian of the laws, thinking that the city, held by these two councils like anchors, would be less likely to be tossed by tumults, and the people would be more tranquil....

20. Among Solon's other laws, one is very peculiar and surprising—it disfranchises any citizen who remains neutral in a revolution. Evidently he did not want anyone to remain apathetic or indifferent to the public good, safeguarding his private affairs while congratulating himself for having no concern for the distresses of his country. One should promptly join the good and righteous cause, assist it and share its dangers, rather than wait in safety to see which side wins....

Long-term Economic Reforms

22. Solon observed that the city was filling up with people who streamed from all areas into Attica for greater security of living, and at the same time he realized that most of the country was poor and unproductive, and that sea traders send no goods to those who can give them nothing in exchange. Therefore he

turned the attention of the citizens to manufactures. He made a law that no son was obliged to support his father unless he had been taught a trade.... and seeing that the soil of Attica was scarcely rich enough to maintain those who tilled it and was incapable of feeding an idle and leisured multitude, he sought to dignify all trades and ordered the Council of the Areopagus to inquire how every man made a living and to punish those who had no occupation....

24. Of the products of the soil, Solon allowed only oil to be exported, and those who exported any other product were to be solemnly cursed by the archon, or else were to pay a hundred drachmas into the public treasury.... His law concerning naturalized citizens is of doubtful wisdom, because he permitted the naturalization only of those who had been permanently exiled from their country or who came with their families to ply a trade. This he did, we are told, not to discourage all immigrants but rather to invite these particular types with the sure hope of their becoming citizens. He also thought that those who had been forced to leave their country, or who had left it for a particular purpose, would prove to be more faithful citizens.

23 Pisistratus

The Rise of Tyranny at Athens

Solon's admonition that "the hardest thing of all is to recognize the invisible Mean of Judgment" was borne out by the developments in Athens after he departed from the city. His compromise legislation satisfied neither of the contending groups, and strife broke out along regional lines with noble-led factions connected respectively to the Plains, the Coasts, and the Hill regions of Attica. The resulting factional fighting paralyzed the Athenian state—no magistrates could be elected in 590 or 580 B.C. The resulting anarchy (*anarchia*, literally "without rulers") led in 560 B.C. to the first of a series of tyrannies imposed by Pisistratus, a famed military hero and leader of the Hill faction who favored the redistribution of land within Attica.[1] To Solon, this was the "retribution of Zeus" that he had foretold in the poems would be visited upon the Athenians should they not heed the lesson of moderation and compromise: "From the clouds come snow and hail, thunder follows the lightning, and by powerful

---

1. During the French Revolution, the moderate republicans, who were avid readers of Plutarch and constantly saw parallels between ancient times and their own, called the party supporting the radical future dictator Robespierre *la Montagne* ("hill," or "mountain"). They may have done so because of a perceived parallel with Pisistratus and his Hill party supporters.

From Plutarch, "Life of Solon," based on the translation by John and William Langhorne (Solon's poetry translated by John Dryden).

men the city is brought low and the people in its ignorance comes into the power of a despot." It is important to remember that Pisistratus' tyranny was widely considered by later Athenians as a moderate regime and indeed a glorious reign that advanced the city's power and prestige.

The following account, which Plutarch fittingly appended to the end of his "Life of Solon," remains one of the clearest expositions of the political techniques employed by ambitious men to acquire dictatorial forms of power and of the often avoidable conditions that time and again have given rise to dictatorships in human societies.

The Renewal of Social Struggle

29. During Solon's absence the Athenians were again divided into factions. Lycurgus headed the Plain, Megacles the son of Alcmaeon the Shore, and Pisistratus the Hill. Among the latter was the multitude of laboring people whose enmity was directed at the rich. Hence it was that though the city did observe Solon's laws, all factions expected a revolution and wanted a different form of government, not to obtain equality but with a view to be gainers by the change and to dominate those who differed from them.

While matters stood thus Solon arrived at Athens [after a ten-year absence]. He was revered and honored by all, but because of his great age he had neither the strength nor the spirit to act or speak in public as he had done. He, therefore, appealed in private to the heads of the factions and endeavored to appease and reconcile them. Pisistratus seemed more amenable than the rest. He had an affable and engaging manner, was a great friend of the poor, and behaved with generosity even to his enemies. He counterfeited so successfully the good qualities which nature had denied him that he gained more credit than those who actually possessed them. He was thought to be cautious and law-abiding, zealous for equality and the present government, and opposed to all who clamored for a change. On these points he deceived most people, but Solon soon discovered his real character and was the first to discern his insidious designs. Yet he did not completely break with him but endeavored to soften him and advise him better, declaring both to him and to others that if ambition could be banished from his soul and he could be cured of his desire for absolute power, there would not be a man better disposed to virtue or a more worthy citizen of Athens.

Thespis Develops Tragedy

About this time Thespis began to develop tragedy and the novelty of the thing attracted many spectators, although this was before any prize was given in competition. Solon, who was always willing to listen and to learn, and now in his old age was more inclined to anything that might divert and entertain, even wine and song, went to see Thespis act in his own play, as was the custom of the ancient poets. After the performance, he asked Thespis if he was not ashamed to tell so many lies before so many people. Thespis answered that there was no harm in speaking and acting that way in a play. To which Solon exclaimed, striking the ground violently with his staff: "If we encourage such make-believe as this, we shall soon find it in our contracts and agreements."

The Technique of Establishing Tyranny

30. Soon afterwards, Pisistratus deliberately wounded himself and drove in a chariot to the marketplace where he tried to arouse the people by telling them that his enemies had plotted to kill him because of his political views. When the multitude loudly expressed their indignation, Solon came up and said to him: "Son of Hippocrates, you act Homer's Odysseus very badly; for he wounded himself to deceive his enemies, but you have done it to mislead your countrymen."

After this the people were ready to fight for Pisistratus, and at a general assembly Ariston made a motion that a bodyguard of fifty club-bearers should be assigned to him. Solon formally opposed it with many arguments similar to those he has left us in his poems:

> You dote upon the words of a wily man.
> True, you are singly each a crafty soul.
> But all together make one empty fool.

But when he saw the poor become riotous and determined to support Pisistratus, while the rich out of fear declined to oppose him, Solon left the assembly, saying that he was wiser than the one party in discerning the plot, and braver than the other, which understood what was happening but was afraid to oppose a tyrant. So the people passed the decree and did not limit the number of guards which Pisistratus employed, but allowed him to keep as many as he pleased until at last he seized the Acropolis.

Solon Reproves the Athenians

When this had been done and the city was in great confusion, Megacles immediately took flight with the rest of the Alcmaeonidae family. But Solon, though he was now very old and had none to support him, appeared in public and addressed the citizens, both upbraiding them for their stupidity and cowardice, and exhorting and encouraging them not to surrender their liberty. Then it was that he spoke those memorable words, that it would have been easier for them to repress the advance of tyranny and prevent its establishment, but now that it was established and fully grown it would be more glorious to destroy it. However, finding that no one had the courage to support him, he returned to his own house and placed his weapons at the street door with these words: "I have done all in my power to defend my country and its laws."

This was his last public effort. Though some urged him to fly, he took no notice of their advice but continued to write poems in which he reproached the Athenians:

> If now you suffer, do not blame the Powers,
> For they are good, and all the fault was ours,
> All the strongholds you put into his hands,
> And now his slaves must do what he commands.

31. Many of his friends, alarmed at this, told him the tyrant would certainly put him to death for it and asked him to what he trusted that he went to such

imprudent lengths. He answered: "To my old age." However, when Pisistratus had fully established himself he paid court to Solon. He treated his with kindness and respect and invited him to his house, until Solon actually became his adviser and approved many of his acts. He retained most of Solon's laws, observing them himself and compelling his friends to do so. For example, when he was accused of murder after he had become tyrant, he appeared in due form before the court of the Areopagus to defend himself, but his accuser did not appear. He also added some laws of his own, one of which provides that persons maimed in war should be maintained at public expense.

War and Peace in the Classical Age

As Greek civic communities responded to the challenges of overpopulation, domestic political strife, and wars with neighbors, they did so within the framework of a developing set of institutions that came to be associated with the classical city-state, or *polis*. The needs of fighting battles in the manner of hoplite warfare not only turned Sparta into an armed camp, it shaped the mores and values of all other Greek cities. Hoplites were citizens, and adult male citizens served as hoplites. The superiority of the Greek hoplite soldier came to be tested in the course of a set of wars with the Achaemenid Persian empire, which had extended its power to western Asia Minor and northwestern Greece. The ensuing wars between Greeks and Persians, in which the Greek emerged victorious, would usher in far-reaching changes and, according to modern historians, mark the transition between the Archaic and Classical periods of Greece.

24 Herodotus

Greece Saved from Persian Conquest

If history can be defined as an "honest attempt first to find out what happened, then to explain why it happened," then Herodotus (ca. 484–ca. 425 B.C.) deserves to be called "the father of history." His forerunners in this endeavor

From Herodotus, *History of the Persian Wars*, Bk. VII, Chs. 8–10, 19–21, 33–37, 44–46, 56, 60, 100–105, 131–33, 138–39, 145–47, 175, 184, 201–205, 207–13, 219–26, 228, based on the translation by George Rawlinson.

were the logographers—"writers of tales (*logoi*)"—who arose during the late sixth century B.C. in Greek Asia Minor (where Herodotus was born) and in their lost works assembled a multitude of disarrayed facts on such diverse subjects as genealogy, local history, and geography. Herodotus was also a collector of facts and a teller of tales, but he went far beyond the logographers in the broad scope and unifying theme of his investigations—the clash of two rival cultures that culminated in the Greek and Persian Wars—and in his concern for explaining causation. All this is clearly stated in his very first sentence, which could well serve as the title to his great work of narrative history: "The researches [*historia*] of Herodotus of Halicarnassus, here set down, that the deeds of men may not be forgotten, and that the great and noble actions of the Greeks and Asiatics may not lose their fame; and, especially, the causes of the war between them."

The theme that gives unity to Herodotus' *History* is the age-old conflict between East and West, which began with the Trojan War and climaxed with the Persian king Xerxes' colossal attempt to conquer Greece in 480 B.C., just a generation before Herodotus' prime. Ten years earlier, the hoplites of Athens (Herodotus' adopted city) had humbled Xerxes' father Darius by pushing into the sea at Marathon the expeditionary force sent to punish the Athenians for aiding the abortive Ionian Revolt of the Greek city-states in Asia Minor. Now Xerxes had readied a combined land and sea operation (according to Herodotus, it ultimately totaled 2,317,610 men and 1,207 warships) and was intent on ending for all time the troublesome meddling of the free Greeks in Persian affairs. By the time the Persians were ready to cross from Asia to Europe on two remarkable pontoon bridges thrown across the mile-wide Hellespont, thirty-one Greek states had put aside their petty quarrels and formed a confederation, the Hellenic League, for the defense of their liberty against an alien despotism.

The following selections from Book VII of Herodotus' *History* begin with some of the preparatory activities of Xerxes and the Greeks and end with the initial clash between the two armies at the narrow pass between sea and mountain at Thermopylae, where a hastily assembled Greek advance force of around seven thousand men were on the verge of being encircled. The Greeks had to pull back to another defensible position and left a small band of elite Spartans and Thespians as a "forlorn hope" to slow Persian advance to buy time for the main army's withdrawal. Commanded by King Leonidas of Sparta, this small force fought against the odds even after treachery allowed their position to be turned. The last stand of this rearguard came to be celebrated as one of the most glorious defeats in history. The Battle at Thermopylae was followed by two immense Greek victories: a naval battle off Salamis in which the Greek allied fleet, under Athenian leadership, routed the Persian navy and a land battle the following year (479 B.C.) at Plataea where the skill and spirit of Spartan hoplites dispersed and slaughtered the enemy until, in the words of Herodotus, "of 300,000 troops, less the 40,000 who fled ..., not 3,000 escaped."

Many scholars have maintained that Herodotus' acceptance of grossly-inflated estimates of the size of the Persian land forces discredits him as a historian. Some, however, noting that the *History* was meant to be read aloud before festival-attending audiences, have argued that he uses these figures because they had become part of Greek tradition and because they were in keeping with the epic sweep and grandeur of his stated purpose—"that the great and noble actions of the Greeks and Asiatics may not lose their fame." Furthermore, such huge figures suited Herodotus' view of causation in history. They underlay his explanation of why a few tiny Greek states were able to defeat a mighty empire that stretched across three thousand miles and commanded the resources of forty-six nations—to Herodotus, as to all Greeks, overweening pride (*hubris*) inevitably leads to destruction (*nemesis*) because "God tolerates pride in none but himself."

Debate at the Persian Court

After Egypt [which had revolted] was subdued, Xerxes, being about to take in hand the expedition against Athens, called together a council of the noblest Persians to learn their opinions and to lay before them his own designs. When the men met, the king spoke thus to them:

"... What need have I to tell you of the deeds of Cyrus and Cambyses, and my own father Darius, how many nations they conquered and added to our dominions? You know right well what great things they achieved. But for myself, I will say that from the day on which I mounted the throne, I have not ceased to consider by what means I may rival those who have preceded me in this post of honor and increase the power of Persia as much as any of them. I have pondered on this, and now at last I have found a way whereby we may win glory and also get possession of a land which is as large and as rich as our own—no, is even richer—while at the same time we obtain satisfaction and revenge. For this reason I have called you together—that I may make known to you what I propose to do. My intent is to throw a bridge over the Hellespont and march an army through Europe against Greece, and thereby punish the Athenians for the wrongs committed by them against the Persians and against my father. Your own eyes saw the preparations of Darius against these men, but death thwarted his hopes of revenge. On his behalf, therefore, and on behalf of all the Persians, I pledge not to rest till I have taken and burnt Athens, which has dared, unprovoked, to injure me and my father. Long ago [498 B.C.] they came to Asia with Aristagoras of Miletus, who was one of our slaves, and entering Sardis, burnt its temples and its sacred groves. More recently, when we made a landing upon their coast under Datis and Artaphernes, how roughly they handled us at Marathon you do not need to be told. For these reasons, therefore, I have decided upon this war, and I see also the following advantages: Once we subdue them and their Spartan neighbors who hold the land of Pelops the Phrygian, we shall extend the Persian territory as far as God's heaven reaches. The sun will then shine on no land beyond our borders, for I will march through Europe from one end to the other and with your aid make it all one country. For if what I hear is true, once Athens and Sparta are swept away, there is no city or country left in all the world which will be able to withstand us. Thus we shall bring all mankind under our yoke, both those who are guilty and those who are innocent of doing us wrong. And you, if you wish to please me, do as follows: When I announce the time for the army to meet together, hasten to the muster with good will, every one of you, and to the man who brings with him the best-equipped troops I will give the gifts which our people consider the most honorable. This is what you have to do. But to show that I am no self-willed tyrant, I lay the business before you and give you full leave to speak your mind openly."

Having so spoken, Xerxes held his peace. Whereupon Mardonius said: "Truly, my lord, you surpass not only all living Persians, but also those yet unborn. Most true and right is each word that you have uttered; but best of all is your resolve not to let the Ionians who live in Europe—a worthless crew—mock us any more. It would indeed be a terrible thing if, after conquering and enslaving the Sacae, the Indians, the Ethiopians, the Assyrians, and many other mighty nations, not for any wrong that they had done us but only to increase our empire, we should then allow the Greeks, who have done us such unprovoked injury, to escape our vengeance. What is it that we fear in them? Not surely their numbers. Not the greatness of their wealth. We know how they fight—we know how weak their power is; already have we subdued their children who dwell in our country, the Ionians, Aeolians, and Dorians. I myself have had the experience of these men when I marched against them by the orders of your father; and though I went as far as Macedonia and came but a little short of reaching Athens itself, yet not a soul ventured to come out against me to battle. And yet, I am told, these same Greeks often wage war against one another in the most foolish way, through sheer ignorance and obstinacy. For no sooner is war declared than they search out the smoothest and most level plain and there they meet and fight, with the result that even the victors depart with great losses—to say nothing of the losers, who are wiped out. Who then is likely, O king, to meet you in arms when you come with all Asia's warriors at your back, and with all her ships? For my part, I do not believe the Greek people will be so foolhardy. Grant, however, that I am mistaken and that they are foolish enough to meet us in open fight; in that case they will learn that we are the best soldiers in the whole world. Nevertheless let us spare no pains; nothing comes without trouble, but all that men acquire is got by painstaking toil."

When Mardonius had in this way smoothed over the harsh speech of Xerxes, he held his peace. The other Persians were silent, for all feared to raise their voice against the plan proposed to them. But Artabanus, the son of Hystaspes and uncle of Xerxes, trusting to this relationship, was bold to speak:

"O king, it is impossible, if no more than one opinion is uttered, to choose the best; a man is forced to follow whatever advice is given him. But if opposite opinions are delivered, then a choice can be made.... You say that you will bridge the Hellespont and lead your troops through Europe against Greece. Now suppose some disaster befall you by land or sea, or both. It may be so, for the Greeks are reputed to be valiant. Indeed one may deduce that from what they have already done. When Datis and Artaphernes led their huge army against Attica, the Athenians alone defeated them. But grant they are not successful on both elements. Still, if they man their ships, and defeating us by sea, sail to the Hellespont and there destroy our bridge, that, sire, would be perilous.... See how God with his lightning always strikes the bigger animals and will not allow them to grow insolent, while the smaller do not offend him. How likewise his bolts fall always on the highest houses and the tallest trees. So clearly does he love to bring down everything that exalts itself. Thus often a mighty army is destroyed by a smaller one, when God in his jealousy sends fear or storm from heaven, and they perish in a way unworthy of them. For God tolerates pride in none but himself. Again, hurry always brings disaster, from which huge sufferings arise; but in delay lie many advantages, not apparent, it may be, at first sight, but such as in the course of time are seen by all. Such is my advice, O king...."

The Persian Army Is Mustered

After Xerxes had decided to go to war,... all the assembled Persian nobles departed to their own provinces, where each displayed the greatest zeal, on the faith of the king's offers, for all hoped to obtain for themselves the gifts which had been promised. And so Xerxes gathered together his army, ransacking every corner of the continent.

Reckoning from the recovery of Egypt, Xerxes spent four years in collecting his army and making ready all things that were needed for his soldiers. It was not till the close of the fifth year that he set forth on his march, accompanied by a mighty multitude. For of all the armies whereof any mention has reached us, this was by far the greatest; no other expedition compared to this seems of any account.... For was there a nation in all Asia which Xerxes did not bring with him against Greece? Or was there a river, except those of unusual size, which sufficed for his troops to drink? One nation furnished ships; another foot-soldiers; a third had to supply horses; a fourth, transports for the horses and men; a fifth, ships for the floating bridges; a sixth, ships with provisions....

Bridging the Hellespont

Xerxes [having led his army to Sardis] made preparations to advance to Abydos, where the bridge across the Hellespont from Asia to Europe was already finished. Midway between Sestos and Madytus in the Hellespontine Chersonese and opposite Abydos, there is a rocky tongue of land which runs out for some distance into the sea.... Towards this tongue of land the men whose business it was carried out a double bridge from Abydos. The Phoenicians constructed one with cables of white flax, the Egyptians in the other used ropes made of papyrus. It is about a mile across from Abydos to the opposite coast. When the channel had been bridged successfully, a great storm broke the whole work to pieces, destroying all that had been done.

When Xerxes heard of it, he was furious and gave orders that the Hellespont should receive three hundred lashes and that a pair of fetters should be cast into it. Indeed, I have even heard it said that he bade the branders take their irons and brand the Hellespont. It is certain that he commanded those who scourged the water to utter these barbarian and arrogant words: "You bitter water, your master lays on you this punishment because you have wronged him without cause, having suffered no evil at his hands. But King Xerxes will cross you, whether you will or not. Well do you deserve that no man honor you with sacrifice, for you are a treacherous and unsavory river." While the sea was thus punished by his orders, he also commanded that the overseers of the work should lose their heads.

Those whose business it was executed the unpleasant order, and other engineers were appointed who accomplished the task in the way which I will now describe.

They joined together triremes and fifty-oared ships, 360 to support the bridge on the side of the Black Sea, and 314 to sustain the other; and these they placed at right-angles to the sea and in the direction of the current of the Hellespont, relieving by these means the strain on the shore cables. Having joined the vessels, they moored them with anchors of unusual size so that the vessels of the bridge towards the Black Sea might resist the winds which blow from within the straits, and that those of the more western bridge facing the Aegean might withstand the winds which set in from the south and from the southeast.... When the strait was bridged, trunks of trees were sawn into planks cut to the width of the bridge, and these were laid side by side upon the tightened cables and fastened on the top. This done, brushwood was arranged upon the planks, after which earth was heaped upon the brushwood and the whole trodden down into a solid mass. Lastly a bulwark was set up on each side of this causeway of a height to prevent the mules and horses from seeing over it and taking fright at the water.

And when all was prepared ..., then the army, having wintered at Sardis, began its march towards Abydos fully equipped, on the first approach of spring. At the moment of departure, the sun suddenly left his seat in the heavens and disappeared, though there were no clouds in sight, the sky being clear and serene. Day was thus turned into night; whereupon Xerxes was seized with alarm, and sending at once for the Magi, inquired of them the meaning of the portent. They replied, "God is foreshowing to the Greeks the eclipse of their cities; for the sun foretells for them and the moon for us." So Xerxes, thus instructed, proceeded on his way with great gladness of heart....

Xerxes Reviews His Army

Arriving at Abydos, Xerxes wished to review his army. There was a throne of white marble on a hill near the city, which the people of Abydos had prepared beforehand at the king's bidding. Xerxes took his seat on it, and gazing upon the shore below was able to view all his land forces and all his ships. Then he felt a desire to see a sailing-match among his ships, which accordingly took place and was won by the Phoenicians of Sidon, much to the joy of Xerxes, who was delighted both with the race and with his army. And as he looked and saw the whole Hellespont covered with the vessels of his fleet, and all the shore and every plain about Abydos as full as could be of men, Xerxes congratulated himself on his good fortune; but after a little while he wept.

Then Artabanus, the king's uncle (the same who first freely spoke his mind to the king and advised him not to lead his army against Greece), when he heard that Xerxes was in tears, went to him and said, "How different, sire, is what you are now doing from what you did a little while ago! Then you congratulated yourself, and now you weep."

"There came upon me," Xerxes replied, "a sense of pity when I thought of the shortness of man's life and considered that of all this army, so numerous as it is, not one will be alive when a hundred years are gone by."...

As soon as Xerxes had reached the European side, he watched his army as it crossed under the lash. The crossing continued for seven days and seven nights without rest or pause. It is said that after Xerxes had made the passage, a Hellespontian exclaimed, "Why, O Zeus, do you, in the likeness of a Persian man, and with the name of Xerxes instead of your own, lead the whole race of mankind to the destruction of Greece? It would have been as easy for you to destroy it without their aid!"...

What the exact number of the troops of each nation was I cannot say with certainty—for it is not mentioned by anyone—but the whole land army together was found to amount to 1,700,000 men. The manner in which the counting took place was the following. A body of 10,000 men was brought to a certain place, and the men were made to stand as close together as possible; then a circle was drawn around them and they were let go. Where the circle had been, a fence was built about the height of a man's middle. The enclosure was filled continually with fresh troops till the whole army had in this way been counted. When the counting was over, the troops were drawn up according to their several nations....

Demaratus' Praise of Sparta

Now when the counting and marshalling of the troops was ended ... Xerxes ... sent for [the Spartan exile] Demaratus the son of Ariston, who had accompanied him on his march against Greece, and addressed him thus:

"Demaratus, it is my pleasure at this time to ask you certain things which I wish to know. You are a Greek, and, as I hear from the other Greeks with whom I converse, no less than from your own lips, you are a native of a city which is not the least or the weakest in their land. Tell me, therefore, what do you think? Will the Greeks lift a hand against us? My own judgment is that even if all the Greeks and all the barbarians of the west were gathered together in one place, they would not be able to withstand my army, not being really united. But I would like to know what you think."

Thus Xerxes questioned and the other replied in his turn, "O king, do you wish me to give you a true answer, or do you wish for an agreeable one?"

The king bade him speak the truth and promised that he would not on that account hold him in less favor than before. So Demaratus, when he heard the promise, spoke as follows: "O king, since you bid me speak the truth and not say what will one day prove to be a lie, thus I answer: Poverty has at all times been a fellow-dweller with us in our land, while Valor is an ally whom we have gained by dint of wisdom and strict laws. Her aid enables us to drive out poverty and escape tyranny. Brave are all the Greeks who dwell in any Dorian land, but what I am about to say does not concern all Dorians, but only the Spartans. First then, come what may, they will never accept your terms, which would reduce

Greece to slavery; and further, they are sure to join battle with you, even though all the rest of the Greeks should submit to your will. As for their numbers, do not ask how many they are; for if only a thousand should take the field, they will meet you in battle, and so will any number, be it less than this or be it more."

When Xerxes heard this answer, he laughed. "What wild words, Demaratus! One thousand men join battle with such an army as this!... How could one thousand men, or ten thousand, or even fifty thousand, particularly if they were all free and not under one master, how could such a force stand against an army like mine? Let them be five thousand, and we shall have more than one thousand men to each one of theirs. If, indeed, like our troops they had a single master, their fear of him might make them courageous beyond their natural bent, or they might be urged on by lashes against an enemy which far outnumbered them. But left to their own free choice, assuredly they will act differently. For my part, I believe that if the Greeks had to contend with the Persians only, and the numbers were equal on both sides, the Greeks would find it hard to stand their ground. We too have among us such men as those of whom you spoke—not many indeed, but still we possess a few. For instance, some of my bodyguard would be willing to engage singly with three Greeks. But this you did not know, and therefore you talked so foolishly."

Demaratus answered, "I knew, O king, at the outset that if I told you the truth my speech would displease you. But as you required me to answer you truthfully, I informed you what the Spartans will do. And in this I speak not from any love that I bear them—for you know what my love towards them is likely to be at the present time, when they have robbed me of my rank and my ancestral honors [claiming he was by birth a bastard] and made me a homeless exile whom your father received, bestowing on me both shelter and sustenance. What likelihood is there that a sensible man should be unthankful for kindness shown him and not cherish it in his heart? For myself, I prefer not to cope with ten men, or with two; indeed, had I the choice I would rather not fight even with one. But if necessary, if there were any great cause urging me on, I would readily contend against one of those persons who boast themselves a match for any three Greeks. So likewise the Spartans when they fight singly are as good men as any in the world, and then they fight in a body are the bravest of all. For though they be free men, they are not in all respects free; Law is their master, and this master they fear more than your subjects fear you. Whatever it commands they do, and its command is always the same: it forbids them to flee in battle, whatever the number of their foes, and requires them to stand firm and to conquer or die. If in these words, O king, I seem to you to speak foolishly, I am content from this time forward to hold my peace. I spoke because I was compelled by you. But I pray that all may turn out according to your wishes."

Such was the answer of Demaratus, and Xerxes was not angry with him at all, but laughed and sent him away with words of kindness. After this interview ... Xerxes started with his army and marched upon Greece through Thrace....

Athens the Savior of Greece

At this time the heralds who had been sent into Greece to demand submission to the king returned to the camp, some of them empty-handed, others with earth and water. Among the number of those from whom earth and water were brought were the Thessalians, Dolopians, Enianians, Perrhaebians, Locrians, Magnetians, Malians, Achaeans of Phthiotis, Thebans, and Boeotians generally, except those of Plataea and Thespiae. Against these the Greeks who had taken up arms to resist the barbarians swore this oath: "From all those of Greek blood who yielded to the Persians without necessity, we will take a tenth of their goods and give it to the god at Delphi."

King Xerxes had sent no heralds to Athens or Sparta to demand earth and water for the reason I will now relate. When Darius had once before sent messengers for the same purpose, they were thrown at Athens into the Pit of Punishment, at Sparta into a well, and bidden to take therefrom earth and water and carry it to their king. On this account Xerxes sent no demand....

To return to my main subject, the expedition of the Persian king, though it was in name directed against Athens, it threatened really the whole of Greece. Of this the Greeks were aware, but they did not all view the matter in the same light. Some had given the Persians earth and water, and so were in good spirits, thinking themselves secure against harm from the barbarian army; others, who had refused compliance, were thrown into a panic—they considered all the ships in Greece too few to engage the enemy, and it was evident that most states would take no part in the war but warmly favor the Persians.

And here I feel compelled to deliver an opinion which most men, I know, will dislike, but which, as it seems to me to be true, I am determined not to withhold. Had the Athenians, from fear of the approaching danger, quit their country, or had they without quitting it submitted to the power of Xerxes, there would certainly have been no attempt to resist the Persians by sea. In which case the course of events by land would have been the following: Though the Spartans might have constructed many breastworks across the Isthmus, their allies would have fallen away, not by voluntary desertion but because town after town would have been taken by the fleet of the barbarians. So the Spartans would at last have stood alone, and, standing alone, would have displayed prodigies of valor and died nobly. Either they would have done this, or else, before it came to that extremity, seeing one Greek state after another embrace the cause of the Persians, they would have come to terms with Xerxes. Thus either way Greece would have been brought under Persia. For I cannot understand of what possible use the walls across the Isthmus could have been if the Persians had the mastery of the sea. If then a man should say that the Athenians were the saviors of Greece, he would not exceed the truth. For they truly held the balance, and whichever side they joined would have prevailed. They, too, it was who, when they had determined to maintain the freedom of Greece, roused up those Greeks who had not yet gone over to the Persians. They, together with the gods, repulsed the invader. Even the terrible oracles which reached them from Delphi and struck fear into their hearts failed to persuade them to fly from Greece.

They had the courage to remain faithful to their land and await the coming of the foe....

Actions of the Greek Confederacy

The Greeks who were loyal to the Grecian cause consulted together and exchanged pledges. They agreed that before any other step was taken the quarrels which existed between the various states should be settled....

When these resolutions had been agreed upon and the quarrels between the states made up, they sent into Asia three men as spies. These men reached Sardis and took note of the king's forces, but, being discovered, were questioned by order of the Persian generals and condemned to death. Xerxes, however, when the news reached him, disapproved the sentence and sent some of his bodyguard with instructions to bring the spies into his presence if they found them still alive. The messengers found the spies alive and brought them before the king, who, when he heard the purpose for which they had come, gave orders to his guards to take them round the camp and show them all the infantry and cavalry, letting them gaze at everything to their heart's content, and then send them away unharmed.

For these orders, Xerxes gave afterwards the following reasons: Had the spies been put to death, the Greeks would have continued ignorant of the vastness of his army, while he would have done them little harm by killing three of their men. On the other hand, by the return of the spies to Greece, his power would become known, the Greeks would surrender their freedom before he began his march, and his troops would be saved all the trouble of an expedition. This reasoning was like that he used on another occasion. While he was staying at Abydos, he saw some grain ships passing through the Hellespont from the Black Sea on their way to Aegina and the Peloponnesus. His attendants, hearing that they were the enemy's, were ready to capture them and looked to see when Xerxes would give the signal. He, however, merely asked, "Where are the ships bound?" and when they answered, "For your foes, master, with grain on board," he replied, "We too are bound there laden with grain, among other things. What harm is it, if they carry our provisions for us?"...

Greeks and Persians at Thermopylae

The Greeks ... considered where they should make a stand and what places they should occupy. The opinion which prevailed was that they should guard the pass of Thermopylae since it was narrower than the Thessalian defile and nearer to them. (Of the pathway by which the Greeks who later fell at Thermopylae were intercepted, they had no knowledge until, on their arrival at Thermopylae, it was revealed to them by the Trachinians.) They decided both to guard the pass in order to prevent the barbarians from penetrating into Greece and to send the fleet to Artemisium in the region of Histiacotis. Those places are near to one another, and it would be easy for the fleet and army to communicate....

The sea force brought by the king from Asia amounted in all to 517,610 men. The number of the foot soldiers was 1,700,000; that of the horsemen

80,000, to which must be added the Arabs who rode on camels and the Libyans who fought in chariots, whom I reckon at 20,000. The whole number, therefore, of the land and sea forces added together was 2,317,610. Such was the force brought from Asia, without including the camp followers or taking account of the men on the provision ships....

King Xerxes pitched his camp in the region of Malis called Trachinia, while the Greeks occupied the pass which the Greeks in general call Thermopylae [literally "Hot Gates"], but which the natives call Pylae. Here the two armies took their stand, the one master of all the region lying north of Trachis, the other of the country extending south of that place.

The Greeks who here awaited the coming of Xerxes were the following: 300 heavy infantry from Sparta, 500 from Tegea, 500 from Mantinea, 120 from Orchomenus in Arcadia, 1,000 from other Arcadian cities, 400 from Corinth, 200 from Philius, and 80 from Mycenae. All these were from the Peloponnesus. There were also from Boeotia 700 Thespians and 400 Thebans. The Locrians of Opus and the Phocians had also obeyed the call to arms; the former sent all the men they had, the latter one thousand. Envoys from the Greeks at Thermopylae had gone to the Locrians and Phocians to ask for aid, claiming that they themselves were only the vanguard sent to precede the main body which was expected any day, and that the sea was being closely watched by the Athenians, the Aeginetans, and the rest of the fleet. Thus there was no cause for alarm, for after all the invader was not a god but a man who, like all men, was liable to misfortunes from the very day of his birth—and the greater the man the greater his misfortune. So the invader, being only a mortal, must surely fall from glory. Hearing this, the Locrians and the Phocians had sent their troops to Trachis.

The various contingents had their own commanders, under whom they served; but the one to whom all looked up, and who commanded the entire force, was the Spartan, Leonidas.... He had come to Thermopylae accompanied by the three hundred men which the law assigned him, whom he had himself chosen from among the citizens and who were all fathers with sons living. On his way he had taken the troops from Thebes, whose number I have already mentioned, and who were under the command of Leontiades the son of Eurymachus. The reason why he made a point of taking their troops from Thebes and Thebes only was that the Thebans were strongly suspected of favoring the Persians. Leonidas therefore called on them to enter the war, wishing to see whether they would comply with his demand or openly refuse to join the Greek alliance. Though they leaned the other way, they nevertheless sent the men....

The Greek forces at Thermopylae, when the Persian army drew near to the entrance of the pass, were seized with fear, and a council was held to consider a retreat. It was the wish of the Peloponnesians generally that the army should fall back upon the Peloponnesus and there guard the Isthmus. But Leonidas, who saw with what indignation the Phocians and Locrians heard of this plan, gave his voice for remaining where they were while they sent envoys to the other cities to ask for help, since they were too few to make a stand against an army like that of the Persians.

While this debate was going on, Xerxes sent a mounted spy to observe the Greeks and note how many they were and what they were doing. He had heard before he came out of Thessaly that a few men were assembled at this place, and that at their head were Spartans under Leonidas, a descendant of Heracles. The horseman rode up to the camp and looked about him, but did not see the whole army, for they were out of sight on the further side of the wall which had been rebuilt and was now carefully guarded. But he observed those on the outside who were encamped in front of the rampart. It chanced that at this time the Spartans held the outer guard and were seen by the spy. Some of them were engaged in gymnastic exercises, others were combing their long hair. This astonished the spy, but he counted their number, and when he had taken accurate note of everything, he rode back quietly. No one pursued him, or paid any heed to his visit. So he returned and told Xerxes all that he had seen.

Xerxes, who had no means of surmising the truth—that the Spartans were preparing to do or die manfully—but thought it laughable that they should be engaged in such employments, sent for Demaratus the son of Ariston, who still remained with the army. Xerxes told him all that he had heard and questioned him concerning the report, being anxious to understand the meaning of such behavior on the part of the Spartans. Then Demaratus said, "I spoke to you, O king, concerning these men when we began our march upon Greece; you, however, only laughed when I told you what would come to pass. Earnestly do I strive at all times to speak truth to you, sire; now listen to it once more. These men have come to dispute the pass with us, and it is for this that they are now making ready. It is their custom, when they are about to risk their lives, to fix their hair with care. Be assured, however, that if you can subdue the men who are here and the Spartans who remain in Sparta, there is no other people in all the world who will venture to lift a hand against you. You have now to deal with the finest kingdom in Greece, and with the bravest men."

Then Xerxes, to whom what Demaratus said seemed beyond belief, asked, "How is it possible for so small an army to contend with mine?" "O king," Demaratus answered, "treat me as a liar, if matters fall not out as I say." But Xerxes was not convinced.

The Fighting Begins

Four whole days Xerxes waited, expecting that the Greeks would run away. When he found on the fifth that they were not gone, thinking that their firm stand was mere impudence and recklessness, he grew angry and sent against them the Medes and Cissians with orders to take them alive and bring them into his presence. The Medes rushed forward and charged the Greeks, but fell in vast numbers; others took the places of the slain and refused to be beaten off, though they suffered terrible losses. In this way it became clear to all, and especially to the king, that though he had plenty of men, he had very few soldiers. The struggle, however, continued the whole day.

The Medes, having met so rough a reception, withdrew from the fight and their place was taken by the band of Persians under Hydarnes whom the king called his Immortals; they, it was thought, would soon finish the business. But when they joined battle with the Greeks, it was with no better success than the Median detachment—things went much as before—the two armies fighting in a narrow space, the barbarians using shorter spears than the Greeks and having no advantage from their numbers.

The Spartans fought memorably and showed themselves far more skillful in battle than their adversaries: often turning their backs and making as though they were flying away, causing the barbarians to rush after them with much noise and shouting; then they would wheel round and face their pursuers, destroying vast numbers of the enemy. Some Spartans also fell, but only a few. At last the Persians, finding that all their efforts to gain the pass availed nothing, whether they attacked by divisions or in any other way, withdrew to their own quarters. During these assaults, it is said that Xerxes, who was watching the battle, three times leaped from the throne on which he sat, in terror for his army.

Next day the combat was renewed, but with no better success for the barbarians. The Greeks were so few that the barbarians hoped to find them disabled by their wounds and offering no further resistance. But the Greeks were drawn up in detachments according to their cities and bore the brunt of the battle in turns, all except the Phocians, who had been stationed on the mountain to guard the pathway. So when the Persians found no difference between that day and the preceding, they again retired to their quarters.

Now, while the king was at a loss how to deal with the situation, Ephialtes, the son of Eurydemus, a man of Malis, came to him and was admitted to a conference. Stirred by the hope of receiving a rich reward at the king's hands, he had come to tell him of the pathway which led across the mountain to Thermopylae. By this disclosure he was to bring destruction on the Greeks who held the pass....

Leonidas Dismisses the Allies

The Greeks at Thermopylae received the first warning of the destruction which the dawn would bring on them from the seer Megistias, who read their fate in the victims as he was sacrificing. After this deserters came in and brought the news that the Persians were marching round by the hills. It was still night when these men arrived. Last of all, scouts came running down from the heights, bringing the same account, as the day was beginning to break. Then the Greeks held a council to consider what they should do, and here opinions were divided: some were strongly against quitting their post, while others contended to the contrary. So part of the troops departed and made their way homeward to their various states; part, however, resolved to remain and stand by Leonidas to the last.

Some say that Leonidas himself sent away the troops who departed because he was concerned for their safety, but thought it unseemly that either he or his Spartans should quit the post which they had been specially sent to guard. I incline to think that Leonidas gave the order because he perceived the allies to be out of heart and unwilling to face the danger. He therefore commanded them to retreat, but said that he himself could not withdraw with honor. He knew that if he stayed, glory awaited him and Sparta would not lose her prosperity—for when the Spartans at the very beginning of the war went to consult the Delphic oracle, the answer they received from the priestess was that either Sparta must be laid waste by the barbarians or one of her kings must perish. The prophecy was in hexameter verse and ran thus:

> Oh! ye men who dwell in the streets of broad Lacedaemon,
> Either your glorious town shall be sacked by the children of
>   Perseus,
> Or, in exchange, must all through the whole Laconian
>   country
> Mourn for the loss of a king, descendant of great Heracles.
> He [Xerxes] cannot be withstood by the courage of bulls or
>   of lions,
> Strive as they may; he is mighty as Zeus; there is nought that
>   shall stay him,
> Till he have got for his prey your king, or your glorious city.

The memory of this answer, I think, and the wish to secure the whole glory for the Spartans, caused Leonidas to send the allies away. This is more likely than that they quarrelled with him and took their departure in such unruly fashion.

To me it seems no small argument in favor of this view that the seer who accompanied the army, Megistias the Acarnanian, said to have been of the blood of Melampus, and the one who was led by the appearance of the sacrificial victims to warn the Greeks of the danger which threatened them, received orders to retire (as it is certain he did) from Leonidas, that he might escape the coming destruction. Megistias, however, though bidden to depart, refused and stayed with the army; but he had an only son present with the expedition, whom he now sent away.

So the allies, when Leonidas ordered them to retire, obeyed him and departed. Only the Thespians and the Thebans remained with the Spartans, and of these the Thebans were kept back by Leonidas as hostages, very much against their will. The Thespians, on the contrary, stayed entirely of their own accord, refusing to retreat and declaring that they would not forsake Leonidas and his men. So they remained with the Spartans and died with them. Their leader was Demophilus, the son of Diadromes.

"Go Tell the Spartans ..."

At sunrise Xerxes made a libation, after which he waited until the usual time for the marketplace to fill, and then began his advance. Ephialtes had so instructed him, for the descent of the mountain is much quicker, and the distance much shorter, than the ascent. As the barbarians under Xerxes began to draw near, the Greeks under Leonidas, determined to die, advanced much further than on previous days until they reached the more open portion of the pass. Hitherto they had remained within the wall and had gone forth to fight where the pass was the narrowest. Now they joined battle beyond the narrows. The invaders fell in heaps, for behind them the captains, armed with whips, urged them forward with continual blows. Many fell into the sea and perished; a still greater number were trampled to death by their own soldiers; no one heeded the dying. The Greeks, reckless of their own safety and desperate, since they knew that the mountain had been crossed and their destruction was near at hand, fought with furious valor against the barbarians. By this time most of their spears were broken, and with their swords they were killing Persians.

Leonidas fell fighting bravely, with many famous Spartans at his side. Their names I have taken care to learn on account of their great worthiness, as indeed I have those of all the three hundred. There fell, too, at the same time many famous Persians, among them two brothers of Xerxes....

And now there arose a fierce struggle over the body of Leonidas. The Greeks four times drove back the enemy, and at last by their great bravery succeeded in bearing off the body. This combat was scarcely ended when the Persians with Ephialtes approached. The Greeks, informed that they were near, made a change in the manner of their fighting. Drawing back into the narrowest part of the pass behind the wall, they posted themselves on a little hill, where they stood drawn up in one close body, all except the Thebans. The hill is at the entrance of the pass, where today the stone lion stands which was set up in honor of Leonidas. Here they defended themselves to the last, those who still had swords using them and the others resisting with their hands and teeth till the barbarians, who had pulled down the wall and encircled them on every side, overwhelmed them.

Thus nobly did all the Spartans and Thespians behave, but one man is said to have distinguished himself above all the rest: Dieneces the Spartan. Before the battle, one of the Trachinians told him that so great was the number of barbarians, that when they shot their arrows the sun would be darkened. Dieneces was not frightened by these words. Making light of the Persian numbers, he answered, "Our Trachinian friend brings us excellent tidings. If the Persians darken the sun, we shall have our battle in the shade."...

The slain were buried where they fell. In their honor, and no less in honor of those who died before Leonidas sent the allies away, an inscription was set up which read:

> Here four thousand men from Pelops' land
> Against three million did bravely stand.

Another inscription was for the Spartans alone:

> Go tell the Spartans, you who pass us by,
> That here, obedient to their laws, we lie.

The seer had the following inscription:

> The great Megistias' tomb you here may view,
>   Whom slew the Medes, fresh from Spercheius' fords.
> Well the wise seer the coming death foreknew,
>   Yet scorned he to forsake his Spartan lords.

25 Pericles' Funeral Oration

An Idealized View of Athenian Democracy and Its Empire

No finer expression of the ideals of democracy exists than the famous Funeral Oration delivered by Pericles in honor of the Athenians who fell fighting Sparta during the first year (431 B.C.) of the Peloponnesian War (See Selection 27). Along with U.S. President Abraham Lincoln's Gettysburg Address, with which it is frequently compared, the oration is considered one of the greatest speeches in literature. Pericles appeals to the patriotism of his listeners, confronted by the crisis of a great war, by describing the superior qualities and advantages of their democracy as a heritage won for them by their ancestors and worthy of any sacrifice to preserve. He emphasizes as the outstanding feature of Athenian democracy—and, we can add, of any democracy—the harmonious blending of opposite tendencies in politics, economics, and culture that it contains. This is perhaps the finest expression of the Greek ideal of a mean between extremes. All this is described in sharp contrast to what Pericles presented as the rigid totalitarianism of Sparta, which regulated every detail of its citizens' existence. An outstanding example of this happy blending of control and freedom in all phases of life was the Athenian acceptance of the leadership of Pericles as the recognized superior individual voted into power by the people to "lead them," as Thucydides noted, "instead of being led by them."

Pericles extends the same argument, that order and liberty are compatible, to justify the existence of the Athenian Empire, which had emerged after the Persian Wars as a defensive naval league of Greek states, the Delian League, that in time became increasingly dominated by Athens and eventually transformed by it into an instrument of imperial control over other Greek states. This growth of this Athenian naval empire alarmed other Greek states, including Sparta and Corinth, a rival trading city jealous of Athenian naval prowess. Charging Athens as a "tyrant city" that extinguished the liberties of many Greek states and was threatening that of the remainder, the Peloponessian League led by these two cities made war on Athens, demanding that it dismantle its empire and free the Greeks it had subjugated to itself. The Peloponnesian War was therefore a war on several dimensions, being not only one among rivals for hegemony in the Greek world but also a contest between rival ideologies. Ironically, "totalitarian" Sparta fought for the principle of Greek civic autonomy while "democratic" Athens stood by its own right to dominate others, to have an empire. Pericles gave voice to such the Athenian belief in their own right to rule: "We secure our friends not by accepting favors but by doing them.... We are alone among mankind in doing men

From Thucydides, *History of the Peloponnesian War*, Book II, 36–46; in *The Greek Commonwealth: Politics and Economics in Fifth-Century Athens*, translated by Alfred Zimmern, 4th edition (Oxford: the Clarendon Press, 1924), pp. 202–209.

Marble bust of Pericles wearing a war helmet; now in the British Museum.
"We are alone among mankind in doing men benefits, not on calculations of self-interest, but in the fearless confidence of freedom. In a word I claim that our city as a whole is an education to Greece."

benefits, not on calculations of self-interest, but in the fearless confidence of [bringing] freedom. In a word I claim that our city as a whole is an education to Greece...."

The Spirit, Constitution, and Manners of Athens

II, 36. My first words shall be for our ancestors; for it is both just to them and seemly that on an occasion such as this our tribute of memory should be paid them. For, dwelling always in this country, generation after generation in unchanging and unbroken succession, they have handed it down to us free by their exertions. So they are worthy of our praises; and still more so are our fathers. For they enlarged the ancestral patrimony by the Empire which we hold today and delivered it, not without labor, into the hands of our own generation; while it is we ourselves, those of us who are now in middle life, who consolidated our power throughout the greater part of the Empire and secured the city's complete independence both in war and peace.

Of the battles which we and our fathers fought, whether in the winning of our power abroad or in bravely withstanding the warfare of barbarian or Greek at home, I do not wish to say more: they are too familiar to you all. I wish rather to set forth the spirit in which we faced them, and the constitution and manners with which we rose to greatness, and to pass from them to the dead; for I think it not unfitting that these things should be called to mind at today's solemnity, and expedient too that the whole gathering of citizens and strangers should listen to them.

37. For our government is not copied from those of our neighbors: we are an example to them rather than they to us. Our constitution is named a democracy, because it is in the hands not of the few but of the many. But our laws secure equal justice for all in their private disputes, and our public opinion welcomes and honors talent in every branch of achievement, not as a matter of privilege but on grounds of excellence alone. And as we give free play to all in our public life, so we carry the same spirit into our daily relations with one another. We have no black looks or angry words for our neighbor if he enjoys himself in his own way, and we abstain from the little acts of churlishness which, though they leave no mark, yet cause annoyance to whoso notes them. Open and friendly in our private intercourse, in our public acts we keep strictly within the control of law. We acknowledge the restraint of reverence; we are obedient to whomsoever is set in authority, and to the laws, more especially to those which offer protection to the oppressed and those unwritten ordinances whose transgression brings shame.

38. Yet ours is no work-a-day city only. No other provides so many recreations for the spirit—contests and sacrifices all the year round, and beauty in our public buildings to cheer the heart and delight the eye day by day. Moreover, the city is so large and powerful that all the wealth of all the world flows in to her, so that our own Attic products seem no more homelike to us than the fruits of the labors of other nations.

39. Our military training too is different from our opponents'. The gates of our city are flung open to the world. We practice no periodical deportations, nor do we prevent our visitors from observing or discovering what an enemy might usefully apply to his own purposes. For our trust is not in the devices of material equipment, but in our own good spirits for battle.

So too with education. They toil from early boyhood in a laborious pursuit after courage, while we, free to live and wander as we please, march out none the less to face the self-same dangers....

40. We are lovers of beauty without extravagance, and lovers of wisdom without unmanliness. Wealth to us is not mere material for vainglory but an opportunity for achievement; and poverty we think it no disgrace to acknowledge but a real degradation to make no effort to overcome. Our citizens attend both to public and private duties, and do not allow absorption in their own various affairs to interfere with their knowledge of the city's. We differ from other states in regarding the man who holds aloof from public life not as "quiet" but as useless; we decide or debate, carefully and in person, all matters of policy, holding, not that words and deeds go ill together, but that acts are foredoomed to failure when undertaken undiscussed. For we are noted for being at once adventurous in action and most reflective beforehand. Other men are bold in ignorance, while reflection will stop their onset. But the bravest are surely those

who have the clearest vision of what is before them, glory and danger alike, and yet notwithstanding go out to meet it.

Apology for the Athenian Empire

In doing good, too, we are the exact opposite of the rest of mankind. We secure our friends not by accepting favors but by doing them. And so we are naturally more firm in our attachments: for we are anxious, as creditors, to cement by kind offices our relation towards our friends. If they do not respond with the same warmness it is because they feel that their services will not be given spontaneously but only as the repayment of a debt. We are alone among mankind in doing men benefits, not on calculations of self-interest, but in the fearless confidence of freedom. (41.) In a word I claim that our city as a whole is an education to Greece, and that her members yield to none, man by man, for independence of spirit, many-sidedness of attainment, and complete self-reliance in limbs and brain.

That this is no vainglorious phrase but actual fact the supremacy which our manners have won us itself bears testimony. No other city of the present day goes out to her ordeal greater than ever men dreamed; no other is so powerful that the invader feels no bitterness when he suffers at her hands, and her subjects no shame at the indignity of their dependence. Great indeed are the symbols and witnesses of our supremacy, at which posterity, as all mankind today, will be astonished. We need no Homer or other man of words to praise us; for such give pleasure for a moment, but the truth will put to shame their imaginings of our deeds. For our pioneers have forced a way into every sea and every land, establishing among all mankind, in punishment or beneficence, eternal memorials of their settlement.

The Worthy Dead

Such then is the city for whom, lest they should lose her, the men whom we celebrate died a soldier's death: and it is but natural that all of us, who survive them, should wish to spend ourselves in her service. (42.) That, indeed, is why I have spent many words upon the city. I wished to show that we have more at stake than men who have no such inheritance, and to support my praise of the dead by making clear to you what they have done. For if I have chanted the glories of the city it was these men and their like who set hand to array her. With them, as with few among Greeks, words cannot magnify the deeds that they have done. Such an end as we have here seems indeed to show us what a good life is, from its first signs of power to its final consummation. For even where life's previous record showed faults and failures it is just to weigh the last brave hour of devotion against them all. There they wiped out evil with good and did the city more service as soldiers than they did her harm in private life. There no hearts grew faint because they loved riches more than honor; none shirked the issue in the poor man's dreams of wealth. All these they put aside to strike a blow for the city. Counting the quest to avenge her honor as the most glorious of all ventures, and leaving Hope, the uncertain goddess, to send them what she would, they faced the foe as they drew near them in the strength of their own manhood; and when the shock of battle came, they chose rather to suffer the uttermost than to win life by weakness. So their memory has escaped the reproaches of men's lips, but they bore instead on their bodies the marks of men's hands, and in a moment of time, at the climax of their lives, were rapt away from a world filled, for their dying eyes, not with terror but with glory.

43. Such were the men who lie here and such the city that inspired them. We survivors may pray to be spared their bitter hour, but must disdain to meet the foe with a spirit less triumphant. Let us draw strength, not merely from twice-told arguments—how fair and noble a thing it is to show courage in battle—but from the busy spectacle of our great city's life as we have it before us day by day, falling in love with her as we see her, and remembering that all this greatness she owes to men with the fighter's daring, the wise man's understanding of his duty, and the good man's self-discipline in its performance—to men who, if they failed in any ordeal, disdained to deprive the city of their services, but sacrificed their lives as the best offerings on her behalf. So they gave their bodies to the commonwealth and received, each for his own memory, praise that will never die, and with it the grandest of all sepulchers, not that in which their mortal bones are laid, but a home in the minds of men, where their glory remains fresh to stir to speech or action as the occasion comes by. For the whole earth is the sepulcher of famous men; and their story is not graven only on stone over their native earth, but lives on far away, without visible symbol, woven into the stuff of other men's lives. For you now it remains to rival what they have done and, knowing the secret of happiness to be freedom and the secret of freedom a brave heart, not idly to stand aside from the enemy's onset. For it is not the poor and luckless, as having no hope of prosperity, who have most cause to reckon death as little loss, but those for whom fortune may yet keep reversal in store and who would feel the change most if trouble befell them. Moreover, weakly to decline the trial is more painful to a man of spirit than death coming sudden and unperceived in the hour of strength and enthusiasm.

Advice to the Survivors

44. Therefore I do not mourn with the parents of the dead who are here with us. I will rather comfort them. For they know that they have been born into a world of manifold chances and that he is to be accounted happy to whom the best lot falls—the best sorrow, such as is yours today, or the best death, such as fell to these, for whom life and happiness were cut to the self-same measure. I know it is not easy to give you comfort. I know how often in the joy of others you will have reminders of what was once your own, and how men feel sorrow, not for the loss of what they have never tasted, but when something that has grown dear to them has been snatched away. But you must keep a brave heart in the hope of other children, those who are still of age to bear them. For the newcomers will help you to forget the gap in your own circle, and will help the city to fill up the ranks of its workers and its soldiers.

For no man is fitted to give fair and honest advice in council if he has not, like his fellows, a family at stake in the hour of the city's danger. To you who are past the age of vigor I would say: count the long years of happiness so much gain to set off against the brief space that yet remains, and let your burden be lightened by the glory of the dead. For the love of honor alone is not staled by age, and it is by honor, not, as some say, by gold, that the helpless end of life is cheered.

45. I turn to those amongst you who are children or brothers of the fallen, for whom I foresee a mighty contest with the memory of the dead. Their praise is in all men's mouths, and hardly, even for supremest heroism, you will be adjudged to have achieved, not the same but a little less than they. For the living have the jealousy of rivals to contend with, but the dead are honored with unchallenged admiration.

If I must also speak a word to those who are now in widowhood on the powers and duties of women, I will cast all my advice into one brief sentence. Great will be your glory if you do not show more weakness than is natural to your sex—hers greatest of all who is not talked about for good or for evil among men.

46. I have spoken such words as I had to say according as the law prescribes, and the graveside offerings to the dead have been duly made. Henceforward the city will take charge of their children till manhood: such is the crown and benefit she holds out to the dead and to their kin for the trials they have undergone for her. For where the prize is highest, there, too, are the best citizens to contend for it.

And now, when you have finished your lamentation, let each of you depart.

26 The Old Oligarch

A Critical View of Athenian Democracy and Its Empire

Pericles perished in the epidemic that broke out in Athens when the city was besieged by the Peloponnesian League army in 429 B.C. His death and the experience of war marked the beginning of a new era of Athenian politics when passion increasingly triumphed over wisdom in the making of policy and demagogues, who played on the emotions and cupidity of the masses, replaced the courageous and far-sighted statesmen of the stamp of Pericles as leaders of the democracy. Critical voices that questioned the conduct of Athenian political figures and even the democratic system and empire began

From *The Old Oligarch, Being the Constitution of the Athenians Ascribed to Xenophon*, translated by James A. Petch (Oxford: Basil Blackwell, 1926).

to come to the fore. One unknown Athenian aristocrat or oligarch delivered a political speech (we have what appears to be a stenographic copy) to an audience of like-minded oligarchs in some unknown Greek city. Despite its sarcastic tone, it balances the idealized picture of Athenian democracy and its empire contained in Pericles' Funeral Oration with a realistic and penetrating description of the shortcomings of that democracy and the self-interested economic basis of its imperialism. The Old Oligarch's views are in some part valid for the Periclean age, but they are especially pertinent to the decade or two following the death of Pericles. Although he spoke with the bitterness and exaggeration of a narrow partisan, much of the Old Oligarch's criticism of the character of the Athenian masses and the motives of their imperialism resonates with judgment pronounced by other contemporaries. More than twenty centuries later, another aristocrat, the French Alexis de Tocqueville, visited the United States to observe its new democracy in action. Some of the conclusions in his *Democracy in America* (1835), though expressed with far more reserve, are similar to those of the Old Oligarch:

> Are you concerned with refining mores, elevating manners, and causing the arts to bloom? Do you desire poetry, renown and glory? ... If in your view that should be the main object of men in society, do not support democratic government; it surely will not lead you to that goal. But if ... in your view the main object of government is ... to provide for every individual therein the utmost well-being, protecting him as far as possible from all afflictions, then it is good to make conditions equal and to establish a democratic government.

"Rascals Fare Better Than Good Citizens"

I, 1. As for the constitution of the Athenians, their choice of this type of constitution I do not approve, for in choosing thus they chose that rascals should fare better than good citizens. This then is why I do not approve. However, this being their decision, I shall show how well they preserve their constitution, and how well otherwise they are acting where the rest of Greece thinks that they are going wrong.

2. First of all then I shall say that at Athens the poor and the commons seem justly to have the advantage over the well-born and the wealthy; for it is the commons which mans the fleet and has brought the state her power, and the steersmen and the boatswains and the shipmasters and the lookout-men and the ship-builders—these have brought the state her power much rather than the infantry and the well-born and the good citizens. This being so it seems just that all should have a share in offices filled by lot or by election, and that any citizen who wishes should be allowed to speak. (3.) Then in those offices which bring security to the whole commons if they are in the hands of good citizens, but if not ruin, the commons desires to have no share. They do not think that they ought to have a share through the lot in the supreme commands or in the cavalry commands, for the commons realizes that it reaps greater benefit by not having these offices in its own hands, but by allowing men of standing to hold them. All those offices however whose end is pay and family benefits the commons does seek to hold.

4. Secondly, some folk are surprised that everywhere they give the advantage to rascals, the poor, and the democrats rather than to good citizens. This is just where they will be seen to be preserving the democracy. For if the poor and the common folk and the worse elements are treated well, the growth of these classes will exalt the democracy; whereas if the rich and the good citizens are treated well the democrats strengthen their own opponents.

"In Every Land the Best Element Is Opposed to Democracy"

5. In every land the best element is opposed to democracy. Among the best elements there is very little license and injustice, very great discrimination as to what is worthy, while among the commons there is very great ignorance, disorderliness and rascality; for poverty tends to lead them to what is disgraceful as does lack of education and the ignorance which befalls some men as a result of lack of means.

6. It may be said that they ought not to have allowed everyone in turn to make speeches or sit on the Council, but only those of the highest capability and quality. But in allowing even rascals to speak they are also very well advised. For if the good citizens made speeches and joined in deliberations, good would result to those like themselves and ill to the democrats. As it is, anyone who wants, a rascally fellow maybe, gets up and makes a speech, and devises what is to the advantage of himself and those like him. (7.) Someone may ask how such a fellow would know what is to the advantage of himself or the commons. They know that this man's ignorance, rascality and goodwill are more beneficial than the good citizen's worth, wisdom, and ill will.

8. From such procedure then a city would not attain the ideal, but the democracy would be best preserved thus. For it is the wish of the commons not that the state should be well ordered and the commons itself in complete subjection, but that the commons should have its freedom and be in control; disorderliness is of little consequence to it. From what you consider lack of order come the strength and the liberty of the commons itself. (9.) If on the other hand you investigate good order, first of all you will see that the most capable make laws for them; then the good citizens will keep the rascals in check and will deliberate on matters of state, refusing to allow madmen to sit on the Council or make speeches or attend the general assemblies. Such advantages indeed would very soon throw the commons into complete subjection.

"License Allowed to Slaves and Aliens"

10. The license allowed to slaves and aliens at Athens is extreme and a blow is forbidden there, nor will a slave make way for you. I shall tell you why this is the custom of the country. If it were legal for a slave or an alien or a freedman to be beaten by a freeman, you would often have taken the Athenian for a slave and struck him; for the commons there does not dress better than the slaves and the aliens, and their general appearance is in no way superior. (11.) If anyone is surprised also at their allowing slaves, that is some of them, to live luxuriously and magnificently there, here too they would be seen to act with wisdom. In a

naval state slaves must serve for hire, that we may receive the fee for their labor, and we must let them go free. Where there are rich slaves it is no longer profitable that my slave should be afraid of you. In Sparta my slave is afraid of you. If your slave is afraid of me there will be a danger even of his giving his own money to avoid personal risks. (12.) This then is why we placed even slaves on a footing of equality with free men; and we placed aliens on a footing of equality with citizens because the state has need of aliens, owing to the number of skilled trades and because of the fleet. For this reason then we were right to place even the aliens on a footing of equality....

"The Allies Are in the Position of Slaves"

14. As for the allies, that the Athenians leave home and, as it is thought, bring false accusations against the good citizens and hate them—they know that the ruler cannot help but be hated by the ruled, and that if the rich and the good citizens in the various cities have control the rule of the commons at Athens will be very short-lived. This then is why they disfranchise the good citizens, rob them of their wealth, drive them into exile, or put them to death, while they exalt the rascals. The good citizens of Athens protect the good citizens in the allied cities, realizing that it is to their own advantage always to protect the best elements in the various cities. (15.) It might be suggested that the ability of the allies to pay tribute is the strength of Athens. The democrats think it more advantageous that each individual Athenian should possess the wealth of the allies and the allies only enough to live on, and continue working without having the power to conspire.

16. The commons of Athens is also thought to be ill-advised in compelling the allies to travel to Athens to have their law-suits tried. They meet this criticism by reckoning up all the benefits to the Athenian commons that this involves: first of all the receipt of pay out of the court fees all the year round; then while remaining at home without sending out ships they manage the allied cities, and protect the party of the commons while they ruin their opponents in the courts. If each of the allies tried their law-suits at home, out of hatred for Athenians they would have destroyed those of their own people most friendly to the Athenian commons. (17.) In addition the commons of Athens gains the following advantages from having the allied law-suits tried at Athens. First the five percent duty levied at the Peiraeus brings more in to the state; (18.) next, anyone who has a lodging-house is more prosperous, and so is the man who has a couple of hacks or a slave for hire; then the heralds are more prosperous as a result of the visits of the allies. Above all this, if the allies did not come to Athens for their law-suits they would honor only those Athenians who leave home—the generals, the naval commanders, and envoys. As it is, all the allies individually must fawn upon the Athenian commons, realizing that they must come to Athens and appear as defendant or prosecutor before the commons and the commons alone, for that forsooth is the law at Athens; and in the law-courts they must make supplications and grasp so-and-so by the hand as he enters. This then is why the allies are rather in the position of slaves of the Athenian commons....

Control of the Sea

II, 3. Of such mainland states as are subject to Athenian rule the large are in subjection because of fear, the small simply because of need; there is not a city which does not require both import and export trade, and it will not have that unless it is subject to the rulers of the sea....

7. If there is any need to mention less important facts too, command of the sea and contact with the different people of different countries were the first means of introducing luxurious ways of living. The delicacies of Sicily, Italy, Cyprus, Egypt, Lydia, Pontus, the Peloponnesus, in fact of any country, all converge upon one point as a result of the command of the sea. (8.) Then hearing every tongue they adopted a phrase from this tongue and a phrase from that. The Greeks as a whole enjoy a language, a way of life, and a general appearance which is rather their own, the Athenians a hotch-potch of those of all the Greeks and foreigners....

11. They alone can possess the wealth of Greeks and foreigners. If a city is rich in shipbuilding timber where will it dispose of it unless it win the consent of the ruler of the sea? What if some city is rich in iron or bronze or cloth? Where will it dispose of it unless it win the consent of the ruler of the sea? These however are just the very things of which my ships are made—somebody's wood, somebody's iron, somebody's bronze, somebody's cloth and somebody's wax. (12.) Moreover they will not allow our rivals to take their goods elsewhere or (if they try) they will not use the sea. I pass my time in idleness, and because of the sea I have all these products of the earth, whereas no other single city has two of these commodities; the same city does not possess both timber and cloth, but where cloth is plentiful the country is flat and treeless, nor do bronze and iron come from the same city, nor does one city possess two or three of the other commodities, but one has one, another has another....

Democracies Are Irresponsible

17. Again oligarchical states must abide by their alliances and their oaths. If they do not keep to the agreement, penalties can be exacted from the few who made it. But whenever the commons makes an agreement it can lay the blame on the individual speaker or proposer, and say to the other party that it was not present and does not approve what they know was agreed upon in full assembly; and should it be decided that this is not so, the commons has discovered a hundred excuses for not doing what they may not wish to do. If any ill result from a decision of the commons it lays the blame on a minority for opposing and working its ruin, whereas if any good results they take the credit to themselves.

18. They do not allow caricature and abuse of the commons, lest they should hear themselves evilly spoken of, but they do allow you to caricature any individual you wish to. They well know that generally the man who is caricatured is not of the commons or of the crowd, but someone rich or well-born or influential, and that few of the poor and democrats are caricatured, and they only because they are busy-bodies and try to overreach the commons; so they are not angry when such men are caricatured either.

Recapitulation

19. I say then that the commons at Athens realizes which citizens are good citizens and which rascals. With this knowledge they favor those who are friendly and useful to them, even if they are rascals, whereas they hate rather the good citizens.... (20.) I pardon the commons itself its democracy, for it is pardonable that everyone should seek his own interest. But the man who is not of the commons yet chose to live in a democratic rather than in an oligarchical state sought opportunity for wrongdoing, and realized that it was more possible for his wickedness to go unnoticed in a democratic state than in an oligarchical.

III, 1. The type of the constitution of the Athenians I do not approve, but as they saw fit to be a democracy in my opinion they preserve their democracy well by employing the means I have pointed out....

10. The Athenians are also thought to be ill advised because they take sides with the worst elements in cities divided by faction. They do this with good reason. If they sided with the better elements they would not side with those who hold the same opinions as themselves, for in no city is the better element well inclined to the commons, but in each the worse element is well inclined to the commons; like favors like. This then is why the Athenians side with the elements akin to themselves.

27 Thucydides, *History*

The Statesman's Handbook

"My history has been composed to be an everlasting possession, not the showpiece of an hour," wrote Thucydides (no doubt with reference to Herodotus) in the introduction to his history of the great war (431–404 B.C.) between the Athenian Empire and the Peloponnesian League led by Sparta. Posterity has ever been in agreement with this appraisal. He knew that this war, in which he was a participant, represented a momentous crisis to which the political and economic development of the Greek world had led. His aim was to analyze this first Greek "world war" in order to acquire an exact knowledge of the facts that would be useful to future statesmen confronted by a like situation; in similar situations, Thucydides insisted, like causes are always followed by like effects. "I shall be content," he wrote of his *History of the Peloponnesian War,* "if it is judged useful by all who wish to study the plain truth of the events which have happened, and which will according to human nature recur in much the same way."

This emphasis upon "the plain truth of the events which have happened" is the foundation for Thucydides' reputation as a great historian. He is, far more than Herodotus, the first critical writer of history and his standard of scientific objectivity with regard to facts has never been surpassed. During the previous century and a half, Greek thought had divorced itself from religion and myth-making and by substituting reason and experience had culminated in the critical thinking of the sophists, who were Thucydides' teachers. This new viewpoint, with its emphasis upon observed facts, also had produced in Thucydides' day the new science of medicine. It is not mere coincidence that the two contemporaries, Hippocrates of Cos in medicine and Thucydides in history, were the champions of the scientific approach in their respective fields. Hippo-crates' famous aphorism, "Every disease has a natural cause, and without natu-ral causes nothing ever happens," is echoed by Thucydides in his *History:* "As for my narrative, it is not derived from any chance source, nor have I trusted to my own impressions only. It rests partly on my own experiences and things which I have seen with my own eyes, partly on the witness of others, which I have verified by the severest and most minute tests possible. This has been labo-rious; for eye-witnesses had not always the same tale to tell of identical events; sometimes, too, memory served badly, or there was prejudice in one direction or another." Thucydides' masterly analysis of his own times was written to serve as a guide for future generations possessed of the wit to profit by the lessons of the Greek example. More than two millennia later, the British, themselves rulers of a great naval empire that reached its high point in the late nineteenth cen-tury, came to see much of their own history in light of Athens' experience. Accordingly, they conferred on Thucycides' *History* the title of "the statesman's handbook" for its cautionary and penetrating study of the themes of war, democracy and empire.

A. THE REVOLT OF MITYLENE

"Democracy is incapable of empire."

In 428 B.C., one year after the death of Pericles, an event that reveals the char-acter of Athenian democracy when stripped of Periclean idealism and states-manship took shape on the other side of the Aegean Sea. The island of Lesbos, encouraged by Sparta and led by the oligarchs of its chief city, Mity-lene, withdrew from its alliance with Athens. This revolt—for so the Athenians saw it—was crushed, and the Athenian assembly voted to make an example of Lesbos to discourage future rebellions within the Empire. A ship was sent with orders to the Athenian commander on Lesbos to put to death all the men of Mitylene and sell the women and children into slavery. "The next day," reports Thucydides, "there was a feeling of repentance; they reflected that the decree was cruel and indiscriminate, to slay a whole city and not the guilty only." The debate was reopened, and the speech delivered on the occa-sion by Cleon, who favored meting out strict punishment as a deterrent to others, is given below in Thucydides' version. It is a typical example of Thucy-dides' use of speeches as a means of penetrating behind the facts to reveal and interpret the character and motives of both individuals and states. He admitted his inability to give verbatim reports of what was said, explaining

From Thucydides, *History of the Peloponnesian War,* based on the translation by Richard Crawley.

that "the speeches have been composed as it seemed to me each speaker would say what was most necessary about the various situations, keeping as close as possible to the general intent of what actually was said."

Cleon represents the new type of democratic leader, "the most violent of the citizens," says Thucydides, given to using "unmeasured language" to inflame the passions of the people. He prided himself on being a practical man—he was a leather manufacturer—who distrusted intellectuals of Pericles' type. Though cynically brutal, his convictions were honestly held, and he had enough statesmanlike courage to oppose the views of his audience. His description of the fickleness of the Athenian populace was warranted. By a narrow margin, the assembly reversed itself and sent another order that arrived in time to halt the wholesale massacre of the Mitylenians.

"Your Empire Is a Despotism"

III, 37. "I have often before now been convicted that a democracy is incapable of empire, and never more so than by your present change of mind in the matter of Mitylene. Fears or plots being unknown to you in your daily relations with each other, you feel just the same with regard to your allies, and never reflect that the mistakes into which you may be led by listening to their appeals, or by giving way to your compassion, are full of danger to yourselves, and bring you no thanks for your weakness from your allies; entirely forgetting that your empire is a despotism and your subjects disaffected conspirators, whose obedience is insured not by your suicidal concessions, but by the superiority given you by your own strength and not their loyalty. The most alarming feature in the case is the constant change of measures with which we appear to be threatened, and our seeming ignorance of the fact that bad laws which are never changed are better for a city than good ones that have no authority; that unlearned loyalty is more serviceable than quick-witted insubordination; and that ordinary men usually manage public affairs better than their more gifted fellows. The latter are always wanting to appear wiser than the laws, and to overrule every proposition brought forward, thinking that they cannot show their wit in more important matters, and by such behavior too often ruin their country; while those who mistrust their own cleverness are content to be less learned than the laws, and less able to pick holes in the speech of a good speaker; and being fair judges rather than rival athletes, generally conduct affairs successfully. These we ought to imitate, instead of being led on by cleverness and intellectual rivalry to advise people contrary to our better judgment.

"The Persons to Blame"

38. "For myself, I adhere to my former opinion, and wonder at those who have proposed to reopen the case of the Mitylenians, and who are thus causing a delay which is all in favor of the guilty, by making the sufferer proceed against the offender with the edge of his anger blunted; although where vengeance follows most closely upon the wrong, it best equals it and most amply repays it. I wonder also who will be the man who will maintain the contrary, and will pretend to show that the crimes of the Mitylenians are of service to us, and our misfortunes

injurious to the allies. Such a man must plainly either have such confidence in his rhetoric as to venture to prove that what has been once for all decided is still undetermined, or be bribed to try to delude us by elaborate sophisms. In such contests the state gives the rewards to others, and takes the dangers for herself. The persons to blame are you who are so foolish as to institute these contests; who go to see an oration as you would to see a sight, take your facts on hearsay, judge of the practicability of a project by the wit of its advocates, and trust for the truth as to past events not to the fact which you saw more than to the clever strictures which you heard; the easy victims of new-fangled arguments, unwilling to follow accepted conclusions; slaves to every new paradox, despisers of the commonplace; the first wish of every man being that he could speak himself, the next to rival those who can speak by seeming to be quite up with their ideas by applauding every hit almost before it is made, and by being as quick in catching an argument as you are slow in foreseeing its consequences; asking, if I may so say, for something different from the conditions under which we live, and yet comprehending inadequately those very conditions; veritable slaves to the pleasure of the ear, and more like the audience of a rhetorician than the assembly of a city.

"Not Revolt but Deliberate and Wanton Aggression"

39. "In order to keep you from this, I proceed to show that no one state has ever injured you as much as Mitylene. I can make allowance for those who revolt because they cannot bear our empire, or who have been forced to do so by the enemy. But for those who possessed an island with fortifications; who could fear our enemies only by sea, and there had their own force of galleys to protect them; who were independent and held in the highest honor by you—to act as these have done, this is not revolt—revolt implies oppression; it is deliberate and wanton aggression; an attempt to ruin us by siding with our bitterest enemies; a worse offense than a war undertaken on their own account in the acquisition of power. The fate of those of their neighbors who had already rebelled and had been subdued was no lesson to them; their own prosperity could not dissuade them from facing danger; but blindly confident in the future, and full of hopes beyond their power though not beyond their ambition, they declared war and made their decision to prefer might to right, their attack being determined not by provocation but by the moment which seemed propitious.... Our mistake has been to distinguish the Mitylenians as we have done: had they been long ago treated like the rest, they never would have so far forgotten themselves, human nature being as surely made arrogant by consideration as it is awed by firmness. Let them now therefore be punished as their crime requires, and do not, while you condemn the aristocracy, absolve the people. This is certain, that all attacked you without distinction, although they might have come over to us, and been now again in possession of their city. But no, they thought it safer to throw in their lot with the aristocracy and so joined their rebellion! Consider therefore! if you subject to the same punishment the ally who is forced to rebel by the enemy, and him who does so by his own free choice, which of them, think you, is there that will not rebel upon the slightest pretext when the reward of success is freedom, and the penalty of failure nothing

so very terrible? We meanwhile shall have to risk our money and our lives against one state after another; and if successful, shall receive a ruined city from which we can no longer draw the revenue upon which our strength depends; while if unsuccessful, we shall have another enemy on our hands, and shall spend the time that might be employed in combating our existing foes in warring with our own allies.

"Three Failings Most Fatal to Empire"

40. "No hope, therefore, that rhetoric may instill or money purchase, of the mercy due to human weakness must be held out to the Mitylenians. Their offense was not involuntary, but of malice and deliberate; and mercy is only for unwilling offenders. I therefore now as before persist against your reversing your first decision, or giving way to the three failings most fatal to empire—pity, sentiment, and indulgence.... To sum up briefly, I say that if you follow my advice you will do what is just towards the Mitylenians, and at the same time expedient; while by a different decision you will not oblige them so much as pass sentence upon yourselves. For if they were right in rebelling, you must be wrong in ruling. However, if right or wrong, you determine to rule, you must carry out your principles and punish the Mitylenians as your interest requires; or else you must give up your empire and cultivate honesty without danger. Make up your minds, therefore, to give them like for like; and do not let those who were unaware of the plot be more guiltless than the conspirators who hatched it; but reflect what they would have done if victorious over you, especially as they were the aggressors.... Punish them as they deserve, and teach your other allies by a striking example that the penalty of rebellion is death. Let them once understand this and you will not have so often to neglect your enemies while you are fighting with your own confederates." Such were the words of Cleon.

B. THE CORCYREAN REVOLUTION:
THE PSYCHOLOGY OF CIVIL WAR

Although the Peloponnesian War began as an attempt on the part of Sparta and its allies to dismantle the Athenian Empire and put an end to the emerging economic and political unification of the Greek world under Athenian leadership, it soon became a struggle between the two rival ideologies of democracy and oligarchy throughout the Greek world.

The genesis of the Peloponnesian War partly lay in Sparta's fear that democratic ideas would undermine its own regime by inspiring revolt among the large mass of subject peoples over whom a small minority of Spartiates ruled. To keep tyranny, democracy and other radical ideas as far away as possible, the Spartans created an "iron curtain" by joining forces with the aristocrats in neighboring states and providing them with military aid to establish and maintain oligarchic regimes of their own. The resulting Peloponnesian

From Thucydides, *The History of the Peloponnesian War,* translated by R. W. Livingstone (Oxford: the Clarendon Press, 1943), pp. 189–92.

League was thus a confederation of oligarchic governments devoted to maintaining the status quo and the political subjugation of the common people. The Athenians used the same technique in reverse in extending and holding their empire. Being a democracy, Athens favored and maintained in power the democratic elements in its allied states, and these, in constant fear of their own aristocratic fellow-citizens, welcomed Athenian friendship and leadership.

The Peloponnesian War, therefore, involved a struggle between two opposed ideologies, and it was inevitable that both sides should seek to use the social tensions between rich and poor existing in every state as a weapon in the conflict. The Spartan-inspired and oligarchic-led revolt of Mitylene from Athens has already been noted. A more famous example concerned the island of Corcyra, modern Corfu, located off the northwestern coast of Greece. The Athenians had earlier engineered an alliance with the democratic government of Corcyra, and as this state was well within the Spartan sphere of influence, the event was one of several incidents in Athenian expansion causing the fear that originally motivated Sparta to declare war. Finally, in 427 B.C., the Peloponnesian League intrigued with the oligarchic party at Corcyra, and a bloody civil war resulted. Both Athens and Sparta sent aid to their respective factions, but the democrats won the day and proceeded to liquidate all who were suspected of oligarchic sympathies. This and similar events inspired Thucydides to write the following brilliant analysis of the psychology of class war and its evil effects.

"Ties of Party Were Closer Than Ties of Blood"

III, 82. Such was the pitch of savagery reached by the revolution; and it made the greater impression because it was the first of such incidents. Later, practically the whole Greek world was affected; there was a struggle everywhere between the leaders of the democratic and oligarchic parties, the former wishing to secure the support of Athens, the latter that of Lacedaemon. In peace there would have been neither the desire nor the excuse for appealing to them, but the war gave both sides, if they wished for a revolution, a ready chance to invoke outside help in order to injure their opponents and to gain power. Revolution brought on the cities of Greece many calamities, such as exist and will exist till human nature changes, varying in intensity and character with changing circumstances. In peace and prosperity states and individuals are governed by higher ideals because they are not involved in necessities beyond their control, but war deprives them of their easy existence and is a rough teacher that brings most men's dispositions down to the level of their circumstances.

So civil war broke out in the cities, and the later revolutionaries, with previous examples before their eyes, devised new ideas which went far beyond earlier ones, so elaborate were their enterprises, so novel their revenges. Words changed their ordinary meanings and were construed in new senses. Reckless daring passed for the courage of a loyal partisan, far-sighted hesitation was the excuse of a coward, moderation was the pretext of the unmanly, the power to see all sides of a question was complete inability to act. Impulsive rashness was held the mark of a man, caution in conspiracy was a specious excuse for avoiding action.

A violent attitude was always to be trusted, its opponents were suspect. To succeed in a plot was shrewd, it was still more clever to divine one: but if you devised a policy that made such success or suspicion needless, you were breaking up your party and showing fear of your opponents. In fine, men were applauded if they forestalled an injury or instigated one that had not been conceived. Ties of party were closer than those of blood, because a partisan was readier to take risks without asking why; for the basis of party association was not an advantage consistent with the laws of the state but a self-interest which ignored them, and the seal of their mutual good faith was complicity in crime and not the divine law. If a stronger opponent made a fair proposal, it was met with active precautions and not in a generous spirit. Revenge was more prized than self-preservation. An agreement sworn to by either party, when they could do nothing else, was binding as long as both were powerless, but the first side to pluck up courage, when they saw an opening and an undefended point, took more pleasure in revenge on a confiding enemy than if they had achieved it by an open attack; apart from considerations of security, a success won by treachery was a victory in a battle of wits. Villainy is sooner called clever than simplicity good, and men in general are proud of cleverness and ashamed of simplicity.

"The Cause of All These Evils Was Love of Power"

The cause of all these evils was love of power due to ambition and greed, which led to rivalries from which party spirit sprung. The leaders of both sides used specious phrases, championing a moderate aristocracy or political equality for the masses. They professed to study public interests but made them their prize, and in the struggle to get the better of each other by any means committed terrible excesses and went to still greater extremes in revenge. Neither justice nor the needs of the state restrained them, their only limit was the caprice of the hour, and they were prepared to satisfy a momentary rivalry by the unjust condemnation of an opponent or by a forcible seizure of power. Religion meant nothing to either party, but the use of fair phrases to achieve a criminal end was highly respected. The moderates were destroyed by both parties, either because they declined to cooperate or because their survival was resented.

83. So civil war gave birth to every kind of iniquity in the Greek world. Simplicity, the chief ingredient in a noble nature, was ridiculed and disappeared, and society was divided into rival camps in which no man trusted his fellow. There was no reconciling force—no promise binding, no oath that inspired awe. Each party in its day of power despairing of security was more concerned to save itself from ruin than to trust others. Inferior minds were as a rule the more successful; aware of their own defects and of the intelligence of their opponents, to whom they felt themselves inferior in debate, and by whose versatility of intrigue they were afraid of being surprised, they struck boldly and at once. Their enemies despised them, were confident of detecting their plots and thought it needless to effect by violence what they could achieve by their brains, and so were taken off guard and destroyed.

84. It was in Corcyra that most of these crimes were first perpetrated: the reprisals taken by subjects when their hour came on rulers who had governed them

oppressively; the unjust designs of those who wished to escape from a life of poverty and who were stung by passion and covetous of their neighbors' wealth; the savage and pitiless excesses of those with whom greed was not a motive, but who were carried away by undisciplined rage in the struggle with their equals.

In the chaos of city life under these conditions human nature, always rebellious against the law and now its master, was delighted to display its uncontrolled passions, its superiority to justice, its hostility to all above itself; for vengeance would not have been set above religion, or gain above justice, had it not been for the fatal power of envy. But in their revenges men are reckless of the future and do not hesitate to annul those common laws of humanity on which everyone relies in the hour of misfortune for his own hope of deliverance; they forget that in their own need they will look for them in vain.

C. THE MELIAN DIALOGUE

"The strong do what they can and the weak submit."

In 416 B.C., the Athenians demanded the submission of Melos, a small island-state in the south Aegean that had remained both outside her empire and neutral up to this point in the war. The Melians, as Dorian Greeks, were related to the Spartans. During the Peloponnesian War, they sought to remain neutral and unaligned but Athens refused to accept this neutrality. When the Melians refused to surrender to Athens, they were overpowered after a six-month siege; all the men were slaughtered, and the women and children enslaved. This incident would be historically unimportant but for the striking dialogue that Thucydides presents as having occurred between the Melians and the Athenian envoys who brought the original demand for submission. Far removed from the idealism of Pericles, the Athenians here justify their empire solely on the grounds of power—power that accepts no limitation from claims of religious piety, or justice, or even, in contrast with the earlier Mitylenian revolt, pity. It is a classic example of Thucydides' use of dialogues, including paired speeches, to comment upon the disjuncture between words and deeds, opinion and truth, and his desire that his readers discern the relationship between public rhetoric, true motives, and human actions. In this particular masterpiece of political commentary, he eternalizes the conflict of the two irreconcilable principles of might and right.

V, 84. The next summer the Athenians made an expedition against the isle of Melos. The Melians are a colony of Lacedaemon that would not submit to the Athenians like the other islanders, and at first remained neutral and took no part in the struggle, but afterwards, upon the Athenians using violence and plundering their territory, assumed an attitude of open hostility. The Athenian generals encamped in their territory with their army, and before doing any harm to their land sent envoys to negotiate. These the Melians did not bring before the

From Thucydides, *The History of the Peloponnesian War*, translated by R. W. Livingstone (Oxford: the Clrendon Press, 1943), pp. 266–74.

people, but told them to state the object of their mission to the magistrates and the council; the Athenian envoys then said:

85. *Athenians:* "As we are not to speak to the people, for fear that if we made a single speech without interruption we might deceive them with attractive arguments to which there was no chance of replying—we realize that this is the meaning of our being brought before your ruling body—we suggest that you who sit here should make security doubly sure. Let us have no long speeches from you either, but deal separately with each point, and take up at once any statement of which you disapprove, and criticize it."

86. *Melians:* "We have no objection to your reasonable suggestion that we should put our respective points of view quietly to each other, but the military preparations which you have already made seem inconsistent with it. We see that you have come to be yourselves the judges of the debate, and that its natural conclusion for us will be slavery if you convince us, and war if we get the better of the argument and therefore refuse to submit."

87. *Ath.:* "If you have met us in order to make surmises about the future, or for any other purpose than to look existing facts in the face and to discuss the safety of your city on this basis, we will break off the conversations; otherwise, we are ready to speak."

88. *Mel.:* "In our position it is natural and excusable to explore many ideas and arguments. But the problem that has brought us here is our security, so, if you think fit, let the discussion follow the line you propose."

89. *Ath.:* "Then we will not make a long and unconvincing speech, full of fine phrases, to prove that our victory over Persia justifies our empire, or that we are now attacking you because you have wronged us, and we ask you not to expect to convince us by saying that you have not injured us, or that, though a colony of Lacedaemon, you did not join her. Let each of us say what we really think and reach a practical agreement. You know and we know, as practical men, that the question of justice arises only between parties equal in strength, and that the strong do what they can, and the weak submit."

90. *Mel.:* "As you ignore justice and have made self-interest the basis of discussion, we must take the same ground, and we say that in our opinion it is in your interest to maintain a principle which is for the good of all—that anyone in danger should have just and equitable treatment and any advantage, even if not strictly his due, which he can secure by persuasion. This is your interest as much as ours, for your fall would involve you in a crushing punishment that would be a lesson to the world."

91. *Ath.:* "We have no apprehensions about the fate of our empire, if it did fall; those who rule other peoples, like the Lacedaemonians, are not formidable to a defeated enemy. Nor is it the Lacedaemonians with whom we are now contending: the danger is from subjects who of themselves may attack and conquer their rulers. But leave that danger to us to face. At the moment we shall prove that we have come in the interest of our empire and that in what we shall say we are seeking the safety of your state; for we wish you to become our subjects with least trouble to ourselves, and we would like you to survive in our interests as well as your own."

92. *Mel.:* "It may be your interest to be our masters: how can it be ours to be your slaves?"

93. *Ath.:* "By submitting you would avoid a terrible fate, and we should gain by not destroying you."

94. *Mel.:* "Would you not agree to an arrangement under which we should keep out of the war, and be your friends instead of your enemies, but neutral?"

95. *Ath.:* "No: your hostility injures us less than your friendship. That, to our subjects, is an illustration of our weakness, while your hatred exhibits our power."

96. *Mel.:* "Is this the construction which your subjects put on it? Do they not distinguish between states in which you have no concern, and peoples who are most of them your colonies, and some conquered rebels?"

97. *Ath.:* "They think that one nation has as good rights as another, but that some survive because they are strong and we are afraid to attack them. So, apart from the addition to our empire, your subjection would give us security: the fact that you are islanders (and weaker than others) makes it the more important that you should not get the better of the mistress of the sea."

98. *Mel.:* "But do you see no safety in our neutrality? You debar us from the plea of justice and press us to submit to your interests, so we must expound our own, and try to convince you, if the two happen to coincide. Will you not make enemies of all neutral powers when they see your conduct and reflect that some day you will attack them? Will not your action strengthen your existing opponents, and induce those who would otherwise never be your enemies to become so against their will?"

99. *Ath.:* "No. The mainland states, secure in their freedom, will be slow to take defensive measures against us, and we do not consider them so formidable as independent island powers like yourselves, or subjects already smarting under our yoke. These are most likely to take a thoughtless step and bring themselves and us into obvious danger."

100. *Mel.:* "Surely, then, if you are ready to risk so much to maintain your empire, and the enslaved peoples so much to escape from it, it would be criminal cowardice in us, who are still free, not to take any and every measure before submitting to slavery?"

101. *Ath.:* "No, if you reflect calmly: for this is not a competition in heroism between equals, where your honor is at stake, but a question of self-preservation to save you from a struggle with a far stronger power."

102. *Mel.:* "Still, we know that in war fortune is more impartial than the disproportion in numbers might lead one to expect. If we submit at once, our position is desperate; if we fight, there is still a hope that we shall stand secure."

103. *Ath.:* "Hope encourages men to take risks; men in a strong position may follow her without ruin, if not without loss. But when they stake all that they have to the last coin (for she is a spendthrift), she reveals her real self in the hour of failure, and when her nature is known she leaves them without means of self-protection. You are weak, your future hangs on a turn of the scales; avoid the mistake most men make, who might save themselves by human means, and then, when visible hopes desert them, in their extremity turn to

the invisible—prophecies and oracles and all those things which delude men with hopes, to their destruction."

104. *Mel.:* "We too, you can be sure, realize the difficulty of struggling against your power and against Fortune if she is not impartial. Still we trust that Heaven will not allow us to be worsted by Fortune, for in this quarrel we are right and you are wrong. Besides, we expect the support of Lacedaemon to supply the deficiencies in our strength, for she is bound to help us as her kinsmen, if for no other reason, and from a sense of honor. So our confidence is not entirely unreasonable."

105. *Ath.:* "As for divine favor, we think that we can count on it as much as you, for neither our claims nor our actions are inconsistent with what men believe about Heaven or desire for themselves. We believe that Heaven, and we know that men, by a natural law, always rule where they are stronger. We did not make that law nor were we the first to act on it; we found it existing, and it will exist forever, after we are gone; and we know that you and anyone else as strong as we are would do as we do. As to your expectations from Lacedaemon and your belief that she will help you from a sense of honor, we congratulate you on your innocence but we do not admire your folly. So far as they themselves and their national traditions are concerned, the Lacedaemonians are a highly virtuous people; as for their behavior to others, much might be said, but we can put it shortly by saying that, most obviously of all people we know, they identify their interests with justice and the pleasantest course with honor. Such principles do not favor your present irrational hopes of deliverance."

106. *Mel.:* "That is the chief reason why we have confidence in them now; in their own interest they will not wish to betray their own colonists and so help their enemies and destroy the confidence that their friends in Greece feel in them."

107. *Ath.:* "Apparently you do not realize that safety and self-interest go together, while the path of justice and honor is dangerous; and danger is a risk which the Lacedaemonians are little inclined to run.... (111) Here experience may teach you like others, and you will learn that Athens has never abandoned a siege from fear of another foe. You said that you proposed to discuss the safety of your city, but we observe that in all your speeches you have never said a word on which any reasonable expectation of it could be founded. Your strength lies in deferred hopes; in comparison with the forces now arrayed against you, your resources are too small for any hope of success. You will show a great want of judgment if you do not come to a more reasonable decision after we have withdrawn. Surely you will not fall back on the idea of honor, which has been the ruin of so many when danger and disgrace were staring them in the face. How often, when men have seen the fate to which they were tending, have they been enslaved by a phrase and drawn by the power of this seductive word to fall of their own free will into irreparable disaster, bringing on themselves by their folly a greater dishonor than fortune could inflict! If you are wise, you will avoid that fate. The greatest of cities makes you a fair offer, to keep your own land and become her tributary ally: there is no dishonor in that. The choice between war and safety is given you; do not obstinately take the worse alternative.

The most successful people are those who stand up to their equals, behave properly to their superiors, and treat their inferiors fairly. Think it over when we withdraw, and reflect once and again that you have only one country, and that its prosperity or ruin depends on one decision."

112. The Athenians now withdrew from the conference; and the Melians, left to themselves, came to a decision corresponding with what they had maintained in the discussion, and answered, "Our resolution, Athenians, is unaltered. We will not in a moment deprive of freedom a city that has existed for seven hundred years; we put our trust in the fortune by which the gods have preserved it until now, and in the help of men, that is, of the Lacedaemonians; and so we will try and save ourselves. Meanwhile we invite you to allow us to be friends to you and foes to neither party, and to retire from our country after making such a treaty as shall seem fit to us both."

113. Such was the answer of the Melians. The Athenians broke up the conference saying, "To judge from your decision, you are unique in regarding the future as more certain than the present and in allowing your wishes to convert the unseen into reality; and as you have staked most on, and trusted most in, the Lacedaemonians, your fortune, and your hopes, so will you be most completely deceived."

114. The Athenian envoys now returned to the army; and as the Melians showed no signs of yielding the generals at once began hostilities, and drew a line of circumvallation round the Melians … and besieged the place.…

116. Summer was now over … and the siege was now pressed vigorously; there was some treachery in the town, and the Melians surrendered at discretion to the Athenians, who put to death all the grown men whom they took, and sold the women and children for slaves; subsequently they sent out five hundred settlers and colonized the island.

D. THE SICILIAN EXPEDITION

"Most glorious to the victors, most calamitous
to the conquered."

Thucydides' *History of the Peloponnesian War* has often been called a tragedy for it deals with the fall of a proud empire. The historian's narrative is thus most powerful with describing the ill-fated Sicilian expedition of 415–413 B.C., where the tragedy reaches its climax. The purpose of the expedition was to use economic pressure to bring Sparta and its allies to their knees by conquering the source of much of their food supply and markets on the populous island of Sicily. This accomplished, the Athenians believed that they would be strong enough, as Thucydides reports, "to conquer the whole world." The blame for the failure of the project can be laid to the folly of the Athenian masses who appointed, against his will, a virtuous but overly cautious elderly

From Thucydides, *History of the Peloponnesian War*, based on the translation by Richard Crawley.

general named Nicias to head an ambitious foreign adventure that only daring leadership could have rendered successful. This is the view of Thucydides, who saw the disaster as a product of the low quality of Athenian leadership since the glory days under Pericles when "what was nominally a democracy became in his hands government by the first citizen. With Pericles' successors it was different. More on a level with one another, and each grasping at supremacy, they ended by committing even the conduct of state affairs to the whims of the multitude. This, as might have been expected in a large imperial state, produced a host of blunders, among them the Sicilian expedition...."

The Sicilian expedition began auspiciously but over time Athenian victories turned to stalemate and finally to defeat. After its navy was bested, Athens' besieging army became itself trapped and was eventually forced to capitulate. In the following selections, the mingled feelings of pride and apprehension among the citizens as they see the expedition off are contrasted with the *pathos* of the tragic fate of the beaten army and the arrival of the news of the disaster at Athens.

Motives of the Athenians

VI, 24. ... All alike fell in love with the enterprise. The older men thought that they would either subdue the places against which they were to sail, or at all events, with so large a force, meet with no disaster; those in the prime of life felt a longing for foreign sights and spectacles, and had no doubt that they should come safe home again; while the idea of the common people and the soldiery was to earn wages at the moment, and make conquests that would supply a neverending fund of pay for the future. With this enthusiasm of the majority, the few that liked it not feared to appear unpatriotic by holding up their hands against it, and so kept quiet....

The Departure

30. After this the departure for Sicily took place, it being now about midsummer. Most of the allies, with the grain transports and the smaller craft and the rest of the expedition, had already received orders to muster at Corcyra, to cross the Ionian sea from thence in a body to the Iapygian promontory. But the Athenians themselves, and such of their allies as happened to be with them, went down to Piraeus on the day appointed at daybreak, and began to man the ships for putting out to sea. With them also went down the whole population, one may say, of the city, both citizens and foreigners; the inhabitants of the country each escorting those that belonged to them, their friends, their relatives, or their sons, with hope and lamentation upon their way, as they thought of the conquests which they hoped to make, or of the friends whom they might never see again, considering the long voyage which they were going to make from their country. Indeed, at this moment, when they were now upon the point of parting from one another, the danger came more home to them than when they voted for the expedition; although the strength of the armament, and the abundant provisions, was a sight that could not but comfort them. As for the

Departure scene on an Athenian vase of about 450 B.C. A hoplite warrior takes leave of his wife in a ritual of farewell. Their restrained expression of sorrow is witnessed by the warrior's father and mother (or sister).

foreigners and the rest of the crowd, they simply went to see a sight worth looking at and passing all belief....

Two Years Later, the Inaction of Nicias Before Syracuse, the Chief Sicilian City, Results in a Reversal of Roles— the Besiegers Become the Besieged

VII, 50. ... The Athenian generals seeing a fresh army come to the aid of the enemy, and that their own circumstances, far from improving, were becoming daily worse, and above all distressed by the sickness of the soldiers, now began to repent of not having moved before; and Nicias no longer offering opposition, except for urging that there should be no open voting, they gave orders as secretly as possible for all to be prepared to sail out from the camp at a given signal. All was at last ready, and they were on the point of sailing away when an eclipse of the moon, which was then at the full, took place. Most of the Athenians, deeply impressed by this occurrence, now urged the generals to wait; and Nicias, who was somewhat over-addicted to divination and practices of that kind, refused from that moment even to take the question of departure into consideration, until they had waited the thrice nine days prescribed by the soothsayers....

When the Athenians Become Completely Surrounded, They Try to Break out of the Harbor to the Open Sea

71. Meanwhile the two armies on shore, while victory hung in the balance, were a prey to the most agonizing and conflicting emotions; the natives thirsting

for more glory than they had already won, while the invaders feared to find themselves in even worse plight than before. The last hope of the Athenians being their fleet, their fear for the event was like nothing they had ever felt; while their view of the struggle was as varied as the battle itself. Close to the scene of action and not all looking at the same point at once, some saw their friends victorious and took courage and called upon Heaven not to deprive them of salvation, while others who had their eyes turned upon the losers wailed and cried aloud, and, although spectators, were more overcome than the actual combatants. Others were gazing at some spot where the battle was even; as the strife continued without decision, their swaying bodies reflected the agitation of their minds and they suffered the worst agony of all, ever just within reach of safety or just on the point of destruction. In short, in that one Athenian army as long as the seafight remained in doubt there was every sound to be heard at once—shrieks, cheers, "We win," "We lose," and all the other exclamations that a great host would necessarily utter in great peril. With the men in the fleet it was nearly the same, until at last the Syracusans and their allies, after the battle had lasted a long while, put the Athenians to flight and with much shouting and cheering chased them in open rout to the shore. The remaining naval force, in confusion, now ran ashore and rushed to their camp; while the army, no more divided in feeling but carried away by one impulse, with shrieks and groans deplored the event and ran, some to save the ships, others to guard what was left of their wall, while the most numerous part began to consider how they should save themselves. Indeed, the panic of that moment had never been surpassed.... now the Athenians had no hope of escaping by land, without the help of some extraordinary happening....

With Escape by Sea Shut off, and Preparations to Break out by Land Completed, the Pathetic Lot of the Expedition Is Surveyed

75. Nicias and Demosthenes now thinking that enough had been done in the way of preparation, the removal of the army took place on the second day after the seafight. It was a lamentable scene, not merely from the fact that they were retreating after having lost all their ships, their great hopes gone, and themselves and the state in peril; but also in leaving the camp there were things most grievous for every eye and heart to contemplate. The dead lay unburied, and each man as he recognized a friend among them shuddered with grief and horror; while the wounded or sick, whom they were leaving behind, were to the living far more shocking than the dead, and more to be pitied than those who had perished. These fell to entreating and bewailing until their friends knew not what to do, begging them to take them and loudly calling to each individual comrade or relative whom they could see, hanging upon the necks of their tent-fellows in the act of departure, and following as far as they could, and when their bodily strength failed them, calling again and again upon Heaven and shrieking aloud as they were left behind. So the whole army, being filled with tears and distracted, found it not easy to go, even from an enemy's land where they had already suffered evils too great for tears, and in the unknown

future before them feared to suffer more. Dejection and self-condemnation were also rife among them. Indeed they could only be compared to a starved-out town, and that no small one, escaping; the whole multitude on the march being not less than forty thousand men. All carried anything they could which might be of use; even the heavy infantry and cavalry, contrary to their practice when under arms, carried their own food, in some cases for lack of servants, in others through not trusting them, as they had long been deserting and now did so in greater numbers than ever. Yet they did not carry enough, since there was no longer food in the camp. Moreover, their disgrace and the universality of their misery, although to a certain extent alleviated by being borne in company, were felt at that moment a heavy burden, especially when they contrasted the splendor and glory of their setting out with the humiliation in which it had ended. For this was by far the greatest reverse that ever befell an Hellenic army. They had come to enslave others, and were departing in fear of being enslaved themselves; they had sailed out with prayer and paeans, and now started to go back with omens directly contrary; they were travelling by land instead of by sea, and trusting not in their fleet but in their heavy infantry. Nevertheless the greatness of the danger still impending made all this appear tolerable.

76. Nicias, seeing the army dejected, passed along the ranks and encouraged and comforted them as far as was possible under the circumstances, raising his voice still higher and higher as he went from one company to another in his anxiety that the benefit of his words might reach as many as possible:

77. "Athenians and allies, even in our present position we must hope on, since men have before now been saved from worse straits than this. You must not condemn yourselves too severely either because of your disasters or because of your present unmerited sufferings. I myself who am not superior to any of you in strength—indeed you see how I am in my sickness—and who in the gifts of fortune am, I think, whether in private life or otherwise, the equal of any, am now exposed to the same danger as the humblest among you. Yet my life has been one of much devotion towards the gods, and of much justice and without offense towards men. I have, therefore, still a strong hope for the future, and our misfortunes do not terrify me as much as they might. Indeed we may hope that they will be lightened: our enemies have had good fortune enough; and if any of the gods was offended at our expedition, we have been already amply punished. Others before us have attacked their neighbors and have done what men will do without suffering more than they could bear; and we may now rightly expect to find the gods more kind, for we have become fitter objects for their pity than their jealousy. And then look at yourselves, mark the numbers and efficiency of the heavy infantry marching in your ranks, and do not give way too much to despondency, but reflect that you are yourselves a city wherever you sit down, and that there is no other in Sicily that could easily resist your attack or expel you when once established. The safety and order of the march is for yourselves to look to; the one thought of each man being that the spot on which he may be forced to fight must be conquered and held as his country and stronghold. Meanwhile we shall hasten on our way night and day alike, for our provisions are scanty; and if we can reach some friendly place of

the Sicels, whom fear of the Syracusans still keeps true to us, you may then con-sider yourselves safe. A message has been sent on to them with directions to meet us with supplies and food. To sum up, be convinced, soldiers, that you must be brave, as there is no place near for your cowardice to take refuge in, and that if you now escape from the enemy, you may all see again what your hearts desire, while those of you who are Athenians will raise up again the great power of the state, fallen though it be. Men make the city and not walls or ships without men in them."…

Half of the Athenian Forces Under Demosthenes Having Been Forced to Surrender, the Rest Under Nicias Come to the Same End

84. As soon as it was day Nicias put his army in motion, pressed as before by the Syracusans and their allies, pelted from every side by their missiles, and struck down by their javelins. The Athenians pushed on for the Assinarus, impelled by the attacks made upon them from every side by a numerous cavalry and the swarm of other troops, hoping that they should breathe more freely if once across the river, and driven on also by their exhaustion and craving for water. Once there they rushed in and all order was at an end, each man wanting to cross first, and the attacks of the enemy making it difficult to cross at all. Forced to huddle together, they fell against and trod down one another, some dying immediately, pierced by their own javelins; others got entangled in the articles of baggage, unable to rise again. Meanwhile the opposite bank, which was steep, was lined by the Syracusans, who showered missiles down upon the Athenians, most of them drinking greedily and heaped together in disorder in the hollow bed of the river. The Spartans also came down and butchered them, especially those in the water, which was thus immediately spoiled, but which they went on drinking just the same, mud and all, bloody as it was, most even fighting to have it.

85. At last, when many dead lay piled one upon another in the stream, part of the army had been destroyed at the river and the few that escaped cut off by the cavalry, Nicias surrendered himself to [the Spartan general] Gylippus, whom he trusted more than he did the Syracusans, and told him and the Spartans to do what they liked with him but to stop the slaughter of the soldiers.…

Treatment of the Prisoners

86. The Syracusans and their allies now mustered their forces and gathered the spoils and as many prisoners as they could and went back to the city. The rest of their Athenian and allied captives were deposited in the quarries, this seeming the safest way of keeping them; but Nicias and Demosthenes were butchered, against the will of Gylippus, who thought that it would be the crown of his triumph if he could take the enemy's generals to Sparta.…

87. The prisoners in the quarries were at first treated harshly by the Syracu-sans. Crowded in a narrow hole, without any roof to cover them, the heat of the sun and the stifling closeness of the air tormented them during the day, and then the nights, which came on autumnal and chilly, made them ill by the extreme

change. Because they had to do everything in the same place for lack of room, and the bodies of those who died of their wounds or from the variation in the temperature, or from other causes, were left heaped together one upon another, intolerable stenches arose. Hunger and thirst never ceased to afflict them, each man during eight months having only half a pint of water and a pint of grain given him daily. In short, no suffering known to men thrust into such a place was spared them. For some seventy days they thus lived all together, after which all, except the Athenians and any Sicilian or Italian Greeks who had joined in the expedition, were sold. The total number of prisoners taken would be difficult to state exactly, but it could not have been less than seven thousand.

This was the greatest Hellenic achievement in this war, or, in my opinion, in Hellenic history—most glorious to the victors, most calamitous to the conquered. They were utterly and at all points defeated; all that they suffered was great. There was total destruction, their fleet, their army—everything was destroyed, and few out of many returned home. Thus ended the Sicilian expedition.

The News Arrives at Athens

VIII, 1. When the news was brought to Athens, for a long while they disbelieved even the most respectable of the soldiers who had themselves escaped from the scene of action and clearly reported the matter, a destruction so complete not being thought credible. When the conviction was forced upon them, they were angry with the orators who had joined in promoting the expedition—as if they had not themselves voted it—and enraged at the reciters of oracles and soothsayers and all other omen-mongers of the time who had encouraged them to hope that they would conquer Sicily. Overwhelmed by what had happened, they were seized by fear and consternation quite without example. It was grievous enough for the state and for every man to lose so many heavy infantry, cavalry, and able-bodied troops, and to see none left to replace them; but when they saw also that they had not sufficient ships in their docks, or money in the treasury, or crews for the ships, they began to despair of salvation. They thought that their enemies in Sicily would immediately sail with their fleet against Piraeus, inflamed by so signal a victory; while their adversaries in Greece, redoubling all their preparations, would vigorously attack them by sea and land at once, aided by their own revolted allies. Nevertheless, with such means as they had, it was determined to resist to the last, to provide timber and money, to equip a fleet as they best could, to take steps to secure their allies and above all Euboea, to reform things in the city upon a more economical footing, and to elect a board of older men to advise upon the state of affairs as occasion should arise. In short, as is the way of a democracy, in the panic of the moment they were ready to be as prudent as possible.

Society, Culture, and Intellectual Life

Athens during the Classical period may be described as a still largely oral society that also sustained cultures of literacy. The art of rhetoric or public speaking permeated its civic discourse and performances, and evidence for this has come down to us in the form of texts. From the legal speeches given by contending speakers in lawcourts or political assemblies, to historical works that embed "reported" speeches, to tragedic and comedic plays presented before the assembled citizenry, the values and identity of the civic body became the topic of representation and reflection. While this discourse was largely produced by male authors for a fellow citizen male audience, it at times attempts to deal with women and family as well as women's relationship to the civic community or *polis* which ancient Greeks tended to define as an exclusively male club.

28 Lysias, The Murder of Eratosthenes

An Athenian Woman's Life

"... I began to trust her...."

During the Classical period, it was generally believed that a respectable Athenian citizen woman should neither be seen nor heard by others; the only proper place for her was indoors, within the house of her father or husband. Athenian men of substance provided their womenfolk with slaves or servants who carried out daily tasks that involved contact with people outside the house. Citizen women left the house only on special occasions, such as during the funeral of a relative or a religious festival that involved the participation of women. For this and other reasons, Athenian women rarely made their presence felt in the historical record. Even from writings that discuss Athenian women, we learn mostly what the males thought and how the women ought to behave. Indeed, most ancient texts that mention women's lives

From *Lysias*, Loeb Classical Library Vol. 244, translated by W. R. M. Lamb (Cambridge, Mass.: Harvard University Press, 1930). The Loeb Classical Library® is a registered trademark of the President and Fellows of Harvard College. Reprinted by permission of the publishers and the Trustees of the Loeb Classical Library.

have other expressed aims in mind. This is very much the case with the following selection, which happens to reveal aspects of the secluded lives that many
citizen Athenian women lived.

Athenians accused of a crime defended themselves by delivering a speech
before a jury. Those who did not have the expertise to compose good forensic
speeches hired experts to write speeches for them. Lysias (died ca. 380 B.C.) was
a famous orator in Athens who was often commissioned by others to compose
such legal speeches. Toward the end of the fifth and the beginning of the
fourth century B.C., Euphiletus had caught another Athenian, Eratosthenes, in
the act of adultery with his wife and had killed him. The relatives of Eratosthenes then brought a legal action against Euphiletus, claiming that he had
committed murder instead. Athenian law granted a cuckolded husband the
right to kill the adulterer if he caught him in the act, but the relatives of
Eratosthenes claimed that Euphiletus had deliberately entrapped Eratosthenes
with the intention of killing him. Euphiletus had to prove that he killed Eratosthenes legally or else pay a heavy penalty. To persuade the Athenian jury of
his innocence, he had to show that the adultery was not a setup and that he
himself was genuinely taken by surprise. In his defense speech, he revealed
many telling details about the daily life of Athenian citizen women and the
domestic arrangements of an Athenian household. Toward the end of his
speech, Euphiletus made a calculated appeal to the civic patriotism and prejudices of the all-male jury: "I therefore, sirs, do not regard this requital as having
been exacted in my own private interest, but in that of the whole city.... Otherwise it were far better to erase our established laws, and ordain others which
will inflict the penalties on men who keep watch on their own wives, and
allow full immunity to those who would debauch them."

... When I, Athenians, decided to marry, and brought a wife into my house, for
some time I was disposed neither to vex her nor to leave her too free to do just
as she pleased; I kept a watch on her as far as possible, with such observation of
her as was reasonable. But when a child was born to me, thenceforward I began
to trust her, and placed all my affairs in her hands, presuming that we were now
in perfect intimacy. It is true that in the early days, Athenians, she was the most
excellent of wives; she was a clever, frugal housekeeper, and kept everything in
the nicest order. But as soon as I lost my mother, her death became the cause of
all my troubles. For it was in attending her funeral that my wife was seen by this
man, who in time corrupted her. He looked out for the servant-girl who went
to market, and so paid addresses to her mistress by which he wrought her ruin.
Now in the first place I must tell you, sirs (for I am obliged to give you these
particulars), my dwelling is on two floors, the upper being equal in space to the
lower, with the women's quarters above and the men's below. When the child
was born to us, its mother suckled it; and in order that, each time that it had to
be washed, she might avoid the risk of descending by the stairs, I used to live
above, and the women below. By this time it had become such an habitual
thing that my wife would often leave me and go down to sleep with the child,
so as to be able to give it the breast and stop its crying. Things went on in this
way for a long time, and I never suspected, but was simpleminded enough to
suppose that my own was the chastest wife in the city. Time went on, sirs; I
came home unexpectedly from the country, and after dinner the child started

crying in a peevish way, as the servant-girl was annoying it on purpose to make it so behave; for the man was in the house,—I learnt it all later. So I bade my wife go and give the child her breast, to stop its howling. At first she refused, as though delighted to see me home again after so long; but when I began to be angry and bade her go,—"Yes, so that you," she said, "may have a try here at the little maid. Once before, too, when you were drunk, you pulled her about." At that I laughed, while she got up, went out of the room, and closed the door, feigning to make fun, and she took the key away with her. I, without giving a thought to the matter, or having any suspicion, went to sleep in all content after my return from the country. Towards daytime she came and opened the door. I asked why the doors made a noise in the night; she told me that the child's lamp had gone out, and she had lit it again at our neighbour's. I was silent and believed it was so. But it struck me, sirs, that she had powdered her face, though her brother had died not thirty days before; even so, however, I made no remark on the fact, but left the house in silence. After this, sirs, an interval occurred in which I was left quite unaware of my own injuries; I was then accosted by a certain old female, who was secretly sent by a woman with whom that man was having an intrigue, as I heard later. This woman was angry with him and felt herself wronged, because he no longer visited her so regularly, and she was keeping a watch on him until she should discover what was the cause. So the old creature accosted me where she was on the look-out, near my house, and said,— "Euphiletus, do not think it is from any meddlesomeness that I have approached you; for the man who is working both your and your wife's dishonour happens to be our enemy. If, therefore, you take the servant-girl who goes to market and waits on you, and torture her, you will learn all. It is," she said, "Eratosthenes of Oë who is doing this; he has debauched not only your wife, but many others besides; he makes an art of it." With these words, sirs, she took herself off; I was at once perturbed; all that had happened came into my mind, and I was filled with suspicion,—reflecting first how I was shut up in my chamber, and then remembering how on that night the inner and outer doors made a noise, which had never occurred before, and how it struck me that my wife had put on powder. All these things came into my mind, and I was filled with suspicion. Returning home, I bade the servant-girl follow me to the market, and taking her to the house of an intimate friend, I told her I was fully informed of what was going on in my house: "So it is open to you," I said, "to choose as you please between two things,—either to be whipped and thrown into a mill, and to be irrevocably immersed in that sort of misery, or else to speak out the whole truth and, instead of suffering any harm, obtain my pardon for your transgressions. Tell no lies, but speak the whole truth." The girl at first denied it, and bade me do what I pleased, for she knew nothing; but when I mentioned Eratosthenes to her, and said that he was the man who visited my wife, she was dismayed, supposing that I had exact knowledge of everything. At once she threw herself down at my knees, and having got my pledge that she should suffer no harm, she accused him, first, of approaching her after the funeral, and then told how at last she became his messenger; how my wife in time was persuaded, and by what means she procured his entrances, and how at the Thesmophoria while I was in the country, she went off to the temple with his mother. And the girl gave an exact account of everything else that had occurred. When her tale was all told, I said,—"Well now, see that nobody in the world gets knowledge of this; otherwise, nothing in your arrangement with me will hold good. And I require that you show me their guilt in the very act; I want no words, but manifestation of the fact, if it really is so." She agreed to do this. Then came an interval of four or five days ... as I shall bring strong evidence to show. But first I wish to relate what took place on the last day. I had an intimate friend named Sostratus. After sunset I met him coming from the country. As I knew that, arriving at that hour, he would find none of his circle at home, I invited him to dine with me; we came to my house, mounted to the upper room, and had dinner. When he had made a good meal, he left me and departed; then I went to bed. Eratosthenes, sirs, entered, and the maid-servant roused me at once, and told me that he was in the house. Bidding her look after the door, I descended and went out in silence; I called on one friend and another, and found some of them at home, while others were out of town. I took with me as many as I could among those who were there, and so came along. Then we got torches from the nearest shop, and went in; the door was open, as the girl had it in readiness. We pushed open the door of the bedroom, and the first of us to enter were in time to see him lying down by my wife; those who followed saw him standing naked on the bed. I gave him a blow, sirs, which knocked him down, and pulling round his two hands behind his back, and tying them, I asked him why he had the insolence to enter my house. He admitted his guilt; then he besought and implored me not to kill him, but to exact a sum of money. To this I replied,—"It is not I who am going to kill you, but our city's law, which you have transgressed and regarded as of less account than your pleasures, choosing rather to commit this foul offence against my wife and my children than to obey the laws like a decent person."...

29 Euripides, *Medea*

Greek Tragic Vision of Women and the City

Euripides composed the play *Medea* for the Great Dionysia, the Athenian civic festival dedicated to Dionysus that combined religious rites and the staging of theatrical performances. The festival involved a competition in which *trageodoi*,

From Euripides, *Medea*; in *Euripides, Volume 1: Cyclops, Alcestis, Medea*, translated by David Kovac, Loeb Classical Library 12 (Cambridge, Mass.: Harvard University Press, 1994), pp. 295–99, 315–23, 327–29. The Loeb Classical Library® is a registered trademark of the President and Fellows of Harvard College. Reprinted by permission of the publishers and the Trustees of the Loeb Classical Library.

writers of tragic plays that treat the themes of gods and heroes, would each offer up to the assembled citizen audience three tragedies and one satyr play. According to one tradition, Euripides produced *Medea* as part of his entry in 431 B.C. Greek playwrights offer particular interpretations of mythological stories that were generally quite well-known to their contemporaries. The story of *Medea* was part of the tales of Jason and the Argonauts. In Jason's quest to reclaim the kingdom of his father Aison, the ousted king of Iolcus, Jason led a group of intrepid hero-sailors—the Argonauts—in a venture to find and seize the Golden Fleece of a magical ram that was said to be in Colchis on the shores of the Black Sea. After braving many hazards along his journey, Jason arrived, and after further winning the adoring support of the local princess Medea, niece of the sorceress Circe well-known from Homer's *Odyssey*, he managed to steal the Fleece from her fellow countrymen. Medea favored her new lover so much so that she supposedly killed her own brother to aid Jason's escape. Returning to Iolcus with the prize, Jason's uncle Pelias refused to honor his bargain to return the kingdom to Jason, and Medea used her reputation for magical powers to persuade Pelias' daughters to help restore their father to youthfulness by chopping up his body and mixing its parts with special magical ingredients in a cauldron. (This story was the subject of an earlier Euripidean drama [now mostly lost] known as *The Daughters of Pelias*.) This act in turn required Jason and Medea to flee in exile, and they came to Corinth where Creon was king. There Jason began to form an attachment to the king's daughter while Medea's reputation as a worker of magic and her status as a foreign woman rendered her an outcast.

The selection below begins with the exchanges between Medea and the Chorus that comprised fifteen Corinthian women who were her neighbors. The voices of the Chorus offer a somewhat detached outside commentary on the background of the story and the events as they occurred; they also gave voice to a critique of a Greek literary tradition that blames women for men's misdeeds and infidelities. Creon, described as clever and wise in the play, then entered and used Medea's reputation and history to accuse her of plotting mischief. He commanded Medea to depart from the city, but Medea supplicated with him and was given a brief reprieve, which she turned into the opportunity for carrying out gruesome revenge against Jason. Euripides' *Medea* reflects a man's attempt at imagining the viewpoint of the ultimate stranger to an Athenian/Greek citizen: a foreign, barbarian woman.

Enter NURSE from the house.

NURSE

Would that the Argo had never winged its way to the land of Colchis through the dark blue Symplegades [clashing rocks guarding the entrance to the Black Sea]! Would that pine trees had never been felled in the glens of Mount Pelion and furnished oars for the hands of the heroes who at Pelias' command set forth in quest of the Golden Fleece! For then my lady Medea would not have sailed to the towers of Iolcus, her heart smitten with love for Jason, or persuaded the daughters of Pelias to loll their father and hence now be inhabiting this land of Corinth, separated from her loved ones and country. At first, to be sure, she had, even in Corinth, a good life with her husband and children, an exile loved by the citizens to whose land she had come, and lending to Jason himself all her support. This it is that most keeps a life free of trouble, when a woman is not at variance with her husband.

But now all is enmity, and love's bonds are diseased. For Jason, abandoning his own children and my mistress, is bedding down in a royal match, having married the daughter of Creon, ruler of this land. Poor Medea, finding herself thus cast aside, calls loudly on his oaths, invokes the mighty assurance of his sworn right hand, and calls the gods to witness the unjust return she is getting from Jason. She lies fasting, giving her body up to pain, spending in ceaseless weeping all the hours since she learned that she was wronged by her husband, neither raising her face nor taking her eyes from the ground. She is as deaf to the advice of her friends as a stone or a wave of the sea, saying nothing unless perchance to turn her snow-white neck and weep to herself for her dear father, her country, and her ancestral house. All these she abandoned when she came here with a man who has now cast her aside. The poor woman has learned at misfortune's hand what a good thing it is not to be cut off from one's native land.

She loathes the children and takes no joy in looking at them. I am afraid that she will hatch some sinister plan. She has a terrible temper and will not put up with bad treatment (I know her), and I fear she may thrust a whetted sword through her vital, [slipping quietly into the house where the bed is laid out,] or kill die royal family and the bridegroom and then win some greater calamity. For she is dangerous. I tell you, no one who clashes with her will find it easy to crow in victory....

Enter MEDEA with the Nurse from the house.

MEDEA

Women of Corinth, I have come out of the house lest you find fault with me. For I know that though many mortals are haughty both in private and in public, others get a *reputation* for indifference to their neighbors from their retiring manner of Me. There is no justice in the eyes of mortals: before they get sure knowledge of a man's true character, they hate him on sight, although he has done them no harm. Now a foreigner must be quite compliant with the city, nor do I have any words of praise for the citizen who is self-willed and causes his fellow citizens pain by his lack of breeding, In my case, however, this sudden blow that has struck me has destroyed my Me. I am undone, I have resigned all joy in Me, and I want to die. For the man in whom all I had was bound up, as I well know—my husband—has proved the basest of men.

Of all creatures that have breath and sensation, we women are the most unfortunate. First at an exorbitant price we must buy a husband and take a master for our bodies. For this is what makes one misfortune even more galling than another, to suffer loss and be insulted to boot. The outcome of our life's striving hangs on this, whether we take a bad or a good husband. For divorce is discreditable for women and it is not possible to refuse wedlock. When a woman comes into the new customs and practices of her husband's house, she must somehow divine, since she has not learned it at home, how she shall best deal with her husband. If after we have spent great efforts on these tasks our husbands live with us without resenting the marriage yoke, our life is enviable. Otherwise, death is preferable. A man, whenever he is annoyed with the company of those in the house, goes elsewhere and thus rids his soul of its boredom [turning to some male friend or agemate]. But we must fix our gaze on one person only. Men say that we live a life free from danger at home while *they* fight with the spear. How wrong they are! I would rather stand three times with a shield in battle than give birth once.

But your story and mine are not the same: you have a city and a father's house, the enjoyment of life and the company of friends, while I, without relatives or city, am suffering outrage from my husband. I was carried off as booty from a foreign land and have no mother, no brother, no kinsman to shelter me from this calamity. And so I shall ask this much from you as a favor: if I find any means or contrivance to punish my husband for these wrongs [and die bride's father and the bride], keep my secret. In all other things a woman is full of fear, incapable of looking on battle or cold steel; but when she is injured in love, no mind is more murderous than hers.

CHORUS LEADER

I will do so. For you will be justified in punishing your husband, Medea, and I am not surprised that you grieve at what has happened.

Enter CREON by Eisodos B.

But I see Creon coming, ruler of this land. He will have some new deliberation to report.

CREON

You, Medea, scowling with rage against your husband, I order you to leave this land and go into exile, taking your two children with you, and instantly! I am the executor of this decree, and I will not return home again until I expel you from the country.

MEDEA

Oh, I am undone, wholly lost! My enemies are making full sail against me, and there is no haven from disaster that I can reach. Still, though I am ill-treated, I will ask you: Why are you exiling me, Creon?

CREON

I am afraid (no need to dissemble) that you will do some deadly harm to my daughter. Many indications of this combine: you are a clever woman and skilled in many evil arts, and you are smarting with the loss of your husband's love. And I hear that you are threatening—such is the report people bring—to harm the bride, her father, and her husband. So I shall take precautions before the event. It is better for me to incur your hatred now, woman, than to be soft now and regret it later.

MEDEA

Ah me! This is not the first time, Creon, but often before now my reputation has done me great harm. No man who is sensible ought ever to have his children educated beyond the common run. For apart from the charge of idleness they incur, they earn hostility and ill will from their fellow citizens. If you bring novel wisdom to fools, you will be regarded as useless, not wise; and if the city regards you as greater than those with a reputation for cleverness, you will be thought vexatious. I myself am a sharer in this lot, for since I am clever, some regard me with ill will, [others find me retiring, others the opposite, others an obstacle, yet I am not so very wise,] while you on the other hand fear me. What harm are you afraid of? Have no fear, Creon: I am not the land of person to commit crimes against my rulers. What injustice have you done me? You married your daughter to the man your heart bade you to. It is my husband I hate, while you, I think, acted with perfect good sense in this. And now I do not begrudge you prosperity. Make your marriage, all of you, and may good fortune attend you! But let me stay in this land. For although I have been wronged, I will hold my peace, yielding to my superiors.

CREON

Your words are soothing to listen to, but I am afraid that in your heart you are plotting some harm, and I trust you that much the less than before. A hot-tempered woman—and a hot-tempered man likewise—is easier to guard against than a clever woman who keeps her own counsel. No, go into exile at once—no more talk: my resolve is fixed and there is no way you can remain in our midst since you are hostile to me.

Medea kneels before him in the attitude of a suppliant,
grasping his knees and hand....

MEDEA

Allow me to remain this one day and to complete my plans for exile and how I may provide for my children, since their father does not care to do so. Have pity on them. You too are a parent: it would be natural for you to show kindness toward them. I do not care if I myself go into exile. It is *their* experience of misfortune I weep for.

CREON

My nature is not at all a tyrant's, and by showing consideration I have often suffered loss. And now, though I see that I am making a serious mistake, nonetheless, woman, you shall have your request. But I warn you, if tomorrow's sun sees you and your children within the borders of this land, you will be put to death. I mean what I have said. Now stay, if stay you must, for one more day. You will not do the mischief I fear by then.

Exit CREON by Eisodos B. Medea rises to her feet....

30 Socrates

Philosophy Shifts from Nature to Man

The history of Greek philosophy falls broadly into two divisions, one beginning with Thales of Miletus about 600 B.C. and the other with Socrates of Athens (469–399 B.C.) almost two hundred years later. The pre-Socratic thinkers, usually termed natural philosophers, turned their attention almost exclusively to the world of nature and sought to understand its origin and meaning. They rejected the naive and fantastic fables of Homer and Hesiod and looked for causes not in the gods but in nature itself. Heraclitus (late sixth century B.C.) spoke for the whole group when he rejected the traditional lore with the proud boast, "I have sought for myself." Thus the early Greek philosophers progressed beyond the limits reached by the speculative thinkers of the ancient Near East and are rightly credited with being the first to establish the independence of philosophy by separating thought from religion and myth.

The detached curiosity of these philosophers first led them to seek out and identify the one element that was the primordial stuff out of which the manifold variety of the universe had been formed. No agreement was reached by the various investigators who segregated and championed as the primary material or first cause of all things such elements as water, air, or fire. A second problem arose out of this original preoccupation with the material substance of the universe: the problem of change. How could something be and still change? Some denied the reality of change, others the reality of being. This controversy led to a further problem: the problem of knowledge. How can something be knowable if it changes from moment to moment? The method of finding truth was thus called into question. To replace the now questioned evidence of the senses, appeal was made to reason, and there followed a great emphasis upon deductive logic as a technique for expounding and proving various theories on the origin and nature of the universe. But these proofs were not satisfying, and the cumulative effect of two centuries of philosophical speculation was the growing conviction that neither sense experience nor human reason could find truths that could be universally accepted.

This individualism and skepticism in thought coincided, in the last half of the fifth century B.C. with the economic and political crisis that produced the Peloponnesian War, and the interaction of these various factors brought Greek thought to the dead end represented by the teachings of the sophists. These highly critical thinkers largely turned their attention to man and society and away from fruitless speculations about the physical world. All religious, ethical, and political values fell before their attack: the gods were invented as "a clever device of some prehistoric statesman as a means of preventing crime"; "justice is simply the interest of the stronger (see Selection 27C)." All agreed in interpreting the famous dictum of Protagoras, "man is the measure of all things," to mean that truth and morality were relative and individual matters, and many went on to accept the extreme skepticism regarding truth formulated by Gorgias: "Nothing exists; if anything did exist, it could not be known; if a man should chance to apprehend it, it would still be a secret: he would be unable to communicate it to his fellows."

Socrates' place in the history of philosophy rests upon his success in reversing the destructive trend of Greek thought and constructing the foundation upon which Plato and Aristotle later built their philosophical systems. Like the sophists, Socrates refused to spend time investigating the physical world, and Plato reports his reason: "I have no leisure for such enquiries; shall I tell you why? I must first know myself, as the inscription at Delphi says; it would be absurd to be curious about what is no business of mine, while I don't know my own self." In other words, because Greek thought had reasoned all traditional values out of existence, the resulting void of meaning demanded his attention. It is therefore the world within man that concerns Socrates, or, as he preferred to call it, the care of the soul. To Socrates, the soul is identified with the mind; it is the seat of reason and capable of finding the ethical truths that will restore meaning and value to life. He did not doubt that such truths could be found and that they would be universally accepted. If people would place themselves under the rule of reason, they would recognize and desire what is good and true, for the nature of goodness and truth is such that all who recognize it will want it; all evil and error are the products of ignorance. This is the meaning of his well-known statements that "virtue is knowledge" and "nobody errs willingly."

To remove ignorance and to demonstrate that, if people will think strenuously and honestly, they will find themselves in agreement on what is true and good, Socrates developed the famous method that has since borne his name and made him recognized as one of the world's great teachers. The Socratic method employs the two devices of examination and exhortation,

Socrates.
"Dire are the pangs which my art is able to arouse and to allay in those who consort with me, just like the pangs of women in childbirth; night and day they are full of perplexity and travail which is even worse than that of the women."

with emphasis upon the former. Exhortation to seek wisdom can have little effect so long as people are satisfied with the beliefs they hold, so Socrates felt compelled to go about cross-examining men, using the dialectical technique of question and answer to demonstrate the inadequacies of their beliefs—the inconsistencies, the half-truths, and the errors. Only after the ground has been prepared in this fashion can the seed planted by exhortation grow into fruit. But the destruction or deconstruction involved in preparing the ground brought upon Socrates the charge of radicalism and subversion of the young, and at the age of seventy, he was condemned and put to death by an Athenian jury on the charge of introducing new gods and corrupting the youth. His optimistic belief in the existence of eternal moral truths and the search for them was left to his most famous pupil, Plato, and to posterity.

A. THE SOCRATIC METHOD

"The unexamined life is not worth living."

Plato's Dialogues, our chief source for understanding the personality and work of Socrates, who himself never committed his teaching writing, owe their origin and form to the questions-and-answer method of Socrates that they imitate. In the two selections that follow, Plato portrays Socrates in the act of describing to his friends the nature, purpose, and results of his method. Socrates calls it a "rough" method, for in no other way can he remove that great barrier to intellectual growth he terms the "spirit of conceit," itself the product of "great prejudices and harsh notions." He also calls it a type of "midwifery" in that it assists the mind in giving birth to ideas but does not itself produce them. Eternal truths exist, Socrates believes, and his method is a technique for the right use of reason to discover them. This means the use of inductive reasoning, and Aristotle credits Socrates with being the founder of inductive logic. The naive and superficial views of the examinee serve as hypotheses that are tested by reference to specific facts known to be true. The contradictions that result force the revision or abandonment of the original hypotheses and make possible movement in the direction of valid hypotheses and ultimate agreement on fundamental truths.

"A Rough and a Smooth Method"

There is a rough and a smooth method in intellectual education. There is a time-honored mode which our fathers commonly practiced towards their sons, and which is still adopted by many—either of roughly reproving their errors, or of gently advising them; these two methods may be correctly described as admonition. But some thinkers appear to have arrived at the conclusion that all ignorance is involuntary, and that no one who thinks himself wise is willing to learn

From Richard W. Livingstone, ed., *Plato: Selected Passages*, translated by Benjamin Jowett, The World's Classics (Oxford: the Clarendon Press, 1940), pp. 19–21.

anything in the subjects in which he believes himself clever, and that the admonitory sort of instruction gives much trouble and does little good. So they set to work to eradicate the spirit of conceit in another way. They cross–examine a man's words, when he thinks that he is talking sense but really is not, and easily convict him of inconsistencies in his opinions; these they then place side by side, and show that they contradict one another. He, seeing this, is angry with himself, and grows gentle toward others, and thus is entirely delivered from great prejudices and harsh notions, in a way which is most amusing to the hearer, and produces the most lasting good effect on the person who is the subject of the operation. For as the physician considers that the body will receive no benefit from taking food until internal obstacles have been removed, so the purifier of the soul is conscious that his patient will receive no benefit from the application of knowledge until he is refuted, and from refutation learns modesty; he must be purged of his prejudices first and made to think that he knows only what he knows, and no more. For all these reasons, Theaetetus, we must admit that refutation is the greatest and chiefest of purifications, and he who has not been refuted, though he be the King of Persia himself, is in an awful state of impurity; he is uneducated and ugly just where purity and beauty are essential to happiness.

(*Sophist*, 229f.)

"Dire Are the Pangs"

My art is like that of midwives, but differs from theirs, in that I attend men and not women, and I look after their souls when they are in labor, and not after their bodies: and the triumph of my art is in thoroughly examining whether the thought which the mind of a young man brings forth is a phantom and a lie, or a fruitful and true birth. And like the midwives, I am barren, and the reproach often made against me, that I ask questions of others and have not the wit to answer them myself, is very just—the reason is, that the god compels me to be a midwife, but does not allow me to have children. So I myself am not at all wise, nor have I any invention or child of my own soul to show, but those who talk with me profit. Some of them appear dull enough at first, but afterwards, as our acquaintance ripens, if God is gracious to them, they all make astonishing progress; and this in the opinion of others as well as in their own. It is quite clear that they never learned anything from me; all that they master and discover comes from themselves. But to me and the god they owe their delivery. And the proof of my words is, that many of them in their ignorance, either in their self-conceit despising me, or falling under the influence of others, have gone away too soon; and have not only lost by an ill upbringing the children of whom I had previously delivered them, but have had subsequent miscarriages owing to evil associates, prizing lies and shams more than the truth; and they have at last ended by seeing themselves, as others see them, to be great fools. Dire are the pangs which my art is able to arouse and to allay in those who consort with me, just like the pangs of women in childbirth; night and day they are full of perplexity and travail which is even worse than that of the women. So much for them. And there are others, Theaetetus, who come to me apparently having nothing in them; and as I know that they have no need of my art, I coax them into marrying some one, and by the grace of God I can generally tell who is likely to do them good. Many of them I have given away to Prodicus, and many to other inspired sages. I tell you this long story, friend Theaetetus, because I suspect, as indeed you seem to think yourself, that you are in labor—great with some conception. Come then to me, who am a midwife's son and myself a midwife, and do your best to answer the questions which I will ask you. And if I expose your first-born, because I discover upon inspection that the conception which you have formed is a blind shadow, do not quarrel with me on that account, as women do when their first children are taken from them. For I have actually known some who were ready to bite me when I deprived them of a darling folly, they did not see that I acted from goodwill, not knowing that no god is the enemy of man; neither am I their enemy in all this, but it would be wrong for me to admit falsehood, or to stifle the truth.

(*Theatetus*, 150f.)

B. ARISTOPHANES, *CLOUDS:* SOCRATES AS TROUBLEMAKER

"You will now believe in no god but those we believe in...."

Socrates was a well-known and easily recognized public figure in Classical Athens. His activities became the object of ridicule at the hands of the comic dramatist Aristophanes, who in 423 B.C. put on a play called the *Clouds* at the Great Festival of the god Dionysus. The topic of the *Clouds* was rather untraditional: it pokes fun at the culture of scientific inquiry and the educational training that contemporary Athenian young men were receiving at the hands of professional teachers called sophists. Sophists were so called because they professed to teach various branches of knowledge, or wisdom, *sophia*. Critics made fun of their pretensions and lamented the devastating effect they were having on the moral formation of Athenian young men. In common opinion, Socrates was grouped with the sophists, even though he himself would have resisted this association because he did not teach for money and even denied he had any real knowledge to impart to his listeners.

In this play, Socrates is the master sophist who inhabits a "think tank," to which ambitious young men look to learn the means by which they can become powerful and rich. Strepsiades, his interlocutor and the father of a young man who is a student of the place, represents the older generation of Athenians who were much more skeptical of the new-fangled ideas. Here Socrates professes a belief in the rather amorphous "clouds" as the feminine deities whom one ought to worship instead of the traditional Olympian gods

From *Aristophanes. Vol. II: the Clouds, Wasps, Peace,* Loeb Classical Library Vol. 488, translated by Jeffrey J. Henderson (Cambridge, Mass.: Harvard University Press, 1988). The Loeb Classical Library® is a registered trademark of the President and Fellows of Harvard College. Reprinted by permission of the publishers and the Trustees of the Loeb Classical Library.

such as Zeus. This notion was connected to the later charge that Socrates sought to introduce new gods into Athens. While such a portrait is an unfair and inaccurate description of what Socrates believed in or sought to accomplish, it gives us an important glimpse into a prevailing image that the Athenian public had of him. The image of Socrates as a troublemaker serves as an important context for his trial and execution in 399 B.C.

… Socrates. The old man must keep silence and listen to the prayer. O Lord and Master, measureless Air, who hold the earth aloft, and you, shining Empyrean, and ye Clouds, awesome goddesses of thunder and lightning, arise, appear aloft, o Mistresses, to the thinker!

Strepsiades. (covering himself with his cloak) Not yet, not until I get this over me, so I don't get soaked. To think I left home, poor fool, without even a cap!

Socrates. Come then, illustrious Clouds, in an exhibition for this man, whether you now sit on Olympus' holy snow-struck peaks, or start up a holy dance for the Nymphs in father Ocean's gardens, or whether again at the Nile's mouths you scoop its waters in golden pitchers, or inhabit Lake Maeotis or the snowy steeps of Mimas: hear my prayer, accept my sacrifice and enjoy these holy rites.
    Chorus. (from afar)
    Clouds everlasting,
    let us arise, revealing our dewy bright form,
    from deep roaring father Ocean
    onto high mountain peaks.,,,

Socrates. Most stately Clouds, you have clearly heard my summons. (to Strepsiades) Did you mark their voice and, in concert, the bellowing thunder that prompts holy reverence?

Strepsiades. I do revere you, illustrious ones, and I'm ready to answer those thunderclaps with a fart; that's how much I fear and tremble at them. And right now, if it's sanctioned, and even if it isn't, I need to shit!

Socrates. Don't be scurrilous and act like those hapless comedians! Now keep silence, for a great swarm of gods is on the move, in song.
    Chorus. (closer)
    Rainbearing maidens,
    let us visit the gleaming land of Pallas [i.e., Athens], to see the ravishing country
    of Cecrops with its fine men….

Strepsiades. By Zeus, I beg you, tell me who they are, Socrates, these females who intoned that awesome song? They're not lady heroes of some sort, are they?

Socrates. Not at all; they're heavenly Clouds, great goddesses for idle gentlemen, who provide us with judgment and dialectic and intelligence, fantasy and circumlocution and verbal thrust and parry.

STREPSIADES. So that's why my soul has taken flight at the sound of their voice, and now seeks to split hairs, prattle narrowly about smoke, and meet argument with counterargument, puncturing a point with a pointlet. So if at all possible, I want to see them now in person.

SOCRATES. Then look over here, toward Mount Parnes, because now I see them quietly descending.

STREPSIADES. Where? Come on, show me!
        The Chorus files along the wings toward the orchestra.

SOCRATES. They're on the march, quite a lot of them, though the hollows and thickets—there, to the side.

STREPSIADES. What's going on? I don't see them.

SOCRATES. In the wings!

STREPSIADES. Yes, now I can almost see them.

SOCRATES. By now you must see them, unless you've got styes like pumpkins!

STREPSIADES. Yes, now I see them. Heaven be praised, they're permeating everything!

SOCRATES. And you didn't realize that they're goddesses, or believe it?

STREPSIADES. God no; I thought they were mist and dew and smoke.

SOCRATES. You didn't because you're unaware that they nourish a great many sophists, diviners ..., medical experts, long-haired idlers with onyx signet rings, and tune bending composers of dithyrambic choruses, men of highflown pretension, whom they maintain as do–nothings, because they compose music about these Clouds.

STREPSIADES. So that's why they compose verses like "dire downdraft of humid clouds zigzaggedly braceleted," and "locks of hundred-headed Typhus," and "blasting squalls," and then "airy scudders crooked of talon, birds swimming on high," and "rain of waters from dewy clouds." Then, as their reward, they get to gulp down nice big mullet fillets and avian thrush cutlets!

SOCRATES. Certainly, thanks to these Clouds. Isn't that fair?

STREPSIADES. So tell me, if these really are Clouds, how is it that they look like mortal women? (pointing skyward) Because those clouds aren't like that.

SOCRATES. Well, what do they look like?

STREPSIADES. I don't know exactly, but they look like fleeces spread out, not like women, no, surely not in any way. And these Clouds have noses!

SOCRATES. Now answer some questions for me.

STREPSIADES. Ask away, whatever you like.

SOCRATES. Have you ever looked up and seen a cloud resembling a centaur, or a leopard, or a wolf, or a bull?

STREPSIADES. Certainly I have. So what?

SOCRATES. Clouds turn into anything they want. Thus, if they see a savage with long hair, one of these furry types, like the son of Xenophantus, they mock his obsession by making themselves look like centaurs.

STREPSIADES. And what if they look down and see a predator of public funds like Simon, what do they do?

SOCRATES. To expose his nature they immediately turn into wolves....

STREPSIADES. Then hail, Mistresses! And now, almighty Queens, if you've ever so favored another man, break forth for me too a sound that spans the sky!

CHORUS LEADER. Hail, oldster born long ago, stalker of erudite arguments, and you too, priest of subtlest hogwash, tell us what you desire; for we would pay no attention to any other contemporary sophist of celestial studies except for Prodicus, for his wisdom and intelligence, and you, because you strut like a popinjay through the streets and cast your eyes sideways and, unshod, endure many woes and wear a haughty expression for our sake.

STREPSIADES. Mother Earth, what a voice! How holy and august and marvelous!

SOCRATES. That's because they are only true goddesses; all the rest are rubbish.

STREPSIADES. Come now, by Earth, doesn't Olympian Zeus count as a god with you people?

SOCRATES. What do you mean, Zeus? Do stop driveling. Zeus doesn't even exist!

STREPSIADES. What are you talking about? Then who makes it rain? Answer me that one, first of all.

SOCRATES. These do, of course! And I'll teach you how, with grand proofs. Now then: where have you ever yet seen rain without Clouds? Though according to you, Zeus should make rain himself on a clear day, when the Clouds are out of town.

STREPSIADES. By Apollo, you've nicely spliced that point with what you were saying a moment ago. And imagine, before now I thought than rain is Zeus pissing through a sieve! But tell me who does the thundering that makes me tremble.

SOCRATES. These do the thundering, by rolling around.

STREPSIADES. In what way, you daredevil?

SOCRATES. When they fill up with lots of water and are forced to drift, by natural compulsion sagging down with rain, then run into one other, and become sodden, they explode and crash.

STREPSIADES. But who is it that forces them to drift? Doesn't Zeus?

SOCRATES. Not at all; it's cosmic whirl.

STREPSIADES. Whirl? That's a new one on me, that Zeus is gone and Whirl now rules in his place. But you still haven't taught me anything about the thunder's crash.

SOCRATES. Didn't you hear me? I repeat: when the clouds are full of water and run into one another, they crash because of their density.

STREPSIADES. Come now, why should anyone believe that?

SOCRATES. I'll teach you from your own person. Have you ever gorged yourself with soup at the Panathenaea [a major Athenian festival], and then had an upset stomach, and a sudden turmoil sets it all arumble?

STREPSIADES. By Apollo I have! It does carry on terribly and shake me up, and like thunder that bit of soup crashes and roars terribly, gently at first, pappax pappax, and then stepping up the pace, papapappax, and when I shit it absolutely thunders, papapappax, just like those Clouds!

SOCRATES. Now then, consider what farts you let off from such a little tummy; isn't it natural that this sky, being limitless, should thunder mightily?

STREPSIADES. So that's why the words are similar, bronte "thunder" and porde "fart!"! But now explain this: where does the lightning bolt come from, blazing with fire, that incinerates us on contact and badly burns the survivors? It's quite obvious that Zeus hurls it against perjurers.

SOCRATES. How's that, you moron redolent of the Cronia, you mooncalf! If he really strikes perjurers, then why hasn't he burned up Simon or Cleonymus or Theorus, since they're paramount perjurers? On the other hand, he strikes his own temple, and Sunium headland of Athens, and the great oaks. What's his point? An oak tree certainly doesn't perjure itself!

STREPSIADES. I don't know; but you seem to have a good argument. Very well, what is the thunderbolt, then?

SOCRATES. When a dry wind rises skyward and gets locked up in these Clouds, it blows them up from within like a bladder, and then by natural compulsion it bursts them and is borne out in a whoosh by dint of compression, burning itself up with the friction and velocity.

STREPSIADES. By Zeus, exactly the same thing happened to me one time at the Diasia, when I was cooking a haggis for my relatives and forgot to make a slit. So it bloated up, then suddenly it exploded, spattering gore in my eyes and burning my face.

CHORUS LEADER. Ah, creature who yearn for grand wisdom from us, how blessed you will become among the Athenians and all Greeks, if you're retentive and a cogitator, if endurance abides in your soul, if you don't tire out either standing or walking, if you're not too annoyed by the cold or too keen on having breakfast, if you stay away from wine and gymnasiums and all other follies, and if, as befits a clever man, you consider absolute excellence to be victory in action, in counsel, and in tongue warfare.

STREPSIADES. Well, if it has to do with a rigorous soul, and restless anxiety, and a belly that's stingy, poorly nourished, and able to make a meal out of herbs, never fear: on these counts I'd dauntlessly present myself for hammering into shape.

SOCRATES. Then I take it you will now believe in no god but those we believe in: this Void, and the Clouds, and the Tongue, and only these three?

STREPSIADES. I wouldn't speak a word to the other gods even if I met them in the street; and I won't sacrifice to them, or pour them libations, or offer them incense....

C. THE APOLOGY OF SOCRATES

"I am that gadfly which God has attached to the state."

In addition to being one of the most moving pieces in the history of world literature, written as it was under the emotional impact of the great wrong done to Socrates, Plato's *Apology* deals with a question that has ever since haunted advanced societies: How much intellectual freedom can a state allow its citizens? For these reasons, the *Apology* has become part of the cultural tradition of the Western world.

In 399 B.C., five years after the fall of the Athenian Empire and three years after democracy had been restored following the overthrow of the dictatorship of Critias and the Thirty (Selection 30), Socrates was brought to trial on the following charge: "Socrates is guilty of crime, because he does not believe in the gods recognized by the state, but introduces strange supernatural beings; he is also guilty, because he corrupts the youth." The first part of the charge, denying the state gods, was brought by a religious fanatic named Meletus. The more serious charge, that of corrupting the youth, was brought by Anytus, a wealthy manufacturer whose son possessed a fine mind and had wanted to become a pupil of Socrates. When Anytus refused and insisted that his son enter his business, the young man took to drink and ended up an alcoholic.

From *The Dialogues of Plato*, translated by Benjamin Jowett (3rd ed.).

Anytus was also a colleague of Thrasybulus and a leading democratic politician. He saw Socrates as the intellectual leader of the antidemocratic faction at Athens, the evil genius behind the scene whose disciples, like Critias and Xenophon, were mostly young noblemen whom he had indoctrinated with his conviction that only knowledge and wisdom entitled one to rule and that ordinary people and democratic politicians did not possess this knowledge and wisdom. In other words, Socrates' teaching destroyed the foundation on which the democratic way of life was built.

Plato was present at the trial, and his version of Socrates' speech before the court falls into three parts. Socrates first defends himself against the charge that he is either a sophist or a philosopher of nature and so a promoter of influences subversive to traditional beliefs and to the welfare of the state. He describes himself as the "gadfly" of the state seeking to sting men into mental activity by opening their eyes to their own ignorance and thereby promoting "wisdom and truth and the greatest improvement of the soul." After a small majority of sixty of the 501 judges find Socrates guilty of the charges, he next exercises his right under Athenian law of proposing a lighter penalty than the sentence of death urged by his accusers. His ironic suggestion (not included in the following selection) that he deserves to be supported at public expense as a reward for his service to the state, and at the worst should pay only a small fine, further antagonizes his judges and he is condemned to death. In the final part of his speech, Socrates discourses on the significance of his case and prophesies—correctly, as it turned out—that he will have disciples who will assume his role of a "gadfly, ... arousing and persuading and reproaching" the citizens of Athens.

"What Do the Slanderers Say?"

How you, O Athenians, have been affected by my accusers, I cannot tell; but I know that they almost made me forget who I was—so persuasively did they speak; and yet they have hardly uttered a word of truth....

I will begin at the beginning, and ask what is the accusation which has given rise to the slander of me, and in fact has encouraged Meletus to prefer this charge against me. Well, what do the slanderers say? They shall be my prosecutors, and I will sum up their words in an affidavit: "Socrates is an evildoer, and a curious person, who searches into things under the earth and in heaven, and he makes the worse appear the better cause; and he teaches the aforesaid doctrines to others." Such is the nature of the accusation: it is just what you have yourselves seen in the comedy of Aristophanes, who has introduced a man whom he calls Socrates, going about and saying that he walks in air, and talking a deal of nonsense concerning matters of which I do not pretend to know either much or little—not that I mean to speak disparagingly of anyone who is a student of natural philosophy. I should be very sorry if Meletus could bring so grave a charge against me. But the simple truth is, O Athenians, that I have nothing to do with physical speculations....

"What Is the Origin of These Accusations?"

I dare say, Athenians, that some one among you will reply, "Yes, Socrates, but what is the origin of these accusations which are brought against you; there must have been something strange which you have been doing? All these rumors and this talk about you would never have arisen if you had been like other men: tell us, then, what is the cause of them, for we should be sorry to judge hastily of you." Now I regard this as a fair challenge, and I will endeavor to explain to you the reason why I am called wise and have such evil fame. Please to attend then. And although some of you think that I am joking, I declare that I will tell you the entire truth. Men of Athens, this reputation of mine has come of a certain sort of wisdom which I possess. If you ask me what kind of wisdom, I reply, wisdom such as may perhaps be attained by man, for to that extent I am inclined to believe that I am wise; whereas the persons of whom I was speaking have a superhuman wisdom, which I may fail to describe, because I have it not myself; and he who says that I have speaks falsely and is taking away my character. And here, O men of Athens, I must beg you not to interrupt me, even if I seem to say something extravagant. For the word which I will speak is not mine. I will refer you to a witness who is worthy of credit; that witness shall be the God of Delphi—he will tell you about my wisdom, if I have any, and of what sort it is. You must have known Chaerephon; he was early a friend of mine, and also a friend of yours. He went into exile with you [democrats], and returned from exile with you. Well, Chaerephon, as you know, was very impetuous in all his doings, and he went to Delphi and boldly asked the oracle to tell him whether—as I was saying, I must beg you not to interrupt—he asked the oracle to tell him whether anyone was wiser than I was, and the Pythian prophetess answered, that there was no man wiser. Chaerephon is dead himself; but his brother, who is in court, will confirm the truth of what I am saying.

Why do I mention this? Because I am going to explain to you why I have such an evil name. When I heard the answer, I said to myself, What can the god mean? and what is the interpretation of his riddle? for I know that I have no wisdom, small or great. What then can he mean when he says that I am the wisest of men? And yet he is a god, and cannot lie; that would be against his nature. After long consideration, I thought of a method of trying the question. I reflected that if I could only find a man wiser than myself, then I might go to the god with a refutation in my hand. I should say to him, "Here is a man who is wiser than I am; but you said that I was the wisest." Accordingly I went to one who had the reputation of wisdom, and observed him—his name I need not mention; he was a politician whom I selected for examination—and the result was as follows: When I began to talk with him, I could not help thinking that he was not really wise, although he was thought wise by many, and still wiser by himself; and thereupon I tried to explain to him that he thought himself wise, but was not really wise; and the consequence was that he hated me, and his enmity was shared by several who were present and heard me. So I left him, saying to myself, as I went away: Well, although I do not suppose that either of us knows anything really beautiful and good, I am better off than he is—for he knows nothing, and thinks that he knows; I neither know nor think that I know. In this latter particular, then, I seem to have slightly the advantage of him. Then I went to another who had still higher pretensions to wisdom, and my conclusion was exactly the same. Whereupon I made another enemy of him, and of many others besides him.

Then I went to one man after another, being not unconscious of the enmity which I provoked, and I lamented and feared this: but necessity was laid upon me—the word of God, I thought, ought to be considered first. And I said to myself, Go I must to all who appear to know, and find out the meaning of the oracle. And I swear to you, Athenians, by the dog I swear!—for I must tell you the truth—the result of my mission was just this: I found that the men most in repute were all but the most foolish; and that the others less esteemed were really wiser and better. I will tell you the tale of my wanderings and of the "Herculean" labors, as I may call them, which I endured only to find at last the oracle irrefutable.

After the politicians, I went to the poets; tragic, dithyrambic, and all sorts. And there, I said to myself, you will be instantly detected; now you will find out that you are more ignorant than they are. Accordingly, I took them some of the most elaborate passages in their own writings, and asked what was the meaning of them—thinking that they would teach me something. Will you believe me? I am almost ashamed to confess the truth, but I must say that there is hardly a person present who would not have talked better about their poetry than they did themselves. Then I knew that not by wisdom do poets write poetry, but by a sort of genius and inspiration; they are like diviners or soothsayers who also say many fine things, but do not understand the meaning of them. The poets appeared to me to be much in the same case; and I further observed that upon the strength of their poetry they believed themselves to be the wisest of men in other things in which they were not wise. So I departed, conceiving myself to be superior to them for the same reason that I was superior to the politicians.

At last I went to the artisans. I was conscious that I knew nothing at all, as I may say, and I was sure that they knew many fine things; and here I was not mistaken, for they did know many things of which I was ignorant, and in this they certainly were wiser than I was. But I observed that even the good artisans fell into the same error as the poets—because they were good workmen they thought that they also knew all sorts of high matters, and this defect in them overshadowed their wisdom; and therefore I asked myself on behalf of the oracle, whether I would like to be as I was, neither having their knowledge nor their ignorance, or like them in both; and I made answer to myself and to the oracle that I was better off as I was.

This inquisition has led to my having many enemies of the worst and most dangerous kind, and has given occasion also to many calumnies....

There is another thing: young men of the richer classes, who have not much to do, come about me of their own accord; they like to hear the pretenders examined, and they often imitate me, and proceed to examine others; there are plenty of persons, as they quickly discover, who think that they know something, but really know little or nothing; and then those who are examined by them instead of being angry with themselves are angry with me: This confounded Socrates, they say; this villainous misleader of youth!—and then if somebody asks them, Why, what evil does he practice or teach? they do not know, and cannot tell; but in order that they may not appear to be at a loss, they repeat the ready-made charges which are used against all philosophers about teaching things up in the clouds and under the earth, and having no gods, and making the worse appear the better cause; for they do not like to confess that their pretense of knowledge has been detected—which is the truth; and as they are numerous and ambitious and energetic, and are drawn up in battle array and have persuasive tongues, they have filled your ears with their loud and inveterate calumnies. And this is the reason why my three accusers, Meletus and Anytus and Lycon, have set upon me; ...

"I Shall Obey God Rather Than You"

Some one will say: And are you not ashamed, Socrates, of a course of life which is likely to bring you to an untimely end? To him I may fairly answer: There you are mistaken: a man who is good for anything ought not to calculate the chance of living or dying; he ought only to consider whether in doing anything he is doing right or wrong—acting the part of a good man or of a bad.... And therefore is you let me go now, and are not convinced by Anytus, who said that since I had been prosecuted I must be put to death; ... and that if I escape now, your sons will all be utterly ruined by listening to my words—if you say to me, Socrates, this time we will not mind Anytus, and you shall be let off, but upon one condition, that you are not to enquire and speculate in this way any more, and that if you are caught doing so again you shall die; if this was the condition on which you let me go, I should reply: Men of Athens, I honor and love you; but I shall obey God rather than you, and while I have life and strength I shall never cease from the practice and teaching of philosophy, exhorting anyone whom I meet and saying to him after my manner: You, my friend a citizen of the great and mighty and wise city of Athens—are you not ashamed of heaping up the greatest amount of money and honor and reputation, and caring so little about wisdom and truth and the greatest improvement of the soul, which you never regard or heed at all? And if the person with whom I am arguing, says: Yes, but I do care; then I do not leave him or let him go at once; but I proceed to interrogate and examine and cross-examine him, and if I think that he has no virtue in him, but only says that he has, I reproach him with undervaluing the greater, and overvaluing the less.... This is my teaching, and if this is the doctrine which corrupts youth, I am a mischievous person....

And now, Athenians, I am not going to argue for my own sake, as you may think, but for yours, that you may not sin against God by condemning me, who am his gift to you. For if you kill me you will not easily find a successor to me, who, if I may use such a ludicrous figure of speech, am a sort of gadfly, given to the state by God; and the state is a great and noble steed who is tardy in his motions owing to his very size, and requires to be stirred into life. I am that gadfly which God has attached to the state, and all day long and in all places am always fastening upon you, arousing and persuading and reproaching you. You will not easily find another like me, and therefore I would advise you to spare me. I dare say that you may feel out of temper (like a person who is suddenly awakened from sleep), and you think that you might easily strike me dead as Anytus advises, and then you would sleep on for the remainder of your lives, unless God in his care of you sent you another gadfly....

"What Deters Me from Being a Politician"

Some one may wonder why I go about in private giving advice and busying myself with the concerns of others but do not venture to come forward in public and advise the state. I will tell you why. You have heard me speak at sundry times and in divers places of an oracle or sign which comes to me, and is the divinity which Meletus ridicules in the indictment. This sign, which is a kind of voice, first began to come to me when I was a child; it always forbids but never commands me to do anything which I am going to do. This is what deters me from being a politician. And rightly, as I think. For I am certain, O men of Athens, that if I had engaged in politics, I should have perished long ago, and done no good either to you or to myself. And do not be offended at my telling you the truth: for the truth is, that no man who goes to war with you or any other multitude, honestly striving against the many lawless and unrighteous deeds which are done in a state, will save his life; he who will fight for the right, if he would live even for a brief space, must have a private station and not a public one.

I can give you convincing evidence of what I say, not words only, but what you value far more—actions. Let me relate to you a passage of my own life which will prove to you that I should never have yielded to injustice from any fear of death.... When the oligarchy of the Thirty was in power, they sent for me and four others into the rotunda, and bade us bring Leon the Salaminian for Salamis, as they wanted to put him to death. This was a specimen of the sort of commands which they were always giving with the view of implicating as many as possible in their crimes; and then I showed, not in word only but in deed, that, if I may be allowed to use such an expression, I cared not a straw for death, and that my great and only care was lest I should do an unrighteous or unholy thing. For the strong arm of that oppressive power did not frighten me into doing wrong; and when we came out of the rotunda the other four went to Salamis and fetched Leon, but I went quietly home. For which I might have lost my life, had not the power of the Thirty shortly afterwards come to an end. And many will witness to my words.

Now do you really imagine that I could have survived all these years if I had led a public life, supposing that like a good man I had always maintained the right and had made justice, as I ought, the first thing? No indeed, men of Athens, neither I nor any other man. But I have been always the same in all my actions, public as well as private, and never have I yielded any base compliance to those who are slanderously termed my disciples, or to any other. Not that I have any regular disciples. But if anyone likes to come and hear me while I am pursuing my mission, whether he be young or old, he is not excluded. Nor do I converse only with those who pay; but anyone, whether he be rich or poor, may ask and answer me and listen to my words; and whether he turns out to be a bad man or a good one, neither result can be justly imputed to me; for I never taught or professed to teach anything. And if anyone says that he has ever learned or heard anything from me in private which all the world has not heard, let me tell you that he is lying....

"I Prophesy to You"

And now, O men who have condemned me, I would like to prophesy to you; for I am about to die, and in the hour of death men are gifted with prophetic power. And I prophesy to you who are my murderers, that immediately after my departure punishment far heavier than you have inflicted on me will surely await you. Me you have killed because you wanted to escape the accuser, and not to give an account of your lives. But that will not be as you suppose: far otherwise. For I say that there will be more accusers of you than there are now; accusers whom hitherto I have restrained: and as they are younger they will be more inconsiderate with you, and you will be more offended at them. If you think that by killing men you can prevent someone from censuring your evil lives, you are mistaken; that is not a way of escape which is either possible or honorable; the easiest and the noblest way is not to be disabling others, but to be improving yourselves. This is the prophecy which I utter before my departure to the judges who have condemned me....

Still I have a favor to ask of them. When my sons are grown up, I would ask you, O my friends, to punish them; and I would have you trouble them, as I have troubled you if they seem to care about riches, or anything, more than about virtue; or if they pretend to be something when they are really nothing—then reprove them, as I have reproved you, for not caring about that for which they ought to care, and thinking that they are something when they are really nothing. And if you do this, both I and my sons will have received justice at your hands.

The hour of departure has arrived, and we go on our ways—I to die, and you to live. Which is better God only knows.

31 Plato

"Turning the eye of the soul toward the light"

The dialogues of Plato (427–348 B.C.) have always charmed readers with their extraordinary literary beauty and stimulated them by raising fundamental problems in many fields, notably in religion, ethics, and politics. The pupil of Socrates and inheritor of his optimistic view that universal truths exist and can be found, Plato went beyond his master in asserting the existence of universal truths (the Platonic ideas) and constructing upon them a philosophical system. Known as Idealism, this system has exerted an incalculable influence on the history of Western philosophy and religion. It takes its name from its central doctrine known as the "Theory of Ideas," a metaphysical conception that is extremely difficult to explain simply and adequately. It has been said that Platonists are born and not made, and Plato himself tells us in his *Seventh Letter* that he was unable to describe his philosophy in ordinary narrative language: "There neither is nor ever will be a treatise of mine on the subject.

For it does not admit of exposition like other branches of knowledge; but after much converse about the matter and a life lived together, suddenly a light, as it were, is kindled in one soul by a flame that leaps to it from another, and thereafter sustains itself." It will be understood and accepted only by "some few who are able with a little teaching to find it out for themselves."

Plato's metaphysical doctrine is founded upon the belief that the things that are seen are temporal, whereas the things that are not seen are eternal. These last are the Platonic Ideas, the universal truths that have an independent existence separate from the world of sense experience. All objects perceived by the senses, whether they be material things like horses and chairs or intangibles like beauty and justice, are all imperfect and transitory manifestations of the only truly real and perfect things, the eternal Ideas. The senses inform us about what is unreal and imperfect, whereas only the reason, identified by Plato with the soul, can grasp what is perfect and eternal. Confronted by these two worlds, the task of humans is to follow the dictates of their reason—or soul—and concern themselves as far as possible with the higher and real world, the world of thought or spirit.

Such, in brief, is the doctrine developed by Plato as his answer to the crisis that confronted his civilization in which the traditional beliefs had been undermined by scientific thought and the material fabric had been rent by war and depression. Its importance for the history of philosophy can be judged by the remark of one scholar that all subsequent philosophy is but a series of footnotes to Plato's writing. But emphasizing the later influence of Platonic theory should not blind us to the fact that Plato was essentially a practical philosopher whose theories were intended both to serve as guideposts along the road whose goal is the good life and to inspire men to create a state in which that life could be lived. The following lines from his *Timaeus* give the essence of Plato's whole view, which integrates both theory and practice, the ideal and the actual:

> God [or the Good, the supreme Idea, the source of all goodness, beauty, and truth] invented and gave us sight to the end that we might behold the courses of intelligence in the heavens and apply them to the courses of our own intelligence which are akin to them, the unperturbed to the perturbed, and that we, learning them and partaking of the natural truth of reason, might imitate the unerring courses of God and regulate our own vagaries.

A. THE THEORY OF IDEAS: THE ALLEGORY OF THE CAVE

Plato frequently employs the language of poetry, using myths, parables, and allegories to transmit to his readers the profound truths of his idealistic philosophy that, to quote again from his *Seventh Letter*, "does not admit of exposition like other branches of knowledge." The most famous and brilliant example of Plato's use of this device is the allegory of the cave from the

From Plato, *Republic*, VII, 514–21 (abridged), translated by Benjamin Jowett.

Republic, his description of an ideal state. Its purpose is to illustrate graphically the importance of moving away from the "shadows" of the world of appearances to the world of eternal nonmaterial realities beyond. This is the realm of the Ideas, the highest of which is the Idea of Good, here compared with the sun. Like the sun, it causes all things to exist, to be visible, and to become intelligible. The passage also contains evidence of Plato's practical side as a moralist and political thinker. He insists that men who have been converted from error to truth—men who are the true philosophers—despite their understandable reluctance must descend again into the cave to serve and enlighten their fellow men. Only when this happens will the state be ruled by the best and most intelligent men. "Until philosophers are kings," writes Plato in another passage in the *Republic*, "or the kings and rulers of this world have the spirit of philosophy, until political power and wisdom are united, until those commoner natures, who pursue either to the exclusion of the other, stand aside, states will never have rest from their evils—no, nor, I believe, will the human race...."

SOCRATES: And now, let me show in a parable how far our nature may be enlightened or unenlightened: Behold! human beings living in an underground den, which has a mouth open toward the light and reaching all along the den; here they have been from their childhood, and have their legs and necks chained so that they cannot move, and can only see before them, being prevented by the chains from turning round their heads. Above and behind them a fire is blazing at a distance, and between the fire and the prisoners there is a raised way; and you will see, if you look, a low wall built along the way, like the screen which marionette players have in front of them, over which they show the puppets. And do you see men passing along the wall carrying all sorts of vessels, and statues and figures of animals made of wood and stone and various materials, which appear over the wall? Some of them are talking, others silent.

GLAUCON: You have shown me a strange image, and they are strange prisoners.

SOC.: Like ourselves, and they see only their own shadows, or the shadows of one another, which the fire throws on the opposite wall of the cave?

GLAU.: True, how could they see anything but the shadows if they were never allowed to move their heads?

SOC.: And of the objects which are being carried in like manner they would only see the shadows. And if they were able to converse with one another, would they not suppose that they were naming what was actually before them?

GLAU.: Very true.

Soc.: And suppose further that the prison had an echo which came from the other side, would they not be sure to fancy when one of the passersby spoke that the voice which they heard came from the passing shadows? To them the truth would be literally nothing but the shadows of the images.

And now look again, and see what will naturally follow if the prisoners are released and disabused of their error. At first, when any of them is liberated and compelled suddenly to stand up and turn his neck round and walk and look toward the light, he will suffer sharp pains; the glare will distress him, and he will be unable to see the realities of which in his former state he had seen the shadows; and then conceive someone saying to him, that what he saw before was an illusion, but that now, when he is approaching nearer to being and his eye is turned toward more real existence, he has a clearer vision—what will be his reply? And you may further imagine that his instructor is pointing to the objects as they pass and requiring him to name them—will he not be perplexed? Will he not fancy that the shadows which he formerly saw are truer than the objects which are now shown him?

And if he is compelled to look straight at the light, will he not have a pain in his eyes which will make him turn away to take refuge in the objects of vision which he can see, and which he will conceive to be in reality clearer than the things which are now being shown to him?

And suppose once more, that he is reluctantly dragged up a steep and rugged ascent, and held fast until he is forced into the presence of the sun himself, is he not likely to be pained and irritated? When he approaches the light his eyes will be dazzled, and he will not be able to see anything at all of what are now called realities. He will require to grow accustomed to the sight of the upper world. And first he will see the shadows best, next the reflections of men and other objects in the water, and then the objects themselves; then he will gaze upon the light of the moon and the stars and the spangled heaven; and he will see the sky and the stars by night better than the sun or the light of the sun by day. Last of all he will be able to see the sun, and not mere reflections of him in the water, but he will see him in his own proper place, and not in another; and he will contemplate him as he is. He will then proceed to argue that this is he who gives the seasons and the years, and is the guardian of all that is in the visible world, and in a certain way the cause of all things which he and his fellows have been accustomed to behold.

And when he remembered his old habitation, and the wisdom of the den and his fellow-prisoners, do you not suppose that he would felicitate himself on the change, and pity them? And if they were in the habit of conferring honors among themselves on those who were quickest to observe the passing shadows and to remark which of them went before, and which followed after, and which were together; and who were therefore best able to draw conclusions as to the future, do you think that he would care for such honors and glories or envy the possessors of them? Would he not say with Homer's Achilles, "Better to be the poor servant of a poor master," and to endure anything, rather than think as they do and live after their manner?

Imagine once more such a one coming suddenly out of the sun to be replaced in his old situation; would he not be certain to have his eyes full of darkness? And if there were a contest, and he had to compete in measuring the shadows with the prisoners who had never moved out of the den, while his sight was still weak, and before his eyes had become steady (and the time which he needed to acquire this new habit of sight might be very considerable), would he not be ridiculous? Men would say of him that up he went and down he came without his eyes; and that it was better not even to think of ascending; and if anyone tried to loose another and lead him up to the light, let them only catch the offender, and they would put him to death.

This entire allegory, you may now append, dear Glaucon, to the previous argument; the prison-house is the world of sight, the light of the fire is the sun, and you will not misapprehend me if you interpret the journey upwards to be the ascent of the soul into the intellectual world according to my poor belief, which, at your desire, I have expressed—whether rightly or wrongly God knows. But, whether true or false, my opinion is that in the world of knowledge the idea of Good appears last of all, and is seen only with great difficulty: and, when seen, is also inferred to be the universal author of all things good and right in this visible world, and the immediate source of reason and truth in the intellectual; and that this is the power upon which he would act with wisdom either in public or private life must have his eye fixed.

GLAU.: I agree, as far as I am able to understand you.

SOC.: Moreover, you must not wonder that those who attain to this beatific vision are unwilling to descend to human affairs; for their souls are ever hastening into the upper world where they desire to dwell; which desire of theirs is very natural, if our allegory may be trusted.

GLAU.: Yes, very natural.

SOC.: Then the business of us who are the founders of the state will be to compel the best minds to attain that knowledge which has been already declared by us to be the greatest of all—they must continue to ascend until they arrive at the good; but when they have ascended and seen enough we must not allow them to do as they do now.

GLAU.: What do you mean?

SOC.: I mean that they remain in the upper world: but this must not be allowed; they must be made to descend again among the prisoners in the den, and partake of their labors and honors, whether they are worth having or not.

GLAU.: But is not this unjust? Ought we to give them an inferior life, when they might have a superior one?

SOC.: You have forgotten, my friend, the intention of the legislator, who did not aim at making any one class in the state happy above the rest; the happiness was to be in the whole state, and he held the citizens together by persuasion or force, making them benefactors of the state, and therefore benefactors of one another; to this end he created philosophers, not that they should please themselves, but they were to be his instruments in binding the community together.

GLAU.: True, I had forgotten.

SOC.: Observe, Glaucon, that there will be no injustice in compelling our philosophers to watch over and care for others; we shall explain to them that in other states, men of their class are not obliged to share in the toils of politics: and this is reasonable, for they grow up at their own sweet will, and the government would rather not have them. Now the wild plant which owes culture to nobody, has nothing to pay for culture. But we have brought you into the world to be rulers of the hive, kings of yourselves and of the other citizens, and have educated you far better and more perfectly than they have been educated, and you are better able to share in the double duty. Wherefore each of you, when his turn comes, must go down to the general underground abode, and get the habit of seeing in the dark; for all is habit; and by accustoming yourselves you will see ten thousand times better than the dwellers in the den, and you will know what the images are, and of what they are images, because you have seen the beautiful and just and good in their truth. And thus the good order of our state, and of yours, will be a reality, and not a dream only, as the order of states too often is, for in most of them men are fighting with one another about shadows and are distracted in the struggle for power, which in their eyes is a great good. Whereas the truth is that the state in which the rulers are most reluctant to govern is best and most quietly governed, and the state in which they are most willing, the worst.

GLAU.: Quite true.

SOC.: And will our pupils, when they hear this, refuse to share in turn the toils of state, when they are allowed to spend the greater part of their time with one another in the heaven of ideas?

GLAU.: Impossible; for they are just men, and the commands which we impose upon them are just; there can be no doubt that every one of them will take office as a stern necessity, and not like our present ministers of state.

SOC.: Yes, my friend, and there lies the point. You must contrive for your future rulers another and a better life than that of a ruler, and then you may have a well-ordered state; for only in the state which offers this, will they rule who are truly rich, not in silver and gold, but in virtue and wisdom, which are the true blessings of life. Whereas if they go to the administration of public affairs, poor and hungering after their own private advantage, thinking that hence they are to snatch the good of life, order there can never be; for they will be fighting about office, and the civil and domestic broils which thus arise will be the ruin of the rulers themselves and of the whole state.

GLAU.: Most true.

B. THE SPIRITUAL LIFE:
DUALISM OF BODY AND SOUL

Through the centuries it has been the mystical rather than the practical side of Plato's thought that has exerted the greatest influence. His poetic tendency to exaggerate the distinction between the two worlds of truth and error at times led him to deny the existence of any reality to the material world. This prepared the way for the mystical otherworldliness and the dualism of soul and body that characterized much of later Greco-Roman thought—especially in the form known as Neoplatonism—and influenced Christianity.

In the following passages from the *Phaedo*, named for the disciple of Socrates who recounts the story of his master's last hours in prison, Socrates is found welcoming death and arguing for the immortality of the soul and the supremacy of the spiritual life. As this differs from the more realistic picture of Socrates portrayed in the *Apology*, where Socrates' chief concern is his right to live, it is generally believed that the views expressed are more Platonic than Socratic. Support for this contention is given by Plato himself, who has *Phaedo* remark that "Plato, if I am not mistaken, was ill" and not present and so unable in this dialogue to give a literal account of what Socrates said.

Phaedo, 66–68, 79, abridged, translated by Benjamin Jowett. From Richard W. Livingstone, ed., *Plato: Selected Passages*, The World's Classics (Oxford: the Clarendon Press, 1940), pp. 41–43.

Have we not found a path of thought which seems to bring us and our argument to the conclusion, that while we are in the body, and while the soul is infected with the evils of the body, our desire will not be satisfied? and our desire is of the truth. For the body is a source of endless trouble to us by reason of the mere requirement of food; and is liable also to diseases which overtake and impede us in the search after reality; it fills us full of loves, and lusts, and fears, and fancies of all kinds, and endless nonsense, and in fact takes away from us the power of thinking at all. Whence come wars, and fighting, and factions, if not from the body and the body's desires? Wars are caused by the love of money, and money has to be acquired for the sake and in the service of the body; and as a result of all these hindrances we have no time to give to philosophy; and, last and worst of all, even if we are at leisure and devote ourselves to some speculation, the body is always breaking in on us, causing turmoil and confusion in our inquiries, and so upsetting us that we are prevented from seeing the truth. Experience has shown us that if we would have pure knowledge of anything we must be quit of the body—the soul in herself must behold things in themselves; and then we shall attain the wisdom which we desire, and of which we say that we are lovers; not while we live, but after death; for if while in company with the body, the soul cannot have pure knowledge, one of two things follows—either knowledge is not to be attained at all, or, if at all, after death. For then, and not till then, the soul will be parted from the body and exist in herself alone.

In this present life, I reckon that we make the nearest approach to knowledge when we have the least possible intercourse or communion with the body, and are not contaminated with the bodily nature, but keep ourselves pure until the hour when God himself is pleased to release us. And so having got rid of the foolishness of the body we shall be pure and hold converse with the pure, and know of ourselves the clear light everywhere, which is no other than the light of truth. If this be true, there is great reason to hope that when I have come to the end of my journey, I shall attain that which has been the pursuit of my life. So I go on my way rejoicing, and not I only, but every other man who believes that his mind is prepared and purified.

True philosophers, Simmias, are always occupied in the practice of dying, and no one finds death so little formidable as they. Look at the matter thus: if they have been in every way at issue with the body, and are wanting to be alone with the soul, when this desire of theirs is granted, how inconsistent would they be if they trembled and repined, instead of rejoicing at their departure to that place where they hope to gain that which in life they desired—and this was wisdom—and at the same time to be rid of the company of their enemy. Many a man has been willing to go to the world below animated by the hope of seeing there an earthly love, or wife, or son, and talking with them. And will a true lover of wisdom, convinced that only in the world below he can worthily enjoin her, still complain of death? Will he not depart with joy? Surely he will, my friend, if he is a true philosopher. For he will have a firm conviction that there, and there only, he can find wisdom in her purity. And if this be true, he would be very absurd, as I was saying, if he were afraid of death....

When the soul uses the body as an instrument of perception, that is to say, when it uses the sense of sight or hearing or some other sense, she is dragged by the body into the region of the changeable, and wanders and is confused; the world spins round her, and she is like a drunkard, when she touches change. But when she contemplates in herself and by herself, then she passes into the other world, the region of purity, and eternity, and immortality, and unchange-ableness, which are her kindred, and with them she ever lives, when she is by herself and is not let or hindered; then she ceases from her erring ways, and being in communion with the unchanging is unchanging. And this state of the soul is called wisdom.

32 Aristotle, *The Nicomachaean Ethics*

"The philosophy of human affairs"

Possessing neither the vivid personality of Socrates nor the vision and imagination of Plato, Aristotle (384–322 B.C.) nevertheless has exerted an equal if not stronger influence upon posterity compared to his two predecessors. A contemporary and teacher of Alexander the Great, he lived at the end of the great period of Greek creative effort and the independent city-state that had nourished the Greek genius. He looked back upon the accomplishments of the past, and in a large number of works—forty-six, about three-quarters of which have survived—he collected, classified, and analyzed the intellectual heritage of Greece and transmitted it to succeeding civilizations. Much of his philosophy was a continuation of that of Plato, differing from his master only in degree and emphasis. He systematized scientifically and logically material that Plato in his dialogues had dealt with only imaginatively and informally. Where Plato poetically described the relationship between the universal Ideas and the transitory world of appearances in a manner that allowed some of his followers to deny the importance of the world of sense impressions, Aristotle insisted that the universal truths, which he called Forms, do not have a separate existence apart from the world of matter. (Only God, or the Unmoved Mover, is pure Form, existing independently of matter.) Form transforms matter by giving it meaning and purpose, pattern and character. The object of inquiry is still the discovery of these Forms, but this can be done only by first observing the objects of sense and then discerning inductively their universal characteristics, or Forms. From this follows Aristotle's characteristic concern with the world of observed phenomena. He has been called a "practical Platonist" because he insisted that "theories must be abandoned unless their teachings tally with the indisputable results of observation."

From Aristotle, *Nicomachean Ethics*, translated by Martin Ostwald (Upper Saddle River, New Jersey: Prentice-Hall, 1962).

Aristotle's extant writings have the merits and the defects of lectures, which they are. They are logical but hard to read and usually uninspired. Yet what they lack in style is compensated for by illuminating generalizations, most of which, especially in his *Ethics* and his *Politics,* are pertinent to our own age. The two works are concerned with an investigation of human character and conduct to discover and establish the good life for humankind. Together they constitute the two halves of what is essentially a single treatise on the subject he called the "philosophy of human affairs." The practical goal of this philosophy is the greatest happiness for the greatest number of people. The *Ethics* discusses the nature of good character, which is the essential ingredient of happiness, whereas the *Politics* describes the political institutions and laws that can best produce the greatest amount of good character and hence the highest degree of happiness. The first work centers its attention on individuals and the virtues that can make them happy; the second looks to the state as a powerful educative agency necessary for the attainment of the greatest amount of human happiness.

A. THE SUBJECT OF *THE NICOMACHAEAN ETHICS*

"The good for man"

Aristotle tells us at the beginning of the *Ethics* that the subject of his inquiry, which must be considered a subdivision of political philosophy, is "the good for man." He rejects Plato's abstract and universal Idea of Good as being too vague and unreal to have practical value, and maintains that there are many "goods." The good for man is a final end or goal that is always chosen for its own sake. This end is happiness.

I, 1. Every art or applied science and every systematic investigation, and similarly every action and choice, seem to aim at some good; the good, therefore, has been well defined as that at which all things aim....

Since there are many activities, arts, and sciences, the number of ends is correspondingly large: of medicine the end is health, of shipbuilding a vessel, of strategy, victory, and of household management, wealth. In many instances several such pursuits are grouped together under a single capacity: the art of bridle-making, for example, and everything else pertaining to the equipment of a horse are grouped together under horsemanship; horsemanship in turn, along with every other military action, is grouped together under strategy; and other pursuits are grouped together under other capacities. In all these cases the ends of the master sciences are preferable to the ends of the subordinate sciences, since the latter are pursued for the sake of the former. This is true whether the ends of the actions lie in the activities themselves or, as is the case in the disciplines just mentioned, in something beyond the activities.

2. Now, if there exists an end in the realm of action which we desire for its own sake, an end which determines all our other desires, ... then obviously this

end will be the good, that is, the highest good. Will not the knowledge of this good, consequently, be very important to our lives? Would it not better equip us, like archers who have a target to aim at, to hit the proper mark? If so, we must try to comprehend in outline at least what this good is and to which branch of knowledge or to which capacity it belongs.

This good, one should think, belongs to the most sovereign and most comprehensive master science, and politics clearly fits this description. For it determines which sciences ought to exist in states, what kind of sciences each group of citizens must learn, and what degree of proficiency each must attain. We observe further that the most honored capacities, such as strategy, household management, and oratory, are contained in politics. Since this science uses the rest of the sciences, and since, moreover, it legislates what people are to do and what they are not to do, its end seems to embrace the ends of the other sciences. Thus it follows that the end of politics is the good for man. For even if the good is the same for the individual and the state, the good of the state clearly is the greater and more perfect thing to attain and to safeguard. The attainment of the good for one man alone is, to be sure, a source of satisfaction; yet to secure it for a nation and for states is nobler and more divine. In short, these are the aims of our investigation, which is in a sense an investigation of social and political matters....

4. To resume the discussion: since all knowledge and every choice is directed toward some good, let us discuss what is in our view the aim of politics, i.e., the highest good attainable by action. As far as its name is concerned, most people would probably agree: for both the common run of people and cultivated men call it happiness, and understand by "being happy" the same as "living well" and "doing well." But when it comes to defining what happiness is, they disagree, and the account given by the common run differs from that of the philosophers. The former say it is some clear and obvious good, such as pleasure, wealth, or honor; some say it is one thing and others another, and often the very same person identifies it with different things at different times: when he is sick he thinks it is health, and when he is poor he says it is wealth; and when people are conscious of their own ignorance, they admire those who talk above their heads in accents of greatness. Some thinkers [Plato and his followers] used to believe that there exists over and above these many goods another good, good in itself and by itself, which also is the cause of good in all these things. An examination of all the different opinions would perhaps be a little pointless....

7. Let us return again to our investigation into the nature of the good which we are seeking. It is evidently something different in different actions and in each art: it is one thing in medicine, another in strategy, and another again in each of the other arts. What, then, is the good of each? Is it not that for the sake of which everything else is done? That means it is health in the case of medicine, victory in the case of strategy, a house in the case of building, a different thing in the case of different arts, and in all actions and choices it is the end. For it is for the sake of the end that all else is done. Thus, if there is some one end for all that

we do, this would be the good attainable by action; if there are several ends, they will be the goods attainable by action.

Our argument has gradually progressed to the same point at which we were before, and we must try to clarify it still further. Since there are evidently several ends, and since we choose some of these—e.g., wealth, flutes, and instruments generally—as a means to something else, it is obvious that not all ends are final. The highest good, on the other hand, must be something final. Thus, if there is only one final end, this will be the good we are seeking; if there are several, it will be the most final and perfect of them. We call that which is pursued as an end in itself more final than an end which is pursued for the sake of something else; and what is never chosen as a means to something else we call more final than that which is chosen both as an end in itself and as a means to something else. What is always chosen as an end in itself and never as a means to something else is called final in an unqualified sense. This description seems to apply to happiness above all else: for we always choose happiness as an end in itself and never for the sake of something else. Honor, pleasure, intelligence, and all virtue we choose partly for themselves—for we would choose each of them even if no further advantage would accrue from them—but we also choose them partly for the sake of happiness, because we assume that it is through them that we will be happy. On the other hand, no one chooses happiness for the sake of honor, pleasure, and the like, nor as a means to anything at all.

B. THE DEFINITION OF HAPPINESS

The good for man can only be found by observing man's function. The proper and distinctive function of human beings is the exercise of reason, and this alone can produce happiness. Since the seat of reason is in the rational part of the soul, human good or happiness can be defined as "an activity of the soul in conformity with excellence or virtue." In other words, the good or happy person is one whose life is guided by the dictates of reason.

I, 7. To call happiness the highest good is perhaps a little trite, and a clearer account of what it is, is still required. Perhaps this is best done by first ascertaining the proper function of man. For just as the goodness and performance of a flute player, a sculptor, or any kind of expert, and generally of anyone who fulfills some function or performs some action, are thought to reside in his proper function, so the goodness and performance of man would seem to reside in whatever is his proper function. Is it then possible that while a carpenter and a shoemaker have their own proper functions and spheres of action, man as man has none, but was left by nature a good-for-nothing without a function? Should we not assume that just as the eye, the hand, the foot, and in general each part of the body clearly has its own proper function, so man too has some function over and above the function of his parts? What can this function possibly be? Simply living? He shares that even with plants, but we are now looking for something peculiar to man. Accordingly, the life of nutrition and growth must be excluded.

Next in line there is a life of sense perception. But this, too, man has in common with the horse, the ox, and every animal. There remains then an active life of the rational element. The rational element has two parts: one is rational in that it obeys the rule of reason, the other in that it possesses and conceives rational rules....

The proper function of man, then, consists in an activity of the soul in conformity with a rational principle or, at least, not without it. In speaking of the proper function of a given individual we mean that it is the same in kind as the function of an individual who sets high standards for himself: the proper function of a harpist, for example, is the same as the function of a harpist who has set high standards for himself. The same applies to any and every group of individuals: the full attainment of excellence must be added to the mere function. In other words, the function of the harpist is to play the harp; the function of the harpist who has high standards is to play it well. On these assumptions, if we take the proper function of man to be a certain kind of life, and if this kind of life is an activity of the soul and consists in actions performed in conjunction with the rational element, and if a man of high standards is he who performs these actions well and properly, and if a function is well performed when it is performed in accordance with the excellence appropriate to it; we reach the conclusion that the good of man is an activity of the soul in conformity with excellence or virtue, and if there are several virtues, in conformity with the best and most complete.

But we must add "in a complete life." For one swallow does not make a spring, nor does one sunny day; similarly, one day or a short time does not make a man blessed and happy.

C. INTELLECTUAL AND MORAL VIRTUE

Human excellence or virtue (*aretē*) is not of the body but of the soul, and the soul has two parts, the rational and the irrational. Intellectual virtues, such as wisdom and intelligence, are those of the rational part of the soul, which alone possesses reason and has its perfection in the contemplative life. Moral virtues, such as justice and temperance, stem from that part of the irrational side of the soul that is emotional but not vegetative, that does not possess or understand reason but is capable of obedience to reason. This side of the soul has its perfection in the moral life. Intellectual virtue originates in and is fostered by teaching, whereas moral virtue is created by habit.

The chief concern of the *Ethics* is with moral rather than intellectual virtue, for Aristotle desires to provide for the majority of citizens a practical guide to the happiness to be found in the world of everyday activity. Moral virtue is described in terms of what we would call character. Good character is produced, as has been seen, through the habitual performance of right acts until the power of doing them freely and willingly becomes second nature. But what are right acts? Here Aristotle brings in his famous doctrine of the mean as the rational principle that can and should guide people in determining those acts whose habitual practice will produce moral virtue and thus happiness. Acts are right and virtuous when they are means or "medians" lying between two extremes. This is the old Greek doctrine of moderation, or "nothing too much," and it illustrates how moral virtue, though not possessing reason, is nevertheless obedient to reason without which it would be blind. It is, in Aristotle's words, "defined by a rational principle, such as a man of practical wisdom would use to determine it." Thus bravery, for example, is the rational mean between the two extreme emotions of rashness and cowardice.

To achieve happiness, people must practice those moral virtues that are acquired when the emotional and impulsive functioning of the irrational part of the soul is guided by the rational principle of the Golden Mean. But those whose reason is thus only indirectly and partially employed with the practical and moral concerns of life fall short of complete happiness. The rational part of the soul, as distinct from the irrational part, is the seat of reason, whose speculative activity is the highest faculty of man's nature. Only this pure reason can contemplate the eternal truths found in philosophy, science, art, and theology, and concern with such truths gives the person who is capable of such activity the greatest pleasure and happiness. As Aristotle states elsewhere, "It is only in a secondary sense that the life that accords with other [moral] virtue can be said to be happy; for the activities of such virtue are human, they have no divine [that is, eternal] element." This section of the *Ethics* reflects the strong influence of Plato, and yet even while praising the life of thought as the ideal life, Aristotle still keeps his feet on the ground and insists that contemplative happiness also requires a certain amount of material goods.

I, 13. Since happiness is a certain activity of the soul in conformity with perfect virtue, we must now examine what virtue or excellence is. For such an inquiry will perhaps better enable us to discover the nature of happiness. Moreover, the man who is truly concerned about politics seems to devote special attention to excellence, since it is his aim to make the citizens good and law-abiding. We have an example of this in the lawgivers of Crete and Sparta and in other great legislators. If an examination of virtue is part of politics, this question clearly fits into the pattern of our original plan.

There can be no doubt that the virtue which we have to study is human virtue. For the good which we have been seeking is a human good and the happiness a human happiness. By human virtue we do not mean the excellence of the body, but that of the soul, and we define happiness as an activity of the soul....

Some things that are said about the soul in our less technical discussions are adequate enough to be used here; for instance, that the soul consists of two elements, one irrational and one rational....

Of the irrational element, again, one part seems to be common to all living things and vegetative in nature: I mean that part which is responsible for nurture and growth. We must assume that some such capacity of the soul exists in everything that takes nourishment, in the embryonic stage as well as when the organism is fully developed; for this makes more sense than to assume the existence of some different capacity at the latter stage. The excellence of this part of the soul is, therefore, shown to be common to all living things and is not exclusively human.... But enough of this subject: we may pass by the nutritive part, since it has no natural share in human excellence or virtue.

In addition to this, there seems to be another integral element of the soul which, though irrational, still does partake of reason in some way.... at any rate, in a morally strong man it accepts the leadership of reason, and is perhaps more obedient still in a self-controlled and courageous man, since in him everything is in harmony with the voice of reason.

Thus we see that the irrational element of the soul has two parts: the one is vegetative and has no share in reason at all, the other is the seat of the appetites and of desire in general and partakes of reason insofar as it complies with reason and accepts its leadership; it possesses reason in the sense that we say it is "reasonable" to accept the advice of a father and of friends, not in the sense that we have a "rational" understanding of mathematical propositions. That the irrational element can be persuaded by the rational is shown by the fact that admonition and all manner of rebuke and exhortation are possible. If it is correct to say that the appetitive part, too, has reason, it follows that the rational element of the soul has two subdivisions: the one possesses reason in the strict sense, contained within itself, and the other possesses reason in the sense that it listens to reason as one would listen to a father.

Virtue, too, is differentiated in line with this division of the soul. We call some virtues "intellectual" and others "moral": theoretical wisdom, understanding, and practical wisdom are intellectual virtues, generosity and self-control moral virtues. In speaking of a man's character, we do not describe him as wise or understanding, but as gentle or self-controlled; but we praise the wise man, too, for his characteristics, and praiseworthy characteristics are what we call virtues....

X, 7. Now, if happiness is activity in conformity with virtue, it is to be expected that it should conform with the highest virtue, and that is the virtue of the best part of us.... That it is an activity concerned with theoretical knowledge or contemplation has already been stated.

This would seem to be consistent with our earlier statements as well as the truth. For this activity is not only the highest—for intelligence is the highest possession we have in us, and the objects which are the concern of intelligence are the highest objects of knowledge—but also the most continuous: we are able to study continuously more easily than to perform any kind of action. Furthermore, we think of pleasure as a necessary ingredient in happiness. Now everyone agrees that of all the activities that conform with virtue activity in conformity with theoretical wisdom is the most pleasant. At any rate, it seems that (the pursuit of wisdom or) philosophy holds pleasures marvelous in purity and certainty, and it is not surprising that time spent in knowledge is more pleasant than time spent in research. Moreover, what is usually called "self-sufficiency" will be found in the highest degree in the activity which is concerned with theoretical knowledge. Like a just man and any other virtuous man, a wise man requires the necessities of life; once these have been adequately provided, a just man still needs people toward whom and in company with whom to act justly, and the same is true of a self-controlled man, a courageous man, and all the rest. But a wise man is able to study even by himself, and the wiser he is the more is he able to do it. Perhaps he could do it better if he had colleagues to work with him, but he still is the most self-sufficient of all. Again, study seems to be the only activity which is loved for its own sake.... it follows that the activity of our intelligence constitutes the complete happiness of man, provided that it encompasses a complete span of life; for nothing connected with happiness must be incomplete.

33 Aristotle, *The Politics*

"A state exists for the sake of the good life."

It is often stated that Aristotle in his *Politics* was blind to the political facts of life in his day because he ignored the imperial state of the future that Philip and Alexander of Macedon were creating and dealt only with the political life of the small city-states whose independent existence was largely over. But this view ignores the fact that the *Politics* was meant to be a continuation of the *Ethics,* that the purpose of the state is to promote and maintain the well-being of its citizens and that this "good and honorable life" would seem to him to be impossible of achievement in a huge and heterogeneous empire in which people could not act as free citizens participating in a shared life. Yet what Aristotle writes in the *Politics* remains an excellent summary and interpretation of Greek political experience, and most of its penetrating generalizations on political and social behavior remain valid and illuminating today.

The eight books of the *Politics* fall into two main divisions to which Book I serves as an introduction. In Books II, III, VII, and VIII, Aristotle gives evidence of the influence of Plato as he describes the characteristics of an ideal state, but in books thought to have been written last (IV, V, VI), he puts aside considerations of an ideal commonwealth and more realistically deals with practical matters relating to the nature and stability of the existing Greek states of his day. The conclusions reached in this second part of his treatise were supported by the multitude of facts gleaned from his analysis of the constitutions of one hundred and fifty-eight Greek states.

A. NATURE, ORIGIN, AND PURPOSE OF THE STATE

In Book I, Aristotle indicates the relationship of the *Politics* to the *Ethics* by insisting upon the necessary connection between the state and the individual's goal of a virtuous and happy life. The state is not an artificial creation, as the sophists argued, but is the natural culmination of earlier and simpler forms of

From *The Politics of Aristotle,* translated by Benjamin Jowett, edited by H. W. C. Davis (Oxford: Oxford University Press, 1905).

society, the family and the village, which people naturally and instinctively create to satisfy their immediate and elementary wants. But a life of moral virtue and happiness, the highest of their wants, can only be provided by the final manifestation of the "social instinct ... implanted in all men by nature," namely, the state. So "the state comes into existence, originating in the bare needs of life, and continuing in existence for the sake of the good life." The modern concept of man versus the state would be unthinkable to Aristotle, for "man is by nature a political animal" who can realize his highest ideals only as a member of society.

I, 1. Every state is a community of some kind, and every community is established with a view to some good; for mankind always act in order to obtain that which they think good. But, if all communities aim at some good, the state or political community, which is the highest of all, and which embraces all the rest, aims, and in greater degree than any other, at the highest good....

Governments differ in kind, as will be evident to anyone who considers the matter according to the method which has hitherto guided us. As in other departments of science, so in politics, the compound should always be resolved into the simple elements or least parts of the whole. We must therefore look at the elements of which the state is composed, in order that we may see in what they differ from one another, and whether any scientific distinction can be drawn between the different kinds of rule.

2. He who thus considers things in their first growth and origin, whether a state or anything else, will obtain the clearest view of them. In the first place (1) there must be a union of those who cannot exist without each other; for example, of male and female, that the race may continue; and this is a union which is formed, not of deliberate purpose, but because, in common with other animals and with plants, mankind have a natural desire to leave behind them an image of themselves. And (2) there must be a union of natural ruler and subject, that both may be preserved. For he who can foresee with his mind is by nature intended to be lord and master, and he who can work with his body is a subject, and by nature a slave; hence master and slave have the same interest. Nature, however, has distinguished between the female and the slave. For she is not niggardly, like the smith who fashions the Delphian knife for many uses; she makes each thing for a single use, and every instrument is best made when intended for one and not for many uses. But among barbarians no distinction is made between women and slaves, because there is no natural ruler among them: they are a community of slaves, male and female. Wherefore the poets say, "It is meet that Hellenes should rule over barbarians"; as if they thought that the barbarian and the slave were by nature one.

Out of these two relationships, between man and woman, master and slave, the family first arises, and Hesiod is right when he says "First house and wife and an ox for the plow," for the ox is the poor man's slave. The family is the association established by nature for the supply of men's everyday wants.... But when several families are united, and the association aims at something more than the supply of daily needs, then comes into existence the village. And the most natural form of a village seems to be that of a colony from the family, composed of the children and grandchildren, who are said to be "suckled with the same milk." And this is the reason why Greek states were originally governed by kings; because the Greeks were under royal rule before they came together, as the barbarians still are.... Wherefore men say that the Gods have a king, because they themselves either are or were in ancient times under the rule of a king. For they imagine, not only the forms of the Gods, but their ways of life to be like their own.

When several villages are united in a single community, perfect and large enough to be nearly or quite self-sufficing, the state comes into existence, originating in the bare needs of life, and continuing in existence for the sake of a good life. And therefore, if the earlier forms of society are natural, so is the state, for it is the end of them, and the completed nature is the end. For what each thing is when fully developed, we call its nature, whether we are speaking of a man, a horse, or a family. Besides, the final cause and end of the thing is the best, and to be self-sufficing is the end and the best.

Hence it is evident that the state is a creation of nature, and that man is by nature a political animal. And he who by nature and not by mere accident is without a state is either above humanity or below it; he is the "tribeless, lawless, heartless one," whom Homer denounces—the outcast who is a lover of war; he may be compared to a bird which flies alone....

Thus the state is by nature clearly prior to the family and to the individual, since the whole is of necessity prior to the part; for example, if the whole body be destroyed, there will be no foot or hand, except in an equivocal sense, as we might speak of a stone hand; for when destroyed the hand will be no better than that. But things are defined by their working and power; and we ought not to say that they are the same when they are no longer the same, but only that they have the same name. The proof that the state is a creation of nature and prior to the individual is that the individual, when isolated, is not self-sufficing; and therefore he is like a part in relation to the whole. But he who is unable to live in society, or who has no need because he is sufficient for himself, must be either a beast or a god; he is not part of a state.

A social instinct is implanted in all men by nature, and he who first founded the state was the greatest of benefactors. For man, when perfected, is the best of animals, but when separated from law and justice, he is the worst of all; since armed injustice is the more dangerous, and he is equipped at birth with the arms of intelligence and with moral qualities which he may use for the worst ends. Wherefore, if he have not virtue, he is the most unholy and the most savage of animals, and most full of lust and gluttony. But justice is the bond of men in states, and the administration of justice, which is the determination of what is just, is the principle of order in political society.

B. GOOD AND BAD CONSTITUTIONS

Aristotle's classification of governments has remained standard for nearly 2,500 years. His division into six types is based upon his study of Greek political experience, while his criterion for distinguishing between good and bad governments is derived from his views on the nature and purpose of the state. The true end of the state is well-being and happiness, and this is the common interest. Good governments are devoted to the common interest, while bad or "perverted" governments place the selfish interest of a ruling class above "the common good of all."

III, 6. ... We have next to consider whether there is only one form of government or many; and if many, what they are, and how many; and what are the differences between them.

A constitution is the arrangement of powers in a state, especially of the supreme power, and the constitution is the government. For example, in democracies the people are supreme, but in oligarchies, the few; therefore, we say that the two constitutions are different; and so in other cases.

First let us consider what is the purpose of a state and how many forms of government there are by which human society is regulated. We have already said, earlier in this treatise, when drawing a distinction between household management and the rule of a governor, that man is by nature a political animal. And therefore men, even when they do not require one another's help, desire to live together all the same, and are in fact brought together by their common interests in proportion as they severally attain to any measure of well-being. Well-being is certainly the chief end of individuals and of states....

The conclusion is evident: governments which have a regard to the common interest are constituted in accordance with strict principles of justice, and are therefore true forms; but those which regard only the interest of the rulers are all defective and perverted forms. For they are despotic, whereas a state is a community of free men.

7. Having determined these points, we have next to consider how many forms of constitution there are, and what they are; and in the first place what are the true forms, for when they are determined the perversions of them will at once be apparent. The words constitution and government have the same meaning; and the government, which is the supreme authority in states, is necessarily in the hands either of one, or of a few, or of many. The true forms of government, therefore, are those in which the one, or the few, or the many, govern with a view to the common interest; but governments which rule with a view to the private interest, whether of the one, or of the few, or of the many, are perversions. For citizens, if they are truly citizens, ought all to participate in the advantages of a state. We call that form of government in which one rules, and which regards the common interest, kingship or royalty; that in which more than one, but not many, rule, aristocracy. It is so called, either because the rulers are the best men, or because they have at heart the best interest of the state and of the citizens. But when the citizens at large administer the state for the common interest, the government is called by the generic name—constitutional government. And there is a reason for this use of language. One man or a few may excel in virtue; but of virtue there are many kinds. As the number of rulers increases it becomes more difficult for them to attain perfection in every kind, though they may in military virtue, for this is found in the masses. Hence, in a constitutional government the fighting men have the supreme power, and those who possess arms are citizens.

Of the above-mentioned forms, the perversions are as follows: of royalty, tyranny; of aristocracy, oligarchy; of constitutional government, democracy. For tyranny is a kind of monarchy which has in view the interest of the monarch only; oligarchy has in view the interest of the wealthy; democracy, of the needy; none of them the common good of all.

C. THE IDEAL STATE: ITS TRUE OBJECT

The true object of the state is neither trade nor empire nor the prevention of crime nor anything but the good life. By "state" Aristotle does not mean "country," but "government" or "constitution," and the best states are those in which the rulers are best fitted by their possession of virtue to rule "in such a manner as to attain the most desirable life." Whether this is to be the rule of one (kingship), or few (aristocracy), or many (constitutionalism) depends upon the nature and temperament of the people. In any case, in an ideal state the laboring and business classes will not be citizens, for "the virtue of a good man is necessarily the same as the virtue of a citizen in a perfect state," and these classes have not the "leisure necessary both for the development of virtue and the performance of political duties."

III, 9. ... But a state exists for the sake of a good life, and not for the sake of life only. If life only were the object, slaves and brute animals might form a state, but they cannot, for they have no share in happiness or in a life of free choice. Nor does a state exist merely for the sake of alliance and security from injustice, nor yet for the sake of trade and mutual intercourse; for then the Tyrrhenians and the Carthaginians, and all who have commercial treaties with one another, would be citizens of one state.... Those who care for good government take into consideration the larger questions of virtue and vice in states. Whence it may be further inferred that virtue must be the serious care of a state which truly deserves the name. Otherwise the community becomes a mere alliance, which differs only in place from alliances of which the members live apart. And law is only a convention, "a surety to one another of justice," as the sophist Lycophron says, and has no real power to make the citizens good and just....

Clearly then a state is not a mere society, having a common place, established for the prevention of crime and for the sake of trade. These are conditions without which a state cannot exist; but all of them together do not constitute a state, which is a community of families and aggregations of families in well-being for the sake of a perfect and self-sufficing life. Such a community can only be established among those who live in the same place and intermarry. Hence arise in states family connections, brotherhoods, common sacrifices, amusements which draw men together. They are created by friendship, for friendship is the motive of society. The end is the good life, and these are the means towards it. And the state is the union of families and villages having for an end a perfect and self-sufficing life, by which we mean a happy and honorable life.

Our conclusion, then, is that political society exists for the sake of noble actions, and not of mere companionship. And they who contribute most to such a society have a greater share in it than those who have the same or a greater freedom or nobility of birth but are inferior to them in political virtue; or than those who exceed them in wealth but are surpassed by them in virtue....

18. We maintain that the true forms of government are three, and that the best must be that which is administered by the best, and in which there is one man, or a whole family, or many persons, excelling in virtue, and both rulers and subjects are fitted, the one to rule, the others to be ruled, in such a manner as to attain the most eligible life. We showed at the commencement of our inquiry that the virtue of the good man is necessarily the same as the virtue of the citizen of the perfect state. Clearly then in the same manner, and by the same means through which a man becomes truly good, he will frame a state which will be truly good whether aristocratical, or under kingly rule, and the same education and the same habits will be found to make a good man a good statesman and king....

VIII, 9. ... Now, since we are here speaking of the best form of government, and that under which the state will be most happy (and happiness, as has been already said, cannot exist without virtue), it clearly follows that in the state which is best governed the citizens who are absolutely and not merely relatively just men must not lead the life of mechanics or tradesmen, for such a life is ignoble and inimical to virtue. Neither must they be husbandmen, since leisure is necessary both for the development of virtue and the performance of political duties.

D. THE IDEAL STATE: EDUCATION

Like so much in Aristotle's writings, his discussion of the central importance of public education is pertinent to our modern civilization where state versus private education has long been a subject of controversy. He also distinguishes between liberal education (he was the first to use the term) and vocational education, and his arguments in favor of the former stem from his all-pervading desire to provide the good life for everyone. It should be noted that what Aristotle terms "music" includes all the arts and literature, or what we today call the "humanities."

VIII, 1. No one will doubt that a lawgiver should direct his attention above all to the education of youth, or that the neglect of education does harm to states. The citizen should be molded to suit the form of government under which he lives. For each government has a peculiar character, which originally formed and which continues to preserve it. The character of democracy creates democracy, and the character of oligarchy creates oligarchy. The better the character, always the better the government.

Now for the exercise of any faculty or art a previous training and practice are required; clearly then they are required for the exercise of virtue. And since the entire state has one end, manifestly education should be one and the same for all, and should be public and not private. It should not be as at present, when everyone looks after his own children separately, and gives them separate instruction of the sort he thinks best. The training in things of common interest should be the same for all. Neither must we suppose that any one of the citizens belongs to himself, for they all belong to the state, and are each of them a part of the state, and the care of each part is inseparable from the care of the whole. In this particular the Spartans are to be praised, for they take the greatest pains about their children, and make education the business of the state.

2. That education should be regulated by law and should be an affair of state is not to be denied; but what should be the character of this public education, and how young persons should be educated, are questions yet to be considered. For men are by no means agreed about the things to be taught, whether we aim at virtue or the best life. Neither is it clear whether education should be more concerned with intellectual or with moral virtue. Existing practice is perplexing; no one knows on what principle we should proceed. Should the useful in life, or should virtue, or should higher knowledge, be the aim of our training? All three opinions have been entertained. Again, about method there is no agreement; for different persons, starting with different ideas about the nature of virtue, naturally disagree about the practice of it.

Undoubtedly children should be taught those useful things that are really necessary, but not all useful things. For occupations are divided into liberal and illiberal, and to young children should be imparted only such kinds of knowledge as will be useful to them without vulgarizing them. Any occupation, art, or science, which makes the body or soul or mind of the free man less fit for the practice or exercise of virtue, is vulgar. Therefore we call those arts vulgar which tend to deform the body, and likewise all paid employments; they absorb and degrade the mind....

3. The customary branches of an education are four, namely, (1) reading and writing, (2) gymnastic exercises, (3) music, to which is sometimes added (4) drawing. Of these, reading, writing, and drawing are regarded as useful for the purposes of life in a variety of ways, and gymnastic exercises are thought to infuse courage. As to music a question may be raised. In our own day most men cultivate it for pleasure, but originally it was included in education because nature herself, as has been often said, requires that we should be able, not only to work well, but to use our leisure well. For, as I must repeat once again, the prime end of all action is leisure. Both are necessary, but leisure is better than labor.

Hence now the question must be asked in good earnest, what ought we to do when at leisure? Clearly we ought not to be always amusing ourselves, for then amusement would be the end of life....

Apparently then there are branches of learning and education which we should study solely with a view to the enjoyment of leisure, and these are to be valued for their own sake; whereas the kinds of knowledge which are useful in business are necessary, and exist for the sake of other things. Therefore our fathers admitted music into education, not on the ground of either its necessity or its utility; for it is not necessary, nor even useful in the same way that reading and writing are useful in wealth getting, in the management of a household, in the acquisition of knowledge, and in political life. Nor is it, like drawing, useful for a more correct judgment of the works of artists, nor again, like gymnastics, does it give health and strength, for neither of these is to be gained from music. There is, however, a use of music for intellectual enjoyment in leisure, which seems indeed to have been the reason of its introduction into education. For music is one of the ways in which, it is thought, a freeman might pass his leisure....

Evidently, then, there is a sort of education in which parents should train their sons, not because it is useful or necessary, but because it is liberal or noble.

E. THE PRACTICABLE STATE: THE BEST CONSTITUTION

In that part of his *Politics* which Aristotle seems to have written last (Books IV, V, VI), he turns from a discussion of the ideal state to deal realistically with the subject of practicable constitutions for existing states. "For the best is often unobtainable, and therefore the true lawmaker or statesmen ought to be acquainted ... with that which is best considering the circumstances." In keeping with his doctrine of the Golden Mean, he defines the best such constitution as one that combines the best features of democracy and oligarchy and rests upon the social foundation of a large middle class. This represents the practicable form of that ideal type of state that Aristotle had called "constitutional government," and is often called today a "republic" as distinct from a "democracy" by those who share Aristotle's fear of the excesses of democracy.

IV, 11. We have now to inquire what is the best constitution for most states, and the best life for most men, neither assuming a standard of virtue which is above ordinary persons, nor an education which is exceptionally favored by nature and circumstances, nor yet an ideal state which is an inspiration only, but having regard to the life in which the majority are able to share, and to the form of government which states in general can attain.... If it was truly said in the Ethics that the happy life is the life according to unimpeded virtue and that virtue is a mean, then the life which is a mean and a mean attainable by everyone must be best. And the same criteria of virtue and vice are characteristic of cities and of constitutions; for the constitution is in pattern the life of the city.

Now in all states there are three elements; one class is very rich, another very poor, and a third in the mean. It is admitted that moderation and the mean are best, and therefore it will clearly be best to possess the gifts of fortune in moderation; for in that condition of life men are most ready to listen to reason.... Those who have too much of the goods of fortune, strength, wealth, friends, and the like, are neither willing nor able to submit to authority. The evil begins at home; for when they are boys, by reason of the luxury in which they are brought up, they never learn, even at school, the habit of obedience. On the other hand, the very poor, who are in the opposite extreme, are too degraded. So that the one class cannot obey, and can only rule despotically; the other knows not how to command and must be ruled like slaves. Thus arises a city, not of freemen, but of masters and slaves, the one despising, the other envying. Nothing can be more fatal to friendship and good fellowship in states than this; for good fellowship starts from friendship. When men are at enmity with one another, they would rather not even share the same path.

But a city ought to be composed, as far as possible, of equals and similars; and these are generally the middle classes. Wherefore a city which is composed of middle-class citizens is necessarily best constituted with respect to what we call the natural elements of a state. And this class of citizens is most secure in a state, for they do not, like the poor, covet their neighbors' goods; nor do others covet theirs, as the poor covet the goods of the rich. And as they neither plot against others nor are themselves plotted against, they pass through life safely....

Thus it is manifest that the best political community is formed by citizens of the middle class, and that those states are likely to be well administered in which the middle class is large, and if possible larger than both the other classes, or at any rate than either singly, for the addition of the middle class turns the scale and prevents either of the extremes from being dominant. Great then is the good fortune of a state in which the citizens have a moderate and sufficient property. For where some possess much and the rest nothing, there may arise an extreme democracy, or a pure oligarchy; or a tyranny may grow out of either extreme— out of either the most rampant democracy or out of an oligarchy. But it is not so likely to arise out of a middle and nearly equal condition. I will explain the reason for this hereafter when I speak of revolutions in states....

Democracies are safer and more permanent than oligarchies, because they have a middle class which is more numerous and has a greater share in the government. For when there is no middle class and the poor greatly exceed in number, troubles arise and the state soon comes to an end. A proof of the superiority of the middle class is that the best legislators have been of a middle rank; for example, Solon, as his own verses testify, and Lycurgus, for he was not a king....

What then is the best form of government, and what makes it the best is evident. Of other states, since we say there are many kinds of democracy and oligarchy, it is not difficult to see which has the first and which the second or any other place in the order of excellence, now that we have determined which is best. For that which is nearest to the best must of necessity be the better, and that which is furthest from it the worse, if we are judging absolutely and not with reference to given conditions. I say "with reference to given conditions," since a particular government may be preferable for some, but another form may be better for others.

F. THE PRACTICABLE STATE: CAUSES OF REVOLUTION

Aristotle seems to feel that even the best practicable constitution, described above, was too visionary for the Greeks of his day whose governments were actually examples of the worst types of constitutions, either turbulent democracies or selfish oligarchies. He therefore turns his attention to these bad or "perverted" constitutions and realistically describes methods for making them more stable and, equally important, less liable of degenerating further. He turns first to analyze the nature of the danger that constantly threatened the governments of his day—revolution. His account of the causes of revolutions, particularly in democracies, has particular relevance for us today.

V, 1. The design which we proposed to ourselves is now nearly completed. Next in order follow the causes of revolutions in states, how many they are, and what is their nature; what elements work ruin in particular states, and out of what and into what they mostly change; also what methods there are of preserving states generally, or a particular state, and by what means each state may be best preserved: these questions remain to be considered....

2. In considering how dissensions and political revolutions arise, we must first of all ascertain the beginnings and causes of them which affect constitutions generally. They may be said to be three in number; and we have now to give an outline of each. We want to know (1) what is the feeling and (2) what are the motives of those who make them and (3) what causes political disturbances and quarrels. The universal and chief cause of revolutionary feeling has already been mentioned; namely, either the desire for equality, when men think that they are equal to others who have more than themselves; or, the desire for inequality and superiority, when they believe themselves superior and think they have not more but the same or less than their inferiors, pretensions which may or may not be just. Inferiors revolt in order that they may be equal, and equals that they may be superior. Such is the state of mind which creates revolutions.

The motives for making them are the desire for gain and for honor, or the fear of dishonor and loss. The authors of them want to divert punishment or dishonor from themselves or their friends.... Other causes are insolence, fear, love of superiority, contempt, disproportionate increase in some part of the state. Causes of another sort are election intrigues, carelessness, neglect about trifles, dissimilarity of elements....

4. In revolutions the occasions may be trifling, but great interests are at stake.... Revolutions are accomplished in two ways, by force and by fraud. Force may be applied either at the time of making the revolution or afterwards. Fraud, again, is of two kinds; for (1) sometimes the citizens are deceived into accepting a change of government, and afterwards held in subjection against their will.... (2) In other cases the people are persuaded at first, and afterwards, by a repetition of the persuasion, their good will and allegiance are still retained....

5. ... Revolutions in democracies are often caused by the intemperance of demagogues, who either in a private capacity report information against rich men until they compel them to combine (for a common danger unites even the bitterest enemies), or else come forward in public and stir up the people against them. The truth of this remark is proved by a variety of examples. At Cos the democracy was overthrown because wicked demagogues arose and the nobles combined.... Much in the same manner the democracy at Megara was overturned. There the demagogues drove out many of the nobles in order that they

might be able to confiscate their property. At length the exiles, becoming numerous, returned, engaged and defeated the people, and established an oligarchy....

Of old, the demagogue was also a general, and then democracies changed into tyrannies. Most of the ancient tyrants were originally demagogues. They are not so now, but they were then; and the reason is that they were generals and not orators, for oratory had not yet come into fashion. Whereas in our day, when the art of rhetoric has made such progress, orators lead the people.... These are the principal causes of revolutions in democracies.

G. THE PRACTICABLE STATE: PRESERVING CONSTITUTIONS

How to preserve existing constitutions from revolution, and even how to cure them of their defects and make them more workable, is the last task that Aristotle sets for himself in the *Politics*. His views on the preservation of democracy are drawn from his observation of Greek politics, and their evident applicability to our present world indicates how fundamentally similar were the political developments of these specific periods in the history of the two civilizations. At the end, Aristotle returns again to the importance of education. He insists that in a democracy it is fatal to educate people to believe in an extreme and hence "false idea of freedom," which leads men to "think it slavery to live by the rules of the constitution." Respect for law is the fundamental safeguard of any constitution.

V, 8. We have next to consider what means there are of preserving states in general, and also in particular cases. In the first place, it is evident that if we understand the causes which destroy states, we shall also understand the causes which preserve them; for opposites produce opposites, and destruction is the opposite of preservation.

In all well-organized governments there is nothing which should be more jealously maintained than the spirit of obedience to law, more especially in small matters; for lawlessness creeps in unperceived and at last ruins the state, just as the constant repetition of small expenses in time eats up a fortune. The change does not take place all at once, and therefore is not observed. The mind is deceived, as by the fallacy which says, "if each part is little, then the whole is little."...

VI, 5. The mere establishment of a democracy is not the only or the principal business of the lawgiver, or of those who wish to create such a state, for any state, however badly constituted, may last one, two or three days. A far greater task is the preservation of it. The lawgiver should therefore endeavor to lay a firm foundation according to the principles already described of the preservation and destruction of states. He should guard against the destructive elements, and make laws, written or unwritten, which will contain all measures preservative of states. He must not think that the truly democratic or oligarchic measure is whatever will give the greatest amount of democracy or oligarchy, but what will make them last longest. The demagogues of our own day often get property confiscated in the law-courts in order to please the people....

Now, in the last and worst form of democracy the citizens are very numerous, and can hardly be made to assemble unless they are paid; and to pay them when there are no revenues presses hard upon the upper class, for the money must be obtained by property taxes and confiscations and corrupt practices of the courts, things which have before now overthrown many democracies.... Where there are revenues, the demagogues should not be allowed after their fashion to distribute the surplus. The poor are always receiving and always wanting more and more, for such help is like water poured into a leaky cask. Yet the true friend of the people should see that they be not too poor, for extreme poverty lowers the character of the democracy. Measures should also be taken which will give them lasting prosperity, and since this is equally to the interest of all classes, the proceeds of public revenues should be accumulated and distributed among the poor, if possible, in such quantities as may enable them to purchase a little farm, or, at any rate, make a beginning in trade or agriculture. And if this benevolence cannot be extended to all, money should be distributed by tribes or other divisions....

V, 9. ... But of all the things I have mentioned, that which most contributes to the permanence of constitutions is the adaptation of education to the form of government, and yet in our own day this principle is universally neglected. The best laws, though sanctioned by every citizen of the state, will be of no avail unless the young are trained by habit and education in the spirit of the constitution, if it is democratic, democratically, or if it is oligarchic, oligarchically. For there may be a want of self-discipline in states as well as in individuals....

In democracies of the more extreme type there has arisen a false idea of freedom which is contradictory to the true interests of the state. For two principles are characteristic of democracy, government by the majority and freedom. Men think that what is equal is just, and that equality is the supremacy of the popular will, and that freedom and equality mean doing what a man likes. In such democracies everyone lives as he pleases, or in the words of Euripides, "according to his fancy." But this is all wrong; men should not think it slavery to live according to the rule of the constitution, for it is their salvation.

I have now discussed generally the causes of the revolutions and destruction of states, and the means of their preservation and continuance.

Late Classical Greece

The half-century that followed the defeat and destruction of the Athenian Empire in 404 B.C. was characterized by almost continuous warfare punctuated by futile peace conferences as the chief Greek states—Sparta, Thebes, and Athens, aided and abetted by the intervention of Persia in Greek affairs—successfully used the principle of the balance of power to prevent any one state from dominating Greece. The resulting political anarchy interfered disastrously with interstate trade and produced within the Greek states a continuing economic depression that manifested itself in bitter civic strife. The plight of the poor led them to promote radical socialistic attacks on the property of the rich, while the resulting fears of the rich produced in them a reactionary opposition to even moderate reform. Isocrates (436–388 B.C.) noted the bitter and uncompromising character of this struggle between rich and poor at Athens as he contrasted the conditions of this later period with those that had prevailed during the prosperous days of the Athenian Empire: "In their mutual relations they are so mistrustful and hostile that they fear their fellow citizens more than their enemies; and whereas, during the period of our supremacy, they were united and readily assisted one another, they have now become so unsocial that those who are possessed of wealth would rather throw their property into the sea than assist the needy, while the poor would prefer to take what they want from the rich by force rather than find a treasure."

Unity and stability for the Greek world were finally achieved in 338 B.C., but they were imposed from outside Greece by Philip II of Macedon and at the point of a sword. All the Greek states except Sparta[1] were forced into a federal union, the so-called League of Corinth, under Macedonian leadership. Each state retained its local autonomy but was required to renounce the right both to make war on its neighbors and to engage in civil strife at home. No tribute was required, but each state was to supply military assistance for a projected war on Persia, which Philip's son Alexander later carried out.

34 Demosthenes Versus Isocrates

"Nationalism" Versus "Internationalism"

During the critical years preceding Philip's conquest of Greece, the political life of Athens was enlivened by a great debate over foreign policy. Isocrates saw that the unification of the Greeks in a common enterprise as the prime necessity of the times; and when the hopelessness of his original plan for a voluntary union became apparent, he turned to Philip and urged him to take the lead in exerting leadership (hegemony) over a free and united Greece and

---

1. Although Sparta was still greatly admired, its Lycurgan system had collapsed and it could no longer play a significant role in interstate relations. By allowing proud Sparta to remain outside the new federation, Philip could maintain the fiction that membership was voluntary.

direct it in a war of conquest in Asia against the Persian Empire. On the other hand, the Athenian orator Demosthenes (384–322 B.C.) regarded Philip's Macedon as the greatest threat to Athens' power in the northern Aegean and its newly re-constituted empire, and indeed to Greek liberty as a whole, and urged on his countrymen a staunch defense against a man whom he abused as a treacherous barbarian. Demosthenes' narrowly nationalistic appeal eventually won the day, and Philip had to defeat Athens and its few allies at the Battle of Chaeronea in 338 B.C. before he could fulfill Isocrates' hopes for a prosperous Greece freed from internal strife and Demosthenes' fears of Macedonian "domination of Greece and the end of the honors and rights of our ancestors." The following selections illustrate the nature of the rival arguments in this great debate over the direction of Athenian foreign policy.

A. DEMOSTHENES, *FIRST PHILIPPIC*

"Athenians, when will you act as becomes you!"

The ambitious, energetic, and shrewd Philip became ruler of Macedon in 359 B.C., and in less than two years he had transformed a Homeric-style kingdom of horse-riding nobles and stalwart peasants into a powerful monarchy. Macedon's army became one of the most capable military machines yet seen in the ancient world. Another result of this national awakening was Philip's conquest of the Greek colonies that had been established along the coast of Macedon during the earlier period of Greek colonization and Macedonian impotence.

Partly because some of these coastal city-states were Athenian colonies and allies, and partly because he feared that Philip's ambition would not stop until he had conquered all of Greece, Demosthenes, in speech after speech, implored the Greeks in general and the Athenians in particular to fight to preserve the free institutions of the city-state from the menace of foreign domination. The most famous of these speeches, the *First Philippic*, urged the Athenians to arouse themselves from apathy and prepare for a war that they little realized had already begun. It was delivered in 351 B.C. when Philip was busily intriguing and intervening in various petty wars among northern Greek states. Demosthenes' impassioned appeal went unheeded for the time being, for the Macedonian danger as yet seemed unreal and far away.

"Your Affairs Are Amiss Because You Do Nothing"

First I say, you must not despair, men of Athens, under your present circumstances, wretched as they are; for that which is worst in the days that are past provides the best hope for the future. What do I mean? That your affairs are amiss, men of Athens, because you do nothing that is needed; for surely if you came into your present predicament while doing all that you should do, we could not then hope for any improvement.

From *First Philippic*, Chs. 2–12, 38–45, 48–50, based on the translation by Charles R. Kennedy.

Consider next, what some of you know by report and others know from experience, how powerful the Spartans were not long ago, yet how nobly and patriotically you did what was worthy of Athens and undertook the war [378–371 B.C.] against them for the rights of Greece. Why do I remind you of this? To show and convince you, men of Athens, that nothing, if you are on your guard, is to be feared, nothing, if you are negligent, goes as you desire. Take for example the strength of the Spartans then, which you overcame by attention to your duties, and the insolence of this man now, by which through neglect of our interests we are confounded. But if there are any among you, men of Athens, who think Philip hard to be conquered in view of the magnitude of his existing power and the loss by us of all our strongholds, they reason rightly. But they should remember that once we held Pydna and Potidaea and Methone and all the region round about Macedonia as our own, and that many of the tribes now leagued with him were then independent and free and preferred our friendship to his. Had Philip then concluded that it was difficult to contend with Athens, when she had so many strong outposts on his borders and he was destitute of allies, he would never have gained his recent successes nor acquired his present power. But he saw clearly, men of Athens, that all these outposts were the open prizes of war, that by natural right the possessions of the absent belong to those on the spot and the possessions of the negligent to those who will venture and toil. Acting on this principle, he has won these places and holds them, either by right of conquest or by means of friendship and alliance—for all men will side with and respect those whom they see prepared and willing to take action.

Men of Athens, if you will adopt this principle now, though you did not do so before, and if each citizen who can and ought to give his service to the state is ready to give it without excuse, the rich to contribute, the able-bodied to enlist; if, put bluntly, you will become your own masters and each cease expecting to do nothing himself while his neighbor does everything for him, then, God willing, you will recover your own, get back what has been frittered away, and turn the tables on Philip. Do not imagine that his power is everlasting like that of a god. There are those who hate and fear and envy him, men of Athens, even among those who now seem most friendly. We can assume that all the feelings that are in other men belong also to his adherents. But now they are all cowed, having no refuge because of your apathy and indolence, which I urge you to abandon at once. For you see, men of Athens, to what pitch of arrogance the man has advanced: he leaves you not even the choice of action or inaction, he threatens and uses outrageous language, he cannot rest content in possession of his conquests but continually widens their circle, and, while we dally and delay, he throws his net around us.

When, then, Athenians, when will you act as becomes you? What are you waiting for? When it is necessary, I suppose. And how should we regard what is happening now? Surely, to free men the strongest necessity is the disgrace of their condition. Or tell me, do you like walking about and asking one another, "Is there any news?" Could there be more startling news than that a Macedonian is subduing Athenians and directing the affairs of Greece? "Is Philip dead?" you ask. "No, but he is sick." What difference does it make? Should anything happen to this man, you will soon create a second Philip if that is the way you attend to affairs. For this Philip has grown great not so much by his own strength as by our negligence....

"Be in Advance of Circumstances"

Shameful it is, men of Athens, to delude ourselves, and by putting off everything unpleasant to miss the time for action and be unable even to understand that skillful makers of war should not follow circumstances, but be in advance of them; for just as a general may be expected to lead his armies, so statesmen must guide circumstances if they are to carry out their policies and not be forced to follow at the heels of events. Yet you, men of Athens, with greater resources than any people—ships, infantry, cavalry, revenue—have never up to this day made proper use of them; instead, your war with Philip differs in no respect from the boxing of barbarians. For among them the party struck moves his hands to the spot; strike him somewhere else, there go his hands again. He neither can nor will parry a blow or look his opponent in the face. So you, if you hear of Philip in the Chersonese, vote to send relief there, if at Thermopylae, the same; if anywhere else, you run up and down after his heels. You take your orders from him; no plan have you devised, no event do you forsee, until you learn that something has happened or is about to happen. Formerly perhaps this was tolerable; now it is come to a crisis and is tolerable no longer. It seems to me, men of Athens, as if some god, ashamed for us because of our conduct, has inspired this activity in Philip. For if he were willing to remain at peace in possession of his conquests and prizes, attempting nothing further, some of you, I think, would be satisfied with a state of things which brands our nation with shame, cowardice, and deep disgrace. But by continually encroaching and grasping after more, he may possibly rouse you, if you have not completely abandoned hope....

One thing is clear: he will not stop, unless someone stops him. Are we to wait for this? Do you think all is well if you dispatch empty ships and the vague hope of some deliverer? Shall we not man the fleet? Shall we not sail with at least a part of our troops, now if never before? Shall we not make a landing on his coast? "Where, then, shall we land?" someone asks. The war itself, men of Athens, will uncover the weak parts of his empire, if we make the effort; but if we sit at home listening to the orators accuse and malign one another, no good can ever be achieved. I believe that wherever you send a force of our own citizens—or even partly ours—there Heaven will bless us and Fortune will aid our struggle; but where you send out a general and an empty decree and high hopes from the debate, nothing that you desire is achieved; your enemies scoff, and your allies die of fright....

"The Future Depends on Ourselves"

Some of us go about saying that Philip is negotiating with Sparta for the destruction of Thebes and the dissolution of the free states; some say that he has sent envoys to the king [of Persia]; others say that he is fortifying cities in

Illyria—thus do we wander about, each inventing his own story. For my part, men of Athens, I solemnly believe that Philip is intoxicated with the magnitude of his exploits and has many such dreams in his mind, for he sees the absence of opponents and is elated by his successes. But most certainly he has no such plan of action as to let the most foolish among us know what his intentions are, and the most foolish are these newsmongers. Let us dismiss such talk and remember only that Philip is our enemy, that he has long been robbing and insulting us, that wherever we have expected aid from others we have found hostility, that the future depends on ourselves, and that unless we are willing to fight him there we shall perhaps be forced to fight here. This let us remember, and then we shall decide wisely and be done with idle conjectures. You need not speculate about the future except to assure yourselves that it will be disastrous unless you face the facts and are willing to do your duty.

B. ISOCRATES, ADDRESS TO PHILIP

"A champion powerful in action"

Isocrates is praised by some as a man of statesmanlike vision who "saw far into the future" and "grasped the situation in its ecumenical aspect," while by others he is condemned as a traitorous advocate whose naïve idealism paved the way for the Macedonian conquest of Greece and the loss of Greek liberty. There are facts to support both estimates.

Just as much a patriotic Athenian as his contemporary Demosthenes, Isocrates' internationalism was based upon a realistic appraisal of the economic and political conditions of his time. He saw that only the removal of economic distress could bring an end to social and political disturbances in the Greek world. To solve this underlying economic problem he urged the Greeks to form a union under the leadership of Athens and Sparta for the purpose of waging war on the Persian Empire and opening Asia to Greek exploitation. This program of imperialistic expansion to solve the ills of Greece was first expressed in 380 B.C. in his Panegyric oration:

> We cannot enjoy a sure peace unless we join together in a war against the barbarians, nor can the Greeks achieve concord until we wrest our material advantages from the same source and wage war against the same enemy. When these things are achieved, when we have been freed from the poverty surrounding our lives—which breaks up friendships, perverts to enmity the ties of kindred, and throws all mankind into wars and seditions—then surely we shall enjoy a spirit of concord and our mutual goodwill will be real.

Years later, in his Address to Philip (346 B.C.), Isocrates' views had undergone one important change. He was now convinced that the Greeks were incapable of voluntarily forming themselves into a union, and he placed the

From "The Philippus," Chs. 8, 9, 12–16, 30, 31, 36–45, 72–75, 89–120, 121, 152–55, based on the translation by J. H. Freese in Orations of Isocrates, Vol. I. By permission of G. Bell & Sons, Ltd.

blame squarely upon the excesses of democracy and the fickleness of the voters who preferred the harangues of demagogues to the reasoned arguments of statesmen. He complained that democracy has become so corrupt that "violence is regarded as democracy, lawlessness as liberty, impudence of speech as equality, and license to act in this manner as happiness." The only possible solution was to put the direction of affairs into the capable hands of a strong and wise leader—"a champion ... powerful ... in action."

We can trace Isocrates' growing disillusionment with democracy in his speeches. He first proposed to stem its radicalism and instability at Athens by a return to the limited democracy of the time of Solon. Then the state had been governed, he declared in his Areopagiticus oration (about 358 B.C.), "not by appointing magistrates from the general body of citizens by lot, but by selecting the best and most capable to fill each office." This, he argued, would put the direction of affairs where it belonged, in the hands of the aristocrats of birth and wealth, for only "those who are able to enjoy ease and who possess sufficient means should attend to public affairs." Security and stability must inevitably follow from the rule of such men, for "their only care was to avoid abolishing any of the institutions of their forefathers."

But all this was wishful thinking, and Isocrates turned gradually to the idea of one-man rule and proceeded to publish three tracts favoring the monarchical system. Above all, he became convinced that only through the efforts of a strong man, and not by such constitutional schemes as he had advocated earlier, could the unification of Greece and conquests in Asia be accomplished. "Great and melancholy indeed is the change that has come over the old age of Isocrates," wrote the nineteenth-century liberal historian George Grote in describing Isocrates' search for a strong man, a search that ended with the appearance of Philip of Macedon. The *Address to Philip* sets forth Isocrates' views in their final form. It contains a good deal of sound political and economic insight mixed with a naïve idealization of Philip's character and his future relations with the Greek states.

By intrigue and aggression, Philip had expanded southward with only inadequate and tardy Athenian resistance, despite Demosthenes' fervid warnings. In 346 this undeclared war was temporarily ended by a peace treaty—the "False Peace" as the Athenians later called it—and Isocrates refers to this peace at the beginning of his *Address to Philip*, composed immediately thereafter.

Rejoicing at the resolutions which were adopted concerning peace, and thinking that they would be to your advantage and to that of all the rest of Hellas as well as to us, I was unable to divert my thoughts from the possibilities connected with it and was in a frame of mind to set to work immediately to consider how to give permanence to what we had achieved and to prevent our state from again, after a short interval, desiring other wars. An examination of these questions in my own mind led me to the conclusion that there was no other way for her to remain at peace except by the determination of the leading states of Hellas to put an end to mutual quarrels and carry the war into Asia, resolving to win from the barbarians the selfish advantages which they now look for at the expense of Hellenes. This was, indeed, the policy I had already advised in the Panegyric oration....

"Speeches Are Ineffectual, Take the Lead"

To trouble the great festivals with oratory, addressing the crowds that come there, is really to speak without an audience; speeches of that kind are as ineffectual as laws and constitutions drawn up by the sophists. Those who wish, on the contrary, to do some practical good instead of idly chattering, and who think they have formed ideas of value to the community, must leave it to others to orate at the festivals while they seek a champion for their cause from among those who are powerful in speech and action and have great reputations—if, that is to say, anyone is to pay attention to them.

With this in mind, I chose to address my discourse to you, not making this choice to win your favor, although it is true that I should consider it of great importance to speak in a manner acceptable to you, but it was not to this end that I came to this decision. It was because I saw that all the other men of high repute were living under the rule of states and laws, without power to do anything but obey orders, and besides were far too weak for the enterprise which I shall propose, while to you alone had Fortune granted full power to send ambassadors to whomsoever you chose and to receive them from whomever you pleased, and to say whatever you thought it expedient to say, and besides this, that you were the possessor to a greater degree than any man in Hellas of wealth and power, the only two things in existence which can both persuade and compel—things which I think will also be required by the enterprise which I am going to propose. For my intention is to advise you to take the lead both in securing the harmony of Hellas and in conducting a campaign against the barbarians; and as persuasion is expedient in dealing with the Greeks, so force is useful in dealing with the barbarians. Such, then, is the general scope of my discourse....

"Persuade Four States to Act Wisely"

I will now direct my remarks to the subject at hand. I say that, while neglecting none of your own interests, you ought to try to reconcile Argos, Sparta, Thebes, and our state; for if you are able to bring these together you will have no difficulty in uniting the others as well, for they are all under the influence of those that I have mentioned and when alarmed take refuge with one or the other of those states and depend on their aid. So if you can persuade four states only to act wisely, you will also release the rest from many evils....

And you have a good opportunity, for ... it is a good thing to appear as the benefactor of the leading states and at the same time to be furthering your own interests no less than theirs. Besides this, you will remove any unpleasant relations that you have had with any of them, for services rendered in the present crisis will cause all of you to forget the wrongs you have committed against each other in the past. Moreover, it is also beyond question that there is nothing which all men remember so well as benefits received in times of trouble. And you can see how they have been reduced to distress by war....

"They Will Prefer the Benefits of Union"

Now perhaps someone will venture to oppose what I have said on the ground that I am endeavoring to persuade you to undertake an impossible task. He may say that the Argives can never be friends with the Spartans, or the Spartans with the Thebans, nor, in a word, can those who have been accustomed always to seek their selfish interests ever cast their lot with one another. I think that nothing of this kind could have been accomplished when our state, or again when Sparta, was supreme in Hellas, for either of them could easily have blocked the attempt; but now I no longer have the same opinion of them. For I know that they have all been brought down to the same level by their misfortunes, so that I think they will much prefer the benefits of union to the selfish advantages of their former policy....

Now I am surprised that those who consider it impossible that any such policy could be carried out do not know from their own experience, or have not heard from others, that there have been indeed many terrible wars after which the participants have been reconciled and done each other great services. What could exceed the enmity between Xerxes and the Hellenes? Yet everyone knows that both we and the Spartans were more pleased with the friendship of Xerxes than of those who helped us to found our respective empires. And need we refer to ancient history or to our relations with the barbarians? ... When the Spartans made war against the Thebans with the intention of ravaging Boeotia and breaking up its league of cities, we gave our help and thwarted their desires; and when fortune changed again and the Thebans and all the Peloponnesians attempted to lay Sparta in ruins, we alone in Hellas made an alliance even with our ancient foes and contributed to their preservation. A man then would be full of folly who could observe such great reversals and see that states care nothing for former enmities or oaths or anything else save what they suppose to be for their advantage, caring only for what is expedient and devoting all their energies to that end, and still suppose that they would be of the same mind now as they always have been, especially with you to preside over the settlement of their disputes, which expediency recommends and present necessity compels. For I think that with these influences fighting on your side everything will turn out as it should....

"You Are Being Slandered"

I should be satisfied with what I have already said on this subject had I not omitted one point, not from forgetfulness, but from a certain unwillingness to mention it. However, I think I ought to disclose it now, for I am of the opinion that it is as much to your advantage to hear what I have to say concerning it as it is becoming to me to speak with my accustomed freedom.

I perceive that you are being slandered by those who are jealous of you and are accustomed to throw their own cities into confusion—men who regard the peace which is for the good of all as a war against their own selfish interests. Unconcerned about everything else, they speak of nothing but your power, asserting that its growth is not for the interests of Hellas but against them, and that you have been already for a long time plotting against us all, and that, while you pretend to be anxious to assist the Messenians as soon as you have settled with the Phocians, you are in reality endeavoring to get the Peloponnesus into your power.... By talking such nonsense and pretending that they possess an accurate knowledge of affairs, and by predicting a speedy overthrow of the whole world, they persuade many....

"In Favor of the Expedition to Asia"

On these points no sensible man would venture to contradict me. And I think that it would occur to any others who should propose to advise in favor of the expedition to Asia to point out that all whose lot it has been to undertake war against the Persian king have risen from obscurity to renown, from poverty to wealth, and from low estate to the ownership of many lands and cities....

What opinion must we think all will have of you if you actually do this; above all, if you endeavor to conquer the whole Persian Empire, or at least to take from it a vast territory, what some call "Asia from Cilicia to Sinope," and in addition to build cities throughout this region and send there as colonists those who are now wanderers from want of their daily bread and who harass all whom they meet? For if we do not stop these men from joining together by providing them with sufficient to live upon, they will before we realize it become so numerous that they will be as great a cause of alarm to the Hellenes as to the barbarians. We, however, pay no attention to them; we ignore the existence of a terrible menace that threatens us all and is increasing day by day....

Conclusion

... When Fortune honorably leads the way, it is a disgrace to lag behind and show yourself unready to advance in whatever direction she wishes.

I think that, while you ought to honor all those who speak well of what you have done, you ought to consider that the most honorable eulogy is that of those who consider your talents worthy of still greater deeds than those which you have already accomplished, great as they are, and who express themselves grateful to you, not only in the present, but who will cause posterity to admire your acts beyond those of all who have lived in former times....

It remains to summarize what I have said in this discourse in order that, in as few words as possible, you may understand the chief point of my advice. I say that you ought to be the benefactor of the Hellenes, the king of Macedonia, and the ruler over as many barbarians as possible. If you succeed in this, all will be grateful to you—the Hellenes by reason of advantages enjoyed; the Macedonians, if you govern them like a king and not like a tyrant; and the rest of mankind, if they are freed by you from barbarian despotism and gain the protection of Hellas. How far my composition is well proportioned in style and in expression, I may reasonably expect to learn from my hearers; but that no one could give you advice that is better than this, or more suited to present circumstances, of that I feel convinced.

SELECTED BACKGROUND READING

Paul Cartledge, *The Cambridge Illustrated History of Ancient Greece* (Cambridge, U.K.: Cambridge University Press, 1998).

Paul Cartledge, *The Spartans: The World of the Warrior-Heroes of Ancient Greece, from Utopia to Crisis and Collapse* (Woodstock, New York: Overlook Press, 2003).

W. Robert Connor, *Thucydides* (Princeton, New Jersey: Princeton University Press, 1984).

Matthew Dillon and Lynda Garland, *Ancient Greece: Social and Historical Documents from Archaic Times to the Death of Socrates (c. 800–399 B.C.)* (London: Routledge, 2000).

Robert Garland, *Daily Life of the Ancient Greeks* (Westport, Conn: Greenwood Press, 2009).

Donald Kagan, *The Peloponnesian War* (New York: Viking, 2003).

Mark Henderson Munn, *The School of History: Athens in the Age of Socrates* (Berkeley: University of California Press, 2000).

Robin Osborne, *Greece in the Making, 1200–479 B.C.* (London: Routledge, 1996).

Sarah B. Pomeroy et al., *Ancient Greece: A Political, Social, and Cultural History* (New York: Oxford University Press, 1999).

H. A. Shapiro, *The Cambridge Companion to Archaic Greece* (Cambridge, U.K.: Cambridge University Press, 2007).

Robert B. Strassler and Richard Crawley, *The Landmark Thucydides: A Comprehensive Guide to the Peloponnesian War* (New York: Free Press, 2008).

CHAPTER III

Hellenistic Civilization

I intended to blend the customs of the Greeks and the
  barbarians;
to cross every continent and tame it;
to search out the farthest points of land and sea;
to make Ocean the boundary of Macedon.

—ALEXANDER THE GREAT

A Hellenistic head of Alexander the Great (about 200 B.C.).

Historians point to the conclusion of the Greek and Persian Wars (490 B.C./480–479 B.C.) as the beginning of the classical age of Greece. They see another set of political-military events as also setting the stage for the following Hellenistic age. The rapid and surprising conquest of the Persian Empire by Alexander III of Macedon (d. 323 B.C.) brought much of the inhabited world under the rule of the Greeks and Macedonians. Within a space of about ten years, Alexander conquered the entire Near East and went as far as northwest India. When he died unexpectedly in Babylon, he was contemplating still greater explorations and conquests.

Much of what Alexander did aroused admiration and wonder, both in antiquity and in more recent times. Some modern scholars have even claimed that Alexander sought to unify humankind by "mixing the races" through a policy of intermarriage between Greeks and non-Greeks (see Selection 35), and that his premature death put an unfortunate end to this fascinating and idealistic experiment. But more recent historians are less certain that Alexander was such an idealist, being more inclined to regard him as a pragmatist and his ethnic policies as motivated by political expedience. While his vast empire did not long survive him, the rulers who succeeded to various parts of his realm continued his legacy in various ways. The great Hellenistic monarchies—the Seleucids in Syria, the Ptolemies in Egypt, and the Antigonids in Macedon, to name only the most powerful—encouraged the spread of Greek culture. During the Hellenistic age, many Greek and Macedonian settlers founded in non-Greek lands Greek-style *poleis*, some of which existed as far east as modern Afghanistan. The diffusion of Greek (Hellenic) culture during this period was accompanied by the development of a written and spoken Greek called the *koinē*, the "common language," which became the *lingua franca* of a cultural zone that extended from Spain in the West and India in the East.

This chapter presents readings that address the following historical themes: From Warrior Kings to Divine Rulers; Hellenistic Rulers and Their Subjects; Hellenistic Culture, Economy, and Thought; and The Limits of Hellenism.

From Warrior Kings to Divine Rulers

While there was much that was new in the Hellenistic age, there was also much that stayed the same. The Greek city-states remained important social and political entities, despite the fact that they were increasingly overshadowed by the power of the Hellenistic kings. Still, these kings frequently paid homage to the ideal of Greek civic autonomy, or freedom, and couched their relationship with city-states in terms of friendship and equality. For their part, Greek cities paid respect to the kings and often voted them divine honors, making the kings gods as well. The idea of divine rulers may appear to exist in tension with the idea of civic freedom, but in fact it allowed the Greeks to rationalize their political subordination. For while it may be shameful to be dominated by a man, who can really complain about being dominated by a god? The spread of the divine cult of the ruler in the Hellenistic period came about as part of the evolving relationship between all-powerful kings and theoretically independent Greek cities. The Hellenistic kings also ruled over many non-Greeks and had to maintain a positive relationship with them. The emerging cult of the divine Hellenistic king became a useful and increasingly universal way for the rulers and the ruled to construct a meaningful relationship with one another. This Hellenistic system of divine ruler cult would later find expression in the cult of divine Roman emperors.

35 Arrian, History of Alexander the Great

Conqueror and Reformer

"We are free men, and they are slaves...."

The career of Alexander the Great (356–323 B.C.) has not lost its ability to fascinate since his death in 323 B.C. His techniques, goals, and ideals are still frequent subject for debates among historians. The nature of his military genius and the attitude he adopted toward the conquered, which some today call his ethnic policy, have often come under scrutiny. Alexander created the Hellenistic world where there was easy mixing of cultures. As historians look back from the cosmopolitan tone of the Hellenistic and Roman periods, it might have appeared that Alexander had planned for the coming together of East and West even before he set foot on the soil of Asia Minor. Some of his military and administrative deeds have been cited in support of this interpretation, for example, the blending of Greeks and Macedonians with "orientals" in his army and administration; the founding of numerous Greek cities in Asia, in which Alexander settled many Greek and Macedonian veterans; his own marriages to two "oriental" princesses, and his encouragement of his officers and men to wed non-Greek wives; and the promotion of East-West trade by the opening up of new trade routes, the founding of port cities, and the minting of a standard coinage.

    Especially relevant to a discussion of his ethnic policy was the dramatic incident at Opis in Babylonia where, following his return from India, Alexander ordered the dismissal of his aged and maimed Macedonian veterans and their

From *The Campaigns of Alexander,* translated by Aubrey de Selincourt, revised with a new introduction and notes by J. R. Hamilton, 112–14, 120–28, 353–67. Copyright © 1971 by Penguin Books. Reproduced by permission of Penguin Books, Ltd.

replacement by Persians who had been trained in Macedonian military techniques. The aggrieved veterans, we are told, mutinied and shouted disapprovingly at Alexander, "You have made Persians your kinsmen!" When order was finally restored, Alexander held a feast of reconciliation, attended by nine thousand Macedonians and Persians and solemnized by Greek seers and Persian magi, or priests. Alexander himself capped the ceremonies with a prayer that one modern scholar has called a revolution in human thought—he prayed "for concord and partnership in the empire between Macedonians and Persians."[1] Today, few if any historians accept that Alexander, although still regarded by many as one of the most romantic figures in history, was aiming to bring about "the Brotherhood of Man."[2]

A Greek who achieved high political office during the Roman Empire (ca. A.D. 86–160), Arrian of Nicomedia made much use of earlier sources to compose a history of the campaigns of Alexander the Great, his most celebrated work. He is generally viewed by modern historians as a credible informant because, in his historical work, he presents himself as a skeptic in the face of the wildly romantic tales that had spread regarding the figure of Alexander. Many modern historians admire Arrian for his sober historical judgment.

… Alexander now sent for his infantry and cavalry commanders and all officers in charge of allied troops and appealed to them for confidence and courage in the coming fight. 'Remember', he said, 'that already danger has often threatened you and you have looked it triumphantly in the face; this time the struggle will be between a victorious army and an enemy already once vanquished. God himself, moreover, by suggesting to Darius to leave the open ground and cram his great army into a confined space, has taken charge of operations in our behalf. We ourselves shall have room enough to deploy our infantry, while they, no match for us either in bodily strength or resolution, will find their superiority in numbers of no avail. Our enemies are Medes and Persians, men who for centuries have lived soft and luxurious lives; we of Macedon for generations past have been trained in the hard school of danger and war. Above all, we are free men, and they are slaves. There are Greek troops, to be sure, in Persian service—but how different is their cause from ours! They will be fighting for pay—and not much of it at that; we, on the contrary, shall fight for Greece, and our hearts will be in it. … And what, finally, of the two men in supreme command? You have Alexander, they—Darius!'

Having thus enumerated the advantages with which they would enter the coming struggle, Alexander went on to show that the rewards of victory would also be great. The victory this time would not be over mere underlings of the Persian King … ; it would be over the fine flower of the Medes and Persians and all the Asiatic peoples which they ruled. The Great King was there in person with his army, and once the battle was over, nothing would remain but to

1. Charles Alexander Robinson, Jr., *Alexander the Great: The Meeting of East and West in World Government and Brotherhood* (New York: E. P. Dutton and Co., 1947), p. 225.

2. Edouard Will, quoted in Chester G. Starr, *Past and Future in Ancient History*, Publications of the Association of Ancient Historians, I (Lanham, Md.: University Press of America, 1987), p. 19.

crown their many labours with the sovereignty of Asia. … Nor did Alexander omit any other words of encouragement such as brave men about to risk their lives might expect from a brave commander; and in response to his address his officers pressed forward to clasp his hand and with many expressions of appreciation urged him to lead them to battle without delay.

[Battle was joined and Alexander emerged victorious.]…

Among the Persian dead were Arsames, Rheomithres, and Atizyes—all three of whom had served as cavalry officers at the battle on the Granicus; also Sabaces, governor of Egypt, and Bubaces, another person of distinguished rank; of the common soldiers, something like 100,000 were killed, including over 10,000 of the cavalry. Ptolemy, son of Lagus, who was serving with Alexander at this time, says in his account of the battle that the Macedonians in their pursuit of Darius actually crossed a ravine on the bodies of the Persian dead.

Darius' headquarters were stormed and captured; his mother was taken, together with his wife (who was also his sister) and his infant son; in addition to these, two of his daughters fell into Alexander's hands with a few noble Persian ladies who were in attendance upon them. The Persian officers had sent their gear and womenfolk to Damascus, and Darius, too, had sent thither most of his treasure and the various paraphernalia which the luxurious life of a great king seems to require, even on campaign, so that a mere 3,000 talents were found at his headquarters. In point of fact, however, the treasure at Damascus, too, was seized not long afterwards by Parmenio, who was ordered there for the purpose. Such, then, was the result of the battle of Issus, fought in the month of November, during the archonship of Nicocrates at Athens.

Alexander had been hurt by a sword-thrust in the thigh, but this did not prevent him from visiting the wounded on the day after the battle, when he also gave a splendid military funeral to the dead in the presence of the whole army paraded in full war equipment. At the ceremony he spoke in praise of every man who by his own observation or from reliable report he knew had distinguished himself in the fighting, and marked his approval in each case by a suitable reward.…

His sympathy was extended, moreover, even to Darius' mother, wife, and children. According to some accounts, on the night when he returned from the pursuit he heard upon entering Darius' tent, which had been set aside as his own special portion of the spoils of war, the confused sound of women's voices raised in lamentation somewhere close at hand. He asked who the women were and why they should be in a tent so close to him. 'Sire,' he was told, 'they are Darius' mother and wife and children. They know that you have his bow and his royal mantle and that his shield has been brought back, and they are mourning for his death.' Alexander at once sent Leonnatus, one of his Companions, to tell them that Darius was alive—his mantle and weapons he had left, as he fled for safety, in his war chariot, and these, and nothing else, had fallen into Alexander's hands. Leonnatus entered their tent, gave the message about Darius, and added that Alexander wished them to retain all the marks, ceremonies, and titles of royalty, as he had not fought Darius with any personal bitterness, but had made legitimate war for the sovereignty of Asia.…

While Alexander was at Marathus, envoys from Darius came with a request for the release of his mother, wife, and children. They also brought a letter from him, of which the substance was as follows:

> Philip and Artaxerxes were on terms of friendship and alliance, but upon the accession of Artaxerxes' son Arses, Philip was guilty of unprovoked aggression against him. Now, since Darius' reign began, Alexander has sent no representative to his court to confirm the former friendship and alliance between the two kingdoms; on the contrary, he has crossed into Asia with his armed forces and done much damage to the Persians. For this reason Darius took the field in defence of his country and of his ancestral throne. The issue of battle was as some god willed; and now Darius the King asks Alexander the King to restore from captivity his wife, his mother, and his children, and is willing to make friends with him and be his ally. For this cause he urges Alexander to send to him, in company with Meniscus and Arsimas who have brought this request, representatives of his own in order that proper guarantees may be exchanged.

Alexander, having written his reply, ordered Thersippus to accompany Darius' envoys on their return, giving him strict instructions to deliver the letter to Darius but to discuss no question whatever which might arise from it. This was the letter:

> Your ancestors invaded Macedonia and Greece and caused havoc in our country, though we had done nothing to provoke them. As supreme commander of all Greece I invaded Asia because I wished to punish Persia for this act—an act which must be laid wholly to your charge. You sent aid to the people of Perinthus in their rebellion against my father; Ochus sent an army into Thrace, which was a part of our dominions; my father was killed by assassins whom, as you openly boasted in your letters, you yourselves hired to commit the crime; ... you sent the Greeks false information about me in the hope of making them my enemies; you attempted to supply the Greeks with money—which only the Lacedaemonians were willing to accept, your agents corrupted my friends and tried to wreck the peace which I had established in Greece—then it was that I took the field against you; but it was you who began the quarrel. First I defeated in battle your generals and satraps; now I have defeated yourself and the army you led. By God's help I am master of your country, and I have made myself responsible for the survivors of your army who fled to me for refuge: far from being detained by force, they are serving of their own free will under my command.
>
> Come to me, therefore, as you would come to the lord of the continent of Asia. Should you fear to suffer any indignity at my hands, then send some of your friends and I will give them the proper guarantees. Come, then, and ask me for your mother, your wife, and your children and anything else you please; for you shall have them, and whatever besides you can persuade me to give you.
>
> And in future let any communication you wish to make with me be addressed to the King of all Asia. Do not write to me as to an

equal. Everything you possess is now mine; so, if you should want anything, let me know in the proper terms, or I shall take steps to deal
with you as a criminal. If, on the other hand, you wish to dispute
your throne, stand and fight for it and do not run away. Wherever
you may hide yourself, be sure I shall seek you out.

Such were the terms of Alexander's answer....

Here at Susa he held wedding ceremonies for his Companions; he also took
a wife himself—Barsine, Darius' eldest daughter, and, according to Aristobulus,
another as well, namely Parysatis, the youngest daughter of Ochus. He had
already married Roxane, daughter of Oxyartes of Bactria. To Hephaestion he
gave Drypetis, another of Darius' daughters and sister of his own wife Barsine,
as he wanted to be uncle to Hephaestion's children; to Craterus he gave
Amastrine, daughter of Darius' brother Oxyatres, and to Perdiccas a daughter
of Atropates, governor of Media. The bride of Ptolemy (of the Guard) was Arta-
cama, daughter of Artabazus, and Eumenes, the King's secretary, had her sister
Artonis; Nearchus was given the daughter of Barsine and Mentor, Seleucus the
daughter of Spitamenes of Bactria. Similarly, the other officers—to the number
of eighty all told—were given as brides young women of the noblest Persian and
Median blood. The marriage ceremonies were in the Persian fashion: chairs were
set for the bridegrooms in order of precedence, and when healths had been
drunk the brides entered and sat down by their bridegrooms, who took them
by the hand and kissed them. The King, who was married just as the others
were, and in the same place, was the first to perform the ceremony—Alexander
was always capable of putting himself on a footing of equality and comradeship
with his subordinates, and everyone felt that this act of his was the best proof of
his ability to do so. After the ceremony all the men took their wives home, and
for every one of them Alexander provided a dowry. There proved to be over
10,000 other Macedonians who had married Asian women; Alexander had
them all registered, and every man of them received a wedding gift.

This also seemed a fitting occasion to clear off the men's debts, and Alexander
ordered a detailed schedule to be prepared, with a promise of settlement. At first
only a few entered their names, suspecting that the order might be a scheme of
Alexander's for detecting the spendthrifts who had failed to make do with their
army pay. Alexander was annoyed when he learned that most of the men were
refusing to enter their names and concealing their possession of covenants to pay,
and told them in no uncertain terms what he thought of their suspicions; a King,
he declared, is in duty bound to speak nothing but the truth to his subjects, who,
in their turn, have no right to suppose that he ever does otherwise. He had tables
set up in the army quarters, with money on them, and instructed the clerks in
charge to pay off the debts of every man who produced an I.O.U. without even
registering their names. After that the troops could not but believe in Alexander's
good faith, and they were even more grateful for the concealment of their names
than for having their debts paid. This gift to his men is said to have amounted to
20,000 talents.

He also made a number of other money awards for distinguished conduct in
the field, or in recognition of a man's reputation for good service generally.

A special decoration consisting of a gold crown was granted to certain officers for conspicuous bravery: the recipients were Peucestas—for saving the King's life; Leonnatus—also for saving the King's life, for hard service in India, for his victory in Oria, for facing and defeating in battle, with the forces left under his command, the rebellious Oreitae and their neighbours, and his satisfactory settlement of affairs in general in Oria; Nearchus (now also arrived at Susa) for his voyage from India along the coasts of the Indian Ocean; Onesicritus, master of the royal galley; and, finally, Hephaestion and the other members of the Personal Guard.

Here in Susa, Alexander received the various officials in charge of affairs in the newly built towns and the governors of the territories he had previously overrun. They brought with them some 30,000 young fellows, all boys of the same age, all wearing the Macedonian battle-dress and trained on Macedonian lines. Alexander called them his Epigoni—'inheritors'—and it is said that their coming caused much bad feeling among the Macedonians, who felt it was an indication of his many efforts to lessen his dependence for the future upon his own countrymen. Already the sight of Alexander in Median clothes had caused them no little distress, and most of them had found the Persian marriage ceremonies by no means to their taste—even some of the actual participants had objected to the foreign form of the ceremony, in spite of the fact that they were highly honoured by being, for the occasion, on a footing of equality with the King. They resented, too, the growing orientalism of Peucestas, Governor of Persia, who, to Alexander's evident satisfaction, had adopted the Persian language and dress, just as they resented the inclusion of foreign mounted troops in the regiments of the Companions. Bactrians, Sogdians, Arachotians; Zarangians, Arians, Parthians, and the so-called Euacae from Persia were all introduced into the crack Macedonian cavalry regiments, provided they had some outstanding personal recommendation, such as good looks, or whatever it might be.... The command over them was given to Hystaspes, a Bactrian, and the orientals were all equipped with the Macedonian spear in place of their native javelin. All this was a cause of deep resentment to the Macedonians, who could not but feel that Alexander's whole outlook was becoming tainted with orientalism, and that he no longer cared for his own people or his own native ways....

At Opis he summoned an assembly of his Macedonian troops and announced the discharge from the army of all men unfit through age or disablement for further service; these he proposed to send home, and promised to give them on their departure enough to make their friends and relatives envy them and to fire their countrymen with eagerness to play a part in similar perilous adventures in the future. Doubtless he meant to gratify them by what he said.

Unfortunately, however, the men already felt that he had come to undervalue their services and to think them quite useless as a fighting force; so, naturally enough, they resented his remarks as merely another instance of the many things which, throughout the campaign, he had done to hurt their feelings, such as his adoption of Persian dress, the issue of Macedonian equipment to the Oriental 'Epigoni', and the inclusion of foreign troops in units of the Companions. The result was that they did not receive the speech in respectful silence, but,

unable to restrain themselves, called for the discharge of every man in the army, adding, in bitter jest, that on his next campaign he could take his father with him—
meaning, presumably, the god Ammon.

Alexander was furious. He had grown by that time quicker to take offence,
and the Oriental subservience to which he had become accustomed had greatly
changed his old open-hearted manner towards his own countrymen. He leapt
from the platform with the officers who attended him, and pointing with his
finger to the ringleaders of the mutiny, ordered the guards to arrest them.
There were thirteen of them, and they were all marched off to execution. A
horrified silence ensued, and Alexander stepped once again on to the rostrum
and addressed his troops in these words: 'My countrymen, you are sick for
home—so be it! I shall make no attempt to check your longing to return. Go
whither you will; I shall not hinder your. But, if go you must, there is one thing
I would have you understand—what I have done for you, and in what coin you
will have repaid me.

'First I will speak of my father Philip, as it is my duty to do. Philip found
you a tribe of impoverished vagabonds, most of you dressed in skins, feeding a
few sheep on the hills and fighting, feebly enough, to keep them from your
neighbours—Thracians and Triballians and Illyrians. He gave you cloaks to
wear instead of skins; he brought you down from the hills into the plains; he
taught you to fight on equal terms with the enemy on your borders, till you
knew that your safety lay not, as once, in your mountain strongholds, but in
your own valour. He made you city-dwellers; he brought you law; he civilized
you. He rescued you from subjection and slavery, and made you masters of the
wild tribes who harried and plundered you; he annexed the greater part of
Thrace, and by seizing the best places on the coast opened your country to
trade, and enabled you to work your mines without fear of attack. Thessaly, so
long your bugbear and your dread, he subjected to your rule, and by humbling
the Phocians he made the narrow and difficult path into Greece a broad and easy
road. The men of Athens and Thebes, who for years had kept watching for their
moment to strike us down, he brought so low—and by this time I myself was
working at my father's side that they who once exacted from us either our
money or our obedience, now, in their turn, looked to us as the means of
their salvation. Passing into the Peloponnese, he settled everything there to his
satisfaction, and when he was made supreme commander of all the rest of Greece
for the war against Persia, he claimed the glory of it not for himself alone, but for
the Macedonian people.

'These services which my father rendered you are, indeed, intrinsically great;
yet they are small compared with my own. I inherited from him a handful of
gold and silver cups, coin in the treasury worth less than sixty talents and over
eight times that amount of debts incurred by him; yet to add to this burden I
borrowed a further sum of eight hundred talents, and, marching out from a
country too poor to maintain you decently, laid open for you at a blow, and
in spite of Persia's naval supremacy, the gates of the Hellespont. My cavalry
crushed the satraps of Darius, and I added all Ionia and Aeolia, the two Phrygias
and Lydia to your empire. Miletus I reduced by siege; the other towns all yielded

of their own free will—I took them and gave them you for your profit and enjoyment. The wealth of Egypt and Cyrene, which I shed no blood to win, now flows into your hands; Palestine and the plains of Syria and the Land between the Rivers are now your property; Babylon and Bactria and Susa are yours; you are masters of the gold of Lydia, the treasures of Persia, the wealth of India—yes, and of the sea beyond India, too. You are my captains, my generals, my governors of provinces.

'From all this which I have laboured to win for you, what is left for myself except the purple and this crown? I keep nothing for my own; no one can point to treasure of mine apart from all this which you yourselves either possess, or have in safe keeping for your future use. Indeed, what reason have I to keep anything, as I eat the same food and take the same sleep as you do? Ah, but there are epicures among you who, I fancy, eat more luxuriously than I; and this I know, that I wake earlier than you—and watch, that you may sleep.

'Perhaps you will say that, in my position as your commander, I had none of the labours and distress which you had to endure to win for me what I have won. But does any man among you honestly feel that he has suffered more for me than I have suffered for him? Come now—if you are wounded, strip and show your wounds, and I will show mine. There is no part of my body but my back which has not a scar; not a weapon a man may grasp or fling the mark of which I do not carry upon me. I have sword-cuts from close fight; arrows have pierced me, missiles from catapults bruised my flesh; again and again I have been struck by stones or clubs—and all for your sakes: for your glory and your gain. Over every land and sea, across river, mountain, and plain I led you to the world's end, a victorious army. I married as you married, and many of you will have children related by blood to my own. Some of you have owed money—I have paid your debts, never troubling to inquire how they were incurred, and in spite of the fact that you earn good pay and grow rich from the sack of cities. To most of you I have given a circlet of gold as a memorial for ever and ever of your courage and of my regard. And what of those who have died in battle? Their death was noble, their burial illustrious; almost all are commemorated at home by statues of bronze; their parents are held in honour, with all dues of money or service remitted, for under my leadership not a man among you has ever fallen with his back to the enemy.

'And now it was in my mind to dismiss any man no longer fit for active service—all such should return home to be envied and admired. But you all wish to leave me. Go then! And when you reach home, tell them that Alexander your King, who vanquished Persians and Medes and Bactrians and Sacae; who crushed the Uxii, the Arachotians, and the Drangae, and added to his empire Parthia, the Chorasmian waste, and Hyrcania to the Caspian Sea; who crossed the Caucasus beyond the Caspian Gates, and Oxus and Tanais and the Indus, which none but Dionysus had crossed before him, and Hydaspes and Acesines and Hydraotes—yes, and Hyphasis too, had you not feared to follow; who by both mouths of the Indus burst into the Great Sea beyond, and traversed the desert of Gedrosia, untrodden before by any army; who made

Carmania his own, as his troops swept by, and the country of the Oreitans; who was brought back by you to Susa, when his ships had sailed the ocean from India to Persia—tell them, I say, that you deserted him and left him to the mercy of barbarian men, whom you yourselves had conquered. Such news will indeed assure you praise upon earth and reward in heaven. Out of my sight!'

As he ended, Alexander sprang from the rostrum and hurried into the palace. All that day he neither ate nor washed nor permitted any of his friends to see him. On the following day too he remained closely confined. On the third day he sent for the Persian officers who were in the highest favour and divided among them the command of the various units of the army. Only those whom he designated his kinsmen were now permitted to give him the customary kiss.

On the Macedonians the immediate effect of Alexander's speech was profound. They stood in silence in front of the rostrum. Nobody made a move to follow the King except his closest attendants and the members of his personal guard; the rest, helpless to speak or act, yet unwilling to go away, remained rooted to the spot. But when they were told about the Persians and Medes— how command was being given to Persian officers, foreign troops drafted into Macedonian units, a Persian Corps of Guards called by a Macedonian name, Persian infantry units given the coveted title of Companions, Persian Silver Shields and Persian mounted Companions, including even a new Royal Squadron, in process of formation—they could contain themselves no longer. Every man of them hurried to the palace; in sign of supplication they flung their arms on the ground before the doors and stood there calling and begging for admission. They offered to give up the ringleaders of the mutiny and those who had led the cry against the King, and swore they would not stir from the spot day or night unless Alexander took pity on them.

Alexander, the moment he heard of this change of heart, hastened out to meet them, and he was so touched by their grovelling repentance and their bitter lamentations that the tears came into his eyes. While they continued to beg for his pity, he stepped forward as if to speak, but was anticipated by one Callines, an officer of the Companions, distinguished both by age and rank. 'My lord,' he cried, 'what hurts us is that you have made Persians your kinsmen—Persians are called "Alexander's kinsmen"—Persians kiss you. But no Macedonian has yet had a taste of this honour.'

'Every man of you,' Alexander replied, 'I regard as my kinsman, and from now on that is what I shall call you.'

Thereupon Callines came up to him and kissed him, and all the others who wished to do so kissed him too. Then they picked up their weapons and returned to their quarters singing the song of victory at the top of their voices.

To mark the restoration of harmony, Alexander offered sacrifice to the gods he was accustomed to honour, and gave a public banquet which he himself attended, sitting among the Macedonians, all of whom were present. Next them the Persians had their places, and next to the Persians distinguished foreigners of other nations; Alexander and his friends dipped their wine from the same bowl and poured the same libations, following the lead of the Greek seers and the Magi. The chief object of his prayers was that Persians and Macedonians might rule together in harmony as an imperial power. It is said that 9,000 people attended the banquet; they unanimously drank the same toast, and followed it by the paean of victory.

After this all Macedonians—about 10,000 all told—who were too old for service or in any way unfit, got their discharge at their own request. They were given their pay not only up to date, but also for the time they would take on the homeward journey. In addition to their pay they each received a gratuity of one talent. Some of the men had children by Asian women, and it was Alexander's orders that these should be left behind to avoid the trouble among their families at home, which might be caused by the introduction of half-caste children; he promised to have them brought up on Macedonian lines, with particular attention to their military training, and added that when they grew up he would himself bring them back to Macedonia and hand them over to their fathers. It was a somewhat vague and unsatisfactory promise; he did, however, give the clearest proof of how warmly he felt for them, and of how much he would miss them when they had gone, by his decision to entrust them on their journey to the leadership and protection of Craterus, the most loyal of his officers and a man he loved as dearly as his own life. When he said good-bye to them, his eyes and the eyes of every man among them were wet with tears....

36 Demetrius

A God Among Men

Son of the Macedonian Antigonus "the One-Eyed," one of Alexander's generals, Demetrius was an active participant in the political intrigues and warfare that characterized the early Hellenistic age. He would eventually become known as a brilliant commander (his moniker "Poliorcetes" means the "besieger of cities"), although a rather poor administrator. The successors were eager to maintain control over the Greek city-states around the Aegean world, and Demetrius, to gain local Greek support for expelling the garrisons imposed by his Macedonian rivals on the cities, proclaimed his respect for the

From *The Age of Alexander: Nine Greek Lives by Plutarch*, translated and annotated by Ian Scott-Kilvert, with an introduction by G. T. Griffith, pp. 336–51. Copyright © 1973 by Penguin Books. Reproduced by permission of Penguin Books, Ltd.

autonomy and freedom of the Greek communities. This was a highly inspired move that resonated with many Greeks. As a result, Demetrius arrived even at Athens not as a conqueror but as a liberator. The local Athenians were delighted to have been "liberated" by one so charming and dashing, and quickly took him in as one of their own. Their warm reception of this young Macedonian warlord even went so far as to lead them to proclaim both Demetrius and Antigonus gods and to vote to institute religious cults for their worship.

A. PLUTARCH, LIFE OF DEMETRIUS

This excerpted biography of Demetrius comes from Plutarch of Chaeronea's *Parallel Lives of Famous Greeks and Romans* (composed around A.D. 100). Plutarch consulted many historical sources that are now lost for his research. Throughout this work, he shows great concern for describing the personal character of his subject and often, in accordance with the conventions of biography at the time, ascribes praise or blame to their particular deeds to arrive at a balanced view of the life in question. The talented and flamboyant Demetrius led an extravagant way of life in his pursuit for the supreme power that ultimately eluded him and his father.

... 2. According to most historians, Antigonus had two sons from Stratonice the daughter of Corrhagus. One of them he named Demetrius after his brother, the other Philip after his father. But some writers tell us that Demetrius was Antigonus' nephew, not his son: they say that his father died when he was quite young, and that his mother married Antigonus, who thus came to be regarded as Demetrius' father. Philip, who was a few years the younger, died at an early age. Demetrius grew up to be a tall man, although not so tall as his father, and both in form and in feature he was so strikingly handsome that no painter or sculptor ever succeeded in fashioning a likeness of him. His features combined charm and seriousness, beauty and a capacity to inspire fear, but hardest of all to represent was the blend in his appearance of the eagerness and fire of youth with a heroic aspect and an air of kingly dignity. In his disposition he was equally capable of making himself loved and feared. He could be the most delightful of companions, more voluptuous than any other ruler of his age in his addiction to drinking and other luxurious habits of life, and yet when action was required, he could show the utmost energy, perseverance and practical ability. It was for this reason that he took Dionysus as his model, since this god was most terrible when waging war, but also most skilful at exploiting the ensuing peace for the pursuit of pleasure and enjoyment....

5. Empedocles tells us that the principles of love and hatred produce perpetual strife among the elements of the universe, especially among those elements which are adjacent to or in contact with one another. In the same way wars continually broke out among the successors of Alexander, and these were particularly violent or bitter when the rival interests or disputed territories happened to lie close to one another. This was the situation in which Antigonus and Ptolemy

found themselves. Antigonus was at that moment in Phrygia, and as soon as he received the news that Ptolemy had crossed over from Cyprus, was ravaging Syria and was compelling or subverting the cities there to transfer their allegiance, he sent his son Demetrius to oppose him. Demetrius was then only twenty-two years of age, and now found himself for the first time on trial as the supreme commander of an expedition in which great interests were at stake. In the event his youth and inexperience proved no match for an opponent who had been trained in the school of Alexander, and who had since fought many great campaigns on his own account. Demetrius was crushingly defeated near the city of Gaza, five thousand of his men were killed, eight thousand taken prisoner, and he lost his tent, his money and all his personal possessions. Ptolemy returned all these to him, together with his friends and added the courteous and humane message that they were not engaged in a struggle for life or death, but only for honour and power. Demetrius accepted this generous gesture: at the same time he uttered a prayer to the gods that he should not remain long in Ptolemy's debt, but should soon repay him in like fashion....

6. When the news of the battle reached Antigonus, he remarked that Ptolemy had so far conquered beardless youths, but would now have to fight with grown men: but he was anxious not to crush or humble the spirit of his son and so he granted the young man's request to be allowed to fight again on his own account. Soon after this Cilles, one of Ptolemy's generals, arrived in Syria. ... But Demetrius launched a sudden attack and achieved complete surprise. He routed Cilles' troops, and seized his camp, generals and all, capturing seven thousand prisoners and a vast quantity of treasure. Demetrius was delighted at this success, not so much for what he had acquired as for what he could give back, and he prized the victory less for the glory and the spoils he had won than for the power it gave him to repay Ptolemy's generosity and return the favours he had received....

7. ... Some years before this Seleucus had been driven out [of] his capital of Babylon by Antigonus, but he had later won back the province and re-established his authority there. He now made an expedition to the east with the intention of annexing the tribes living on the borders of India and the provinces in the neighbourhood of Mount Caucasus. So Demetrius, calculating that he would find Mesopotamia undefended, suddenly crossed the Euphrates and made a surprise attack on Babylon. He captured one of the two citadels of the capital, drove out the garrison left by Seleucus and replaced it with a force of seven thousand of his own troops. Then he gave orders to his soldiers to seize and plunder everything that they could carry or drive out of the country and marched back to the coast. But in the event his action only left Seleucus more firmly established in possession of his kingdom than before, for by ravaging the country he appeared to admit that it no longer belonged to him and his father. Then as Demetrius was returning through Syria, he learned that Ptolemy had laid siege to Halicarnassus, whereupon he swiftly marched to the city and relieved it.

8. This feat won great renown for Demetrius and Antigonus and fired them with the inspiring ambition to restore freedom to the whole of Greece, which had been deprived of its liberty by the rule of Cassander and Ptolemy. None of the kings who succeeded Alexander ever waged a nobler or a juster war than this,

for Demetrius now took the huge quantities of treasure which they had amassed from their victories over the barbarians and devoted it for their own honour and good name to the cause of delivering the Greeks. They decided to begin their campaign by sailing against Athens, whereupon one of Antigonus' friends remarked that if they captured the city they must keep possession of it, since it was the gangway that led to all the rest of Greece. But Antigonus would not hear of this. He declared that he needed no better or steadier gangway than a people's goodwill, that Athens was the watch-tower of the whole world, and that through her reputation she would swiftly beacon forth his deeds to all mankind.

So Demetrius sailed to Athens with a fleet of two hundred and fifty ships and five thousand talents. The city was at this time governed by Demetrius of Phaleron as Cassander's deputy, and a force of Macedonians was garrisoned in Munychia. Demetrius arrived ... and through a combination of good fortune and good management ... took his opponents completely by surprise. When his ships were first sighted off the coast, everybody took them for Ptolemy's fleet and prepared to receive them. ... For Demetrius, as he found the entrances to the harbours undefended, sailed straight in, and was soon in full view of the Athenians on the deck of his ship: he then signalled to the citizens to be quiet and allow him a hearing. When silence had been restored, he ordered a herald standing by his side to announce that he had been sent by his father on what he prayed would prove a happy mission for the Athenians, for his orders were to set the city free, to expel the garrison and to restore to the people the use of their laws and their ancestral constitution.

9. When they heard this proclamation, most of the Athenians immediately threw down their shields at their feet and burst into applause. Then with loud cheers they called upon Demetrius to land, acclaiming him as their benefactor and saviour....

10. ... [H]e called the people together and formally restored to them their ancestral constitution. He also promised that his father would supply one hundred and fifty thousand bushels of wheat and enough timber to build a fleet of a hundred triremes. It was by then fourteen years since the Athenians had been deprived of their democratic constitution, and in the intervening period since the Lamian war and the battle of Crannon they had in theory been governed by an oligarchy but in practice by a single man, because of the continuously growing power of Demetrius of Phalerum.

The benefactions which Demetrius had lavished on the Athenians had made his name great and glorious, but the people themselves now began to make it obnoxious by the extravagance of the honours which they voted him. For example they were the first people in the world to confer upon Antigonus and Demetrius the title of king. Both men had hitherto made it a matter of piety to decline this appellation, for they regarded it as the one royal honour which was still reserved for the lineal descendants of Philip and Alexander and which it would be wrong for others to assume or share. The Athenians were also the only people who described them as saviour-gods, and they even abolished the ancient office of the archon, from whom the year received its name, and elected in his place a priest to officiate at the altar of the saviour-gods. They also decreed that the figures of

Demetrius and Antigonus should be woven into the sacred robe of Athene, together with those of the other gods. They consecrated the spot where Demetrius had first alighted from his chariot and built an altar there, which was known as the altar of the Descending Demetrius. Besides this they created two new tribes and named them Demetrias and Antigonis, and in consequence raised the number of senators from five hundred to six hundred, since each tribe supplies fifty....

15. Soon after this his father sent for him to take command of the operations against Ptolemy with the object of capturing Cyprus. ... [H]e attacked Menelaus, Ptolemy's brother, and immediately defeated him. Soon afterwards Ptolemy himself appeared on the scene with a large fleet and army, and the two commanders exchanged haughty and threatening messages. ... The battle which then followed was of the greatest moment, not only to the combatants themselves but to all the other rulers of the eastern Mediterranean, for apart from the uncertainty of the outcome, they believed that the prize was not merely the possession of Cyprus and Syria, but an absolute supremacy over all their rivals....

16. ... He bore down upon the opposing fleet with great speed and dash and utterly routed Ptolemy, who after his defeat fled with a squadron of eight ships. This was all that remained of his fleet: of the rest, some had been sunk in the battle and seventy had been captured, crews and all.

17. Demetrius added more lustre to his brilliant victory by the generosity and humanity which he showed to his opponents: he not only buried the enemy's dead with full honours but he also set his prisoners free. He then chose twelve hundred complete suits of armour from the spoils and presented them to the Athenians.

He sent Aristodemus of Miletus as his personal messenger to carry the news of the victory to his father....

18. After this success the people for the first time acclaimed Antigonus and Demetrius as kings. Antigonus was immediately crowned, and Demetrius received a diadem from his father with a letter addressing him as king. At the same time when the news reached Ptolemy's followers in Egypt, they also conferred the title of king on him, so as not to appear unduly cast down by their defeat, and this spirit of rivalry proved infectious among the other successors of Alexander. Lysimachus began to wear a diadem, and Seleucus who had already assumed royal prerogatives when he gave audience to the barbarians, now adopted the same practice in his interviews with Greeks. Cassander, however, although others addressed him as king both in letters and in speech continued to sign letters with his own name, as he had always done.

The assumption of these dignities meant something more than the mere addition of a name or a change in appearance. It stirred the spirits of these men, raised their ideas to a different plane and introduced an element of pride and self-importance into their daily lives and their dealings with others, in the same way as tragic actors, when they put on royal robes, alter their gait, their voice, their deportment and their mode of address. As a result they also became harsher in their administration of justice, and they cast off the various disguises whereby they had previously concealed their power and which had made them treat their subjects more gently and tolerantly. Such was the effect of a single word from a flatterer, which in this way brought about a revolution throughout the world....

B. ATHENAEUS, *THE LEARNED BANQUET*:
ITHYLPHALLIC HYMN IN HONOR OF DEMETRIUS

The popular hymns that the Athenians composed to honor Demetrius and his divinity are recorded in *The Learned Banquet*, a collection of entertaining anecdotes by Athenaeus of Naucratis around A.D. 200. Athenaeus united these anecdotes by making them appear as part of a dinner party conversation. Guests describe various topics and in this selection arrive at the theme of flattery. The hymn was cited by a diner as evidence for the Athenians' shameless flattery of Demetrius and presumably of Hellenistic rulers in general. On the other hand, one might see the hymn as rather more playful than serious or sycophantic. In any event, the hymn is interesting for its pragmatic and "down-to-earth" notions about what made someone a god.

[T]he Athenian populace became notorious for flattery. Demochares, at any rate, a relative of the orator Demosthenes, tells a story in the twentieth book of his Histories of the flattering conduct of the Athenians toward Demetrius Poliorcetes, and says that it was not to his liking. He writes as follows: 'Some of these things, it is plain, annoyed him, but other acts were downright disgraceful and humiliating, such as temples to Aphrodite Leaena and Aphrodite Lamia, also altars, shrines, and libations to Burichus, Adeimantus, and Oxythemis, his parasites. ... When Demetrius returned from Leucas and Corcyra to Athens, not only did the Athenians welcome him with offerings of incense and crowns and libations, but processional choruses also, and mummers with the elevated phallus met him with dancing and song; and as they took their places in the crowds they sang and danced, repeating the refrain that he was the only true god, while all the others were asleep or making a journey or non-existent; he, however, was sprung from Poseidon and Aphrodite, pre-eminent in beauty and embracing all in his benevolence. They supplicated him with entreaty ... and offered prayers to him.' This is the amazing account of Athenian flattery. ... And Duris of Samos cites the mummers' song itself ...: ... 'For the highest and dearest of the gods are come to our city. Hither, indeed, the time hath brought together Demeter and Demetrius. She comes to celebrate the solemn mysteries of the Daughter, but he, as is meet for the god, is here in gladness, fair and smiling. Something august he seemeth, all his friends about him, and he himself in their midst, his friends the stars, even as he is the sun. O son of the most mighty god Poseidon and of Aphrodite, hail! For other gods are either far away, or have not ears, or are not, or heed us not at all; but thee we can see in very presence, not in wood and not in stone, but in truth. And so we pray to thee. First bring peace, thou very dear! For thou hast the power....

37 Euhemerus of Messene, *Sacred History*

How Men Became Gods

"... publicly proclaimed him a god"

Individual kings and even whole dynasties received honors and were worshipped by people as divine beings during the Hellenistic age. This feature remained an important aspect of Hellenistic and imperial Roman civilizations. The divinity of the Hellenistic ruler might have had roots in Alexander the Great's career, but the tradition properly took off during the time of his successors. To approach this topic with the right historical perspective, we must first set aside our present-day notions about what is divine and what is not and attempt to see these issues through the eyes of the ancients.

Euhemerus of Messene, a friend of an important Hellenistic ruler, Cassander of Macedon, wrote a work entitled Sacred History (now lost). Euhemerus' work is later quoted by Diodorus of Sicily in his book on universal history entitled *The Library* (begun around 60 B.C.), from which this selection is excerpted. Euhemerus proposed that the gods whom the Greeks worshipped were once mortal and that they received immortality and divinity because of their great deeds and beneficence toward humankind. If one was to accept the idea that even gods such as Zeus used to be mortal, then it should be easy to accept a contemporary Hellenistic king as also capable of being made a god provided that he act in a manner befitting this divine status. Euhemerus' doctrine, while not universally subscribed to, tells us how certain learned men in the early Hellenistic age rationalized to themselves and those around them the new form of political institution that emerged: the Hellenistic god-king.

[Diodorus, citing the words of Euhemerus of Messenē, wrote:] "As regards the gods, then, men of ancient times have handed down to later generations two different conceptions: Certain of the gods, they say, are eternal and imperishable, such as the sun and the moon and the other stars of the heavens, and the winds as well and whatever else possesses a nature similar to theirs; for each of these the genesis and duration are from everlasting to everlasting. But the other gods, we are told, were terrestrial beings who attained to immortal honour and fame because of their benefactions to mankind, such as Heracles, Dionysus, Aristaeus, and the others who were like them. Regarding these terrestrial gods many and varying accounts have been handed down by the writers of history and of mythology; of the historians, Euhemerus, who composed the *Sacred History*, has written a special treatise

From *Diodorus Siculus, Vol. III, Library of History*, Loeb Classical Library Vol. 340, translated by C. H. Oldfather (Cambridge, Mass.: Harvard University Press, 1939). The Loeb Classical Library® is a registered trademark of the President and Fellows of Harvard College. Reprinted by permission of the publishers and the Trustees of the Loeb Classical Library.

about them, while, of the writers of myths, Homer and Hesiod and Orpheus and the others of their kind have invented rather monstrous stories about the gods. But for our part, we shall endeavour to run over briefly the accounts which both groups of writers have given, aiming at due proportion in our exposition.

"Now Euhemerus, who was a friend of King Cassander[1] and was required by him to perform certain affairs of state and to make great journeys abroad, says that he travelled southward as far as the ocean; for setting sail from Arabia the Blest [near modern Yemen] he voyaged through the ocean for a considerable number of days and was carried to the shore of some islands in the sea, one of which bore the name of Panchaea. On this island he saw the Panchaeans who dwell there, who excel in piety and honour the gods with the most magnificent sacrifices and with remarkable votive offerings of silver and of gold. The island is sacred to the gods, and there are a number of other objects on it which are admired both for their antiquity and for the great skill of their workmanship.... There is also on the island, situated upon an exceedingly high hill, a sanctuary of Zeus Triphylius, which was established by him during the time when he was king of all the inhabited world and was still in the company of men. And in this temple there is a stele of gold on which is inscribed in summary, in the writing employed by the Panchaeans, the deeds of Uranus and Cronus and Zeus.

"Euhemerus goes on to say that Uranus was the first to be king, that he was an honourable man and beneficent, who was versed in the movement of the stars, and that he was also the first to honour the gods of the heavens with sacrifices, whence he was called Uranus or "Heaven." There were born to him by his wife Hestia two sons, Titan and Cronus, and two daughters, Rhea and Demeter. Cronus became king after Uranus, and marrying Rhea he begat Zeus and Hera and Poseidon. And Zeus, on succeeding to the kingship, married Hera and Demeter and Themis, and by them he had children, the Curetes by the first named, Persephonê by the second, and Athena by the third. And going to Babylon he was entertained by Belus, and after that he went to the island of Panchaea, which lies in the ocean, and here he set up an altar to Uranus, the founder of his family. From there he passed through Syria and came to Casius, who was ruler of Syria at that time, and who gave his name to Mt. Casius. And coming to Cilicia he conquered in battle Cilix, the governor of the region, and he visited very many other nations, all of which paid honour to him and publicly proclaimed him a god."

After recounting what I have given and more to the same effect about the gods, as if about mortal men, Diodorus goes on to say: "Now regarding Euhemerus, who composed the *Sacred History*, we shall rest content with what has been said, and shall endeavour to run over briefly the myths which the Greeks recount concerning the gods, as they are given by Hesiod and Homer and Orpheus." Thereupon Diodorus goes on to add the myths as the poets give them.

... Regarding the gods, the most learned Diodorus also says in his writings that those gods whom men were wont to address as immortal, considering them to be so

---

1. A general who became king of Macedon after Alexander's death. Cassander reigned from ca. 301 until his death in 297 B.C.

because of their beneficences, had indeed been born human beings; but that certain of them had acquired the appellations they have after the lands they conquered....

Hellenistic Rulers and Their Subjects

The relationship between a Hellenistic king and a Greek city-state was a complicated one. On the one hand, the king held a fearsome amount of power and influence and must be reckoned with. On the other, the tradition of what made a Greek city-state a city-state—its autonomy and sovereignty—would hinder any straightforward attempt to define the relationship between city and king as one of subject and master. A balanced ideological formulation was needed to address both these points. The cult of worship offered by city-state communities to Hellenistic rulers was the inspired mechanism that allowed the kings to be honored as they expected to be and for the cities to maintain their semblance of independence. After all, they were paying honors to gods, as was proper, not men. They were also doing so in deep gratitude for benefits received from the ruler. The regular offer of gold crowns of specified weight rendered the transfer of wealth part of a sacral ritual and not a form of direct taxation, the lack a overt sign of political dubmission and the lack of freedom. This political dynamic remained vitally important throughout the Hellenistic and Roman periods.

38 Antigonus the One-Eyed and Scepsis

"that Antigonus may receive honours worthy of his achievements..."

Antigonus and Demetrius made much capital out of their policy to respect the autonomy and freedom of Greek city-states. Antigonus indeed sent many official messages, in which he would cite his especial care for their welfare, to the Greeks to cement his relationship with them. The Greeks generally responded

From M. M. Austin, *The Hellenistic World from Alexander to the Roman Conquest: A Selection of Ancient Sources in Translation* (Cambridge, U.K.: Cambridge University Press, 1981), pp. 57–61. Reprinted with permission of Cambridge University Press.

positively to his overtures and, one must also add, to those of his rivals, who made similar gestures.

The following exchange (parts A and B of this selection) between Antigonus and one such Greek city-state, Scepsis in the Troad (in modern northwest Turkey), exemplifies a kind of negotiation that probably took place in hundreds of different cities. We are fortunate to have this surviving evidence, which comes from a stone inscription put up by the citizens of Scepsis to commemorate the set of events that led to their setting up of an annual festival in honor of Antigonus.

A. LETTER OF ANTIGONUS TO SCEPSIS

(The beginning of the inscription is lost)

... we displayed [zeal for the] freedom [of the Greeks] and made [for this purpose] many considerable concessions including [the gift of?] money, and to this end we sent out jointly Aeschylus [and Demarchus?]. As long as there was agreement on [this] point, we took part in the meeting at the [Hellespont], and if [certain] men had not raised difficulties, the matter would have been settled then. [But now] when Cassander and [Ptolemy] were discussing a truce and Prepelaus and Aristodemus came to see us [on] this matter, although we saw that some of Cassander's demands were excessive, we thought we ought to overlook them since there was agreement about the Greeks, so that the essential points should be implemented as soon as possible; we should have thought it a great achievement to arrange something for the Greeks as we had wished, but because this would have been a rather lengthy process and delay can often bring about many unforeseen consequences, and because we were anxious to see the affairs of the Greeks settled in our lifetime, we thought it imperative that questions of detail should not prevent the implementation of the essential points. How great is the zeal we have displayed over this will, I think, be clear to you and to all others from the actual dispositions taken. When we had reached agreement with Cassander and Lysimachus, for which purpose they had sent Prepelaus with full powers, Ptolemy sent ambassadors to us requesting a truce with himself and his inclusion in the same agreement. We saw that it was no small matter to give up part of the goal for which we had taken great trouble and spent much money, and that when we had reached a settlement with Cassander and Lysimachus and the rest of the task was easier; nevertheless, because we understood that a settlement with him too (Ptolemy) would speed up a solution to the question of Polyperchon, since he would have no allies, and because of our relationship with him, and also because we saw that you and the other allies were burdened by military service and by expenses, we thought it was right to give way and to conclude a truce with him too. We despatched Aristodemus, Aeschylus and Hegesias to conclude the agreement; they have returned after receiving pledges, and the envoys from Ptolemy, Aristobulus and his colleagues, have arrived to receive pledges from us. Know therefore that the truce has been concluded and that peace has been made. We have written a clause into the agreement that all

the Greeks should join together in protecting their mutual freedom and autonomy, in the belief that in our lifetime they would in all human expectation be
preserved, but that in future with all the Greeks and the men in power bound by
oath, the freedom of the Greeks would be much more securely guaranteed. To
join in the oath to protect what we agreed with each other did not seem to us
inglorious or without advantage to the Greeks. It therefore seems to me right
that you should swear the oath which we have sent to you. We shall endeavour
in future to achieve whatever is in your interest and that of the other Greeks.
Concerning these matters I resolved to write to you and to send Acius to discuss
them with you; he brings you copies of the agreement we have made and of the
oath. Farewell.

B. SCEPSIS' RESPONSE TO ANTIGONUS' LETTER

(The beginning of the incription is lost)

[... since Antigonus has sent] Acius who [in every respect shows himself to be] well
disposed [to our city] and continues to [maintain his zeal] and [requests] that the
city declares to him its demands; and since he has also sent news of the agreement
concluded by him with Cassander, Ptolemy and Lysimachus, copies of the oath,
and news of what has been done concerning the peace and the autonomy of the
Greeks; be it resolved by the people: since Antigonus has been responsible for great
benefits to the city and the other Greeks, to praise Antigonus and to rejoice with
him in what has been accomplished; let the city also rejoice with the other Greeks
that they shall live in peace henceforward enjoying freedom and autonomy, and so
that Antigonus may receive honours worthy of his achievements and the people
should be seen to be returning thanks for the benefits it has received, let it mark
off a sacred enclosure ... for him, build an altar and set up a cult statue as beautiful
as possible, and let the sacrifice, the competition, the wearing of the wreath and the
rest of the festival be celebrated every [year] in his honour as they were before. Let
it [crown] him with a gold crown [weighing] 100 gold [staters], and crown Demetrius and Philippus with crowns weighing each 50 drachmas; and let it proclaim the
crowns [at the] contest during the festival; let the city offer a sacrifice for the good
tidings sent by Antigonus; let all the citizens wear wreaths, and let the treasurer
provide the money for this expense. Let friendly gifts be sent to Antigonus, and
let there be inscribed on a stele the text of the agreement, the letter from Antigonus
and the oath which he sent, as he instructed, and place it in the sanctuary of
Athena; let the secretary [supervise] the task, [and] let the treasurer provide the
money for the expenditure; let all the citizens [swear] the [oath which was sent],
as [instructed by Antigonus]; and let those who have been chosen...

(the rest of the inscription is lost)

From ibid. pp. 59–60. Reprinted with permission of Cambridge University Press.

39 Athenaeus, *The Learned Banquet*

Hellenistic Pomp and Circumstance

"What monarchy ... has ever been so rich in gold?"

The Hellenistic kings did not invent pomp and circumstance but they certainly refined the art. The deliberate use of magnificent and sumptuous public displays as a form of royal self-representation was a common feature in all the successor kingdoms. It was copied by the Romans later when they attained their empire. Careful to maintain a positive and potent public image and reputation, most often in stiff competition with their rivals, these god-kings spared no expense to put on the best show possible. Often these displays took place during annual festivals of the ruler cult and featured impressive parades involving gloriously decked-out soldiers, mythological "floats," and even elephants.

The following account comes from *The Learned Banquet*, a collection of entertaining anecdotes drawn from history by Athenaeus of Naucratis (around A.D. 200). It represents the attempts by two rival Hellenistic dynasties, the Seleucids and the Ptolemies, to put on marvelous shows to impress foreigners and subjects alike. The first story is of a Seleucid king's grand parade in Daphne, a luxurious suburb of Antioch in Syria, his royal capital. The second concerns the grand spectacles found in Alexandria, by Egypt during the time of the Ptolemaieia, the festival of the divine Ptolemy I Soter put on by his son and successor, Ptolemy II Philadelphus. The festival was neither staid nor strictly formal because a bacchanalian atmosphere also reigned as all the festival-goers made merry amidst the pomp and circumstance.

... This same king, hearing about the games instituted in Macedonia by Aemilius Paulus, the Roman general, and wishing to outdo Paulus in magnificence, dispatched envoys and delegates to the cities to proclaim the games which were to be given by him near Daphne; hence great interest arose on the part of the Greeks in meeting him. As a beginning to the meeting he got up a parade which was carried out in the following manner. It was led by certain men in the prime of their youth, five thousand in number, who wore Roman armour of chain-mail; after them came five thousand Mysians; close to these were three thousand Cilicians equipped in the fashion of light-armed troops, and wearing gold crowns. After these came three thousand Thracians and five thousand Celts. These were followed by twenty thousand Macedonians, ten thousand of them with gold shields, five thousand with bronze shields, and the rest with silver shields; close upon these came two hundred and forty pairs of gladiators. Behind them were one thousand Nisaean horsemen and three thousand citizen soldiers, of whom the majority wore gold cheek-coverings and gold crowns, the rest had cheek-coverings of silver. After them came the so-called "mounted companions"; there were about a thousand of these, all with gold cheek-pieces. Next to these was the division made up of his friends, equal in numbers and in beauty of equipment. After them were a thousand picked men, followed by the so-called Agema ("Guard"), which has the reputation of being the best organization of horsemen, numbering about a thousand. Last of all was the armoured cavalry, both horses and men being completely covered with armour in accordance with their name. They numbered alone one thousand five hundred. And all these mentioned wore purple cloaks, many also cloaks woven with gold and embroidered with figures. After them were a hundred chariots drawn by six horses, and forty drawn by four horses; next a chariot drawn by four elephants, and another by a pair of elephants; and in single file followed thirty-six caparisoned elephants.

It would be difficult to pursue the description of the rest of the procession, and it must be described summarily. Young men who had just come of age, to the number of eight hundred, and wearing gold crowns, marched in the line; fatted oxen, about one thousand; sacrificial tables, little short of three hundred; elephants' tusks, eight hundred. It is not possible to enumerate the quantity of sacred images; for statues of all beings who are said or held to be gods, demigods, or even heroes among mankind were borne along, some gilded, others draped in garments of gold thread. And beside all of them lay the sacred myths pertaining to each, according to the traditional accounts, in sumptuous editions. They were followed by representations of Night and Day, Earth and Heaven, and Dawn and Noon. One might guess how great was the number of gold and silver vessels in the following way: of only one of the king's friends, the secretary Dionysius, one thousand slaves marched in the procession carrying silver vessels, none of which weighed less than a thousand drachms. Then came six hundred royal slaves with gold vessels. After them nearly two hundred women sprinkled scented oil from gold pitchers. Close upon these in the procession were eighty women seated in litters having gold supports, and five hundred in litters with silver supports, all richly dressed. These were the most conspicuous features of the parade. The games, gladiatorial contests, and hunts took thirty days to conclude; during the first five days in which spectacles were carried out, all persons in the gymnasium anointed themselves with saffron oil from golden basins; these numbered fifteen, and there was an equal number of bowls with oil of cinnamon and nard. Similarly there were brought in, on the succeeding days, oil of fenugreek, marjoram, and orris, all of them rare in their fragrance. For a banquet on one occasion there were spread a thousand triclinia, on another fifteen hundred, with the most extravagant deckings. The management of these matters was undertaken by the king himself. Riding on a poor horse, he ran up and down the procession, commanding one division to advance, another to halt. At the symposia he stood at the entrance introducing some, assigning couches to others, and he himself brought in the servants who carried in the dishes served. And going round he would seat himself in one place, or throw himself down in another. At one moment he would throw aside a morsel or a cup just as he had put them to his lips, and jumping up suddenly, he would change his place or walk round among the drinkers, receiving toasts standing sometimes by one, sometimes by another, at the same time laughing at the entertainments. When the party had been going on a long time and many had already withdrawn, the king was brought in by the mime-performers entirely wrapped up, and deposited on the ground as though he were one of the performers. When the symphony sounded the challenge, he would leap up and dance naked and act with the clowns, so that every one departed in shame. All these celebrations were paid for partly from funds which he had appropriated in Egypt when he broke his treaty with King Ptolemy Philometor, who was then a lad, and partly from contributions by his friends. He had also plundered most of the temples.

The guests expressed their wonder at the state of the king's mind, judging that he was not illustrious, but really insane,... Masurius then added an account of the procession which was arranged in Alexandria by the most excellent king Ptolemy Philadelphus; this is recorded by Callixeinus of Rhodes in the fourth book of his work on Alexandria....

... [W]e will now give an account of the procession. It was held in the city stadium. At the head marched the 'division of the Morning Star' because the procession began at the time that star appears. Then came that part of the procession which was named from the parents of the king and queen. After these came the divisions named from all the gods, having decorative symbols appropriate to the story of each divinity. The last division, as it happened, was that of the Evening Star, since the season of the year brought the time consumed by the procession down to that point. If anyone wishes to learn the details, let him take and study the records of the quadrennial games. In the Dionysiac procession, there marched at the head Sileni who kept back the crowds; they were dressed in purple riding-cloaks, some in red. These were closely followed by Satyrs, twenty at each end of the stadium, carrying torches ornamented with gilt ivy-leaves. After these came Victories with gold wings. These carried censers nine feet high, ornamented with gilt ivy-sprays; the women had on embroidered tunics, and their persons were covered with much gold jewelry. After them followed a double altar nine feet long, ornamented in high relief with gilt ivy-foliage, and having a gold crown of grape-leaves twined with striped white ribbons. Following this came one hundred and twenty boys in purple tunics, carrying frankincense and myrrh, and, moreover, saffron upon gold trenchers. After them marched forty Satyrs crowned with gold crowns in ivy pattern; their bodies were smeared in some cases with purple, in others with vermilion and other colours. These also wore a gold crown wrought in grape and ivy patterns. After them came two Sileni in purple riding-cloaks and white shoes. One of them wore a broad-brimmed hat and held a herald's staff of gold, the other carried a trumpet. Between these walked a man over six feet tall, in tragic costume and mask, carrying a gold horn of plenty; he was called 'The Year.' He was followed by a very beautiful woman as tall as he, dressed in a striking tunic and adorned with much gold, and carrying in one hand a crown of persea, in the other a palm-branch; she was called 'Lustrum.' She was closely followed by the four Seasons gaily dressed and each carrying the fruits appropriate to her. Next these were two censers, nine feet tall, ornamented with ivy pattern in gold; also a square altar between them, of gold. Again came Satyrs wearing gold ivy-crowns and clad in red tunics; some carried a gold wine-pitcher, others a gold goblet. After them marched the poet Philiscus, who was a priest of Dionysus, and all the guild of the artists of Dionysus. Next were borne Delphic tripods, being prizes for the managers of the athletes; the one intended for the manager of the boys' class was thirteen and a half feet high, the other, for the manager of the adults' class, was eighteen feet. After these came a four-wheeled cart, twenty-one feet long and twelve feet wide, drawn by one hundred and eighty men; in this stood a statue of Dionysus, fifteen feet tall, pouring a libation from a gold goblet, and wearing a purple tunic extending to the feet, over which was a transparent saffron coat; but round his shoulders was thrown a purple mantle spangled with gold. In front of him lay a gold Laconian mixing-bowl holding one hundred and fifty gallons; also a gold tripod, on which lay a gold censer and two saucers of gold full of cassia and saffron. Over him stretched a canopy decorated with ivy, grape-vine, and the other cultivated fruits, and hanging to it also were wreaths, ribbons, Bacchic wands, tambourines, fillets, and satyric, comic, and tragic masks. The cart (was followed) by priests and priestesses and those who had charge of the sacred vestments, sacred guilds of every description, and women carrying the winnowing-fans. Next came Macedonian bacchants, the so-called 'Mimallones,' and 'Bassarae' and 'Lydian women,' with hair streaming down and crowned with wreaths, some of snakes, others of smilax and vine-leaves and ivy; in their hands some held daggers, others snakes.... Next came a four-wheeled cart thirty-seven and a half feet long, twenty-one feet wide, and drawn by six hundred men; in it was a wine skin holding thirty thousand gallons, stitched together from leopard pelts; this also trickled over the whole line of march as the wine was slowly let out. Following the skin came a hundred and twenty crowned Satyrs and Sileni, some carrying wine-pitchers, others shallow cups, still others large deep cups—everything of gold. [A large number of magnificent gold and silver vessels holding food and drinks are described in great detail.] After all this there marched one thousand six hundred boys who had on white tunics and wore crowns, some of ivy, others of pine; two hundred and fifty of them carried gold pitchers, four hundred, silver pitchers; while another band of three hundred and twenty bore gold or silver wine-coolers. After them other boys carried jars intended to be used for sweetmeats; twenty of these were of gold, fifty of silver, and three hundred were adorned with encaustic paintings in all sorts of colours. And since the mixtures had already been made in the water-jars and casks, all persons in the stadium were duly showered with sweetness."

Next to these in his catalogue were six-foot tables on which were borne remarkable scenes lavishly represented. Among these was included the bridal chamber of Semele, in which certain characters wear tunics of gold bejewelled with the costliest gems. And it would not be right to omit the following mention of "the four-wheeled cart, in length thirty-three feet, in width twenty-one, drawn by five hundred men; it it was a deep cavern profusely shaded with ivy and yew. From this pigeons, ring-doves, and turtle-doves flew forth along the whole route, with nooses tied to their feet so that they could be easily caught by the spectators. And from it also gushed forth two fountains, one of milk, the other of wine. And all the nymphs standing round him wore crowns of gold, and Hermes had a staff of gold, and all in rich garments. In another cart, which contained 'the return of Dionysus from India,' there was a Dionysus measuring eighteen feet who reclined upon an elephant's back, clad in a purple coat and wearing a gold crown, of ivy and vine pattern; he held in his hands a gold wand-lance, and his feet were shod with shoes fastened by gold straps. Seated in front of him on the elephant's neck was a Satyr measuring seven and a half feet, crowned with a gold pine-wreath, his right hand holding a goat-horn of gold, as though he were signalling with it. The elephant had trappings of gold and round its neck an ivy-crown in gold. This cart was followed by five hundred young girls dressed in purple tunics with gold girdles. Those who were in the lead, numbering one hundred and twenty, wore gold pine-crowns; following them came one hundred and twenty Satyrs, some in gold, some in silver, and some in bronze panoply. After them marched five troops of asses on which were mounted Sileni and Satyrs wearing crowns. Some of the asses had frontlets and harness of gold, others, of silver. After them were sent forth twenty-four elephant chariots, sixty teams of he-goats, twelve of saiga antelopes, seven of beisa antelopes, fifteen of leucoryse, eight teams of ostriches, seven of Père David deer, four of wild asses, and four four-horse chariots. On all of these were mounted little boys wearing the tunics and wide-brimmed hats of charioteers, and beside them stood little girls equipped with small crescent shields and wand-lances, dressed in robes and decked with gold coins. The lads driving the chariots wore pine crowns, the girls wore ivy. Next after them came six teams of camels, three on either side. These were immediately followed by carts drawn by mules. These contained barbaric tents, under which sat Indian and other women dressed as captives. Then came camels, some of which carried three hundred pounds of frankincense, three hundred of myrrh, and two hundred of saffron, cassia, cinnamon, orris, and all other spices. Next to these were negro tribute-bearers, some of whom brought six hundred tusks, others two thousand ebony logs, others sixty mixing-bowls full of gold and silver coins and gold dust. After these, in the procession, marched two hunters carrying gilded hunting-spears. Dogs were also led along, numbering two thousand four hundred, some Indian, the others Hyrcanian or Molossian or of other breeds. Next came one hundred and fifty men carrying trees on which were suspended all sorts of animals and birds. Then were brought, in cages, parrots, peacocks, guinea-fowls, and birds from the Phasis and others from Aethiopia, in great quantities."

After he has spoken of very many other things, and enumerated many droves of animals he adds: "One hundred and thirty Aethiopian sheep, three hundred Arabian, twenty Euboean; also twenty-six Indian zebus entirely white, eight Aethiopian, one large white she-bear, fourteen leopards, sixteen genets, four caracals, three bear-cubs, one giraffe, one Aethiopian rhinoceros. Next in a four-wheeled cart was Dionysus at the altar of Rhea, having found refuge there while being pursued by Hera; he had on a gold crown, and Priapus stood at his side, with a gold ivy-crown. The statue of Hera had a gold diadem. Then there were statues of Alexander and Ptolemy, crowned with ivy-crowns made of gold. The statue of Goodness which stood beside Ptolemy had a gold olive-crown.

Priapus stood beside them also wearing an ivy-crown made of gold. The city of Corinth, standing beside Ptolemy, was crowned with a gold band. Beside all these figures were placed a stand for cups, full of gold vessels, and a gold mixing-bowl of fifty gallons capacity. Following this cart were women who wore very rich robes and ornaments; they bore the names of cities, some from Ionia, while all the rest were the Greek cities which occupied Asia and the islands and had been under the rule of the Persians; they all wore gold crowns. In other carts, also, were carried a Bacchic wand of gold, one hundred and thirty-five feet long, and a silver spear ninety feet long; in another was a gold phallus one hundred and eighty feet long, painted in various colours and bound with fillets of gold; it had at the extremity a gold star, the perimeter of which was nine feet."

Many and varied though the things are which have been mentioned as belonging to these processions, yet I have selected for mention only those things which contained gold and silver. For there were numerous articles worth mentioning, and quantities of wild beasts and horses, and twenty-four huge lions. "There were other carts besides, which carried images of kings and of gods as well, many of them. After them marched a choral band of six hundred men; among them three hundred harp-players performed together, carrying harps gilded all over, and wearing gold crowns. After them two thousand steers, all of the same colour and with gilded horns, came by, having gold stars on their foreheads, wreaths between the horns, and necklaces and aegises on their breasts; all these were of gold. And after this came marching in the carnival a division in honour of Zeus and one of other gods in great number, and following all one devoted to Alexander, whose effigy in gold was borne, Victory and Athena on either side, in a chariot drawn by live elephants. In the procession also were many thrones constructed of ivory and gold; on one of these lay a gold diadem, on another a gilded horn, on still another a gold crown, and on another a horn of solid gold. Upon the throne of Ptolemy Soter lay a crown made of ten thousand gold coins. In the procession also were three hundred and fifty gold censers, and gilded altars wreathed with gold crowns; on one of these, four gold torches fifteen feet long were affixed. And two gilded braziers were also carried in the procession, of which one was eighteen feet in circumference and sixty in height, the other measured twenty-two and a half feet. There were also nine Delphic tripods of gold of six feet each, eight more of nine feet, another of forty-five feet; on this were figures in gold seven and a half feet high, and a vine-wreath of gold encircled it. There went by also seven gilded palm-trees twelve feet high and a gilded herald's staff sixty-seven and a half feet long, a gilded thunderbolt sixty feet long, also a gilded temple measuring sixty feet all round; there was a double horn in addition, twelve feet high. A very large number of gilded figures were in the procession, the most of which were eighteen feet high; and there were figures of wild beasts of extraordinary size, and eagles thirty feet high. Three thousand two hundred gold crowns were shown in the procession, and there was another mystic crown of gold one hundred and twenty feet in circumference, adorned with precious stones; this was hung round the portal of Berenice's shrine; there was similarly a gold aegis. And there were also very many gold diadems in the procession, carried by girls richly dressed; one diadem was three feet high, and it had a perimeter of twenty-four feet. There was paraded also a gold breastplate eighteen feet in length, and another of silver, twenty-seven feet, with two gold thunderbolts on it fifteen feet long, and an oak crown of gold studded with jewels. Twenty gold shields, sixty-four suits of armour in gold, two pairs of gold greaves four and a half feet long, twelve gold hods, saucer-shaped cups in very great number, thirty wine-pitchers, ten large ointment-holders, twelve water-jars, fifty bread-platters, various tables, five stands of gold vessels, a horn of solid gold forty-five feet long. And these articles of gold were exclusive of those carried by in the division of Dionysus. Further, there were four hundred cartloads of silver vessels, twenty of gold vessels, and eight hundred of spices. After all these marched the cavalry and infantry forces, all wonderfully armed cap-à-pie. The infantry numbered about 57,600, the cavalry 23,200. All of these marched dressed in the garments proper to each, and in their appropriate panoply. But beside the panoplies worn by all these troops, there were very many others stored in chests, of which it is not easy to set down even the number." Yet Callixeinus gave the list. "And in the games twenty persons were crowned with gold crowns; Ptolemy was first, then Berenice, who were honoured with three portrait-statues in gold chariots, and with precincts at Dodona. The total expense, in currency, amounted to two thousand, two hundred and thirty-nine talents and fifty minas; and all this sum was paid in to the managing officials before the exhibition was over, through the enthusiastic zeal of those who gave the crowns. And their son Ptolemy Philadelphus, was awarded two gold portrait-statues, in gold chariots, mounted on columns, one of nine feet, five of seven and a half feet, and six of six feet."

What monarchy, fellow-banqueters, has ever been so rich in gold? Surely not any that appropriated the wealth of Persia or Babylon, or that had mines to work, or that owned the Pactolus river, washing down gold-dust. No; for it is only the Nile, the river truly called "gold-flowing," that with its boundless crops of food actually washes down unadulterated gold which is harvested with no risk, so that it can supply all men sufficiently; being, like Triptolemus, sent forth into every land. For this reason the Byzantian poet by the name of Parmenon says "Thou Nile, Egypt's Zeus!"

Hellenistic Culture, Economy, and Thought

Hellenistic societies were diverse and pluralistic. The major cities became centers of a cosmopolitan culture that expressed itself in Greek language and idioms. This was a time when Greek culture bore the cachet of the victorious and was widely seen as a symbol of privilege and status. Some non-Greeks aspired to imitate their conquerors and become more Greek (*hellenizein* in Greek; hence the word Hellenistic) in speech, dress, and outlook. The Hellenistic age was therefore a time when Greek culture became universalized and local peoples facing its insistent claims found it necessary to assert themselves culturally and politically in ways that intensified both interethnic contacts and conflicts. On a more pragmatic level, Hellenistic rulers were concerned about their own image and power, which relied on their ability to extract wealth from subject territories. The Ptolemies, in particular, continued pharaonic Egyptian administrative practices and scrupulously husbanded their resources to maximize royal revenues. Meanwhile, Hellenistic society encouraged the growth of new philosophical traditions, including those of the Cynics and Stoics whose views of themselves as "citizens of the world," or *kosmopolitai*, were an expected response to the widened cultural horizons of the time. A fierce Greek ethos of competition continued to drive innovation in the areas of culture and learning during this time, and Hellenistic science and technology reached heights that would often not be surpassed during the ancient world.

40 Rosetta Stone Inscription

"Ptolemy the everliving, beloved of Ptah"

Temple priesthoods were a major institution in Egypt. The priests carried out religious rituals and sacrifices and served in the temple that were home to native Egyptians deities. They supervised important cults, including the worship of the Apis Bulls in Memphis and the bulls of Mnevis in Heliopolis, both of which came to be associated with Ptah and Osiris, gods of the Egyptian underworld. The priests' roles and high standing in Egyptian society made their loyalty and support especially sought after when the Ptolemaic kings needed to establish themselves more firmly as legitimate pharaohs in Egypt. The following translation is derived from the Greek text of the decree passed by a council of Egyptian priests that met in Memphis in 196 B.C. to honor the very young king Ptolemy V in recognition of his acts of beneficence towards the people of Egypt. The child Ptolemy had assumed royal power at a time when unrests were widespread throughout the land of Egypt, particularly in the Delta and the Thebaid (the region around Thebes) in Upper or northern Egypt and the various provisions referred to in the decree may be read as concessions to native demands that stemmed from the king's position of weakness. The decree was inscribed on stone stelae set up throughout Egypt in the three written languages of Ptolemaic Egypt: hieroglyphics (sacred letters

From M. M. Austin, *The Hellenistic World from Alexander to the Roman Conquest: A Selection of Ancient Sources in Translation* (Cambridge, U.K.: Cambridge University Press, 1981), pp. 374–77. Reprinted with permission of Cambridge University Press.

used on pharaonic and priestly monuments), demotic (or popular native Egyptian script in common everyday use), and Greek (the language of the court and high administration). The language of the decree also illustrates the comingling of native and Greek names, institutions and concepts that became a feature of life in Ptolemaic Egypt. The trilingual character of the inscription and knowledge of ancient Greek enabled this inscription, the Rosetta Stone, rediscovered during Napoleonic's campaign to Egypt in 1799, to be used as the key to the decipherment of hieroglyphics by Jean François Champollion in the 19th century. This in turn allowed the modern science of Egyptology to emerge. A spoil of war taken from a French ship in 1802, the Rosetta Stone current resides in the British Museum.

In the reign of the young one [Ptolemy V who became king at thirteen], who has received royalty from his father, the lord of crowns, whose glory is great, who established Egypt and is pious towards the gods, the conqueror of his enemies, who restored the life of men, the lord of the Thirty-Year festivals, like Hephaestus [=Egyptian god Ptah] the Great, a king like the Sun [Rā], the great king of the upper and lower regions, son of the Father-Loving Gods..., approved by Hephaestus, to whom the Sun granted victory, the living image of Zeus [=Egyptian god Amun] son of the Sun, Ptolemy the everliving, beloved of Ptah, in the 9th year, when Aetus son of Aetus was priest of Alexander, the Saviour Gods, the Brother-Sister Gods, the Benefactor Gods, the Father-Loving Gods and / the God Manifest and Beneficent..., when Pyrrha daughter of Philinus was *athlophoros* ["prize-bearer" or priestess] of Berenice Euergetis, when Areia daughter of Diogenes was basket-bearer (*canephoros*) of Arsinoe Philadelphus, when Irene daughter of Ptolemy was priestess of Arsinoe Philopator, on the 4th of the month Xandicus and the 18th of the Egyptian month Mecheir (27 March 196); decree; the chief priests, the prophets, those who enter the holy of holies for the robing of the gods, the *pterophoroi* ["wing-bearers"], the sacred scribes and all the other priests who assembled before the king from the temples throughout the land to Memphis for the festival of the reception of royalty to the everliving Ptolemy, beloved of Ptah, God Manifest and Beneficent, which he received from his father, having come together in the temple at Memphis on this day, declared: since King Ptolemy the everliving, beloved of Ptah, God Manifest and Beneficent, born of King Ptolemy and Queen Arsinoe Father-Loving Gods, has conferred many benefits on the temples and / those who dwell in them and on all the subjects in his kingdom, being a god and goddess—just as Horus son of Isis and Osiris, who avenged his father Osiris—and being benevolently disposed towards the gods, has dedicated to the temples revenues in money and corn, and has sustained many expenses to bring Egypt to a state of prosperity and to establish the temples, and has given away freely from his own means, and of the revenues and dues he receives from Egypt some he has completely remitted and others he has reduced, so that the people and all others might enjoy prosperity during his reign, and he has remitted the debts to the crown which were owed by the people in Egypt and those in the rest of his kingdom, which were considerable, and he has freed those who were in the prisons and who were under accusation for a long time from the charges against them; and he has ordered that the revenues of the temples and the grants which are made to them annually in corn / and money, and also the proper quota ... which is assigned to the gods from vineyards and gardens and the other possessions of the gods, should remain as they were in his father's time; and with regard to the priests he has ordered that they should pay no more as their fee for consecration than they were required to pay under his father and up to the first year [of Ptolemy V's reign]; and he has released the members of the priestly class from the annual obligation to sail down the river [the Nile] to Alexandria; and he has ordered that men shall no longer be pressganged for the navy, and has remitted two-thirds of the tax on byssus cloth paid by the temples to the royal treasury, and has restored to order whatever things were neglected in former times, taking care that the customary celebrations should be offered to the gods as is fitting; and he has also dispensed justice to everybody, just like Hermes (=Egyptian god Thoth) the Great and Great; and he has ordered further that those [native Egyptian] soldiers *(machimoi)* who come back, and the others who were rebellious / during the period of disturbances, should return and keep possession of their own property; and he has made sure that the cavalry and infantry forces and ships should be sent out against those attacking Egypt by sea and by land, and has sustained great expenses in money and corn so that the temples and all the people in the land might be in safety; and having gone to Lycopolis in the Busirite nome, which had been occupied and fortified for a siege with an abundant stock of weapons and other supplies—for the disaffection was now of long standing among the impious men [i.e., rebels] who had gathered there and who had done much harm to the temples and the inhabitants of Egypt—and having encamped against it he surrounded it with mounds and trenches and massive fortifications; and when the Nile rose to a great height in the 8th year (198/7 B.C.) and was about to flood the plains as usual, / he held it in check by damming in many places mouths of the canals, for which he spent no small sum of money, having stationed cavalry and infantry to guard them, in a short while he took the city by storm and destroyed all the impious men in it, just as Hermes (=Thoth) and Horus, the son of Isis and Osiris, subdued formerly those who had rebelled in the same places. When he came to Memphis to avenge his father and his own royalty, he punished in a fitting way all the leaders of those who rebelled in his father's time, who had [disturbed] the country and done harm to the temples, at the time when he came there for the performance of the appropriate ceremonies for his reception of royalty; and he has remitted the debts of the temples to the royal treasury up to the 8th year (198/7), which was no small amount of corn and money, [and] similarly the dues on the byssus cloth which had not been delivered to the royal treasury / and of those delivered (he has remitted) the cost of checking them, up to the same period; and he has freed the temples from the (tax of one) artaba for each arura of sacred land, and also the (tax of one) jar of wine for each arura of vineyards; and he has bestowed many gifts on Apis and Mnevis and the other sacred animals in Egypt, much more than the kings before him, showing consideration for what belonged [to] them in every respect, and for their burials he gave what was needed lavishly and splendidly, and what was paid to their special shrines, with sacrifices and religious assemblies and the other [customary observances], and he has maintained the privileges of the temples and of Egypt in accordance with the laws, and has adorned the temple of Apis with lavish work, spending on it no small sum of gold [and silver] and precious stones, and he has founded temples and shrines and altars, and has restored those in need of repair, in the spirit of a beneficent god in matters relating [to] / religion; and having discovered what temples were held in the highest honour, he has restored them during his own reign, as is fitting; in return for these things the gods have granted him health, victory, power and [all] other blessings, and his royalty shall remain with him and his children for all time.

With good fortune. The priests of all the temples throughout the land have resolved to increase greatly the [honours] existing [in the temples] for King Ptolemy the everliving, beloved of Ptah, God Manifest and Beneficent, and also those for his parents the Father-Loving Gods, and those for his grandparents the Benefactor Gods [and those] for the Brother-Sister Gods and those for the Saviour Gods. A statue of King Ptolemy the everliving, God Manifest and Beneficent, shall be set up in each temple in the [most] distinguished [place], to be called (statue) of Ptolemy the avenger of Egypt, and beside it shall stand the chief god of each temple presenting to him the weapon of victory, which shall be constructed [in the Egyptian] / fashion and the priests shall worship the statues three times a day and shall put upon them the sacred dress, and perform the customary rites as for the other gods at [festivals and] religious assemblies. A statue and a [golden] shrine shall be established for King Ptolemy, God Manifest and Beneficent, born from King Ptolemy and Queen Arsinoe, the Father-Loving Gods, [in each] temple and they shall be placed in the innermost sanctuaries together with the other shrines, and in the great religious assemblies, in which the shrines are carried in procession, the [shrine] of the God Manifest and [Beneficent shall also] be carried. And so that the shrine may be clearly marked now and in future, it shall be surmounted by the ten golden crowns of the king, with an asp fixed on them [as with all] the crowns with asps in the other shrines. In the centre of them shall be the crown called *Pschent,* which he [the king] put on when he entered the [temple] at Memphis [to] celebrate [there] / the ceremonies for the reception of royalty. And there shall be placed on the square around the crowns, beside the above-mentioned crown, [golden] symbols [which shall proclaim that] they are those of the king who made illustrious the upper and the lower country. And since the 30th of Mesore (*ca.* 7 October), on which the king's birthday is celebrated, and also [the 17th of Phaophi] (*ca.* 28 November) on which he received the royalty from his father, have been recognised as name-days in the temples, for they were the sources of many blessings, these days shall be celebrated as festivals [and religious assemblies in the] temples [throughout] Egypt every month, and in them sacrifices, libations and the other customary celebrations shall be performed, as in other religious assemblies ... in the temples. And a festival and religious assembly shall be celebrated every [year] for the everliving, beloved of Ptah, King Ptolemy, God Manifest and Beneficent [in the temples throughout the] / country from the first day of Thoth for five days, during which they shall wear wreaths as they perform the sacrifices, libations and other appropriate rites. And [all the priests] shall also be called priests of the God Manifest and Beneficent in addition to the other names of the gods whom they serve, and his priesthood shall be entered in all documents and [engraved on the rings they wear]. And private individuals may also celebrate the festival and set up the shrine mentioned above and keep it in their houses, celebrating [the customary rites in the monthly and] annual [festivals], in order that it may be well known that the people in Egypt magnify and honour the God Manifest and Beneficent, as is customary [for them. This decree shall be inscribed on stelae] of hard stone, in sacred, native and Greek letters, and placed in every [temple] of the first, second [and third rank, next to the statue].

41 Papyri on Greek and Non-Greek Interactions

"I do not know how to speak Greek."

The conquests of Alexander and subsequent Greco-Macedonian rule over different subject peoples intensified the social and cultural interactions between Greeks and non-Greeks in a variety of ways. On the level of interpersonal and intergroup relationships, a Greek identity could become a badge of pride for some and a source of ethnic contentions when this feeling translated into what others regarded as arrogance and unjust treatment. The following two texts are translation from Hellenistic papyri that speak to these cultural tensions. The first (A) is part of a collection of texts from the archive of Zenon, the manager of large estates in the middle of the third century B.C. this collection was discovered in Egypt in 1914–15. The selection is a petition dated ca. 256–55 B.C. by one of Zenon's underlings who claimed that, because he was not a Greek, he came to be mistreated by Zenon's other agents who despised him as a non-Greek or barbarian. The second text (B) dates from a century later (161 B.C.) and is part of the correspondence by Ptolemaios, a Greek (or Macedonian, then a formal status claimed by descendants of Greek and Macedonian colonists) who lived in Ptolemaic Egypt. Ptolemaios had established himself in the Egyptian temple of Serapis in the former pharaonic capital of Memphis as a *katochos*, or recluse commanded by a deity to dwell in his or her temple. He addressed his complaint, written in his native Greek, to Dionysius, the *strategos*, or royal Ptolemaic governor of the region, reporting that he was being mistreated by the native Egyptian cleaning staff at the Serapeum, who even "tried to kill me because I was Greek." Greek was the administrative language of the Hellenistic kingdom, and Ptolemaios' cultural background gave him clear advantages and an even clearer sense of his privilege with respect to the native population.

Zenon Papyri II.66; in Roger S. Bagnall and Peter Derow, *The Hellenistic Period: Historical Sources in Translation* (Oxford: Blackwell, 2004), pp. 230–33, 278–84.

A.

... dab ... to Zenon, greeting. You do well if you are healthy. I too am well. You know that you left me in Syria with Krotos and I did everything that was ordered with respect to the camels and was blameless towards you. When you sent an order to give me pay, he gave nothing of what you ordered. When I asked repeatedly that he give me what you ordered and Krotos gave me nothing, but kept telling me to remove myself, I held out for it long time waiting for you; but when I was in want of necessities and could not get anything anywhere, I was compelled to run away into Syria so that I might not perish of hunger. So I wrote you that you might know that Krotos was the cause of it. When you sent me again to Philadelphia to Jason, although I did everything that is ordered, for nine months now he gives me nothing of what you ordered me to have, neither oil nor grain, except at two-month periods: when he also pays the clothing (allowance). And I am toiling away both summer and winter. And he orders me to accept sour wine for my ration Well, they have treated me with scorn because I am a 'barbarian'. I beg you therefore, if it seems good to you, to give them orders that I am to obtain what is owing and that in future they pay me in full, in order that I may not perish of hunger because I do not know how to speak Greek. You, therefore, please pay attention to me. I pray to all the gods and to the guardian divinity of the king that you remain well and come to us soon so that you may yourself see that I am blameless. Farewell. (Address) To Zenon.

B.

To Dionysios one of the friends and *strategos,* from Ptolemaios son of Glaukias, Macedonian, one of those in *katoche* in the great Serapeum in Memphis in my 12th year. Being outrageously wronged and often put in danger of my life by the below-listed cleaners from the sanctuary, I am seeking refuge with you thinking that I shall thus particularly receive justice. For in the 21st wear, on Phaophi 8, they came to the Astartieion in the sanctuary, in which I have been in *katoche* for the aforesaid years, some of them holding stones in their hands, others sticks, and tried to force their way in, so that with this opportunity they might plunder the temple and kill me because I am a Greek, attacking me in concerted fashion. And when I made it to the door of the temple before them and shut it with a great crash, and ordered them to go away quietly, they did not depart; but they struck Diphilos, one of the servants *compelled to remain* by Sarapis, who showed his indignation at the way they were behaving in the sanctuary, robbing him outrageously and attacking him violently and beating him, so that their illegal violence was made obvious to everybody. When the same men did the same things to me in *Phaophi of the 19th year,* I petitioned you at that time, but because I had no one to wait on you it happened that when they went unwarned they conceived an even greater scorn for me. I ask you, therefore, if it seems good to you, to order them brought before you, so that they may get the proper punishment for all these things. Farewell.

Mys the clothing-seller, Psosnaus the yoke-bearer, Imouthes the baker, Harembasnis the grain-seller, Stotoetis the porter, Harchebis the doucher, Po ... os the carpet-weaver, and others with them, whose names I do not know.

42 Oil Monopoly of Ptolemy II Philadelphus

Toward a Command Economy

"… exact payment from them …"

While Hellenistic kings and Greek cities often maintained a cordial and mutually supportive relationship, using the rituals of divine ruler cult as the language of communication, both were devoted to the extraction of agricultural surplus from the land they controlled. Their very existence and power depended on the basis of this wealth. The Ptolemaic kings held large swathes of the country of Egypt as "spear-won" land and employed royal stewards and laborers to make that land productive. They imposed administrative guidelines, sometimes described as "revenue laws," to regulate the generation of royal revenues from these sources. The royal administration also sought to maximize its own profits by imposing a monopoly on the production of certain products, including all kinds of vegetable oils.

The following selection is an official document from 259 B.C. that outlines the control that the Ptolemaic officials had over the production of oils during the reign of Ptolemy II Philadelphus. Almost everything was fixed ahead of time by this administration: prices, schedules for sowing and harvesting, and the various duties of the different administrative personnel. The goal of these measures was to increase the kings' income and not necessarily to make production more scientific or efficient. The overall effort to exert central control over every aspect of agricultural production that emerges in this document remains impressive.

Year 27, Loius 10. Corrected in the office of Apollonius the dioecetes....

The cultivators ... shall sell the oil in the country at the rate of 48 drachmaein copper for a metretes of sesame oil or cnecus oil containing 12 choes, and at the rate of 30 drachmae for a metretes of castor oil, colocynth oil, or lamp oil. (Altered to ... both sesame and cnecus oil and castor oil, colocynth oil and lamp

From *Select Papyri: Volume II, Official Documents*, Loeb Classical Library Vol. 282, translated by A. S. Hunt and C. C. Edgar (Cambridge, Mass.: Harvard University Press, 1934). The Loeb Classical Library® is a registered trademark of the President and Fellows of Harvard College. Reprinted by permission of the publishers and the Trustees of the Loeb Classical Library.

oil at the rate of 48 drachmae in copper for a metretes of 12 choes, and 2 obols for a cotyla.)

In Alexandria and the whole of Libya they shall sell it at the rate of 48 drachmae for a metretes of sesame oil and 48 drachmae for a metretes of castor oil. (Altered to ... 48 drachmae for a metretes of sesame oil or castor oil, and 2 obols for a cotyla.)...

They shall exhibit the land sown to the director of the contract with the oeconomus and the controller, and if after measuring it they find that the right number of arurae has not been sown, the nomarch and the toparch and the oeconomus and the controller shall, each who is responsible, forfeit to the Crown 2 talents, and to the holders of the contract for each artaba of sesame which they ought to have received 2 drachmae, and for each artaba of croton 1 drachma, together with the profit which would have been made on the sesame oil and the castor oil. The dioecetes shall exact the payment from them....

When it is time to harvest the sesame and the croton and cnecus, the cultivators shall give notice to the nomarch and the toparch, or, where there are no nomarchs or toparchs, to the oeconomus, and these officials shall summon the holder of the contract, and the director of the contract shall visit the acreage with them and make an assessment.

The native peasants and the other cultivators shall assess their own crops severally by kind before they harvest them, and they shall make a duplicate sealed agreement with the contractor concerning the assessment, and every peasant shall write down on oath the amount of land which he has sown with each kind of seed, and the amount of his assessment, and shall seal the agreement, and the delegate sent by the nomarch or toparch shall also seal it.

The nomarch or the official in charge in the nome shall report the number of arurae sown, cultivator by cultivator, sixty days before the crop is harvested. If he fails to report or to show that the cultivators have sown the amount of land appointed, he shall forfeit to the purchaser of the contract the prescribed penalty, and shall himself exact payment from the disobedient cultivators....

They shall not allow the oil-makers appointed in each nome to migrate to another nome. Any oil-maker who goes elsewhere shall be subject to arrest by the director of the contract and the oeconomus and the controller.

No one shall harbour oil-makers (from another nome). If anyone does so knowingly or fails to bring them back when ordered, he shall forfeit for each oil-maker 3000 drachmae, and the oil-maker shall be liable to arrest....

If the oeconomus or his representative fails to pay the oil-makers their wages or their share in the profits from the sale, he shall forfeit to the Crown 3000 drachmae, and to the oil-makers their pay, and twice the amount of any loss incurred by the contract on account of the workmen.

If they fail to set up oil factories in accordance with these regulations, or to deposit a sufficient quantity of produce, and in consequence the contract incurs a loss, the oeconomus and the controller shall forfeit the amount of the deficit thus caused, and shall pay to the purchasers of the contract twice the amount of their loss....

They shall compel the oil-makers to work every day and shall stay beside them, and they shall each day make into oil not less than 1 artaba of sesame at each mortar, and 4 artabae of croton, and 1 of cnecus, and they shall pay as wages for crushing 4 artabae of sesame ... drachmae, and for ... artabae of croton 4 drachmae, and for ... artabae of cnecus 8 drachmae....

If anyone is detected manufacturing oil from sesame or croton or cnecus in any manner whatsoever, or buying sesame oil or cnecus oil or castor oil from any quarter except from the contractors, the king shall decide his punishment, but he shall forfeit to the contractors 3000 drachmae and be deprived of the oil and the produce; and payment of the penalty shall be exacted by the oeconomus and the controller, and if he is without means, he shall be committed...

... on any pretext, nor bring oil into Alexandria apart from the government supply. If any persons bring in more than they are likely to use for their own consumption in three days, they shall be deprived both of the goods and of the means of transport, and shall in addition forfeit 100 drachmae for each metretes, and for more or less in proportion....

It shall not be lawful to bring [foreign oil] into the interior for sale, either from Alexandria or Pelusium or any other place. Whoever does so shall be deprived of the oil, and shall in addition pay a fine of 100 drachmae for each metretes, and for more or less in proportion....

43 Hellenistic Philosophy

Greek Thought in a Wider World

Soon after the death of Socrates, his pupils began to differ radically from one another concerning the content of his teaching, and several distinct philosophical schools eventually arose. Plato held that Socrates was a systematic philosopher who created the theory of Ideas, the doctrine of immortality of the soul, and the concept of an ideal state. Other pupils, influenced by the impact of Socrates' teaching on their own lives, argued that he was not a philosopher in that sense at all, but a moral hero whose character and manner of living should be emulated.

From *Lucian, Vol. VIII*, Loeb Classical Library Vol. 432, translated by M. D. Macleod (Cambridge, Mass.: Harvard University Press, 1967). The Loeb Classical Library® is a registered trademark of the President and Fellows of Harvard College. Reprinted by permission of the publishers and the Trustees of the Loeb Classical Library.

A. THE CYNIC COUNTERCULTURE

"May I consider the universe my house"

Whereas Plato held that Socrates' pretense of knowing nothing was only the first step on the way to a knowledge of the eternal Ideas that were preexistent in the soul, Antisthenes, who together with his more radical disciple Diogenes is considered the founder of the Cynic school of philosophy, denied that it was possible to know anything. And while Plato went on to develop Socrates' basic assumption that all education must be political, training Athenians to be either good rulers or good subjects, Antisthenes preached the need to be a "citizen of the world" (*kosmopolitēs*) in a new society free of the conventional laws and mores of the Greek city-states. Diogenes, an older contemporary of Alexander the Great, exaggerated Socrates' criticism of the values pursued by his fellow citizens and his ideal of frugality and independence of external things—autarky, or self-sufficiency. Frugality became in Diogenes asceticism—he looked and acted the part of a beggar and lived in a large wine cask—and self-sufficiency meant the severence of all human ties. He and many other Cynics were exhibitionists who dramatized their counterculture and scandalized sober citizens by their biting attacks on the Establishment and by their unconventional appearance and behavior. ("When my body needs sexual satisfaction," Antisthenes once said, "whatever lies close to hand is good enough for me. So the women I associate with are exceedingly grateful to me, for no one else will approach them.")

As with the other major Hellenistic philosophies—Skepticism (Selection 52A), Epicureanism (Selection 53), and Stoicism (Selection 63)—Cynicism later spread through much of the Roman world when conditions similar to those of the Hellenistic Age prevailed. The second century A.D., in particular, witnessed large numbers of Cynic philosophers crisscrossing the Empire and preaching and actively demonstrating the Cynic ideal of the virtuous wise man who has achieved perfect happiness by freeing himself from conventional society. The Syrian-born and Greek-educated Lucian of Samosata (ca. A.D. 120–190), rhetorician and man of letters, rationalist and skeptic, frequently excoriated those Cynic philosophers whom he considered to be charlatans. But in his dialogue "The Cynic," which purports to be a conversation between himself ("Lycinus") and a Cynic philosopher, Lucian presents a sympathetic picture of the Cynic wise man whose patron saint is that energetic battler against overwhelming odds, the mythical hero Heracles, and who has achieved true self-sufficiency by rejecting the values and conventions of society. He is most like the gods because he, too, needs nothing.

Lycinus: You there, why in heaven's name have you the beard and the long hair, but no shirt? Why do you expose your body to view, and go barefooted, adopting by choice this nomadic anti-social and bestial life? Why unlike all others do you abuse your body by ever inflicting on it what it likes least, wandering around and prepared to sleep anywhere at all on the hard ground, so that your old cloak carries about a plentiful supply of filth, though it was never fine or soft or gay?

CYNIC: I need no such cloak. Mine is the kind that can be provided most easily and affords least trouble to its owner. Such a cloak is all I need. But you tell me something, I beg you. Don't you think that there's vice in extravagance?

LYCINUS: Yes indeed.

CYNIC: And virtue in economy?

LYCINUS: Yes indeed.

CYNIC: Why, then, when you see me living a more economical life than the average man, and them living a more extravagant life, do you find fault with me rather than with them?

LYCINUS: Because—by Zeus!—I do not think your manner of life more economical than that of the average man, but more wanting—or rather completely wanting and ill-provided. For you're no better than the paupers who beg for their daily bread....

CYNIC: Do you think that Heracles, the best of all mankind, a godlike man and rightly considered a god, was compelled by an evil star to go around naked, wearing only a skin and needing none of the same things as you do? No, he was not ill-starred, he who brought the rest of men relief from their bane, nor was he destitute who was the master of both land and sea; for no matter what he essayed, he prevailed over all everywhere, and never encountered his equal or superior, till he left the realm of men. Do you think that he couldn't provide blankets and shoes, and that was why he went around in the state he did? No one could say that; no, he had self-control and hardness; he wished to be powerful, not to enjoy luxury. ... These men of old therefore are the ones that I admire and should like to emulate, but the men of today I do not admire for the "wonderful" prosperity they enjoy in the matter of food and clothing, and when they smooth and depilate every part of their bodies, not even allowing any of their private parts to remain in its natural condition.

I pray that I may have feet no different from horses' hooves, as they say were those of Chiron [the Centaur], and that I myself may not need bedclothes any more than do the lions, nor expensive fare any more than do the dogs. But may I have for bed to meet my needs the whole earth, may I consider the universe my house, and choose for food that which is easiest to procure, gold and silver may I not need, neither I nor any of my friends. For from the desire for these grow up all men's ills—civic strife, wars, conspiracies and murders. All these have as their fountainhead the desire for more. But may this desire be far from us, and never may I reach out for more than my share, but be able to put up with less than my share.

Such, you see, are our wishes, wishes assuredly far different from those of most men. Nor is it any wonder that we differ from them in dress when we differ so much from them in principles too. But you surprise me by the way that you think that a lyre-player has a particular uniform and garb, but, when it comes to a good man, you don't think that he has his own dress and garb, but should wear the same as the average man, and that too although the average man is depraved. If good men need one particular dress of their own, what one would be more suitable than this dress which seems quite shameless to debauched men and which they would most deprecate for themselves?

Therefore my dress is, as you see, a dirty shaggy skin, a worn cloak, long hair and bare feet, but yours is just like that of the sodomites and no one could tell yours from theirs either by the color of your cloaks, or by the softness and number of your tunics, or by your wraps, shoes, elaborate hair-styles, or your scent. For nowadays you reek of scent just like them—you, who are the most fortunate of men! Yet of what value can one think a man who smells the same as a sodomite? So it is that you are no more able to endure hardships than they are, and no less amenable to pleasures than they. Moreover, your food is the same as theirs, you sleep like them and walk like them—or rather just like them prefer not to walk but are carried like baggage, some of you by men, others by beasts. But I am carried by my feet wherever I need to go, and I am able to put up with cold, endure heat and show no resentment at the works of the gods, because I am unfortunate, whereas you, because of your good fortune, are pleased with nothing that happens, and always find fault, unwilling to put up with what you have, but eager for what you have not, in winter praying for summer, and in summer for winter, in hot weather for cold, and in cold weather for hot, showing yourselves as hard to please and as querulous as invalids. But whereas the cause of their behavior is illness, the cause of yours is your character.

Again you would have us change and you would reform our manner of life for us because we often are ill-advised in what we do, though you yourselves bestow no thought on your own actions, basing none of them on rational judgment, but upon habit and appetite. Therefore you are exactly the same as men carried along by a torrent; for they are carried along wherever the current takes them, and you wherever your appetites take you. Your situation is just like what they say happened to the man who mounted a mad horse. For it rushed off, carrying him with it; and he couldn't dismount again because the horse kept running. Then someone who met him asked him where he was off to, and he replied, "Wherever this fellow decides," indicating the horse. Now if anyone asks you where you're heading for, if you wish to tell the truth, you will say simply that it's where your appetites choose, or more specifically where pleasure chooses, or now where ambition, or now again where avarice chooses; and sometimes temper, sometimes fear, or sometimes something else of the sort seems to carry you off. For you are carried along on the back not of one but of many horses, and different ones at different times—but all of them mad. As a result they carry you away towards cliffs and chasms. But before you fall you are quite unaware of what is going to happen to you.

But this worn cloak which you mock, and my long hair and my dress are so effective that they enable me to live in peace of mind doing what I want to do and keeping the company of my choice. For the fools and the uninstructed do not wish to associate with one who dresses as I do, while the fops turn away while they're still a long way off. But my associates are the most intelligent and decent of men, and those with an appetite for virtue. These men are my particular associates, for I rejoice in the company of men like them. But I dance no attendance at the doors of the so-called fortunate, but consider their golden crowns and their purple robes mere pride, and I laugh at the fellows who wear them.

And I'd have you know that my style of dress becomes not only good men but also gods, though you go on to mock it; and so consider the statues of the gods. Do you think they are like you or like me? And don't confine your attentions to the statues of the Greeks, but go round examining foreigners' temples too, to see whether the gods themselves have long hair and beards as I do, or whether their statues and paintings show them close-shaven like you. What's more, you will see they are just like me not only in these respects but also in having no shirt. How then can you still have the effrontery to describe my style of dress as contemptible, when it's obvious that it's good enough even for gods?

B. STOICS AND THEIR WORLDVIEW

"The wise man does all things well."

One of the major schools of ancient philosophy was that of the Stoics. From the Hellenistic period through the Roman period, Stoic philosophy became the dominant intellectual current that found especial favor among the Roman elite, including several Roman emperors, as well as greatly influenced the development of Christian ideas. The school's founder was Zeno (334 B.C.–262 B.C.), who came to Athens around 312/11 and learned from different philosophers.

Diogenes Laertius, "Life of Zeno," 7.84–90, 110–18, 121–23; in *Diogenes Laertius. Lives of Eminent Philosophers*, edited by R. D. Hicks, Loeb Classical Library (Cambridge, Mass.: Harvard University Press, 1979), v. 2, pp. 193–99, 215–23, 225–29.

He then taught and established his own school just before 300 on the site of the "Painted Colonnades," or *Stoa Poikilē,* from which the philosophy would derive its name of Stoa. Stoics engaged in a broad range of intellectual inquiries: logic as a discipline to ascertain truth or reality from falsehood or *phantasia,* physics that posit a fundamental cosmology that regards the present world as the construct of the elements of Air, Water, and Earth, and ethics that relate the notion of the good to one's ability to live in conformity to that which is real. Accordingly, Stoics pursued a rigorous intellectual and moral regimen that entailed both the acquisition of clear discernment and the moral fortitude to endure even suffering as they attempted to live lives in light of the truth without fear or false hopes.

The teachings of Zeno gained wide currency, but information about his life is mainly preserved in Diogenes Laertius' *Lives of Famous Philosophers,* a work from late third century A.D. that offers biographical sketches of key figures in the development of major strands of Greek philosophical thought from the pre-Socratic philosophers to influential late Classical and Hellenistic philosophers such as Zeno.

According to the Stoics there is an eight-fold division of the soul: the five senses, the faculty of speech, the intellectual faculty, which is the mind itself, and the generative faculty, being all parts of the soul. Now from falsehood there results perversion, which extends to the mind; and from this perversion arise many passions or emotions, which are causes of instability. Passion, or emotion, is defined by Zeno as an irrational and unnatural movement in the soul, or again as impulse in excess.

The main, or most universal, emotions, according to Hecato in his treatise *On the Passions,* book ii., and Zeno in his treatise with the same title, constitute; four great classes, grief, fear, desire or craving, pleasure. They hold the emotions to be judgements, as is stated by Chrysippus in his treatise *On the Passions:* avarice being a supposition that money is a good, while the case is similar with drunkenness and profligacy and all the other emotions.

And grief or pain they hold to be an irrational mental contraction. Its species are pity, envy, jealousy, rivalry, heaviness, annoyance, distress, anguish, distraction. Pity is grief felt at undeserved suffering; envy, grief at others' prosperity; jealousy, grief at the possession by another of that which one desires for oneself; rivalry, pain at the possession by another of what one has oneself. Heaviness or vexation is grief which weighs us down, annoyance that which coops us up and straitens us for want of room, distress a pain brought on by anxious thought that lasts and increases, anguish painful grief, distraction irrational grief, grasping and hindering us from viewing the situation as a whole.

Fear is an expectation of evil. Under fear are ranged the following emotions: terror, nervous shrinking, shame, consternation, panic, mental agony. Terror is a fear which produces fright; shame is fear of disgrace; nervous shrinking is a fear that one will have to act; consternation is fear due to a presentation of some unusual occurrence; panic is fear with pressure exercised by sound; mental agony is fear felt when some issue is still in suspense.

Desire or craving is irrational appetency, and under it are ranged the following states: want, hatred, contentiousness, anger, love, wrath, resentment. Want, then, is a craving when it is baulked and, as it were, cut off from its object, but kept at full stretch and attracted towards it in vain. Hatred is a growing and lasting desire or craving that it should go ill with somebody. Contentiousness is a craving or desire connected with partisanship; anger a craving or desire to punish one who is thought to have done you an undeserved injury. The passion of love: is a craving from which good men are free; for it is an effort to win affection due to the visible presence of beauty. Wrath is anger which has long rankled and has become malicious, waiting for its opportunity, as is illustrated by the lines:

> Even though for the one day he swallow his anger, yet doth he still keep his displeasure thereafter in his heart, till he accomplish it.

Resentment is anger in an early stage.

Pleasure is an irrational elation at the accruing of what seems to be choice-worthy; and under it are ranged ravishment, malevolent joy, delight, transport. [Ravishment is pleasure which charms the ear. Malevolent joy is pleasure at another's ills. Delight is the mind's propulsion to weakness, its name in Greek ... [terpsis] being akin to ... [trepsis] or turning. To be in transports of delight is the melting away of virtue.

And as there are said to be certain infirmities in the body, as for instance gout and arthritic disorders, so too there is in the soul love of fame, love of pleasure, and the like. By infirmity is meant disease accompanied by weakness; and by disease is meant a fond imagining of something that seems desirable. And as in the body there are tendencies to certain maladies such as colds and diarrhoea, so it is with the soul, there are tendencies like enviousness, pitifuless, quarrelsomeness, and the like.

Also they say that there are three emotional states which are good, namely, joy, caution, and wishing. Joy, the counterpart of pleasure, is rational elation; caution, the counterpart of fear, rational avoidance; for though the wise man will never feel fear, he will yet use caution. And they make wishing the counterpart of desire (or craving), inasmuch as it is rational appetency. And accordingly, as under the primary passions are classed certain others subordinate to them, so too is it with the primary eupathies or good emotional states. Thus under wishing they bring well-wishing or benevolence, (friendliness, respect, affection; under caution, reverence and modesty; under joy, delight, mirth, cheerfulness.

Now they say that the wise man is passionless, because he is not prone to fall into such infirmity. But they add that in another sense the term apathy is applied to the bad man, when, that is, it means that he is callous and relentless. Further, the wise man is said to be free from vanity; for he is indifferent to good or evil report. However, he is not alone in this, there being another who is also free from vanity, he who is ranged among the rash, and that is the bad man. Again, they tell us that all good men are austere or harsh, because they neither have dealings with pleasure themselves nor tolerate those who have. The term harsh is applied, however, to others as well, and in much the same sense as a wine is said to be harsh when it is employed medicinally and not for drinking at all.

Again, the good are genuinely in earnest and vigilant for their own improvement, using a manner of life which banishes evil out of sight and makes what good there is in things appear. At the same time they are free from pretence; for they have stripped off all pretence or "make-up" whether in voice or in look. Free too are they from all business cares, declining to do anything which conflicts with duty. They will take wine, but not get drunk. Nay more, they will not be liable to madness either; not but what there will at times occur to the good man strange impressions due to melancholy or delirium, ideas not determined by the principle of what is choiceworthy but contrary to nature. Nor indeed will the wise man ever feel grief; seeing that grief is irrational contraction of the soul, as Apollodorus says in his *Ethics.*

They are also, it is declared, godlike; for they have a something divine within them; whereas the bad man is godless. And yet of this word—godless or ungodly—there are two senses, one in which it is the opposite of the term "godly," the other denoting the man who ignores the divine altogether: in this latter sense, as they note, the term does not apply to every bad man. The good, it is added, are also worshippers of God; for they have acquaintance with the rites of the gods, and piety is the knowledge of how to serve the gods. Further, they will sacrifice to the gods and they keep themselves pure; for they avoid all acts that are offences against the gods, and the gods think highly of them: for they are holy and just in what concerns the gods. The wise too are the only priests; for they have made sacrifices their study, as also the building of temples, purifications, and all the other matters appertaining to the gods.

The Stoics approve also of honouring parents and brothers in the second place next after the gods. They further maintain that parental affection for children is natural to the good, but not to the bad.

Again, the Stoics say that the wise man will take part in politics, if nothing hinders him—so, for instance, Chrysippus in the first book of his work *On Various Types of Life*—since thus he will restrain vice and promote virtue. Also (they maintain) he will marry, as Zeno says in his *Republic,* and beget children. Moreover, they say that the wise man will never form mere opinions, that is to say, he will never give assent to anything that is false; that he will also play the Cynic, Cynicism being a short cut to virtue, as Apollodorus calls it in his *Ethics;* that he will even turn cannibal under stress of circumstances. They declare that he alone is free and bad men are slaves, freedom being power of independent action, whereas slavery is privation of the same: though indeed there is also a second form of slavery consisting in subordination, and a third which implies possession of the slave as well as his subordination; the correlative of such servitude being lordship; and this too is evil. Moreover, according to them not only are the wise free, they are also kings; kingship being irresponsible rule, which none but the wise can maintain: so Chrysippus in his treatise vindicating Zeno's use of terminology. For he holds that knowledge of good and evil is a necessary attribute of the ruler, and that no bad man is acquainted with this science. Similarly the wise and good alone are fit to be magistrates, judges, or orators, whereas among the bad there is not one so qualified. Furthermore, the wise are infallible, not being liable to error. They are also without offence; for they do no hurt to others or to themselves. At the same time they are not pitiful and make no allowance for anyone; they never relax the penalties fixed by the laws, since indulgence and pity and even equitable consideration are marks of a weak mind, which affects kindness in place of chastizing. Nor do they deem punishments too severe. Again, they say that the wise man never wonders at any of the things which appear extraordinary, such as Charon's mephitic caverns,[1] ebbings of the tide, hot springs or fiery eruptions. Nor yet, they go on to say, will the wise man

---

1. Underground caverns that lead down to Hades.

live in solitude; for he is naturally made for society and action. He will, however, submit to training to augment his powers of bodily endurance.

And the wise man, they say, will offer prayers, and ask for good things from the gods: so Posidonius in the first book of his treatise *On Duties,* and Hecato in his third book *On Paradoxes.* Friendship, they declare, exists only between the wise and good, by reason of their likeness to one another. And by friendship they mean a common use of all that has to do with life, wherein we treat our friends as we should ourselves. They argue that a friend is worth having for his own sake and that it is a good thing to have many friends. But among the bad there is, they hold, no such thing as friendship, and thus no bad man has a friend. Another of their tenets is that the unwise are all mad, inasmuch as they are not wise but do what they do from that madness which is the equivalent of their folly....

44 Hellenistic Science

Archimedes

Science and mathematics reached their highest point of development in ancient times during the Hellenistic Age. The debt of Western civilization to the Hellenistic workers in medicine, botany, geography, astronomy, physics, and mathematics is large. In all antiquity the greatest name in physics and mathematics—which was the most extensive and enduring contribution of the Hellenistic scientists—is Archimedes of Syracuse (ca. 287–212 B.C.), who had studied at the Museum in Alexandria, the famed research center endowed by the Ptolemies. Everyone has heard of his famous boast on discovering the principle of the lever, "Give me a place to stand, and I will move the earth"; and of his rushing naked from his bath with the cry, "Eureka!" on discovering the principle of specific gravity.

Archimedes was killed during an incident in the Second Punic War when the Romans under Marcellus besieged and sacked Syracuse after it had sided with the Carthaginians. Plutarch's "Life of Marcellus" contains a description of this event along with an account of Archimedes' scientific genius. Here one finds a striking statement of the Greek devotion to knowledge for its own sake, typical of both Hellenic and Hellenistic times. But the achievements of Archimedes show that the Greeks could, when they wished, make practical application of their theoretical knowledge. Their failure to achieve the spectacular material progress more characteristic of the Roman and especially of our own modern civilization is here attributed to a disdainful regard for "the whole business of engineering and the useful arts as base and vulgar."

From "Life of Marcellus," translated by Aubrey Stewart and George Long.

14. ... He [Marcellus] now attacked the city both by sea and land, Appius commanding the land forces, while Marcellus directed a fleet of sixty quinqueremes full of armed men and missile weapons. He raised a vast engine upon a raft made by lashing eight ships together, and sailed with it to attack the wall, trusting to the numbers and excellence of his siege engines and to his own personal prestige. But Archimedes and his machines cared nothing for this, though he did not speak of any of these engines as being constructed by serious labor, but as the mere holiday sports of a geometrician. He would not indeed have constructed them but at the earnest request of King Hiero [of Syracuse], who entreated him to leave the abstract for the concrete and bring his ideas within the comprehension of the people by embodying them in tangible forms.

Eudoxus and Archytas were the first who began to treat of this renowned science of mechanics, cleverly illustrating it, and proving such problems as were hard to understand, by means of solid and actual instruments. ... Plato was much vexed at this, and inveighed against them for destroying the real excellence of geometry by making it leave the region of pure intellect and come within that of the senses and become mixed up with bodies which require much base servile labor. So mechanics became separated from geometry, and, long regarded with contempt by philosophy, was reckoned among the military arts.

However Archimedes, who was a relative and friend of Hiero, wrote that with a given power he could move any given weight whatever, and, as if rejoicing in the strength of his demonstration, he is said to have declared that if he were given another world to stand upon, he could move this upon which we live. Hiero wondered at this, and begged him to put this theory into practice and show him something great moved by a small force. Archimedes took a three-masted ship, a transport in the king's army, which had just been dragged up on land with great labor and many men; in this he placed her usual complement of men and cargo, and then sitting at some distance, without any trouble, by gently pulling with his hand the end of a system of pullies, he dragged it towards him with as smooth and even a motion as if it were passing over the sea. The king wondered greatly at this, and perceiving the value of his arts, prevailed upon Archimedes to construct for him a number of machines, some for the attack and some for the defence of a city, of which he himself did not make use, as he spent most of his life in unwarlike and literary leisure, but now these engines were ready for use in Syracuse, and the inventor also was present to direct their working.

15. So when the Romans attacked by sea and land at once, the Syracusans were at first terrified and silent, dreading that nothing could resist such an armament. But Archimedes opened fire from his machines, throwing upon the land forces all manners of darts and great stones, with an incredible noise and violence, which no man could withstand; but those upon whom they fell were struck down in heaps, and their ranks thrown into confusion, while some of the ships were suddenly seized by iron hooks, and by a counter-balancing weight were drawn up and then plunged to the bottom. Others they caught by irons like hands or claws suspended from cranes, and first pulled them up by their bows till they stood upright upon their sterns, and then cast down into the

water, or by means of windlasses and tackles worked inside the city, dashed them against the cliffs and rocks at the base of the walls, with terrible destruction to their crews. Often was seen the fearful sight of a ship lifted out of the sea into the air, swaying and balancing about, until the men were all thrown out or over-whelmed with stones from slings, when the empty vessel would either be dashed against the fortifications or dropped into the sea by the claws being let go.

The great engine which Marcellus was bringing up on the raft, called the Harp from some resemblance to that instrument, was, while still at a distance, struck by a stone of ten talents weight [about 830 pounds], and then another and another, which fell with a terrible crash, breaking the platform on which the machine stood, loosening its bolts, and tearing asunder the hulks which sup-ported it. Marcellus, despairing of success, drew off his ships as fast as possible and sent orders to the land forces to retreat. In a council of war, it was determined to make another assault by night; for they argued that the straining cords which Archimedes used to propel his missiles required a long distance to work in, and would make the shot fly over them at close quarters, and be practically useless, as they required a long stroke. But he, it appears, had long before prepared engines suited for short as well as long distances, and short darts to use in them; and from many small loop-holes pierced through the wall small scorpions, as they are called, stood ready to shoot the enemy, though invisible to them.

16. When they attacked, expecting that they would not be seen, they again encountered a storm of blows from stones which fell perpendicularly upon their heads and darts which were poured from all parts of the wall. They were forced to retire, and when they came within range of the larger machines missiles were showered upon them as they retreated, destroying many men and throwing the ships into great disorder, without their being able to retaliate. For most of the engines on the walls had been devised by Archimedes, and the Romans thought that they were fighting against gods and not men, as destruction fell upon them from invisible hands.

17. However, Marcellus escaped unhurt, and sarcastically said to his own engineers: "Are we to give in to this [hundred-handed] Briareus of a geometri-cian, who sits at his ease by the sea-shore and plays at upsetting our ships, to our lasting disgrace, and surpasses the hundred-handed giant of fable by hurling so many weapons at us at once?" For indeed all the other Syracusans were merely the limbs of Archimedes, and his mind alone directed and guided everything. All other arms were laid aside and the city trusted to his weapons solely for defence and safety. At length Marcellus, seeing that the Romans had become so scared that if only a rope or small beam were seen over the wall they would turn and fly, crying out that Archimedes was bringing some engine to bear upon them, ceased assaulting the place, and trusted to time alone to reduce it.

Yet Archimedes had so great a mind and such immense philosophic specula-tions that although by inventing these engines he had acquired the glory of a more than human intellect, he would not condescend to leave behind him any writings upon the subject, regarding the whole business of engineering and the useful arts as base and vulgar, but placed his whole study and delight in those speculations in which absolute beauty and excellence appear unhampered by the necessities of life, and argument is made to soar above its subject matter, since by the latter only bulk and outward appearance, but by the other accuracy of reasoning and wondrous power, can be attained: for it is impossible in the whole science of geometry to find more difficult problems explained on clearer or more simple principles than in his works. Some attribute this to his natural genius, others say that his indefatigable industry made his work seem as though it had been done without labor, though it cost much. For no man by himself could find out the solution of his problems, but as he reads, he begins to think that he could have discovered it himself, by so smooth and easy a road does he lead one up to the point to be proved.

One cannot therefore disbelieve the stories which are told of him: how he seemed ever bewitched by the song of some indwelling siren of his own so as to forget to eat his food, and neglect his person, and how, when dragged forcibly to the baths and perfumers, he would draw geometrical figures with the ashes on the hearth, and when his body was anointed would trace lines on it with his finger, absolutely possessed and inspired by the joy he felt in his art. He discovered many beautiful problems, and is said to have begged his relatives and friends to place upon his tomb when he died a cylinder enclosing a sphere, and to write on it the proof of the ratio of the containing solid to the contained.

Such was Archimedes, who at this time rendered himself, and as far as lay in him, the city, invincible....

[The Romans finally take and plunder the city.]

19. ... Marcellus was especially grieved at the fate of Archimedes. He was studying something by himself upon a figure which he had drawn, to which he had so utterly given up his thoughts and his sight that he did not notice the assault of the Romans and the capture of the city, and when a soldier suddenly appeared before him and ordered him to follow him into the presence of Marcellus, he refused to do so before he had finished his problem and its solution. The man hereupon in a rage drew his sword and killed him. Others say that the Roman fell upon him at once with a sword and killed him, but he, seeing him, begged him to wait for a little while, that he might not leave his theorem imperfect, and that while he was reflecting upon it, he was slain. A third story is that as he was carrying into Marcellus's presence his mathematical instruments, sundials, spheres, and quadrants, by which the eye might measure the magnitude of the sun, some soldiers met with him, and supposing that there was gold in the boxes, slew him. But all agree that Marcellus was much grieved, that he turned away from his murderer as though he were an object of abhorrence to gods and men, and that he sought out his family and treated them well.

The Limits of Hellenism

Hellenistic civilization was impressive for its geographical reach and its abiding cultural influence, which in many regions of the ancient Mediterranean and Near Eastern world lasted a millennium or even more. Yet the Hellenistic kingdoms that were successors to the conquest state of Alexander the Great would one by one succumb to challengers, not least the rising Mediterranean superpower that was Republican Rome. Successor Hellenistic kingdoms such as the Seleucid realm suffered from a lack of cohesion that came with their geographical expanse and the diversity of their peoples, while efforts to enhance integration through Hellenization brought about a negative backlash in places where certain local populations held on with fierce defiance to particularistic native traditions. These processes and dynamics would continue to play out even after the Hellenistic world drew to a close in political terms when the Ptolemaic kingdom was dissolved and annexed by the Romans because its last queen, Cleopatra VII, fought on the losing side of a Roman civil war.

45 Polybius, *Histories*

Rome and the Hellenistic Kings

"He drew a circle round Antiochus...."

Polybius of Megalopolis (ca. 200–ca. 118 B.C.) was a Greek statesmen and historian who was a leader in a Greek (Achaean League) revolt against Rome. A hostage in Italy after the revolt was defeated, he was befriended by the Roman aristocratic family of the Scipios. When Scipio Aemilianus, son of the Scipio who defeated the Achaeans and Macedonians at Pynda, was charged with the conduct of the final war against Carthage, Polybius likely accompanied him and so witnessed the end of the city of Queen Dido, which the Romans razed to the ground in 146 B.C. The Romans' destruction of two major cities, Carthage in the west and Corinth in the east, within a year or so of each other signaled for Polybius and others the rise of Roman hegemony in the Mediterranean world. Polybius composed his *Histories* in Greek to make sense of the development of Roman power from the time of the First Punic War onward. His principal goal is to explain the reasons for Rome's rise to power through a narrative of political and historical events. He made extensive

Polybius, *Histories*, 29.2, 27; in *Polybius. The Histories of Polybius*, translated from the text of F. Hultsch by Evelyn S. Shuckburgh (Bloomington, Ind.: Indiana University Press, 1962), v. 2, pp. 389, 405–406.

use of written documents from both Greek and Roman archives and applied a critical Greek perspective to their analysis. His overall conclusion is that the Romans benefited from having more discipline and focus than their contemporaries and it is thanks to this particular trait, as well as to their balanced "constitution" and careful military dispositions (topics he breaks his chronological narrative to discuss in Book Six), that they owed their ultimate success. The following account comes from Polybius' description of the Roman responses to the Seleucid king Antiochus IV Epiphanes' second successful invasion of Egypt in 168 B.C. In this case, a mere gesture of "drawing a line in the sand," and the threat of war with the Romans, was enough to send the Hellenistic king hurrying back to his own kingdom.

XXIX

2. The Senate being informed that Antiochus had become master of Egypt, and all but taken Alexandria, and conceiving that the aggrandisement of that king was a matter affecting themselves, appointed Gaius Popilius and others to go as ambassadors to put an end to the war, and generally to inspect the state of affairs....

27. When Antiochus had advanced to attack Ptolemy in order to possess himself of Pelusium, he was met by the Roman commander Gaius Popilius Laenas. Upon the king greeting him from some distance, and holding out his right hand to him, Popilius answered by holding out the tablets which contained the decree of the Senate, and bade Antiochus read that first: not thinking it right, I suppose, to give the usual sign of friendship until he knew the mind of the recipient, whether he were to be regarded as a friend or foe. On the king, after reading the despatch, saying that he desired to consult with his friends on the situation, Popilius did a thing which was looked upon as exceedingly overbearing and insolent. Happening to have a vine stick in his hand, he drew a circle round Antiochus with it, and ordered him to give his answer to the letter before he stepped out of that circumference. The king was taken aback by this haughty proceeding. After a brief interval of embarrassed silence, he replied that he would do whatever the Romans demanded. Then Popilius and his colleagues shook him by the hand, and one and all greeted him with warmth. The contents of the despatch was an order to put an end to the war with Ptolemy at once. Accordingly a stated number of days was allowed him, within which he withdrew his army into Syria, in high dudgeon indeed, and groaning in spirit, but yielding to the necessities of the time.

Popilius and his colleagues then restored order in Alexandria; and after exhorting the two kings to maintain peaceful relations with each other, and charging them at the same time to send Polyaratus to Rome, they took ship and sailed towards Cyprus, with the intention of promptly ejecting from the island the forces that were also gathered there. When they arrived, they found that Ptolemy's generals had already sustained a defeat, and that the whole island was in a state of excitement. They promptly caused the invading army to evacuate the country, and remained there to keep watch until the forces had sailed away for Syria. Thus did the Romans save the kingdom of Ptolemy, when it was all but sinking under its disasters. Fortune indeed so disposed of the fate of Perseus and the Macedonians, that the restoration of Alexandria and the whole of Egypt was decided by it; that is to say, by the fate of Perseus being decided previously: for if that had not taken place, or had not been certain, I do not think that Antiochus would have obeyed these orders.

46 First and Second Maccabees

Jewish Responses to Hellenization

Local peoples responded in various ways to the imposition of Hellenistic Greek rule. For the first hundred years of the Hellenistic era, Judaea came under the authority of the Ptolemaic kings and enjoyed considerable local autonomy. The relations between the Ptolemies and the Jewish priestly aristocracy seems to have been a good one. One Hellenistic Jewish text, the so-called *Letter of Aristeas to Philocrates*, even claims that the second Ptolemaic king Philadelphus, desirous that a Greek bible be deposited in the newly founded Great Library at Alexandria, sent to the High Priest in Jerusalem asking for wise men who could translate the Hebrew Bible into Greek. This is the famous story of the Septuagint (LXX), the Greek translation of the Hebrew Bible, which was said to have been the product of seventy sages working independently of each other: the miraculous fully identical translation attests to the divine approval of the Greek text. The defeat of the Ptolemies by their Seleucid rivals in the second century B.C. saw Judaea falling within the latter's sphere of influence. The Seleucids promoted Greek culture as a way to bring about cultural integration in their large and disparate domain and encouraged those of their subjects who wished to adopt Greek customs and identities. Many communities saw embracing Greek culture, or Hellenization, as a way to get ahead in a world dominated by a Greek-speaking ruling elite. In Judaea, this dynamic exacerbated internal tensions within the Jewish community whereby some of the elite, who in this case were members of the priests who served the temple cult, were said to have wanted to join others in adopting Greek ways. Other Jews found this offensive, and the growing tensions soon developed into full-scale civil strife that eventually drew in outsiders in the form of the Seleucid king Antiochus IV Epiphanes. By this point, local Jews led by a Judas "the Hammer" (Maccabaeus) were in open revolt and defeated several Seleucid armies. The Maccabees eventually succeeded in asserting local Jewish autonomy and in turn founded a new native dynasty, that of the Hasmoneans.

The struggle of the Maccabean rebels against the Jewish Hellenizers and the Seleucid forces became part of the formative cultural memory of Judaism. Many different accounts by distinct authors treat the remembered events of this period, and among them are the two separate works that have since come to be known as the First Book of the Maccabees and the Second Book of the Maccabees.

A. FIRST MACCABEES: JEWS WELCOME ROMAN POWER

"They were very strong ..."

First Maccabees was a work that was originally composed in Aramaic or Hebrew for fellow Jews and later translated into Greek to reach a wider audience, including Jews in the Diaspora who could no longer read Hebrew. It treats the struggles of Judas Maccabaeus and his sons against the "Judaizers" among the Jews and their successful revolt against the Seleucid king Antiochus IV Epiphanes after 166 B.C. that eventually reclaimed Jerusalem and overthrew Greek rule over Judaea. The following excerpt recounts a tradition that the rebel Jews managed to conclude a mutual defense treaty with the rising Mediterranean power that was Rome.

8 1. Now Judas heard of the fame of the Romans, that they were very strong and were well-disposed toward all who made an alliance with them, that they pledged friendship to those who came to them, and that they were very strong. Men told him of their wars and of the brave deeds which they were doing among the Gauls, how they had defeated them and forced them to pay tribute, and what they had done in the land of Spain to get control of the silver and gold mines there, and how they had gained control of the whole region by their planning and patience, even though the place was far distant from them. They also subdued the kings who came against them from the ends of the earth, until they crushed them and inflicted great disaster upon them; the rest paid them tribute every year. Philip, and Perseus king of the Macedonians, and the others who rose up against them, they crushed in battle and conquered. They also defeated Antiochus the Great, king of Asia, who went to fight against them with a hundred and twenty elephants and with cavalry and chariots and a very large army. He was crushed by them; they took him alive and decreed that he and those who should reign after him should pay a heavy tribute and give hostages and surrender some of their best provinces, the country of India and Media and Lydia. These they took from him and gave to Eumenes the king. The Greeks planned to come and destroy them, but this became known to them, and they sent a general against the Greeks and attacked them. Many of them were wounded and fell, and the Romans took captive their wives and children; they plundered them, conquered the land, tore down their strongholds, and enslaved them to this day. The remaining kingdoms and islands, as many as ever opposed them, they destroyed and enslaved; but with their friends and those who rely on them they have kept friendship. They have subdued kings far and near, and as many as have heard of their fame have feared them. Those whom they wish to help and to make kings, they make kings, and those whom they wish they depose; and they have been greatly exalted. Yet for all this not one of them has put on a crown or worn purple as a mark of pride, but they have built for themselves a senate chamber, and every day three hundred and twenty

I Maccabees 8.1–31 (Revised Standard Version 1962), pp. 239–41.

senators constantly deliberate concerning the people, to govern them well. They trust one man each year to rule over them and to control all their land; they all heed the one man, and there is no envy or jealousy among them.

17. So Judas chose Eupolemus the son of John, son of Accos, and Jason the son of Eleazar, and sent them to Rome to establish friendship and alliance, and to free themselves from the yoke; for they saw that the kingdom of the Greeks was completely enslaving Israel. They went to Rome, a very long journey; and they entered the senate chamber and spoke as follows: "Judas, who is also called Maccabeus, and his brothers and the people of the Jews have sent us to you to establish alliance and peace with you, that we may be enrolled as your allies and friends." The proposal pleased them, and this is a copy of the letter which they wrote in reply, on bronze tablets, and sent to Jerusalem to remain with them there as a memorial of peace and alliance:

23. "May all go well with the Romans and with the nation of the Jews at sea and on land for ever, and may sword and enemy be far from them. If war comes first to Rome or to any of their allies in all their dominion, the nation of the Jews shall act as their allies wholeheartedly, as the occasion may indicate to them. And to the enemy who makes war they shall not give or supply grain, arms, money, or ships, as Rome has decided; and they shall keep their obligations without receiving any return. In the same way, if war comes first to the nation of the Jews, the Romans shall willingly act as their allies, as the occasion may indicate to them. And to the enemy allies shall be given no grain, arms, money, or ships, as Rome has decided; and they shall keep these obligations and do so without deceit. Thus on these terms the Romans make a treaty with the Jewish people. If after these terms are in effect both parties shall determine to add or delete anything, they shall do so at their discretion, and any addition or deletion that they may make shall be valid.

31. "And concerning the wrongs which King Demetrius is doing to them we have written to him as follows, 'Why have you made your yoke heavy upon our friends and allies the Jews? If now they appeal again for help against you, we will defend their rights and fight you on sea and on land.'"

B. SECOND MACCABEES

"The altar was covered with abominable offerings..."

Second Maccabees is a Hellenistic Greek work that abridges a no longer extant history by Jason of Cyrene. While First Maccabees adheres closely to the Greek genre of historical writing, Second Maccabees focuses more on the religious aspects of the wars, offering a pious interpretation of Judas Maccabaeus as well as an account of the suffering of a family of pious Jews—the so-called seven Maccabean martyrs and their mother—who bore witness

II Maccabees 4.7–17, 5–6.6, 7.1–23, 41–42, 7.41–42, 810.1–8 (Revised Standard Version 1962), pp. 269–70, 272–77, 281.

(*martyria*) to their faith in God by enduring grievous torture and death. Judas and his followers fought against Judaizing Jews and the Seleucids and eventually reclaimed Jerusalem. They restored divine worship to the Temple, which was ritually purified by means of the relighting of the oil lamps, an event that was subsequently commemorated as the festival of Hanukkah.

4 7. When Seleucus died and Antiochus who was called Epiphanes succeeded to the kingdom, Jason the brother of Onias obtained the high priesthood by corruption, promising the king at an interview three hundred and sixty talents of silver and, from another source of revenue, eighty talents. In addition to this he promised to pay one hundred and fifty more if permission were given to establish by his authority a gymnasium and a body of youth for it, and to enrol the men of Jerusalem as citizens of Antioch. When the king assented and Jason came to office, he at once shifted his countrymen over to the Greek way of life. He set aside the existing royal concessions to the Jews, secured through John the father of Eupolemus, who went on the mission to establish friendship and alliance with the Romans; and he destroyed the lawful ways of living and introduced new customs contrary to the law. For with alacrity he founded a gymnasium right under the citadel, and he induced the noblest of the young men to wear the Greek hat. There was such an extreme of Hellenization and increase in the adoption of foreign ways because of the surpassing wickedness of Jason, who was ungodly and no high priest, that the priests were no longer intent upon their service at the altar. Despising the sanctuary and neglecting the sacrifices, they hastened to take part in the unlawful proceedings in the wrestling arena after the call to the discus, disdaining the honors prized by their fathers and putting the highest value upon Greek forms of prestige. For this reason heavy disaster overtook them, and those whose ways of living they admired and wished to imitate completely became their enemies and punished them. For it is no light thing to show irreverence to the divine laws—a fact which later events will make clear....

5 6. About this time Antiochus made his second invasion of Egypt. And it happened that over all the city, for almost forty days, there appeared golden-clad horsemen charging through the air, in companies fully armed with lances and drawn swords—troops of horsemen drawn up, attacks and counter-attacks made on this side and on that, brandishing of shields, massing of spears, hurling of missiles, the flash of golden trappings, and armor of all sorts. Therefore all men prayed that the apparition might prove to have been a good omen.

5. When a false rumor arose that Antiochus was dead, Jason took no less than a thousand men and suddenly made an assault upon the city. When the troops upon the wall had been forced back and at last the city was being taken, Menelaus took refuge in the citadel. But Jason kept relentlessly slaughtering his fellow citizens, not realizing that success at the cost of one's kindred is the greatest misfortune, but imagining that he was setting up trophies of victory over enemies and not over fellow countrymen. He did not gain control of the government, however; and in the end got only disgrace from his conspiracy, and fled again into the country of the Ammonites. Finally he met a miserable end.

Accused before Aretas the ruler of the Arabs, fleeing from city to city, pursued by all men, hated as a rebel against the laws, and abhorred as the executioner of his country and his fellow citizens, he was cast ashore in Egypt; and he who had driven many from their own country into exile died in exile, having embarked to go to the Lacedaemonians in hope of finding protection because of their kinship. He who had cast out many to lie unburied had no one to mourn for him; he had no funeral of any sort and no place in the tomb of his fathers.

11. When news of what had happened reached the king, he took it to mean that Judea was in revolt. So, raging inwardly, he left Egypt and took the city by storm. And he commanded his soldiers to cut down relentlessly every one they met and to slay those who went into the houses. Then there was killing of young and old, destruction of boys, women, and children, and slaughter of virgins and infants. Within the total of three days eighty thousand were destroyed, forty thousand in hand-to-hand fighting; and as many were sold into slavery as were slain.

15. Not content with this, Antiochus dared to enter the most holy temple in all the world, guided by Menelaus, who had become a traitor both to the laws and to his country. He took the holy vessels with his polluted hands, and swept away with profane hands the votive offerings which other kings had made to enhance the glory and honor of the place. Antiochus was elated in spirit, and did not perceive that the Lord was angered for a little while because of the sins of those who dwelt in the city, and that therefore he was disregarding the holy place. But if it had not happened that they were involved in many sins, this man would have been scourged and turned back from his rash act as soon as he came forward, just as Heliodorus was, whom Seleucus the king sent to inspect the treasury. But the Lord did not choose the nation for the sake of the holy place, but the place for the sake of the nation. Therefore the place itself shared in the misfortunes that befell the nation and afterward participated in its benefits; and what was forsaken in the wrath of the Almighty was restored again in all its glory when the great Lord became reconciled.

21. So Antiochus carried off eighteen hundred talents from the temple, and hurried away to Antioch, thinking in his arrogance that he could sail on the land and walk on the sea, because his mind was elated. And he left governors to afflict the people: at Jerusalem, Philip, by birth a Phrygian and in character more barbarous than the man who appointed him; and at Gerizim, Andronicus; and besides these Menelaus, who lorded it over his fellow citizens worse than the others did. In his malice toward the Jewish citizens, Antiochus sent Apollonius, the captain of the Mysians, with an army of twenty-two thousand, and commanded him to slay all the grown men and to sell the women and boys as slaves. When this man arrived in Jerusalem, he pretended to be peaceably disposed and waited until the holy sabbath day; then, finding the Jews not at work, he ordered his men to parade under arms. He put to the sword all those who came out to see them, then rushed into the city with his armed men and killed great numbers of people.

27. But Judas Maccabeus, with about nine others, got away to the wilderness, and kept himself and his companions alive in the mountains as wild animals

do; they continued to live on what grew wild, so that they might not share in the defilement.

6 Not long after this, the king sent an Athenian senator to compel the Jews to forsake the laws of their fathers and cease to live by the laws of God, and also to pollute the temple in Jerusalem and call it the temple of Olympian Zeus, and to call the one in Gerizim the temple of Zeus the Friend of Strangers, as did the people who dwelt in that place.

3. Harsh and utterly grievous was the onslaught of evil. For the temple was filled with debauchery and reveling by the Gentiles, who dallied with harlots and had intercourse with women within the sacred precincts, and besides brought in things for sacrifice that were unfit. The altar was covered with abominable offerings which were forbidden by the laws. A man could neither keep the sabbath, nor observe the feasts of his fathers, nor so much as confess himself to be a Jew....

7 It happened also that seven brothers and their mother were arrested and were being compelled by the king, under torture with whips and cords, to partake of unlawful swine's flesh. One of them, acting as their spokes-man, said, "What do you intend to ask and learn from us? For we are ready to die rather than transgress the laws of our fathers."

3. The king fell into a rage, and gave orders that pans and caldrons be heated. These were heated immediately, and he commanded that the tongue of their spokes-man be cut out and that they scalp him and cut off his hands and feet, while the rest of the brothers and the mother looked on. When he was utterly helpless, the king ordered them to take him to the fire, still breathing, and to fry him in a pan. The smoke from the pan spread widely, but the brothers and their mother encouraged one another to die nobly, saying, "The Lord God is watching over us and in truth has compassion on us, as Moses declared in his song which bore witness against the people to their faces, when he said, 'And he will have compassion on his servants.'"

7. After the first brother had died in this way, they brought forward the second for their sport. They tore off the skin of his head with the hair, and asked him, "Will you eat rather than have your body punished limb by limb?" He replied in the language of his fathers, and said to them, "No." Therefore he in turn underwent tortures as the first brother had done. And when he was at his last breath, he said, "You accursed wretch, you dismiss us from this present life, but the King of the universe will raise us up to an everlasting renewal of life, because we have died for his laws."

10. After him, the third was the victim of their sport. When it was demanded, he quickly put out his tongue and courageously stretched forth his hands, and said nobly, "I got these from Heaven, and because of his laws I disdain them, and from him I hope to get them back again." As a result the king himself and those with him were astonished at the young man's spirit, for he regarded his sufferings as nothing.

13. When he too had died, they maltreated and tortured the fourth in the same way. And when he was near death, he said, "One cannot but choose to die

at the hands of men and to cherish the hope that God gives of being raised again by him. But for you there will be no resurrection to life!"

15. Next they brought forward the fifth and maltreated him. But he looked at the king, and said, "Because you have authority among men, mortal though you are, you do what you please. But do not think that God has forsaken our people. Keep on, and see how his mighty power will torture you and your descendants!"

18. After him they brought forward the sixth. And when he was about to die, he said, "Do not deceive yourself in vain. For we are suffering these things on our own account, because of our sins against our own God. Therefore astounding things have happened. But do not think that you will go unpunished for having tried to fight against God!"

20. The mother was especially admirable and worthy of honorable memory. Though she saw her seven sons perish within a single day, she bore it with good courage because of her hope in the Lord. She encouraged each of them in the language of their fathers. Filled with a noble spirit, she fired her woman's reasoning with a man's courage, and said to them, "I do not know how you came in my womb. It was not I who set in order the elements within each of you. Therefore the Creator of the world, who shaped the beginning of man and devised the origin of all things, will in his mercy give life and breath back to you again, since you now forget yourselves for the sake of his laws."...

41. Last of all, the mother died, after her sons.

42. Let this be enough, then, about the eating of sacrifices and the extreme tortures....

10 Now Maccabeus and his followers, the Lord leading them on, recovered the temple and the city; and they tore down the altars which had been built in the public square by the foreigners, and also destroyed the sacred precincts. They purified the sanctuary, and made another altar of sacrifice; then, striking fire out of flint, they offered sacrifices, after a lapse of two years, and they burned incense and lighted lamps and set out the bread of the Presence. And when they had done this, they fell prostrate and besought the Lord that they might never again fall into such misfortunes, but that, if they should ever sin, they might be disciplined by him with forbearance and not be handed over to blasphemous and barbarous nations. It happened that on the same day on which the sanctuary had been profaned by the foreigners, the purification of the sanctuary took place, that is, on the twenty-fifth day of the same month, which was Chislev. And they celebrated it for eight days with rejoicing, in the manner of the feast of booths, remembering how not long before, during the feast of booths, they had been wandering in the mountains and caves like wild animals: Therefore bearing ivy-wreathed wands and beautiful branches and also fronds of palm, they offered hymns of thanksgiving to him who had given success to the purifying of his own holy place. They decreed by public ordinance and vote that the whole nation of the Jews should observe these days every year.

47 Plutarch, The Life of Antony

The Portrait of Queen Cleopatra

"… putting her greatest confidence in herself …"

The last queen of the Ptolemaic Dynasty that ruled Egypt, Cleopatra VII (69–30 B.C.) was truly a woman to be reckoned with. Best known to most of us today through Shakespeare's portrayal of her and her Roman lover Mark Antony, Cleopatra was less a great beauty (she supposedly had an odd-looking nose) and seductress than a highly intelligent and sophisticated political figure. She certainly needed all these skills to survive in the tumultuous political climate of the time.

Cleopatra was the first in the Greco-Macedonian Ptolemaic dynasty to have learned how to speak Egyptian. This may seem surprising to us because the Ptolemies had governed Egypt for more than two centuries by then, but like other Hellenistic kings, the Ptolemies saw themselves mainly as Greek kings who ruled over native peoples. Cleopatra also took pains to appeal to native Egyptian sentiments by supporting traditional Egyptian religions and (although she was not the first Ptolemy to do so) adopting the royal symbols of the native Egyptian pharaohs. Cleopatra's elaborate use of "oriental" royal pomp and circumstance, which Hollywood movies have sought to capture, was part of this deliberate strategy to capitalize on native Egyptian traditions.

When the Romans made their presence felt in the East, Cleopatra played her hand as best she could. First, she became an ally and lover of Julius Caesar and, with Caesar's death, she formed a new liaison with Mark Antony. When Mark Antony fought Octavian for supremacy in the Roman world and was defeated at the Battle of Actium in 31 B.C., Cleopatra fled to Egypt and took her own life.

The Hellenistic age witnessed the presence of many important royal women, queens, and princesses. Yet none of their royal Hellenistic women ruled in her own right, as Cleopatra did for a time, or exerted as much independent control over the political affairs of a powerful kingdom. All royal women, Cleopatra included, owed their positions to the family in which they were born because dynastic regimes naturally render the women in royal families prominent public figures as well. Many of these women received a divine cult status with their husbands. Notice that the highly public roles played by the Hellenistic royal women neatly oppose the ideals that classical Athenian men set for their own women. The following biographical sketch of Cleopatra comes from Plutarch of Chaeronea's biography of the Roman warlord Mark Antony: in his *Parallel Lives of Famous Greeks and Romans*.

From Plutarch, "Life of Antony," in *Plutarch's Lives: Demetrius and Anthony, Pyrrhus and Caius Marius,* translated by Bernadette Perrin, Loeb Classical Library (Cambridge, Mass.: Harvard University Press, 1920), pp. 193–97.

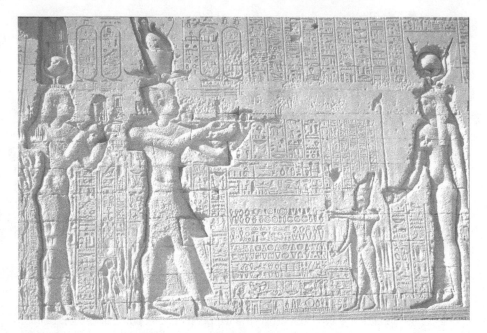

The monumental stone relief featuring Queen Cleopatra VII and her son (with Julius Caesar) Caesarion in the act of worshipping Isis, Hathor, and other Egyptian gods. From the walls of Temple of Hathor at Dendera in southern Egypt. It shows how a Hellenistic ruler came to be represented in Egyptian artistic style and with hieroglyphic writing.

… Caesar and Pompey had known her [Cleopatra] when she was still a girl and inexperienced in affairs, but she was going to visit Antony at the very time when women have most brilliant beauty and are at the acme of intellectual power. Therefore she provided herself with many gifts, much money, and such ornaments as her high position and prosperous kingdom made it natural for her to take; but she went putting her greatest confidence in herself, and in the charms and sorceries of her own person.

26. Though she received many letters of summons both from Antony himself and from his friends, she so despised and laughed the man to scorn as to sail up the river Cydnus in a barge with gilded poop, its sails spread purple, its rowers urging it on with silver oars to the sound of the flute blended with pipes and lutes. She herself reclined beneath a canopy spangled with gold, adorned like Venus in a painting, while boys like Loves in paintings stood on either side and fanned her. Likewise also the fairest of her serving-maidens, attired like Nereids and Graces, were stationed, some at the rudder-sweeps, and others at the reefing-ropes. Wondrous odours from countless incense-offerings diffused themselves along the river-banks. Of the inhabitants, some accompanied her on either bank of the river from its very mouth, while others went down from the city to behold the sight. The throng in the market-place gradually streamed away, until at last Antony himself, seated on his tribunal, was left alone. And a rumour spread on every hand that Venus was come to revel with Bacchus for the good of Asia.

Antony sent, therefore, and invited her to supper; but she thought it meet that he should rather come to her. At once, then, wishing to display his complacency and friendly feelings, Antony obeyed and went. He found there a preparation that beggared description, but was most amazed at the multitude of lights. For, as we are told, so many of these were let down and displayed on all sides at once, and they were arranged and ordered with so many inclinations and adjustments to each other in the form of rectangles and circles, that few sights were so beautiful or so worthy to be seen as this.

27. On the following day Antony feasted her in his turn, and was ambitious to surpass her splendour and elegance, but in both regards he was left behind, and vanquished in these very points, and was first to rail at the meagreness and rusticity of his own arrangements. Cleopatra observed in the jests of Antony much of the soldier and the common man, and adopted this manner also towards him, without restraint now, and boldly. For her beauty, as we are told, was in itself not altogether incomparable, nor such as to strike those who saw her; but converse with her had an irrestistible charm, and her presence, combined with the persuasiveness of her discourse and the character which was somehow diffused about her behaviour towards others, had something stimulating about it. There was sweetness also in the tones of her voice; and her tongue, like an instrument of many strings, she could readily turn to whatever language she pleased, so that in her interviews with Barbarians she very seldom had need of an interpreter, but made her replies to most of them herself and unassisted, whether they were Ethiopians, Troglodytes, Hebrews, Arabians, Syrians, Medes or Parthians. Nay, it is said that she knew the speech of many other peoples also, although the kings of Egypt before her had not even made an effort to learn the native language, and some actually gave up their Macedonian dialect.

28. Accordingly, she made such booty of Antony that, while Fulvia his wife was carrying on war at Rome with Caesar in defence of her husband's interests, and while a Parthian army was hovering about Mesopotamia (over this country the generals of the king had appointed Labienus Parthian commander-in-chief, and were about to invade Syria), he suffered her to hurry him off to Alexandria. There, indulging in the sports and diversions of a young man of leisure, he squandered and spent upon pleasures that which Antiphon calls the most costly outlay, namely, time. For they had an association called The Inimitable Livers, and every day they feasted one another, making their expenditures of incredible profusion....

SELECTED BACKGROUND READING

M. M. Austin, *The Hellenistic World from Alexander to the Roman Conquest: A Selection of Ancient Sources in Translation* (Cambridge, U.K.: Cambridge University Press, 1981).

Roger S. Bagnall and Peter Derow, *The Hellenistic Period: Historical Sources in Translation* (Oxford: Blackwell, 2004).

Glenn R. Bugh, *The Cambridge Companion to the Hellenistic World* (Cambridge, U.K.: Cambridge University Press, 2006).

Andrew Erskine, *A Companion to the Hellenistic World* (Oxford: Blackwell, 2005).

Peter Green, *Alexander to Actium: The Historical Evolution of the Hellenistic Age* (Berkeley: University of California Press, 1990).

Erich S. Gruen, *The Hellenistic World and the Coming of Rome,* 2 vols. (Berkeley: University of California Press, 1984).

Naphtali Lewis, *Greeks in Ptolemaic Egypt: Case Studies in the Social History of the Hellenistic World* (Oxford: Clarendon Press, 1986).

Arnaldo Momigliano, *Alien Wisdom: The Limits of Hellenization* (Cambridge, U.K.: Cambridge University Press, 1975).

Susan M. Sherwin-White and Amélie Kuhrt, *From Samarkhand to Sardis: A New Approach to the Seleucid Empire* (London: Duckworth, 1993).

Graham Shipley, *The Greek World After Alexander 323–30 B.C.* (London: Routledge, 2000).

Frank W. Walbank, *The Hellenistic World* (Cambridge, Mass: Harvard University Press, 1993).

CHAPTER IV

The Roman Republic

What can be nobler than the government of the state by
    virtue?
For then the man who rules others is not himself a slave to
    any passion,
but has already acquired for himself those qualities
to which he is training and summoning his fellows.

—CICERO, *Republic*

Part of a stone carving depicting the Roman public ritual of the *lustrum,* the taking of
the census, a necessary part in the conscription of citizen soldiers for war. (Scene from the
so-called Altar of Domitius Ahenobarbus, first century B.C.)

As Alexander the Great led his expedition to the East and set in motion the events that gave rise to the universal Hellenistic civilization that came after him, the city of Rome was still a nascent power locked in struggle with its many Italian neighbors. Yet two centuries later, by the middle of the second century B.C., Rome would become the paramount political and military power in the entire Mediterranean world, overshadowing in importance even the Hellenistic monarchies that were successors to Alexander's empire. The growth of Rome from a city-state to a world empire and the evolution of a Roman civilization count as two of the key stories of the ancient world.

Many historians have previously emphasized the intermediary role that Roman civilization played in the development of a Western civilization, which they trace from the ancient Near East through Ancient Greece and Rome to the post-Roman Germanic West that became the kernel of European civilization. In this view, Rome's role is mainly conceived of as that of a bridge over which the heritage of the Greeks and the Ancient Near East passed on to what came to be known as Western Civilization. But today's historians not only question the idea of Western Civilization as a construct but also increasingly prefer to evaluate Roman achievements on their own terms instead of mainly as part of a grand arc of historical evolution.

The story of Roman civilization may conveniently be divided into three different episodes, each with its own characteristics and emphases: the Republic, the (Early and High) Empire, and Early Christianity and Late Antiquity (or the Later Roman Empire). This and the two last chapters of the present reader are structured according to this tripartite division.

Chapter Four focuses on the history of Rome during the period of the monarchy and especially the Republic. From the foundation of the Republic to the series of civil wars in the first century B.C., Rome developed its major institutions and political ideals. Throughout this period, it also gradually expanded its control, first in the Italian peninsula and then to the Mediterranean world as a whole. The growth of Rome from city-state to empire brought with it many social, economic, and political challenges. These challenges created conflicts that, during the course of first century B.C., erupted in large-scale civil wars that brought an end to the republican form of government in Rome and eventually ushered in strong one-person rule. The story of Republican Rome thus raises many important questions. Can a city-state become an empire without itself changing in the process? How did a society that relied heavily on slave labor come to terms with its own traditions that validated the free citizen-farmer-soldier? What was the price of empire for the ancient Romans? Was the fall of the republican form of government an inevitable outcome of Rome's imperial success?

Readings in this chapter will focus on these historical developments with special attention paid to the following themes: Traditions on Early Rome; Rome as a Rising Power; Crises and Transformations; Intellectual Life and Culture; and Late Republic and the Rise of Autocracy.

Traditions on Early Rome

Surviving Roman traditions combined mythical and historical elements in a manner that reflects how Romans in the mid- to late republican period chose to remember their more distant past. Traditional stories often served to reify the cultural values and social institutions that came to be considered core characteristics of Roman identity. One notable aspect of these traditions is how the paradigm of fraternal or civil strife is represented as a central feature of Rome's historical evolution and destiny.

48 Livy

The Early Romans

"The kind of lives our ancestors lived"

Livy (Titus Livius) was born in 59 B.C. at Patavium (Padua) in northern Italy and died in A.D. 17. Little else is known about his life other than that he came to Rome when he was about thirty and spent the next forty years composing his great history of the Roman Republic entitled *Ab Urbe Condita*, "From the Founding of the City." Published in installments, it covered a vast scope of over seven hundred years, from the founding of Rome to A.D. 9, in 142 books—the equivalent, it is estimated, of eight thousand printed pages. Only one-fourth of this enormous work has survived entire: Books I–X (753–293 B.C.) and Books XXI–XLV (218–167 B.C.).

Livy was not a critical historian; he did not possess the tools used by modern historians in picking and evaluating sources. He selected what served his purpose, which was to tell an inspiring story—how the heroic citizens of a small city-state overcame many adversities to become masters of the world. His *History* is a noble prose epic, comparable to the *Aeneid* of Virgil, his contemporary, as a glorification of Rome.

Livy's *History*, a literary masterpiece, became an instant success. No Roman ever attempted to improve upon it, and earlier histories disappeared. Livy's personal fame soon extended to the borders of the empire: "Have you

From *Livy: The Early History of Rome, Books I–V of The History of Rome from Its Foundations*, translated by Aubrey de Sélincourt, pp. 33–34, 96–101, 114–16. Copyright © 1960 by Penguin Books. Reproduced by permission of Penguin Books, Ltd.

never heard the story of the man from Gades (Cadiz)," asked Tacitus, "who was so impressed by the name and reputation of Titus Livius that he journeyed from the end of the inhabited world just to see him, turned about, and went back home?"

A. PREFACE

"The greatest nation in the world"

Livy's account of early Roman history (Books I–V) is a story told in great detail and based on what appears to be exact knowledge. In reality, early Roman history contains more legend than fact, although the legends quite likely preserve a kernel of truth. In his preface, Livy acknowledges the legendary character of the early stories and defends their inclusion: "There is no reason, I feel, to object when antiquity draws no hard line between the human and the supernatural: it adds dignity to the past...."

Livy began his *History* soon after the Republic had fallen, the result, he believed, of the collapse of moral character. Hence his emphasis upon "the dignity of the past"—the way to improve people's character is through the study of history. Augustus, whose permanent dictatorship replaced the fallen Republic, was also concerned with moral regeneration, but through the force of legislation and propaganda. Livy is too steeped in the republican tradition of freedom to favor completely Augustus' program, although he continued to enjoy the emperor's friendship. His brief reference in his preface to Augustus' authoritarian solution, "the dark dawning of our modern day when we can neither endure our vices nor face the remedies needed to cure them," is followed immediately by his own preferred solution for Rome's ills: "The study of history is the best medicine for a sick mind...."

The task of writing a history of our nation from Rome's earliest days fills me, I confess, with some misgiving, and even were I confident in the value of my work, I should hesitate to say so. I am aware that for historians to make extravagant claims is, and always has been, all too common: every writer on history tends to look down his nose at his less–cultivated predecessors, happily persuaded that he will better them in point of style, or bring new facts to light. But however that may be, I shall find satisfaction in contributing—not, I hope, ignobly—to the labor of putting on record the story of the greatest nation in the world. Countless others have written on this theme and it may be that I shall pass unnoticed amongst them; if so, I must comfort myself with the greatness and splendor of my rivals, whose work will rob my own of recognition.

My task, moreover, is an immensely laborious one. I shall have to go back more than seven hundred years, and trace my story from its small beginnings up to these recent times when its ramifications are so vast that any adequate treatment is hardly possible. I am aware, too, that most readers will take less pleasure in my account of how Rome began and in her early history; they will wish to hurry on to more modern times and to read of the period, already a long one, in which the might of an imperial people is beginning to work its own ruin. My own feeling is different; I shall find antiquity a rewarding study, if only because, while I am absorbed in it, I shall be able to turn my eyes from the troubles which for so long have tormented the modern world, and to write without any of that over-anxious consideration which may well plague a writer on contemporary life, even if it does not lead him to conceal the truth.

Events before Rome was born or thought of have come to us in old tales with more of the charm of poetry than of sound historical record, and such traditions I propose neither to affirm nor refute. There is no reason, I feel, to object when antiquity draws no hard line between the human and the supernatural: it adds dignity to the past, and, if any nation deserves the privilege of claiming a divine ancestry, that nation is our own; and so great is the glory won by the Roman people in their wars that, when they declare that Mars himself was their first parent and father of the man [Romulus] who founded their city, all the nations of the world might well allow the claim as readily as they accept Rome's imperial domination.

These, however, are comparatively trivial matters and I set little store by them. I invite the reader's attention to the much more serious consideration of the kind of lives our ancestors lived, of who were the men, and what the means both in politics and war by which Rome's power was first acquired and subsequently expanded; I would then have him trace the process of our moral decline, to watch, first, the sinking of the foundations of morality as the old teaching was allowed to lapse, then the rapidly increasing disintegration, then the final collapse of the whole edifice, and the dark dawning of our modern day when we can neither endure our vices nor face the remedies needed to cure them. The study of history is the best medicine for a sick mind; for in history you have a record of the infinite variety of human experience plainly set out for all to see; and in that record you can find for yourself and your country both examples and warnings; fine things to take as models, base things, rotten through and through, to avoid.

I hope my passion for Rome's past has not impaired my judgment; for I do honestly believe that no country has ever been greater or purer than ours or richer in good citizens and noble deeds; none has been free for so many generations from the vices of avarice and luxury; nowhere have thrift and plain living been for so long held in such esteem. Indeed, poverty, with us, went hand in hand with contentment. Of late years wealth has made us greedy, and self-indulgence has brought us, through every form of sensual excess, to be, if I may so put it, in love with death both individual and collective.

But bitter comments of this sort are not likely to find favor, even when they have to be made. Let us have no more of them, at least at the beginning of our great story. On the contrary, I should prefer to borrow from the poets and begin with good omens and with prayers to all the host of heaven to grant a successful issue to the work which lies before me.

B. THE RAPE OF LUCRETIA: MONARCHY
ABOLISHED

In tradition, Rome was ruled by kings from its founding by the legendary Romulus in 753 B.C. until an oligarchic revolution ended monarchy and established a republic in 509 B.C. The ethnic makeup of the Roman people is reflected in the fact that some of these kings were Latin, others were Sabine, and others—after Rome came under Etruscan influence about 600 B.C.—were Etruscan.

The power of the Roman kings was limited by an advisory council of their fellow nobles (the Senate), which resisted any attempt by the kings to act arbitrarily. Livy reports (I, 49, 50) that Tarquin (Livius Tarquinius), the last Etruscan king of Rome, "was the first king to break the established tradition of consulting the Senate on all matters of public business, and to govern by the mere authority of himself and his household." For this reason he was called the Proud, "though at first none dared more than to whisper it." (Compare the Sumerian nobles who were "gloomy in their chambers" because Gilgamesh's "arrogance" was "unbridled" [Selection 1A], Samuel's fulminations against strong monarchy in Israel [Selection 10D], and the opposition to King Agamemnon, "steeped in insolence," in the *Iliad* [Selection 16].

The following account of Tarquin the Proud's "arrogant and tyrannical behavior," and the melodramatic story of "the hideous rape of the innocent Lucretia" resulting from "the brutal and unbridled lust of Sextus Tarquinius," his son, remind us of the complaints of the nobles of Sumerian Uruk:

> Gilgamesh leaves not the son to his father;
> Day and night is unbridled his arrogance....
> Gilgamesh leaves not the maid to her mother,
> The warrior's daughter, the noble's spouse!

In 510 B.C. the Roman nobles expelled Tarquin the Proud and abolished monarchy. The name they gave to their new oligarchic government, *res publica* ("republic" or "commonwealth"), may have been adopted for propagandistic reasons—to gain the support of the common people.

I, 56.... About this time an alarming and ominous event occurred: a snake slid out from a crack in a wooden pillar in the palace. Everyone ran from it in fright; even the king was scared, though in his case it was not fear so much as foreboding. About signs and omens of public import the custom had always been to consult only Etruscan soothsayers; this, however, was a different matter: it was in the king's own house that the portentous sight had been seen; and that, Tarquin felt, justified the unusual step of sending to Delphi, to consult the most famous oracle in the world. Unwilling to entrust the answer of the oracle to anybody else, he sent on the mission two of his sons, Titus and Arruns, who accordingly set out for Greece through country which Roman feet had seldom trod and over seas which Roman ships had never sailed. With them went Lucius Junius Brutus, son of the king's sister Tarquinia.

Now Brutus had deliberately assumed a mask to hide his true character. When he learned of the murder by Tarquin of the Roman aristocrats, one of the victims being his own brother, he had come to the conclusion that the only way of saving himself was to appear in the king's eye as a person of no account. If there were nothing in his character for Tarquin to fear, and nothing in his fortune to covet, then the sheer contempt in which he was held would be a better protection than his own rights could ever be. Accordingly he pretended to be a half-wit and made no protest at the seizure by Tarquin of everything he possessed. He even submitted to being known publicly as the "Dullard" (which is what his name signifies), that under cover of that opprobrious title the great spirit which gave Rome her freedom might be able to bide its time. On this occasion he was taken by Arruns and Titus to Delphi less as a companion than as a butt for their amusement; and he is said to have carried with him, as his gift to Apollo, a rod of gold inserted into a hollow stick of cornel-wood—symbolic, it may be, of his own character.

The three young men reached Delphi, and carried out the king's instructions. That done, Titus and Arruns found themselves unable to resist putting a further question to the oracle. Which of them, they asked, would be the next king of Rome? From the depths of the cavern came the mysterious answer: "He who shall be the first to kiss his mother shall hold in Rome supreme authority." Titus and Arruns were determined to keep the prophecy absolutely secret, to prevent their other brother, Tarquin, who had been left in Rome, from knowing anything about it. Thus he, at any rate, would be out of the running. For themselves, they drew lots to determine which of them, on their return, should kiss his mother first.

Brutus, however, interpreted the words of Apollo's priestess in a different way. Pretending to trip, he fell flat on his face, and his lips touched the Earth—the mother of all living things.

Back in Rome, they found vigorous preparations in progress for war with the Rutuli. (57) The chief town of the Rutuli was Ardea, and they were a people, for that place and period, of very considerable wealth. Their wealth was, indeed, the reason for Tarquin's preparations: he needed money to repair the drain on his resources resulting from his ambitious schemes of public building and he knew, moreover, that the commons were growing ever more restive, not only in view of his tyrannical behavior generally but also, and especially, because they had been so long employed in manual labor such as belonged properly to slaves, and the distribution of plunder from a captured town would do much to soften their resentment.

The attempt was made to take Ardea by assault. It failed; siege operations were begun, and the army settled down into permanent quarters. With little prospect of any decisive action, the war looked like being a long one, and in these circumstances leave was granted, quite naturally, with considerable freedom, especially to officers. Indeed, the young princes, at any rate, spent most of their leisure enjoying themselves in entertainments on the most lavish scale. They were drinking one day in the quarters of Sextus Tarquinius—Collatinus, son of Egerius, was also present—when someone chanced to mention the subject of wives. Each of them, of course, extravagantly praised his own; and the rivalry got hotter and hotter, until Collatinus suddenly cried: "Stop! What need is there of words, when in a few hours we can prove beyond doubt the incomparable superiority of my Lucretia? We are all young and strong: why shouldn't we ride to Rome and see with our own eyes what kind of women our wives are? There is no better evidence, I assure you, than what a man finds when he enters his wife's room unexpectedly."

They had all drunk a good deal, and the proposal appealed to them; so they mounted their horses and galloped off to Rome. They reached the city as dusk was falling; and there the wives of the royal princes were found enjoying themselves with a group of young friends at a dinner-party, in the greatest of luxury. The riders then went on to Collatia, where they found Lucretia very differently employed: it was already late at night, but there, in the hall of her house, surrounded by her busy maid-servants, she was still hard at work by lamplight upon her spinning. Which wife had won the contest in womanly virtue was no longer in doubt.

With all courtesy Lucretia rose to bid her husband and the princes welcome, and Collatinus, pleased with his success, invited his friends to sup with him. It was at that fatal supper that Lucretia's beauty, and proven chastity, kindled in Sextus Tarquinius the flame of lust, and determined him to debauch her.

Nothing further occurred that night. The little jaunt was over, and the young men rode back to camp.

58. A few days later Sextus, without Collatinus's knowledge, returned with one companion to Collatia, where he was hospitably welcomed in Lucretia's house, and, after supper, escorted, like the honored visitor he was thought to be, to the guest-chamber. Here he waited till the house was asleep, and then, when all was quiet, he drew his sword and made his way to Lucretia's room determined to rape her. She was asleep. Laying his left hand on her breast, "Lucretia," he whispered, "not a sound! I am Sextus Tarquinius, I am armed—if you utter a word, I will kill you." Lucretia opened her eyes in terror; death was imminent, no help at hand. Sextus urged his love, begged her to submit, pleaded, threatened, used every weapon that might conquer a woman's heart. But all in vain; not even the fear of death could bend her will. "If death will not move you," Sextus cried, "dishonor shall. I will kill you first, then cut the throat of a slave and lay his naked body by your side. Will they not believe that you have been caught in adultery with a servant—and paid the price?" Even the most resolute chastity could not have stood against this dreadful threat.

Lucretia yielded. Sextus enjoyed her, and rode away, proud of his success.

The unhappy girl wrote to her father in Rome and to her husband in Ardea, urging them both to come at once with a trusted friend—and quickly, for a frightful thing had happened. Her father came with Valerius, Volesus's son, her husband with Brutus, with whom he was returning to Rome when he was met by the messenger. They found Lucretia sitting in her room, in deep distress. Tears rose to her eyes as they entered, and to her husband's question, "Is it well with you?" she answered, "No. What can be well with a woman who has lost her honor? In your bed, Collatinus, is the impress of another man. My body only has been violated. My heart is innocent, and death will be my witness. Give me your solemn promise that the adulterer shall be punished—he is Sextus Tarquinius. He it was who last night came as my enemy disguised as my guest, and took his pleasure of me. That pleasure will be my death—and his, too, if you are men."

The promise was given. One after another they tried to comfort her. They told her she was helpless, and therefore innocent; that he alone was guilty. It was the mind, they said, that sinned, not the body: without intention there could never be guilt.

"What is due to *him*," Lucretia said, "is for you to decide. As for me I am innocent of fault, but I will take my punishment. Never shall Lucretia provide a precedent for unchaste women to escape what they deserve." With these words she drew a knife from under her robe, drove it into her heart, and fell forward, dead.

Her father and husband were overwhelmed with grief. (59) While they stood weeping helplessly, Brutus drew the bloody knife from Lucretia's body, and holding it before him cried: "By this girl's blood—none more chaste till a tyrant wronged her—and by the gods I swear that with sword and fire, and whatever else can lend strength to my arm, I will pursue Lucius Tarquinius the Proud, his wicked wife, and all his children, and never again will I let them or any other man be King in Rome."

He put the knife into Collatinus's hands, then passed it to Lucretius, then to Valerius. All looked at him in astonishment: a miracle had happened—he was a changed man. Obedient to his command, they swore their oath. Grief was forgotten in the sudden surge of anger, and when Brutus called upon them to make war, from that instant, upon the tyrant's throne, they took him for their leader.

Lucretia's body was carried from the house into the public square. Crowds gathered, as crowds will, to gape and wonder—and the sight was unexpected enough, and horrible enough, to attract them. Anger at the criminal brutality of the king's son and sympathy with the father's grief stirred every heart; and when Brutus cried out that it was time for deeds not tears, and urged them, like true Romans, to take up arms against the tyrants who had dared to treat them as a vanquished enemy, not a man amongst them could resist the call. The boldest spirits offered themselves at once for service; the rest soon followed their lead. Lucretia's father was left to hold Collatia; guards were posted to prevent news of the rising from reaching the palace, and with Brutus in command the armed populace began their march on Rome.

In the city the first effect of their appearance was alarm and confusion, but the sight of Brutus, and others of equal distinction, at the head of the mob, soon convinced people this was, at least, no mere popular demonstration. Moreover the horrible story of Lucretia had had hardly less effect in Rome than in Collatia. In a moment the Forum was packed, and the crowds, by Brutus's order, were immediately summoned to attend the Tribune of Knights—an office held at the time by Brutus himself. There, publicly throwing off the mask under which he had hitherto concealed his real character and feelings, he made a speech painting in vivid colors the brutal and unbridled lust of Sextus Tarquinius, the hideous rape of the innocent Lucretia and her pitiful death, and the bereavement of her father, for whom the cause of her death was an even bitterer and more dreadful thing than the death itself. He went on to speak of the king's arrogant and tyrannical behavior; of the sufferings of the commons condemned to labor underground clearing or constructing ditches and sewers; of gallant Romans—soldiers who had beaten in battle all neighboring peoples—robbed of their swords and turned into stone-cutters and artisans. He reminded them of the foul murder of Servius Tullius [Tarquin's predecessor], of the daughter [Tullia, Tarquin's queen] who drove her carriage over her father's corpse, in violation of the most sacred of relationships—a crime which God alone could punish. Doubtless he told them of other, and worse, things, brought to his mind in the heat of the moment by the sense of this latest outrage, which still lived in his eye and pressed upon his heart; but a mere historian can hardly record them.

The effect of his words was immediate: the populace took fire, and were brought to demand the abrogation of the king's authority and the exile of himself and his family.

With an armed body of volunteers Brutus then marched for Ardea to rouse the army to revolt. Lucretius, who some time previously had been appointed by the king Prefect of the City, was left in command in Rome. Tullia fled from the palace during the disturbances; wherever she went she was met with curses; everyone, men and women alike, called down upon her head the vengeance of the furies who punish sinners against the sacred ties of blood.

60. When news of the rebellion reached Ardea, the king immediately started for Rome, to restore order. Brutus got wind of his approach, and changed his route to avoid meeting him, finally reaching Ardea almost at the same moment as Tarquin arrived at Rome. Tarquin found the city gates shut against him and his exile decreed. Brutus the Liberator was enthusiastically welcomed by the troops, and Tarquin's sons were expelled from the camp. Two of them followed their father into exile at Caere in Etruria. Sextus Tarquinius went to Gabii—his own territory, as he doubtless hoped; but his previous record there of robbery and violence had made him many enemies, who now took their revenge and assassinated him.

Tarquin the Proud reigned for twenty-five years. The whole period of monarchical government, from the founding of Rome to its liberation, was 244 years. After the liberation two consuls were elected by popular vote, under the presidency of the Prefect of the City; the voting was by "centuries," according to the classification of Servius Tullius.[1] The two consuls were Lucius Junius Brutus and Lucius Tarquinius Collatinus.

C. HORATIUS AT THE BRIDGE

"A noble piece of work"

The new Roman Republic had not seen the last of Tarquin the Proud. Roman tradition holds that he made several attempts to regain his throne, the last with the help of Lars Porsena, the Etruscan king of Clusium. The oligarchic

---

1. Although the popular assembly continued to operate, its composition and voting sequence were rigged in such a way as to allow the wealthier Roman citizens to dominate it.

revolution at Rome was the first of a series that would eventually end monarchy in all the Etruscan city-states, and Porsena no doubt feared for his own throne.

Modern historians believe that about 506 B.C. Porsena did conquer Rome and hold it for a short time, but Roman patriotic tradition pretended that his attack was foiled by the heroic efforts of a single Roman soldier, Horatius Cocles—"one man against an army." Livy reports this tradition, and it is a good example of the many vivid, dramatic stories that he tells to exemplify the virtues of the early Romans for the edification and enjoyment of his readers. Livy's continual emphasis on the national character of "the greatest nation in the world" should sound familiar to modern Americans: "The national character of our own country has been a favorite subject of presidents and politicians, who over the years have untiringly instructed the nation and the world about the American work ethic, American know-how, and American values."[2]

II, 9. The Tarquins, meanwhile, had taken refuge at the court of Lars Porsena, the king of Clusium. By every means in their power they tried to win his support, now begging him not to allow fellow Etruscans, men of the same blood as himself, to continue living in penniless exile, now warning him of the dangerous consequences of letting republicanism go unavenged. The expulsion of kings, they urged, once it had began, might well become common practice; liberty was an attractive idea, and unless reigning monarchs defended their thrones as vigorously as states now seemed to be trying to destroy them, all order and subordination would collapse; nothing would be left in any country but flat equality; greatness and eminence would be gone for ever. Monarchy, the noblest thing in heaven or on earth, was nearing its end. Porsena, who felt that his own security would be increased by restoring the monarchy in Rome, and also that Etruscan prestige would be enhanced if the king were of Etruscan blood, was convinced by these arguments and lost no time in invading Roman territory.

Never before had there been such consternation in the Senate, so powerful was Clusium at that time and so great the fame of Porsena. Nor was the menace of Porsena the only cause for alarm: the Roman populace itself was hardly less to be feared, for they might well be scared into admitting the Tarquins into the city and buying peace even at the price of servitude. To ensure their support, therefore, the Senate granted them a number of favors, especially in the matter of food supplies. Missions were sent to Cumae and the Volscians to purchase grain; the monopoly in salt, the price of which was high, was taken from private individuals and transferred wholly to state control; the commons were exempted from tolls and taxes, the loss of revenue being made up by the rich, who could afford it; the poor, it was said, made contribution enough if they reared children. These concessions proved wonderfully effective, for during the misery and privation of the subsequent blockade the city remained united—so closely, indeed, that the poorest in Rome hated the very name of

2. T. J. Luce, *Livy: The Composition of His History* (Princeton, New Jersey: Princeton University Press, 1977), p. 277.

"king" as bitterly as did the great. Wise government in this crisis gave the Senate greater popularity, in the true sense of the word, than was ever won by a demagogue in after years.

10. On the approach of the Etruscan army, the Romans abandoned their farmsteads and moved into the city. Garrisons were posted. In some sections the city walls seemed sufficient protection, in others the barrier of the Tiber. The most vulnerable point was the wooden bridge, and the Etruscans would have crossed it and forced an entrance into the city, had it not been for the courage of one man, Horatius Cocles—that great soldier whom the fortune of Rome gave to be her shield on that day of peril. Horatius was on guard at the bridge when the Janiculum was captured by a sudden attack. The enemy forces came pouring down the hill, while the Roman troops, throwing away their weapons, were behaving more like an undisciplined rabble than a fighting force. Horatius acted promptly: as his routed comrades approached the bridge, he stopped as many as he could catch and compelled them to listen to him. "By God," he cried, "can't you see that if you desert your post escape is hopeless? If you leave the bridge open in your rear, there will soon be more of them in the Palatine and the Capitol than on the Janiculum." Urging them with all the power at his command to destroy the bridge by fire or steel or any means they could muster, he offered to hold up the Etruscan advance, so far as was possible, alone. Proudly he took his stand at the outer end of the bridge; conspicuous amongst the rout of fugitives, sword and shield ready for action, he prepared himself for close combat, one man against an army. The advancing enemy paused in sheer astonishment at such reckless courage. Two other men, Spurius Lartius and Titus Herminius, both aristocrats with a fine military record, were ashamed to leave Horatius alone, and with their support he won through the first few minutes of desperate danger. Soon, however, he forced them to save themselves and leave him; for little was now left of the bridge, and the demolition squads were calling them back before it was too late. Once more Horatius stood alone; with defiance in his eyes he confronted the Etruscan chivalry, challenging one after another to single combat, and mocking them all as tyrants' slaves who, careless of their own liberty, were coming to destroy the liberty of others. For a while they hung back, each waiting for his neighbor to make the first move, until shame at the unequal battle drove them to action, and with a fierce cry they hurled their spears at the solitary figure which barred their way. Horatius caught the missiles on his shield and, resolute as ever, straddled the bridge and held his ground. The Etruscans moved forward, and would have thrust him aside by the sheer weight of numbers, but their advance was suddenly checked by the crash of the falling bridge and the simultaneous shout of triumph from the Roman soldiers who had done their work in time. The Etruscans could only stare in bewilderment as Horatius, with a prayer to Father Tiber to bless him and his sword, plunged fully armed into the water and swam, through the missiles which fell thick about him, safely to the other side where his friends were waiting to receive him. It was a noble piece of work—legendary, maybe, but destined to be celebrated in story through the years to come.

Rome as a Rising Power

The Roman conquest of Italy and then of the Mediterranean world was a long drawn-out process marked by both momentary setbacks and ultimate triumph. Rising Roman militarism combined with a willingness to extend its citizenship to others advanced the Roman cause while contemporary Greek authors marveled at Rome's success and attributed it to Republican Rome's balanced political constitution.

49 Livy

The Foreign Policy of the Roman Republic

"One people in the world which would fight for others' liberties."

Immediately following the victory over Hannibal (201 B.C.), which ended the Second Punic War and left the Roman Republic the dominant power in the western Mediterranean, the Romans were drawn into the maelstrom of eastern Mediterranean power politics. By 189 B.C. Rome had fought and defeated in turn the two most powerful Hellenistic states, Antigonid Macedon and the Seleucid Empire, thereby becoming the virtual master of the entire Mediterranean area.

The following selection from Livy's *History of Rome*, written in the reign of Augustus, supports the view that Rome's initial intervention in the East, like her expansion in the West, was motivated by fear. During the darkest days of the Second Punic War following Rome's defeat at Cannae (p. 32), Philip V of Macedon, believing that Rome's earlier establishment of a naval base in the Adriatic Sea to deal with pirates was a prelude to expansion in the Balkans and a threat to his kingdom, allied himself with Hannibal. However, clashes with the Greeks kept him from aiding Hannibal. After the war, following an agreement with the Seleucid ruler Antiochus III to partition the outlying possessions of the declining Ptolemaic rulers of Egypt, he began advancing in the Aegean Sea region. The small states of Pergamum and

From *Livy: Volume IX, History of Rome*, Loeb Classical Library Vol. 295, translated by E. T. Sage (Cambridge, Mass.: Harvard University Press, 1935). The Loeb Classical Library® is a registered trademark of the President and Fellows of Harvard College. Reprinted by permission of the publishers and the Trustees of the Loeb Classical Library.

Rhodes, already at war with Philip, asked Rome's aid in preserving the balance of power in the East, and the Senate decided to act. Philip's refusal to heed a Roman ultimatum was followed by a declaration of war, but only after the Senate had overcome the initial refusal of the popular assembly to approve another war only one year after the end of the "Great War" with Hannibal.

Supported by some Greek allies, notably the Aetolian League and Athens, the Roman commander Quinctius Flamininus routed the Macedonian army at Cynoscephalae in 197 B.C. Rome's lenient peace terms were designed to end Philip's dreams of empire while preserving his state as a buffer against barbarians to the north and Antiochus III to the east. The decision to end Macedon's longstanding attempt to dominate Greece, together with the philhellene sentiments of Flamininus and other leading Romans, led to the theatrical announcement of the freedom of Greece and the withdrawal of Roman forces. The delirious enthusiasm that this declaration evoked among the Greeks was quickly undermined, however, by misunderstandings between the liberators and the liberated. In time the paternalistic attitude of the Romans convinced most Greeks that the Romans were still semi-barbarians, and the Romans in turn lost their early philhellene idealism. In 146 B.C.—the same year in which they razed the city of Carthage at the end of the Third Punic War—the exasperated Romans completely destroyed the city of Corinth, a hotbed of anti-Romanism, and placed all of Greece under the administrative authority of the Roman governor of Macedonia, which had been annexed two years earlier.

Livy's report that the liberated Greeks had eulogized the Romans as "one people in the world which would fight for others' liberties at its own cost, ... ready to cross the sea that there might be no unjust empire anywhere ...," reminds us of Pericles' defense of Athenian imperialism more than two centuries earlier (Selection 25): "We are alone among mankind in doing men benefits ... in the fearless confidence of [bringing] freedom."

Roman Policy Vexes the Aetolians

11. Philip, having collected the straggling fugitives who had followed his trail after the changing fortunes of the battlefield, sent agents to Larisa to burn the royal records, in order to prevent their falling into the hands of the Romans, and retired into Macedonia. Quinctius [Flamininus] sold part of the prisoners and booty and gave part to the soldiers, and marched towards Larisa, still uncertain where the king had gone and what he was planning. There the king's herald met him, ostensibly to ask for a truce, that those who had fallen in the battle might be removed for burial, in reality to ask permission to send an embassy. Both requests were granted by the Roman. The consul, moreover, added that the king should take heart, a phrase which gave great offence to the Aetolians, who were already swollen with pride and complaining that victory had changed the general: before the battle he had been wont to discuss with the allies all matters great and small, but now they were excluded from all his deliberations, and he decided everything according to his own personal judgment, since he was trying to win a place of private influence with the king,

in order that, although the Aetolians had endured the hardships and toils of the war, the Roman might take to himself the credit for the peace and the profits of victory. And beyond doubt something of their honorable position had been lost; but they did not see why they should be utterly ignored. They believed that the consul—a man of a soul unconquerable by such cupidity—was eager to receive gifts from the king; but he was in fact angry at the Aetolians, and with just cause, for their insatiable desire for booty and their arrogance in claiming the glory of the victory for themselves, while with their boasting they had offended the ears of everyone, and he saw that with Philip out of the way and the power of the Macedonian kingdom broken the Aetolians would be held the masters of Greece. For these reasons he deliberately took many steps to cause them to be and to seem of less moment and importance in the eyes of all men.

12. A truce of fifteen days had been granted to the enemy and a conference arranged with the king; but before the time for this arrived, he called a council of the allies and referred to them the terms of peace which they wished to be imposed. Amynander, king of the Athamanes, spoke briefly: the peace should be so arranged that Greece, even in the absence of the Romans, should be strong enough to maintain at once peace and liberty. The language of the Aetolians was more harsh; they said, after a brief preface, that the Roman commander was acting correctly and in order in discussing the conditions of peace with those whom he had had as his allies in the war; but that he was totally wrong if he thought that he would leave either assured peace to the Romans or liberty to the Greeks unless Philip were either killed or dethroned, either of which was easy if he were willing to follow up his good fortune.

In reply, Quinctius asserted that the Aetolians neither remembered Roman policy nor employed arguments consistent with themselves. On the one hand, in all previous conferences and conversations they had always spoken of conditions of peace and not of waging a war of extermination; on the other, the Romans, in addition to observing, from remote antiquity, their custom of sparing conquered peoples, had given striking proof of their mercifulness in the peace granted to Hannibal and the Carthaginians. He would say nothing about the Carthaginians: how often had conferences been held with Philip himself? Never was there any suggestion that he should give up his kingdom. Or, because he had been defeated in the battle, did that make war an unpardonable offense? An armed enemy should be met in hostile mood; towards the conquered, the mildest possible attitude was the greatest thing. The Macedonian kings seemed a menace to Greek liberty; but if that kingdom and people were removed, the Thracians, the Illyrians, and then the Gauls, fierce and untamed peoples, would pour into Macedonia and into Greece. They should not, by breaking up all the nearest states, open the way to themselves for larger and more powerful tribes. Then, when Phaeneas, the Aetolian praetor, interrupted, reminding him that if Philip escaped this time he would soon cause a greater war, Quinctius replied, "Cease causing disturbance when we should be deliberating. The conditions by which the king will be bound will not be such that he will be able to start a war."...

Peace Terms Imposed on Philip

30. [T]en commissioners arrived from Rome, and with their approval peace was granted to Philip on these terms: that all the Greek cities which were in Europe or in Asia should enjoy their liberty and laws; that, whatever cities had been under the sway of Philip, from these Philip should withdraw his garrisons and should hand them over to the Romans, free of his troops, before the time of the Isthmian Games; that he should withdraw also from the following cities in Asia: Euromum and Pedasa and Bargyliae and Iasus and Myrina and Abydus and Thasos and Perinthus (for it was determined that these too should be free); that ... Philip should turn over to the Romans the prisoners and deserters, all his warships except five and one royal galley of almost unmanageable size, which was propelled by sixteen tiers of oars; that he should have a maximum of five thousand soldiers and no elephants at all; that he should wage no war outside Macedonia without the permission of the Senate; that he should pay to the Roman people an indemnity of one thousand talents, half at once and half in ten annual instalments.... Claudius ... mentions an explicit provision that he should not wage war with Eumenes, son of Attalus—he was the new king there [Pergamum]. Hostages were taken to insure performance, among them Demetrius, the son of Philip. Valerius Antias adds that the island of Aegina and the elephants were presented as a gift to Attalus, who was absent, that the Rhodians were given Stratonicea and other cities in Caria which Philip had held, and the Athenians the islands of Paros, Imbros, Delos, and Scyros.

More Grumblings of the Aetolians

31. While all the Greek cities approved this settlement, only the Aetolians with secret grumblings criticized the decision of the ten commissioners: mere words had been trimmed up with the empty show of liberty; why were some cities delivered to the Romans without being named, others specified and ordered to be free without such delivery, unless the purpose was that those which were in Asia, being more secure by reason of their remoteness, should be set free, but those which were in Greece, not being named, should become Roman property, to wit, Corinth and Chalcis and Oreus along with Eretria and Demetrias? Their complaint was not altogether groundless. For there was some uncertainty with respect to Corinth and Chalcis and Demetrias, because in the decree of the Senate, under which the ten commissioners were sent from Rome, the other cities of Greece and Asia were beyond question set free, but regarding these three cities the commissioners were instructed to take such action as the public interest should have proved to demand, in accordance with the general good and their own sense of honor. There was King Antiochus, who, there was no doubt, would invade Europe as soon as his forces seemed adequate; they did not wish to leave these cities, so favorably located, open to his occupancy. Quinctius with the ten commissioners moved from Elatia to Anticyra and thence to Corinth. There plans for the liberation of Greece were discussed almost every day at meetings of the ten commissioners. Quinctius urged repeatedly that all Greece should be set free, if they wished to stop the muttering of the Aetolians and to create

genuine affection and respect for the Roman name among all the Greeks, and if they wished to convince them that they had crossed the sea to liberate Greece and not to transfer dominion from Philip to themselves. The others said nothing opposed to this as regards the freedom of the cities, but they believed it safer for the Greeks themselves to remain for a while under the protection of Roman garrisons than to receive Antiochus as lord in place of Philip. Finally, this decision was reached: Corinth should be given over to the Achaeans, a garrison, however, to be retained in Acrocorinthus; Chalcis and Demetrias should be held until the anxiety about Antiochus should have passed.

The Liberation of Greece

32. The appointed time of the Isthmian Games was at hand, a spectacle always, even on other occasions, attended by crowds, on account of the fondness, native to the race, for exhibitions in which there are trials of skill in every variety of art as well as of strength and swiftness of foot; moreover, they came because, on account of the favorable situation of the place, lying between the two opposite seas and furnishing mankind with abundance of all wares, the market was a meeting-place for Asia and Greece. But at this time they had assembled from all quarters not only for the usual purposes, but especially they were consumed with wonder what thenceforth the state of Greece would be, and what their own conditions; they not only had their own silent thoughts, some believing one thing and others another, but discussed openly what the Romans would do; almost no one was convinced that they would withdraw from all Greece. They had taken their seats at the games and the herald with the trumpeter, as is the custom, had come forth into the midst of the arena, where the games are regularly opened with a ritual chant, and proclaiming silence with a trumpet-call, the herald read the decree: "The Roman Senate and Titus Quinctius, *imperator,* having conquered King Philip and the Macedonians, declare to be free, independent, and subject to their own laws, the Corinthians, the Phocians, all the Locrians, the island of Euboea, the Magnesians, the Thessalians, the Perrhaebians, and the Phthiotic Achaeans." He had named all the states which had been subject to King Philip. When the herald's voice was heard there was rejoicing greater than men could grasp in its entirety. They could scarce believe that they had heard aright, and they looked at one another marvelling as at the empty vision of a dream; they asked their neighbors what concerned each one, unwilling to trust the evidence of their own ears. The herald was recalled, each one desiring not only to hear but to behold the man who brought the tidings of his freedom, and again the herald read the same decree. Then, when the ground for their joy was certain, such a storm of applause began and was so often repeated that it was easily apparent that a throng of good men values nothing more highly than liberty. The contests were then rapidly finished, no man's eyes or thoughts being fixed upon the sight; joy alone had so completely replaced their perception of all other delightful things.

33. When the games were over, almost everyone rushed toward the Roman commander, so that he was endangered by the crowd that rushed to one place,

desiring to draw near him, to touch his hand, and showering garlands and cha-
plets upon him. But he was only about thirty-three years old, and both the vigor
of youth and the joy he felt at so remarkable a reward of fame gave him strength.
Nor did the rejoicing spend itself at once, but was renewed for many days in
thoughts and expressions of gratitude: there was one people in the world
which would fight for others' liberties at its own cost, to its own peril and with
its own toil, not limiting its guarantees of freedom to its neighbors, to men of the
immediate vicinity, or to countries that lay close at hand, but ready to cross the
sea that there might be no unjust empire anywhere and that everywhere justice,
right, and law might prevail. By the single voice of a herald, they said, all the
cities of Greece and Asia had been set free; to conceive hopes of any such
thing as this required a bold mind; to bring it to pass was the proof of immense
courage and good fortune as well.

50 Polybius

The Constitution of the Roman Republic

"It is impossible to find a better"

Second only to Thucydides among Greek historians was Polybius (ca. 200–ca.
117 B.C.). He witnessed and speculated upon the events that marked the
expansion of Rome in the Mediterranean area from Spain to Asia Minor, and
he grasped the fact that Hellenistic history was becoming inextricably inter-
twined with Roman history. He spent sixteen years in Rome as one of a thousand Greek hostages brought to Rome in 167 B.C. to ensure the good
behavior of their compatriots at home. Here he became a firm admirer of the
character and the political and social institutions of his Roman captors. Above
all, he became convinced that the expansion of Rome was natural and inevitable, and he undertook to write a history of his own times in order to reconcile
the Greek world to the reality of Roman domination. He chose as his starting
point the year 220 B.C.—the beginning of the First Punic War—because, as he
put it, "since that time history has been a kind of organic whole, and the
affairs of Italy and Africa have been interconnected with those of Asia and
Greece, all moving toward one end," the Roman world-state. He closed his
history with the events of 146 B.C., the year in which the Third Punic War
was ended with the complete destruction of Carthage, and the year in which
the final step in the subjugation of Greece and Macedonia was signaled by an
equally ruthless destruction of Corinth.

From Polybius, *The Histories*, Book VI, translated by Evelyn S. Shuckburgh.

Polybius was particularly interested in discovering causes and in seeing the interrelation of events, without which history is but a rope of sand with no meaning or value: "Neither the writer nor the reader of history, therefore, should confine his attention to a bare statement of facts.... For if you take from history all explanation of cause, principle, and motive, and of the adaptation of the means to the end, what is left is a mere panorama without being instructive, and though it may please for the moment, has no abiding value."

He attributed Rome's rise to the superior qualities of its citizens and the perfection of its institutions, all of which he contrasted with those of other peoples in the Mediterranean area. His famous description of the Roman constitution at the end of the third century B.C. is a case in point. He divided governments into three types—kingship, aristocracy, and democracy—and he attributed the excellence of the Roman constitution to the fact that it contained elements of these three types in dynamic equilibrium. His emphasis upon the checks and balances of the Roman constitution influenced eighteenth-century French political thinkers and through them entered these ideas into the American constitution.

Introduction

1. I am aware that some will be at a loss to account for my interrupting the course of my narrative for the sake of entering upon the following disquisition on the Roman constitution. But I think that I have already in many passages made it fully evident that this particular branch of my work was one of the necessities imposed on me by the nature of my original design; and I pointed this out with special clearness in the preface which explained the scope of my history. I there stated that the feature of my work which was at once the best in itself, and the most instructive to the students of it, was that it would enable them to know and fully realize in what manner, and under what kind of constitution, it came about that nearly the whole world fell under the power of Rome in somewhat less than fifty-three years—an event certainly without precedent. This being my settled purpose, I could see no more fitting period than the present for making a pause, and examining the truth of the remarks about to be made on this constitution. In private life if you wish to satisfy yourself as to the badness or goodness of particular persons, you would not, if you wish to get a genuine test, examine their conduct at a time of uneventful repose, but in the hour of brilliant success or conspicuous reverse. For the true test of a perfect man is the power of bearing with spirit and dignity violent changes of fortune. An examination of a constitution should be conducted in the same way; and therefore being unable to find in our day a more rapid or more signal change than that which has happened to Rome, I reserved my disquisition on its constitution for this place....

3. Of the Greek republics, which have again and again risen to greatness and fallen into insignificance, it is not difficult to speak, whether we recount their past history or venture an opinion on their future. For to report what is already known is an easy task, nor is it hard to guess what is to come from our knowledge of what has been. But in regard to the Romans it is neither an easy matter to describe their present state, owing to the complexity of their constitution; nor

to speak with confidence of their future, from our inadequate acquaintance with their peculiar institutions in the past whether affecting their public or their private life. It will require then no ordinary attention and study to get a clear and comprehensive conception of the distinctive features of this constitution.

Now, it is undoubtedly the case that most of those who profess to give us authoritative instruction on this subject distinguish three kinds of constitutions, which they designate *kingship, aristocracy, democracy*. But in my opinion the question may be fairly put to them, whether they name these as being the *only* ones, or as the *best*. In either case I think they are wrong. For it is plain that we must regard as the best constitution that which partakes of all these three elements. And this is no mere assertion, but has been proved by the example of Lycurgus, who was the first to construct a constitution—that of Sparta—on this principle....

11. ... I will now endeavor to describe [the constitution] of Rome at the period of their disastrous defeat at Cannae [by Hannibal, 216 B.C.].

I am fully conscious that to those who actually live under this constitution I shall appear to give an inadequate account of it by the omission of certain details. Knowing accurately every portion of it from personal experience, and from having been bred up in its customs and laws from childhood, they will not be struck so much by the accuracy of the description as annoyed by its omissions; nor will they believe that the historian has purposely omitted unimportant distinctions, but will attribute his silence upon the origin of existing institutions or other important facts to ignorance. What is told they depreciate as insignificant or beside the purpose; what is omitted they desiderate as vital to the question: their object being to appear to know more than the writers. But a good critic should not judge a writer by what he leaves unsaid, but from what he says: if he detects misstatement in the latter, he may then feel certain that ignorance accounts for the former; but if what he says is accurate, his omissions ought to be attributed to deliberate judgment and not to ignorance. So much for those whose criticisms are prompted by personal ambition rather than by justice....

Another requisite for obtaining a judicious approval for an historical disquisition, is that it should be germane to the matter in hand; if this is not observed, though its style may be excellent and its matter irreproachable, it will seem out of place, and disgust rather than please....

Three Sovereign Elements

As for the Roman constitution, it had three elements, each of them possessing sovereign powers: and their respective share of power in the whole state had been regulated with such a scrupulous regard to equality and equilibrium, that no one could say for certain, not even a native, whether the constitution as a whole were an aristocracy or democracy or despotism. And no wonder: for if we confine our observation to the power of the Consuls we should be inclined to regard it as despotic; if on that of the Senate, as aristocratic; and if finally one looks at the power possessed by the people it would seem a clear case of democracy. What the exact powers of these several parts were, and still, with slight modifications, are, I will now state.

12. The Consuls, before leading out the legions, remain in Rome and are supreme masters of the administration. All other magistrates, except the Tribunes, are under them and take their orders. They introduce foreign ambassadors to the Senate; bring matters requiring deliberation before it; and see to the execution of its decrees. If, again, there are any matters of state which require the authorization of the people, it is their business to see to them, to summon the popular meetings, to bring the proposals before them, and to carry out the decrees of the majority. In the preparations for war, also, and in a word in the entire administration of a campaign, they have all but absolute power. It is competent to them to impose on the allies such levies as they think good, to appoint the Military Tribunes, to make up the roll for soldiers and select those that are suitable. Besides they have absolute power of inflicting punishment on all who are under their command while on active service: and they have authority to expend as much of the public money as they choose, being accompanied by a Quaestor who is entirely at their orders. A survey of these powers would in fact justify our describing the constitution as despotic—a clear case of royal government. Nor will it affect the truth of my description, if any of the institutions I have described are changed in our time, or in that of our posterity: and the same remarks apply to what follows.

13. The Senate has first of all the control of the treasury, and regulates the receipts and disbursements alike. For the Quaestors cannot issue any public money for the various departments of the state without a decree of the Senate, except for the service of the Consuls. The Senate controls also what is by far the largest and most important expenditure, that, namely, which is made by the censors every *lustrum* [five years] for the repair or construction of public buildings; this money cannot be obtained by the censors except by the grant of the Senate. Similarly all crimes committed in Italy requiring a public investigation, such as treason, conspiracy, poisoning, or willful murder, are in the hands of the Senate. Besides, if any individual or state among the Italian allies requires a controversy to be settled, a penalty to be assessed, help or protection to be afforded—all this is the province of the Senate. Or again, outside Italy, if it is necessary to send an embassy to reconcile warring communities, or to remind them of their duty, or sometimes to impose requisitions upon them, or to receive their submission, or finally to proclaim war against them—this too is the business of the Senate. In like manner the reception to be given foreign ambassadors in Rome, and the answers to be returned to them, are decided by the Senate. With such business the people have nothing to do. Consequently, if one were staying at Rome when the Consuls were not in town, one would imagine the constitution to be a complete aristocracy: and this has been the idea entertained by many Greeks, and by many kings as well, from the fact that nearly all the business they had to do with Rome was settled by the Senate.

14. After this one would naturally be inclined to ask what part is left for the people in the constitution, when the Senate has these various functions, especially the control of the receipts and expenditures of the exchequer; and when

the Consuls, again, have absolute power over the details of military preparation, and an absolute authority in the field? There is, however, a part left the people, and it is a most important one. For the people is the sole fountain of honor and of punishment; and it is by these two things and these alone that dynasties and constitutions and, in a word, human society are held together.... The people then are the only court to decide matters of life and death; an even in cases where the penalty is money, if the sum to be assessed is sufficiently serious, and especially when the accused have held the higher magistracies. And in regard to this arrangement there is one point deserving especial commendation and record. Men who are on trial for their lives at Rome, while sentence is in process of being voted—if even only one of the tribes whose votes are needed to ratify the sentence has not voted—have the privilege at Rome of openly departing and condemning themselves to a voluntary exile. Such men are safe at Naples or Praeneste or at Tibur, and at other towns with which this arrangement has been duly ratified on oath.

Again, it is the people who bestow offices on the deserving, which are the most honorable rewards of virtue. It has also the absolute power of passing or repealing laws; and, most important of all, it is the people who deliberate on the question of peace or war. And when provisional terms are made for alliance, suspension of hostilities, or treaties, it is the people who ratify them or the reverse.

These considerations again would lead one to say that the chief power in the state was the people's, and that the constitution was a democracy.

Checks and Balances

15. Such, then, is the distribution of power between the several parts of the state. I must now show how each of these several parts can, when they choose, oppose or support each other.

The Consul, then, when he has started on an expedition with the powers I have described, is to all appearance absolute in the administration of the business in hand, still he has need of the support both of people and Senate, and, without them, is quite unable to bring the matter to a successful conclusion. For it is plain that he must have supplies sent to his legions from time to time; but without a decree of the Senate they can be supplied neither with grain, nor clothes, nor pay, so that all the plans of a commander must be futile, if the Senate is resolved either to shrink from danger or hamper his plans. And again, whether a Consul shall bring any undertaking to a conclusion or no depends entirely on the Senate: for it has absolute authority at the end of a year to send another Consul to supersede him, or to continue the existing one in his command. Again, even to the successes of the generals, the Senate has the power to add distinction and glory, and on the other hand to obscure their merits and lower their credit. For these high achievements are brought in tangible form before the eyes of the citizens by what are called "triumphs." But in these triumphs the commanders cannot celebrate with proper pomp, or in some cases celebrate at all, unless the Senate concurs and grants the necessary money. As for the people, the Consuls are preeminently obliged to court their favor, however distant from home may be the field of their operations; for it is the people, as I have said before, that ratifies, or refuses to ratify, terms of peace and treaties; but most of all because when laying down their office they have to give an account of their administration before it. Therefore in no case is it safe for the Consuls to neglect either the Senate or the good will of the people.

16. As for the Senate, which possesses the immense power I have described, in the first place it is obliged in public affairs to take the multitude into account, and respect the wishes of the people; and it cannot put into execution the penalty for offences against the republic, which are punishable with death, unless the people first ratify its decrees. Similarly even in matters which directly affect the senators—for instance, in the case of a law depriving senators of certain dignities and offices, or even actually cutting down their property—even in such cases the people have the sole power of passing or rejecting the law. But most important of all is the fact that, if the Tribunes interpose their veto, the Senate not only are unable to pass a decree, but cannot even hold a meeting at all, whether formal or informal. Now, the Tribunes are always bound to carry out the decree of the people, and above all things to have regard to their wishes: therefore, for all these reasons the Senate stands in awe of the multitude, and cannot neglect the feelings of the people.

17. In like manner the people on its part is far from being independent of the Senate, and is bound to take its wishes into account both collectively and individually. For contracts, too numerous to count, are given out by the censors in all parts of Italy, for the repairs or construction of public buildings; there is also the collection of revenue from many rivers, harbors, gardens, mines, and land—everything, in a word, that comes under the control of the Roman government: and in all these the people at large are engaged; so that there is scarcely a man, so to speak, who is not interested either as a contractor or as being employed in the works. For some purchase the contracts from the censors for themselves; and others go partners with them; while others again go security for these contractors, or actually pledge their property to the treasury for them. Now over all these transactions the Senate has absolute control. It can grant an extension of time; and in case of unforeseen accident can relieve the contractors from a portion of their obligation, or release them from it altogether, if they are absolutely unable to fill it.... But the most important point of all is that the judges are taken from its members in the majority of trials, whether public or private, in which the charges are heavy. Consequently, all citizens are much at its mercy; and being alarmed at the uncertainty as to when they may need its aid, are cautious about resisting or actively opposing its will. And for a similar reason men do not rashly resist the wishes of the Consuls, because one and all may become subject to their absolute authority on a campaign.

18. The result of this power of the several estates for mutual help or harm is a union sufficiently firm for all emergencies, and a constitution than which it is impossible to find a better. For whenever any danger from without compels them to unite and work together, the strength which is developed by the State is so extraordinary, that everything required is unfailingly carried out by the eager rivalry

shown by all classes to devote their whole minds to the need of the hour, ... Even when these external alarms are past, and the people are enjoying their good fortune and the fruits of their victories, and, as usually happens, growing corrupt by flattery and idleness, show a tendency to violence and arrogance—it is in these circumstances, more than ever, that the constitution is seen to possess within itself the power of correcting abuses. For when any one of the three classes becomes puffed up, and manifests an inclination to be contentious and unduly encroaching, the mutual interdependency of all the three, and the possibility of the pretensions of any one being checked and thwarted by the others, must plainly check this tendency; and so the proper equilibrium is maintained by the impulsiveness of the one part being checked by its fear of the other.

51 Cato the Elder

Traditional Standards in a New Age

The Romans of the early Republic attributed their military successes, along with the stability of their whole society, to the qualities of character instilled in them by the *mos maiorum*—their ancestral way of life that subordinated the individual to the religious and social traditions of family, state, and gods. Yet, ironically, it was continued military success that did much to destroy the hold of the *mos maiorum*. As one crisis followed another and Rome expanded outside Italy, new situations arose that required a new type of leadership that could only come from self-confident individuals who did not feel tightly bound by tradition. The career of Scipio Africanus (ca. 236–ca. 183 B.C.) illustrates the emergence of this new type of highly individualistic leader. In the darkest days of Roman defeats inflicted by Hannibal in the Second Punic War, Scipio arose to shatter all precedents of caution and restraint and, while often acting contrary to the orders of the Senate, turned the tide of war against the Carthaginians. Self-styled traditionalists such as Cato the Elder (234–149 B.C.) were keenly aware that such individualism was a challenge to the old Roman traditions, and they retaliated later by accusing and convicting Scipio on trumped-up charges of irregularities in military expenditures. Scipio scornfully refused to defend himself and chose to remain in voluntary exile from his "thankless city" for the remainder of his life.

It is significant that Scipio, from one of Rome's most influential aristocratic families, was also one of the earliest Romans to embrace enthusiastically the study of Greek literature. This contributed to the suspicion held by some

From *Plutarch: Vol. II, The Parallel Lives*, Loeb Classical Library Vol. 47, translated by B. Perrin, (Cambridge, Mass.: Harvard University Press, 1914). The Loeb Classical Library® is a registered trademark of the President and Fellows of Harvard College. Reprinted by permission of the publishers and the Trustees of the Loeb Classical Library.

of his opponents that Greek thought was subversive of the established order. Did not the Hellenistic philosophies, for example, with their emphasis on reason and individual happiness, undermine the traditional subordination of the individual to family, state, and gods? It is no wonder that strenuous attempts were made by Roman conservatives, led by Cato, a "new man" from a modest background, to prevent the seemingly unchecked advance of Greek culture among the Roman aristocracy in particular. In 181 B.C., the Senate ordered the public burning of a treatise on Pythagorean philosophy. Again, in 173 B.C., two Epicurean philosophers were ordered out of Rome, and a more general decree twelve years later expelled all Greek teachers and philosophers. But all such efforts were futile, and by the end of the second century the cosmopolitan culture of Greece seemed to many to have absorbed and transformed the ancestral Roman way of life. In Horace's well-known line, "Captive Greece captured in turn her untutored conqueror."

The following selection from Plutarch's "Life of Marcus Cato" illustrates two main reasons for Cato's claim to fame: his personification of early Roman character, and his leadership in the struggle against Greek learning. He fought hard for an old ideal he realized was fast slipping away, and in one of his last speeches he finally and sadly acknowledged that his cause was lost. "It is hard," he said, "to have to give an account of your life to men of another age than that in which you have lived."

A "New Man" but "Oldest of the Old"

1. The family of Marcus Cato, it is said, was of Tusculan origin, though he lived, previous to his career as soldier and statesman, on an inherited estate in the country of the Sabines. His ancestors commonly passed for men of no note whatever, but Cato himself extols his father, Marcus, as a brave man and good soldier. He also says that his grandfather, Cato, often won prizes for soldierly valor, and received from the state treasury, because of his bravery, the price of five horses which had been killed under him in battle. The Romans used to call men who had no family distinction, but were coming into public notice through their own achievements, "new men," and such they called Cato. But he himself used to say that as far as office and distinction went, he was indeed new, but having regard to ancestral deeds of valor, he was oldest of the old....

2. Near his fields was the cottage which had once belonged to Manius Curius, a hero of three triumphs. To this he would often go, and the sight of the small farm and the mean dwelling led him to think of their former owner, who, though he had become the greatest of the Romans, had subdued the most warlike nations, and driven Pyrrhus out of Italy, nevertheless tilled this little patch of ground with his own hands and occupied this cottage, after three triumphs. Here it was that the ambassadors of the Samnites once found him seated at his hearth cooking turnips, and offered him much gold; but he dismissed them, saying that a man whom such a meal satisfied had no need of gold, and for his part he thought that a more honorable thing than the possession of gold was the conquest of its possessors. Cato would go away with his mind full of these things, and on viewing again his own house and lands and servants and mode of life, would increase the labors of his hands and lop off his extravagancies....

"New Modes of Life of Every Sort"

4. The influence which Cato's oratory won for him waxed great, and men called him a Roman Demosthenes; but his manner of life was even more talked about and noised abroad. For his oratorical ability only set before young men a goal which many already were striving eagerly to attain; but a man who wrought with his own hands, as his fathers did, and was contented with a cold breakfast, a frugal dinner, simple raiment, and a humble dwelling—one who thought more of not wanting the superfluities of life than of possessing them—such a man was rare. The Commonwealth had now grown too large to keep its primitive integrity; the sway over many realms and peoples had brought a large admixture of customs, and the adoption of examples set in new modes of life of every sort. It was natural, therefore, that men should admire Cato, when they saw that, whereas other men were broken down by toils and enervated by pleasures, he was victor over both, and this too, not only while he was still young and ambitious, but even in his hoary age, after consulship and triumph. Then, like some victorious athlete, he persisted in the regimen of his training, and kept his mind unaltered to the last.

He tells us that he never wore clothing worth more than a hundred drachmas; that he drank, even when he was praetor or consul, the same wine as his slaves; that as for fish and meats, he would buy thirty asses' worth for his dinner from the public stalls, and even this for the city's sake, that he might not live on bread alone, but strengthen his body for military service; that he once fell heir to an embroidered Babylonian robe, but sold it at once; that not a single one of his cottages had plastered walls; that he never paid more than fifteen hundred drachmas for a slave, since he did not want them to be delicately beautiful, but sturdy workers, such as grooms and herdsmen, and these he thought it his duty to sell when they got oldish, instead of feeding them when they were useless; and that in general, he thought nothing cheap that one could do without, but that what one did not need, even if it cost but a penny, was dear; also that he bought lands where crops were raised and cattle herded, not those where lawns were sprinkled and paths swept.

5. These things were ascribed by some to the man's parsimony; but others condoned them in the belief that he lived in this contracted way only to correct and moderate the extravagance of others. However, for my part, I regard his treatment of his slaves like beasts of burden, using them to the uttermost, and then, when they were old, driving them off and selling them, as the mark of a very mean nature, which recognizes no tie between man and man but that of necessity....

Cato as Censor: "Still More Strict"

19. ... [After being elected censor, Cato] grew still more strict. He cut off the pipes by which people conveyed part of the public water supply into their private houses and gardens; he upset and demolished all buildings that encroached on public land; he reduced the cost of public works to the lowest, and forced the rent of public lands to the highest possible figure. All these things brought much odium upon him....

Still, it appears that the people approved of his censorship to an amazing extent. At any rate, after erecting a statue to his honor in the temple of Health, they commemorated in the inscription upon it, not the military commands nor the triumph of Cato, but, as the inscription may be translated, the fact "that when the Roman state was tottering to its fall, he was made censor, and by helpful guidance, wise restraints, and sound teachings, restored it again." And yet, before this time he used to laugh at those who delight in such honors, saying that, although they knew it not, their pride was based simply on the work of sculptors and painters, whereas his finest image, of the most exquisite workmanship, was carried in the hearts of his fellow citizens. And to those who expressed their amazement that many men of no fame had statues, while he had none, he used to say: "I would much rather have men ask why I have no statue, than why I have one." In short, he thought a good citizen should not even allow himself to be praised, unless such praise was beneficial to the Commonwealth....

"Good Father, Husband, Economist"

20. He was also a good father, a considerate husband, and an economist of no mean talent, nor did he give only a fitful attention to this, as a matter of little or no importance. Therefore I think I ought to give suitable instances of his conduct in these relations. He married a wife who was of nobler birth than she was rich, thinking that, although the rich and the high-born may be alike given to pride, still, women of high birth have such a horror of what is disgraceful that they are more obedient to their husbands in all that is honorable. He used to say that the man who struck his wife or child, laid violent hands on the holiest of things. Also that he thought it more praiseworthy to be a good husband than a great senator, nay, there was nothing else to admire in Socrates of old except that he was always kind and gentle in his intercourse with a shrewish wife and stupid sons. After the birth of his son, no business could be so urgent, unless it had a public character, as to prevent him from being present when his wife bathed and swaddled the babe. For the mother nursed it herself, and often gave suck also to the infants of her slaves, that so they might come to cherish a brotherly affection for her son. As soon as the boy showed signs of understanding, his father took him under his own charge and taught him to read, although he had an accomplished slave, Chilo by name, who was a school-teacher, and taught many boys. Still, Cato thought it not right, as he tells us himself, that his son should be indebted to his slave for such a priceless thing as education. He was therefore himself not only the boy's reading-teacher, but his tutor in law, and his athletic trainer, and he taught his son not merely to hurl the javelin and fight in armor and ride the horse, but also to box, to endure heat and cold, and to swim lustily through the eddies and billows of the Tiber. His *History of Rome*, as he tells us himself, he wrote out with his own hand and in large characters, that his son might have in his own home an aid to acquaintance with his country's ancient traditions. He declares that his son's presence put him on his guard against indecencies of speech as much as that of the so-called Vestal Virgins, and that he never bathed with him. This, indeed, would seem to have been a general custom

with the Romans, for even fathers-in-law avoided bathing with their sons-in-law, because they were ashamed to uncover their nakedness. Afterwards, however, when they had learned from the Greeks their freedom in going naked, they in turn infected the Greeks with the practice even when women were present.

So Cato wrought at the fair task of molding and fashioning his son to virtue....

21. ... However, as he applied himself more strenuously to money-getting, he came to regard agriculture as more entertaining than profitable, and invested his capital in business that was safe and sure. He bought ponds, hot springs, places producing fuller's earth, pitch factories, land with natural pasture and forest, all of which brought him in large profits, and "could not," to use his own phrase, "be ruined by Jupiter." He used to loan money also in the most disreputable of all ways, namely, on ships, and his method was as follows. He required his borrowers to form a large company, and when there were fifty partners and as many ships for his security, he took one share in the company himself, and was represented by Quintio, a freedman of his, who accompanied his clients in all their ventures. In this way his entire security was not imperilled, but only a small part of it, and his profits were large. He used to lend money also to those of his slaves who wished it, and they would buy boys with it, and after training and teaching them for a year, at Cato's expense, would sell them again. Many of the boys Cato would retain for himself, crediting to the slave the highest price bid for the boy. He tried to incite his son also to such economies, by saying that it was not the part of a man, but of a widow woman, to lessen his capital. But that surely was too vehement a speech of Cato's, when he went so far as to say that a man was to be admired and glorified like a god if the final inventory of his property showed that he had added to it more than he had inherited.

"He Made Mock of All Greek Culture"

22. When he was now well on in years, there came as ambassadors from Athens to Rome, Carneades the Academic, and Diogenes the Stoic philosopher.... Upon the arrival of these philosophers, the most studious of the city's youth hastened to wait upon them, and became their devoted and admiring listeners. The charm of Carneades especially, which had boundless power, and a fame not inferior to its power, won large and sympathetic audiences, and filled the city, like a rushing mighty wind, with the sound of his praises. Report spread far and wide that a Greek of amazing talent, who disarmed all opposition by the magic of his eloquence, had infused a tremendous passion into the youth of the city, in consequence of which they forsook their other pleasures and pursuits and were "possessed" about philosophy. The other Romans were pleased at this, and glad to see their young men lay hold of Greek culture and consort with such admirable men. But Cato, at the very outset, when this zeal for discussion came pouring into the city, was distressed, fearing lest the young men, by giving this direction to their ambition, should come to love a reputation based on mere words more than one achieved by martial deeds. And when the fame of the visiting philosophers rose yet higher in the city, and their first speeches before

the Senate were interpreted, at his own instance and request, by so conspicuous a man as Gaius Acilius, Cato determined, on some decent pretext or other, to rid and purge the city of them all. So he rose in the Senate and censured the magistrates for keeping in such long suspense an embassy composed of men who could easily secure anything they wished, so persuasive were they. "We ought," he said, "to make up our minds one way or another, and vote on what the embassy proposes, in order that these men may return to their schools and lecture to the sons of Greece, while the youth of Rome give ear to their laws and magistrates, as heretofore."

23. This he did, not, as some think, out of personal hostility to Carneades, but because he was wholly averse to philosophy, and made mock of all Greek culture and training, out of patriotic zeal. He says, for instance, that Socrates was a mighty prattler, who attempted, as best he could, to be his country's tyrant, by abolishing its customs, and by enticing his fellow citizens into opinions contrary to the laws. He made fun of the school of Isocrates, declaring that his pupils kept on studying with him till they were old men, as if they were to practice their arts and plead their cases before Minos in Hades. And seeking to prejudice his son against Greek culture, he indulged in an utterance all too rash for his years, declaring, in the tone of a prophet or a seer, that Rome would lose her empire when she had become infected with Greek letters. But time has certainly shown the emptiness of this ill-boding speech of his, for while the city was at the zenith of its empire, she made every form of Greek learning and culture her own.

52 Pseudo-Cicero

How to Get Elected to Public Office in Rome

"You must take pains to solicit the votes of all these men...."

The consulship represented the summit of Roman political office. Every self-respecting and properly ambitious member of the aristocracy aspired to that position. By the first century B.C., new consuls took office on January 1 when they presided over the festival of the Kalends of January and gave their names to the year itself. They also exercised broad political powers in addition to their ceremonial roles. In the final years of the Roman Republic, two consuls were elected annually by the Centuriate Assembly, one of the two popular assemblies in Rome. The following selection, which was written in the form of a letter, describes the steps that an aspiring candidate had to take to ensure a

From *Roman Civilization: Selected Readings*, Volume 1, 3rd ed., edited by Naphtali Lewis and Meyer Reinhold. © 1990 by Columbia University Press. Reprinted with the permission of the publisher.

successful outcome to his candidacy. The letter claims that it was itself written by Quintus Tullius Cicero, the foremost orator and important political figure in the last generation of the Republic, to his younger brother Marcus Tullius Cicero regarding the latter's bid for the consulship in the election of 64 B.C. Modern scholars are inclined to believe, however, that the letter was composed by an anonymous individual, possibly even a century later.

The selection refers to the candidate as a "new man" (Latin: *novus homo*), that is, a Roman who was the first of his family to gain entrance into the senatorial order through holding high political office. Such a person would not have had the political advantages that noble birth and name recognition conferred and, when trying to promote his own career, would have had to compensate for such deficiencies by taking the various measures described in the letter. This writing gives us welcome insight into the electoral politics of the Late Republic generally and the political calculations of the elite in particular. The uncertain relationship between an ambitious elite candidate and the mass of Roman citizens in the letter hints at the social and political tensions that eventually led to the downfall of the Republic.

Consider these three things: what state this is, what you are seeking and who you are. Then every day, as you descend to the Forum, you must say to yourself, "I am a new man; I am standing for the consulship; this is Rome."

The political newness of your name you will overcome to a large extent by your reputation as a speaker. That is an accomplishment which has always carried with it the highest distinction. The man who is considered a worthy advocate for men of consular rank cannot be reckoned unworthy of the consulship....

Next, let the number and quality of your friends be apparent. For you have in your favor what not many new men have had: all the publicans, nearly all the equestrian order, many faithful municipalities, many individuals of every class who have been defended by you, some private groups, also a large number of young men won over by their pursuit of eloquence, and the diligent daily concourse of your personal friends. Take care to retain all these supporters by reminding them, asking for their votes, and taking all steps to make them understand—those who are under obligation to you—that they will never have another opportunity of showing their gratitude, and those who desire your services, that they will never have another opportunity of placing you in their debt.

Another thing, it seems to me, that can be of great assistance to a new man is the good will of the nobles, especially those of consular rank. It is well to be considered worthy of that rank by those into whose rank and number you wish to enter. You must take pains to solicit the votes of all these men, you must assure and convince them that we have always sided with the *optimates* in politics and have never been supporters of the *populares*; that if we appear to have given utterance to any popular sentiments, we did so with a view to winning the support of Gnaeus Pompey in order to have the most powerful man in the state friendly to our candidacy, or at least not hostile to it. Further, make a special effort to win over the young nobles, and to keep the ones you have won over devoted to you; they will bring you great esteem. You have many such friends; see to it that they know how important you consider them. If you can convert them from passive to active supporters, they will do you the greatest good....

Therefore take care to secure all the centuries by your many varied friendships. First of all, it is obvious you must conciliate the senators and *equites*, and the active and influential men of the other orders. There are many industrious men in the city, many freedmen influential and active in the Forum. Some you can reach in person, some through mutual friends: exercise the greatest diligence, bend every effort to make them your active supporters—court them, assure them, point out that they will be doing you the greatest service. Next, take into account the whole city, all the private groups, country districts, and neighborhoods. If you can win over the leading men in these to your friendship, you will through them easily gain the crowd. After that, see that you imprint on your mind and memory the whole of Italy, divided and catalogued by tribes, so that you may let no municipality, colony, or prefecture, in short no place at all in Italy exist in which you have not sufficient support. Seek out and discover men in every district, make their acquaintance, solicit them, give them assurances, and see to it that they canvass for you in their neighborhoods and become, as it were, candidates themselves in your cause. They will wish to have you for a friend if they see that their friendship is sought for by you, and you can bring this home to them by suitable address; for men who live in the municipal towns and in the country think themselves friends of ours if they can gain in addition some assistance for themselves from our friendship, they lose no opportunity of earning it. The others, and in particular your rivals, don't even know these men, but you have some acquaintance, and will easily be able to increase it....

The centuries of *equites*, it seems to me, can be much more easily won over by diligence. First, make their acquaintance (they are but few), then court them (they are mostly young men, and youth is much more easily won to friendship), and then you will have with you all of the best of the youth and the most assiduous in kindnesses.... And the zeal of the young men in your behalf, in voting, in canvassing, in spreading reports, and in attending you about the city, is of wonderful importance and very honorable.

And speaking of attending you about the city, you must take care to have a daily company of attendants, of every class, order, and age. From their numbers it will be possible to conjecture how much power and support you are likely to have at the election itself. Now, there are three parts to this matter: the first, those who wait upon you at your house in the morning; the second, those who escort you from your house, and the third, those who accompany you about the city. In the case of the first, who are the most ordinary kind of attendants and, in the current fashion, come in great numbers, you must take care to make even this trifling service of theirs appear most acceptable to you. Let those who come to your house know that you notice it: tell it to them often, and to their friends, who will report it to them. In this way, when there are several rival candidates and people see that there is one man who takes especial notice of these acts of attention, they often desert the others and swing over to him....

Now as to those who escort you from your house, show them and let them know that you are the more grateful for their attention, since it is greater than that of your morning greeters, and as far as possible come down into the Forum at regular times. A great company escorting you every day lends great reputation and distinction. The third group of this kind are those who attend you constantly. See to it that those among them who do so of their own volition understand that they are placing you in their perpetual debt by the greatest favor. From those who are under obligation to you, you can simply require this service, that those whose age and business permit be in constant attendance upon you, and those who cannot attend in person assign relatives to this service....

As enough has now been said about contracting friendships, we must proceed to speak of that other branch of a candidate's concerns, his popularity among the common people. That requires calling everyone by his name, flattery, assiduity, courtesy, reputation, and confidence in your political career. As to the first, knowing men's names, let it be evident that you do, and improve so as to be better at it day by day. Nothing seems to me to be so popular or so pleasing. Next, though flattery is not in your nature, convince yourself that you must pretend to practice it naturally, for though character is more important, still in a business of a few months [i.e., an election campaign] pretense can prevail over character. You are not lacking in the complaisance worthy of a good and agreeable person, but you particularly need the gift of flattery, which, though vicious and repulsive in the rest of one's life, is indispensable in an election campaign. Indeed, it is bad only when, by "yessing" a man, it makes him worse; when it renders him more friendly it is not so blamable; but in any case it is indispensable for a candidate, whose expression, countenance, and language must be constantly changed and adapted to the feelings and inclinations of everyone he meets....

Courtesy has a wide range. It appears in a man's family life, which cannot directly reach the multitude, to be sure, but pleases the multitude if praised by his friends. It appears at banquets, which you should take care to have celebrated both by yourself and by your friends on many occasions and for each tribe. It appears in services, which you must offer to all: see that there is ready access to you night and day, and that not only the doors of your house are open, but also your countenance and expression, which are the doors of your mind; and if the latter indicate that your intentions are concealed and hidden, it is little use for your house door to be open. For men like not only to be promised things, especially such things as they ask of a candidate, but to have them promised liberally and honorably. Accordingly, this rule, at least, is easy to practice: always to make it clear that you will be doing eagerly and cheerfully whatever you are going to do. But it is more difficult, and more suited to the requirements of the occasion than to your nature, to promise what you may not be able to perform, instead of refusing politely. The second is the conduct of a good man, the first of a good campaigner.... Gaius Cotta, a past master at canvassing, used to say that he would promise his services to all, so long as nothing contrary to his duty was asked of him, but would really render them only to those on whom he thought they were best bestowed; that he would refuse no one, because it often happened that the man to whom he had given a promise did not avail himself of it, or that he himself had more free time than he had expected; and that the man who only promised what he was sure he could perform would never have a house full of well-wishers.... If you make a promise, the thing is still uncertain, is a matter for a future day, and concerns but few people; but if you refuse, you alienate many people definitely and at once....

Lastly, see that your whole campaign is full of pomp, illustrious, splendid, and pleasing to the people, that it has the greatest honor and dignity, so that your rivals may reproach you with no wickedness, lust, or bribery such as they practice. And in this campaign it is necessary to take especial care that people shall have confidence in your political career and an honorable opinion of you. A political career is achieved neither in a campaign nor in the senate nor in the assembly; the things that count are that the senate shall judge that you will be a defender of its authority because you have been so hitherto, that the *equites* (and virtuous and wealthy men in general) shall judge from your past life that you will be a lover of peace and tranquillity, and that the multitude shall judge, from the fact that in your speeches at least you have been a supporter of popular causes in the assembly and in the courts, that you will not be unfriendly to its interests.

These are the thoughts which occurred to me with respect to the first two of the morning meditations that I said you ought to ponder every day as you were descending to the Forum: "I am a new man; I am standing for the consulship." The third point remains, "The city is Rome," a state formed of an assemblage of all nations, a state in which many intrigues, much deceit, many vices of every kind abound, in which the arrogance of many, the contumacy of many, the malevolence of many, the pride of many, the hatred and vexation of many must be endured. I see that it requires great prudence and tact for one, living amid so many and such great vices of men of every sort, to avoid giving offense, to avoid gossip, to avoid treachery; and that there is but one man adapted to such a variety of manners, talk and dispositions. Wherefore, continue constantly to walk in that path in which you have set out: excel in speaking. This is the means by which men are controlled at Rome, won over and kept from hindering or harming you. And since this is the point in which the state is most at fault, that it is apt to forget virtue and worth when bribery intervenes, in this see that you fully realize your own power, i.e., that you are a man who can cause your rivals the greatest fear of the risks of a trial. Let them know that they are being watched and observed by you, and they will fear not only your diligence, authority, and powerful eloquence, but also the zeal of the equestrian order in your behalf. And I wish you to put this to them, not so as to appear to be actually planning prosecution, but merely in order, by alarming them thus, to attain your goal more easily. In a word, strive in this way with all your strength and ability, so that we may obtain what we seek.

Crises and Transformations

Rome's rise in the aftermath of the Punic Wars and the introduction of large-scale slavery transformed the nature of the economy and society in Sicily and Italy. The tensions between social groups within the Roman polity became further accentuated. Each sought to advance their own interests against the backdrop of a Roman senatorial aristocracy that sought to maintain its monopoly over wealth and power during the changing and challenging times.

53 Tiberius Gracchus

The Republic at the Crossroads

It is an ironic but outstanding lesson of history that the Roman constitution of the middle of the second century B.C., whose stability and permanence seemed so apparent to Polybius (Selection 50), was soon to weaken and collapse. Polybius' verdict on the history of the Greek states, that "while they still thought themselves prosperous, and likely to remain so, they found themselves involved in circumstances completely the reverse," applies equally well to the last century of the Roman Republic (133–31 B.C.).

The hundred years preceding 31 B.C. witnessed great changes not only in Rome's political institutions, but in every other important aspect of Roman civilization as well. Historians following Sir Ronald Syme have aptly named the period the "Roman Revolution," for at its end Cicero could sadly contemplate the radical changes it had brought and ask, "What remains of the old ways in which Ennius [239–169 B.C., whose poetry celebrated the old traditions] said the Roman state stood rooted?" The forces that destroyed the old ways came out of the new environment produced by Rome's expansion in the Mediterranean area. (By 133 B.C., Rome ruled provinces in western Europe, North Africa, and Asia Minor.) The political, economic, social, and cultural ideas and institutions that had served a small city-state well underwent radical change when Rome emerged as a world power.

The impact of the new forces that were destined to change Roman civilization was manifested in politics for the first time during the tribunate of

From Plutarch, *Parallel Lives*, "Life of Tiberius Gracchus," based on the translation by John Dryden and revised by Arthur H. Clough.

Tiberius Gracchus in 133 B.C. Tiberius was a young aristocrat in whom the influence of the liberal learning of Greece, newly imported and popular in the best-educated circles of Roman higher society, combined with an awareness that the old Roman way of life was fast slipping away and inspired him to become a reformer. He proposed an agrarian reform law aimed at solving all the problems that had arisen out of the new environment created by Rome's expansion; he hoped to recapture the traditional Roman ways by restoring the old environment that had originally produced them. By breaking up the newly formed large estates worked by a slave-labor force plentifully provided by Rome's wars, he would reverse the trend of events that had brought troubles to the Roman state: the dangerous and still-growing proletariat of the city would be dispersed to become again a large class of small landowners, the old Roman morale and traditional values would reappear, a citizen-army of sturdy yeomen would be possible as of old, and a stable foundation for democratic government would be provided. In his hopes for these beneficial results of land reform, Tiberius reflected a traditional Roman viewpoint. A generation earlier, Marcus Cato the Elder (see Selection 51) had written of the old Romans that "when they praised a man as good, they called him 'a good farmer' and 'a good tiller of the soil,'" and he had insisted that "from among the tillers of the soil both the strongest men and the most efficient soldiers come, and that way of gaining a livelihood carries with it beyond all others fidelity to gods and men, and stability and freedom from envy, and those occupied in it are least liable to evil thoughts."

The opposition to Tiberius' agrarian law centered in the Senate, not only because its members constituted the great landholding class whose economic interests were threatened, but above all because the political supremacy of that body was challenged by the tactics used by the reformer. Since the passage of the Hortensian Law in 287 B.C., by which all bills passed by the popular assembly became fully valid without the approval of the Senate, Rome had been functioning much as a democracy. But during the unsettled period following the passage of the Hortensian Law, Rome had in fact remained an oligarchy in which the senatorial nobility continued to rule. During these critical years, Rome fought the Punic Wars and expanded in Italy and the Mediterranean, and the Roman populace willingly allowed the Senate, composed largely of experienced former magistrates, to exercise all legislative authority. When Tiberius Gracchus revived the legislative activity of the popular assembly to bypass his opposition in the Senate, the continuation of the senatorial oligarchy was threatened.

In the ensuing struggle, it is difficult to determine the degree of guilt or innocence of the rival factions, for both resorted to illegal or ill-considered measures; but the use of violence by the senatorial faction was the great error that ultimately reaped the whirlwind of civil war and led to the fall of the Republic. History is filled with similar instances in which men blinded by fear and hate have unwittingly destroyed that which they sought to preserve. It was the head of the Roman state religion, the *pontifex maximus* Nasica, who incited the mob to kill Tiberius and his followers, and he did so with a cry that could be the epitome of misguided patriotism: "Let those who would save our country follow me!"

The selections that follow are from Plutarch's "Life of Tiberius Gracchus," generally considered to favor the reform party or the *Populares*.

The Land Problem

8. Of the land that the Romans gained [in Italy] by conquest of their neighbors, part they sold and part they added to the public domain. This latter common land they assigned to those of the citizens who were poor and landless, on payment of a small rent into the public treasury. But when the wealthy began to offer larger rents and to drive the poorer people out, a law was enacted [367 B.C.] that no person could hold more than three hundred acres of public land. This act for some time checked the avarice of the rich and aided the poor, who retained the land they had rented in the past. Later, however, the rich men of the neighborhood managed to get these lands into their possession by using fictitious names, and finally they claimed most of the public land as their own. The poor, who were thus deprived of their farms, no longer registered for service in war, nor did they care about the education of their children. In a short time there were comparatively few free laborers left in Italy, which swarmed with gangs of foreign slaves. These the rich used in cultivating the lands from which they had driven the free citizens. Gaius Laelius, the close friend of Scipio, tried to reform this abuse; but meeting with opposition from men of influence he soon desisted, fearing a disturbance; as a result he received the name of "the Wise" or "the Prudent," both meanings belonging to the Latin word *Sapiens*.

Tiberius' Land Law

Tiberius, however, being elected tribune of the people, embarked on the same venture without delay, at the instigation, most people say, of Diophanes the rhetorician and Blossius the philosopher. Diophanes was a refugee from Mitylene, the other was an Italian from Cumae…. Some have also charged that Cornelia, the mother of Tiberius, was partly responsible because she frequently upbraided her sons by saying that the Romans called her the daughter of Scipio Africanus rather than the mother of the Gracchi. Others say that Spurius Postumius was to blame. He was a man of the same age as Tiberius and his rival as a public speaker. When Tiberius returned from the army he found that Postumius had far outdistanced him in fame and influence and was much looked up to. Tiberius thought to outdo him by promoting a political measure of great daring and great consequence for the people. But his brother Gaius stated in one of his writings that when Tiberius went through Tuscany to Numantia and found the country almost depopulated, there being hardly any free farmers or shepherds but for the most part only imported barbarian slaves, he then first conceived the public policy which in its sequel proved so fatal to his family. However, it is very certain that the people themselves did most to kindle his zeal and determination by writing appeals on porticoes, walls, and monuments, calling upon him to return the public lands to the poor.

9. He did not, however, draw up his law without the advice and assistance of those citizens who were most eminent for their virtue and reputation, among whom were Crassus the *pontifex maximus,* Mucius Scaevola the jurist, who was then consul, and Appius Claudius, his father-in-law. Never did any law appear more moderate and mild, especially in view of such great injustice and avarice.

For men who ought to have been punished for transgressing the law, and who should at least have lost title to lands which they illegally enjoyed, were nevertheless to receive compensation for quitting their unlawful claims and giving up the lands to those citizens who needed help. But even though this reform was very moderate—the people were satisfied and ready to forget the past if they could prevent abuses of like nature in the future—the rich hated the law because of their greed and the lawgiver because of their anger and party spirit. They therefore endeavored to confuse the people, declaring that Tiberius was designing a general redivision of lands in order to overthrow the government and put all things in confusion.

But they had no success. For Tiberius, supporting an honorable and just measure with an eloquence sufficient to make a far less credible cause appear plausible, was quite invincible. Whenever the people crowded around the rostra, he would take his place there and speak on behalf of the poor. "The wild beasts of Italy," he would say, "have their own dens as places of repose and refuge, but the men who fight and die for their country enjoy nothing more in it than the air and light; having no houses or settlements of their own, they must wander from place to place with their wives and children. The army commanders are guilty of a ridiculous error when they exhort the common soldiers to defend their sepulchers and altars, for not one among so many Romans has an ancestral altar or tomb. They fight and die to maintain the luxury and wealth of other men. They are called the masters of the world, but they have not one foot of ground to call their own."

Veto and Impeachment of Octavius

10. Eloquence of this nature, spoken to an enthusiastic and sympathetic audience by a person of commanding spirit and genuine feeling, none of the opponents of Tiberius could successfully oppose. Abandoning therefore all discussion and debate, they turned to Marcus Octavius, one of the tribunes, a young man of steady and orderly character and a close friend of Tiberius. For this reason Octavius at first declined the task of opposing him; but finally, under pressure from numerous influential people, he was prevailed upon to do so by vetoing the bringing of the law to a vote. (It is the law that any tribune has the power to veto an act, and that all the other tribunes can do nothing if one of them dissents.) Angered by this procedure, Tiberius withdrew his mild bill and introduced another which was more pleasing to the common people and more severe against the wrongdoers, since it ordered the latter to immediately surrender without compensation all lands which they held contrary to former laws....

Observing that Octavius himself would be an offender against this law, for he held a great deal of public land, Tiberius begged him to stop his opposition, offering to pay the price of Octavius' land out of his own pocket, although he was not rich. But when Octavius refused this offer, Tiberius issued an edict prohibiting all magistrates from exercising their public functions until such time as his law was voted on....

11. When the appointed day came and Tiberius was summoning the people to vote, the rich men carried off the voting urns and thus caused great confusion. But when Tiberius' party appeared strong enough to oppose the other faction and banded together with the intention to do so, Manlius and Fulvius, men of consular rank, threw themselves before Tiberius, took him by the hand, and with tears in their eyes begged him to desist. Tiberius, considering the dangers that were now threatening and having great respect for two such eminent men, asked them what they would advise him to do. They acknowledged themselves unfit to advise on a matter of so great importance, and earnestly entreated him to refer the question to the Senate. He agreed; but when the Senate assembled it could accomplish nothing, owing to the influence of the rich faction. Tiberius then resorted to a course neither legal nor fair, the removal of Octavius from his tribunate, for it was impossible for him in any other way to bring his law to a vote....

12. When the people again met, Tiberius mounted the rostra and tried a second time to persuade Octavius. But when Octavius could not be persuaded, Tiberius referred the whole matter to the people, calling on them to vote at once on whether Octavius should be deposed or not. When seventeen of the thirty-five tribes had already voted against Octavius and there was needed only the votes of one more tribe for his deposition, Tiberius called a halt to the proceedings and once more renewed his entreaties, embracing and kissing Octavius before the assembly, earnestly begging him not to allow himself to be so dishonored or force Tiberius to be known as the promoter of so severe and odious a measure. Octavius, we are told, did seem a little softened and moved by these entreaties; his eyes filled with tears and he stood silent for a long time. But when he looked toward the men of wealth and substance who stood gathered in a body together, partly for shame and partly for fear of disgracing himself with them, he boldly bid Tiberius to do what he pleased. The law was passed and Tiberius ordered one of his freedmen to remove Octavius from the rostra. The use of a freedman as a public official made the action seem all the sadder— Octavius being dragged out in such an ignominious manner. The people immediately assaulted him, while the rich men ran to his assistance. With some difficulty, Octavius was snatched away and safely conveyed out of the crowd, though one of his faithful slaves, who had placed himself in front of his master to protect him, had his eyes torn out, much to the displeasure of Tiberius who, when he perceived the disturbance, ran with all haste to stop the violence.

13. The land law was then passed, and three commissioners were appointed to make a survey and distribute the public land. These were Tiberius himself, his father-in-law Appius Claudius, and his brother Gaius, who was not in Rome but in the army serving with Scipio against Numantia. These appointments Tiberius arranged quietly and without disturbance; in addition he had a new tribune chosen, not a person of distinction but a certain Mucius, one of his own clients. The great men of the city resented all this and, fearing lest he grow even more powerful, they took every opportunity to insult him in the Senate. When he requested to have the customary tent provided at public expense for his use while dividing the land, though it was a favor commonly granted to persons

employed in business of much less importance, it was refused him; and the allowance made him for his daily expenses was fixed at nine sesterces [about two days' wages]. The chief promoter of these affronts was Publius Nasica, who completely surrendered himself to his hatred of Tiberius, for he was a large holder of public lands and greatly resented being forced to give them up. The people, on the other hand, became more and more excited....

The Senate's Control of Foreign Policy Endangered

14. About this time Attalus Philometor [the last king of Pergamum] died, and Eudemus of Pergamum brought his will to Rome. In it the king had made the Roman people his heirs. Tiberius courted popular favor by immediately proposing a law to distribute the money of Attalus among the citizens who were receiving public land, to enable them to stock and cultivate their farms. As for what was to be done with the cities in the kingdom of Attalus, he declared that this matter did not belong to the Senate but to the people, and that he would refer to the judgment of the people. By this proposal he offended the Senate more than ever, and Pompeius arose and told that body that he was a neighbor of Tiberius and so he knew that Eudemus the Pergamenian had presented Tiberius with a royal diadem and a purple robe, since he intended to be king of Rome....

Tiberius Justifies the Impeachment of Octavius

15. Tiberius soon realized that the action he had taken against Octavius had alarmed not only the nobility, but the people as well, because they felt that the dignity of the tribunes, so carefully guarded up to that time, had been insulted and destroyed. He therefore made a speech to the people, from which it may be proper to quote some of the argument to illustrate his force and persuasiveness as a speaker. He admitted that a tribune was sacred and inviolable because he was consecrated to be the guardian and protector of the people, "but if he degenerates so far as to harm the people, reducing their power and taking away their right to vote, he stands deprived of his immunity by the neglect of the conditions on which it was bestowed upon him. Otherwise we should be obliged to allow a tribune to do what he wished, even though he should try to destroy the Capitol or set fire to the arsenal. He who attempts such acts would be a bad tribune; he who attacks the power of the people is no tribune at all. Is it not inconceivable that a tribune should have power to imprison a consul, while the people who gave him that power have no right to take it from him when he uses it to their detriment? For tribunes and consuls alike are elected by the people. The rule of a king, which embraces all power in itself, is also sanctified by the most solemn religious ceremonies. Yet the citizens deposed Tarquin when he acted wrongfully; because of one man's arrogance, the ancient government under which Rome was founded was abolished [Selection 48B]. What is there in all Rome so sacred and venerable as the Vestal Virgins, who tend the eternal fire? Yet if one of them breaks her vows, she is buried alive; the sanctity granted her for the gods' sake is forfeited when she offends against the gods. So likewise a

tribune loses his inviolability, which was granted him for the people's sake, when he offends against the people by attacking that very power from which he derives his own. We consider him to be a legally chosen tribune who is elected by a majority of votes; is it not equally legal to depose him by a unanimous vote? Nothing is so sacred and inviolable as religious offerings; yet the people were never prohibited from using them, or removing and carrying them wherever they pleased. So, just like some sacred object, they have the power to transfer the tribunate from one man to another. Nor can that office be considered inviolable and irremovable which so many of those who have held have of their own accord asked to be discharged from."

A Second Term and Other Proposals

16. These were the principal points of Tiberius' defense. But his friends, discerning the threats and the hostile combination against him, were of the opinion that the safest way would be for him to be reelected tribune for the following year. Accordingly he again sought to secure popular support with fresh laws: reducing the term of military service, granting the right of appeal from the judges to the people, and adding to the judges, who at that time were all senators, an equal number of citizens of the equestrian [capitalist] order. Indeed, he endeavored as much as possible to weaken the power of the Senate, being influenced more by passion and partisanship than by any regard for justice and the public good....

The Senate Resorts to Force

17. ... Several men ran to Tiberius with a message from his friends on the Capitol, saying that all things there [at the polls] went according to expectation. And indeed Tiberius' appearance there went well at first, for as soon as he appeared the people welcomed him with loud cheers, and as he went up the hill they repeated their expressions of joy, gathering around him so that no stranger might approach.

18. Mucius then began again to call the roll of the tribes, but he could do nothing in proper order because a disturbance caused by those who were on the edge of the crowd, where there was a struggle going on with those of the opposite party, who were pushing and trying to force their way in. In the midst of this confusion, Flavius Flaccus, a senator ... finally reached Tiberius and informed him that the rich men, having failed to win over the consul in a meeting of the Senate, had decided among themselves to assassinate him, and for that purpose had armed a great number of their clients and slaves.

19. Tiberius reported this to those around him, and they immediately tucked up their togas and seized the fasces with which the officers keep back the crowd. These they broke and distributed the pieces to use against attack. Those who stood at a distance wondered at this and asked what was going on. Tiberius, knowing that they could not hear him at that distance, lifted his hand to his head to indicate the great danger he was in. His opponents, noticing this,

ran off at once to the senate house and reported that Tiberius desired the people to bestow a crown upon him, claiming this was the meaning of his touching his head. This news enraged the senators, and Nasica demanded that the consul should rescue the state and destroy the tyrant. The consul quietly replied that he would resort to no violence, nor would he allow any citizen to be put to death without a trial; neither would he allow any measure to go into effect, if by persuasion or compulsion on the part of Tiberius the people voted to do anything illegal. Thereupon Nasica jumped from his seat and cried out: "Since the consul has betrayed the state, let those who would save our country follow me!" He then threw the edge of his toga over his head and ran to the Capitol. Those who followed him wrapped their togas around their left arms and forced their way through the crowd. Since they were men of great dignity, the common people did not obstruct their passing; instead they pushed one another aside and fled.... Tiberius tried to save himself by flight. As he was running he was stopped by a senator who caught hold of his toga, but he threw it off and fled in his tunic. Then he stumbled and fell over the bodies of those who had been knocked down. As he struggled to rise, everyone saw Publius Satureius, one of his fellow tribunes, give him the first fatal blow by hitting him on the head with the leg of a bench. Lucius Rufus claimed the second blow, as though it had been a deed to be proud of. And of the rest more than three hundred were killed with clubs and stones, but not one with a sword.

Conclusion

20. This, we are told, was the first disturbance at Rome since the expulsion of the kings to end in bloodshed and the murder of citizens. All others—neither small nor about trivial matters—were amicably settled by mutual concessions, the Senate yielding for fear of the commons, and the commons out of respect for the Senate. And it is probable that Tiberius could easily have been persuaded to compromise, and he certainly would have yielded if his opponents had not resorted to violence and bloodshed, since he had not more than three thousand followers. It is probable that this rising against him was fomented more out of the hatred and anger of the rich than for the reasons they alleged. In support of this we may cite the barbarous and inhuman treatment of his dead body: they would not allow his own brother to bury it at night, as he requested, but they threw it, along with the other corpses, into the river. Nor was this all; they banished some of his friends without trial, and they arrested and killed others.... Blossius of Cumae was brought before the consuls, and when he was asked about what had happened, he admitted that he had done whatever Tiberius requested. "What," cried Nasica, "then if Tiberius had ordered you to burn the Capitol, would you have burned it?" His first answer was that Tiberius never would have given such an order; but being pressed with the same question by several others, he declared: "If Tiberius had ordered it, it would have been right for me to do it, for he never would have given such an order if it had not been for the peoples' good." Blossius was acquitted....

54 Gaius Gracchus

The Republic at the Crossroads, Continued

To an even greater degree than his older brother, Gaius Gracchus labored to bring government back to the common people. He was elected tribune in 124 B.C., and until he failed to be reelected for a third term he consistently ignored the Senate in presenting his comprehensive program of legislation before the popular assembly. When the use of legitimate but quite unethical means of stopping him failed, the senatorial oligarchy contributed to the precedent of force, which it had already established in dealing with his elder brother, by forcing Gaius' death and decreeing death without trial for some three thousand of his supporters. After this there remained little hope of solving Rome's problems by constitutional means.

Although mixed with an amount of political opportunism, Gaius Gracchus' legislative program was far more constructive and statesmanlike than the simple land law of his more visionary brother. Where Tiberius hoped to eliminate present problems in one fell swoop with the restoration of the old Roman agricultural society, Gaius realistically sought to solve each specific problem by remedial legislation fitted to the demands of the situation.

People will always debate the validity of much of Gaius Gracchus' major legislation, but few will doubt, after reading Plutarch's account of the constructive energy with which he faced Rome's problems, that he deserves the name of statesman. it should not be difficult to understand why the Roman people, as Plutarch reports, "looked with amazement at the man himself, seeing him attended by crowds of building contractors, artisans, ambassadors, magistrates, soldiers, and learned men, to all of whom he was of easy access."

Character and Popularity

1. Gaius Gracchus at first, either for fear of his brother's enemies or because he wanted to make them more odious to the people, withdrew from public life and lived quietly at home like a humbled man who wanted to pass his life in inaction. Some, indeed, went so far as to say that he disliked his brother's program and had repudiated it. He was also still a youth, being nine years younger than his brother, and Tiberius was not yet thirty when he was slain. In time, however, his true character asserted itself—an utter aversion to indolence, effeminacy, drinking, and moneymaking. And it became clear from the emphasis he placed on the study of oratory as wings upon which he might aspire to public office, that he did not intend to pass his days in obscurity....

From Plutarch, *Parallel Lives*, "Life of Gaius Gracchus," based on the translation by John Dryden and revised by Arthur H. Clough.

3. ... Gaius now came forward to ask for the tribuneship. Though he was universally opposed by all men of distinction, so many people from all parts of Italy came to vote for him that lodgings for many could not be supplied in the city; and the Campus Martius not being large enough to contain the assembly, many climbed upon the roofs and the tilings of the houses to shout their support. However, the nobility so far forced the people to their will and disappointed Gaius' hopes that he was not returned the first, as was expected, but the fourth tribune. But after entering into his office, he quickly made himself first tribune, for he was a better orator than any of his contemporaries, and the passion with which he still lamented his brother's death made him bold in speaking....

Legislative Program

5. Of the laws which he introduced to win the favor of the people and undermine the power of the Senate, the first concerned the public lands, which were to be divided among the poor citizens; another concerned the soldiers, who were to be clothed at public expense without any deduction from their pay, and no one was to be conscripted into the army who was under seventeen years old; another gave Italians the same voting rights as the citizens of Rome; a fourth related to the supply of grain and the lowering of its price to the poor; and a fifth regulated the courts of justice. This last law greatly reduced the power of the senators. Hitherto they alone sat as judges and were therefore much feared by the common people and the equestrian order. Gaius added three hundred citizens of equestrian rank to the senators, who also numbered three hundred, and entrusted the judicial authority to the whole six hundred.

In arguing for this law he showed in many ways unusual earnestness; whereas other popular leaders had always turned their faces toward the Senate and the place called the *comitium,* he now for the first time turned the other way, toward the people, and he continued to do so thereafter—an insignificant change of posture, yet it marked no small revolution in state affairs, in a way transforming the constitution from an oligarchy to a democracy, his action implying that speakers should address themselves to the people and not to the Senate.

6. When the people not only ratified this law but gave him power to select the equestrians of his choice to be judges, he acquired almost kingly power, and even the Senate listened to his advice. Nor did he advise any measure that might lessen the honor of that body. For example, his decree concerning the grain which the propraetor Fabius sent from Spain was very just and honorable; for he persuaded the Senate to sell the grain and return the money to the Spanish provinces, and also to censure Fabius for making the Roman government odious and burdensome to its subjects. This earned him great respect and good will in the provinces.

He also introduced bills to found colonies, construct roads, and establish public granaries. He himself undertook the management and superintendence of all these works and was never too busy to attend to the execution of all these different and great undertakings, in each instance doing so with wonderful rapidity and industry as though it were his only task. Even those who hated or feared him were astonished to see what a capacity he had for effecting and completing all he undertook. As for the people themselves, they looked with amazement at the man himself, seeing him attended by crowds of building contractors, artisans, ambassadors, magistrates, soldiers, and learned men, to all of whom he was of easy access. Yet he preserved his dignity while being affable, and he adapted his own nature to those who addressed him. Thus he demonstrated that those who had represented him as a terrible, overbearing, and violent person, were ugly slanderers. He was thus a more skillful popular leader in his private conduct and dealings with men than in his public speeches.

7. He was especially interested in constructing roads, laying stress on beauty and grace as well as utility. They were carried through the country in a perfectly straight line, and were paved with hewn stone laid upon solid masses of gravel. Depressions were filled and intersecting watercourses were bridged; and the roads were so well-levelled—being of equal height on both sides—that the work presented a uniform and beautiful sight. In addition, he had the roads measured in miles..., and erected stone pillars to mark the distance. He placed other stones at short intervals on both sides of the road to help travellers mount their horses without needing a groom.

Tactics of the Senate

8. When the people praised him for these services and were ready to express their affection for him in any way, he said in a speech that he had one favor to ask, which, if it were granted, he would value greatly, but if it were denied he would not blame them. This statement led people to believe that his ambition was to be consul, and everyone expected that he would be a candidate for the consulship and the tribunate at the same time. But when the day for the election of consuls was at hand and everyone was in great expectation, he appeared in the Campus Martius with Gaius Fannius, canvassing for him with his friends. This turned the tide in Fannius' favor. He was chosen consul, and Gaius was elected tribune for the second time on a wave of popular enthusiasm, though he was not a candidate and did not seek the office. But when he saw the Senate openly hostile and Fannius weakening his friendship toward him, he again wooed the people with other laws. He proposed that colonists be sent to repeople Tarentum and Capua, and that the Latins should enjoy the same privileges as Roman citizens. The Senate, fearing that he would become invincible, made a new and unusual attempt to alienate the people from him by playing the demagogue and offering them favors contrary to the best interests of the state. One of Gaius' fellow tribunes was Livius Drusus, a man of as good a family and as well-educated as any Roman, and the equal in eloquence and wealth to the most honored and powerful men of the time. To him the nobles turned, urging him to attack Gaius and join them against him, not by resorting to violence or clashing with the people, but by using his office to gratify and please them....

9. So Livius devoted his tribunate to the Senate's interests, introducing laws that were neither honorable nor advantageous but had one purpose only, to outdo Gaius in winning the favor of the mob, as in a comedy. The Senate thus showed clearly that it was not angry with Gaius' program but desired to destroy

him completely—or at least to humble him. For when Gaius proposed to found two colonies, to which he would admit only the better class of citizens, they accused him of being a demagogue. But when Livius proposed to found twelve colonies, each to consist of three thousand poor citizens, they supported him. When Gaius divided the public land among the needy and charged each of them a small rent to be paid into the treasury, they were angry and accused him of truckling to the mob. Yet they commended Livius when he proposed to exempt the allotment holders from paying any rent. They were angry with Gaius for offering the Latins equal voting rights, but when Livius proposed that it be made unlawful for a Roman to flog a Latin soldier, they supported his law. In his speeches to the people, Livius always said that the laws he proposed were agreeable to the Senate, which was concerned with the people's welfare. This really was the only good result of his political activities, for the people now looked more kindly on the Senate....

12. After Gaius' return to Rome [from Carthage, where he supervised the founding of a colony], he gave up his house on the Palatine hill and went to live near the forum, which he thought more democratic since most of the poor and humble citizens lived there. He then announced the rest of his laws, intending to have them ratified by popular vote. A vast number of people gathered from all parts of Italy, but the Senate persuaded the consul Fannius to order out of the city all who were not Roman citizens. Accordingly a new and unusual proclamation was made, prohibiting any of the allies and friends of Rome to appear in the city during that time. Gaius published a counter-edict, denouncing the consul and promising the allies his support if they remained in Rome. However, he did not keep his word, for though he saw one of his friends and companions dragged to prison by Fannius' officers, he passed by without aiding him, either because he was afraid to put to test his power which was already on the decline, or because he was unwilling, as he said, to give his enemies the opportunity they were seeking of coming to a violent collision. He had also, for the following reason, incurred the anger of his fellow tribunes. An exhibition of gladiators was to be held for the people in the forum, and most of the magistrates had erected seats round about with the intention of renting them. Gaius ordered them to dismantle the seats so the poor might see the show without cost. When no one obeyed this order, he collected a group of city employees and removed the seats the night before the spectacle. By the next morning the forum was clear, and in accomplishing this the common people thought he had acted the part of a man. But he had annoyed his colleagues, who regarded him as audacious and violent.

Last Days

This act, it was believed, cost him the election to the tribunate for the third time; although he received the most votes, his colleagues out of revenge caused false returns to be made. This story is disputed, however. It is certain that he greatly resented this failure and behaved with unusual arrogance toward some of his adversaries who exulted over his defeat, telling them that their laughter was a false sardonic mirth since they little realized how much his political measures threw them into obscurity.

13. After effecting the election of Opimius to the consulship, Gaius' enemies began to repeal many of his laws and to meddle with the organization of his colony at Carthage. They omitted nothing that was likely to irritate him, in order that his reaction might give them grounds to get rid of him. Gaius at first endured all this patiently; but finally, at the urging of his friends, especially Fulvius, he organized his supporters to oppose the consul....

On the day when Opimius intended to repeal the laws of Gaius, both parties met very early on the Capitol. After the consul had offered sacrifice, one of his officers named Quintus Antyllius was carrying out the entrails of the sacrificed victim when he cried out to the partisans of Fulvius, "Make way for honest citizens, you rascals!" Some say that when he uttered these words he extended his bare arm in an insulting gesture. At any rate he was killed on the spot, stabbed with large writing styles said to have been made expressly for this purpose. The murder caused sudden panic in the assembly, and it produced exactly opposite effects on the leaders of the two parties. Gaius was much distressed and severely reprimanded his followers for providing their adversaries with a pretense for action which they had long awaited; but Opimius was elated, having found the opportunity he wanted, and he urged the people to get revenge. A shower of rain occurred just then, and the assembly was dissolved.

14. Early the next morning the consul convened the Senate and proceeded to transact business. In the meantime the corpse of Antyllius was laid upon a bier and, as prearranged, carried through the forum and past the senate house with loud cries and lamentations. Opimius knew what was happening, but as he pretended to be surprised at the noise, the Senate went out to investigate.... On returning to the senate house, they passed a decree[1] investing the consul Opimius with extraordinary power to protect the state and suppress the tyrants. The consul immediately ordered the senators to arm themselves, and each member of the equestrian order was directed to appear early the next morning accompanied by two well-armed slaves. Fulvius also made his preparations and collected a rabble; but Gaius, as he left the forum, stopped in front of his father's statue and looked at it for some time without speaking, then he burst into tears and departed with a groan....

16. When [next day] the people were assembled, Gaius advised Fulvius to send his youngest son to the forum with a herald's staff in his hand. He was a very handsome and modest youth, and with tears in his eyes he addressed conciliatory words to the consul and the Senate. The majority of those present were inclined to come to terms; but Opimius declared that the petitioners should not send messengers in an attempt to persuade the Senate, but should surrender themselves for trial, like law-abiding citizens, and then beg for mercy. He ordered the youth not to come back again unless he came on those terms. Gaius, it is reported, was willing to go and clear himself before the Senate; but no one else agreed with him, so Fulvius sent his son a second time to plead in their behalf as before. But Opimius, who

---

1. Called the "final decree" (*senatus consultum ultimum*), it is the first appearance, apparently, of the concept of martial laws or state of emergency.

was eager for a fight, ordered the youth to be seized and imprisoned, and then he advanced on Fulvius' supporters with many legionary soldiers and Cretan archers. These archers inflicted so many wounds that panic and flight quickly followed. Fulvius fled into an unused bath where he was soon discovered and slain, together with his oldest son. Gaius was not observed taking part in the violence; greatly disturbed by what was happening, he withdrew into the Temple of Diana. There he attempted to kill himself, but was prevented by his faithful friends, Pomponius and Licinius, who took away his sword and urged him to fly. It is reported that, falling upon his knees and lifting his hands to the goddess, he prayed that the Roman people might always remain in slavery as a punishment for their ingratitude and treachery, for a proclamation of amnesty had been announced and most of them were openly deserting him.

17. Gaius then fled, closely pursued by his enemies…. All the onlookers, as though at a race, urged him to run faster, but no one came to his aid, nor did anyone lend him a horse when he asked for one, for his pursuers were close behind him. He barely had time to hide in a sacred grove of the Furies. There he fell by the hand of his slave Philocrates, who then killed himself on the body of his master….

They say that when Gaius' head had been cut off and was being carried away by someone, a friend of Opimius named Septimuleius forcibly took it from him because, just as the fighting began, they had issued a proclamation that whoever brought in the head of Gaius or Fulvius would receive its weight in gold. So Septimuleius fixed Gaius' head on his spear and presented it to Opimius. Scales were brought in and it was found to weigh seventeen and two-thirds pounds. Septimuleius was as great a knave as he was a scoundrel, for he had taken out the brain and replaced it with lead. But those who brought in the head of Fulvius got nothing, because they belonged to the lower class. The bodies of Gaius and Fulvius and their followers—they numbered three thousand— were thrown into the Tiber. Their property was confiscated, their wives forbidden to go into mourning, and Gaius' wife Licinia was deprived of her widow's portion. Most inhumane of all was their treatment of Fulvius' youngest son. He had not taken up arms against them or been present at the fighting, but had only tried to effect an agreement; for this he was first imprisoned, then slain.

But what angered the common people most was that Opimius built a temple to Concord, which was viewed as evidence of his insolence and arrogance— a kind of triumph for the slaughter of so many citizens. One night someone added this verse under the inscription on the temple: "Folly and Discord Concord's temple built."

18. This Opimius, the first consul to exercise the power of a dictator, who condemned without trial three thousand citizens, among them Gaius Gracchus and Fulvius Flaccus, one of whom had been consul and had celebrated a triumph, while the other far excelled all his contemporaries in virtue and honor—this Opimius was afterwards incapable of keeping his hands from fraud. When he was sent as ambassador to Jugurtha, King of Numidia, he accepted bribes. On his return, he was found guilty of shameful corruption. He grew old in infamy, hated and insulted by the people, who, though humbled and frightened for a time, did not fail before long to let everybody know the respect

and veneration they had for the memory of the Gracchi. They ordered statues of the brothers to be made and set up in public view, and they declared the places where they were slain to be holy ground and brought there the first-fruits of the season as offerings. Many came daily to worship there, as at a temple of the gods.

A Mother's Noble Nature

19. It is reported that Cornelia, their mother, bore the loss of her two sons in a noble and undaunted spirit, and to have said in reference to the sacred places where they were slain that their bodies were worthy of such sepulchres. Later she moved to Misenum [on the Bay of Naples], but did not change her former way of life. She had many friends and hospitably received many guests. Greeks and other learned men frequently visited her, and all the kings of foreign lands exchanged gifts with her. All who visited her were much interested when she entertained them with her recollections of the life and habits of her father, Scipio Africanus [Selection 51, Introduction], but what they admired most was to hear her speak of her sons without any tears or signs of grief, giving a full account of their deeds and misfortunes as though she were relating the history of some early Roman heroes. This made some people imagine that old age or the weight of her misfortunes had affected her mind and dulled her normal feelings. But those who so thought were themselves too insensible to understand how a noble nature and upbringing can conquer any grief, and that though fate may defeat the efforts of virtue to avert misfortune, it cannot prevent us from enduring it with composure.[2]

55 The Social War

Rome's Italian Allies in Revolt

"They considered it no longer tolerable"

Appian of Alexandria (ca. A.D. 95–ca. A.D. 165) wrote a history of the Roman Civil Wars along with several other works that failed to survive. A Greek aristocrat by birth, he received a traditional education in rhetoric, or public

---

2. The following anecdote illustrates why the Romans and the people of later ages remembered Cornelia as the standard by which Roman matrons were judged: "When a Campanian matron who was staying with Cornelia, mother of the Gracchi, was showing off her jewels—the most beautiful of that period—Cornelia managed to prolong the conversation until her children got home from school. Then she said, 'These are *my* jewels.'" (Quoted in Mary R. Lefkowitz and Maureen B. Fant, eds., *Women's Life in Greece and Rome* [London: Gerald Duckworth & Co. Ltd., 1982], p. 138.)

From Appian, *Civil Wars* 1.7, 9, 11; in *Appian's Roman History, Vol. III*, edited by Horace White, Loeb Classical Library, Vol. 4 (Cambridge, Mass.: Harvard University Press, 1913), pp. 149–53, 175.

speaking, and was said to have pleaded cases before Roman emperors, possibly Antoninus Pius. A distinguished provincial from the privileged city of Alexandria, Appian was admitted into the Roman equestrian order and received the office of procurator some time after 147.

The Social War (91–88 B.C.) was the revolt of Rome's Italian allies (*socii*) who were protesting their perceived mistreatment and unmet demands for a greater share of the war spoils while fighting alongside the Romans. In the middle Republic, Rome made alliances with numerous Italic communities, and the allies were obliged to contribute contingents to Rome's wars as well to pay tribute to Rome. Still, expectations of financial gain through shared war booty offset the burden of the exactions, and the allies remained loyal. But in the second century B.C., Roman political leaders altered the arrangement so that war spoils were channeled to Rome, leading to acute disgruntlement on the part of Roman allies. The precipitating event that caused the ill feelings to surface and erupt in open revolt was the murder of the tribune of the people Marcus Livius Drusus in 91 B.C. Drusus had championed the cause of granting Roman citizenship to Rome's Italian allies, and his murder at the hand of opponents ended hopes that the Roman political process could bring about this outcome. Revolt in one city after another in Italy broke out. Only in Latium, where Rome's oldest allies and the ones to which it felt the closest bonds of kinship were to be found, was there no revolt—save by one city, Venusia. The rebels, foremost among whom were the central Italic tribes of the Marsi and Samnites, created their own state called Italia, with its capital at Corfinum, which was then renamed Italica, and they waged a long and damaging war against the Romans. In the fighting between the *Italici* and the *Romani*, both sides claimed victories as well as suffered grievous reverses. Over time, the Roman military forces, led by able generals such as Gaius Marius and Sulla, prevailed, and one by one the rebels were reduced until only the Samnites held out. Instead of crushing the rebels and imposing draconian terms, the Romans extended concessions that effectively granted all Latin-right cities that did not revolt Roman citizenship, bringing about the outcome for which the murdered Roman tribune Drusus had previously agitated for in vain.

Such was the third civil strife (that of Apuleius) which succeeded those of the two Gracchi, and such the results it brought to the Romans. 34. While they were thus occupied the so-called Social War, in which many Italian peoples were engaged, broke out. It began unexpectedly, grew rapidly to great proportions and extinguished the Roman seditions for a long time by a new terror. When it was ended it also gave rise to new seditions under more powerful leaders, who did not work by introducing new laws, or by the tricks of the demagogue, but by matching whole armies against each other. I have treated it in this history because it had its origin in the sedition in Rome and resulted in another much worse. It began in this way.

Fulvius Flaccus in his consulship first and foremost openly excited among the Italians the desire for Roman citizenship, so as to be partners in the empire instead of subjects. When he introduced this idea and strenuously persisted in it, the Senate, for that reason, sent him away to take command in a war, in the course of which his consulship expired; but he obtained the tribuneship after that and contrived to have the younger Gracchus for a colleague, with whose co-operation he brought forward other measures in favour of the Italians. When they were both killed, as I have previously related, the Italians were still more excited. They could not bear to be considered subjects instead of equals, or to think that Flaccus and Gracchus should have suffered such calamities while working for their political advantage.

35. After them the tribune Livius Drusus, a man of most illustrious birth, promised the Italians, at their urgent request, that he would bring forward a new law to give them citizenship. They especially desired this because by that one step they would become rulers instead of subjects. In order to conciliate the plebeians to this measure he led out to Italy and Sicily several colonies which had been voted some time before, but not yet planted. He endeavoured to bring together by an agreement the Senate and the equestrian order, who were then in sharp antagonism to each other, in reference to the law courts. As he was not able to restore the courts to the Senate openly, he tried the following artifice to reconcile them. As the senators had been reduced by the seditions to scarcely 300 in number, he brought forward a law that an equal number, chosen according to merit, should be added to their enrolment from the knights, and that the courts of justice should be made up thereafter from the whole number. He added a clause in the law that they should make investigations about bribery, as accusations of that kind were almost unknown, since the custom of bribe-taking prevailed without restraint.

This was the plan that he contrived for both of them, but it turned out contrary to his expectations, for the senators were indignant that so large a number should be added to their enrolment at one time and be transferred from knighthood to the highest rank. They thought it not unlikely that they would form a faction in the Senate by themselves and contend against the old senators more powerfully than ever. The knights, on the other hand, suspected that, by this doctoring, the courts of justice would be transferred from their order to the Senate exclusively. Having acquired a relish for the great gains and power of the judicial office, this suspicion disturbed them. Most of them, too, fell into doubt and distrust toward each other, discussing which of them seemed more worthy than others to be enrolled among the 300; and envy against their betters filled the breasts of the remainder. Above all the knights were angry at the revival of the charge of bribery, which they thought had been ere this entirely suppressed, so far as they were concerned.

36. Thus it came to pass that both the Senate and the knights, although opposed to each other, were united in hating Drusus. Only the plebeians were gratified with the colonies. Even the Italians, in whose especial interest Drusus was devising these plans, were apprehensive about the law providing for the colonies, because they thought that the Roman public domain (which was still undivided and which they were cultivating, some by force and others clandestinely) would at once be taken away from them, and that in many cases they might even be disturbed in their private holdings. The Etruscans and the Umbrians had the same fears as the Italians, and when they were summoned

to the city, as was thought, by the consuls, for the ostensible purpose of complaining against the law of Drusus, but actually to kill him, they cried down the
law publicly and waited for the day of the comitia. Drusus learned of the plot
against him and did not go out frequently, but transacted business from day to
day in the atrium of his house, which was poorly lighted. One evening as he was
sending the crowd away he exclaimed suddenly that he was wounded, and
fell down while uttering the words. A shoemaker's knife was found thrust into
his hip.

37. Thus was Drusus also slain while serving as tribune. The knights, in
order to make his policy a ground of vexatious accusation against their enemies,
persuaded the tribune Quintus Varius to bring forward a law to prosecute those
who should, either openly or secretly, aid the Italians to acquire citizenship, hoping thus to bring all the senators under an odious indictment, and themselves to
sit in judgment on them, and that when they were out of the way they themselves would be more powerful than ever in the government of Rome.

38. As this malice against the aristocracy grew more and more, the people
were grieved because they were deprived all at once of so many distinguished
men who had rendered such great services. When the Italians learned of the
murder of Drusus and of the reasons alleged for banishing the others, they
considered it no longer tolerable that those who were labouring for their
political advancement should suffer such outrages, and as they saw no other
means of acquiring citizenship they decided to revolt from the Romans altogether, and to make war against them with might and main. They sent envoys
secretly to each other, formed a league, and exchanged hostages as a pledge of
good faith.

The Romans were in ignorance of these facts for a long time, being busy
with the trials and the seditions in the city. [A young man was seen taken as
hostage from Asculum to another town, and this was reported to the Roman
praetor Sevilius.] Servilius hastened to Asculum and indulged in very menacing
language to the people, who were celebrating a festival, and they, supposing that
the plot was discovered, put him to death. They also killed Fonteius, his legate
(for so they call those of the senatorial order who accompany the governors
of provinces as assistants). After these were slain none of the other Romans in
Asculum were spared. The inhabitants fell upon them, slaughtered them all,
and plundered their goods.

39. When the revolt broke out all the neighbouring peoples declared war at
the same time, the Marsi, the Peligni, the Vestint, the Marrucini; and after them
the Picentines, the Frentani, the Hirpini, the Pompeiians, the Venusini, the Apu-
lians, the Lucanians, and the Samnites, all of whom had been hostile to the
Romans before; also all the rest extending from the river Liris (which is now, I
think, the Liternus) to the extremity of the Adriatic gulf, both inland and on the
sea coast. They sent ambassadors to Rome to complain that although they had
cooperated in all ways with the Romans in building up the empire, the latter
had not been willing to admit their helpers to citizenship. The Senate answered
sternly that if they repented of what they had done they could send ambassadors,

otherwise not. The Italians, in despair of any other remedy, went on with their mobilization. Besides the soldiers which were kept for guards at each town, they had forces in common amounting to about 100,000 foot and horse. The Romans sent an equal force against them, made up of their own citizens and of the Italian peoples who were still in alliance with them.

40. The Romans were led by the consuls Sextus Julius Caesar and Publius Rutilius Lupus, for in this great civil war both consuls marched forth at once, leaving the gates and walls in charge of others, as was customary in cases of danger arising at home and very near by. When the war was found to be complex and many-sided, they sent their most renowned men as lieutenant-generals to aid the consuls: to Rutilius, Gnaeus Pompeius, the father of Pompey the Great, Quintus Caepio, Gaius Perpenna, Gaius Marius, and Valerius Messala; to Sextus Caesar, Publius Lentulus, a brother of Caesar himself, as well as Titus Didius, Licinius Crassus, Cornelius Sulla, and Marcellus. All these served under the consuls and the country was divided among them. The consuls visited all parts of the field of operations, and the Romans sent them additional forces continually, realizing that it was a serious conflict. The Italians had generals for their united forces besides those of the separate towns. The chief commanders were Titus Lafrenius, Gaius Pontilius, Marius Egnatius, Quintus Pompaedius, Gaius Papius, Marcus Lainponius, Gaius Vidacilius, Herius Asinius, and Vettius Scaton. They divided their army in equal parts, took their positions against the Roman generals, performed many notable exploits, and suffered many disasters. The most memorable events of either kind I shall here summarize.

49. While these events were transpiring on the Adriatic side of Italy, the inhabitants of Etruria and Umbria and other neighbouring peoples on the other side of Rome heard of them and all were excited to revolt. The Senate, fearing lest they should be surrounded by war, and unable to protect themselves, garrisoned the sea-coast from Cumae to the city with freedmen, who were then for the first time enrolled in the army on account of the scarcity of soldiers. The Senate also voted that those Italians who had adhered to their alliance should be admitted to citizenship, which was the one thing they all desired most. They sent this decree around among the Etruscans, who gladly accepted the citizenship. By this favour the Senate made the faithful more faithful, confirmed the wavering, and mollified their enemies by the hope of similar treatment. The Romans did not enroll the new citizens in the thirty-five existing tribes, lest they should outvote the old ones in the elections, but incorporated them in ten new tribes, which voted last. So it often happened that their vote was useless, since a majority was obtained from the thirty-five tribes that voted first. This fact was either not noticed by the Italians at the time or they were satisfied with what they had gained, but it was observed later and became the source of a new conflict.

50. The insurgents along the Adriatic coast, befote they learned of the change of sentiment among the Etruscans, sent 15,000 men to their assistance by a long and difficult road. Gnaeus Pompeius, who was now consul, fell upon them and killed 5000 of them. The rest made their way homeward through a trackless region, in a severe winter; and half of them after subsisting on acorns

perished. The same winter Poreius Cato, the colleague of Pompeius, was killed while fighting with the Marsians.

Such was the course of events throughout Italy as regards the Social War, which had raged with violence thus far, until the whole of Italy came into the Roman state except, for the present, the Lucanians and the Samnites, who also seem to have obtained what they desired somewhat later. Each body of allies was enrolled in tribes of its own, like those who had been admitted to citizenship before, so that they might not, by being mingled with the old citizens, vote them down in the elections by force of numbers.

56 The Revolt of Spartacus

The Dangers of a Slave Society

"... the slaves leaped and began to fight...."

The influx of large numbers of cheap foreign slaves after the Punic Wars transformed the demography and economy of Sicily and Italy in a dramatic fashion. Large agricultural estates or *latifundia* used this slave labor to grow food for the ever-growing urban populations swollen by the flight of dispossessed peasants to the towns and cities. The concentration of slaves in the countryside combined with abusive conditions led to a number of slave revolts, notably in Sicily. While the Romans took great pains to control their slaves, they were not always successful. Even the prospect of extremely severe punishment failed to prevent several important slave rebellions during the Late Republic. The most famous slave revolt, sometimes referred to as the Third Servile or Slave War, was the one led by Spartacus, a gladiator from Thrace, in 73–71 B.C. Having gathered other gladiators from southern Italy, slaves from the rural estates, and even some of the free poor, he defeated several Roman armies sent against him. His successes and style of leadership drew many to him. The circumstances of the revolt reflect the tensions in the Italian countryside decades after the failed reforms by the Gracchi brothers, who were indeed apprehensive of the effects of the large-scale introduction of slave labor. The following account of the "war of Spartacus" comes from Plutarch's "Life of Crassus." Crassus is the general who was principally responsible for Spartacus' defeat.

... VIII. The insurrection of the gladiators and their devastation of Italy, which is generally called the war of Spartacus, had its origin as follows. A certain Lentulus Batiatus had a school of gladiators at Capua, most of whom were Gauls and Thracians. Through no misconduct of theirs, but owing to the injustice of their

From *Plutarch, Lives. Pericles and Fabius Maximus, Nicias and Crassus*, with an English translation by Bernadette Perrin, pp. 335–51. Copyright © 1916 by Harvard University Press.

owner, they were kept in close confinement and reserved for gladiatorial combats. Two hundred of these planned to make their escape, and when information was laid against them, those who got wind of it and succeeded in getting away, seventy-eight in number, seized cleavers and spits from some kitchen and sallied out. On the road they fell in with waggons conveying gladiators' weapons to another city; these they plundered and armed themselves. Then they took up a strong position and elected three leaders. The first of these was Spartacus, a Thracian of Nomadic stock, possessed not only of great courage and strength, but also in sagacity and culture superior to his fortune, and more Hellenic than Thracian. It is said that when he was first brought to Rome to be sold, a serpent was seen coiled about his face as he slept, and his wife, who was of the same tribe as Spartacus, a prophetess, and subject to visitations of the Dionysiac frenzy, declared it the sign of a great and formidable power which would attend him to a fortunate issue. This woman shared in his escape and was then living with him.

IX. To begin with, the gladiators repulsed the soldiers who came against them from Capua, and getting hold of many arms of real warfare, they gladly took these in exchange for their own, casting away their gladiatorial weapons as dishonourable and barbarous. Then Clodius the praetor was sent out from Rome against them with three thousand soldiers, and laid siege to them on a hill which had but one ascent, and that a narrow and difficult one, which Clodius closely watched; everywhere else there were smooth and precipitous cliffs. But the top of the hill was covered with a wild vine of abundant growth, from which the besieged cut off the serviceable branches, and wove these into strong ladders of such strength and length that when they were fastened at the top they reached along the face of the cliff to the plain below. On these they descended safely, all but one man, who remained above to attend to the arms. When the rest had got down, he began to drop the arms, and after he had thrown them all down, got away himself also last of all in safety. Of all this the Romans were ignorant, and therefore their enemy surrounded them, threw them into consternation by the suddenness of the attack, put them to flight, and took their camp. They were also joined by many of the herdsmen and shepherds of the region, sturdy men and swift of foot, some of whom they armed fully, and employed others as scouts and light infantry.

In the second place, Publius Varinus, the praetor, was sent out against them, whose lieutenant, a certain Furius, with two thousand soldiers, they first engaged and routed; then Spartacus narrowly watched the movements of Cossinius, who had been sent out with a large force to advise and assist Varinus in the command, and came near seizing him as he was bathing near Salinae. Cossinius barely escaped with much difficulty, and Spartacus at once seized his baggage, pressed hard upon him in pursuit, and took his camp with great slaughter. Cossinius also fell. By defeating the praetor himself in many battles, and finally capturing his lictors and the very horse he rode, Spartacus was soon great and formidable; but he took a proper view of the situation, and since he could not expect to overcome the Roman power, began to lead his army toward the Alps, thinking it necessary for them to cross the mountains and go to their respective homes, some to Thrace, and some to Gaul. But his men were now strong in numbers and full of confidence, and would not listen to him, but went ravaging over Italy.

It was now no longer the indignity and disgrace of the revolt that harassed the senate, but they were constrained by their fear and peril to send both consuls into the field, as they would to a war of the utmost difficulty and magnitude. Gellius, one of the consuls, fell suddenly upon the Germans, who were so insolent and bold as to separate themselves from the main body of Spartacus, and cut them all to pieces; but when Lentulus, the other consul, had surrounded the enemy with large forces, Spartacus rushed upon them, joined battle, defeated the legates of Lentulus, and seized all their baggage. Then, as he was forcing his way towards the Alps, he was met by Cassius, the governor of Cisalpine Gaul, with an army of ten thousand men, and in the battle that ensued, Cassius was defeated, lost many men, and escaped himself with difficulty.

X. On learning of this, the Senate angrily ordered the consuls to keep quiet, and chose Crassus to conduct the war, and many of the nobles were induced by his reputation and their friendship for him to serve under him. Crassus himself, accordingly, took position on the borders of Picenum, expecting to receive the attack of Spartacus, who was hastening thither; and he sent Mummius, his legate, with two legions, by a circuitous route, with orders to follow the enemy, but not to join battle nor even skirmish with them. Mummius, however, at the first promising opportunity, gave battle and was defeated; many of his men were slain, and many of them threw away their arms and fled for their lives. Crassus gave Mummius himself a rough reception, and when he armed his soldiers anew, made them give pledges that they would keep their arms. Five hundred of them, moreover, who had shown the greatest cowardice and been first to fly, he divided into fifty decades, and put to death one from each decade, on whom the lot fell, thus reviving, after the lapse of many years, an ancient mode of punishing the soldiers. For disgrace also attaches to this manner of death, and many horrible and repulsive features attend the punishment, which the whole army witnesses.

When he had thus disciplined his men, he led them against the enemy. But Spartacus avoided him, and retired through Lucania to the sea. At the Straits, he chanced upon some Cilician pirate craft, and determined to seize Sicily. By throwing two thousand men into the island, he thought to kindle anew the servile war there, which had not long been extinguished, and needed only a little additional fuel. But the Cilicians, after coming to terms with him and receiving his gifts, deceived him and sailed away. So Spartacus marched back again from the sea and established his army in the peninsula of Rhegium. Crassus now came up, and observing that the nature of the place suggested what must be done, he determined to build a wall across the isthmus, thereby at once keeping his soldiers from idleness, and his enemies from provisions. Now the task was a huge one and difficult, but he accomplished and finished it, contrary to all expectation, in a short time, running a ditch from sea to sea through the neck of land three hundred furlongs in length and fifteen feet in width and depth alike. Above the ditch he also built a wall of astonishing height and strength. All this work Spartacus neglected and despised at first; but soon his provisions began to fail, and when he wanted to sally forth from the peninsula, he saw that he was walled in, and that there was nothing more to be had there. He therefore waited for a snowy night and a wintry storm, when he filled up a small portion of the ditch with earth and timber and the boughs of trees, and so threw a third part of his force across.

XI. Crassus was now in fear lest some impulse to march upon Rome should seize Spartacus, but took heart when he saw that many of the gladiator's men had seceded after a quarrel with him, and were encamped by themselves on a Lucanian lake. This lake, they say, changes from time to time in the character of its water, becoming sweet, and then again bitter and undrinkable. Upon this detachment Crassus fell, and drove them away from the lake, but he was robbed of the slaughter and pursuit of the fugitives by the sudden appearance of Spartacus, who checked their flight.

Before this Crassus had written to the senate that they must summon Lucullus from Thrace and Pompey from Spain, but he was sorry now that he had done so, and was eager to bring the war to an end before those generals came. He knew that the success would be ascribed to the one who came up with assistance, and not to himself. Accordingly, in the first place, he determined to attack those of the enemy who had seceded from the rest and were campaigning on their own account (they were commanded by Caius Canicius and Castus), and with this in view, sent out six thousand men to preoccupy certain eminence, bidding them keep their attempt a secret. And they did try to elude observation by covering up their helmets, but they were seen by two women who were sacrificing for the enemy, and would have been in peril of their lives had not Crassus quickly made his appearance and given battle, the most stubbornly contested of all; for although he slew twelve thousand three hundred men in it, he found only two who were wounded in the back. The rest all died standing in the ranks and fighting the Romans.

After the defeat of this detachment, Spartacus retired to the mountains of Petelia, followed closely by Quintus, one of the officers of Crassus, and by Scrophas, the quaestor, who hung upon the enemy's rear. But when Spartacus faced about, there was a great rout of the Romans, and they barely managed to drag the quaestor, who had been wounded, away into safety. This success was the ruin of Spartacus, for it filled his slaves with over-confidence. They would no longer consent to avoid battle, and would not even obey their leaders, but surrounded them as soon as they began to march, with arms in their hands, and forced them to lead back through Lucania against the Romans, the very thing which Crassus also most desired. For Pompey's approach was already announced, and there were not a few who publicly proclaimed that the victory in this war belonged to him; he had only to come and fight and put an end to the war. Crassus, therefore, pressed on to finish the struggle himself, and having encamped near the enemy, began to dig a trench. Into this the slaves leaped and began to fight with those who were working there, and since fresh men from both sides kept coming up to help their comrades, Spartacus saw the necessity that was upon him, and drew up his whole army in order of battle.

In the first place, when his horse was brought to him, he drew his sword, and saying that if he won the day he would have many fine horses of the enemy's, but if he lost it he did not want any, he slew his horse. Then pushing his way towards Crassus himself through many flying weapons and wounded men, he did not indeed reach him, but slew two centurions who fell upon him together. Finally, after his companions had taken to flight, he stood alone, surrounded by a multitude of foes, and was still defending himself when he was cut down. But although Crassus had been fortunate, had shown most excellent generalship, and had exposed his person to danger, nevertheless, his success did not fail to enhance the reputation of Pompey. For the fugitives from the battle encountered that general and were cut to pieces, so that he could write to the senate that in open battle, indeed, Crassus had conquered the slaves, but that he himself had extirpated the war. Pompey, accordingly, for his victories over Sertorius and in Spain, celebrated a splendid triumph; but Crassus, for all his self-approval, did not venture to ask for the major triumph, and it was thought ignoble and mean in him to celebrate even the minor triumph on foot, called the ovation, for a servile war....

57 The Conspiracy of Catiline

The Roman Republic in Decay

The story of the conspiracy of Catiline (63 B.C.) is an excellent commentary on the political, social, and moral conditions of the late Roman Republic. The prodigal living of the nobility, growing out of the taste for luxury that accompanied Roman expansion, and the enormous cost of campaigning for public office, caused by the prevalence of bribery and corruption, had created a chronic condition of debt and bankruptcy among many patrician families. The brilliant but dissolute Catiline became the leader of this group and, having failed three times to win the consulship by constitutional means—on his third attempt, in 63 B.C., he advocated a general cancellation of debts—he conspired to gain it by causing disruption and employing force. He may have been influenced by the example of Sulla, who in 82 B.C. had used his army to establish a dictatorship in the interest of the Optimates or "best people," as the senatorial oligarchy was now called. Catiline had served under Sulla, but now he posed as a leader of the *Populares* ("peoples' party") and successor to Gaius Gracchus, although his democratic sentiments appear to have been a sham to cover his own selfish interests and those of his followers, debt-ridden young nobles—descendants of the stern and simple fathers of the Republic—whose fortunes had been dissipated by sophisticated city living, and the city mob, now largely composed of non-Roman freedmen who

From Sallust, *Conspiracy of Catiline*, based on the translation by John Selby Watson.

equated democracy with governmental handouts. The corrupt character of the Roman masses and the nature of their interest in Catiline's program was noted by Plutarch, who reports that in the year following the suppression of the conspiracy, "Cato [the Younger], seeing the people greatly stirred up by Caesar in the affair of Catiline and dangerously inclined toward a revolution, persuaded the Senate to vote a dole to the poor, and the giving of this halted the disturbance and checked the insurrection."

The following account of the conspiracy, written by Sallust (86–34 B.C.), is considered more reliable than that found in the famous *Catilinarian Orations* of Cicero, who as consul had suppressed Catiline. Yet neither was Sallust impartial, despite his claim to writing objective history with Thucydides as his model. He had been an active partisan of Julius Caesar and the popular party and, after Caesar's assassination, had turned to writing the history of his time in a manner that highlighted the incompetence and corruption of the Optimates. To some modern scholars, Catiline was motivated mainly by wounded pride and fierce ambition thwarted by the Establishment and the electoral process; to Sallust he was a demagogue whose true character, typical of the whole aristocracy, was ultimately recognized by even the common people, whose hatred of the Roman upper classes was so profound that they idolized any politician who opposed them.

Sallust's view of Republican history, a story of degeneration and moral decay resulting from Roman expansion, became the favorite reading of the Romans of the later Empire, and especially of the Christians. The famous character sketch of the conspiratress Sempronia, the mother of Caesar's assassin Decimus Brutus, illustrates both Sallust's skill in depicting the vices of the nobility and the degree of his bias in favor of Caesar. His moving description of the death of Catiline contributes to the suspicion that Catiline may deserve better of history than ancient and unfavorable sources of information allow.

Sallust's Purpose

... 4. When I had found peace of mind after many troubles and trials and had determined to pass the remainder of my days unconnected with politics, it was not my intention to waste my valuable leisure in indolence and inactivity, or to engage in the slavish occupations of farming or hunting. Rather, I decided to return to those studies from which a misguided ambition had lured me—the writing of monographs on episodes worthy of record in the history of the Roman people, a task for which I felt myself well-qualified as my mind was uninfluenced by the hopes and fears of political partisanship. I shall accordingly give as true and brief an account as I can of the conspiracy of Catiline, for I think it a subject eminently deserving of record because of the unusual nature of the crime and its danger to the state. But before beginning my narrative, I must give a short description of the character of the man.

Personality and Motives of Catiline

5. Lucius Catiline was a man of noble birth and of eminent mental and physical endowments, but he had a vicious and depraved nature. From his youth he had delighted in civil war, bloodshed, pillage, and political strife, and

in such activities he had spent his early manhood. His body could endure hunger, cold, and lack of sleep to an incredible degree. His mind was daring, crafty, versatile, and capable of any kind of pretense or cover-up. He was covetous of other men's property and prodigal of his own. A man of violent passions, he had abundant eloquence but little wisdom. His insatiable ambition was always pursuing objects extravagant, romantic, and unattainable.

After Sulla's dictatorship, a strong desire of seizing the government had possessed him, nor did he care by what means he might achieve it. His violent spirit was goaded more and more every day by poverty and a consciousness of guilt, both of which were aggravated by those evil practices which I have mentioned. He was spurred on, too, by the corrupt morals of society, which were thoroughly depraved by two pernicious and opposite vices, extravagance and avarice.

"The Conduct of Our Ancestors"

Since the occasion has thus brought public morals to my attention, it seems appropriate to look back and briefly describe the conduct of our ancestors in peace and war, how they governed the state, which they made so great before leaving it to us, and how by gradual degeneration it changed from the most virtuous of states to the most vicious and corrupted....

8. Surely Fortune rules all things; she makes all events famous or obscure according to caprice rather than merit. The exploits of the Athenians, as far as I can judge, were very great and glorious, but somewhat less important than her fame indicates. But because writers of great talent flourished there, the actions of the Athenians are celebrated over the world as the most splendid achievements. Thus the merit of men in action is rated as high as illustrious intellects exalt it in their writings. But the Romans never had that advantage, because with them the most able men were the most actively engaged in affairs. No one exercised the mind independently of the body; every man of ability preferred action to words and thought that his own deeds should be celebrated by others rather than that he should record theirs.

9. Good morals, accordingly, were cultivated at home and in the camp. There was the greatest possible harmony and the least possible avarice. Justice and probity prevailed, not so much from the influence of laws as from natural inclination. They displayed animosity, enmity, and resentment only against the enemy. Citizens contended with citizens in nothing but honor. They were lavish in their religious services, frugal in their homes, and loyal to their friends.

By these two virtues, boldness in war and justice in peace, they maintained themselves and their state. I consider the following to be convincing proof of this: in time of war punishment was more often inflicted on those who attacked an enemy contrary to orders and retired too slowly when commanded to retreat than on those who had dared to abandon their standards or give ground when pressed by the enemy; in time of peace they governed more by conferring benefits than by exciting terror, and when wronged they would rather pardon than avenge the injury.

"Universal Innovation"

10. But when by perseverance and integrity the Republic had increased its power, when mighty kings had been vanquished in war, when barbarous tribes and populous states had been reduced to subjection, when Carthage, the rival of Rome's dominion, had been utterly destroyed and sea and land lay everywhere open, Fortune became unkind and introduced universal innovation. Those who had easily endured toil, danger, anxiety, and adversity had found leisure and wealth—usually the objects of desire—to be a burden and a curse. Now first the love of money, then of power, began to prevail, and these became the sources of every evil. For avarice destroyed honesty, integrity, and other honorable principles, and in their stead inculcated pride, inhumanity, contempt of religion, and the belief that everything has its price. Ambition prompted many to become deceitful, to keep one thing concealed in the breast and another ready on the tongue, to judge friendships and enmities not by merit but by profit, and to value a good front more than a good heart. These vices at first grew slowly and were sometimes punished. But later, when the infection had spread like a plague, the state was entirely changed, and the government, once so just and admirable, became cruel and intolerable.

11. At first, however, it was ambition rather than avarice that influenced the minds of men. Ambition is a vice which comes nearer to being a virtue than avarice. For glory, honor, and power are desired by the worthy and the worthless; but the one pursues them by just methods, while the other, being destitute of honorable qualities, works with fraud and deceit. But avarice has only money for its object, which no wise man has ever desired. It is like a deadly poison, which enervates whatever is manly in body or mind. It is always unbounded and insatiable, and is abated neither by abundance nor by want.

But after Lucius Sulla, having taken over the state by force of arms, proceeded after a good beginning to a bad end, all became robbers and plunderers. Some coveted houses, others land. His victorious troops knew neither restraint nor moderation, but inflicted on the citizens disgraceful and inhuman outrages. Their rapacity was increased by the fact that Sulla had sought to secure the loyalty of the forces which he commanded in Asia by allowing them, contrary to the practice of our ancestors, extraordinary luxury and exemption from discipline, and pleasant resorts had easily enervated the warlike spirits of soldiers on leave. There it was that the army of the Roman people first became habituated to women and wine, and to admire statues, paintings, and sculptured vases which they stole from public edifices and private dwellings, plundering temples and lacking all respect for everything both sacred and profane. Such troops, accordingly, when once they obtained a victory, left nothing to the vanquished. Since success undermines the principles even of philosophers, how should these depraved men show moderation in victory?

12. As soon as wealth came to be considered an honor, and fame, privilege, and power depended on it, honesty lost its influence, poverty was thought a disgrace, and a blameless life was regarded as a sign of ill-nature. The result of the influence of riches was that high living, selfishness, and insolence began to prevail

among the young. They stole and squandered, cared little for what was their own and coveted what was another's, set aside modesty and continence, lost all distinction between sacred and profane, and threw off all consideration of self-restraint.

It is worthwhile to compare our modern mansions and villas, some of which are the size of cities, with the temples which our god-fearing ancestors erected. Our forefathers adorned the temples of the gods with piety and their homes with their own glory, and they took nothing from those whom they conquered except the power of doing harm. Their base descendants, on the contrary, have even wrested from our allies, with the most flagrant injustice, whatever our brave and victorious ancestors had left them, as though the only use of power were to inflict injury.

13. Need I mention those displays of extravagance which can be believed only by those who have seen them? Mountains have been leveled and seas covered over by private citizens for their building operations. Such men I consider to have made a sport of their wealth, since they were impatient to squander shamelessly what they might have enjoyed with honor.

The passion for lust, vice, and all kinds of sensuality had spread with equal force. Men forgot their sex; women threw off all the restraints of modesty. To gratify their appetites, they sought out every kind of delicacy by land and by sea; they slept before there was any need for sleep; they did not wait to feel hunger, thirst, cold, or fatigue, but anticipated them all with decadent indulgence. Such practices drove the young, when their patrimonies were exhausted, to criminal practices, for minds impregnated with evil habits could not easily abstain from gratifying their passions, and so were even more recklessly devoted to all kinds of rapacity and extravagance.

"Accomplices and Adherents"

14. In so populous and so corrupt a city, Catiline could easily keep around him, like a bodyguard, gangs of the unprincipled and desperate. For all these shameless, libertine, and profligate characters who had dissipated their patrimonies by gambling, luxury, and sensuality; all who had contracted heavy debts to purchase immunity for their crimes or offenses; all assassins or sacrilegious persons from every quarter, convicted or dreading conviction for their evil deeds; all, in addition, who maintained themselves by perjury or civil bloodshed; all, in short, who were wicked, poor, or had a guilty conscience, were the associates and intimate friends of Catiline. And if anyone still innocent fell into his company, by daily contact and temptation he soon became similar to the rest. It was the young whose acquaintance he chiefly sought; their minds, being still impressionable and unsettled, were easily ensnared. In order to gratify their youthful desires, he furnished mistresses to some, bought horses and dogs for others, and spared neither his purse nor his honor to make them his devoted followers. Some, I know, have thought that the youth who frequented the house of Catiline were guilty of crimes against nature, but this report arose rather from other causes than from any evidence of the fact....

16. ... Depending on such accomplices and adherents, and knowing that load of debt was everywhere great and that Sulla's veterans had spent their money too freely and, remembering the loot acquired from past victories, were longing for civil war, Catiline planned a revolution. There was no army in Italy; Pompey was fighting in a distant part of the world; he himself had great hopes of being elected consul; the Senate was wholly off its guard; everything was quiet and tranquil—all these circumstances were exceedingly favorable for Catiline....

After His Failure at the Polls, Catiline Addresses His Comrades

20. "... What I have been planning you have already heard individually. My own ardor for action is daily more and more excited when I consider what our lot will be unless we ourselves assert our claims to liberty. Ever since the state has come under the power and jurisdiction of a few, foreign kings and princes have constantly paid them tribute and nations and tribes have paid them taxes. All the rest of us, however brave and worthy, whether noble or plebeian, have been regarded as a mere mob, without influence or authority, and subject to those who in a true state would be afraid of us. Thus all influence, power, honor, and wealth are in their hands or where they choose to bestow them; to us they leave only insults, dangers, persecutions, and poverty. How long, brave comrades, will you submit to such indignities? Is it not better to die in a glorious attempt, than, after having been the sport of other men's insolence, to lose a miserable and dishonored existence like cowards?

"But success—I call gods and men to witness!—is in our grasp. We are young and our spirit is unbroken, whereas our oppressors are enfeebled by age and wealth. We have only to make a start; the course of events will accomplish the rest.

"Who in the world who is a man at heart can endure that they should have a surplus of wealth to squander in building out over the seas and in leveling mountains, while we lack the means to buy even the necessities of life? They join together two houses or more, and we have not a home to call our own. Though they purchase paintings, statues, and sculptured vases, pull down new buildings to erect others, and lavish and abuse their wealth in every possible way, yet with all their extravagance they cannot exhaust it. But for us there is poverty at home and debts everywhere; our present circumstances are bad, our prospects much worse; what, in fact, have we left but a miserable existence?

"Wake up, then! Look! Liberty, that liberty of which you have so often dreamed is set before your eyes, together with wealth, honor and glory. All these prizes Fortune offers to the victorious. Let the facts, the opportunity, your poverty, your peril, and the rich spoils of war animate you far more than my words. Use me as your leader or as your fellow-soldier; neither my heart nor my hand will ever desert you. These objects I hope to achieve with your help when I am consul—unless indeed my hopes deceive me and you prefer to be slaves rather than masters."...

The Conspiratress Sempronia

24. ... At this time Catiline is said to have gained the support of a great number of men of all classes and even of some women. The latter had, in their earlier days, supported an expensive lifestyle by prostitution, but later, when age had lessened their incomes but not their extravagances, had contracted huge debts. Through their influence Catiline hoped to induce the slaves in Rome to set the city on fire, and either secure the support of their husbands or murder them.

25. Among the number of female adherents was Sempronia, a woman who had committed many crimes with the spirit of a man. In birth and beauty, in her husband and her children, she was extremely fortunate. Well-educated in Greek and Roman literature, she could sing, play, and dance with greater skill than became a respectable woman, and she possessed many other accomplishments that tend to excite the passions. Nothing was of less value to her than honor or chastity. Whether she was more careless of her money or her reputation would have been difficult to decide. Her desires were so ardent that she more often made advances to men than waited for solicitation. She had frequently, before this period, broken her word, repudiated debts, been an accessory to murder, and been propelled into the utmost excesses by her extravagance and poverty. Yet her abilities were not to be despised; she could compose verses, jest, and join in conversation either modest, tender, or licentious. In a word, she was a woman of considerable wit and charm....

"The Common People Favored Catiline"

37. Nor was this madness confined only to the ringleaders of the conspiracy; the common people as a whole, in their eagerness for change, favored the scheme of Catiline. This one would expect from their general character. In every state the poor envy the better class of citizens and make heroes of agitators; they hate the established order and long for something new; they are discontented with their own lot and desire a general upheaval; they can support themselves in the midst of tumult and revolution without worry, since poverty has nothing to lose.

The common people of the city had become disaffected for various reasons. Those who everywhere took the lead in crime and audacity, those who had wasted their substance in dissipation, and all whom vice and villainy had driven from their homes, had poured into Rome as though it were a sewer. Many, remembering the victory of Sulla, when they had seen some raised from common soldiers to senators and others so enriched as to live in luxury and pomp like kings, hoped for similar rewards of victory if they took up arms. Young men from the country, who barely earned a living by manual labor, had been attracted by public and private doles and preferred idleness in the city to hard labor in the field. These and all the others would benefit from public disorders. It is not at all surprising, therefore, that paupers with low principles and high hopes should have considered their country's interest subservient to their own. Those also whose parents had been proscribed by Sulla, whose property had been confiscated, and whose civil rights had been curtailed, looked forward to the event of a war with precisely the same feelings. Again, all the factions opposed to the Senate preferred to see the government overturned than themselves out of power. Such was the evil which, after many years, again threatened the state....

After Cicero's Disclosure of the Plot, the Common People Desert Catiline

48. The disclosure of the plot caused the common people, who had at first, in their desire for a change in the government, been only too eager for war, to change their minds. They now cursed Catiline's scheme and praised Cicero to the skies, showing as much joy and happiness as if they had been rescued from slavery. Other acts of civil war they thought would bring gain rather than loss, but the proposed burning of the city they thought inhuman, outrageous, and especially ruinous to themselves, whose whole property consisted of articles of everyday use and the clothes they wore....

Defeat and Death of Catiline

60. ... Catiline, when he saw his army routed and himself left with only a few supporters, remembering his birth and former dignity, rushed into the thickest of the enemy, where he was slain, fighting to the last.

61. When the battle was over it became plainly evident how boldly and courageously Catiline's army had fought. For almost every soldier covered with his body when he died the spot he had occupied when alive. A few in the center, whom the praetorian cohort had routed, had fallen some distance away, but all had wounds in front. Catiline himself was found far in advance of his men among dead bodies of the enemy. He was not quite dead, his face expressing the spirit of haughty defiance that he had shown all his life. Of his whole army not one free-born citizen was taken prisoner either in battle or in flight, for they had spared their own lives no more than those of the enemy. Nor did the army of the Roman people obtain a joyful or bloodless victory; all the bravest men were either killed in the battle or left the field severely wounded. Many who went from the camp to view the ground or plunder the slain, in turning over the bodies of the enemy found a friend, an acquaintance, or a relative. Some also recognized an enemy. Thus gladness and sorrow, grief and joy, were variously felt throughout the whole army.

Intellectual Life and Culture

Greek philosophical traditions found favorable reception among members of the Roman elite who sought to adapt late Classical and Hellenistic Greek thought to their own new Latin-speaking milieu.

58 Lucretius

Epicurean Philosophy at Rome

Titus Lucretius Carus (ca. 99–55 B.C.) was born of aristocratic parents amidst the social and moral decline of the Roman Republic's fatal last century. He saw his fellow citizens, he tells us, "in their greed for gain swelling their possessions out of civil war, doubling their wealth by piling murder on murder, and welcoming a brother's tragic death with heartless glee." He rejected the normal political career open to men of his class, "for to seek power, an empty thing which is never gained, and ever to labor sore in that pursuit, is but struggling to push up a mountain a stone that rolls back from the very top and rushes down to the level of the open plain." Thoroughly disillusioned with life, Lucretius withdrew into the seclusion of what he called the "ivory tower" ("quiet citadel" in the translation presented here).

But retreat from the world did not mean for Lucretius an indifference to the welfare of his fellow citizens. There had come to him, as a sudden revelation of truth comes to one who has long been without truth, a new faith and a new ideal. With the impassioned enthusiasm of a prophet he presented his views in a long didactic poem, *De rerum natura* (On the Nature of Things). His new faith was founded on the belief that science could destroy ignorance, from which came all the evil in the world; and his new ideal was the tranquillity that men could achieve in their lives if they would only be guided by reason.

The source of this revelation was the Hellenistic philosophy of Epicurus (ca. 342–270 B.C.), who taught that the happiness people sought consisted simply of being free from pain in body and mind. ("By pleasure we mean the absence of pain in the body and of trouble in the soul.") Epicurus, in turn, based his simple ethical philosophy upon the physics of Democritus (fifth century B.C.), who taught that the universe is composed of tiny particles of matter called atoms that come together and then fall apart, thus providing the constant flux and change that is characteristic of all material things and all life. There is, according to Epicurus, no meaning or purpose to be found in the workings of the natural world. Although people have free will—the result of the ability of atoms to "swerve," a concept added by Epicurus to Democritus' purely deterministic atomic theory—they are still a part of nature. Their birth and death represent the temporary coalescence and final disintegration of a group of atoms. The gods do not concern themselves with mundane affairs but spend their time pursuing happiness, like good Epicureans. When people understand that the world has no purpose, they can be freed from the fears, the errors, and the vain pursuits—including love, both physical and romantic—that produce unhappiness.

All this Lucretius expounds to his friend Memmius with the fervor of a convert to a new faith, enriching the dry arguments of Epicurus with a wealth of illustrations and a poetic enthusiasm that is evident even in a prose translation. The result is both a work of art and the best existing description of Epicurean philosophy.

The Nature of Happiness

What joy it is, when out at sea the stormwinds are lashing the waters, to gaze from the shore at the heavy stress some other man is enduring! Not that anyone's afflictions are in themselves a source of delight; but to realize from what troubles you yourself are free is joy indeed. What joy, again, to watch opposing hosts marshalled on the field of battle when you have yourself no part in their peril! But this is the greatest joy of all: to stand aloof in a quiet citadel, stoutly fortified by the teaching of the wise, and to gaze down from that elevation on others wandering aimlessly in a vain search for the way of life, pitting their wits one against another, disputing for precedence, struggling night and day with unstinted effort to scale the pinnacles of wealth and power. O joyless hearts of men! O minds without vision! How dark and dangerous the life in which this tiny span is lived away! Do you not see that nature is clamoring for two things only, a body free from pain, and a mind released from worry and fear for the enjoyment of pleasurable sensations?

So we find that the requirements of our bodily nature are few indeed, no more than is necessary to banish pain. To heap pleasure upon pleasure may heighten man's enjoyment at times. But what matter if there are no golden images of youths about the house, holding flaming torches in their right hands to illumine banquets prolonged into the night? What matter if the hall does not sparkle with silver and gleam with gold, and no carved and gilded rafters ring to the music of the lute? Nature does not miss these luxuries when men recline in company on the soft grass by a running stream under the branches of a tall tree and refresh their bodies pleasurably at small expense. Better still if the weather smiles upon them and the season of the year stipples the green herbage with flowers. Burning fevers flee no swifter from your body if you toss under figured counterpanes and coverlets of crimson than if you must lie in rude homespun....

Praise of Epicurus

When human life lay grovelling in all men's sight, crushed to the earth under the dead weight of superstition whose grim features lowered menacingly upon mortals from the four quarters of the sky, a man of Greece was first to raise mortal eyes in defiance, first to stand erect and brave the challenge. Fables of the gods did not crush him, nor the lightning flash and the growling menace of the sky. Rather, they quickened his manhood, so that he, first of all men, longed to smash the constraining locks of nature's doors. The vital vigor of his mind prevailed. He ventured far out beyond the flaming ramparts of the world and voyaged in mind throughout infinity. Returning victorious, he proclaimed to us what can be and what cannot: how a limit is fixed to the power of everything and an immovable frontier post. Therefore superstition in its turn lies crushed beneath his feet, and we by his triumph are lifted level with the skies.

"Superstition Is the Mother of Sinful Deeds"

One thing that worries me is the fear that you may fancy yourself embarking on an impious course, setting your feet on the path of sin. Far from it. More often it is this very superstition that is the mother of sinful and impious deeds. Remember how at Aulis the altar of the Virgin Goddess was foully stained with the blood of Iphigeneia by the leaders of the Greeks, the patterns of chivalry. The headband was bound about her virgin tresses and hung down evenly over both her cheeks. Suddenly she caught sight of her father standing sadly in front of the altar, the attendants beside him hiding the knife and her people bursting into tears when they saw her. Struck dumb with terror, she sank on her knees to the ground. Poor girl, at such a moment it did not help her that she had been first to give the name of father to a king. Raised by the hands of men, she was led trembling to the altar. Not for her the sacrament of marriage and the loud chant of Hymen. It was her fate in the very hour of marriage to fall a sinless victim to a sinful rite, slaughtered to her greater grief by a father's hand, so that a fleet might sail under happy auspices. Such are the heights of wickedness to which men are driven by superstition.

You yourself, if you surrender your judgment at any time to the bloodcurdling declamations of the prophets, will want to desert our ranks. Only think what phantoms they can conjure up to overturn the tenor of your life and wreck your happiness with fear. And not without cause. For, if men saw that a term was set to their troubles, they would find strength in some way to withstand the hocus-pocus and intimidations of the prophets. As it is, they have no power of resistance, because they are haunted by the fear of eternal punishment after death. They know nothing of the nature of the spirit. Is it born, or is it implanted in us at birth? Does it perish with us, dissolved by death, or does it visit the murky depths and dreary sloughs of Hades? Or is it transplanted by divine power into other creatures, as described in the poems of our own Ennius, who first gathered on the delectable slopes of Helicon an evergreen garland destined to win renown among the nations of Italy? Ennius indeed in his immortal verses proclaims that there is also a Hell, which is peopled not by our actual spirits or bodies but only by shadowy images, ghastly pale. It is from this realm that he pictures the ghost of Homer, of unfading memory, as appearing to him, shedding salt tears and revealing the nature of the universe....

First Principles

I am well aware that it is not easy to elucidate in Latin verse the obscure discoveries of the Greeks. The poverty of our language and the novelty of the theme compel me often to coin new words for the purpose. But your merit and the joy I hope to derive from our delightful friendship encourage me to face any task however hard. This it is that leads me to stay awake through the quiet of the night, studying how by choice of words and the poet's art I can display before your mind a clear light by which you can gaze into the heart of hidden things.

This dread and darkness of the mind cannot be dispelled by the sunbeams, the shining shafts of day, but only by an understanding of the outward form and inner workings of nature. In tackling this theme, our starting-point will be this principle: *Nothing can ever be created by divine power out of nothing.* The reason why all mortals are so gripped by fear is that they see all sorts of things happening on the earth and in the sky with no discernible cause, and these they attribute to the will of God. Accordingly, when we have seen that nothing can be created out of nothing, we shall then have a clearer picture of the path ahead, the problem of how things are created and occasioned without the aid of the gods....

The second great principle is this: *nature resolves everything into its component atoms and never reduces anything to nothing.* If anything were perishable in all its parts, anything might perish all of a sudden and vanish from sight. There would be no need of any force to separate its parts and loosen their links. In actual fact, since everything is composed of indestructible seeds, nature obviously does not allow anything to perish till it has encountered a force that shatters it with a blow or creeps into chinks and unknits it....

Well, Memmius, I have taught you that things cannot be created out of nothing nor, once born, be summoned back to nothing. Perhaps, however, you are becoming mistrustful of my words, because these atoms of mine are not visible to the eye. Consider, therefore, this further evidence of *bodies whose existence you must acknowledge though they cannot be seen.* First, wind, when its force is roused, whips up waves, founders tall ships and scatters cloud-rack. Sometimes scouring plains with hurricane force it strews them with huge trees and batters mountain peaks with blasts that hew down forests. Such is wind in its fury, when it whoops aloud with a mad menace in its shouting. Without question, therefore, there must be invisible particles of wind which sweep sea and land and the clouds in the sky, swooping upon them and whirling them along in a headlong hurricane. In the way they flow and the havoc they spread they are no different from a torrential flood of water when it rushes down in a sudden spate from the mountain heights, swollen by heavy rains, and heaps together wreckage from the forest and entire trees. Soft though it is by nature, the sudden shock of oncoming water is more than even stout bridges can withstand, so furious is the force with which the turbid, storm-flushed torrent surges against their piers. With a mighty roar it lays them low, rolling huge rocks under its waves and brushing aside every obstacle from its course. Such, therefore, must be the movement of blasts of wind also. When they have come surging along some course like a rushing river, they push obstacles before them and buffet them with repeated blows; and sometimes, eddying round and round, they snatch them up and carry them along in a swiftly circling vortex. Here then is proof upon proof that winds have invisible bodies, since in their actions and behavior they are found to rival great rivers, whose bodies are plain to see....

... It follows that nature works through the agency of invisible bodies....

... Since the atoms are moving freely through the void, they must all be kept in motion either by their own weight or on occasion by the impact of another atom. For it must often happen that two of them in their course knock together and immediately bounce apart in opposite directions, a natural consequence of their hardness and solidity and the absence of anything behind to stop them....

This process, as I might point out, is illustrated by an image of it that is continually taking place before our very eyes. Observe what happens when sunbeams are admitted to a building and shed light on its shadowy places. You will see a multitude of tiny particles mingling in a multitude of ways in the empty space within the light of the beam, as though contending in everlasting conflict, rushing into battle rank upon rank with never a moment's pause in a rapid sequence of unions and disunions. From this you may picture what it is for the atoms to be perpetually tossed about in the illimitable void. To some extent a small thing may afford an illustration and an imperfect image of great things. Besides, there is a further reason why you should give your mind to these particles that are seen dancing in a sunbeam: their dancing is an actual indication of underlying movements of matter that are hidden from our sight....

"The Atoms Swerve—The Source of Free Will"

In this connection there is another fact that I want you to grasp. *When the atoms are traveling straight down through empty space by their own weight, at quite indeterminate times and places they swerve ever so little from their course,* just so much that you can call it a change of direction. If it were not for this swerve, everything would fall downwards like raindrops through the abyss of space. No collision would take place and no impact of atom on atom would be created. Thus nature would never have created anything.

If anyone supposes that heavier atoms on a straight course through empty space could outstrip lighter ones and fall on them from above, thus causing impacts that might give rise to generative motions, he is going far astray from the path of truth. The reason why objects falling through water or thin air vary in speed according to their weight is simply that the matter composing water or air cannot obstruct all objects equally, but is forced to give way more speedily to heavier ones. But empty space can offer no resistance to any object in any quarter at any time, so as not to yield free passage as its own nature demands. Therefore, through undisturbed vacuum all bodies must travel at equal speed though impelled by unequal weights. The heavier will never be able to fall on the lighter from above or generate of themselves impacts leading to that variety of motions out of which nature can produce things. We are thus forced back to the conclusion that the atoms swerve a little—but only a very little, or we shall be caught imagining slantwise movements, and the facts will prove us wrong. For we see plainly and palpably that weights, when they come tumbling down, have no power of their own to move aslant, so far as meets the eye. But who can possibly perceive that they do not diverge in the very least from a vertical course?

Again, if all movement is always interconnected, the new arising from the old in a determinate order—if the atoms never swerve so as to originate some new movement that will snap the bonds of fate, the everlasting sequence of cause and effect—what is the source of the free will possessed by living things throughout the earth? What, I repeat, is the source of that willpower snatched from the fates, whereby we follow the path along which we are severally led by pleasure, swerving from our course at no set time or place but at the bidding of our hearts? There is no doubt that on these occasions the will of the individual originates the movements that trickle through his limbs.... Although many men are driven by an external force and often constrained involuntarily to advance or to rush headlong, yet there is within the human breast something that can fight against this force and resist it. At its command the supply of matter is forced to take a new course through our limbs and joints or is checked in its course and brought once more to a halt. So also in the atoms you must recognize the same possibility: besides weight and impact there must be a third cause of movement, the source of this inborn power of ours, since we see that nothing can come out of nothing. For the weight of an atom prevents its movements from being completely determined by the impact of other atoms. But the fact that the mind itself has no internal necessity to determine its every act and compel it to suffer in helpless passivity—this is due to the slight swerve of the atoms at no determinate time or place....

"Spirit Is Mortal"

My next point is this: you must understand that the *minds of living things and the light fabric of their spirits are neither birthless nor deathless.* To this end I have long been mustering and inventing verses with a labor that is also a joy. Now I will try to set them out in a style worthy of your career.

Please note that both objects are to be embraced under one name. When, for instance, I proceed to demonstrate that "spirit" is mortal, you must understand that this applies equally to "mind" since the two are so conjoined as to constitute a single substance.

First of all, then, I have shown that spirit is flimsy stuff composed of tiny particles. Its atoms are obviously far smaller than those of swift-flowing water or mist or smoke, since it far outstrips them in mobility and is moved by a far slighter impetus. Indeed, it is actually moved by images of smoke and mist. So, for instance, when we are sunk in sleep, we may see altars sending up clouds of steam and giving off smoke; and we cannot doubt that we are here dealing with images. Now, we see that water flows out in all directions from a broken vessel and the moisture is dissipated, and mist and smoke vanish into thin air. Be assured, therefore, that spirit is similarly dispelled and vanishes far more speedily and is sooner dissolved into its component atoms once it has been let loose from the human frame. When the body, which served as a vessel for it, is by some means broken and attenuated by loss of blood from the veins, so as to be no longer able to contain it, how can you suppose that it can be contained by any kind of air, which must be far more tenuous than our bodily frame?

Again, we are conscious that mind and body are born together, grow up together and together decay. With the weak and delicate frame of wavering childhood goes a like infirmity of judgment. The robust vigor of ripening years is accompanied by a steadier resolve and a maturer strength of mind. Later, when the body is palsied by the potent forces of age and the limbs begin to droop with blunted vigor, the understanding limps, the tongue falters and the mind totters: everything weakens and gives way at the same time. It is thus natural that the vital spirit should all evaporate like smoke, soaring into the gusty air, since we have seen that it shares the body's birth and growth and wearies with the weariness of age....

... You must admit, therefore, that when the body has perished there is an end also of the spirit diffused through it. It is surely crazy to couple a mortal object with an eternal and suppose that they can work in harmony and mutually interact. What can be imagined more incongruous, what more repugnant and discordant, than that a mortal object and one that is immortal and everlasting should unite to form a compound and jointly weather the storms that rage about them? ...

"Nothing to Fear in Death"

From all this it follows that *death is nothing to us* and no concern of ours, since our tenure of the mind is mortal....

If any feeling remains in mind or spirit after it has been torn from our body, that is nothing to us, who are brought into being by the wedlock of body and spirit, conjoined and coalesced. Or even if the matter that composes us should be reassembled by time after our death and brought back into its present state—if the light of life were given to us anew—even that contingency would still be no concern of ours once the chain of our identity had been snapped. We who are now are not concerned with ourselves in any previous existence: the sufferings of those selves do not touch us. When you look at the immeasurable extent of time gone by and the multiform movements of matter, you will readily credit that these same atoms that compose us now must many a time before have entered into the self-same combinations as now. But our mind cannot recall this to remembrance. For between then and now is interposed a breach in life, and all the atomic motions have been wandering far astray from sentience.

If the future holds travail and anguish in store, the self must be in existence, when that time comes, in order to experience it. But from this fate we are redeemed by death, which denies existence to the self that might have suffered these tribulations. Rest assured, therefore, that we have nothing to fear in death. One who no longer is cannot suffer, or differ in any way from one who has never been born when once this mortal life has been usurped by death the immortal....

... The old is always thrust aside to make way for the new, and one thing must be built out of the wreck of another. There is no murky pit of Hell awaiting anyone. There is need of matter, so that later generations may arise; when they have lived out their span, they will all follow you. Bygone generations have taken your road, and those to come will take it no less. So one thing will never cease to spring from another. To none is life given in freehold; to all on lease. Look back at the eternity that passed before we were born, and mark how utterly it counts to us as nothing. This is a mirror that Nature holds up to us, in which we may see the time that shall be after we are dead. Is there anything terrifying in the sight—anything depressing—anything that is not more restful than the soundest sleep? ...

"The Thing Called Love—Be on Your Guard!"

This, then, is what we term Venus. This is the origin of the thing called love—that drop of Venus' honey that first drips into our heart, to be followed by numbing heartache. Though the object of your love may be absent, images of it still haunt you and the beloved name chimes sweetly in your ears. If you find yourself thus passionately enamoured of an individual, you should keep well away from such images. Thrust from you anything that might feed your passion, and turn your mind elsewhere. Vent the seed of love upon other objects. By clinging to it you assure yourself the certainty of heartsickness and pain....

To avoid enticement into the snares of love is not so difficult as, once entrapped, to escape out of the toils and snap the tenacious knots of Venus. And yet, be you never so tightly entangled and embrangled, you can still free yourself from the curse unless you stand in the way of your own freedom. First, you should concentrate on all the faults of mind or body of her whom you covet and sigh for. For men often behave as though blinded by love and credit the beloved with charms to which she has no valid title. How often do we see blemished and unsightly women basking in a lover's adoration! ... It would be a wearisome task to run through the whole catalogue. But suppose her face in fact is all that could be desired and the charm of Venus radiates from her whole body. Even so, there are still others. Even so, we lived without her before. Even so, in her physical nature she is no different, as we well know, from the plainest of her sex. She is driven to use foul-smelling fumigants. Her maids keep well away from her and snigger behind her back. The tearful lover, shut out from the presence, heaps the threshold with flowers and garlands, anoints the disdainful doorposts with perfume, and plants rueful kisses on the door. Often enough, were he admitted, one whiff would promptly make him cast around for some decent pretext to take his leave. His fond complaint, long-pondered and far-fetched, would fall dismally flat. He would curse himself for a fool to have endowed her with qualities above mortal imperfection.

To the daughters of Venus themselves all this is no secret. Hence they are at pains to hide all the back-stage activities of life from those whom they wish to keep fast bound in the bonds of love. But their pains are wasted, since your mind has power to drag all these mysteries into the daylight and get at the truth behind the sniggers.

59 Cicero

Advocate of Property Rights, Greek Philosophy, and the Status Quo

The speeches and writings of Marcus Tullius Cicero (106–43 B.C.) contain numerous passages justifying the assassination of Julius Caesar as well as the role of the conservative party (Optimates, "best people") in Roman politics. Born near Rome into a non-noble equestrian family, Cicero achieved such great fame as a courtroom lawyer that in 63 B.C. he was elected to the consulship with the backing of the Optimates, who desired at all costs to defeat the bid of the radical Catiline for that office. Following his counsulship, during which he suppressed the Catilinarian conspiracy (Selection 57) and was eulogized as "father of his country" by the Senate, Cicero was unable to take an active part in the turbulent politics of the dying Republic, being but a "new man" (Selection 51) among the senatorial nobility, and lacking the essential support of either great wealth or legions. In his desire "never to stop seeking the good of the community," he turned to the writing of popular treatises on political theory and moral philosophy. These treatises became the medium through which much of the best of Greek thought on these subjects was transmitted to the Romans.

Running as a thread through all of Cicero's writings and speeches is his concern for freedom and order in society and, conversely, his opposition to despotism. With such fervor and eloquence does he expound this theme, together with the Roman ideal of virtue as dedication to social and civic duty, that his views have become an integral part of the Western heritage. On the evidence of Plutarch's "Life of Cicero," it appears that even Caesar's heir and successor, Augustus, recognized Cicero's contribution: "I have heard that Caesar [Augustus] a long time after once went to see one of his daughter's sons, and as the youth had in his hand one of Cicero's writings, he was afraid and hid it in his vest; which Caesar observing took the book and read a good part of it while standing, and then returning the book said, 'An eloquent man, my son, and one who loved his country well.'"

From *Cicero*, Vol. XII, Loeb Classical Library Vol. 309, translated by R. Gardner (Cambridge, Mass.: Harvard University Press, 1958). The Loeb Classical Library® is a registered trademark of the President and Fellows of Harvard College. Reprinted by permission of the publishers and the Trustees of the Loeb Classical Library.

As shown by the following selections—from a courtroom speech delivered in 56 B.C., and from his last treatise on philosophy, *On Duties*, written in 44 B.C.—Cicerco's concern for freedom and order often took on a strong conservative slant. On such occasions he is little more than a propagandist for vested interests, concerned with preserving property rights and the status quo, and not averse to slanting the evidence to serve his purpose. This narrowness of outlook is a reflection of Cicero's supposition that the Republic's ills were caused by the "seditious" activities of a few "mad revolutionaries." The selections also include Cicero's views on the value of philosophy and why he turned to it—in particular to the Academic school founded by Plato but which under the leadership of men like Carneades had rejected Plato's dogmatism and adopted the views of the Skeptic school of philosophy, founded by Socrates' disciple Antisthenes. The Skeptics' liberal, open-minded approach to truth required that it be tested by experience and exposed to the possibility of contradiction. As Cicero put it in another of his philosophical writings, "The only difference between us and the dogmatists is that they have no doubt of the truth of their case, whereas we consider many doctrines probable and are prepared to act on them, but hardly to affirm them as certain."

Marcus Tullius Cicero
"And this is the highest statesmanship and the soundest wisdom on the part of a good citizen, not to divide the interests of the citizens but to unite all on the basis of impartial justice."

"Two Classes of Men Eager to Engage in Politics"

You made a special point of asking me what was the meaning of our "breed of *optimates,*" to use your own term. You ask about a matter which is vital for our younger generation to learn and not difficult for me to offer some instruction....

There have always been two classes of men in this state eager to engage in politics and to distinguish themselves. One group wished to be known, by repute and in reality, as *populares*; the other, *optimates.* The *populares* were those who wished everything they did and said to be agreeable to the masses; the *optimates* acted so as to win by their policy the approval of the best people. Who then are these "best people"? Their numbers, if you ask me, are infinite; for otherwise we could not survive in politics. They include the leaders of opinion in the Senate and those who follow their lead; they include men of the upper classes to whom the Senate is open; they include Romans living in municipal towns and in country districts; they include men of business, too, as well as freedmen— all these are "best people." In its numbers, I repeat, this class is spread far and wide and is variously composed. But, to prevent misunderstanding, the whole class can be summed up and defined in a few words. All are *optimates* who are neither criminal nor vicious in disposition, nor mad revolutionaries, nor embarrassed by their private life. It follows, then, that those who are upright, sound in mind, and good family men, belong to this so-called "breed." Those in the government who serve the wishes, the interests, and the principles of these men are called their champions and are regarded as the most influential of the *optimates,* the most eminent of our citizens, and the leaders of the state. What then is the goal to which those who guide the helm of state ought to direct their course? It is the best and noblest goal of all sound and good and prosperous men—civil peace with honor. Those who desire this are *optimates*; those who achieve it are considered the best of men and the saviors of the state. For just as it is wrong for men to be so carried away by their desire for the honor of public office that they are indifferent to civil peace, so too it is wrong for them to welcome a peace which is inconsistent with honor.

Now civil peace with honor has the following foundations and elements which our leaders ought to protect and defend even at the risk of life itself: religious observances, auspices, powers of the magistrates, authority of the Senate, laws and ancestral custom, criminal and civil justice, credit, our provinces and allies, the prestige of our government and its army and treasury. To be a defender and a protector of so many and so important interests requires great courage, great ability, and great resolution. For, in so large a body of citizens, there are great numbers of men who, either from fear of punishment, being conscious of their crimes, seek to cause chaos and revolution; or who, owing to a sort of inborn anarchistic madness, thrive on civil discord and sedition; or who, on account of private financial embarrassment, prefer a general conflagration to their own ruin. When such men as these have found advisers and leaders to suit their vicious aims, storms are aroused in the Commonwealth, so that those who have hitherto been granted the helm of state must watch and strive with all their

skill and devotion that they may be able, without any damage to those foundations and elements of which I have just spoken, to keep on their course and
reach that haven of peace with honor. If I were to deny, gentlemen, that this
course is stormy and difficult, perilous and treacherous, I should be telling a
lie—especially since not only have I always understood it to be so, but experience
has convinced me more than others.

There are greater forces and means for attacking than for defending the state.
The reason is that reckless and depraved men need only a nod to set them moving, and their own natural disposition incites them against the state. But good
men somehow tend to move slowly, neglect the beginnings of movements,
and are aroused to action at the last moment only by dire necessity. As a result,
thanks to their hesitation and indolence, sometimes even when they wish to
keep civil peace by sacrificing their honor, they lose both....

It is a difficult task; I do not deny it. There an many risks; I confess it. Truly
has it been said, "Many traps are set for the virtuous." ... A law to provide for
voting by secret ballot was proposed by Lucius Cassius [137 B.C.]. The people
thought that their liberty was at stake. The leading men in the state held a different opinion; they were concerned over the interests of the *optimates* and they
dreaded the irresponsibility of the masses and the license afforded by the secret
ballot. Tiberius Gracchus proposed an agrarian law. The law was popular with
the people, for it seemed to restore the fortunes of the poorer classes. The *optimates* vigorously opposed it, because they thought it would cause dissension and
strip the state of its stoutest champions by evicting the rich from their long-
established holdings. Gaius Gracchus brought forward a grain law. It delighted
the masses, for it provided food in abundance without work. Good citizens
were against it; they thought it was an invitation to the masses to desert work
for idleness, and they saw it as a drain upon the treasury.

★ ★ ★

"I Advocate the Study of Philosophy"

My books have aroused in not a few men the desire not only to read but to
write, and yet I sometimes fear that what we term philosophy is distasteful to
certain worthy gentlemen and that they wonder that I devote so much time
and effort to it.

As long as the state was administered by its own elected representatives, I
devoted all my effort and thought to it. But when it passed under the absolute
control of a despot [Julius Caesar] and there was no longer any room for my
leadership and advice, and when I had lost the eminent friends who had been
associated with me in the task of serving the interests of the state, I neither
resigned myself to despair, which would have overwhelmed me had I not

From *Cicero: Vol. XXI, De Officiis,* Loeb Classical Library Vol. 30, translated by Walter Miller, (Cambridge, Mass.:
Harvard University Press, 1913). The Loeb Classical Library® is a registered trademark of the President and Fellows of
Harvard College. Reprinted by permission of the publishers and the Trustees of the Loeb Classical Library.

struggled against it, nor surrendered myself to a life of sensual pleasure unbecoming to a philosopher.

I would that the state had stood fast in its former position and had not fallen into the hands of men who desired not so much to reform as to abolish the constitution. For then, in the first place, I should now be devoting my energies more to politics than to writing, as I used to do when the Republic existed; and in the second place, I should be committing to written form not these present essays but my public speeches, as I often formerly did. But when the Republic, to which all my care and thought and effort used to be devoted, was no more, then, of course, my voice was silenced in the forum and in the Senate. And since my mind could not be wholly idle, I thought, as I had been well-read along these lines of thought from my early youth, that the most honorable way for me to forget my sorrows would be by turning to philosophy. As a young man, I had devoted a great deal of time to philosophy as a discipline; but after I began to fill the high offices and devoted myself heart and soul to the public service, there was only so much time for philosophical studies as was left over from the claims of my friends and of the state; all of this was spent in reading; I had no leisure for writing.

Therefore, amid all the present most awful calamities I yet flatter myself that I have won this good out of evil—that I may commit to written form matters not at all familiar to our countrymen but still very much worth their knowing. For what, in the name of heaven, is more to be desired than wisdom? What is more to be prized? What is better for a man, what more worthy of his nature? Those who seek after it are called philosophers; and philosophy is nothing else, if one will translate the word into our idiom, than "the love of wisdom." Wisdom, moreover, as the word has been defined by some older philosophers, is "the knowledge of things human and divine and of the causes by which those things are controlled." And if the man lives who would belittle the study of philosophy, I quite fail to see what in the world he would see fit to praise. For if we are looking for mental enjoyment and freedom from care, what can be compared with the pursuits of those who are constantly searching for something that will tend toward and effectively promote a good and happy life? Or, if our concern is for strength of character and virtue, then this is the method by which we can attain to those qualities, or there is none at all. And to say that there is no "method" for securing the highest blessings, when none even of the least important concerns is without its method, is the language of people who talk without due reflection and who blunder in matters of the utmost importance. Furthermore, if there is really a way to learn virtue, where shall one look for it, when one has turned aside from this field of learning? When I advocate the study of philosophy, I usually discuss this subject at greater length, as I have done in another of my books [*Hortensius,* now lost]. For the present I mean only to explain why, deprived of the tasks of public service, I have devoted myself to this particular pursuit.

But people raise other objections against me—and they are philosophers and scholars—asking whether I think I am quite consistent in that, although our school maintains that nothing can be known for certain, yet I make a habit of presenting my opinions on all sorts of subjects and at this very moment am trying to formulate rules of duty. I wish that they had a better understanding of our position. We Academics are not men whose minds wander in uncertainty and never know what principles to adopt. For what sort of mental habit, or rather what sort of life would that be which would dispense with all rules for reasoning or even for living? Not so with us. Other schools maintain that some things are certain, others uncertain; we, differing from them, say that some things are probable, others improbable.

What, then, is to prevent me from pursuing what seems to me to be probable and rejecting what seems to be improbable? Surely by shunning the presumption of dogmatism one keeps clear of that recklessness of assertion which is so far removed from true wisdom. And as to the fact that our school questions the certainty of everything, that is only because we could not get a clear view of what is "probable" unless a comparative analysis were made of all the arguments on both sides....

"No Invasion of Property Rights by the State"

Any man who holds a state office must make it his first care that everyone shall have what belongs to him and that private citizens shall suffer no invasion of their property rights by act of the state. It was a ruinous policy that Philippus proposed when in his tribuneship [104 B.C.] he introduced his agrarian bill. However, when his law was rejected, he took his defeat with good grace and displayed extraordinary moderation. But in his public speeches on the measure he often played the demagogue, and dangerously so when he said that owners of private property in the state numbered less than two thousand. That speech deserves unqualified condemnation, for it favored an equal distribution of property; and what more subversive policy than that can be conceived? For the chief purpose in the establishment of constitutional state and municipal governments was that individual property rights might be protected. Although by nature men are gregarious, it was in the hope of safeguarding their possessions that they sought the protection of cities.

The administration should also put forth every effort to prevent the levying of a property tax, and to this end precautions should be taken long in advance. Such a tax was often levied in the time of our forefathers on account of the depleted state of their treasury caused by incessant wars. But if any state ... ever has to face a crisis requiring the imposition of such a burden, every effort must be made to let all the people realize that they must bow to the inevitable if they wish to survive the crisis....

But they who pose as friends of the people and for that reason either attempt to have agrarian laws passed in order that the occupants may be driven out of their homes, or propose that money loaned should be remitted to the borrowers, are undermining the foundations of the Commonwealth. First of all, they are destroying harmony, which cannot exist when money is taken away from one party and bestowed upon another; and second, they do away with equity, which is utterly subverted if the rights of property are not respected. For, as I said above, it is the peculiar function of the state and the city to guarantee to every man the free and undisturbed control of his own particular property.... And how is it fair that a man who never had any property should take possession of lands that had been occupied for many years or even generations, and that he who had them before should lose possession of them?

Now, it was on account of just this sort of wrongdoing that the Spartans banished their ephor Lysander, and put their king Agis to death [in 241 B.C.]—an act without precedent in the history of Sparta. From that time on—and for the same reason—dissension so serious ensued that tyrants arose, the nobles were sent into exile, and the best-governed state in history crumbled to pieces. Nor did it fall alone; the contagion of the ills that originated in Sparta spread widely and dragged the rest of Greece down to ruin. What shall we say of our own Gracchi, the sons of that famous Tiberius Gracchus and grandsons of Scipio Africanus? Was it not strife over the agrarian issue that caused their downfall and death? ...

And this is the highest statesmanship and the soundest wisdom on the part of a good citizen, not to divide the interests of the citizens but to unite all on the basis of impartial justice. "Let them live in their neighbor's house rent-free." Why so? In order that, when *I* have bought, built, kept up, and spent my money upon a place, you may without my consent enjoy what belongs to me?[1] What else is that but to rob one man of what belongs to him and to give to another what does not belong to him? And what is the meaning of an abolition of debts, except that you buy a farm with my money? You have the farm, and I have not my money.

We must, therefore, take measures that there shall be no indebtedness of a nature to endanger the public safety. It is a menace that can be averted in many ways; but should a serious debt be incurred, we are not to allow the rich to lose their property while the debtors profit by what is their neighbor's. For there is nothing that upholds a government more powerfully than its credit, and it can have no credit unless the payment of debts is enforced by law. Never were measures for the repudiation of debts more strenuously agitated than in my consulship. Men of every sort and rank attempted with arms and armies to force the project through. But I opposed them with such energy that this plague was wholly eradicated from the body politic. Indebtedness was never greater; yet debts were never liquidated more easily or more fully because the hope of defrauding the creditor was cut off and payment was enforced by law....

Those, then, whose office it is to look after the interests of the state will refrain from that form of liberality which robs one man to enrich another. Above all, they will take particular care that everyone shall be protected in the possession of his own property by the fair administration of the law and the courts, that the poorer classes shall not be oppressed because of their helplessness, and that envy shall not stand in the way of the rich to prevent them from keeping or recovering possession of what is theirs.

---

1. Cicero owned several tenements in Rome, from which he received a good income.

Late Republic and
the Rise of Autocracy

Success abroad intensified social and political competition among the Roman aristocracy, which increasingly involved the common people in their mutual struggles. In the process, both the "checks and balances" that Greek authors found in the Roman constitution and Roman Republican aversion to kingship were swept aside in rising civil strife that culminated in the autocratic rule of the emperors.

60 Appian

First Roman Civil War and Proscriptions

"… destruction, death, confiscation, and wholesale
extermination"

Mithridates of Pontus (Asia Minor), a self-styled descendant of Alexander the Great, sought to reestablish a great empire in the eastern Mediterranean. His ambition set him against Roman allies and the rising Roman hegemony in the region even as many local inhabitants welcomed his rise. In Ephesus, eighty thousand Italians and Romans were killed in a single day, an unmistakable expression of Greek resentment toward exploitative Italian merchants and tax collectors. War against Mithridates thus became both certain and imminent, and yet Roman political factions intrigued over who would receive the military command. Some wanted Gaius Marius, victorious general and a *popularis* who championed the cause of the common people, to lead while others favored offering the command to Sulla, as the Senate had originally voted. In 82 B.C., Sulla eventually decided the issue by marching the army under his command upon the Colline gates of Rome, and there dispersed his political enemies, with Marius fleeing to Africa and others hunted down and killed. Sulla assumed the dictatorship and imposed a new order, which included the first open proscriptions in Rome, thereby cementing his subsequent reputation as a tyrant. Proscriptions are so named for the act of inscribing the names of

From Appian, *Civil Wars* 1.5; in *Appian's Roman History, Vol. III*, edited by Horace White, Loeb Classical Library, Vol. 4 (Cambridge, Mass.: Harvard University Press, 1913), pp. 101–103.

condemned persons on a writing tablet. Accounts vary as to the number of Sulla's victims; Appian (See Selection 55) mentions that forty senators, sixteen hundred equestrians, and countless common citizens faced accusations and judicial procedures that stripped them of their possessions. This was a time when *delatores*, informants who accused others in the hope of gaining some of the proscribed man's property as reward, came to the fore. All ancient writers, including Plutarch and Appian who offer accounts of Sulla's life and career, agree that proscriptions were an evil and that men were often killed just so that their wealth could be seized and redistributed to Sulla's supporters, among whom were army veterans who increasingly looked toward their general as patron and their sole guarantor of a secure retirement.

VII

55. Hitherto the murders and seditions had been internal and fragmentary. Afterward the chiefs of factions assailed each other with great armies, according to the usage of war, and their country lay as a prize between them. The beginning and origin of these contentions came about directly after the Social War, in this wise.

When Mithridates, king of Pontus and of other nations, invaded Bithynia and Phrygia and that part of Asia adjacent to those countries, as I have related in the preceding book, the consul Sulla was chosen by lot to the command of Asia and the Mithridatic war, but was still in Rome. Marius, for his part, thought that this would be an easy and lucrative war and desiring the command of it prevailed upon the tribune, Publius Sulpicius, by many promises, to help him to obtain it. He also encouraged the new Italian citizens, who had very little power in the elections, to hope that they should be distributed among all the tribes—not in any way openly suggesting his own advantage, but with the expectation of employing them as loyal servants for all his ends. Sulpicius straightway brought forward a law for this purpose. If it were enacted Marius and Sulpicius would have everything they wanted, because the new citizens far outnumbered the old ones. The old citizens saw this and opposed the new ones with all their might. They fought each other with sticks and stones, and the evil increased continually, till the consuls, becoming apprehensive, as the day for voting on the law drew near, proclaimed a vacation of several days, such as was customary on festal occasions, in order to postpone the voting and the danger....

81. Sulla now had plenty of soldiers and plenty of friends of the higher orders, whom he used as lieutenants. He and Metellus marched in advance, being both proconsuls, for it seems that Sulla, who had been appointed proconsul against Mithridates, had at no time hitherto laid down his command, although he had been voted a public enemy at the instance of Cinna. Now Sulla moved against his enemies with a most intense yet concealed hatred. The people in the city, who formed a pretty fair judgment of the character of the man, and who remembered his former attack and capture of the city, and who took into account the decrees they had proclaimed against him, and who had witnessed the destruction

of his house, the confiscation of his property, the killing of his friends, and the narrow escape of his family, were in a state of terror. Conceiving that there was no middle ground between victory and utter destruction, they united with the consuls to resist Sulla, but with trepidation. They despatched messengers throughout Italy to collect soldiers, provisions, and money, and, as in cases of extreme peril, they omitted nothing that zeal and earnestness could suggest.

82. Gains Norbanus and Lucius Scipio, who were then the consuls, and with them Carbo, who had been consul the previous year (all of them moved by equal hatred of Sulla and more alarmed than others because they knew that they were more to blame for what had been done), levied the best possible army from the city, joined with it the Italian army, and marched against Sulla in detachments. They had 200 cohorts of 500 men at first, and their forces were considerably augmented afterward. For the sympathies of the people were much in favour of the consuls, because the action of Sulla, who was marching against his country, seemed to be that of an enemy, while that of the consuls, even if they were working for themselves, was ostensibly the cause of the republic. Many persons, too, who knew that they had shared the guilt, and who believed that they could not despise the fears, of the consuls, co-operated with them. They knew very well that Sulla was not meditating merely punishment, correction, and alarm for them, but destruction, death, confiscation, and wholesale extermination. In this they were not mistaken, for the war ruined everyone. From 10,000 to 20,000 men were slain in a single battle more than once. Fifty thousand on both sides lost their lives round the city, and to the survivors Sulla was unsparing in severity, both to individuals and to communities, until, finally, he made himself the undisputed master of the whole Roman government, so far as he wished or cared to be.

83. It seems, too, that divine providence foretold to them the results of this war. Mysterious terrors came upon many, both in public and in private, throughout all Italy. Ancient, awe-inspiring oracles were remembered. Many monstrous things happened. A mule foaled, a woman gave birth to a viper instead of a child. There was a severe earthquake divinely sent and some of the temples in Rome were thrown down (the Romans being in any case very seriously disposed towards such things). The Capitol, that had been built by the kings 400 years before, was burned down, and nobody could discover the cause of the fire. All things seemed to point to the multitude of coming slaughters, to the conquest of Italy and of the Romans themselves, to the capture of the city, and to constitutional change.

84. This war began as soon as Sulla arrived at Brundusium, which was in the 174th Olympiad [ca. 83 B.C.]. Considering the magnitude of the operations, its length was not great, compared with wars of this size in general, since the combatants rushed upon each, other with the fury of private enemies. For this special reason greater and more distressing calamities than usual befell those who took part in it in a short space of time, because they rushed to meet their troubles. Nevertheless the war lasted three years in Italy alone, until Sulla had secured the supreme power, but in Spain it continued even after Sulla's death. Battles, skirmishes, sieges, and fighting of all kinds were numerous throughout Italy,

and the generals had both regular battles and partial engagements, and all were noteworthy. The greatest and most remarkable of them I shall mention in brief....

XI

... [N]ow, after thus crushing Italy by war, fire, and murder, Sulla's generals visited the several cities and established garrisons at the suspected places. Pompey was despatched to Africa against Carbo and to Sicily against Carbo's friends who had taken refuge there. Sulla himself called the Roman people together in an assembly and made them a speech, vaunting his own exploits and making other menacing statements in order to inspire terror. He finished by saying that he would bring about a change which would be beneficial to the people if they would obey him, but of his enemies he would spare none, but would visit them with the utmost severity. He would take vengeance by strong measures on the praetors, quaestors, military tribunes, and everybody else who had committed any hostile act after the day when the consul Scipio violated the agreement made with him. After saying this he forthwith proscribed about forty senators and 1600 knights. He seems to have been the first to make a formal list of those whom he punished, to offer prizes to assassins and rewards to informers, and to threaten with punishment those who should conceal the proscribed. Shortly afterward he added the names of other senators to the proscription. Some of these, taken unawares, were killed where they were caught, in their houses, in the streets, or in the temples. Others were hurled through mid-air and thrown at Sulla's feet. Others were dragged through the city and trampled on, none of the spectators daring to utter a word of remonstrance against these horrors. Banishment was inflicted upon some and confiscation upon others. Spies were searching everywhere for those who had fled from the city, and those whom they caught they killed.

96. There was much massacre, banishment, and confiscation also among those Italians who had obeyed Carbo, or Marius, or Norbanus, or their lieutenants. Severe judgments of the courts were rendered against them throughout all Italy on various charges—for exercising military command, for serving in the army, for contributing money, for rendering other service, or even giving counsel against Sulla. Hospitality, private friendship, the borrowing or lending of money, were alike accounted crimes. Now and then one would be arrested for doing a kindness to a suspect, or merely for being his companion on a journey. These accusations abounded mostly against the rich. When charges against individuals failed Sulla took vengeance on whole communities. He punished some of them by demolishing their citadels, or destroying their walls, or by imposing fines and crushing them by heavy contributions. Among most of them he placed colonies of his troops in order to hold Italy under garrisons, sequestrating their lands and houses and dividing them among his soldiers, whom he thus made true to him even after his death. As they could not be secure in their own holdings

unless all Sulla's system were on a firm foundation, they were his stoutest champions even after he died.

While the affairs of Italy were in this state, Pompey sent a force and captured Carbo, who had fled with many persons of distinction from Africa to Sicily and thence to the island of Cossyra. He ordered his officers to kill all of the others without bringing them into his presence; but Carbo, "the three times consul," he caused to be brought before his feet in chains, and after making a public harangue at him, murdered him and sent his head to Sulla.

97. When everything had been accomplished against his enemies as he desired, and there was no longer any hostile force except that of Sertorius, who was far distant, Sulla sent Metellus into Spain against him and seized upon everything in the city to suit himself. There was no longer any occasion for laws, or elections, or for casting lots, because everybody was shivering with fear and in hiding, or dumb. Everything that Sulla had done as consul, or as proconsul, was confirmed and ratified, and his gilded equestrian statue was erected in front of the rostra with the inscription, "Cornelius Sulla, the ever Fortunate," for so his flatterers called him on account of his unbroken success against his enemies. And this flattering title still attaches to him. I have come across a document which relates that Sulla was styled Epaphroditus by a decree of the Senate itself. This does not seem to me to be inappropriate for one of his names was Faustus (lucky), which name seems to have very nearly the same signification as Epaphroditus. There was also an oracle given to him somewhere which, in response to his question concerning the future, assured his prosperous career as follows:—

"Roman, believe me! On Aeneas' line
Cypris, its patron, sheddeth power divine;
To all the Immortals bring thy yearly gifts;
And chief to Delphi. But where Taurus lifts
His snowy side, and Carian men have walled
A far-spread town, from Aphrodite called,
There bring an Axe, and power supreme is thine!"

Whichever inscription the Romans voted when they erected the statue, they seem to me to have inscribed it either by way of jest or cajolery. However, Sulla did actually send a golden crown and axe to Venus with this inscription:—

This Axe to Aphrodite Sulla brought,
For in a dream he saw her as she fought
Queen of his host, full armed, and deeds of knighthood
    wrought.

98. Thus Sulla became king, or tyrant, *de facto,* not elected, but holding power by force and violence. As, however, he needed the pretence of being elected this too was managed in this way. The kings of the Romans in the olden time were chosen for their bravery, and whenever one of them died the senators held the royal power in succession for five days each, until the people should decide who should be the new king. This five-day ruler was called the Interrex, which means king for the time being. The retiring consuls always

presided over the election of their successors in office, and if there chanced to be no consul at such a time an Interrex was appointed for the purpose of holding the consular comitia. Sulla took advantage of this custom. There were no consuls at this time, Carbo having lost his life in Sicily and Marius in Praeneste. So Sulla went out of the city for a time and ordered the Senate to choose an Interrex.

They chose Valerius Flaccus, expecting that he would soon hold the consular comitia. But Sulla wrote ordering Flaccus to represent to the people his own strong opinion that it was to the immediate interest of the city to revive the dictatorship, an office which had now been in abeyance 400 years. He told them not to appoint the dictator for a fixed period, but until such time as he should firmly re-establish the city and Italy and the government generally, shattered as it was by factions and wars. That this proposal referred to himself was not at all doubtful, and Sulla made no concealment of it, declaring openly at the conclusion of the letter that, in his judgment, he could be most serviceable to the city in that capacity.

99. Such was Sulla's message. The Romans did not like it, but they had no more opportunities for elections according to law, and they considered that this matter was not altogether in their own power. So, in the general deadlock, they welcomed this pretence of an election as an image and semblance of freedom, and chose Sulla their absolute master for as long a time as he pleased.

61 Julius Caesar

The Man and the Statesman

"He doth bestride the narrow world/Like a colossus."
Shakespeare, *Julius Caesar* Act 1

Among the complex of problems that destroyed the Roman Republic, the immediate and most apparent one was the rise to supremacy of military leaders strong enough to defy constitution, Senate, and assembly alike. The deep-seated and largely unsolved issues that had arisen during more than a century of Roman expansion were fundamental to the decline of the Republic, but it was on the sword of the victorious and supremely powerful general that the Republic committed suicide.

The First Triumvirate (60–53 B.C.) was formed when three political strongmen—Julius Caesar, Pompey, and Crassus—relinquished their rivalry to

From *Suetonius: Vol. I, Lives of the Caesars*, Loeb Classical Library Vol. 31, translated by J. C. Rolfe, (Cambridge, Mass.: Harvard University Press, 1951, 1998). The Loeb Classical Library® is a registered trademark of the President and Fellows of Harvard College. Reprinted by permission of the publishers and the Trustees of the Loeb Classical Library.

control Rome in their own interests and in defiance of the constitution. After the death of Crassus, however, the Senate, scheming to regain power, won over Pompey with the intent of using him against Caesar and then destroying him. The results of the civil war that followed were not what the Senate had anticipated. Caesar emerged all-powerful and proceeded to manipulate the constitution to give himself absolute power for life. He was convinced that the events of the previous century had made the republican constitution unworkable, that, in his own words, "The Republic is nothing but a name, without substance or reality." It is easy to see a parallel between this situation and the question raised by Thucydides with regard to Athens: Is a democracy capable of running an empire?

During the short period of his dictatorship (46–44 B.C.), Caesar brought order throughout the Roman world. His constructive program of legislation and his colorful personality are described in the following selections from *The Lives of the Caesars* by Suetonius (ca. A.D. 75–ca. 150). Alexis de Tocqueville's famous characterization (1835) of Napoleon, "He was as great as a man can be without morality," is also applicable to Caesar.

The son of an army officer of the equestrian order, Suetonius held various imperial posts, including that of secretary to the emperor Hadrian, before he retired to a life of study and writing. Of his voluminous writings, only the *Lives*—the biographies of Julius Caesar and the first eleven emperors (Augustus to Domitian)—has survived entire, an indication of its early and continuing popularity. It is also an outstanding source of information on the early empire, for despite Suetonius' uncritical fondness for gossip and scandal, he frequently quotes contemporary documents and uses other sources of great value to the historian.

Coin legend proclaiming Julius Caesar as *Dictator perpetuo*, "Dictator in perpetuity." "The Republic is a mere name, without body or form."

Caesar the Statesman

40. Then [46 B.C.] turning his attention to the reorganization of the state, he reformed the calendar, which the pontiffs had long since so disordered, by neglecting to order the necessary intercalations, that the harvest festivals did not come in summer nor those of the vintage in the autumn. He adjusted the year to the sun's course by making it consist of 365 days, abolishing the intercalary month and adding one day every fourth year. Furthermore, that the correct reckoning of time might begin with the next Kalends [first day] of January, he inserted two additional months between November and December. Hence the year in which these arrangements were made was one of fifteen months, including the intercalary month which belonged to that year according to the former custom.

41. He filled the vacancies in the Senate by enrolling additional patricians, and increased the number of praetors, aediles, and quaestors as well as of minor officials. He reinstated those who had been degraded by official action of the censors or found guilty of electoral bribery by verdict of the jurors. He shared the elections with the people on this basis: that except in the case of the consulship, half of the magistrates should be appointed by the people's choice while the rest should be those whom he personally had nominated....

He made the enumeration of the people neither in the usual manner nor place, but from street to street aided by the owners of blocks of houses. He then reduced the number of those who received grain at public expense from 320,000 to 150,000 [adult citizen males], and to prevent the calling of additional meetings at any future time for purposes of enrollment, he provided that the places of such as died should be filled by lot each year by the praetor from those who were not on the list....

42. Moreover, ... he enacted a law ... that those who made a business of grazing should have among their herdsmen at least one third who were men of free birth. He conferred citizenship on all who practiced medicine at Rome, and on all teachers of the liberal arts, to make them more desirous of living in the city and to induce others to resort to it.

As to debts, he disappointed those who looked for their cancellation, which was often agitated, but finally decreed that the debtors should satisfy their creditors according to a valuation of their possessions at the price which they paid for them before the civil war, deducting from principal any interest that had been paid in cash or assigned in writing—an arrangement which wiped out about a fourth part of their indebtedness. He dissolved all associations, except those of ancient foundation. He increased the penalties for crimes; and inasmuch as the rich involved themselves in guilt with less hesitation because they merely suffered exile without any loss of property, he punished murderers of freemen by confiscation of all their goods, and murderers of others by the loss of half.

43. He administered justice with the utmost conscientiousness and strictness. Those convicted of extortion he even expelled from the senatorial order. He annulled the marriage of an ex-praetor who had married a woman the very day after her divorce, although there was no suspicion of adultery. He imposed

duties on foreign wares. He denied the use of litters and the wearing of scarlet robes or pearls to all except those of a designated position or age, and then only on fixed days. In particular he enforced the law against extravagance, setting watchmen in various parts of the market to seize and bring to him dainties which were exposed for sale in violation of the law; and sometimes he sent his lictors and soldiers to take from a dining room any articles which had escaped the vigilance of his watchmen, even after they had been served.

44. In particular, for the adornment and convenience of the city, also for the protection and extension of the empire, he formed more projects and more extensive ones every day: first of all, to rear a temple to Mars, greater than any in existence, filling up and leveling the pool in which he had exhibited the sea-fight, and to build a theater of vast size, sloping down from the Tarpeian rock; to reduce the civil code to fixed limits (of the vast and prolix mass of statutes to include only the best and most essential in a limited number of volumes); to open to the public the greatest possible libraries of Greek and Latin books, assigning to Marcus Varro the charge of procuring and classifying them; to drain the Pomptine marshes; to let out the water from Lake Fucinus; to make a highway from the Adriatic across the summit of the Apennines as far as the Tiber; to cut a canal through the Isthmus [of Corinth]; to check the Dacians, who had poured into Pontius and Thrace; then to make war on the Parthians by way of Lesser Armenia, but not to risk a battle with them until he had first tested their mettle.

All these enterprises and plans were cut short by his death. But before I speak of that, it will not be amiss to describe briefly his personal appearance, his dress, his mode of life, and his character, as well as his conduct in civil and military life.

Caesar the Man

45. He is said to have been tall of stature, with a fair complexion, shapely limbs, a somewhat full face, and keen black eyes; sound of health, except that towards the end he was subject to sudden fainting fits and to nightmare as well. He was twice attacked by the falling sickness during his campaigns. He was some-what overnice in the care of his person, being not only carefully trimmed and shaved, but even having superfluous hair plucked out, as some have charged; while his baldness was a disfigurement which troubled him greatly, since he found that it was often the subject of the gibes of his detractors. Because of it he used to comb forward his scanty locks from the crown of his head, and of all the honors voted him by the Senate and people there was none which he received or made use of more gladly than the privilege of wearing a laurel wreath at all times. They say, too, that he was fantastic in his dress; that he wore a senator's tunic with fringed sleeves reaching to the wrist, and always had a girdle over it, though rather a loose one; and this, they say, was the occasion of Sulla's *mot,* when he often warned the nobles to keep an eye on the ill-girt boy.

46. He lived at first in the Subura in a modest house, but after he became pontifex maximus, in the official residence on the Sacred Way. Many have

written that he was very fond of elegance and luxury; that having laid the foundations of a country-house on his estate at Nemi and finished it at great cost, he tore it all down because it did not suit him in every particular, although at the time he was still poor and heavily in debt; and that he carried tessellated and mosaic floors about with him on his campaigns.

47. They say that he was led to invade Britain by the hope of getting pearls, and that in comparing their size he sometimes weighed them with his own hand; that he was always a most enthusiastic collector of gems, carvings, statues, and pictures by early artists; also of slaves of exceptional figure and training at enormous prices of which he himself was so ashamed that he forbade their entry in his accounts....

50. That he was unbridled and extravagant in his intrigues is the general opinion, and that he seduced many illustrious women, among them Postumia, wife of Servius Sulpicius, Lollia, wife of Aulus Gabinius, Terrulla, wife of Marcus Crassus, and even Gnaeus Pompey's wife Mucia. At all events there is no doubt that Pompey was taken to task by the elder and the younger Curio, as well as by many others, because through a desire for power he had afterwards married the daughter of a man [Caesar] on whose account he divorced a wife who had borne him three children, and whom he had often referred to with a groan as an Aegisthus. But beyond all others Caesar loved Servilia, the mother of Marcus Brutus, for whom in his first consulship he bought a pearl costing six million sesterces. During the civil war, too, besides other presents, he knocked down some fine estates to her in a public auction at a nominal price, and when some expressed their surprise at the low figure, Cicero wittily remarked: "It's a better bargain than you think, for there is a third off." And in fact it was thought that Servilia was prostituting her own daughter Tertia ["Third"] to Caesar.

51. That he did not refrain from intrigues in the provinces is shown in particular by this couplet, which was also shouted by the soldiers in his Gallic triumph:

> Home we bring the bald adulterer: Romans, lock your
> wives away!
> Gold in Gaul he spent in dalliance, which he borrowed here
> in Rome.

52. He had love affairs with queens too, including Eunoe the Moor, wife of Bogudes, on whom, as well as on her husband, he bestowed many splendid presents, as Naso writes; but above all with Cleopatra, with whom he often feasted until daybreak, and he would have gone through Egypt with her in her state-barge almost to Aethiopia, had not his soldiers refused to follow him. Finally he called her to Rome and did not let her leave until he had ladened her with high honors and rich gifts, and he allowed her to give his name to the child which she bore. In fact, according to certain Greek writers, this child was very like Caesar in looks and carriage. Mark Antony declared to the Senate that Caesar had really acknowledged the boy, and that Gaius Matius, Gaius Oppius, and other friends of Caesar knew this. Of these Gaius Oppius, as if admitting that the situation required apology and defense, published a book, to prove that the child whom

Cleopatra fathered on Caesar was not his. Helvius Cinna, tribune of the commons, admitted to several that he had a bill drawn up in due form, which Caesar had ordered him to propose to the people in his absence, making it lawful for Caesar to marry what wives he wished, and as many as he wished, "for the purpose of begetting children." But to remove all doubt that he had an evil reputation both for shameless vice and for adultery, I have only to add that the elder Curio in one of his speeches calls him "every woman's man and every man's woman."

53. That he drank very little wine not even his enemies denied. There is a saying of Marcus Cato that Caesar was the only man who undertook to overthrow the state when sober. Even in the matter of food Gaius Oppius tells us that he was so indifferent, that once when his host served stale oil instead of fresh, and the other guests would have none of it, Caesar partook even more plentifully than usual, not to seem to charge his host with carelessness or lack of manners.

54. Neither when in command of armies nor as a magistrate at Rome did he show a scrupulous integrity; for as certain men have declared in their memoirs, when he was proconsul in Spain, he not only begged money from the allies, to help pay his debts, but also attacked and sacked some towns of the Lusitanians, although they did not refuse his terms and opened their gates to him on his arrival. In Gaul he pillaged shrines and temples of the gods filled with offerings, and oftener sacked towns for the sake of plunder than for any fault. In consequence he had more gold than he knew what to do with, and offered it for sale throughout Italy and the provinces at the [low] rate of three thousand sesterces the pound. In his first consulship he stole three thousand pounds of gold from the Capitol, replacing it with the same weight of gilded bronze. He made alliances and thrones a matter of barter, for he extorted from Ptolemy alone in his own name and that of Pompey nearly six thousand talents, while later on he met the heavy expenses of the civil wars and of his triumphs and entertainments by the most bare-faced pillage and sacrilege.

"The Art of War"

55. In eloquence and in the art of war he either equalled or surpassed the fame of the most eminent. After his accusation of Dolabella, he was without question numbered with the leading advocates. At all events when Cicero reviews the orators in his *Brutus,* he says that he does not see to whom Caesar ought to yield the palm, declaring that his style is elegant as well as brilliant, even grand and in a sense noble.... He is said to have delivered himself in a high-pitched voice with impassioned action and gestures, which were not without grace....

56. He left memoirs too of his deeds in the Gallic war and in the civil strife with Pompey.... With regard to Caesar's memoirs Cicero, also in the *Brutus,* speaks in the following terms: "He wrote memoirs which deserve the highest praise; they are naked in their simplicity, straightforward yet graceful, stripped of all rhetorical adornment, as of a garment; but while his purpose was to supply

material to others, on which those who wished to write history might draw, he perhaps gratified silly folk, who will try to use the curling-irons on his narrative, yet he has kept men of any sense from touching the subject." Of these same memoirs Hirtius uses this emphatic language: "They are so highly rated in the judgment of all men, that he seems to have deprived writers of an opportunity, rather than given them one; yet our admiration for this feat is greater than that of others; for they know how well and faultlessly he wrote, while we know besides how easily and rapidly he finished his task." Asinius Pollio thinks that they were put together somewhat carelessly and without strict regard for truth; since in many cases Caesar was too ready to believe the accounts which others gave of their actions, and he also gave a distorted account of his own, either designedly or perhaps from forgetfulness; and he thinks that he intended to rewrite and revise them....

57. He was highly skilled in arms and horsemanship, and of incredible powers of endurance. On the march he headed his army, sometimes on horseback, but oftener on foot, bareheaded both in the heat of the sun and in rain. He covered great distances with incredible speed, making a hundred miles a day in a hired carriage and with little baggage, swimming the rivers which barred his path or crossing them on inflated skins, and very often arriving before the messengers sent to announce his coming.

58. In the conduct of his campaigns it is a question whether he was more cautious or more daring, for he never led his army where ambuscades were possible without carefully reconnoitering the country, and he did not cross to Britain without making personal inquiries about the harbors, the course, and the approach to the island. But on the other hand, when news came that his camp in Germany was beleaguered, he made his way to his men through the enemies' pickets, disguised as a Gaul....

59. No regard for religion ever turned him from any undertaking, or even delayed him. Though the victim escaped as he was offering sacrifice, he did not put off his expedition against Scipio and Juba. Even when he had a fall as he disembarked, he gave the omen a favorable turn by crying: "I hold thee fast, Africa." Furthermore, to make the prophecies ridiculous which declared that the stock of the Scipios was fated to be fortunate and invincible in that province, he kept with him in camp a contemptible fellow belonging to the [same] Cornelian family, to whom the nickname Salvito ["Greetings! and goodby!"] had been given as a reproach for his manner of life.

60. He joined battle, not only after planning his movements in advance but on a sudden opportunity, often immediately at the end of a march, and sometimes in the foulest weather, when one would least expect him to make a move. It was not until his later years that he became slower to engage, through a conviction that the oftener he had been victor, the less he ought to tempt fate, and that he could not possibly gain as much by success as he might lose by a defeat. He never put his enemy to flight without also driving him from his camp, thus giving him no respite in his panic. When the issue was doubtful, he used to send away the horses, and his own among the first,

to impose upon his troops the greater necessity of standing their ground by taking away that aid to flight....

62. When his army gave way, he often rallied it single-handed, planting himself in the way of the fleeing men, laying hold of them one by one, and even catching them by the throat and forcing them to face the enemy; that, too, when they were in such a panic that an eagle-bearer made a pass at him with the point as he tried to stop him, while another left the standard in Caesar's hand when he would hold him back....

65. He valued his soldiers neither for their personal character nor their fortune, but solely for their prowess, and he treated them with equal strictness and indulgence; for he did not curb them everywhere and at all times, but only in the presence of the enemy. Then he required the strictest discipline, not announcing the time of a march or a battle, but keeping them ready and alert to be led on a sudden at any moment wheresoever he might wish. He often called them out even when there was no occasion for it, especially on rainy days and holidays....

67. He did not take notice of all their offenses or punish them by rule, but he kept a sharp lookout for deserters and mutineers, and chastised them most severely, shutting his eyes to other faults. Sometimes, too, after a great victory he relieved them of all duties and gave them full license to revel, being in the habit of boasting that his soldiers could fight well even when reeking of perfumes. In the assembly he addressed them not as "soldiers" but by the more flattering term "comrades," and he kept them in fine trim, furnishing them with arms inlaid with silver and gold, both for show and to make them hold fast to them in battle, through fear of the greatness of the loss. Such was his love for them that when he heard of the disaster to Titurius, he let his hair and beard grow long, and would not cut them until he had taken vengeance.

68. In this way he made them most devoted to his interests as well as most valiant. When he began the civil war, every centurion of each legion proposed to supply a horseman from his own allowance, and the soldiers one and all offered their service without pay and without rations, the richer assuming the care of the poorer. Throughout the long struggle not one deserted and many of them, on being taken prisoner, refused to accept their lives when offered them on the condition of consenting to serve against Caesar. They bore hunger and other hardships, both when in a state of siege and when besieging others, with such fortitude that when Pompey saw in the works at Dyrrachium a kind of bread made of herbs, on which they were living, he said that he was fighting wild beasts; and he gave orders that it be put out of sight quickly and shown to none of his men for fear that the endurance and resolution of the foe would break their spirit....

"By Nature Most Merciful"

74. Even in avenging wrongs he was by nature most merciful, ... When summoned as a witness against Publius Clodius, the paramour of his wife Pompeia, charged on the same count with sacrilege, Caesar declared that he had no evidence, although both his mother Aurelia and his sister Julia had given the same jurors a faithful account of the whole affair, and on being asked why it

was then that he had put away his wife he replied; "Because I maintain that the members of my family should be free from suspicion, as well as from guilt."

75. He certainly showed admirable self-restraint and mercy, both in his conduct of the civil war and in the hour of victory. While Pompey threatened to treat as enemies those who did not take up arms for the government, Caesar gave out that those who were neutral and of neither party should be numbered with his friends. He freely allowed all those whom he had made centurions on Pompey's recommendation to go over to his rival.... At the battle of Pharsalus he cried out, "Spare your fellow citizens," and afterwards allowed each of his men to save any one man he pleased of the opposite party. And it will be found that no Pompeian lost his life except in battle, save only Afranius and Faustus, and the young Lucius Caesar; and it is believed that not even these men were slain by his wish, even though the two former had taken up arms again after being pardoned, while Lucius Caesar had not only cruelly put to death the dictator's slaves and freedmen with fire and sword, but had even butchered the wild beasts which Caesar had procured for the entertainment of the people. At last, in his later years, he went so far as to allow all those whom he had not yet pardoned to return to Italy and to hold magistracies and the command of armies; and he actually set up the statues of Lucius Sulla and Pompey, which had been broken to pieces by the populace. After this, if any dangerous plots were formed against him, or slanders uttered, he preferred to quash them rather than to punish anyone. Accordingly, he took no further notice of the conspiracies which were detected, and of meetings by night, than to make known by proclamation that he was aware of them; and he thought it enough to give public warning to those who spoke ill of him not to persist in their conduct, bearing with good nature the attacks on his reputation made by the scurrilous volume of Aulus Caecina and the abusive lampoons of Pitholaus.

"He at Last Is Made Our King"

76. Yet after all, his other actions and words so turn the scale that it is thought that he abused his power and was justly slain. For not only did he accept excessive honors, such as an uninterrupted consulship, the dictatorship for life, and the censorship of public morals, as well as the forename Imperator, the surname of Father of his Country, a statue among those of the kings, and a raised couch in the orchestra; but he also allowed honors to be bestowed on him which were too great for mortal man: a golden throne in the Senate House and on the judgment seat; a chariot and litter in the procession at the circus; temples, altars, and statues beside those of the gods; a special priest, an additional college of the Luperci, and the calling of one of the months by his name. In fact, there were no honors which he did not receive or confer at pleasure.

He held his third and fourth consulships in name only, content with the power of the dictatorship conferred on him at the same time as the consulships. Moreover, in both years he substituted two consuls for himself for the last three months, in the meantime holding no elections except for tribunes and plebeian aediles, and appointing praefects instead of the praetors to manage the affairs of the city during his absence. When one of the consuls suddenly died the day before the Kalends of January, he gave the vacant office for a few hours to a man who asked for it. With the same disregard of law and precedent he named magistrates for several years to come, bestowed the emblems of consular rank on ten expraetors, and admitted to the Senate men who had been given citizenship— in some cases half-civilized Gauls. He assigned the charge of the mint and of the public revenues to his own slaves, and gave the oversight and command of the three legions which he had left at Alexandria to a favorite of his called Rufio, son of one of his freedmen.

77. No less arrogant were his public utterances, which Titus Ampius records: that the Republic was nothing, a mere name without body or form; that Sulla did not know his ABCs when he laid down his dictatorship; that men ought now to be more circumspect in addressing him, and to regard his word as law. So far did he go in his presumption that when a soothsayer once reported direful innards without a heart, he said: "They will be more favorable when I wish it; it should not be regarded as a portent, if a beast has no heart."

78. But it was the following action in particular that roused deadly hatred against him. When the Senate approached him in a body with many highly honorary decrees, he received them before the temple of Venus Genetrix without rising. Some think that when he attempted to get up, he was held back by Cornelius Balbus; others, that he made no such move at all, but on the contrary frowned angrily on Gaius Trebatius when he suggested that he should rise. And this action of his seemed the more intolerable, because when he himself in one of his triumphal processions rode past the benches of the tribunes, he was so incensed because a member of the college, Pontius Aquila by name, did not rise, that he cried: "Come then, Aquila, take back the Republic from me, you mighty tribune"; and for several days he would not make a promise to anyone without adding, "That is, if Pontius Aquila will allow me."

79. To an insult which so plainly showed his contempt for the Senate he added an act of even greater insolence. At the Latin Festival, as he was returning to the city amid the extravagant and unprecedented demonstrations of the populace, someone in the press placed on his statue a laurel wreath with a white fillet tied to it; and when Epidius Marullus and Caesetius Flavus, tribunes of the commons, gave orders that the ribbon be removed from the crown and the man taken off to prison, Caesar sharply rebuked and deposed them, either offended that the hint at regal power had been received with so little favor, or, as he asserted, that he had been robbed of the glory of refusing it. But from that time on he could not rid himself of the odium of having aspired to the title of monarch, although he replied to the commons, when they hailed him as king, "I am Caesar and no king," and at the Lupercalia, when the consul Antony several times attempted to place a crown upon his head as he spoke from the rostra, he put it aside and at last sent it to the Capitol to be offered to Jupiter Optimus Maximus. Nay, more, the report had spread in various quarters that he intended to move to Troy or Alexandria, taking with him the resources of the state, draining Italy by levies, and leaving it and the charge of the city to his friends; also that at the next meeting of the Senate Lucius Cotta would announce as the decision of the Fifteen [priests], that inasmuch as it was written in

the books of fate that the Parthians could be conquered only by a king, Caesar should be given that title.

80. It was this that led the conspirators to hasten in carrying out their designs, in order to avoid giving their assent to this proposal. Therefore the plots which had previously been formed separately, often by groups of two or three, were united in a general conspiracy, since even the populace no longer were pleased with present conditions, but both secretly and openly rebelled at his tyranny and cried out for defenders of their liberty. On the admission of foreigners to the Senate, a placard was posted: "God bless the Republic! Let no one consent to point out the Senate House to a newly made senator." The following verses too were sung everywhere:

> Caesar led the Gauls in triumph, led them to the Senate
>   House;
> There the Gauls pulled off their breeches, and put on the
>   purple gown.

When Quintus Maximus, whom he had appointed consul in his place for three months, was entering the theater and his lictor called attention to his arrival in the usual manner, a general shout was raised: "He's no consul!" At the first election after the deposing of Caesetius and Marullus, the tribunes, several votes were found for their appointment as consuls. Some wrote on the base of Lucius Brutus' statue, "If only you were still alive"; and on that of Caesar himself.

> Brutus was elected consul, since he drove the kings from
>   Rome;
> Since this man drove out the consuls, he at last is now our
>   king.

More than sixty joined the conspiracy against him, led by Gaius Cassius and Marcus and Decimus Brutus.

62 Cicero as Champion of Liberty

The Second Philippic

The assassination of Julius Caesar on the Ides (15th) of March, 44 B.C., served only to set the stage for yet another round of civil wars. For a few months, the Senate reasserted control by means of "divide and conquer." With Cicero again playing a leading role, it first outmaneuvered Mark Antony, Caesar's

From *Second Philippic*, 1, 25–30, 112–14, 116–19, based on the translation by C. D. Yonge.

lieutenant and colleague in the consulship, and then, with the decisive assistance of the young Octavian (the future Augustus) and his legions, defeated
him in battle and forced him to flee Italy. Exultant hopes for a new era of
republican constitutionalism were short-lived, however. Once Antony no longer seemed a danger, the Senate slighted Octavian—"The young man is to
be praised, honored, and set aside," advised Cicero—with the result that he
joined with Antony and Lepidus in forming a new military dictatorship, the
Second Triumvirate.

During the struggle with Antony, Cicero assumed the role of a second
Demosthenes fighting for liberty against another Philip (Selection 34A). He
denounced Antony in a series of fourteen *Philippic Orations,* thereby assuring
his own death at the hands of Antony's agents during the proscriptions that
followed the establishment of the Second Triumvirate. The following selection from the *Second Philippic,* the most famous of the series, is both a
good example of the powerful invective directed at Antony (and at the late
Julius Caesar as well), and a last eloquent statement of the higher ideals
that underlay Cicero's attachment to the Republic. Because Cicero's political
career had ended as it had begun, fighting despotism, two generations later
the historian Velleius Paterculus could confidently predict, in a passage
directed against Mark Antony, "He lives and will live in the memory of all succeeding ages.... All posterity will admire his writings against you, and execrate your conduct toward him; and sooner shall the race of man fail in the
world, than his name decay."

To what destiny of mine, gentlemen of the Senate, shall I attribute it that no one
for the last twenty years has been an enemy of the Republic without at the same
time declaring war against me? Nor is there any necessity for naming any particular person; you yourselves recollect instances in proof of my statement. They
have all suffered severer punishments than I could have wished for them; but I
marvel that you, Antony, do not shudder at the end of those men whose conduct you are imitating. And in the case of the others I had less cause for wonder.
None of those men was a personal enemy of mine; all of them were attacked by
me for the sake of the Republic. But you, who have never been injured by me,
not even by a word, in order to appear more audacious than Catiline, more mad
than Clodius, have of your own accord attacked me with abuse, and have considered that your break with me would be a recommendation of you to disloyal
citizens.

What am I to think? That I am despised? I see nothing earlier in my life, or
in my influence in the city, or in my exploits, or even in the moderate abilities
with which I am endowed, which Antony can despise. Did he think that it was
easiest to slander me in the Senate, a body which has borne testimony to many
most illustrious citizens because they governed the Republic well, but to me
alone of all men because I saved it? Or did he wish to contend with me in the
field of oratory? That, indeed, is an act of generosity! For what could be a more
fertile or richer subject for me than to speak in defense of myself and against
Antony?...

Cicero next takes up various charges (omitted here) made by Antony against him, including the charge that Cicero caused the war between Caesar and Pompey.

But that is ancient history. This charge, however, is quite new, that Caesar was slain by my advice. I am afraid, gentlemen of the Senate, lest I should appear to you to have planted a sham accuser against myself (which is a most disgraceful thing to do)—a man not only to distinguish me by the praises which are my due, but to load me also with, those which do not belong to me. For who ever heard my name mentioned as an accomplice in that most glorious deed? And whose name has ever been concealed among the number of that gallant band? Concealed, did I say? Whose name was not at once made public? I would be more inclined to say that some had boasted in order to appear to have been members of that conspiracy, though they had really known nothing of it, than that anyone who had been an accomplice in it would have wished his name concealed. Moreover, how likely is it that among so many men, some obscure, some young, all courting publicity, my name could possibly have escaped notice?

Indeed, if leaders were needed for the liberation of the country, what need was there of my instigating the two Bruti, one of whom saw every day in his house the bust of Lucius Brutus [Selection 48B] and the other that of Ahala [who in 439 B.C. killed Spurius Maelius for aspiring to tyranny]? Were these the men to seek counsel from the ancestors of others rather than their own, and from outside rather than at home? What? Caius Cassius, a man of that family which could not tolerate, I do not say the supremacy, but even the authority of others—he, I suppose, needed my encouragement? ... Was Cnacus Domitius spurred on to seek the recovery of liberty, not by the death of his father, a most illustrious man, nor by the death of his uncle, nor by his own loss of office, but by my influence? Did I persuade Caius Trebonius? I would not have ventured even to suggest it. The Republic owes him even a greater debt of gratitude, because he preferred the liberty of the Roman people to the friendship of one man, and because he preferred overthrowing tyranny to collaborating with it.... It would take a long time to go through all the rest; it is a glorious thing for the Republic, and a most honorable thing for themselves, that they were so numerous.

But consider how this shrewd investigator has convicted me. "When Caesar was slain," he says, "Marcus Brutus immediately lifted high his bloody dagger, called on Cicero by name, and congratulated him on the recovery of liberty." Why on me of all people? Because I knew of the plot? Consider whether this was not his reason for calling on me: when he had performed a deed very like that which I myself had done, he called me especially to witness that he had been an imitator of my glorious exploit.... What does it matter whether I wished it done or rejoiced that it was done? Is there anyone then, except those men who wished him to become a king, who was unwilling that the deed should be done or who disapproved of it after it was done? All men, therefore, are guilty. For all good men, to the best of their ability, had a part in the slaying of Caesar. Some had no plan, some had no courage, some had no opportunity—everyone had the desire....

However, we will say no more of what is past. But today, this very day that now is, this very moment while I am speaking, defend your conduct during this very moment, if you can. Why is the Senate surrounded by a belt of armed men? Why are your henchmen listening to me sword in hand? Why are not the doors of the Temple of Concord open? Why do you bring Ityreans, the most barbarous of all tribes, into the forum armed with arrows? He says he does so as a guard. Is it not better to perish a thousand times than to be unable to live in one's own city without an armed guard? But believe me, there is no protection in that—a man must be defended by the affection and good will of his fellow-citizens, not by arms....

But if you are not afraid of brave men and good citizens because they are prevented from attacking you by an armed guard, still, believe me, your own followers will not long put up with you. And what a life it is, day and night to fear danger from your own followers! Unless, of course, you have men who are bound to you by greater obligations than Caesar had from some of those by whom he was slain; or unless there are any aspects in which you can be compared with him.

In that man were combined genius, logic, memory, literary talent, prudence, deliberation, and industry. He had performed exploits in war which, though calamitous for the Republic, were nevertheless mighty deeds. Having for many years aimed at absolute power, he had with great labor and much personal danger accomplished what he intended. He had conciliated the ignorant crowd by shows, public works, gifts of food, and banquets; he had bound his own party to him by rewards, his adversaries by a show of clemency. In short, he had already brought to a free community the habit of slavery, partly out of fear, partly out of passiveness.

With him I can, indeed, compare you as to your passion for power, but in all other respects you are in no way comparable. Bur from the many evils which he has inflicted upon the Republic there is this good: the Roman people have learned how much to believe each man, to whom to entrust itself, and against whom to be on guard. Do you never think of these things? And do you not realize that it is enough for brave men to have learned how noble in act, how welcome in benefit, how glorious in fame, it is to slay a tyrant? Believe me, the time will come when men will compete with one another to do this deed, and when no one will wait for the tardy arrival of an opportunity.

Recover your senses sometime, I beg of you. Think of the family of which you are born, not of the men with whom you associate. Treat me as you will, but be reconciled to the Republic. But decide on your own conduct; I myself will declare what mine shall be. I defended the Republic in my youth, I will not desert it now that I am old. I scorned the sword of Catiline, I will not dread yours. No, I will gladly offer my body if the liberty of the state can be restored by my death and the pangs of the Roman people at last give birth to that which it has so long been in labor. Indeed, if twenty years ago in this very temple I asserted that death could not come prematurely to a man of consular rank, with how much more truth can I now say the same of an old man? To me,

Conscript Fathers, death is now even desirable, after all the honors I have gained and the deeds I have done. I pray only for these two things: one, that dying I may leave the Roman people free—no greater boon than this can be granted me by the immortal gods. The other, that each man may meet with a fate suitable to his deserts and conduct toward the Republic.

SELECTED BACKGROUND READING

Ernst Badian, *Roman Imperialism in the Late Republic*, 2nd ed. (Oxford: Oxford University Press, 1968).

Mary Beard and Michael Crawford, *Rome in the Late Republic: Problems and Interpretations* (London: Duckworth, 1985).

Peter A. Brunt, *Social Conflicts in the Roman Republic* (London: Chatto & Windus, 1971).

Timothy J. Cornell, *The Beginnings of Rome: Italy and the Rome from the Bronze Age to the Punic Wars* (c. 1000–264 BC) (London: Routledge, 1995).

Michael Crawford, *The Roman Republic*, 2nd ed. (Cambridge, Mass.: Harvard University Press, 1993).

Harriet I. Flower, *The Cambridge Companion of the Roman Republic* (Cambridge, U.K.: Cambridge University Press, 2004).

William V. Harris, *War and Imperialism in Republican Rome, 327–70 B.C.* (Oxford: Oxford University Press, 1979).

Claude Nicolet, *The World of the Citizen in Republican Rome* (Berkeley: University of California Press, 1980).

Elizabeth Rawson, *Intellectual Life in the Late Roman Republic* (Baltimore, Maryland: Johns Hopkins University Press, 1985).

Roman Civilization. Selected Readings, vol. I, *The Republic and the Augustan Age*, edited by Naphthali Lewis and Meyer Reinhold. (New York: Columbia University Press, 1990).

CHAPTER V

The Roman Empire

You, O Roman, remember to rule the nations with might.
This will be your genius—to impose the way of peace,
to spare the conquered and crush the proud.

—VIRGIL, *Aeneid*

Detail of the imperial family on the sculpted frieze of Augustus' "Altar of Peace," Rome.

The victory of Octavian, later known by his portentous title Augustus, put an end to the civil wars of the Late Roman Republic. His arrival also brought an end to republican government itself, even though many of its formal institutions were maintained. Augustus governed the vast Roman world with the cooperation of the Roman senators and ushered in what later historians called the Roman Empire. During the Imperial period, the Romans consolidated their hold over the entire Mediterranean under the rule of the emperors. For those free inhabitants who lived within the protected center of this empire, a remarkable degree of wealth and prosperity prevailed. Rome had transformed the Mediterranean world from an area of many, often warring, states to an integrated and largely peaceful realm—the *Pax Romana*.

Many contemporaries took notice of the importance of such a change. For some, the words of the poet Virgil depicted Rome appropriately as "a new hope for the human race, a hope of peace, of order, of civilization." Both rulers and subjects prided themselves on this ideal, which in the second century A.D. seemed eminently real. The Greek orator Aelius Aristides could thus address the Roman people: "Before the establishment of your empire, the world was in confusion, upside down, adrift and out of control; but as soon as you Romans intervened the turmoil and factions ceased, and life and politics were illumined by the dawn of an era of universal order." This "Roman Peace," backed by military force, allowed for the even greater achievements and prosperity of the High Roman Empire in the second century A.D. Edward Gibbon, the late eighteenth-century rationalist and author of the *Decline and Fall of the Roman Empire*, called this period the "Golden Age of Man."

Readings in this chapter are arranged thematically, as follows: Foundations of the Principate; Romans and Non-Romans in the *Pax Romana*; Society, Women, Family, and Roman Slave Society; and Philosophy and Religion.

Foundations of the Principate

63 Augustus

The Achievements of the Deified Augustus

" … attained supreme power by universal consent."

Octavian came to power in a context of civil wars. He was adopted as son and private heir by his uncle Gaius Julius Caesar. Becoming a warlord at the age of nineteen, he consolidated his own power as he first formed alliances with and later eliminated political rivals. Finally, defeating the forces of Mark Antony and Cleopatra VII, the last Macedonian queen of Ptolemaic Egypt, he became supreme in the Roman world. Octavian adopted the title of Augustus, which was granted to him by the Roman Senate, and claimed that he had restored the Republic. The system of rule he established was called the Principate, and involved—at least on a formal level—the political cooperation between the *princeps* (i.e., himself) and the Roman Senate, traditionally the most influential ruling body during the Republic.

The complicated nature of the Principate is spelled out in the following selection. It is important to understand that, at this time, there was no such thing as a clearly defined office of the emperor. Augustus was involved in the process of inventing that position and did so through a series of ad hoc measures. What he accomplished, and the way in which he accomplished his deeds, became important precedents for Roman emperors for centuries to come. This remarkable document, part autobiography, part *curriculum vitae*, was composed by Augustus toward the end of his long career, when he was seventy-six years old, to document his many contributions to the Roman state. By his order, the text was engraved on stone and the inscriptions were displayed in public in Rome as well as in various cities of the Roman world. The present text is based mainly on the Latin original and Greek translation found on an exterior wall of the Temple of Rome and Augustus in the city of Ancyra (Ankara, Turkey).

… 1. At the age of nineteen, on my own initiative and at my own expense, I raised an army by means of which I liberated the Republic, which was

From *Roman Civilization: Selected Readings*, Volume 1, 3rd ed., edited by Naphtali Lewis and Meyer Reinhold. © 1990 by Columbia University Press. Reprinted with the permission of the publisher.

oppressed by the tyranny of a faction. For which reason the senate, with honor-ific decrees, made me a member of its order in the consulship of Gaius Pansa and Aulus Hirtius [43 B.C.], giving me at the same time consular rank in voting, and granted me the *imperium*. It ordered me as propraetor, together with the consuls, to see to it that the state suffered no harm. Moreover, in the same year, when both consuls had fallen in the war, the people elected me consul and a triumvir for the settlement of the commonwealth.

2. Those who assassinated my father I drove into exile, avenging their crime by due process of law; and afterwards when they waged war against the state, I conquered them twice on the battlefield [the two battles of Phillippi (42 B.C.)].

3. I waged many wars throughout the whole world by land and by sea, both civil and foreign, and when victorious I spared all citizens who sought pardon. Foreign peoples who could safely be pardoned I preferred to spare rather than to extirpate. About 500,000 Roman citizens were under military oath to me. Of these, when their terms of service were ended, I settled in colonies or sent back to their own municipalities a little more than 300,000, and to all of these I allotted lands or granted money as rewards for military service. I captured 600 ships, exclusive of those which were of smaller class than triremes.

4. Twice I celebrated ovations, three times curule triumphs, and I was acclaimed *imperator* twenty-one times. When the senate decreed additional triumphs to me, I declined them on four occasions. I deposited in the Capitol laurel wreaths adorning my *fasces,* after fulfilling the vows which I had made in each war. For suc-cesses achieved on land and on sea by me or through my legates under my auspices the senate decreed fifty-five times that thanksgiving be offered to the immortal gods. Moreover, the number of days on which, by decree of the senate, such thanksgiving was offered, was 890. In my triumphs there were led before my char-iot nine kings or children of kings. At the time I wrote this, I had been consul thir-teen times, and I was in the thirty-seventh year of my tribunician power [A.D. 14].

5. The dictatorship offered to me in the consulship of Marcus Marcellus and Lucius Arruntius [22 B.C.] by the people and by the senate, both in my absence and in my presence, I refused to accept. In the midst of a critical scarcity of grain I did not decline the supervision of the grain supply, which I so administered that within a few days I freed the whole people from imminent panic and danger by my expenditures and efforts. The consulship, too, which was offered to me at that time as an annual office for life, I refused to accept.

6. In the consulship of Marcus Vinicius and Quintus Lucretius, and again in that of Publius Lentulus and Gnaeus Lentulus, and a third time in that of Paullus Fabius Maximus and Quintus Tubero [in 19, 18, and 11 B.C.], though the Roman senate and people unitedly agreed that I should be elected sole guardian of the laws and morals with supreme authority, I refused to accept any office offered me which was contrary to the traditions of our ancestors. The measures which the senate desired at that time to be taken by me I carried out by virtue of the tribunician power....

7. I was a member of the triumvirate for the settlement of the common-wealth for ten consecutive years. I have been ranking senator for forty years, up to the day on which I wrote this document. I have been *pontifex maximus,* augur,

member of the college of fifteen for performing sacrifices, member of the college of seven for conducting religious banquets, member of the Arval Brotherhood, one of the *Titii sodales,* and a fetial [priest].

8. ... By new legislation which I sponsored I restored many traditions of our ancestors which were falling into desuetude in our generation; and I myself handed down precedents in many spheres for posterity to imitate.

9. The senate decreed that vows for my health should be offered up every fifth year by the consuls and priests. In fulfillment of these vows, games were often celebrated during my lifetime.... Moreover, the whole citizen body, with one accord, both individually and as members of municipalities, prayed continuously for my health at all the shrines.

10. My name was inserted, by decree of the senate, in the hymn of the Salian priests. And it was enacted by law that I should be sacrosanct in perpetuity and that I should possess the tribunician power as long as I live. I declined to become *pontifex maximus* in place of a colleague while he was still alive, when the people offered me that priesthood, which my father had held. A few years later, in the consulship of Publius Sulpicius and Gaius Valgius, I accepted the priesthood, when death removed the man who [had] taken possession of it at a time of civil disturbance; and from all Italy a multitude flocked to my election such as had never previously been recorded at Rome....

12. ... When I returned to Rome from Spain and Gaul in the consulship of Tiberius Nero and Publius Quintilius [13 B.C.], after successfully settling the affairs of those provinces, the senate, to commemorate my return, ordered an altar of the Augustan Peace to be consecrated in the Campus Martius, on which it decreed that the magistrates, priests, and Vestal Virgins should make an annual sacrifice.

13. The temple of Janus Quirinus, which our ancestors desired to be closed whenever peace with victory was secured by sea and by land throughout the entire empire of the Roman people, and which before I was born is recorded to have been closed only twice since the founding of the city, was during my principate three times ordered by the senate to be closed.

14. My sons Gaius and Lucius Caesar, whom fortune took from me in their youth, were, in my honor, made consuls designate by the Roman senate and people when they were fifteen years old, with permission to enter that magistracy after a period of five years. The senate further decreed that from that day on which they were introduced into the Forum, they should attend its debates. Moreover, the whole body of Roman *equites* presented each of them with silver shields and spears and saluted each as *princeps iuventutis.*

15. To the Roman plebs I paid 300 sesterces apiece in accordance with the will of my father [i.e., Julius Caesar]; and in my fifth consulship [29 B.C.] I gave each 400 sesterces in my own name out of the spoils of war; and a second time in my tenth consulship [24 B.C.] I paid out of my own patrimony a largess of 400 sesterces to every individual; in my eleventh consulship [23 B.C.] I made twelve distributions of food out of grain purchased at my own expense; and in the twelfth year of my tribunician power [12 B.C.] for the third time I gave 400 sesterces to every individual. These largesses of mine reached never less than 250,000 persons. In the eighteenth year of my tribunician power and my twelfth

consulship [5 B.C.] I gave sixty *denarii* to each of 320,000 persons of the urban plebs. And in my fifth consulship [29 B.C.] I gave out of the spoils of war 1,000 sesterces apiece to my soldiers settled in colonies. This largess on the occasion of my triumph was received by about 120,000 persons in the colonies. In my thirteenth consulship [2 B.C.] I gave sixty *denarii* apiece to those of the plebs who at that time were receiving public grain; the number involved was a little more than 200,000 persons.

16. I reimbursed municipalities for the lands which I assigned to my soldiers in my fourth consulship, and afterwards in the consulship of Marcus Crassus and Gnaeus Lentulus the augur [30 and 14 B.C.]. The sums involved were about 600,000,000 sesterces which I paid for Italian estates, and about 260,000,000 sesterces which I paid for provincial lands....

17. Four times I came to the assistance of the treasury with my own money, transferring to those in charge of the treasury 150,000,000 sesterces. And in the consulship of Marcus Lepidus and Lucius Arruntius [A.D. 6] I transferred out of my own patrimony 170,000,000 sesterces ... for the purpose of providing bonuses for soldiers who had completed twenty or more years of service.

18. From the year in which Gnaeus Lentulus and Publius Lentulus [18 B.C.] were consuls, whenever the provincial taxes fell short, in the case sometimes of 100,000 persons and sometimes of many more, I made up their tribute in grain and in money from my own grain stores and my own patrimony.

19. I built the following structures: the senate house and the Chalcidicum adjoining it; the temple of Apollo on the Palatine with its porticoes; the temple of the deified Julius; the Lupercal; the portico at the Circus Flaminius, which I allowed to be called Octavia after the name of the man who had built an earlier portico on the same site; the state box at the Circus Maximus; the temples of Jupiter the Smiter and Jupiter the Thunderer on the Capitoline; the temple of Quirinus; the temples of Minerva and Queen Juno and of Jupiter Freedom on the Aventine; the temple of the Lares at the head of the Sacred Way; the temple of the Penates on the Velia; the temple of Youth and the temple of the Great Mother on the Palatine.

20. I repaired the Capitol and the theater of Pompey with enormous expenditures on both works, without having my name inscribed on them. I repaired the conduits of the aqueducts which were falling into ruin in many places because of age, and I doubled the capacity of the aqueduct called Marcia by admitting a new spring into its conduit. I completed the Julian Forum and the basilica which was between the temple of Castor and the temple of Saturn, works begun and far advanced by my father.... In my sixth consulship [28 B.C.] I repaired eighty-two temples of the gods in the city, in accordance with a resolution of the senate, neglecting none which at that time required repair. In my seventh consulship [27 B.C.] I reconstructed the Flaminian Way from the city as far as Ariminum, and also all the bridges except the Mulvian and the Minucian....

22. I gave a gladiatorial show three times in my own name, and five times in the names of my sons or grandsons; at these shows about 10,000 fought. Twice I presented to the people in my own name an exhibition of athletes invited from all parts of the world, and a third time in the name of my grandson. I presented

games in my own name four times, and in addition twenty-three times in the place of other magistrates. On behalf of the college of fifteen, as master of that college, with Marcus Agrippa as my colleague, I celebrated the Secular Games in the consulship of Gaius Furnius and Gaius Silanus…. Twenty-six times I provided for the people, in my own name or in the names of my sons or grandsons, hunting spectacles of African wild beasts in the circus or in the Forum or in the amphitheaters; in these exhibitions about 3,500 animals were killed.

23. I presented to the people an exhibition of a naval battle across the Tiber where the grove of the Caesars now is, having had the site excavated 1,800 feet in length and 1,200 feet in width. In this exhibition thirty beaked ships, triremes or biremes, and in addition a great number of smaller vessels engaged in combat. On board these fleets, exclusive of rowers, there were about 3,000 combatants.

24. When I was victorious I replaced in the temples of all the communities of the province of Asia the ornaments which my opponent [Mark Antony] in the war had seized for his private use after despoiling the temples….

25. I brought peace to the sea by suppressing the pirates. In that war I turned over to their masters for punishment nearly 30,000 slaves who had run away from their owners and taken up arms against the state. The whole of Italy voluntarily took an oath of allegiance to me and demanded me as its leader in the war in which I was victorious at Actium. The same oath was taken by the provinces of the Gauls, the Spains, Africa, Sicily, and Sardinia. More than 700 senators served at that time under my standards; of that number eighty-three attained the consulship and about 170 obtained priesthoods, either before that date or subsequently, up to the day on which this document was written.

26. I extended the frontiers of all the provinces of the Roman people on whose boundaries were peoples not subject to our empire. I restored peace to the Gallic and Spanish provinces and likewise to Germany, that is to the entire region bounded by the Ocean from Gades to the mouth of the Elbe river. I caused peace to be restored in the Alps, from the region nearest to the Adriatic Sea as far as the Tuscan Sea, without undeservedly making war against any people. My fleet sailed the Ocean from the mouth of the Rhine eastward as far as the territory of the Cimbrians, to which no Roman previously had penetrated either by land or by sea. The Cimbrians, the Charydes, the Semnones, and other German peoples of the same region through their envoys sought my friendship and that of the Roman people. At my command and under my auspices two armies were led almost at the same time into Ethiopia and into Arabia which is called Felix; and very large forces of the enemy belonging to both peoples were killed in battle, and many towns were captured. In Ethiopia a penetration was made as far as the town of Napata, which is next to Meroe; in Arabia the army advanced into the territory of the Sabaeans to the town of Mariba.

27. I added Egypt to the empire of the Roman people….

28. I established colonies of soldiers in Africa, Sicily, Macedonia, in both Spanish provinces, in Achaea, Asia, Syria, Narbonese Gaul, and Pisidia. Italy, moreover, has twenty-eight colonies established by me, which in my lifetime have grown to be famous and populous.

29. A number of military standards lost by other generals I recovered, after conquering the enemy, from Spain, Gaul, and the Dalmatians. The Parthians I

compelled to restore to me the spoils and standards of three Roman armies and to seek the friendship of the Roman people as suppliants. The standards, moreover, I deposited in the inner shrine of the temple of Mars Ultor [the Avenger]....

31. Royal embassies from India, never previously seen before any Roman general, were often sent to me. Our friendship was sought through ambassadors by the Bastarnians and Scythians and by the kings of the Sarmatians, who live on both sides of the Don River, and by the kings of the Albanians and of the Iberians and of the Medes....

32. ... Under my principate numerous other peoples, with whom previously there had existed no exchange of embassies and friendship, experienced the good faith of the Roman people....

34. In my sixth and seventh consulships, after I had put an end to the civil wars, having attained supreme power by universal consent, I transferred the state from my own power to the control of the Roman senate and the people. For this service of mine I received the title of Augustus by decree of the senate, and the doorposts of my house were publicly decked with laurels, the civic crown was affixed over my doorway, and a golden shield was set up in the Julian senate house, which, as the inscription on this shield testifies, the Roman senate and people gave me in recognition of my valor, clemency, justice, and devotion. After that time I excelled all in authority, but I possessed no more power than the others who were my colleagues in each magistracy.

35. When I held my thirteenth consulship, the senate, the equestrian order, and the entire Roman people gave me the title of "father of the country" and decreed that this title should be inscribed in the vestibule of my house, in the Julian senate house, and in the Augustan Forum on the pedestal of the chariot which was set up in my honor by decree of the senate. At the time I wrote this document I was in my seventy-sixth year.

64 Augustus' Reconstruction of the Roman World

Contrasting Estimates

The murder of Julius Caesar was in part a reaction to his growing leanings toward despotism and, although it led to a resumption of civil war, it was not wholly in vain. It demonstrated the tenacity with which republican or

From *Dio Cassius:* Vol. VI, *Roman History,* Loeb Classical Library Vol. 83, translated by Earnest Cary (Cambridge, Mass.: Harvard University Press, 1917). The Loeb Classical Library® is a registered trademark of the President and Fellows of Harvard College. Reprinted by permission of the publishers and the Trustees of the Loeb Classical Library.

antimonarchic traditions still maintained themselves at Rome and so helped to determine the final settlement established by Augustus after his victory over Antony and Cleopatra at Actium (31 B.C.). That decisive battle, in fact, was pictured by Romans as a victory of the old Roman way of life over the autocratic forces of orientalism represented by Antony's "paramour," Cleopatra, "with her polluted crew of creatures foul with lust." Accordingly, Augustus claimed that his system of government, known in history as the Principate—from *princeps* ("leader"), Augustus' favorite title—was in essence a restoration of the Republic. "May it be my privilege to establish the Republic safe and sound on its foundations," Suetonius reports him as saying, "gathering the fruit of my desire to be known as the author of the best possible constitution, and taking with me to the grave the hope that the foundation that I have laid will be permanent."

The nature of this "best possible constitution" has been the subject of debate ever since. Were Augustus' words sincerely uttered and was he really a true republican who reluctantly kept for himself only such power as would ensure the continued operation of the constitution and prevent a return to anarchy? Or was he at heart a tyrant who skillfully camouflaged his autocratic powers under republican forms? Modern scholars are still debating the question in much the same fashion as did the ancient Romans, whose divergent views are indicated in the following selections.

A. DIO CASSIUS: THE "TRUE DEMOCRACY" OF THE ROMAN EMPIRE

In attempting to understand the constitutional settlement that Augustus imposed upon Rome at the end of the civil wars, the remarkable document that purports to be the advice given to Augustus by Maecenas, the richest capitalist in Rome, deserves study. It is found in the *Roman History* of Dio Cassius (ca. A.D. 155–235), a Greek from Nicaea in Asia Minor who had a long career in governmental service, both at Rome and in the provinces. The speech of Maecenas is Dio's own invention, a favorite device of ancient historians since Herodotus and Thucydides. But because of Dio's insight into political and constitutional matters, even though the words and ideas expressed are his, there is little reason to doubt that they reflect the advice that men like Maecenas gave to Augustus. ("You labor to perfect the pattern of government," Horace, a contemporary, wrote in an ode [III, 29] addressed to Maecenas.) No one in Roman times seems to have doubted their appropriateness, and the reforms of Augustus were in line with such advice.

The essence of Maecenas' argument is that the old-style politics of the Republic is to be distrusted and should be replaced by the joint rule of Augustus and "the other best citizens." The constitution will continue to be called a *res publica* and the emphasis will still be upon liberty, but this will be the "true" liberty that can guarantee order and the welfare of all classes in the state.

Modeled after an early Greek statue by the celebrated sculptor Polykleitus, the imposing first century "Prima Porta Augustus" statue represents the emperor as a semi-divine, heroic figure. His military costume includes an elaborate cuirass or breast-plate, the center of which features a Parthian handing back Roman military standards captured in earlier wars. Now in the Vatican Museum.

"Put an End to the Insolence of the Populace"

14. ... If you feel any concern at all for your country, for which you have fought so many wars and would so gladly given even your life, reorganize it and regulate it in the direction of greater moderation. For while the privilege of doing and saying precisely what one pleases becomes, in the case of sensible persons, if you examine the matter, a cause of the highest happiness to them all, yet in the case of the foolish it becomes a cause for disaster. For this reason he who offers this privilege to the foolish is virtually putting a sword in the hands of a child or a madman.... Therefore I ask you not to fix your gaze upon the specious terms applied to these things and thus be deceived, but to weigh carefully the results which come from the things themselves and then put an end to the insolence of the populace and place the management of public affairs in the hands of yourself and the other best citizens, to the end that the business of deliberation may be performed by the most prudent and that of ruling by those best fitted for command, while the work of serving in the army for pay is left to those who are strongest physically and most needy. In this way each class of citizens will zealously discharge the duties which devolve upon them and will readily render to one another such services as are due, and will thus be unaware of

their inferiority when one class is at a disadvantage as compared with another, and all will gain the true democracy and the freedom which does not fail. For the boasted freedom of the mob proves in experience to be the bitterest servitude of the best element to the other and brings upon both a common destruction; whereas this freedom of which I speak everywhere prefers for honor the men of prudence, awarding at the same time equality to all according to their deserts, and thus gives happiness impartially to all who enjoy this liberty.

15. For I would not have you think that I am advising you to enslave the people and the Senate and then set up a tyranny. This is a thing I should never dare suggest to you nor would you bring yourself to do it. The other course, however, would be honorable and expedient both for you and for the city— that you should yourself, in consultation with the best men, enact all the appropriate laws, without the possibility of any opposition or remonstrance to these laws on the part of anyone from the masses; that you and your counsellors should conduct the wars according to your own wishes, all other citizens rendering instant obedience to your commands; that the choice of the officials should rest with you and your advisers; and that you and they should also determine the honors and the punishments. The advantage of all this would be that whatever pleased you in consultation with your peers would immediately become law; that our wars against our enemies would be waged with secrecy and at the opportune time; that those to whom any task was entrusted would be appointed because of their merit and not as the result of the lot or rivalry for office; that the good would be honored without arousing jealousy and the bad punished without causing rebellion. Thus whatever business was done would be most likely to be managed in the right way, instead of being referred to the popular assembly, or deliberated upon openly, or entrusted to factions, or exposed to ambitious rivalry; and we should be happy in the enjoyment of the blessings which belong to us, instead of being embroiled in hazardous wars abroad or in unholy civil strife. For these are the evils found in every democracy—since the more powerful men, in reaching out after the primacy and hiring the weaker, turn everything upside down—but they have been most frequent in our country, and there is no other way to put a stop to them than the way I propose. And the proof is that we have now for a long time been engaged in wars and civil strife. The cause is the multitude of our population and the magnitude of the business of our government; for the population embraces men of every kind, in respect both to race and to endowment, and both their tempers and their desires are manifold; and the business of the state has become so vast that it can be administered only with the greatest difficulty.

16. Witness to the truth of my words is borne by our past. For while we were but few in number and differed in no important respect from our neighbors, we got along well with our government and subjugated almost all Italy; but ever since we were led outside the peninsula and crossed over to many continents and many islands, filling the whole sea and the whole earth with our name and power, nothing good has been our lot. At first it was only at home and within our walls that we broke up into factions and quarrelled, but afterwards we even carried this plague out into the legions. Therefore our city, like

a great merchantman manned with a crew of every race and lacking a pilot, has now for many generations been rolling and plunging as it has drifted this way and that in a heavy sea, a ship as it were without ballast. Do not, then, allow her to be longer exposed to the tempest; for you see that she is waterlogged. And do not let her be pounded to pieces upon a reef; for her timbers are rotten and she will not be able to hold out much longer. But since the gods have taken pity on her and have set you over her as her arbiter and overseer, prove not false to her, to the end that, even as now she has revived a little by your aid, so she may survive in safety for the ages to come.

"Accept the Leadership"

17. Now I think you have long since been convinced that I am right in urging you to give the people a monarchical government; if this is the case, accept the leadership over them readily and with enthusiasm—or rather do not throw it away. For the question we are deliberating upon is not whether we shall take something, but whether we shall decide not to lose it and by so doing incur danger into the bargain. Who, indeed, will spare you if you thrust the control of the state into the hands of the people, or even if you entrust it to some other man? There are great numbers whom you have injured, and practically all these will lay claim to the sovereignty, and no one of them will wish either that you should go unpunished for what you have done or that you should be allowed to survive as his rival. Pompey, for example, once he had given up the supreme power, became the object of scorn and of secret plotting and consequently lost his life when he was unable to regain his power. Caesar also, your father, lost not only his position but also his life for doing precisely what you are proposing to do. And Marius and Sulla would certainly have suffered a like fate had they not died first. And yet some say that Sulla, fearing this very fate, forestalled it by making away with himself; at any rate, much of his legislation began to be undone while he was yet alive. Therefore you also must expect that there will be many a man who will prove a Lepidus to you and many a man who will prove a Sertorius, a Brutus, or a Cassius.

18. Looking, then, at these facts and reflecting upon all the other considerations involved, do not abandon yourself and your country merely in order to avoid giving the impression to some that you deliberately sought the office. For, in the first place, even if men do suspect this, the ambition is not inconsistent with human nature and the risk involved is a noble one. Again, what man is there who does not know the circumstances which constrained you to assume your present position? Hence, if there be any fault to find with these compelling circumstances, one might with entire justice lay it upon your father's murderers. For if they had not slain him in so unjust and pitiable a fashion, you would not have taken up arms, would not have gathered your legions, would not have made your compact with Antony and Lepidus, and would not have had to defend yourself against these men themselves. That you were right, however, and were justified in doing all this, no one is unaware. Therefore, even if some slight error has been committed, yet we cannot at this time with safety undo

anything that has been done. Therefore, for your own sake and for that of the state let us obey Fortune, who offers you the sole rulership. And let us be very grateful to her that she has not only freed us from our domestic troubles, but has also placed in your hands the organization of the state, to the end that you, by bestowing due care upon it, may prove to all mankind that those troubles were stirred up and that mischief wrought by other men, whereas you are an upright man.

"Administer It as I Shall Advise"

And do not, I beg you, be afraid of the magnitude of the empire. For the greater its extent, the more numerous are the salutary elements it possesses; also, to guard anything is far easier than to acquire it. Toils and dangers are needed to win over what belongs to others, but a little care suffices to retain what is already yours. Moreover, you need not be afraid, either, that you will live quite safely in that office and enjoy all the blessings which men know, provided that you will consent to administer it as I shall advise you. And do not think that I am shifting the discussion from the subject in hand if I speak to you at considerable length about the office. For of course my purpose in doing this will be, not to hear myself talk, but that you may learn by a strict demonstration that it is both possible and easy, for a man of sense at least, to rule well and without danger.

19. I maintain, therefore, that you ought first and foremost to choose and select with discrimination the entire senatorial body, inasmuch as some who have not been fit have, on account of our dissensions, become senators. Such of them as possess any excellence you ought to retain, but the rest you should erase from the roll. Do not, however, get rid of any good man because of his poverty, but even give him the money he requires. In the place of those who have been dropped introduce the noblest, the best, and the richest men obtainable, selecting them not only from Italy but also from the allies and the subject nations. In this way you will have many assistants for yourself and will have in safekeeping the leading men from all the provinces; thus the provinces, having no leaders of established repute, will not begin rebellions, and their prominent men will regard you with affection because they have been made sharers in your empire.

Take these same measures in the case of the knights also, by enrolling in the equestrian order such men as hold second place in their several districts as regard births, excellence and wealth. Register as many new members in both classes as you please, without being over-particular on the score of their number. For the more men of repute you have as your associates, the easier you will find it, for your own part, to administer everything in time of need and, so far as your subjects are concerned, the more easily will you persuade them that you are not treating them as slaves or as in any way inferior to us, but that you are sharing with them, not only all the other advantages which we ourselves enjoy, but also the leadership of the state, and thus make them as devoted to your office as if it were their own. And so far am I from retracting this last statement as rashly made, that I declare that the citizens ought every one actually to be given a share in the government, in order that, being on an equality with us in this respect also, they may be our faithful allies, living as it were in a single city, namely our own, and considering that this is in very truth a city, whereas their own homes are but the countryside and the villages....

23. Let all these men to whom the commands outside the city are assigned receive salaries, the more important officers more, the less important less, and those between an intermediate amount. For they cannot live in a foreign land upon their own resources, nor should they indulge, as they do now, in unlimited and indefinite expenditure. They should hold office not less than three years, unless they are guilty of misconduct, nor more than five. The reason is that offices held for only one year or for short periods merely teach the officials their bare duties and then dismiss them before they can put any of their acquired knowledge into use, while, on the other hand, the longer terms of many years' duration somehow have the effect, in many cases, of filling the officials with conceit and encouraging them to rebellion. Hence, again, I think that the more important posts ought in no case to be given consecutively to the same man....

27. Let this be your procedure, then, in the case of the senators and the knights. A standing army also should be supported, drawn from the citizens, the subject nations, and the allies, its size in the several provinces being greater or less according as the necessities of the case demand; and these troops ought always to be under arms and to engage in the practice of warfare continually. They should have winter-quarters constructed for them at the most advantageous points, and should serve for a stated period, so that a portion of life may still be left for them between their retirement from service and old age. The reason for such a standing army is this: far removed as we are from the frontiers of the empire, with enemies living near our borders on every side, we are no longer able at critical times to depend upon expeditionary forces; and if, on the other hand, we permit all the men of military age to have arms and to practice warfare, they will always be the source of seditions and civil wars....

28. From what source, then, is the money to be provided for these soldiers and for the other expenses that will of necessity be incurred? ... My proposal, therefore, is that you shall first of all sell the property that belongs to the state— and I observe that this has become vast on account of the wars—reserving only a little that is distinctly useful or necessary to you; and that you lend out all the money thus realized at a moderate rate of interest. In this way not only will the land be put under cultivation, being sold to owners who will cultivate it themselves, but also the latter will acquire a capital and become more prosperous, while the treasury will gain a permanent revenue that will suffice for its needs.... The next step is to provide for any deficiency by levying an assessment upon absolutely all property which produces any profit for its possessors, and by establishing a system of taxes among all the peoples we rule. For it is but just and proper that no individual or district be exempt from these taxes, inasmuch as they are to enjoy the benefits derived from the taxation as much as the rest. And you should appoint tax-collectors to have supervision of this business in each district, and cause them to exact the entire amount that falls due during the term of their supervision from all the sources of revenue. This plan will not only render the work of collection easier for these officials, but will in particular

benefit the taxpayers, inasmuch, I mean, as these will bring in what they owe in the small installments appointed, whereas now, if they are remiss for a brief period, the entire sum is added up and demanded of them in a single payment.

I am not unaware that some will object if this system of assessments and taxes is established. But I know this, too—that if they are subjected to no further abuses and are indeed convinced that all these contributions of theirs will make for their own security and for their fearless enjoyment of the rest of their property, and that, again, the larger part of their contributions will be received by none but themselves, as governors, procurators, or soldiers, they will be exceedingly grateful to you, since they will be giving but a slight portion of the abundance from which they derive the benefit without having to submit to abuses. Especially will this be true if they see that you live temperately and spend nothing foolishly. For who, if he saw that you were quite frugal in your expenditures for yourself and quite lavish in those for the commonwealth, would not willingly contribute, believing that your wealth meant his own security and prosperity? ...

30. So far as funds are concerned, therefore, a great abundance would be supplied from these sources. And I advise you to conduct as follows the administration of such matters as have not yet been mentioned. Adorn this capital with utter disregard of expense and make it magnificent with festivals of every kind. For it is fitting that we who rule over many people should surpass all men in all things, and brilliance of this sort, also, tends in a way to inspire our allies with respect for us and our enemies with terror. The affairs of the other cities you should order in this fashion: In the first place, the populace should have no authority in any matter, and should not be allowed to convene in any assembly at all; for nothing good would come out of their deliberations and they would always be stirring up a great deal of turmoil....

None of the cities should be allowed to have its own separate coinage or system of weights and measures; they should all be required to use ours....

34. ... You should, of course, supervise the lives of our subjects, but do not scrutinize them with too much rigor....

Moral Regeneration

36. Therefore, if you desire to become in very truth immortal, act as I advise; and, furthermore, do you not only yourself worship the Divine Power everywhere, and in every way in accordance with the traditions of our fathers, but compel all others to honor it. Those who attempt to distort our religion with strange rites you should abhor and punish, not merely for the sake of the gods (since if a man despises these he will not pay honor to any other being), but because such men, by bringing in new divinities in place of the old, persuade many to adopt foreign practices, from which spring up conspiracies, factions, and secret societies, which are far from profitable to a monarchy. Do not, therefore, permit anybody to be an atheist or a sorcerer.... For such men, by speaking the truth sometimes, but generally falsehood, often encourage a great many to attempt revolutions. The same thing is done also by many who pretend to be philosophers; hence I advise you to be on your guard against them, too. Do not, because you have had experience of good and honorable men like Areius

and Athenodorus, believe that all the rest who claim to be philosophers are like them; for infinite harm, both to communities and to individuals, is worked by certain men who but use this profession as a screen....

"Regarding You with Affection as Father and Savior"

39. These are the things I would have you do—these and others of like nature; for there are many which I must pass over, since it is impossible to include them all in a single discussion. There is, however, one statement which will serve as a summary with respect both to what has been said and to what has been left unsaid: if you of your own accord do all that you would wish another to do if he became your ruler, you will err in nothing and succeed in everything, and in consequence you will find your life most happy and utterly free from danger. For how can men help regarding you with affection as father and savior, when they see that you are orderly and upright in your life, successful in war though inclined to peace; when you refrain from insolence and greed; when you meet them on a footing of equality, do not grow rich yourself while levying tribute on them, do not live in luxury yourself while imposing hardships upon them, are not licentious yourself while reproving licentiousness in them—when, instead of all this, your life is in every way and manner precisely like theirs? Therefore, since you have in your own hands a mighty means of protection— that you never do wrong to another—be of good courage and believe me when I tell you that you will never become the object of hatred or of conspiracy. And since this is so, it follows of necessity that you will also lead a happy life; for what condition is happier, what more blissful, than, possessing virtue, to enjoy all the blessings which men can know and to be able to bestow upon others?

40. Think upon these things and upon all that I have told you, and be per- suaded by me, and let not this fortune slip which has chosen you from all man- kind and has set you up as their ruler. For, if you prefer the monarchy in fact but fear the title of "king" as being accursed, you have but to decline this title and still be sole ruler under the appellation of "Caesar." And if you require still other titles, your people will give you that of *"imperator"* as they gave it to your father; and they will pay reverence to your august position by still another term of address, so that you will enjoy fully the reality of the kingship without the odium which attaches to the name of "king."

B. TACITUS, *ANNALS*

"It was really from a lust for power."

The greatest Roman writer of history was Tacitus (d. ca. A.D. 120), whose *Annals* and *Histories* cover the period of the early empire from the death of Augustus to that of Domitian (A.D. 96) in his own day. He is outstanding for

From Book I, based on the translation by A. J. Church and W. J. Brodribb.

his ability to evaluate and criticize the facts that he carefully collected and verified, and his unique style is characterized by its biting irony and its clipped, epigrammatic sentences filled with a world of meaning. Like Thucydides and Livy, he sought after the lessons that he believed history provided. To Tacitus, these were moral lessons, and he defined the object of history to be "to ensure that merit shall not lack its record and to hold before the vicious word and deed the terrors of posterity and infamy." He idealized the freedom of the old Republic and exaggerated the tyrannical behavior of the early emperors after Augustus. In the following selection from the *Annals,* Tacitus reports two opposing estimates of Augustus, and although he claims to be impartial and does not choose between them, it is not difficult to ascertain his own conclusion: Augustus had fatally undermined republican liberty.

"*Without Either Bitterness or Partiality*"

1. Rome at the beginning was ruled by kings. Freedom and the consulship were established by Lucius Brutus [Selection 48B]. Dictatorships were held for a temporary crisis. The power of the decemvirs did not last beyond two years, nor was the consular jurisdiction of the military tribunes of long duration. The despotisms of Cinna and Sulla were brief; the rule of Pompey and of Crassus soon yielded before Caesar; the arms of Lepidus and Antony yielded before Augustus who, when the world was wearied by civil strife, subjected it to his command under the title of *princeps.* The successes and reverses of the old Roman people have been recorded by famous historians; and fine intellects were not wanting to describe the times of Augustus, till growing sycophancy scared them away. The histories of Tiberius, Germanicus, Claudius, and Nero, while they were in power, were falsified through terror, and after their death were written under the irritation of a recent hatred. Hence my purpose is to relate a few facts about Augustus—more particularly his last acts, then the reign of Tiberius, and all which follows, without either bitterness or partiality, from any motives to which I am far removed.

Augustus Won Over All Men

2. When after the destruction of Brutus and Cassius there was no longer any army of the Republic, ... then, dropping the title of triumvir, and giving out that he was a consul, and was satisfied with a tribune's authority for the protection of the people, Augustus won over the soldiers with gifts, the populace with cheap grain, and all men with allurements of peace, and so grew greater by degrees, while he concentrated in himself the functions of the Senate, the magistrates, and the laws. He was wholly unopposed, for the boldest spirits had fallen in battle, or in the proscription, while the remaining nobles, the readier they were to be slaves, were raised the higher by wealth and promotion, so that, profited by revolution, they preferred the safety of the present to the dangerous past. Nor did the provinces dislike that condition of affairs, for they distrusted the government of the Senate and the people, because of the rivalries between the leading men and the rapacity of the officials, while the protection of the laws was unavailing, as they were continually deranged by violence, intrigue, and finally by corruption.

The Succession: "Safeguards to Rest On"

3. Augustus meanwhile, as supports to his despotism, raised to the pontificate and curule aedileship Marcellus, his sister's son, while a mere stripling, and Marcus Agrippa, of humble birth, a good soldier, and one who had shared his victory, to two consecutive consulships, and as Marcellus soon afterwards died, he also accepted him as his son-in-law. Tiberius and Drusus, his stepsons, he honored with imperial titles, although his own family was yet undiminished. For he had admitted the children of Agrippa, Caius and Lucius, into the house of the Caesars; and before they had yet laid aside the dress of boyhood he had most fervently desired, with an outward show of reluctance, that they should be entitled "Leaders of the Youth," and be consuls-elect. When Agrippa died, and Lucius Caesar as he was on his way to our armies in Spain, and Caius while returning from Armenia, still suffering from a wound, were prematurely cut off by destiny— or by their step-mother Livia's treachery—Drusus too having long been dead, Tiberius remained alone of the stepsons, and in him everything tended to center. He was adopted as a son, as a colleague in command and a partner in the tribunician power, and paraded through all the armies, no longer through his mother's [Livia] secret intrigues, but at her open suggestion. For she had gained such a hold on the aged Augustus that he drove out as an exile into the island of Planasia his only grandson, Agrippa Postumus, who, though devoid of worthy qualities, and having only the brute courage of physical strength, had not been convicted of any gross offense. And yet Augustus had appointed Germanicus, Drusus's offspring, to the command of eight legions on the Rhine, and required Tiberius to adopt him, although Tiberius had a son, now a young man, in his house; but he did it that he might have several safeguards to rest on. He had no war at the time on his hands except against the Germans, which was rather to wipe out the disgrace of the loss of Quintilius Varus and his army than out of an ambition to extend the empire, or for any adequate recompense.

"How Few Were Left Who Had Seen the Republic!"

At home all was tranquil, and there were magistrates with the same title as before; there was a younger generation, sprung up since the victory of Actium, and even many of the older men had been born during the civil wars. How few were left who had seen the Republic!

4. Thus the state had been revolutionized, and there was not a vestige left of the old sound morality. Stripped of equality, all looked up to the commands of a *princeps* without the least apprehension for the present, while Augustus in the vigor of life, could maintain his own position, that of his house, and the general tranquility. When in advanced old age, he was worn out by a sickly frame, and the end was near and new prospects opened, a few voices began idly to discuss the blessings of freedom....

"Men ... Spoke Variously of His Life"

8.... On the day of the funeral [of Augustus] soldiers stood round as a guard, amid much ridicule from those who had either themselves witnessed or who had heard from their parents of the famous day when slavery was still something fresh, and freedom had been resought in vain by the slaying of Caesar, the dictator—to some the vilest, to others the most glorious of deeds. Now, they said, an aged dictator, whose power has lasted long, who has provided his heirs with abundant means to coerce the state, seems to require the defense of soldiers that his burial may be undisturbed.

9. Then followed much talk about Augustus himself, and many expressed an idle wonder that the same day marked the beginning of his assumption of power and the close of his life, and, again, that he had ended his days at Nola in the same house and room as his father Octavius. People extolled too the number of his consulships, in which he had equalled Valerius Corvus and Caius Marius combined, the continuance for thirty-seven years of the tribunician power, the title of Imperator twenty-one times earned, and his other honors which had been either frequently repeated or were wholly new. Sensible men, however, spoke variously of his life with praise and censure. Some said that dutiful feeling towards a father [Julius Caesar], and the necessities of the state in which laws had then no place, drove him into civil war, which can neither be planned nor conducted on any right principles.... the only remedy for his distracted country was the rule of a single man. Yet the state had been organized under neither the name of a kingdom nor a dictatorship, but under that of a *princeps*. The ocean and remote rivers were the boundaries of the empire; the legions, provinces, fleets, all things were linked together; there was law for the citizens; there was respect shown to the allies. The capital had been embellished on a grand scale; only in a few instances had he resorted to force, simply to secure general tranquility.

10. It was said, on the other hand, that filial duty and state necessity were merely assumed as a mask. It was really from a lust for power that he had excited the veterans by bribery, had, when only a youth and without official status, raised an army, tampered with the consul's legions, and feigned an attachment to the faction of Sextus Pompey. Then, when by a decree of the Senate he had usurped the high functions and authority of praetor, ... he wrested the consulate from a reluctant Senate, and turned against the state the arms with which he had been intrusted against Antony. Citizens were proscribed and lands distributed—distasteful even to those who carried out these deeds. Even granting that the deaths of Cassius and Brutus were sacrifices to an inherited feud (though duty requires us to waive private animosities for the sake of the public welfare), still Sextus Pompey had been deluded by the phantom of peace, and Lepidus by the mask of friendship. Subsequently, Antony had been lured on by the treaties of Tarentum and Brundisium, and by the marriage to his sister, and had paid by his death the penalty of a treacherous alliance. No doubt, there was peace after all this, but it was a peace stained with blood....

The domestic life too of Augustus was not spared—how he had abducted Nero's wife ... Livia, terrible to the state as a mother, terrible to the house of the Caesars as a stepmother. No honor was left for the gods when Augustus chose to be himself worshipped with temples and statues, like those of the deities, and with flamens and priests. He had not even adopted Tiberius as his successor out of affection or any regard to the state, but, having thoroughly seen his arrogant and savage temper, he had sought glory for himself by a contrast of extreme wickedness....

However, after the funeral rites had been duly performed, a temple and divine worship was decreed him.

C. VIRGIL, *AENEID*: A ROMAN NATIONAL EPIC

"Behold this nation"

Virgil (70–19 B.C.) was a writer of the Augustan age who used his literary skills to create a number of poetic works, including the *Aeneid*, *Eclogues*, and *Georgics*, that would be usher in a "golden age" in Latin literature. His best known epic poem, the *Aeneid*, centers on its eponymous hero, the Trojan prince Aeneas, who escaped the conflagrations of his native city and fled, via Africa where he had a dalliance with the Carthaginian queen Dido, to Italy where he was destined to found a world-ruling people. Clearly modeled on the Homeric epics of the *Odyssey* and the *Iliad*, Virgil's *Aeneid* regales its audience with the wandering travels of its main protagonist who was also a man of destiny. Aeneas finally alighted in Italy and there encountered the Sibyl, an oracle at Cumae in southern Italy, who inducted him to the underworld where he found the shade of his newly departed father Anchises. Anchises revealed to his son the portentous destiny awaiting him and his descendants, the Roman people. During Virgil's time, Augustus, who was adopted into the Julian clan that claimed ancestry from Aeneas, promoted the idea that his age was the culmination of the centuries of Roman past with its panoply of famous men and heroes, an ideology that found expression at the time in artistic works and monuments, such as the Temple of Mars Ultor ("the Avenger") that Augustus had built in Rome. Virgil's *Aeneid* accordingly functions as a Roman national epic by conferring a "Homeric" cast on aspects of Roman tradition and values that Augustus sought to promulgate throughout his reign.

But deep in a green vale father Anchises was surveying with earnest thought the imprisoned souls that were to pass to the light above and, as it chanced, was counting over the full number of his people and beloved children, their fates and fortunes, their works and ways. And as he saw Aeneas coming towards him over the sward, he eagerly stretched forth both hands, while tears streamed from his eyes and a cry fell from his lips: "Have you come at last, and has the duty that your father expected vanquished the toilsome way? Is it given me to see your face, my son, and hear and utter familiar tones? Even so I mused and deemed the hour would come, counting the days, nor has my yearning failed me. Over what lands, what wide seas have you journeyed to my welcome! What dangers have beset you, my son! How I feared the realm of Libya might work you harm!" But he answered: "Your shade, father, your sad shade, meeting me

From Virgil, *Aeneid* 6.679–853; in *Virgil. Eclogues. Georgics. Aeneid I-VI*, Loeb Classical Library, translated by H. Ruston Fairclough and revised by G. P. Goold, (Cambridge, Mass.: Harvard University Press, 1999), pp. 581–93. The Loeb Classical Library® is a registered trademark of the President and Fellows of Harvard College.

repeatedly, drove me to seek these portals. My ships ride the Tuscan sea. Grant me to clasp your hand, grant me, father, and withdraw not from my embrace!" So he spoke, his face wet with flooding tears. Thrice there he strove to throw his arms about his neck; thrice the form, vainly clasped, fled from his hands, even as light winds, and most like a winged dream.

Meanwhile, in a retired vale, Aeneas sees a sequestered grove and rustling forest thickets, and the river of Lethe drifting past those peaceful homes. About it hovered peoples and tribes unnumbered; even as when, in the meadows, in cloudless summertime, bees light on many-hued blossoms and stream round lustrous lilies and all the fields murmur with the humming. Aeneas is startled by the sudden sight and, knowing not, asks the cause—what is that river yonder, and who are the men thronging the banks in such a host? Then said father Anchises: "Spirits they are, to whom second bodies are owed by Fate, and at the water of Lethe's stream they drink the soothing draught and long forgetfulness. These in truth I have long yearned to tell and show you to your face, yea, to count this, my children's seed, that so you may rejoice with me the more at finding Italy." "But, father, must we think that any souls pass aloft from here to the world above and return a second time to bodily fetters? What mad longing for life possesses their sorry hearts?" "I will surely tell you, my son, and keep you not in doubt," Anchises replies, and reveals each truth in order.

"First, know that heaven and earth and the watery plains, the moon's bright sphere and Titan's star [the Sun] a spirit within sustains; in all the limbs mind moves the mass and mingles with the mighty frame. Thence spring the races of man and beast, the life of winged creatures, and the monsters that ocean bears beneath his marble surface. Fiery is the vigour and divine the source of those seeds of life, so far as harmful bodies clog them not, or earthly limbs and frames born but to die. Hence their fears and desires, their griefs and joys; nor do they discern the heavenly light, penned as they are in the gloom of their dark dungeon. Still more! When life's last ray has fled, the wretches are not entirely freed from all evil and all the plagues of the body; and it needs must be that many a taint, long ingrained, should in wondrous wise become deeply rooted in their being. Therefore are they schooled with punishments, and pay penance for bygone sins. Some are hung stretched out to the empty winds; from others the stain of guilt is washed away under swirling floods or burned out by fire till length of days, when time's cycle is complete, has removed the inbred taint and leaves unsoiled the ethereal sense and pure flame of spirit: each of us undergoes his own purgatory. Then we are sent to spacious Elysium, a few of us to possess the blissful fields. All these that you see, when they have rolled time's wheel through a thousand years, the god summons in vast throng to Lethe's river, so that, their memories effaced, they may once more revisit the vault above and conceive the desire of return to the body."

Anchises paused, and drew his son and with him the Sibyl into the heart of the assembly and buzzing throng, then chose a mound whence he might scan face to face the whole of the long procession and note their faces as they came.

"Now then, the glory henceforth to attend the Trojan race, what children of Italian stock are held in store by fate, glorious souls waiting to inherit our name, this shall I reveal in speech and inform you of your destiny. The youth you see leaning on an untipped spear holds by lot of life the most immediate place: he first shall rise into the upper air with Italian blood in his veins, Silvius of Alban name, last-born of your children, whom late in your old age your wife Lavinia shall rear in the woodlands, a king and father of kings, with whom our race shall hold sway in Alba Longa. He next is Procas, pride of the Trojan nation, then Capys and Numitor and he who will resurrect you by his name, Aeneas Silvius, no less eminent in goodness and in arms, if ever he come to reign over Alba. What fine young men are these! Mark the strength they display and the civic oak that shades their brows! These to your honour will build Nomentum and Gabii and Fidena's town; these shall crown hills with Collatia's towers, and Pometii, the Fort of Inuus, Bola and Cora: one day to be famous names, these now are nameless places. Further, a son of Mars shall keep his grandsire company, Romulus, whom his mother Ilia shall bear of Assaracus' stock. Do you see how twin plumes stand upright on his head and how the Father of the gods stamps him with divine majesty? Lo, under his auspices, my son, shall that glorious Rome extend her empire to earth's ends, her ambitions to the skies, and shall embrace seven hills with a single city's wall, blessed in a brood of heroes; even as the Berecyntian mother, turret-crowned, rides in her chariot through Phrygian towns, happy in a progeny of gods, clasping a hundred grand-sons, all denizens of heaven, all tenants of celestial heights.

"Turn hither now your two-eyed gaze, and behold this nation, the Romans that are yours. Here is Caesar and all the seed of Iulus destined to pass under heaven's spacious sphere. And this in truth is he whom you so often hear prom-ised you, Augustus Caesar, son of a god, who will again establish a golden age in Latium amid fields once ruled by Saturn; he will advance his empire beyond the Garamants and Indians to a land which lies beyond our stars, beyond the path of year and sun, where sky-bearing Atlas wheels on his shoulders the blazing star-studded sphere. Against his coming both Caspian realms and the Maeotic land even now shudder at the oracles of their gods, and the mouths of sevenfold Nile quiver in alarm. Not even Hercules traversed so much of earth's extent, though he pierced the stag of brazen foot, quieted the woods of Erymanthus, and made Lerna tremble at his bow; nor he either, who guides his car with vine-leaf reins, triumphant Bacchus, driving his tigers down from Nysa's lofty peak. And do we still hesitate to make known our worth by exploits or shrink in fear from settling on Western soil?

"But who is he apart, crowned with sprays of olive, offering sacrifice? Ah, I recognize the hoary hair and beard of that king of Rome [Numa| who will make the infant city secure on a basis of laws, called from the needy land of lowly Cures to sovereign might. Him shall Tullus next succeed, the breaker of his country's peace, who will rouse to war an inactive folk and armies long unused to triumphs. Hard on his heels follows over-boastful Ancus, who even now enjoys too much the breeze of popular favour. Would you also see the Tarquin kings, the proud spirit of Brutus the Avenger, and the fasces regained? He first shall receive a consul's power and the cruel axes, and when his sons would stir up revolt, the father will hale them to execution in fair freedom's name, unhappy man, however later ages will extol that deed; yet shall a patriot's love prevail and unquenched thirst for fame.

"Now behold over there the Decii and the Drusi, Torquatus of the cruel axe, and Camillus bringing the standards home! But they whom you see, resplendent in matching arms, souls now in harmony and as long as they are imprisoned in night, alas, if once they attain the light of life, what mutual strife, what battles and bloodshed will they cause, the bride's father swooping from Alpine ramparts and Monoecus' fort, her husband confronting him with forces from the East! Steel not your hearts, my sons, to such wicked war nor vent violent valour on the vitals of your land. And you who draw your lineage from heaven, be you the first to show mercy; cast the sword from your hand, child of my blood! ...

"He yonder, triumphant over Corinth, shall drive a victor's chariot to the lofty Capitol, famed for Achaeans he has slain. Yon other shall uproot Argos, Agamemnon's Mycenae, and even an heir of Aeacus, seed of mighty Achilles: he will avenge his Trojan sires and Minerva's polluted shrine. Who, lordly Cato, could leave you unsung, or you, Cossus; who the Gracchan race or the Scipios twain, two thunderbolts of war and the ruin of Carthage, or Fabricius, in penury a prince, or you, Serranus, sowing seed in the soil? Whither, O Fabii, do ye hurry me all breathless? You are he, the mightiest, who could, as no one else, through inaction preserve our state. Others, I doubt not, shall with softer mould beat out the breathing bronze, coax from the marble features to the life, plead cases with greater eloquence and with a pointer trace heaven's motions and predict the risings of die stars: you, Roman, be sure to rule the world (be these your arts), to crown peace with justice, to spare the vanquished and to crush the proud."

Romans and Non-Romans in the *Pax Romana*

65 The *Pax Romana*

Divergent Views

The Augustan reorganization of the Roman world lasted without major change through the death of Marcus Aurelius in A.D. 180. These two centuries of relative peace and security, the *Pax Romana*, constitute the longest period

From Book IV, based on the translation by A. J. Church and W. J. Brodribb.

of tranquility known in the history of the Western world. It is the judgment of many modern historians that the ideas and practices of Roman imperial administration were generally successful: "Particularly happy was Rome in her methods of Romanization and civilization of backward peoples in Western Europe. By her spirit of practical realism, wise compromise, generous grants of citizenship, and development of local, tribal, or municipal autonomy, she inspired a feeling of loyalty in the Western provinces."[1]

To many of Rome's neighbors, however, the prospect of Roman domination was unattractive. The writings of Tacitus throw light on both sides of the matter.

A. TACITUS, *HISTORIES*

"By the prosperity and order of eight hundred years has this fabric of empire been consolidated...."

The year A.D. 69, known as the "Year of the Four Emperors," witnessed a temporary breakdown of the *Pax Romana* after the death of Nero when a series of civil wars were fought by rival frontier armies seeking to elevate their respective commanders to imperial power. "The secret of empire was now disclosed," wrote Tacitus, "that an emperor could be made elsewhere than at Rome," and the resulting anarchy encouraged a revolt of subject peoples along the lower Rhine. The leader of the revolt was a German Batavian chieftain named Julius Civilis, who had served with his troops in the Roman auxiliary armies for twenty-five years and had been granted Roman citizenship. He and his people had been aroused by Nero's high-handed arrest of their officers on the charge of treason, and he now urged other German tribes in the area to join him in forming an independent Germanic kingdom. Inspired by this example, Belgian tribes in northeastern Gaul, led by the Treveri and the Lingones (the latter having recently received Roman citizenship), also revolted and proclaimed a Gallic national state. The revolts collapsed early in A.D. 70, when a strong Roman expedition arrived on the scene. Tacitus reports in his *Histories* the substance of the speech delivered to the Treveri and Lingones by the Roman commander Cerialis after their surrender. It sums up bluntly and realistically the Roman Empire's policy of "submission and safety" as the alternative to "petty kingdoms and intestine wars."

73. Cerialis then convoked an assembly of the Treveri and Lingones, and thus addressed them: "I have never cultivated eloquence; it is by my sword that I have asserted the excellence of the Roman people. Since, however, words have very great weight with you, since you estimate good and evil, not according to their real value, but according to the representations of seditious men, I have resolved to say a few words, which, as the war is at an end, it may be useful for you to hear rather than for me to speak. Roman generals and emperors entered your territory, as they did the rest of Gaul, with no ambitious purposes, but at the solicitation of your ancestors, who were wearied to the last extremity by intestine strife, while

---

1. Albert Trever, *History of Ancient Civilization*, 2 vols. (New York: Harcourt, Brace and Co., 1948), II, p. 748.

the Germans, whom they had summoned to their help, had imposed their yoke alike on friend and foe. How many battles we have fought against the Cimbri and Teutones, at the cost of what hardships to our armies, and with what result we have waged our German wars, is perfectly well known. It is not to defend Italy that we occupied the borders of the Rhine, but to insure that no second Ariovistus[2] should seize Gaul.... There have ever been the same causes at work to make the Germans cross over into Gaul—lust, avarice, and the longing for a new home, prompting them to leave their own marshes and deserts, and to possess themselves of this most fertile soil and of you its inhabitants. 'Liberty' and similar specious names are their pretexts; but never did any man seek to enslave his fellows and secure dominion for himself without using the very same words.

74. "Gaul always had its petty kingdoms and intestine wars, till you submitted to our authority. We, though so often provoked, have used the right of conquest to burden you only with the cost of maintaining peace. For the tranquillity of nations cannot be preserved without armies; armies cannot exist without pay; pay cannot be furnished without tribute; all else is common among us. You often command our legions. You rule these and other provinces. There is no privilege, no exclusion. From worthy emperors you derive benefits equal to ours, though you dwell so far away, while cruel rulers are most formidable to their neighbors. Endure the passions and rapacity of your masters, just as you bear barren seasons and excessive rains and other natural evils. There will be vices as long as there are men. But they are not perpetual, and they are compensated by the occurrence of better things....

"Should the Romans be driven out—which God forbid—what can result but wars between all these nations? By the prosperity and order of eight hundred years has this fabric of empire been consolidated, nor can it be overthrown without destroying those who overthrow it. Yours will be the worst peril, for you have gold and wealth, and these are the chief incentives to war. Give therefore your love and respect to the cause of peace, and to that capital in which we, conquerors and conquered, claim an equal right. Let the lessons of fortune in both its forms teach you not to prefer rebellion and ruin to submission and safety." With words to this effect he quieted his audience, who feared harsher treatment.

B. TACITUS, *AGRICOLA*

"They create a desert and call it peace."

Shortly after the suppression of the Rhineland revolt, Cerialis was appointed governor of Britain by Vespasian, who had emerged victorious out of the "Year of the Four Emperors." The conquest of Britain was only half-completed; Claudius had begun it in A.D. 43, but under Nero the Romans

---

2. The German tribal king whose crossing of the Rhine and occupation of Alsace triggered the events that led to Caesar's conquest of Gaul.

Chs. 30–32; based on the translation by A. J. Church and W. J. Brodribb.

had been set back by a revolt under famed Queen Boudicca of the Iceni (Essex, England). Cerialis and his successors now resumed the northward march of Roman conquest, which was completed by Agricola, Vespasian's third governor of Britain (A.D. 78–83), who conquered Caledonia (Scotland). But during Domitian's reign, Rome's legions were needed on the Rhine and Danube frontiers; Agricola was recalled and Caledonia abandoned. Tacitus, who was Agricola's son-in-law, wrote a biography of him that is at once a eulogy to a noble Roman, a description of Britain and its conquest, and a case study of Roman imperialism in action. The last point is illustrated by the following selection, the speech that Tacitus attributes to the Caledonian chieftain Calgacus just before his final defeat by the Romans. A description of Roman imperialism as it appeared to freedom-loving people, it balances the Roman picture of the *Pax Romana*.

Whenever I consider the causes of this war and the circumstances of our position, I have sure confidence that this day, and our united efforts, will be the beginning of freedom for the whole of Britain. To all of us slavery is a thing unknown. There are no lands beyond us, and even the sea is not safe, menaced as we are by a Roman fleet. And thus war and battle, in which the brave find glory, offers the only safety even to cowards. Former battles, in which, with varying fortune, the Romans were resisted, still left us as a last hope, because we, being the most renowned nation of Britain, dwelling in the very heart of the country and out of sight of the shores of the conquered, could keep our eyes unpolluted by the contagion of slavery. To us who dwell on the uttermost confines of the earth and of freedom, this remote sanctuary of Britain's glory has up to this time been a defense. Now, however, the furthest limits of Britain are thrown open, and the unknown always passes for the marvellous. But there are no tribes beyond us, nothing indeed but waves and rocks, and the yet more terrible Romans, from whose oppression escape is vainly sought by obedience and submission. Robbers of the world, having by their universal plunder exhausted the land, they ransack the sea. If the enemy be rich, they are rapacious; if he be poor, they lust for dominion. Neither East nor West has been able to satisfy them. Alone among men they cover with equal eagerness the poor and the rich. To robbery, slaughter, plunder, they give the lying name of empire; they create a desert and call it peace.

Nature has willed that every man's children and kindred should be his dearest objects. Yet these are torn from us by conscriptions to be slaves in foreign lands. Our wives and our sisters, even though they may escape being raped by the enemy, are seduced under the names of friendship and hospitality. Our goods and fortunes they collect for their tribute, our harvests for their granaries. Our hands and bodies, under the lash and in the midst of insult, are worn down by the toil of clearing forests and swamps. Creatures born to slavery, once sold, are fed by their masters; but Britain is daily purchasing, daily feeding, her own enslaved people. And as in a household the last comer among the slaves is always the butt of his companions, so we in a world long used to slavery, as the newest and the most contemptible, are marked for destruction. For we have neither fruitful plains, nor mines, nor harbors, for the working of which we may be spared. Valor and high spirit in subjects are offensive to rulers; remoteness and seclusion also, while they give safety, provoke suspicion. Since then you cannot hope for mercy, at least take courage, whether it be safety or honor that you hold most precious. Under a woman's leadership the Brigantes were able to burn a colony, to storm a camp, and had not success made them careless, might have thrown off the yoke. Let us, then, a fresh and unconquered people, eager to maintain our freedom, show at the very first encounter what heroes Caledonia has held in reserve.

Do you suppose the Romans will be as brave in war as they are licentious in peace? To our quarrels and discords they owe their fame; they turn the errors of an enemy to the renown of their own army, an army which, composed as it is of every variety of nations, is held together by success and will be broken up by disaster. These Gauls and Germans, and, I blush to say, these numerous Britons, who, though they lend their lives to support a stranger's rule, have been its enemies longer than its subjects, you cannot really believe to be bound by loyalty and affection. Fear and terror are feeble bonds of attachment; remove them, and those who have ceased to fear will begin to hate. All the incentives to victory are on our side. The Romans have no wives to kindle their courage, no parents to taunt them if they run away; many have either no country or one far away. Few in number, ignorant of the country, looking upon a sky, a sea, and forests which are unfamiliar to them, the gods have delivered them, like caged prisoners, into our hands. Be not frightened by outward show, by the glitter of gold and silver, which can neither protect nor wound. In the ranks of the enemy we shall find hands to help us. The Britons will recognize their own cause; the Gauls will remember their former freedom; the rest of the Germans will desert them, as the Usipi recently did. Behind them there is nothing to dread—the forts are ungarrisoned; the colonies are in the hands of aged men, the towns with their disloyal subjects and oppressive rulers are ill-affected and rife with discord. Here before you is their general and his army; behind are the tribute, the mines, and all the other penalties of an enslaved people. Whether you endure these for ever, or instantly avenge them, this field is to decide. Think, therefore, as you advance to battle, of your ancestors and of those who will come after you.

C. AELIUS ARISTIDES, *ORATION ON ROME*

"How is this form of government not beyond
every democracy?"

The ideal of the classical city-state remained an important one throughout antiquity. An important component of this civic ideal was the notion of freedom or autonomy that derived from self-governance. Another significant ingredient was the ability of city-states to pursue their own agendas and interests, even to the point of going to war with each other. In the post-classical period, many Greek thinkers who reflected on the events since the Peloponnesian War concluded that the rivalry and lack of unity among cities were

From *P. Aelius Aristides: The Complete Works*, Vol. I: Orations XVII–LIII, translated by Charles A. Behr (Leiden: E. J. Brill, 1981). Copyright © 1981 by E. J. Brill. Reprinted by permission.

the principal causes for the political weaknesses of the "culturally superior" Greeks. When the Romans first began to intervene in Greek affairs, the Greek reaction was understandably mixed. But by the second century A.D., Roman power had become deeply entrenched, with no serious alternative to the Roman Empire appearing on the horizon. Greek subjects of the Roman Empire had to adjust themselves to the reality of imperial rule while also trying to reconcile Roman domination with the ideals of Greek civic freedom.

The following selection is a particularly fascinating example of such an attempt. Aelius Aristides (A.D. 117–ca. A.D. 181) was a highly distinguished Greek provincial from Asia Minor and an accomplished orator. The passages below are excerpted from a speech he delivered before the people and Senate of Rome upon his visit to the city. He praised the Romans for their many accomplishments and for the peace and order they brought to the Mediterranean world. A careful reading of this speech can give us important insights into how Greek intellectuals reacted to the ruling power in Rome and how they sought to construct a "strategic partnership" with the Romans to create a classical, Greco-Roman civilization.

(1) It is customary for those traveling by sea or by land to make whatever vows each may conceive of. Some poet once said in jest that he vowed "golden-horned frankincense." But we, gentlemen, during our journey here and our sailing, made this vow, which was not uncultured, out of tune, or separated from our art, that if we should be kept safe, we would publicly address the city. (2) It was impossible to vow a speech equal to the measure of the city, but that truly again required another vow. Perhaps it is even for one greater than I to be able to carry out such a speech, which will equal the great and weighty dignity of the city. Yet we promised to make an address, however we could, since others even use things which are equal to their measure for what is equal to the measure of the gods. (3) But, gentlemen, who inhabit this great city, if you have any concern that my vow not prove false, aid my daring, so that right at the beginning of our praise we can even say that straight off it was possible to meet men of such quality, through whom "if ever one was formerly uncultured," to quote Euripides, he immediately becomes tuneful and clever, and can even speak on subjects beyond his ability. (4) All men sing of and will sing of this city, but they detract from it more than if they were silent, in as much as in silence it can be neither magnified nor diminished from its existing state, but it remains to be known in an uncontaminated condition. Speeches, on the other hand, do the opposite of what they intend. In their praise they do not depict precisely what they admire. But if some painter in endeavoring to depict with artistry a handsome and admired body should fail, everyone would surely say that it would be better if he did not paint it at all, but either let the body itself be seen or not display an inferior imitation to them. So also the same holds true, I think, about this city. (5) Speeches detract from many of its wonders and seem to me to have the same effect as if someone wishing to report the number of an expedition, for example that of Xerxes, and being full of admiration, should say that he saw ten or twenty thousand soldiers and so and so many cavalry, while not even telling a fraction of all the things which amaze him.

(6) This city is the first to have exposed the power of oratory as not entirely sufficient.... (9) ... If one considers the whole empire, he is amazed at the city

when he thinks that a fraction of the world rules over the whole of it. Yet if he regards the city itself and the boundaries of the city, he is no longer amazed that the whole world is ruled by so great a city. (10) A certain prose writer said about Asia that one man "rules all as far as is the course of the sun," untruly since he excluded all Africa and Europe from the sun's rising and setting. But it has now turned out to be true that the course of the sun and your possessions are equal and that the sun's course is always in your land.... (11) ... Here is brought from every land and sea all the crops of the seasons and the produce of each land, river, lake, as well as of the arts of the Greeks and barbarians, so that if someone should wish to view all these things, he must either see them by traveling over the whole world or be in this city. It cannot be otherwise than that there always be here an abundance of all that grows and is manufactured among each people. So many merchant ships arrive here, conveying every kind of goods from every people every hour and every day, so that the city is like a factory common to the whole earth. (12) It is possible to see so many cargoes from India and even from Arabia Felix, if you wish, that one imagines that for the future the trees are left bare for the people there and that they must come here to beg for their own produce if they need anything. Again there can be seen clothing from Babylon and ornaments from the barbarian world beyond, which arrive in much larger quantity and more easily than if merchantmen bringing goods from Naxus or Cythnus had only to put into Athens. Your farmlands are Egypt, Sicily, and all of Africa which is cultivated. (13) The arrivals and departures of the ships never stop, so that one would express admiration not only for the harbor, but even for the sea. Hesiod said about the limits of the Ocean, that it is a place where everything has been channeled into one beginning and end. So everything comes together here, trade, seafaring, farming, the scourings of the mines, all the crafts that exist or have existed, all that is produced and grown. Whatever one does not see here, is not a thing which has existed or exists, so that it is not easy to decide which has the greater superiority, the city in regard to present day cities, or the empire in regard to the empires which have gone before....

(15) Let us consider the Persian empire which once enjoyed much fame among the Greeks and gave to the king who held it the title "Great." I shall omit the empires before it as being of less importance. And let us regard everything in order, its size and what took place in it. We must also examine how they enjoyed their possessions and how they treated their subjects. (16) First of all, what the Atlantic Ocean now means for you, was then simply the Mediterranean for the King. Here were the borders of his empire, so that the Ionians and Aeolians lived on the limits of his territory. When that king "of everything from the rising to the setting sun" once attempted to cross over to Greece, he excited admiration only for his great failure. And he proved his distinction by the fact that he could be stripped of many, great possessions. Indeed, since he was so far from ruling Greece, and Ionia formed the limit of his kingdom, he did not, in fact, fall short of your empire by the throw of a discus or the distance of a bowshot, but by a whole half of the inhabited world and the Mediterranean itself besides....

(24) Again although Alexander possessed the great empire up to the time of yours and overran the earth, truly, as they say, he was more like one who got possession of a kingdom than a king. Just as if some private citizen should acquire

much good land and should die before enjoying the fruits of it, so it seems to me to have befallen him. (25) He advanced over the most territory, subdued all who opposed him, and enjoyed to the full every difficulty. Yet he was unable to establish his empire and to put an end to his toils, but he died in the middle course of his work, so that one would say that he was successful in most battles, but was least a king, and that he was a great competitor for the kingdom, yet enjoyed nothing worthy of his plans and art, but had the same experience as if a contestant in the Olympic games overcame his opponents and then died right after his victory before he had well and fairly fitted the crown to his head. (26) What laws did he institute for each people? Or what lasting arrangements relative to finances, or to the army, or to the fleet did he make? Or with what kind of regular administration, one routinely proceeding in fixed cycles, did he direct affairs? What measures of government did he take among his subjects? He left only one deed and monument worthy of his nature, the city named after him in Egypt. This he generously founded for you, so that you might possess and rule over the greatest city after your own. Therefore he overthrew the Persian rulers, but he himself almost did not rule at all. (27) When he died, the Macedonians were immediately split into innumerable parts, proving in fact that empire was beyond them.... (28) Now, indeed, the boundaries of your empire are of an extent not to be despised, nor such that their interior can be measured. Proceeding westward from the point where the limit of the Persian empire was then fixed, the remainder of your empire is much greater than the whole of that one. Nothing escapes you, neither city, nor nation, nor harbor, nor land, unless you have condemned something as useless. The Red Sea, the cataracts of the Nile, and Lake Maeotis, which former men spoke of as the ends of the earth, are for this city like "the fence of courtyard." As to the Ocean, which certain writers neither believed existed at all nor that it flowed around the earth and whose name they thought that the poets had invented and put in their compositions to please their audience, you have discovered this ocean so thoroughly that not even the island in it has escaped your notice. (29) Although your empire is so large and so great, it is much greater in its good order than in its circumference.... [L]ike the enclosure of a courtyard, cleansed of every disturbance, a circle encompasses your empire. So the whole inhabited world speaks in greater harmony than a chorus, praying that this empire last for all time. So fairly is it forged together by this chorus-leader prince.... (31) Everything is accomplished by edict and by a sign of assent more easily than one would strike the chord of a lyre. And if something must be done, it is enough to decree it and it is accomplished. The rulers who are sent to the cities and to the peoples are each the rulers of those under them, but in regard to their personal position and their relations to each other are equally subjects. And, indeed, one would say that in this respect they differ from their subjects, in that they first teach the duties of a subject. So much fear is instilled in all for the great ruler and president of the whole. (32) Therefore they believe that he has more knowledge of their actions than they do of themselves, and they have more fear and respect for him than anyone would for the presence of his master who was supervising and giving orders. No one is so confident in himself that he is able to remain calm after only hearing his name. But he stands up, praises, and reverences him, and offers a double prayer, one to the gods on the emperor's behalf, the other concerning his personal affairs to the emperor himself. If they should have even some small doubt over suits and the legal privileges of their subjects, either public or private, whether any are entitled to these privileges, they immediately send to him, asking what should be done, and they wait for his signal, no less than a chorus waits upon its teacher. (33) Therefore there is no need for him to wear himself out by journeying over the whole empire, nor by visiting different people at different times to confirm individual matters, whenever he enters their land. But it is very easy for him to govern the whole inhabited world by dispatching letters without moving from the spot. And the letters are almost no sooner written than they arrive, as if borne by winged messengers. (34) Now I shall speak of what is particularly worthy of admiration and of amazement and of gratitude shown in word and deed. Although you hold so great an empire and rule with such authority and power, you have also proved most successful in that quality which is in every way peculiar to you. (36) For you are the only ones ever to rule over free men.... But like those in individual cities, you govern throughout the whole inhabited world as if in a single city and you appoint governors as it were by election for the protection and care of their subjects, not to be their masters. Therefore governor is succeeded by governor whenever his term has expired; and it is improbable that he would even meet his successor—so far would he be from raising a dispute as if the land were his own. (37) Cases under judicial review, like an appeal from one's demesmen[3] to the courts, take place with no less fear in regard to the verdict on the part of those who have handled the cases than on the part of those who institute the appeals, so that one would say that people now are governed by those sent out to them in so far as it pleases them.... (38) How is this form of government not beyond every democracy? ...

66 Tacitus

The Early Germans

When Tacitus wrote his essay "On the Origins, Geography, and Customs of the Germans" (usually called the *Germania*) in A.D. 98, the Germans had become something of a problem for the Romans. The Emperor Trajan was encamped

---

3. The citizen body of Athens (and territory of Attica) was divided into demes that were important for purposes of voting, military service, and religious worship.

Adapted from Arthur C. Howland, ed., *Translations and Reprints from the Original Sources of European History*, Vol. VI, No. 3.

along the Rhine frontier, and there was some talk that he might revive Augustus' ill-fated plan to conquer Germany, which had ended ingloriously in A.D. 9, when three legions were ambushed and destroyed by a German chieftain named Arminius. Tacitus wrote to satisfy Roman curiosity concerning the barbarians of the North for whose martial abilities he had a healthy respect. Nor could he refrain from his inclination to moralize by frequently noting the contrast between the unspoiled, energetic, virtuous Germans—"noble savages" in Tacitus' view—and the decadent, oversophisticated Romans of his own day. Tacitus' work on the Germanic peoples is of inestimable historical value. Most modern accounts of the early Germans are still largely based upon its descriptions.

Origin and Physical Characteristics

2. I regard the Germans themselves as an indigenous people, without any subsequent mixture of blood through immigration or friendly intercourse; for in ancient times it was by sea and not by land that those who wished to change their homes wandered, and the boundless and, so to speak, hostile sea beyond us, is rarely traversed by ships from our part of the world. And not to mention the danger of the terrible and unknown sea, who indeed would leave Asia or Africa or Italy to seek Germany with its wild scenery, its harsh climate, its sullen manners and aspect, unless, indeed, it were his native country? They tell in their ancient songs, the only kind of tradition and history that they have, how Tuisto, a god sprung from the earth and his son Mannus were the originators and founders of their race....

4. I myself subscribe to the opinion of those who hold that the German tribes have never been contaminated by intermarriage with other nations, but have remained peculiar and unmixed and wholly unlike the other people. Hence, the physical type is the same among them all, despite the vastness of their population. They all have fierce blue eyes, reddish hair and large bodies fit only for sudden exertion; they do not submit patiently to work and effort and cannot endure thirst and heat at all, although cold and hunger they are accustomed to because of their climate....

Kings and Leaders

7. They choose their kings on account of their ancestry, their leaders for their valor. The kings do not have free and unlimited power and the leaders lead by example rather than command, winning great admiration if they are energetic and fight in plain sight in front of the line. But no one is allowed to put a culprit to death or to imprison him, or even to beat him with stripes except the priests, and then not by way of a punishment or at the command of the leader but as though ordered by the god who they believe aids them in their fighting. Certain figures and images taken from their sacred groves they carry into battle, but their greatest incitement to courage is that a division of horse or foot is not made up by chance or by accidental association but is formed of families and clans; and their dear ones are close at hand so that the wailings of the women and the crying of the children can be heard during the battle. These are for each warrior the most sacred witnesses of his bravery, these his dearest applauders. They carry their wounds to their mothers and their wives, nor do the latter fear to count and examine the wounds while they bring them food and urge them to deeds of valor....

Religion

9. Among the gods they worship Mercury [Woden] most of all, to whom it is lawful to offer human sacrifices also on stated days. Hercules [Thor] and Mars [Tiu] they placate by the sacrifice of worthy animals. Some of the Suebi sacrifice to Isis. The reason for this foreign rite and its origin I have not discovered, except that the image fashioned like a gallery shows that the cult has been introduced from abroad. On the other hand they hold it to be inconsistent with the sublimity of the celestials to confine the gods in walls made by hands, or to liken them to the form of any human countenance. They consecrate woods and sacred groves to them and give the names of the deities to that hidden mystery which they perceive by faith alone.

10. They pay as much attention as any people to augury and lots. The method of casting lots is uniform. They cut off a branch from a fruitbearing tree and divide it into small wands marked with certain characters. These they throw at random on a white cloth. Then the priest of the tribe, if it is a matter concerning the community, or the father of the family in case it is a private affair, calling on the gods and keeping his eyes raised toward the sky, takes up three of the lots, one at a time, and then interprets their meaning according to the markings before mentioned. If they have proven unfavorable there can be no further consultation that day concerning that particular matter....

Council of Chiefs and Popular Assembly

11. Concerning minor matters the chiefs deliberate, but in important affairs all the people are consulted, although the subjects referred to the common people for judgment are discussed beforehand by the chiefs. Unless some sudden and unexpected events call them together they assemble on fixed days either at the new moon or the full moon, for they think these the most auspicious times to begin their undertakings.... When the crowd is sufficient they take their places fully armed. Silence is proclaimed by the priests, who have on these occasions the right to keep order. Then the king or a chief addresses them, each being heard according to his age, noble blood, reputation in warfare and eloquence, though more because he has the power to persuade than the right to command. If an opinion is displeasing they reject it by shouting; if they agree to it they clash their spears. The most complimentary form of assent is that which is expressed by means of their weapons.

Law

12. It is also allowable in the assembly to bring up accusations, and to prosecute capital offenses. Penalties are distinguished according to crime. Traitors and deserters are hung to trees. Weaklings and cowards and those guilty of infamous vices are cast into the mire of swamps with a wattled hurdle placed over their heads. This difference of penalty indicates that violent crimes should be punished publicly while shameful acts should be hidden out of sight. Lighter offenses also are punished according to their degree, the guilty parties being fined a certain number of horses or cattle. A part of the fine goes to the king or the tribe,

part to the injured party or his relatives. In these same assemblies are chosen the magistrates who decide suits in the cantons and villages. Each one has a hundred associates, chosen from the people, who support them with their advice and influence.

The "Following" (Comitatus)

13. They undertake no public or private business without being armed. But it is not customary for anyone to bear arms until the tribe has recognized his competence to use them. Then in a full assembly some one of the chiefs or the father or relatives of the youth invest him with shield and spear. This is the sign that the lad has reached the age of manhood; this is his first honor. Before this he was only a member of a household, hereafter he is a member of the tribe. Distinguished rank or the great services of their parents secure even for lads the rank of chief. They attach themselves to certain more experienced chiefs of approved merit; nor are they ashamed to be looked upon as belonging to their followings. There are even different grades among the followers, assigned by the judgment of its leader. There is a great rivalry among these companions as to who shall rank first with the chief, and among the chiefs as to who shall have the most and the bravest followers. It is an honor and a source of strength always to be surrounded by a great band of chosen youths, for they are an ornament in peace and a defense in war. It brings reputation and glory to a leader not only in his own tribe but also among the neighboring peoples if his following is superior in numbers and courage: for he is courted by embassies and honored by gifts, and often the fame attached to his name decides wars.

Values

14. When they go into battle it is a disgrace for the chief to be outdone in deeds of valor and for the following not to match the courage of their chief; furthermore, for any one of the followers to have survived his chief and come unharmed out of a battle is life-long infamy and shame. It is in accordance with their most sacred oath of allegiance to defend and protect him and to ascribe their bravest deeds to his renown. The chief fights for victory; the men of his following for their chief. If the tribe to which they belong sinks into the lethargy of long peace and quiet, many of the noble youth voluntarily seek other tribes that are still carrying on war, because a quiet life is irksome to the Germans and they gain renown more rapidly in the midst of perils, and a large following cannot be maintained except by violence and war. For they look to the generosity of their chief for their war-horse and their deadly and victorious spear; the feasts and entertainments, however, furnished them on a homely but liberal scale, they count as mere pay. The means for this bounty are acquired through war and plunder. Nor could you persuade them to till the soil and await the yearly produce as easily as you could induce them to stir up an enemy and earn glorious wounds. They think it tame and stupid to acquire by sweat what they can win by their blood.

15. In the intervals of peace they spend some time in hunting but more in idleness, giving themselves over to sleep and eating. All the bravest and most warlike do nothing, while the hearth and home and the care of the fields is given over to the women, the old men, and the weakest members of the family. The warriors lie buried in sloth because of that strange contradiction in their nature that causes them to love indolence and hate peace....

Customs

16. It is well known that none of the German tribes live in cities, nor even allow their dwellings to be set close together. They live separated and in various places, as a spring or a meadow or a grove strikes their fancy. They lay out their villages not as with us in connected or closely-jointed houses, but each one surrounds his dwelling with an open space, either as a protection against fire or because of their ignorance of the art of building. They do not even make use of rough stones or tiles. They use for all purposes undressed timber, giving no beauty or comfort. Some parts they plaster carefully with earth of such purity and brilliancy as to form a substitute for painting and designs in color....

17. ... The women dress the same as the men except that they often wear linen undergarments which they adorn with purple stripes and do not lengthen the upper part into sleeves, but leave the arms bare. The upper part of their breasts is also exposed. However, their marriage code is strict, and in no other part of their manners are they to be praised more than in this. For almost alone among barbarian peoples they are content with one wife each, excepting those few who because of their high position rather than out of lust enter into more than one marriage engagement.

18. The wife does not bring a dowry to the husband, but the husband to the wife. The parents and relatives are present at the ceremony and examine and accept the gifts—gifts not suited to female luxury nor such as a young bride would deck herself with, but oxen, a horse and bridle, a shield, a spear, and a sword. In consideration of such gifts the man gets a wife, and she in her turn brings her husband a gift of weapons. This they consider the strongest bond, these are their mystic rites, their gods of marriage. Lest the woman think herself immune from sharing in heroic deeds and in the dangers of war, she is reminded by the initiatory ceremonies of matrimony that she is becoming the partner of her husband's labors and dangers, destined to suffer and to dare with him alike in peace and in war. The yoke of oxen, the horse and bridle, the gift of arms, give this warning. So must she live, so must she die. What things she receives she must hand down to her children worthy and untarnished so that her future daughters-in-law may receive them and pass them on to her grandchildren.

19. Thus they live in well-protected virtue, uncorrupted by the allurements of public shows or the enticement of banquets. Men and women alike know nothing of clandestine love letters. Though the nation is so populous, adultery is very rare, its punishment being immediate and inflicted by the injured husband. He cuts off the woman's hair in the presence of her kinsfolk, drives her naked from his house and flogs her through the whole village. Indeed, the loss of

chastity meets with no mercy; neither beauty, youth, nor wealth can procure the guilty woman a husband, for no one there laughs at vice, nor is corrupting and being corrupted spoken of as the way of the world. Those tribes do better still where only the virgins marry and where the hopes and aspirations of a bride are settled once and for all. They accept one husband, just as they have one body and one life; they must have no thought beyond this, no further desire. Their love must not be for the married state itself but for the husband. To limit the number of children or to put any late children to death is considered a crime, and with them good customs are more effective than good laws elsewhere.

20. In every household the children grow up naked and dirty with those stout bodies and sturdy limbs that we admire. Each mother nurses her own children; they are not handed over to servants and paid nurses. The master and the slave are in no way to be distinguished by the quality of their upbringing. They live among the same flocks and lie on the same ground until age separates them and valor distinguishes the free born. The young men marry late and their vigor is thereby unimpaired. Nor is the marriage of girls hastened. They have the same youthful vigor, the same stature as the young men. Thus well-matched and strong when they marry, the children reproduce the robustness of their parents.... A man's heirs and successors are his own children; there is no such thing as a will. If there are no children the next heirs are the brothers, then come the paternal and maternal uncles. The more relatives a man has and the greater the number of his relations by marriage, the more honored in his old age. Childlessness in Germany has no advantages.

21. A German is required to adopt not only the feuds of his father or of a relative, but also their friendships, though feuds are not irreconcilable. Even homicide is expiated by the payment of a certain number of cattle, and the whole family accepts the satisfaction—a useful practice for the community because feuds are more dangerous when there is much freedom.

No other nation indulges more freely in entertainment and hospitality. It is considered a crime to turn any man away from one's door. According to his means each one receives those who come with a well-furnished table. When all his food has been eaten, he who had been the host becomes the guide and companion of his guest to the next house, which they enter uninvited. It does not matter; they are received just as warmly. No one distinguishes between friend and stranger so far as concerns the right of hospitality. If the departing guest asks for any gift, it is customary to grant to it to him. The host, too, feels the same freedom in making a request. They take great pleasure in presents, but they ask no favor for giving them, nor do they feel any obligation in accepting them.

22. As soon as they awake from sleep, which they generally prolong until late in the day, they bathe, usually in warm water as their winter lasts a great part of the year. After the bath they take food, each sitting in a separate seat and having a table to himself. Then they proceed to their business or not less often to feasts, fully armed. It is no disgrace to spend the whole day and night in drinking. Quarreling is frequent enough as is natural among drunken men, though their disputes are rarely settled by mere wrangling but oftener by

bloodshed and wounds. Yet it is at their feasts that they consult about reconciling enemies, forming family alliances, electing chiefs, and even regarding war and peace, as they think that at no other time is the mind more open to fair judgment or more inflamed to mighty deeds....

23. A liquor for drinking bearing a certain resemblance to wine is made by the process of fermentation from barley or other grain. Those next to the border also buy wine. Their food is of a simple kind—wild fruit, fresh game, or curdled milk. They satisfy their hunger without elaborate preparation and without the use of condiments. In the matter of thirst they do not use the same moderation. If you indulge their love of drink by furnishing them as much as they wanted, they will be conquered as easily by their vices as by your arms.

26. Loaning money at interest and increasing it by compound interest is unknown, and so it is ignorance rather than legal prohibition that protects them. Land is held by the villages as communities according to the number of the cultivators, and is then divided among the freemen according to their rank. The vast extent of their territories makes this partition easy. They cultivate fresh fields every year and there is still land to spare....

27. There is no pomp in the celebration of their funerals. The only custom they observe is that the bodies of illustrious men should be burned with certain kinds of wood. They do not heap garments and perfumes upon the funeral pile. In every case a man's arms are burned with him, and sometimes his horse also. They believe that stately monuments and sculptured columns oppress the dead with their weight; a mound of turf covers their graves. Tears and lamentations are quickly laid aside; sadness and grief linger long. It is fitting for women to mourn, for men to remember.

Such in general are the facts I have obtained concerning the origin and customs of the Germans as a whole.

67 Claudius' *Letter to the Alexandrians*

Greeks, Jews, and Romans

"A solicitude of very long standing for the city"

Since the founding of the city of Alexandria, Jews had been a major constituent of the city and yet had not been accepted by the original Greek inhabitants as fully members—or citizens—of the polity. Instead, Jews had their

From *Select Papyri II. Official Documents*, edited by A. S. Hunt and C. C. Edgard, Loeb Classical Library, Vol. 282 (Cambridge Mass.: Harvard University Press, 1934), pp. 79–89. The Loeb Classical Library® is a registered trademark of the President and Fellows of Harvard College.

own *politeia* and were said to have been governed by their own ancestral laws. Over time, the attempts by Alexandrian Jews to gain civic rights and citizenship caused serious fractures that resulted even in bloody riots in the city. After one such riot, the Greeks and Jews of Alexandria sent separate delegations to the Roman emperor Claudius in an attempt to enlist his support of their respective causes. Claudius' response to these appeals is captured in his *Letter to the Alexandrians*. While we have known about this interaction from the historian Josephus, the full text of this document, dated to A.D. 41, only came to light with a discovery of a copy on papyri from the Fayum region in Egypt. The Roman Prefect at the time published this letter in Greek, having presumably translated it from an original Latin version sent by the emperor, and had the decree copied on papyri so that its content could be widely perused throughout Egypt. The emperor took up a number of different issues, including the underlying disputes that caused the recent riots, and urged on all the addressees a spirit on moderation.

LETTER OF CLAUDIUS TO THE ALEXANDRIANS

Proclamation by Lucius Aemilius Rectus [Roman prefect of Egypt]. Seeing that all the populace, owing to its numbers, was unable to be present at the reading of the most sacred and most beneficent letter to the city, I have deemed it necessary to display the letter publicly in order that reading it one by one you may admire the majesty of our god Caesar and feel gratitude for his goodwill towards the city. Year 2 of Tiberius Claudius Caesar Augustus Germanicus Imperator, the 14th of Neus Sebastus.

Tiberius Claudius Caesar Augustus Germanicus Imperator, Pontifex Maximus, holder of the Tribunician Power, consul designate, to the city of Alexandria greeting. Tiberius Claudius Barbillus, Apollonius son of Artemidorus, Chaeremon son of Leonidas, Marcus Julius Asclepiades, Gaius Julius Dionysius, Tiberius Claudius Phanias, Pasion son of Potamon, Dionysius son of Sabbion, Tiberius Claudius Archibius, Apollonius son of Ariston, Gaius Julius Apollonius, Hermaiscus son of Apollonius, your ambassadors, having delivered to me the decree, discoursed at length concerning the city, directing my attention to your goodwill towards us, which from long ago, you may be sure, had been stored up to your advantage in my memory; for you are by nature reverent towards the Augusti, as I know from many proofs, and in particular have taken a warm interest in my house, warmly reciprocated, of which fact (to mention the last instance, passing over the others) the supreme witness is my brother Germanicus addressing you in words more clearly stamped as his own. Wherefore I gladly accepted the honours given to me by you, though I have no weakness for such things. And first I permit you to keep my birthday as a *dies Augustus*[1] as you have yourselves proposed, and I agree to the erection in their several places of the statues of myself and my family; for I see that you were anxious to establish on every side memorials of your reverence for my house. Of the two golden statues

---

1. Or *dies Augusti*, a religious holiday dedicated to the Roman imperial house.

the one made to represent the Pax Augusta Claudiana, as my most honoured Barbillus suggested and entreated when I wished to refuse for fear of being thought too offensive, shall be erected at Rome, and the other according to your request shall be carried in procession on name-days in your city; and it shall be accompanied by a throne, adorned with trappings you choose. It would perhaps be foolish, while accepting such great honours, to refuse the institution of a Claudian tribe and the establishment of groves after the manner of Egypt; wherefore I grant you these requests as well, and if you wish you may also erect the equestrian statues given by Vitrasius Pollio my procurator. As for the erection of those in four-horse chariots which you wish to set up to me at the entrances into the country, I consent to let one be placed at Taposiris, the Libyan town of that name, another at Pharos in Alexandria, and a third at Pelusium in Egypt. But I deprecate the appointment of a high-priest to me and the building of temples, for I do not wish to be offensive to my contemporaries, and my opinion is that temples and such forms of honour have by all ages been granted as a prerogative to the gods alone.

Concerning the requests which you have been anxious to obtain from me, I decide as follows. All those who have become ephebi[2] up to the time of my principate I confirm and maintain in possession of the Alexandrian citizenship with all the privileges and indulgences enjoyed by the city, excepting such as by beguiling you have contrived to become ephebi though born of servile mothers; and it is equally my will that all the other favours shall be confirmed which were granted to you by former princes and kings and praefects, as the deified Augustus also confirmed them. It is my will that the *neocori*[3] of the temple of the deified Augustus in Alexandria shall be chosen by lot in the same way as those of the said deified Augustus in Canopus are chosen by lot. With regard to the civic magistracies being made triennial your proposal seems to me to be very good; for through fear of being called to account for any abuse of power your magistrates will behave with greater circumspection during their term of office. Concerning the senate, what your custom may have been under the ancient kings I have no means of saying, but that you had no senate under the former Augusti you are well aware. As this is the first broaching of a novel project, whose utility to the city and to my government is not evident, I have written to Aemilius Rectus to hold an inquiry and inform me whether in the first place it is right that a senate should be constituted and, if it should be right to create one, in what manner this is to be done.

As for the question which party was responsible for the riots and feud (or rather, if the truth must be told, the war) with the Jews, although in confrontation with their opponents your ambassadors, and particularly Dionysius son of Theon, contended with great zeal, nevertheless I was unwilling to make a strict inquiry, though guarding within me a store of immutable indignation against whichever party renews the conflict; and I tell you once for all that unless you put a stop to this ruinous and obstinate enmity against each other, I shall be driven to show

---

2. Ephebes were Greek citizen youths between the ages of 18 and 20.

3. Those who supervised the maintenance of temples.

what a benevolent prince can be when turned to righteous indignation. Wherefore once again I conjure you that on the one hand the Alexandrians show themselves forbearing and kindly towards the Jews who for many years have dwelt in the same city, and dishonour none of the rites observed by them in the worship of their god, but allow them to observe their customs as in the time of the deified Augustus, which customs I also, after hearing both sides, have sanctioned; and on the other hand I explicitly order the Jews not to agitate for more privileges than they formerly possessed, and not in future to send out a separate embassy as if they lived in a separate city, a thing unprecedented, and not to force their way into gymnasiarchic or cosmetic games, while enjoying their own privileges and sharing a great abundance of advantages in a city not their own, and not to bring in or admit Jews who come down the river from Syria or Egypt, a proceeding which will compel me to conceive serious suspicions; otherwise I will by all means take vengeance on them as fomenters of what is a general plague infecting the whole world. If desisting from these courses you consent to live with mutual forbearance and kindliness, I on my side will exercise a solicitude of very long standing for the city, as one which is bound to us by traditional friendship. I bear witness to my friend Barbillus of the solicitude which he has always shown for you in my presence and of the extreme zeal with which he has now advocated your cause, and likewise to my friend Tiberius Claudius Archibius. Farewell.

68 Rebels Against Rome

The territorial expansion of Rome was not always met with success or local acquiescence. On several notable occasions, indigenous peoples resisted Roman power, particularly when it was exercised in an abusive manner by provincial governors who paid little heed to local sentiments. During the reign of Emperor Nero, major rebellions on opposite sides of the Roman Empire broke out in Britain and Judaea. They presage the unrest that would eventually bring an end to the Julio-Claudian dynasty.

A. TACITUS, *ANNALS*: THE REBELLION OF
BOUDICCA IN BRITAIN

"That is what I, a woman, plan to do!"

During the reign of Emperor Claudius, in A.D. 43, the Romans established a province in southern Britain after several previous attempts had failed.

From *Tacitus: The Annals of Imperial Rome*, Revised Edition, translated by Michael Grant, pp. 326–31. Reprinted by permission of Penguin Books, Ltd.

The process of romanization was well under way, with towns such as Camulodunum (Colchester), Verulamium (St. Albans), and Londinium (London) serving as centers of Roman influence. Some Roman governors, such as Agricola, the father-in-law of the historian Tacitus, ruled wisely and gained the trust and support of local inhabitants; others took undue advantage of their power and increased local resistance to Roman rule.

In A.D. 60, the chief of the tribe of the Iceni, who had been a Roman client-king, passed away. The local Roman authorities took advantage of the situation to seize his goods and violate the persons of his daughters. Boudicca, the indignant queen and widow of the late king, led the Iceni in a desperate war of independence against the Romans and enjoyed some early successes. There was much slaughter on both sides. In the end, the Romans were triumphant in battle, and the revolt was suppressed by the following year. This selection, from the *Annals* of Tacitus, illustrates a rather sympathetic Roman portrayal of this revolt against Roman rule.

... The following year, when the consuls were Lucius Caesennius Paetus and Publius Petronius Turpilianus, witnessed a serious disaster in Britain. The imperial governor Aulus Didius Gallus had, as I have said, merely held his own. His successor Quintus Veranius had only conducted minor raids against the Silures when death terminated his operations. His life had been famous for its austerity. But his testamentary last words were glaringly self-seeking, for they grossly flattered Nero and added that Veranius, if he had lived two years longer, would have presented him with the whole province.

The new imperial governor of Britain was Gaius Suetonius Paulinus. Corbulo's rival in military science, as in popular talk—which makes everybody compete—he was ambitious to achieve victories as glorious as the reconquest of Armenia. So Suetonius planned to attack the island of Mona, which although thickly populated had also given sanctuary to many refugees.

Flat-bottomed boats were built to contend with the shifting shallows, and these took the infantry across. Then came the cavalry; some utilized fords, but in deeper water the men swam beside their horses. The enemy lined the shore in a dense armed mass. Among them were black-robed women with dishevelled hair like Furies, brandishing torches. Close by stood Druids, raising their hands to heaven and screaming dreadful curses.

This weird spectacle awed the Roman soldiers into a sort of paralysis. They stood still—and presented themselves as a target. But then they urged each other (and were urged by the general) not to fear a horde of fanatical women. Onward pressed their standards and they bore down their opponents, enveloping them in the flames of their own torches. Suetonius garrisoned the conquered island. The groves devoted to Mona's barbarous superstitions he demolished. For it was their religion to drench their altars in the blood of prisoners and consult their gods by means of human entrails.

While Suetonius was thus occupied, he learnt of a sudden rebellion in the province. Prasutagus, king of the Iceni, after a life of long and renowned prosperity, had made the emperor co-heir with his own two daughters. Prasutagus hoped by this submissiveness to preserve his kingdom and household from attack. But it turned out otherwise. Kingdom and household alike were plundered like prizes of war, the one by Roman officers, the other by Roman slaves. As a beginning, his widow Boudicca was flogged and their daughters raped. The Icenian chiefs were deprived of their hereditary estates as if the Romans had been given the whole country. The king's own relatives were treated like slaves.

And the humiliated Iceni feared still worse, now that they had been reduced to provincial status. So they rebelled. With them rose the Trinobantes and others. Servitude had not broken them, and they had secretly plotted together to become free again. They particularly hated the Roman ex-soldiers who had recently established a settlement at Camulodunum. The settlers drove the Trinobantes from their homes and land, and called them prisoners and slaves. The troops encouraged the settlers' outrages, since their own way of behaving was the same—and they looked forward to similar licence for themselves. Moreover, the temple erected to the divine Claudius was a blatant stronghold of alien rule, and its observances were a pretext to make the natives appointed as its priests drain the whole country dry.

It seemed easy to destroy the settlement; for it had no walls. That was a matter which Roman commanders, thinking of amenities rather than needs, had neglected. At this juncture, for no visible reason, the statue of Victory at Camulodunum fell down—with its back turned as though it were fleeing the enemy. Delirious women chanted of destruction at hand. They cried that in the local senate-house outlandish yells had been heard; the theatre had echoed with shrieks; at the mouth of the Thames a phantom settlement had been seen in ruins. A blood-red colour in the sea, too, and shapes like human corpses left by the ebb tide, were interpreted hopefully by the Britons—and with terror by the settlers.

Suetonius, however, was far away. So they appealed for help to the imperial agent Catus Decianus. He sent them barely two hundred men, incompletely armed. There was also a small garrison on the spot. Reliance was placed on the temple's protection. Misled by secret pro-rebels, who hampered their plans, they dispensed with rampart or trench. They omitted also to evacuate old people and women and thus leave only fighting men behind. Their precautions were appropriate to a time of unbroken peace.

Then a native horde surrounded them. When all else had been ravaged or burnt, the garrison concentrated itself in the temple. After two days' siege, it fell by storm. The ninth Roman division, commanded by Quintus Petilius Cerialis Caesius Rufus, attempted to relieve the town, but was stopped by the victorious Britons and routed. Its entire infantry force was massacred, while the commander escaped to his camp with his cavalry and sheltered behind its defences. The imperial agent Catus Decianus, horrified by the catastrophe and by his unpopularity, withdrew to Gaul. It was his rapacity which had driven the province to war.

But Suetonius, undismayed, marched through disaffected territory to Londinium. This town did not rank as a Roman settlement, but was an important centre for business-men and merchandise. At first, he hesitated whether to stand and fight there. Eventually, his numerical inferiority—and the price only too clearly paid by the divisional commander's rashness—decided him to sacrifice the single city of Londinium to save the province as a whole. Unmoved by lamentations and appeals, Suetonius gave the signal for departure. The inhabitants were allowed to accompany him. But those who stayed because they were women, or old, or attached to the place, were slaughtered by the enemy. Verulamium suffered the same fate.

The natives enjoyed plundering and thought of nothing else. Bypassing forts and garrisons, they made for where loot was richest and protection weakest. Roman and provincial deaths at the places mentioned are estimated at seventy thousand. For the British did not take or sell prisoners, or practise other wartime exchanges. They could not wait to cut throats, hang, burn, and crucify— as though avenging, in advance, the retribution that was on its way.

Suetonius collected the fourteenth brigade and detachments of the twentieth, together with the nearest available auxiliaries—amounting to nearly ten thousand armed men—and decided to attack without further delay. He chose a position in a defile with a wood behind him. There could be no enemy, he knew, except at his front, where there was open country without cover for ambushes. Suetonius drew up his regular troops in close order, with the light-armed auxiliaries at their flanks, and the cavalry massed on the wings. On the British side, cavalry and infantry bands seethed over a wide area in unprecedented numbers. Their confidence was such that they brought their wives with them to see the victory, installing them in carts stationed at the edge of the battlefield.

Boudicca drove round all the tribes in a chariot with her daughters in front of her. 'We British are used to woman commanders in war,' she cried. 'I am descended from mighty men! But now I am not fighting for my kingdom and wealth. I am fighting as an ordinary person for my lost freedom, my bruised body, and my outraged daughters. Nowadays Roman rapacity does not even spare our bodies. Old people are killed, virgins raped. But the gods will grant us the vengeance we deserve! The Roman division which dared to fight is annihilated. The others cower in their camps, or watch for a chance to escape. They will never face even the din and roar of all our thousands, much less the shock of our onslaught. Consider how many of you are fighting—and why. Then you will win this battle, or perish. That is what I, a woman, plan to do!—let the men live in slavery if they will.'

Suetonius trusted his men's bravery. Yet he too, at this critical moment, offered encouragement and appeals. 'Disregard the clamours and empty threats of the natives!' he said. 'In their ranks, there are more women than fighting men. Unwarlike, unarmed, when they see the arms and courage of the conquerors who have routed them so often, they will break immediately. Even when a force contains many divisions, few among them win the battles—what special glory for your small numbers to win the renown of a whole army! Just keep in close order. Throw your javelins, and then carry on: use shield-bosses to fell them, swords to kill them. Do not think of plunder. When you have won, you will have everything.'

The general's words were enthusiastically received: the old battle-experienced soldiers longed to hurl their javelins. So Suetonius confidently gave the signal for battle. At first the regular troops stood their ground. Keeping to the defile as a natural defence, they launched their javelins accurately at the approaching enemy. Then, in wedge formation, they burst forward. So did the auxiliary infantry. The cavalry, too, with lances extended, demolished all serious resistance. The remaining Britons fled with difficulty since their ring of wagons blocked the outlets. The Romans did not spare even the women. Baggage animals too, transfixed with weapons, added to the heaps of dead.

It was a glorious victory, comparable with bygone triumphs. According to one report almost eighty thousand Britons fell. Our own casualties were about four hundred dead and a slightly larger number of wounded. Boudicca poisoned herself....

B. JOSEPHUS, *HISTORY OF THE JEWISH WAR*: RESISTANCE IS FUTILE

"So there is no refuge left except to make God your ally."

As with most imperial peoples, the Romans relied on military as well as psychological force to maintain the stability of their far-flung domains. For this reason, Rome aimed to make a strong impression around the world so that none of its subjects, realizing the futility of resistance, would even contemplate rebellion. Instead they would be persuaded that continued obedience was the safest and best course of action. Although Roman rule promised many benefits in the form of peace and prosperity, this Roman policy was not always and everywhere effective.

In A.D. 66, a full-scale rebellion broke out in the Roman province of Judaea. According to the Jewish general and writer Josephus, whose *History of the Jewish War* remains the most important source for the war, it was the combined result of Roman misrule, Jewish internal dissensions, and an escalating series of tense confrontations between the Jews, Greeks, and Romans. On the eve of the revolt, the Roman client-king Agrippa II tried unsuccessfully to persuade the Jews to abandon their plan. Josephus, himself a contemporary and participant in the events, used the speech of Agrippa to outline his own subsequent view of the futility of resisting Rome.

The war of the Jews against the Romans was the greatest of our time; greater too, perhaps, than any recorded struggle whether between cities or nations. Yet persons with no first-hand knowledge, accepting baseless and inconsistent stories on hearsay, have written garbled accounts of it, while those of eyewitnesses have been falsified either to flatter the Romans or to vilify the Jews, eulogy or abuse

From *Josephus: The Jewish War*, translated by G. A. Williamson, pp. 28, 149–52, 156–62. Reproduced by permission of Penguin Books, Ltd.

Spoils from the Temple of Jerusalem were paraded by the Romans in the triumph of Titus. A stone relief from the Arch of Titus in the Forum of the city of Rome.

being substituted for factual record. So for the benefit of the Emperor's subjects I have decided to translate into Greek the books which I wrote some time ago in my native language for circulation among non-Greek speakers inland. I myself, Josephus, son of Matthias, am a Hebrew by race, and a priest from Jerusalem; in the early stages I fought against the Romans, and of the later events I was an unwilling witness.

This upheaval, as I said, was the greatest of all time; and when it occurred Rome herself was in a most unsettled state. Jewish revolutionaries took advantage of the general disturbance; they had vast resources of men and money; and so widespread was the ferment that some were filled with hope of gain, others with fear of loss, by the state of affairs in the East; for the Jews expected all their Mesopotamian brethren to join their insurrection. From another side Roman supremacy was being challenged by the Gauls on their borders, and the Celts were restive—in fact after Nero's death disorder reigned everywhere. Presented with this opportunity many aspired to the imperial throne, while the soldiery were eager for a transference of power as a means of enriching themselves.

I therefore thought it inexcusable, when such issues were involved, to see the truth misrepresented and to take no notice. Parthians, Babylonians, Southern Arabians, Mesopotamian Jews, and Adiabenians, thanks to my labours, were accurately informed of the causes of the war, the sufferings it involved, and its disastrous ending. Were the Greeks and those Romans who took no part in it to remain ignorant of the facts, deluded with flattery or fiction? Yet the writers I have in mind claim to be writing history, though besides getting all their facts wrong they seem to me to miss their target altogether. For they wish to establish the greatness of the Romans while all the time disparaging and deriding the actions of the Jews. But I do not see how men can prove themselves great by overcoming feeble opponents! Again, they are not impressed by the length of the war, the vastness of the Roman forces which endured such hardships, and the genius of their commanders, whose strenuous endeavours before Jerusalem will bring them little glory if the difficulties they overcame are belittled.

However, it is not my intention to counter the champions of the Romans by exaggerating the heroism of my own countrymen: I shall state the facts accurately and impartially. At the same time the language in which I record the events will reflect my own feelings and emotions; for I must permit myself to bewail my country's tragedy. She was destroyed by internal dissension.... For it so happened that of all the cities under Roman rule our own reached the highest summit of prosperity, and in turn fell into the lowest depths of misery; the misfortunes of all other races since the beginning of history, compared with those of the Jews, seem small; and for our misfortunes we have only ourselves to blame....

The Escalation of Local Tensions

The next procurator, Festus, tackled the chief curse of the country; he killed a considerable number of the bandits and captured many more. Albinus, who followed him, acted very differently, being guilty of every possible misdemeanour. Not content with official actions that meant widespread robbery and looting of private property, or with taxes that crippled the whole nation, he allowed those imprisoned for banditry by local courts or his own predecessors to be bought out by their relatives, and only the man who failed to pay was left in jail to serve his sentence. Now too the revolutionary party in Jerusalem cast off all restraint, and its leaders bribed Albinus to shut his eyes to their subversive activities, whilst any of the common people who did not care for peace and quiet joined forces with the procurator's associates. Every scoundrel, surrounded by his own gang, stood out from his followers like a bandit chief or dictator and used his henchmen to rob respectable citizens. The result was that the victims kept their wrongs to themselves while those still immune, through fear of the same fate, flattered those they should have battered. In short, free speech was completely suppressed and tyranny reigned everywhere; from then on the seeds of the coming destruction were being sown in the City.

Such a man was Albinus, but his successor Gessius Florus made him appear an angel by comparison. Albinus for the most part did his mischief with secrecy and dissimulation; Gessius boasted of the wrongs he did to the nation and, as if sent as public executioner to punish condemned criminals, indulged in every kind of robbery and violence. When pitiable things happened, he showed himself the most heartless of men; when disgraceful things, the most disgusting.

No one ever had less use for truth or thought out more subtle methods of crime. Making a profit out of individuals he considered poor sport: he stripped whole cities, ruined complete communities, and virtually announced to the entire country that everyone might be a bandit if he chose, so long as he himself received a rake-off. The result of his avarice was that every district was denuded, and many people left their old homes and fled to foreign provinces.

As long as Cestius Gallus was in Syria administering his province, no one dared even to approach him with complaints against Florus; but when he appeared in Jerusalem on the eve of the Passover, the people crowded round— at least 3,000,000 of them—imploring him to pity the nation in its distress and shouting against Florus, the ruin of their country. Florus, who was present and stood at Cestius' side, laughed at their protests. Cestius, however, quieted the excited crowd by assuring them that he would guarantee more reasonable conduct on Florus' part in the future. Then he returned to Antioch. But Florus accompanied him as far as Caesarea, disguising the intention he had already formed of making war on the nation, his only hope of diverting attention from his own crimes; for if peace lasted, he foresaw that he would have the Jews accusing him to Caesar, but if he contrived to make them revolt, the greater outrage would forestall any enquiry into lesser ones. So to ensure a nation-wide revolt he daily added to the general distress.

... War broke out in the twelfth year of Nero's reign and the seventeenth of Agrippa's, in the month of Artemisios. In comparison with the fearful disasters to which it led its pretext was insignificant. The Jews in Caesarea had a synagogue alongside a piece of ground belonging to a Greek citizen. This they had repeatedly tried to acquire, offering many times the real value. Scorning their requests, the Greek further insulted them by beginning to build a factory right up to the dividing line, leaving them a narrow and utterly inadequate passage. The immediate result was that the more hot-headed of the young men jumped in and interfered with the builders. When this display of force was suppressed by Florus, the leading Jews, among them John the tax-collector, having no other way out, gave Florus a bribe of eight silver talents to put a stop to the work. As nothing mattered to him but money, he promised full co-operation; but as soon as the money was his, he left Caesarea for Sebaste, allowing party strife to take its course as if he had sold the Jews permission to fight it out!

The next day was a Sabbath, and when the Jews gathered in the synagogue a Caesarean partisan had placed a chamber-pot upside down at the entrance and was sacrificing birds on it. This infuriated the Jews, who felt that their Law had been violated and the site desecrated. The steadier, gentler people advised an appeal to the authorities; the quarrelsome element and youthful hotheads burned for a fight. The Caesarean partisans stood waiting for them, for they had sent the men to sacrifice by prearrangement, and the clash soon came. Jucundus, the cavalry officer detailed to prevent it, stepped forward, picked up the pot, and attempted to end the strife. But he was no match for the violence of the Caesareans, so the Jews seized the rolls of the Law and retired to Narbata, a Jewish area seven miles from Caesarea....

This new outrage caused anger in Jerusalem, but passions were still kept under control. Florus, however, as if he had contracted to fan the war into flame, sent to the Temple treasury and removed seventeen talents on the pretext that Caesar required it. Uproar followed at once and the people rushed in a body into the Temple, where with piercing yells they called on the name of Caesar, imploring him to free them from Florus' misrule. Some of the rioters shouted the most scandalous abuse at the latter, and going round with a basket begged coppers for the poor starveling! This did not cure his avarice but increased his determination to get rich quickly. So instead of going to Caesarea to extinguish the conflagration that was breaking out there and to remove the causes of the trouble—as he had been paid to do—he dashed off to Jerusalem with an army of horse and foot, in order that he might get what he wanted with the help of Roman arms, and by intimidation skin the City. The people, anxious to make him ashamed of his attempt, met the soldiers with friendly greetings and prepared to receive Florus submissively. He, however, sent ahead fifty horsemen commanded by Capito, ... and when Capito's troops charged into their midst, they scattered before they could salute Florus or convince the soldiers of their readiness to obey. Returning to their homes they passed the night in fear and dejection.

Florus slept in the Palace, and the next day had a dais erected outside and took his seat. The chief priests, political leaders, and eminent citizens lined up before this tribunal. Florus ordered them to give up the men who had abused him, declaring that they themselves would feel the weight of his hand if the culprits were not forthcoming. The Jewish leaders insisted that the people were peacefully disposed and apologized for the offending remarks; in such a mass of people there were bound to be some impudent juveniles, and it was impossible to identify the miscreants when everyone was conscience-stricken and afraid to confess his guilt. If Florus cared anything about the peaceful state of the nation and wished to save the City for the Romans, it would be better for the sake of the innocent to pardon the few guilty than because of a few scamps to wreck the lives of so many loyal subjects....

The Eve of War

The Jewish crowd now turned to the king [Agrippa] and the chief priests, begging them to send envoys to Nero to denounce Florus, and by protesting against his wholesale massacres to end suspicions of a Jewish revolt. For they would be thought to have started hostilities if they were not quick to point out the real aggressor. It was evident that they would not take it quietly if anyone tried to block the embassy. Agrippa realized that to choose men to accuse Florus would be to ask for trouble, but that to stand by till Jewish fury flared up into actual hostilities was dangerous even for himself. So he summoned the crowd into the Gymnasium and placed his sister Berenice conspicuously on the roof of the Hasmonaean Palace. This was above the Gymnasium on the other side of the Upper City; the Gymnasium was linked with the Temple by a bridge. Then he began:

'If I had found you all eager for war with the Romans, whereas in fact the most honest and sincere section of the people are bent on keeping the peace, I should not have come forward to address you or ventured to give advice, for it is a waste of breath to say anything in favour of a wise course when the audience is unanimously in favour of a foolish one. But some of you are young men with no experience of the horrors of war, others are too sanguine about the prospects of independence, and others are led on by selfish ambition and the profit to be made out of weaker men if the explosion occurs. So in the hope that these men may learn sense and change their ways, and that the folly of a few may not be visited on good citizens, I felt obliged to call you all together and tell you what I think is best. Please do not interrupt me if you disapprove of what I say; for those who have absolutely made up their mind to revolt will be free to feel the same after hearing my views, but my words will be lost even on those who want to listen unless everyone keeps quiet.

'Now I am aware that many rant against the insolence of the procurators and rhapsodize about the wonders of liberty; but before I go into the question of who you are and whom you are planning to fight, I must first sort out your jumble of pretexts. If you are trying to avenge your wrongs, why do you prate about liberty? If on the other hand slavery seems unbearable, it is a waste of time to blame your rulers; if they were the mildest of men, it would still be disgraceful to be slaves.

'Consider these pretexts one at a time, and see how feeble are your grounds for war. First, the charges against the procurators. You should flatter, not provoke, the authorities; when for trifling errors you pile on reproaches, it is yourselves you hurt by your denunciation of the offenders; instead of injuring you secretly and shamefacedly they plunder you openly. Nothing damps an aggressor like patient submission, and the meekness of the persecuted puts the persecutor to shame. I grant that the ministers of Rome are unbearably harsh; does it follow that all the Romans are persecuting you, including Caesar? Yet it is on them that you are going to make war! It is not by their wish that an unscrupulous governor comes from Rome, and western eyes cannot see the goings-on in the east; it is not easy in Rome even to get up-to-date news of what happens here. It would be absurd because of the trifling misdemeanours of one man to go to war with a whole nation, and such a nation—a nation that does not even know what it is all about! Our grievances can be quickly put right; the same procurator will not be here for ever, and his successors are almost sure to be more reasonable. But once set on foot, war cannot easily be either broken off or fought to a conclusion without disaster.

'As for your new passion for liberty, it comes too late; you ought to have made a supreme effort to retain it long ago. For the experience of slavery is a painful one, and to escape it altogether any effort is justified; but the man who has once submitted and then revolts is a refractory slave, not a lover of liberty. Thus the time when we ought to have done everything possible to keep the Romans out was when the country was invaded by Pompey. But our ancestors and their kings, with material, physical, and mental resources far superior to yours, faced a mere fraction of the Roman army and put up no resistance; will you, who have learnt submission from your fathers and are so ill provided compared with those who first submitted, stand up to the whole Roman Empire? ...

'Where are the men, where are the weapons you count on? Where is the fleet that is to sweep the Roman seas? Where are the funds to pay for your expeditions? Do you think you are going to war with Egyptians and Arabs? Look at the far-flung empire of Rome and contrast your own impotence. Why, our forces have been worsted even by our neighbours again and again, while their arms have triumphed over the whole world! And even the world is not big enough to satisfy them; the Euphrates is not far enough to the east, or the Danube to the north, or Libya and the desert beyond to the south, or Cadiz to the west; but beyond the Ocean they have sought a new world, carrying their arms as far as Britain, that land of mystery. Why not face facts? Are you richer than the Gauls, stronger than the Germans, cleverer than the Greeks, more numerous than all the nations of the world? What gives you confidence to defy the power of Rome?

'It is terrible to be enslaved, it will be said. How much worse for Greeks, who surpass every nation under the sun in nobility and fill such a wide domain, and yet bow before the *fasces* of a Roman governor, as do the Macedonians, who have a better right than you to demand their liberty! And what of the five hundred cities of Asia? Do they not without a garrison bow before one governor and the consular *fasces*? Need I mention the Heniochi, the Colchians, and the Tauric race, the peoples near the Bosporus, the Black Sea, and the Sea of Azov? At one time they recognized not even a native ruler, and now they submit to 3,000 legionaries, while forty warships keep the peace on the sea where before none but pirates sailed. How justly Bithynia, Cappadocia, Pamphylia, Lycia, and Cilicia might demand liberty! Yet without armed pressure they pay their dues.

'Then there are the Thracians, spread over a country five days' march in width and seven in length, more rugged and much more defensible than yours, a country whose icy blasts are enough to halt an invader. Yet 2,000 Roman guards suffice to maintain order. Their neighbours the Illyrians, whose land extends from Dalmatia to the Danube frontier, need only two legions to keep them quiet; in fact Illyrians unite with Romans to halt Dacian raids. The Dalmatians again, who have so often tried to shake off the yoke and have always been driven by defeat to rally their forces and revolt again, now live peaceably under one Roman legion!

'But if any people might reasonably be tempted to rebel by its peculiar advantages, that people is the Gauls, provided as they are with such marvellous natural defences, on the east the Alps, on the north the Rhine, on the south the Pyrenees, and on the west the Ocean. Yet in spite of these immense obstacles, in spite of their huge total of three hundred and five tribes, in spite of the prosperity that wells up from their soil and enables them to flood the whole world with their goods, they submit to being the milch cow of Rome and receiving from her hands what they themselves have produced! And this they tolerate, not from effeminacy or racial inferiority—they fought for eighty years to save their liberty—but because they are overawed by the might of Rome and still more by her destiny, which wins her more victories than do her arms. So Gaul is kept in order by 1,200 soldiers—hardly more men than she has cities!

'Then Spain—in the fight for independence the gold from her soil could not save her, nor could the vast stretch of land and sea that separates her from Rome, nor the tribes of Lusitania and Cantabria with their passion for fighting, nor the neighbouring Ocean that terrifies even the natives with its tides. Crossing the cloud-capped Pyrenees and advancing their arms beyond the Pillars of Hercules, the Romans enslaved Spain too. Yet to guard this remote and almost invincible nation requires but one legion!

'Which of you has not heard of the Germans, with their inexhaustible man-power? You have, I am sure, seen their magnificent physique on many occasions, for on every side Roman masters have German slaves; yet this people occupies an immense area, their physique is surpassed by their pride, from the bottom of their hearts they despise death, and when enraged they are more dangerous than the fiercest of wild beasts. Yet the Rhine is the limit of their aggression and the Romans with eight legions have tamed them, enslaving the prisoners and driving the entire nation to seek refuge in flight.

'Consider the defences of the Britons, you who feel so sure of the defences of Jerusalem. They are surrounded by the Ocean and inhabit an island as big as the land which we inhabit; yet the Romans crossed the sea and enslaved them, and four legions keep that huge island quiet. But why should I say more about that, when even the Parthians, the most warlike race of all, rulers of so many nations and protected by such vast forces, send hostages to Rome, and on Italian soil may be seen, humbly submitting for the sake of peace, the aristocrats of the east.

'Almost every nation under the sun bows down before the might of Rome; and will you alone go to war, not even considering the fate of the Carthaginians, who boasted of great Hannibal and their glorious Phoenician ancestors, but fell beneath Scipio's hand? The Cyrenians (Spartans by descent), the Marmaridae (a race that extends to the waterless desert), Syrtes, whose very mention terrifies, Nasamonians, Moors, Numidians with their vast numbers—none of them could resist Roman skill at arms. This third of the whole world, whose nations could hardly be counted, bounded by the Atlantic and the Pillars of Hercules, and supporting the millions of Ethiopia as far as the Indian Ocean, is subdued in its entirety; and apart from the regular crops which for eight months of the year feed the whole population of Rome, these people pay tribute of every kind, and for the needs of the Empire willingly submit to taxation; and unlike you they take no offence when given orders, though only a single legion is quartered in their midst.

'But why should we go so far for evidence of the Roman power when we can find it in Egypt, our nearest neighbour? She stretches as far as Ethiopia and Arabia Felix; she is the port for India; she has a population of seven and a half million (excluding the citizens of Alexandria), as is shown by the poll-tax returns. But she does not repudiate the rule of Rome—yet what a stimulus to revolt she has in Alexandria with its size, its population and its wealth! a city three and a half miles long and over a mile wide, which pays Rome every month more tribute than you pay in a year, and apart from money sends her corn for four months, and which is protected on every side by trackless deserts or harbourless seas or rivers or marshes. Yet none of these things proved equal to the fortune of Rome, and two legions stationed in the city curb the remotest parts of Egypt and the nobility of Macedon as well.

'Whom, I ask you, will you find in the uninhabited wilds to be your allies in this war? for in the inhabited world all are Romans—unless you extend your hopes beyond the Euphrates and imagine that your kinsmen from Adiabene will come to your aid! But they will not without good reason get involved in a full-scale war, and if they should decide on anything so foolish, the Parthian king would put a stop to it; for he is anxious to preserve his armistice with the Romans, and will consider it a breach of the truce if any of his tributaries takes the field against them.

'So there is no refuge left except to make God your ally. But He too is ranged on the Roman side, for without His help so vast an empire could never have been built up. Think too how difficult it would be, even if you were fighting feeble opponents, to preserve the purity of your religion, and how you will be forced to transgress the very laws which furnish your chief hope of making God your ally, and so will alienate Him. If you observe the custom of the Sabbath with its complete cessation of activity, you will promptly be crushed, as were your ancestors by Pompey, who was most active in pressing the siege on the days when the besieged were passive. But if in the war you transgress your ancestral Law I don't see what you have left to fight for, since your one desire is that none of your ancestral customs should be broken. How will you be able to call the Deity to your aid, if you deliberately deny Him the service that is due?

'Everyone who engages in war relies on either divine or human help; but when, as is probable, both are denied, the aggressor is bringing certain destruction on himself. What prevents you from killing your wives and children with your own hands and from consigning your ancestral home, the most beautiful in the world, to the flames? By such madness you would at least avoid the shame of defeat! It is wise, my friends, it is wise, while the vessel is still in harbour, to foresee the approaching storm, and not to sail out into the middle of the hurricane to sure destruction. For those on whom disaster falls out of the blue are at least entitled to pity, but a man who plunges into destruction with his eyes open earns only contempt.

'Possibly some of you suppose that you are making war in accordance with agreed rules, and that when the Romans have won they will be kind to you, and will not think of making you an example to other nations by burning down your Holy City and destroying your entire race. I tell you, not even if you survive will you find a place of refuge, since every people recognizes the lordship of Rome or fears that it will have to do so. Again, the danger threatens not only ourselves here but also those who live in other cities; for there is not a region in the world without its Jewish colony. All these, if you go to war, will be massacred by your opponents, and through the folly of a few men every city will run with Jewish blood. There would be an excuse for such a massacre; but if it did not take place, think how wicked it would be to take up arms against such kindly people! Pity your wives and children, or at least pity your mother city and its sacred precincts. Spare the Temple and preserve for your use the Sanctuary with its sacred treasures. For the Romans will no longer keep their hands off when they have captured these, since for sparing them hitherto they have received no thanks at all. I call to witness all you hold sacred, the holy angels of God, and the Fatherland we all share, that I have not kept back anything that is for your safety; if you make a right decision, you will share with me the blessings of peace, but if you are carried away by your passion, you will go without me to your doom.'

At the end of his speech he burst into tears as did his sister, and with his tears considerably damped the ardour of his hearers. But they shouted that it was not Rome they were fighting, it was Florus—the man who had done them such wrong....

69 Pliny's Correspondence with Trajan

Rome as Benevolent Ruler

"Worthy of ... the splendor of your reign"

Pliny the Younger (62–ca. 115) rose in Roman imperial service under his friend the emperor Trajan and reached the high office of consul. He admired Trajan as an ideal prince, and in addition to composing a *Panegyric* in the emperor's praise, Pliny published a body of correspondence between himself and the emperor. In 109, Trajan appointed him the special governor of Bithynia-Pontus, a territory on the southern shores of the Black Sea that was experiencing severe local problems. Pliny dutifully traveled from one city to the next trying to resolve outstanding social and financial issues, tackling one nettlesome problem after another. He wrote on a regular basis to his emperor and friend asking for advice and affirmation for his decisions; the emperor's replies show a careful attentiveness to his friend's missives and the minutiae of the many local issues Pliny raised in them. Pliny and Trajan's correspondence offers a fascinating glimpse into the mind-set of the high Roman elite and its attitudes toward the people it ruled. Historians often hold this correspondence up as an example of the admirable official Roman concern for the welfare of the governed. Trajan's reign is accordingly considered a prime example of an enlightened imperial regime when governing well was seen as both the duty and the glory of the ruler.

From Pliny the Younger, *Letters* 10.15–18, 23–24, 31–38, 65–66; in *Pliny. Letters and Panegyric*, translated by Betty Radice, Loeb Classical Library, Vol. 5 (Cambridge Mass.: Harvard University Press, 1969), v. 2, pp. 187–91, 197, 203–13, 249–51. The Loeb Classical Library® is a registered trademark of the President and Fellows of Harvard College.

XV

PLINY TO THE EMPEROR TRAJAN

I feel sure, Sir, that you will be interested to hear that I have rounded Cape Malea and arrived at Ephesus with my complete staff, after being delayed by contrary winds. My intention now is to travel on to my province partly by coastal boat and partly by carriage. The intense heat prevents my travelling entirely by road and the prevailing Etesian winds make it impossible to go all the way by sea.

XVI

TRAJAN TO PLINY

You did well to send me news, my dear Pliny, for I am much interested to know what sort of journey you are having to your province. You are wise to adapt yourself to local conditions and travel either by boat or carriage.

XVII A

PLINY TO THE EMPEROR TRAJAN

I kept in excellent health, Sir, throughout my voyage to Ephesus, but I found the intense heat very trying when I went on to travel by road and developed a touch of fever which kept me at Pergamum. Then, when I had resumed my journey by coastal boat, I was further delayed by contrary winds, so that I did not reach Bithynia until 17 September. I had hoped to arrive earlier, but I cannot complain of the delay as I was in time to celebrate your birthday in my province, and this should be a good omen.

   I am now examining the finances of the town of Prusa, expenditure, revenues, and sums owing, and finding the inspection increasingly necessary the more I look into their accounts; large sums of money are detained in the hands of private individuals for various reasons, and further sums are paid out for quite illegal purposes, I am writing this letter, Sir, immediately after my arrival here.

XVII B

PLINY TO THE EMPEROR TRAJAN

I entered my province, Sir, on 17 September, and found there the spirit of obedience and loyalty which is your just tribute from mankind.

   Will you consider, Sir, whether you think it necessary to send out a land surveyor? Substantial sums of money could, I think, be recovered from contractors of public works if we had dependable surveys made. I am convinced of this by the accounts of Prusa, which I am handling with all possible care.

XVIII

TRAJAN TO PLINY

I wish you could have reached Bithynia without any illness yourself or in your party, and that your journey from Ephesus had been as easy as your voyage there. The date of your arrival in Bithynia, my dear Pliny, I have noted from your letter. The people there will appreciate, I think, that I am acting in their own interests, and you too will see that it is made clear to them that you were chosen as my representative for a special mission. Your first task must be to inspect the accounts of the various towns, as they are evidently in confusion.

As for land surveyors, I have scarcely enough for the public works in progress in Rome or in the neighbourhood, but there are reliable surveyors to be found in every province and no doubt you will not lack assistance if you will take the trouble to look for it....

XXIII

PLINY TO THE EMPEROR TRAJAN

The public bath at Prusa, Sir, is old and dilapidated, and the people are very anxious for it to be rebuilt. My own opinion is that you could suitably grant their petition. There will be money available for building it, first from the sums I have begun to call in from private individuals, and secondly because the people are prepared to apply to building the bath the grants they usually make towards financing the distribution of olive oil. This is, moreover, a scheme which is worthy of the town's prestige and the splendour of your reign.

XXIV

TRAJAN TO PLINY

If building a new bath at Prusa will not strain the city's finances, there is no reason why we should not grant their petition; provided that no new tax is imposed and there is no further diversion of funds of theirs intended for essential services....

XXXI

PLINY TO THE EMPEROR TRAJAN

You may stoop when necessary, Sir, to give ear to my problems, without prejudice to your eminent position, seeing that I have your authority to refer to you when in doubt.

In several cities, notably Nicomedia and Nicaea, there are people who were sentenced to service in the mines or the arena, or to other similar punishments, but are now performing the duties of public slaves and receiving an annual salary for their work. Since this was told me I have long been debating what to do. I felt it was too hard on the men to send them back to work out their sentences after a lapse of many years, when most of them are old by now, and by all accounts are quietly leading honest lives, but I did not think it quite right to retain criminals in public service; and though I realized there was nothing to be gained by supporting these men at public expense if they did no work, they might be a potential danger if they were left to starve. I was therefore obliged to leave the whole question in suspense until I could consult you.

You may perhaps want to know how they came to be released from the sentences passed on them. I asked this question myself, but received no satisfactory answer to give you, and although the records of their sentences were produced, there were no documents to prove their release. But people have stated on their behalf that they had been released by order of the previous governors or their deputies, and this is confirmed by the unlikelihood that any unauthorized person would take this responsibility.

XXXII

TRAJAN TO PLINY

Let us not forget that the chief reason for sending you to your province was the evident need for many reforms. Nothing in fact stands more in need of correction than the situation described in your letter, where criminals under sentence have not only been released without authority but are actually restored to the status of honest officials. Those among them who were sentenced within the last ten years and were released by no proper authority must therefore be sent back to work out their sentences. But if the men are elderly and have sentences dating back farther than ten years, they can be employed in work not far removed from penal labour, cleaning public baths and sewers, or repairing streets and highways, the usual employment for men of this type.

XXXIII

PLINY TO THE EMPEROR TRAJAN

While I was visiting another part of the province, a widespread fire broke out in Nicomedia which destroyed many private houses and also two public buildings (the Elder Citizens' Club and the Temple of Isis) although a road runs between them. It was fanned by the strong breeze in the early stages, but it would not have spread so far but for the apathy of the populace; for it is generally agreed that people stood watching the disaster without bestirring themselves to do anything to stop it. Apart from this, there is not a single fire engine anywhere in the town, not a bucket nor any apparatus for fighting a fire. These will now be provided on my instructions.

Will you, Sir, consider whether you think a company of firemen might be formed, limited to 150 members? I will see that no one shall be admitted who is not genuinely a fireman, and that the privileges granted shall not be abused: it will not be difficult to keep such small numbers under observation.

XXXIV

TRAJAN TO PLINY

You may very well have had the idea that it should be possible to form a company of firemen at Nicomedia on the model of those existing elsewhere, but we must remember that it is societies like these which have been responsible for the political disturbances in your province, particularly in its towns. If people assemble for a common purpose, whatever name we give them and for whatever reason, they soon turn into a political club. It is a better policy then to provide the equipment necessary for dealing with fires, and to instruct property owners to make use of it, calling on the help of the crowds which collect if they find it necessary.

XXXV

PLINY TO THE EMPEROR TRAJAN

We have made our annual vows, Sir, to ensure your safety and thereby that of the State, and discharged our vows for the past year, with prayers to the gods to grant that those vows may be always thus discharged and confirmed. There seems to have been a general ban on any form *of collegium* in the eastern cities.

XXXVI

TRAJAN TO PLINY

I was glad to hear from your letter, my dear Pliny, that you and the provincials have discharged your vows to the immortal gods on behalf of my health and safety, and have renewed them for the coming year.

XXXVII

PLINY TO THE EMPEROR TRAJAN

The citizens of Nicomedia, Sir, have spent 3,318,000 sesterces on an aqueduct which they abandoned before it was finished and finally demolished. Then they made a grant of 200,000 sesterces towards another one, but this too was abandoned, so that even after squandering such enormous sums they must still spend more money if they are to have a water supply.

I have been myself to look at the spring which could supply pure water to be brought along an aqueduct, as originally intended, if the supply is not to be confined to the lower-lying parts of the town. There are very few arches still standing, but others could be built out of the blocks of stone taken from the earlier construction, and I think some ought to be made of brick, which would be easier and cheaper.

But the first essential is for you to send out a water-engineer or an architect to prevent a third failure. I will add only that the finished work will combine utility with beauty, and will be well worthy of your reign.

XXXVIII

TRAJAN TO PLINY

Steps must be taken to provide Nicomedia with a water supply, and I am sure you will apply yourself to the task in the right way. But for goodness' sake apply yourself no less to finding out whose fault it is that Nicomedia has wasted so much money up to date. It may be that people have profited by this starting and abandoning of aqueducts. Let me know the result of your inquiry....

LXV

PLINY TO THE EMPEROR TRAJAN

A serious problem, Sir, which affects the whole province, concerns the status and cost of maintenance of the persons generally known as foundlings. I have looked at the orders of your predecessors, but was unable to find either a particular case or a general rule which could apply to Bithynia; so I decided I must ask you for directions, as I felt it was not sufficient to be guided only by precedents in a matter which required your authoritative opinion.

An edict referring to Andania [a city in Greece] was quoted to me, which was said to be one issued by the deified Emperor Augustus, also letters of the deified Emperors Vespasian and Titus to the Spartans, and another from Titus to the Achaeans. There were also letters from Domitian to the governors Avidius Nigrinus and Armenius Brocchus, and yet another to the Spartans from Domitian. I have not sent copies of them to you as they seemed to be inaccurate, and some of them of doubtful authenticity; and I felt sure that you had accurate and genuine versions among your official files.

LXVI

TRAJAN TO PLINY

The question you raise of free persons who were exposed at birth, but then brought up in slavery by those who rescued them, has often been discussed, but I can find nothing in the records of my predecessors which could have applied to all provinces. There are, it is true, the letters from Domitian to Avidius Nigrinus and Annenius Brocchus, which ought possibly to give us guidance, but Bithynia is not one of the provinces covered by his ruling. I am therefore of the opinion that those who wish to claim emancipation on this ground should not be prevented from making a public declaration of their right to freedom, nor should they have to purchase their freedom by refunding the cost of their maintenance.

Women, Family, and Roman Slave Society

70 The Legal Status of Roman Women

The Roman family and Roman society more generally are often described, with considerable justification, as patriarchal. The male head of the household, the *paterfamilias,* exercised tremendous authority over his children, including adult sons, even to the point of putting them to death. This incredible power of the Roman patriarch, called *patria potestas,* was recognized by law and may be seen as a factor that colored all Roman social and even political relationships. But while Roman males expected to come out eventually from under this *patria potestas* later in life, most Roman females had male legal guardians their entire lives. Women were seen as needing male protection (from other males) due to what the Romans called the infirmity of their sex and the levity of their souls. Because the Roman state was committed to the protection and integrity of the family, Roman law therefore helped define the proper legal roles, status, and rights of women, particularly concerning the ownership of property such as the marriage dowry. The following sources from Roman legal texts reveal some of the official Roman attitudes toward women, their roles in the life of the family, and the nature of marriage.

Patria Potestas and Guardianship

[(i) Justinian, *Institutes* 1. 9; 1.11. pr., 10; *Codex* 9. 10. 1: *Digest* 23. 2. 36 (Paulus); 48. 5. 7. pr. (Marcianus). 6th cent. A.D. Translated by D. C. Munro, S. P. Scott.]

Our children whom we have begotten in lawful wedlock are in our power. Wedlock or matrimony is the union of male and female, involving the habitual intercourse of daily life. The power which we have over our children is peculiar to Roman citizens and is found in no other nation. The offspring then of you and your wife is in your power, and so too is that of your son and his wife, that is to say, your grandson and granddaughter, and so on. But the offspring of your daughter is not in your power, but in that of its own father.

Not only our natural children under our authority as we have already stated, but those whom we adopt as well.... Women also cannot adopt because they have

Funeral portrait of a young woman in
Roman Egypt. Fayum, Egypt.

not even control over their own children, but by the indulgence of the Emperor
they can do so by way of consolation for the children they have lost.

When a guardian violates the chastity of his female ward, he shall be sentenced
to deportation, and all his property shall be confiscated to the treasury, although
he must still suffer the penalty which the laws inflict upon ravishers.

A guardian or a curator cannot marry a grown woman who is committed to his care,
unless she has been betrothed to, or intended for him by her father, or where the
marriage takes place in accordance with some condition mentioned in his will.

A man who contracts matrimony with his own female ward in violation of the
decree of the senate is not legally married; and he who was her guardian or curator can be prosecuted for adultery if he marries a girl under twenty-six years of
age who has not been betrothed to him, or destined for him, or mentioned for
this purpose in a will.

[Ulpian, *Rules* 5. 8–10; 11.1. Rome, 3rd cent. A.D. Translated by S. P. Scott.]

When legal marriage takes place, the children always follow the father, but if it
does not take place, they follow the condition of the mother; except where a

child is born of an alien father, and a mother who is a Roman citizen, as the *lex Minicia* directs that where a child is born of parents one of whom is an alien, it shall follow the condition of the inferior parent.

A child born of a father who is a Roman citizen and a Latin mother is a Latin; one born of a freeman and a female slave is a slave; since the child follows the mother as in cases where there is no legal marriage.

In the case of children who are the issue of a legally contracted marriage, the time of conception is considered; in the case of those who were not legitimately conceived, the time of their birth is considered; for instance, if a female slave conceives and brings forth a child after having been manumitted, the child will be free; for while she did not lawfully conceive, as she was free at the time the child was born the latter will also be free.

Guardians are appointed for males as well as for females, but only for males under puberty, on account of their infirmity of age; for females, however, both under and over puberty, on account of the weakness of their sex as well as their ignorance of business matters.

Marriage and Property

[Paulus, *Opinions* 2. 1–9; 2. 20.1; 3. 10. 1–2; 2. 22. 1. Rome, 3rd cent. A.D. Translated by S. P. Scott.]

Betrothal can take place between persons over or under the age of puberty. Marriage cannot legally be contracted by persons who are subject to the control of their father, without their consent; such contracts, however, are not dissolved, for the consideration of the public welfare is preferred to the convenience of private individuals. Marriage cannot be contracted, but cohabitation can exist between slaves and persons who are free. An insane person of either sex cannot contract marriage, but where marriage has been contracted it is not annulled by insanity. An absent man can marry a wife; an absent woman, however, cannot marry. It has been decided that a freedman who aspires to marry his patroness, or the daughter of the wife of his patron, shall be sentenced to the mines, or to labour on the public works, according to the dignity of the person in question.

A man cannot keep a concubine at the same time that he has a wife. Hence a concubine differs from a wife only in the fact that she is entertained for pleasure.

On the Orphitian decree of the senate:

Children born of promiscuous intercourse are not prevented from claiming the estate of their mother, if she died intestate; because, as their estates pass to their mother, so the estate of their mother should vest in them.

Through the operation of the Claudian decree of the senate, the estate of a mother who died intestate cannot pass to a daughter who is either a female slave, or a freedwoman; because neither slaves nor freedmen are understood to have mothers under the civil law.

The crops of dotal land are gathered for the benefit of the husband during the existence of the marriage, and also proportionately during the year in which a divorce takes place.

[Justinian, *Institutes* 1. 10. pr. (excerpt); *Codex* 9. 12. 1; *Digest* 23. 2. 3. 1, 3 (Papinian); 23. 2. 42. pr.–1 (Modestinus); 24. 2. 1, 3 (Paulus); 23. 2. 70 (Paulus); 24. 1. 31. pr.–1 (Pomponius); 12. 4. 9. pr. (Paulus). 6th cent. A.D. Translated by S. P. Scott.]

Roman citizens unite in legal marriage when they are joined according to the precepts of the law, and the males have attained the age of puberty and the females are capable of childbirth, whether they are the heads of families or the children of families; if the latter have also the consent of the relatives under whose authority they may be, for this should be obtained and both civil and natural law require that it should previously be secured.

Those who seize the property of a wife on account of a debt of her husband, or because of some public civil liability which he has incurred, are considered to have been guilty of violence.

Where a man has accused his wife of adultery in accordance with his right as a husband, he is not forbidden, after the annulment of the marriage, to marry again. If, however, he does not accuse his wife as her husband, it will be held that the marriage which has been contracted will remain valid.

Where the daughter of a senator marries a freedman, this unfortunate act of her father does not render her a wife, for children should not be deprived of their rank on account of an offence of their parent.

In unions of the sexes, it should always be considered not only what is legal, but also what is decent. If the daughter, granddaughter, or great-granddaughter of a senator should marry a freedman, or a man who practises the profession of an actor, or whose father or mother did so, the marriage will be void.

Marriage is dissolved by divorce, death, captivity, or by any other kind of servitude which may happen to be imposed upon either of the parties....

It is not a true or actual divorce unless the purpose is to establish a perpetual separation. Therefore, whatever is done or said in the heat of anger is not valid, unless the determination becomes apparent by the parties persevering in their intention, and hence where repudiation takes place in the heat of anger and the wife returns in a short time, she is not held as to have been divorced.

Where doubtful questions arise, it is better to decide in favour of the dowry.

Where a husband makes clothing for his wife out of his own wool, although this is done for his wife and through solicitude for her, the clothing, nevertheless, will belong to the husband; nor does it make any difference whether the wife assisted in preparing the wool, and attended to the matter for her husband.

Where a wife uses her own wool, but makes garments for herself with the aid of female slaves belonging to her husband, it will belong to him, if he paid his wife the value of the wool.

If I intend to give money to a woman, and pay it to her betrothed as dowry by her direction but the marriage does not take place, the woman has a right of action for its recovery....

[Ulpian, *Rules* 6. 1, 2, 4, 6, 7, 9, 10, 12; 7. 2. Rome, 3rd cent. A.D. Translated by S. P. Scott.]

A dowry is either given, expressly stated, or promised.

A woman who is about to be married can state her dowry, and her debtor can do so, at her direction; a male ascendant of the woman related to her through the male sex, such as her father or paternal grandfather, can likewise so do. Any person can give or promise a dowry....

When a woman dies during marriage, her dowry given by her father reverts to him, a fifth of the same for each child she leaves being retained by the husband, no matter what the number may be. If her father is not living, the dowry remains in the hands of the husband....

When a divorce takes place, if the woman is her own mistress, she herself has the right to sue for the recovery of the dowry. If, however, she is under the control of her father, he having been joined with her daughter, can bring the action for the recovery of the dowry; nor does it make any difference whether it is adventitious or profectitious.

If the woman dies after the divorce, no right of action will be granted to her heir, unless her husband has been in default in restoring her dowry....

Portions of a dowry are retained either on account of children, on account of bad morals, on account of expenses, on account of donations, or on account of articles which have been abstracted.

A portion is retained on account of children, when the divorce took place either through the fault of the wife, or her father; for then a sixth part of the dowry shall be retained in the name of each child, but not more than three-sixths altogether....

A sixth of the dowry is also retained on the ground of a flagrant breach of morals; an eighth, where the offence is not so serious. Adultery alone comes under the head of a flagrant breach of morals; all other improper acts are classed as less serious.

If a husband in anticipation of divorce abstracts anything belonging to his wife, he will be liable to an action for the clandestine removal of property.

Children and Slaves

[Paulus, *Opinions* 2. 24. 1–9; 2. 21. 1–4, 9–13, 16. Rome, 3rd cent. A.D. Translated by S. P. Scott.]

If a female slave conceives, and has a child after she has been manumitted, the child will be free.

If a free woman conceives and has a child after having become a slave, the child will be free; for this is demanded by the favour conceded to freedom.

If a female slave conceives, and in the meantime is manumitted, but, having subsequently again become a slave, has a child, it will be free; for the intermediate time can benefit, but not injure freedom.

A child born to a woman who should have been manumitted under the terms of a trust, is born free, if it comes into the world after the grant of freedom is in default.

If, after a divorce has taken place, a woman finds herself to be pregnant, she should within three hundred days notify either her husband, or his father to send witnesses for the purpose of making an examination of her condition: and if this is not done, they shall, by all means, be compelled to recognise the child of the woman.

If the woman should not announce that she is pregnant, and should not permit the witnesses sent to make an examination of her, neither the father nor the grandfather will be compelled to support the child; but the neglect of the mother will not offer any impediment to the child being considered the proper heir of his father.

Where a woman denies that she is pregnant by her husband, the latter is permitted to make an examination of her, and appoint persons to watch her.

The physical examination of the woman is made by five midwives, and the decision of the majority shall be held to be true.

It has been decided that a midwife who introduces the child of another in order that it may be substituted shall be punished with death.

If a freeborn woman, who is also a Roman citizen or a Latin, forms a union with the slave belonging to another, and continues to cohabit with him against the consent and protest of the owner of the slave, she becomes a female slave.

If a freeborn woman forms a union with a slave who is a ward, she becomes a female slave by the denunciation of the guardian.

Although a woman cannot permit her freedwoman to cohabit with the slave of another without the permission of her guardian, still, by denouncing her who has formed such a union with her slave, she will acquire the woman as her slave.

An attorney, a son under parental control, and a slave, by the order of his father, master, or principal, makes a woman a female slave under such circumstances by denouncing her.

If a daughter under paternal control, without the consent or knowledge of her father, forms a union with a slave belonging to another she will retain her position, even after being denounced; for the reason that the condition of a parent cannot become worse through any act of his children.

If a daughter under paternal control, by order of her father, and against the will of his master, forms a union with the slave of another she becomes a female slave; because parents can render the condition of their children worse.

A freedwoman who forms a union with the slave of her patron will remain in the same condition after having been denounced, because she is considered to have been unwilling to abandon the house of her patron.

Any woman who erroneously thinks that she is a female slave, and on this account forms a union with the slave of another, and, after having ascertained that she is free, continues in the same relation with him, becomes a female slave.

If a patroness forms a union with the slave of her freedman, it has been decided that she does not become a female slave by his denunciation....

If a mother forms a union with the slave of her son, the Claudian decree of the senate does not abolish the filial reverence which should be entertained for a mother; even though she should blush on account of her disgrace, as in the case of her who cohabits with the slave of her freedman.

[Justinian, *Codex* 11. 11. pr.; *Digest* 23. 2. 13 (Ulpian); 5. 3. 27. pr.–1 (Ulpian). 6th cent. A.D. Translated by S. P. Scott.]

When a woman is convicted of having secretly had sexual intercourse with her slave, she shall be sentenced to death, and the rascally slave shall perish by fire....

Where a patroness is so degraded that she even thinks that marriage with her freedman is honourable, it should not be prohibited by a judge to whom application is made to prevent it.

The issue of female slaves and the offspring of their female children are not considered to be profits, because it is not customary for female slaves to be acquired for breeding purposes; their offspring are, nevertheless, an increase of the estate; and since all these form part of the estate, there is no doubt that the possessor should surrender them, whether he is the actual possessor, or, after suit was brought, he acted fraudulently to avoid being in possession. Moreover, rents which have been collected from persons who leased buildings, are included in the action; even though they may have been collected from a brothel, for brothels are kept on the premises of many reputable persons.

71 Juvenal, *Satires*

The Emancipated Women of the Early Empire

Juvenal (ca. A.D. 55–ca. 130) has been called "the greatest satiric poet who ever lived" for his sixteen *Satires* that poke fun at the vices and follies of Roman society at the end of the first century A.D. He had started on a career in the Imperial civil service when his property was confiscated and he was exiled in A.D. 92 for lampooning the political influence of a foreign ballet dancer in the entourage of the emperor Domitian. Four years later political exiles were recalled by Nerva, the first of the Five Good Emperors whose last member was Marcus Aurelius (Selection 73), and a penniless and embittered Juvenal returned to Rome where he set himself the task of denouncing his age. He saw himself as a member of the silent majority of thrifty, hard-working, patriotic, and virtuous citizens speaking out against those who were disrupting the old pattern of society—those of the upper class who lowered their standards and neglected their traditional duties, and those of the common people, here derided as "the mob," who demanded and received free "bread and circuses" or rose "from the gutter" to become "top people." To Juvenal, all this was the result of too many years of debilitating peace, the influx of foreign customs, and the corrupting power of wealth. He was convinced that money had corroded everything, particularly social conventions and morality, and that moral degeneracy had reached its zenith in the Rome of his day.

In his Sixth Satire, Juvenal denounces the emancipated upper-class women of Rome for breaching social conventions and moral standards. Because of the resulting collapse of sexual morality and family life, a good woman is a *rara avis* ("rare bird"), as "uncommon as a black swan." To prove his case, he sets forth a series of horrid examples of ruthless, strong-willed women motivated by ambition, selfishness, and lust.

> Yet a musical wife's not so bad as some presumptuous
> Flat-chested busybody who rushes around the town
> Gate-crashing all-male meetings, talking back straight-faced
> To a uniformed general—*and* in her husband's presence.
> She knows all the news of the world, what's cooking in
>   Thrace
> Or China, just what the stepmother did with her stepson
> Behind closed doors, who's fallen in love, which gallant
> Is all the rage. She'll tell you who got the widow
> Pregnant, and in which month; she knows each woman's
> Pillow endearments, and all the positions she favors.
> She's the first to spot any comet presaging trouble
> For some eastern prince, in Armenia, maybe, or Parthia.
> She's on to the latest gossip and rumors as soon as
> They reach the city-gates, or invents her own, informing
> Everyone she meets that Niphates has overflowed
> And is inundating whole countries—towns are cut off,
> She says, and the land is sinking: flood and disaster!
>   Yet even this is not so insufferable
> As her habit, when woken up, of grabbing some poor-class
> Neighbor and belting into him with a whip. If her precious
> Sleep is broken by barking, 'Fetch me the cudgels,'
> She roars, 'and be quick about it!' The dog gets a thrashing,
> But its master gets one first. She's no joke to cross,
> And her face is a grisly fright. Not till the evening
> Does she visit the baths: only then are her oil-jars and

The rest of her clobber transferred there. First she works out
With the weights and dumb-bells. Then, when her arms are
    aching,
The masseur takes over, craftily slipping one hand
Along her thigh, and tickling her up till she comes.
Lastly she makes for the sweat-room. She loves to sit there
Amid all that hubbub, perspiring. Meanwhile at home
Her unfortunate guests are nearly dead with hunger.
At last she appears, all flushe, with a three-gallon thirst,
Enough to empty the brimming jar at her feet
Without assistance. She knocks back two straight pints
On an empty stomach, to sharpen her appetite: then
Throws it all up again, souses the floor with vomit
That flows in rivers across the terrazzo. She drinks
And spews by turns, like some big snake that's tumbled
Into a wine-vat, till her gilded jordan brims
Right over with sour and vinous slops. Quite sickened,
Eyes shut, her husband somehow holds down his bile.
    Worse still is the well-read menace, who's hardly settled
      for dinner.
Before she starts praising Virgil, making a moral case
For Dido (death justifies all), comparing, evaluating
Rival poets, Virgil and Homer suspended
In opposite scales, weighed up one against the other.
Critics surrender, academics are routed, all
Fall silent, not a word from lawyer or auctioneer—
Or even another woman. Such a rattle of talk,
You'd think all the poets and bells were being clashed
    together
When the moon's in eclipse....
                So avoid a dinner-partner
With an argumentative style, who hurls well-rounded
Syllogisms like slingshots, who has all history pat:
Choose someone rather who doesn't understand *all* she reads.
I hate these authority-citers, the sort who are always thumbing
Some standard grammatical treatise, whose every utterance
Observes all the laws of syntax, who with antiquarian zeal
Quote poets I've never heard of. Such matters are men's
    concern.
If she wants to correct someone's language, she can always
Start with her unlettered girl-friends.

72 Aspects of Roman Slavery

The Romans distinguished between those slaves engaged in large enterprises and farms and those who were domestic servants. The latter usually received better treatment than the former, although much depended on the master. The growth of large Roman estates worked predominantly by slaves made prudent management a matter of public discussion in elite Roman circles. Several handbooks furnished advice regarding the proper running of such plantations. The first two sources in this selection come from these handbooks. While they express the ideology of the slave-owning Romans, they also reveal something about the nature and conditions of Roman slavery. The third source in this selection addresses the treatment of slaves who were employed in domestic service. It suggests a humanitarian streak, admittedly a thin one, in elite Roman attitudes toward slaves and slavery.

A. VARRO, *ON AGRICULTURE*: SETTING UP A SLAVE PLANTATION

"Slaves should be neither cowed nor high-spirited."

For the ancient Romans, slaves, especially rural or farm slaves, were a necessary means of production. Their labor made the land produce. Varro, a prolific Roman author from the Late Republic (ca. 116–27 B.C.), discusses the role played by farm slaves in the large Roman country estate and how a master should select, organize, and treat his labor force. Varro's work, *On Agriculture,* set out in literary dialogue form the collected wisdom regarding farming and husbandry and was aimed at elite Roman landowners such as himself.

"All Agriculture Is Carried on by Men"

... All agriculture is carried on by men—slaves, or freemen, or both; by freemen, when they till the ground themselves, as many poor people do with the help of their families; or hired hands, when the heavier farm operations, such as the vintage and the haying, are carried on by the hiring of freemen.... With regard to these in general this is my opinion: it is more profitable to work unwholesome lands with hired hands than with slaves; and even in wholesome places it is more profitable thus to carry out the heavier farm operations, such as storing the products of the vintage or harvest.... [S]uch hands should be selected as can bear heavy work, are not less than twenty-two years old, and show some aptitude for farm labour. You may judge of this by the way they carry out their other

From *Marco Porcius Cato: On Agriculture,* Loeb Classical Library Vol. 283, translated by W. D. Hooper and H. B. Ash (Cambridge, Mass.: Harvard University Press, 1934). The Loeb Classical Library® is a registered trademark of the President and Fellows of Harvard College.

orders, and, in the case of new hands, by asking one of them what they were in the habit of doing for their former master.

"Slaves should be neither cowed nor high-spirited. They ought to have men over them who know how to read and write and have some little education, who are dependable and older than the hands whom I have mentioned; for they will be more respectful to these than to men who are younger. Furthermore, it is especially important that the foremen be men who are experienced in farm operations; for the foreman must not only give orders but also take part in the work, so that his subordinates may follow his example, and also understand that there is good reason for his being over them—the fact that he is superior to them in knowledge. They are not to be allowed to control their men with whips rather than with words, if only you can achieve the same result. Avoid having too many slaves of the same nation, for this is a fertile source of domestic quarrels. The foremen are to be made more zealous by rewards, and care must be taken that they have a bit of property of their own, and mates from among their fellow-slaves to bear them children; for by this means they are made more steady and more attached to the place. Thus, it is on account of such relationships that slave families of Epirus have the best reputation and bring the highest prices. The good will of the foremen should be won by treating them with some degree of consideration; and those of the hands who excel the others should also be consulted as to the work to be done. When this is done they are less inclined to think that they are looked down upon, and rather think that they are held in some esteem by the master. They are made to take more interest in their work by being treated more liberally in respect either of food, or of more clothing, or of exemption from work, or of permission to graze some cattle of their own on the farm, or other things of this kind; so that, if some unusually heavy task is imposed, or punishment inflicted on them in some way, their loyalty and kindly feeling to the master may be restored by the consolation derived from such measures.

"Experiment and Imitation"

XVIII. "With regard to the number of slaves required, Cato has in view two bases of calculation: the size of the place, and the nature of the crop grown. Writing of oliveyards and vineyards, he gives two formulas. The first is one in which he shows how an oliveyard of 240 iugera should be equipped; on a place of this size he says that the following thirteen slaves should be kept: an overseer, a housekeeper, five labourers, three teamsters, one muleteer, one swineherd, one shepherd. The second he gives for a vineyard of 100 iugera, on which he says should be kept the following fifteen slaves: an overseer, a housekeeper, ten labourers, a teamster, a muleteer, a swineherd. Saserna states that one man is enough for eight iugera, and that he ought to dig over that amount in forty-five days, although he can dig over a single iugerum with four days' work; but he says that he allows thirteen days extra for such things as illness, bad weather, idleness, and laxness. Neither of these writers has left us a very clearly expressed rule. For if Cato wished to do this, he should have stated it in such a way that we add or subtract from the number proportionately as the farm is larger or smaller.

Further, he should have named the overseer and the housekeeper outside of the number of slaves; for if you cultivate less than 240 iugera of olives you cannot get along with less than one overseer, nor if you cultivate twice as large a place or more will you have to keep two or three overseers. It is only the labourers and teamsters that are to be added proportionately to larger bodies of land; and even then only if the land is uniform. But if it is so varied that it cannot all be ploughed, as, for instance, if it is very broken or very steep, fewer oxen and teamsters will be needed. I pass over the fact that the 240 iugera instanced is a plot which is neither a unit nor standard (the standard unit is the century, containing 200 iugera); when one-sixth, or 40 iugera, is deducted from this 240, I do not see how, according to this rule, I shall take one-sixth also from thirteen slaves, or, if I leave out the overseer and the housekeeper, how I shall take one-sixth from the eleven. As to his saying that on 100 iugera of vineyard you should have fifteen slaves; if one has a century, half vineyard and half oliveyard, it will follow that he should have two overseers and two housekeepers, which is absurd. Wherefore the proper number and variety of slaves must be determined by another method, and Saserna is more to be approved in this matter; he says that each iugerum is enough to furnish four days' work for one hand. But if this applied to Saserna's farm in Gaul, it does not necessarily follow that the same would hold good for a farm in the mountains of Liguria. Therefore you will most accurately determine the number of slaves and other equipment which you should provide if you observe three things carefully: the character of the farms in the neighbourhood and their size; the number of hands employed on each; and how many hands should be added or subtracted in order to keep your cultivation better or worse. For nature has given us two routes to agriculture, experiment and imitation. The most ancient farmers determined many of the practices by experiment, their descendants for the most part by imitation. We ought to do both—imitate others and attempt by experiment to do some things in a different way, following not chance but some system: as, for instance, if we plough a second time, more or less deeply than others, to see what effect this will have. This was the method they followed in weeding a second and third time, and those who put off the grafting of figs from spring-time to summer....

B. COLUMELLA, *ON AGRICULTURE*:
MASTERS AND SLAVES

"Their unending toil was lightened by such friendliness ..."

Many Roman landlords were absent from their estates and lived in the large towns and cities such as Rome. They had to appoint overseers or stewards as the managers to be responsible for the day-to-day operations of their farms.

From *Columella, Vol. I,* Loeb Classical Library Vol. 361, translated by Harrison B. Ash (Cambridge, Mass.: Harvard University Press, 1934). The Loeb Classical Library® is a registered trademark of the President and Fellows of Harvard College.

Many of these overseers were themselves chosen from among the slaves. The following excerpt from Columella's *On Agriculture* discusses how a master selects a good overseer, what the latter's duties consist of, as well as the proper relationship between a master and his slaves. Such advice gives a relatively favorable image of Roman slave masters, although one can easily imagine that not too many were in fact such ideal masters. Columella was an early Imperial Roman author (mid-first century A.D.) who composed one of the most comprehensive manuals on ancient agriculture.

"Appoint an Overseer"

... VIII. The next point is with regard to slaves—over what duty it is proper to place each and to what sort of tasks to assign them. So my advice at the start is not to appoint an overseer from that sort of slaves who are physically attractive, and certainly not from that class which has busied itself with the voluptuous occupations of the city. This lazy and sleepy-headed class of servants, accustomed to idling, to the Campus, the Circus, and the theatres, to gambling, to cookshops, to bawdy-houses, never ceases to dream of these follies; and when they carry them over into their farming, the master suffers not so much loss in the slave himself as in his whole estate. A man should be chosen who has been hardened by farm work from his infancy, one who has been tested by experience. If, however, such a person is not available, let one be put in charge out of the number of those who have slaved patiently at hard labour; and he should already have passed beyond the time of young manhood but not yet have arrived at that of old age, that youth may not lessen his authority to command, seeing that older men think it beneath them to take orders from a mere stripling, and that old age may not break down under the heaviest labour. He should be, then, of middle age and of strong physique, skilled in farm operations or at least very painstaking, so that he may learn the more readily; for it is not in keeping with this business of ours for one man to give orders and another to give instructions, nor can a man properly exact work when he is being tutored by an underling as to what is to be done and in what way. Even an illiterate person, if only he have a retentive mind, can manage affairs well enough....

... [T]he overseer ... should be given a woman companion to keep him within bounds and yet in certain matters to be a help to him; and this same overseer should be warned not to become intimate with a member of the household, and much less with an outsider, yet at times he may consider it fitting, as a mark of distinction, to invite to his table on a holiday one whom he has found to be constantly busy and vigorous in the performance of his tasks. He shall offer no sacrifice except by direction of the master. Soothsayers and witches, two sets of people who incite ignorant minds through false superstition to spending and then to shameful practices, he must not admit to the place. He must have no acquaintance with the city or with the weekly market, except to make purchases and sales in connection with his duties. For, as Cato says, an overseer should not be a gadabout; and he should not go out of bounds except to learn something new about farming, and that only if the place is so near that he can come back. He must allow no foot-paths or new crosscuts to be made in the farm; and he shall entertain no guest except a close friend or kinsman of his master.

As he must be restrained from these practices, so must he be urged to take care of the equipment and the iron tools, and to keep in repair and stored away twice as many as the number of slaves requires, so that there will be no need of borrowing from a neighbour; for the loss in slave labour exceeds the cost of articles of this sort. In the care and clothing of the slave household he should have an eye to usefulness rather than appearance, taking care to keep them fortified against wind, cold, and rain, all of which are warded off with long-sleeved leather tunics, garments of patchwork, or hooded cloaks. If this be done, no weather is so unbearable but that some work may be done in the open. He should be not only skilled in the tasks of husbandry, but should also be endowed, as far as the servile disposition allows, with such qualities of feeling that he may exercise authority without laxness and without cruelty, and always humour some of the better hands, at the same time being forbearing even with those of lesser worth, so that they may rather fear his sternness than detest his cruelty. This he can accomplish if he will choose rather to guard his subordinates from wrongdoing than to bring upon himself, through his own negligence, the necessity of punishing offenders. There is, moreover, no better way of keeping watch over even the most worthless of men than the strict enforcement of labour, the requirement that the proper tasks be performed and that the overseer be present at all times; for in that case the foremen in charge of the several operations are zealous in carrying out their duties, and the others, after their fatiguing toil, will turn their attention to rest and sleep rather than to dissipation.

Would that those well-known precepts, old but excellent in morality, which have now passed out of use, might be held to to-day: That an overseer shall not employ the services of a fellow-slave except on the master's business; that he shall partake of no food except in sight of the household, nor of other food than is provided for the rest; for in so doing he will see to it that the bread is carefully made and that other things are wholesomely prepared. He shall permit no one to pass beyond the boundaries unless sent by himself, and he shall send no one except there is great and pressing need. He shall carry on no business on his own account, nor invest his master's funds in livestock and other goods for purchase and sale; for such trafficking will divert the attention of the overseer and will never allow him to balance his accounts with his master, but, when an accounting is demanded, he has goods to show instead of cash. But, generally speaking, this above all else is to be required of him—that he shall not think that he knows what he does not know, and that he shall always be eager to learn what he is ignorant of; for not only is it very helpful to do a thing skilfully, but even more so is it hurtful to have done it incorrectly. For there is one and only one controlling principle in agriculture, namely, to do once and for all the thing which the method of cultivation requires; since when ignorance or carelessness has to be rectified, the matter at stake has already suffered impairment and never recovers thereafter to such an extent as to regain what it has lost and to restore the profit of time that has passed.

"... the overseer must be most observant ..."

In the case of the other slaves, the following are, in general, the precepts to be observed, and I do not regret having held to them myself: to talk rather familiarly with the country slaves, provided only that they have not conducted themselves unbecomingly, more frequently than I would with the town slaves; and when I perceived that their unending toil was lightened by such friendliness on the part of the master, I would even jest with them at times and allow them also to jest more freely. Nowadays I make it a practice to call them into consultation on any new work, as if they were more experienced, and to discover by this means what sort of ability is possessed by each of them and how intelligent he is. Furthermore, I observe that they are more willing to set about a piece of work on which they think their opinions have been asked and their advice followed. Again, it is the established custom of all men of caution to inspect the inmates of the workhouse, to find out whether they are carefully chained, whether the places of confinement are quite safe and properly guarded, whether the overseer has put anyone in fetters or removed his shackles without the master's knowledge. For the overseer should be most observant of both points—not to release from shackles anyone whom the head of the house has subjected to that kind of punishment, except by his leave, and not to free one whom he himself has chained on his own initiative until the master knows the circumstances; and the investigation of the householder should be the more painstaking in the interest of slaves of this sort, that they may not be treated unjustly in the matter of clothing or other allowances, inasmuch as, being liable to a greater number of people, such as overseers, taskmasters, and jailers, they are the more liable to unjust punishment, and again, when smarting under cruelty and greed, they are more to be feared. Accordingly, a careful master inquires not only of them, but also of those who are not in bonds, as being more worthy of belief, whether they are receiving what is due to them under his instructions; he also tests the quality of their food and drink by tasting it himself, and examines their clothing, their mittens, and their foot-covering. In addition he should give them frequent opportunities for making complaint against those persons who treat them cruelly or dishonestly. In fact, I now and then avenge those who have just cause for grievance, as well as punish those who incite the slaves to revolt, or who slander their taskmasters; and, on the other hand, I reward those who conduct themselves with energy and diligence. To women, too, who are unusually prolific, and who ought to be rewarded for the bearing of a certain number of offspring, I have granted exemption from work and sometimes even freedom after they had reared many children. For to a mother of three sons exemption from work was granted; to a mother of more her freedom as well.

Such justice and consideration on the part of the master contributes greatly to the increase of his estate. But he should also bear in mind, first to pay his respects to the household gods as soon as he returns from town; then at once, if time permits, if not, on the next day, to inspect his lands and revisit every part of them and judge whether his absence has resulted in any relaxation of discipline and watchfulness, whether any vine, any tree, or any produce is missing; at the same time, too, he should make a new count of stock, slaves, farm-equipment, and furniture. If he has made it a practice to do all this for many years, he will maintain a well-ordered discipline when old age comes; and whatever his age, he will never be so wasted with years as to be despised by his slaves.

C. SENECA, *MORAL EPISTLE*

"... see in him a freeborn man ..."

While slavery was widely accepted as a normal social institution by the ancient Greeks and Romans, more philosophical writers questioned and spoke out against the often inhumane treatment of slaves. An important adviser to Emperor Nero, Seneca (ca. A.D. 1–A.D. 40) was not just a man of affairs but had studied philosophy in Rome and was generally sympathetic to the teachings of the Stoics. He wrote a moral essay that, like others of his treatises, uses the outward form of a letter to a friend named Lucillus. In it, he articulates how the traditional Stoic philosophical belief in the fundamental equality of all humankind should moderate one's attitude toward slaves. Seneca's sentiments on the humane treatment of slaves find an echo in the writing of later Christian authors. Note, however, that this plea for humanity did not translate into a case for the actual emancipation of all slaves. Such a cause had few, if any, known champions in antiquity.

I am glad to learn, through those who come from you, that you live on friendly terms with your slaves. This befits a sensible and well-educated man like yourself. "They are slaves," people declare. Nay, rather they are men. "Slaves!" No, comrades. "Slaves!" No, they are unpretentious friends. "Slaves!" No, they are our fellow-slaves, if one reflects that Fortune has equal rights over slaves and free men alike.

That is why I smile at those who think it degrading for a man to dine with his slave. But why should they think it degrading? It is only because purse-proud etiquette surrounds a householder at his dinner with a mob of standing slaves. The master eats more than he can hold, and with monstrous greed loads his belly until it is stretched and at length ceases to do the work of a belly; so that he is at greater pains to discharge all the food than he was to stuff it down. All this time the poor slaves may not move their lips, even to speak. The slightest murmur is repressed by the rod; even a chance sound,—a cough, a sneeze, or a hiccup—is visited with the lash. There is a grievous penalty for the slightest breach of silence. All night long they must stand about, hungry and dumb.

The result of it all is that these slaves, who may not talk in their master's presence, talk about their master. But the slaves of former days, who were permitted to

From Seneca, *Moral Epistle*, 77, in *Seneca, Epistles 1–65,* translated by Richard M. Gummere, Loeb Classical Library, Vol. 76 (Cambridge, Mass.: Harvard University Press, 1917), pp. 301–13. The Loeb Classical Library® is a registered trademark of the President and Fellows of Harvard College.

converse not only in their master's presence, but actually with him, whose mouths were not stitched up tight, were ready to bare their necks for their master, to bring upon their own heads any danger that threatened him; they spoke at the feast, but kept silence during torture. Finally, the saying, in allusion to this same highhanded treatment, becomes current: "As many enemies as you have slaves." They are not enemies when we acquire them; we make them enemies.

I shall pass over other cruel and inhuman conduct towards them; for we maltreat them, not as if they were men, but as if they were beasts of burden. When we recline at a banquet, one slave mops up the disgorged food, another crouches beneath the table and gathers up the left-overs of the tipsy guests. Another carves the priceless game birds; with unerring strokes and skilled hand he cuts choice morsels along the breast or the rump. Hapless fellow, to live only for the purpose of cutting fat capons correctly,—unless, indeed, the other man is still more unhappy than he, who teaches this art for pleasure's sake, rather than he who learns it because he must. Another, who serves the wine, must dress like a woman and wrestle with his advancing years; he cannot get away from his boyhood; he is dragged back to it; and though he has already acquired a soldier's figure, he is kept beardless by having his hair smoothed away or plucked out by the roots, and he must remain awake throughout the night, dividing his time between his master's drunkenness and his lust; in the chamber he must be a man, at the feast a boy. Another, whose duty it is to put a valuation on the guests, must stick to his task, poor fellow, and watch to see whose flattery and whose immodesty, whether of appetite or of language, is to get them an invitation for to-morrow. Think also of the poor purveyors of food, who note their masters' tastes with delicate skill, who know what special flavours will sharpen their appetite, what will please their eyes, what new combinations will rouse their cloyed stomachs, what food will excite their loathing through sheer satiety, and what will stir them to hunger on that particular day. With slaves like these the master cannot bear to dine; he would think it beneath his dignity to associate with his slave at the same table! Heaven forfend! ...

Kindly remember that he whom you call your slave sprang from the same stock, is smiled upon by the same skies, and on equal terms with yourself breathes, lives, and dies. It is just as possible for you to see in him a free-born man as for him to see in you a slave. As a result of the massacres in Marius's day, many a man of distinguished birth, who was taking the first steps toward senatorial rank by service in the army, was humbled by fortune, one becoming a shepherd, another a care-taker of a country cottage. Despise, then, if you dare, those to whose estate you may at any time descend, even when you are despising them.

I do not wish to involve myself in too large a question, and to discuss the treatment of slaves, towards whom we Romans are excessively haughty, cruel, and insulting. But this is the kernel of my advice: Treat your inferiors as you would be treated by your betters....

Associate with your slave on kindly, even on affable, terms; let him talk with you, plan with you, live with you. I know that at this point all the exquisites will cry out against me in a body; they will say: "There is nothing more debasing, more disgraceful, than this." But these are the very persons whom I sometimes surprise kissing the hands of other men's slaves. Do you not see even this,—how our ancestors removed from masters everything invidious, and from slaves everything insulting? They called the master "father of the household," and the slaves "members of the household," a custom which still holds in the mime. They established a holiday on which masters and slaves should eat together,—not as the only day for this custom, but as obligatory on that day in any case. They allowed the slaves to attain honours in the household and to pronounce judgment; they held that a household was a miniature commonwealth.

"Do you mean to say," comes the retort, "that I must seat all my slaves at my own table?" No, not any more than that you should invite all free men to it. You are mistaken if you think that I would bar from my table certain slaves whose duties are more humble, as, for example, yonder muleteer or yonder herdsman; I propose to value them according to their character, and not according to their duties. Each man acquires his character for himself, but accident assigns his duties. Invite some to your table because they deserve the honour, and others that they may come to deserve it. For if there is any slavish quality in them as the result of their low associations, it will be shaken off by intercourse with men of gentler breeding. You need not, my dear Lucilius, hunt for friends only in the forum or in the Senate-house; if you are careful and attentive, you will find them at home also. Good material often stands idle for want of an artist; make the experiment, and you will find it so. As he is a fool who, when purchasing a horse, does not consider the animal's points, but merely his saddle and bridle; so he is doubtly a fool who values a man from his clothes or from his rank, which indeed is only a robe that clothes us.

"He's a slave." His soul, however, may be that of a freeman. "He is a slave." But shall that stand in his way? Show me a man who is not a slave; one is a slave to lust, another to greed, another to ambition, and all men are slaves to fear. I will name you an ex-consul who is slave to an old hag, a millionaire who is slave to a serving-maid; I will show you youths of the noblest birth in serfdom to pantomime players! No servitude is more disgraceful than that which is self-imposed.

... Some may maintain that I am now offering the liberty-cap to slaves in general and toppling down lords from their high estate, because I bid slaves respect their masters instead of fearing them.... [Yet] respect means love, and love and fear cannot be mingled. So I hold that you are entirely right in not wishing to be feared by your slaves, and in lashing them merely with the tongue; only dumb animals need the thong....

D. PETRONIUS, *SATYRICON*: BANQUET OF TRIMALCHIO, EX-SLAVE AND SELF-MADE MILLIONAIRE

The Augustan era saw many aspects of Roman civilization, including its economy, enter a golden age. The new security, together with the *laissez-faire* policy of Augustus (touched on in the advice given him by Maecenas in Selection 64A) led to a remarkable expansion of large-scale agriculture, commerce, and industry, particularly in Italy. Abundant capital circulated freely, large fortunes were easily made, and a new class of bourgeois rich men, many of whom started life as slaves, arose to rival the old aristocracy. Typical of this *nouveau riche* class is the fictional ex-slave or freedman character Trimalchio, whose swift rise to riches and bourgeois outlook on life were amusingly satirized in the picaresque novel, *Satyricon,* written by Gaius Petronius (d. A.D. 65), a member of the old aristocracy and arbiter of taste at the court of the emperor Nero. Like many other self-made men of this and similar ages, Trimalchio accumulated his first fortune by shrewd trading, then turned to money-lending and the purchase of numerous estates. Lacking culture and good breeding, he sought compensation in a vulgar and ostentatious display of his wealth.

The setting of the following selection from *Satyricon* is a banquet given by Trimalchio and attended by some of his newly rich fellow capitalists, their wives, and a professor of rhetoric who has brought along two rapscallion students, one of whom narrates the scene.

At last we took our places. Immediately slaves from Alexandria came in and poured ice water over our hands. These were followed by other slaves who knelt at our feet and with extraordinary skill pedicured our toenails. Not for an instant, moreover, during the whole of this odious job, did one of them stop singing. This made me wonder whether the whole *ménage* was given to bursts of song, so I put it to the test by calling for a drink. It was served immediately by a boy who trilled away as shrilly as the rest of them. In fact, anything you asked for was invariably served with a snatch of song, so that you would have thought you were eating in a concert-hall rather than a private dining room.

Now that the guests were all in their places, the *hors d'oeuvres* were served, and very sumptuous they were. Trimalchio alone was still absent, and the place of honor—reserved for the host in the modern fashion—stood empty. But I was speaking of the *hors d'oeuvres*. On a large tray stood a donkey made of rare Corinthian bronze; on the donkey's back were two panniers, one holding green olives, the other, black. Flanking the donkey were two side dishes, both engraved with Trimalchio's name and the weight of the silver, while in dishes shaped to resemble little bridges there were dormice, all dipped in honey and rolled in poppyseed. Nearby, on a silver grill, piping hot, lay small sausages, while beneath the grill black damsons and red pomegranates had been sliced up and arranged so as to give the effect of flames playing over charcoal.

We were nibbling at these splendid appetizers when suddenly the trumpets blared a fanfare and Trimalchio was carried in, propped up on piles of miniature pillows in such a comic way that some of us couldn't resist impolitely smiling. His head, cropped close in a recognizable slave cut, protruded from a cloak of blazing scarlet; his neck, heavily swathed already in bundles of clothing, was wrapped in a large napkin bounded by an incongruous senatorial purple stripe with little tassels dangling down here and there. On the little finger of his left hand he sported an immense gilt ring; the ring on the last joint of his fourth finger looked to be solid gold of the kind the lesser nobility wear, but was actually, I think, an imitation, pricked out with small steel stars. Nor does this exhaust the inventory of his trinkets. At least he rather ostentatiously bared his arm to show us a large gold bracelet and an ivory circlet with a shiny metal plate.

He was picking his teeth with a silver toothpick when he first addressed us. "My friends," he said, "I wasn't anxious to eat just yet, but I've ignored my own wishes so as not to keep you waiting. Still, perhaps you won't mind if I finish my game." At these words a slave jumped forward with a board of juniper wood and a pair of crystal dice. I noticed one other elegant novelty as well: in place of the usual black and white counters, Trimalchio had substituted gold and silver coins. His playing, I might add, was punctuated throughout with all sorts of vulgar exclamations....

By this time Trimalchio had finished his game. He promptly sent for the same dishes we had had and with a great roaring voice offered a second cup of mead to anyone who wanted it. Then the orchestra suddenly blared and the trays were snatched away from the tables by a troupe of warbling waiters. But in the confusion a silver side dish fell to the floor and a slave quickly stooped to retrieve it. Trimalchio, however, had observed the accident and gave orders that the boy's ears should be boxed and the dish tossed back on the floor. Immediately the servant in charge of the dishware came pattering up with a broom and swept the silver dish out of the door with the rest of the rubbish. Two curly-haired Ethiopian slaves followed him as he swept, both carrying little skin bottles like the circus attendants who sprinkle the arena with perfume, and poured wine over our hands. No one was offered water.

We clapped enthusiastically for this fine display of extravagance. "The god of war," said Trimalchio, "is a real democrat. That's why I gave orders that each of us should have a table to himself. Besides, these stinking slaves will bother us less than if we were all packed in together."

Glass jars carefully sealed and coated were now brought in. Each bore this label:

GENUINE FALERNIAN WINE
GUARANTEED ONE HUNDRED YEARS OLD!
BOTTLED
IN THE CONSULSHIP
OF OPIMIUS

While we were reading the labels, Trimalchio clapped his hands for attention. "Just think, friends, wine lasts longer than us poor suffering humans. So soak it up, it's the stuff of life. I give you, gentlemen, the genuine Opimian vintage. Yesterday I served much cheaper stuff and the guests were much more important." While we were commenting on it and savoring the luxury, a slave brought in a skeleton, cast of solid silver, and fastened in such a way that the joints could be twisted and bent in any direction. The servants threw it down on the table in front of us and pushed it into several suggestive postures by twisting its joints, while Trimalchio recited this verse of his own making:

> Nothing but bones, that's what we are.
> Death hustles us humans away.
> Today we're here and tomorrow we're not,
> So live and drink while you may! ...

Suddenly the orchestra gave another flourish and four slaves came dancing in and whisked off the top of the tray. Underneath, in still another tray, lay fat capons and sowbellies and a hare tricked out with wings to look like a little Pegasus. At the corners of the tray stood four little gravy boats, all shaped like the satyr Marsyas, with phalluses for spouts and a spicy hot gravy dripping down over several large fish swimming about in the lagoon of the tray. The slaves burst out clapping, we clapped too and turned with gusto to these new delights. Trimalchio, enormously pleased with the success of his little *tour de force,* roared for a slave to come and carve. The carver appeared instantly and went to work, thrusting with his knife like a gladiator practicing to the accompaniment of a water-organ. But all the time Trimalchio kept mumbling in a low voice, "Carver, carver, carver, carver ..." I suspected that this chant was somehow connected with a trick, so I asked my neighbor, an old hand at these party surprises. "Look," he said, "you see that slave who's carving? Well, he's called Carver, so every time Trimalchio says, 'Carver,' he's also saying 'Carve'er!' and giving him orders to carve."

This atrocious pun finished me: I couldn't touch a thing. So I turned back to my neighbor to pick up what gossip I could and soon had him blabbing away, especially when I asked him about the woman who was bustling around the room. "Her?" he said, "why, that's Fortunata, Trimalchio's wife. And the name couldn't suit her better. She counts her cash by the cartload. And you know what she used to be? Well, begging your Honor's pardon, but you wouldn't have taken bread from her hand. Now, god knows how or why, she's sitting pretty: has Trimalchio eating out of her hand. If she told him at noon it was night, he'd crawl into bed. As for him, he's so loaded he doesn't know how much he has. But that bitch has her finger in everything—where you'd least expect it too. A regular tightwad, never drinks, and sharp as they come. But she's got a nasty tongue; get her gossiping on a couch and she'll chatter like a parrot. If she likes you, you're lucky; if she doesn't, god help you.

"As for old Trimalchio, that man's got more farms than a kite could flap over. And there's more silver plate stuffed in his porter's lodge than another man's got in his safe. As for slaves, whoosh! So help me, I'll bet not one in ten has ever seen his master. Your ordinary rich man is just peanuts compared to him; he could knock them all under a cabbage and you'd never know they were gone.

"And buy things? Not him. No sir, he raises everything right on his own estate. Wool, citron, pepper, you name it. By god, you'd find hen's milk if you looked around. Now take his wool. The home-grown strain wasn't good enough. So you know what he did? Imported rams from Tarentum, bred them into the herd. Attic honey he raises at home. Ordered the bees special from Athens. And the local bees are better for being crossbred too. And, you know, just the other day he sent off to India for some mushroom spawn. Every mule he owns has a wild ass for a daddy. And you see those pillows there? Every last one is stuffed with purple or scarlet wool. That boy's loaded!

"And don't sneer at his friends. They're all ex-slaves, but every one of them's rich. You see that guy down there on the next to last couch? He's worth a cool half-million. Came up from nowhere. Used to tote wood on his back. People say, but I don't know, he stole a cap off a hobgoblin's head and found a treasure. He's the god's fair-haired boy. That's luck for you, but I don't begrudge him. Not so long ago he was just a slave. Yes sir, he's doing all right. Just a few days ago he advertised his apartment for rent. The ad went like this:

APARTMENT FOR RENT AFTER THE FIRST OF JULY.
AM BUYING A VILLA. SEE G. POMPEIUS DIOGENES.

"And you see that fellow in the freedman's seat? He's already made a pile and lost it. What a life! But I don't envy him. After the first million the going got sticky. Right now I'll bet he's mortgaged every hair on his head. But it wasn't his fault. He's too honest, that's his trouble, and his crooked friends stripped him to feather their own nests. One thing's sure: once your little kettle stops cooking and the business starts to slide, you get the brushoff from your friends. And, you know, he had a fine, respectable business too. Undertaking. Ate like a king: boars roasted whole, pastry as tall as buildings, pheasants, chefs, pastrycooks—the whole works. Why, he's had more wine spilled under his table than most men have in their cellars. Life? Hell, it was a dream! Then when things started sliding, he got scared his creditors would think he was broke. So he advertised an auction:

GAIUS JULIUS PROCULUS
WILL HOLD
AN AUCTION
OF HIS
SPARE FURNITURE! ...

"For god's sake," the ragseller Echion broke in, "cut out the damned gloom, will you? 'Sometimes it's good, sometimes it's bad,' as the old peasant said when he sold the spotted pig. Luck changes. If things are lousy today, there's always tomorrow. That's life, man. Sure, the times are bad, but they're no better any-where else. We're all in the same boat, so what's the fuss? If you lived anywhere else, you'd be swearing the pigs here went waddling around already roasted. And don't forget, there's a big gladiator show coming up the day after tomorrow. Not the same old fighters either; they've got a fresh shipment in and there's not a slave in the batch. You know how old Titus works. Nothing's too good for him when he lets himself go. Whatever it is, it'll be something special. I know the old boy well, and he'll go whole hog. Just wait. There'll be cold steel for the crowd, no quarter, and the amphitheater will end up looking like a slaughterhouse. He's got what it takes too....

"Well, Agamemnon, I can see you're thinking, 'What's that bore blabbing about now?' You're the professor here, but I don't catch you opening your mouth. No, you think you're a cut above us, don't you, so you just sit there and smirk at the way we poor men talk. Your learning's made you a snob.

Still, let it go. I tell you what. Someday you come down to my villa and look it over. We'll find something to nibble on, a chicken, a few eggs maybe. This crazy weather's knocked everything topsy-turvy, but we'll come up with something you like. Don't worry your head about it, there'll be loads to eat.

"You remember that little shaver of mine? Well, he'll be your pupil one of these days. He's already doing division up to four, and if he comes through all right, he'll sit at your feet someday. Every spare minute he has, he buries himself in his books. He's smart all right, and there's good stuff in him. His real trouble is his passion for birds.... The older boy now, he's a bit slow. But he's a hard worker and teaches the others more than he knows. Every holiday he spends at home, and whatever you give him, he's content. So I brought him some of those big red lawbooks. A smattering of law, you know, is a useful thing around the house. There's money in it too. He's had enough literature, I think. But if he doesn't stick it out in school, I'm going to have him taught a trade. Barbering or auctioneering, or at least a little law. The only thing that can take a man's trade away is death. But every day I keep pounding the same thing into his head: 'Son, get all the learning you can. Anything you learn is money in the bank. Look at Lawyer Phileros. If he hadn't learned his law, he'd be going hungry and chewing on air. Not so long ago he was peddling his wares on his back; now he's running neck and neck with old Norbanus. Take my word for it, son, there's a mint of money in books, and learning a trade never killed a man yet.'"

Conversation was running along these lines when Trimalchio returned, wiping the sweat from his brow. He splashed his hands in perfume and stood there for a minute in silence. "You'll excuse me, friends," he began, "but I've been constipated for days and the doctors are stumped. I got a little relief from a prescription of pomegranate rind and resin in a vinegar base. Still, I hope my tummy will get back its manners soon. Right now my bowels are bumbling around like a bull. But if any of you has any business that needs attending to, go right ahead; no reason to feel embarrassed. There's not a man been born yet with solid insides. And I don't know any anguish on earth like trying to hold it in. Jupiter himself couldn't stop it from coming—what are you giggling about, Fortunata? You're the one who keeps me awake all night with your trips to the potty. Well, anyone at table who wants to go has my permission, and the doctors tell us not to hold it in. Everything's ready outside—water and pots and the rest of the stuff. Take my word for it, friends, the vapors go straight to your brain. Poison your whole system. I know of some who've died from being too polite and holding it in." We thanked him for his kindness and understanding, but we tried to hide our snickers in repeated swallows of wine.

As yet we were unaware that we had slogged only halfway through this "forest of refinements," as the poets put it....

By now Trimalchio was drinking heavily and was, in fact, close to being drunk. "Hey, everybody!" he shouted, "nobody's asked Fortunata to dance. Believe me, you never saw anyone do grinds the way she can." With this he raised his hands over his forehead and did an impersonation of the actor Syrus singing one of his numbers, while the whole troupe of slaves joined in on the chorus. He was just about to get up on the table when Fortunata went and whispered

something in his ear, probably a warning that these drunken capers were undignified. Never was a man so changeable: sometimes he would bow down to Fortunata
in anything she asked; at other times, as now, he went his own way.

But it was the secretary, not Fortunata, who effectively dampened his desire
to dance, for quite without warning he began to read from the estate records as
though he were reading some government bulletin.

"Born," he began, "on July 26th, on Trimalchio's estate at Cumae, thirty
male and forty female slaves.

"Item, 500,000 bushels of wheat transferred from the threshing rooms into
storage.

"On the same date, the slave Mithridates crucified alive for blaspheming the
guardian spirit of our master Gaius.

"On the same date, the sum of 300,000 returned to the safe because it could
not be invested.

"On the same date, in the gardens at Pompeii, fire broke out in the house of
the bailiff Nasta ..."

"What?" roared Trimalchio. "When did I buy any gardens at Pompeii?"

"Last year," the steward replied. "That's why they haven't yet appeared on
the books."

"I don't care what you buy," stormed Trimalchio, "but if it's not reported
to me within six months, I damn well won't have it appearing on the books at
all!" ...

... Trimalchio suddenly ... ordered his will brought out and read aloud from
beginning to end while the slaves sat there groaning and moaning. At the close of
the reading, he turned to Habinnas. "Well, old friend, will you make me my tomb
exactly as I order it? First, of course, I want a statue of myself. But carve my dog at
my feet, and give me garlands of flowers, jars of perfume and every fight in Pet-
raites' career. Then, thanks to your good office, I'll live on long after I'm gone. In
front, I want my tomb one hundred feet long, but two hundred feet deep. Around
it I want an orchard with every known variety of fruit tree. You'd better throw in a
vineyard too. For it's wrong, I think, that a man should concern himself with the
house where he lives his life but give no thought to the home he'll have forever.
But above all I want you to carve this notice:

THIS MONUMENT DOES NOT PASS INTO
THE POSSESSION OF MY HEIRS.

In any case I'll see to it in my will that my grave is protected from damage after
my death. I'll appoint one of my ex-slaves to act as custodian to chase off the
people who might come and crap on my tomb. Also I want you to carve me
several ships with all sail crowded and a picture of myself sitting on the judge's
bench in official dress with five gold rings on my fingers and handing out a sack
of coins to the people. For it's a fact, and you're my witness, that I gave a free
meal to the whole town and a cash handout to everyone. Also make me a dining
room, a frieze maybe, but however you like, and show the whole town celebrating at my expense. On my right I want a statue of Fortunata with a dove in her

hand. And oh yes, be sure to have her pet dog tied to her girdle. And don't forget my pet slave. Also I'd like huge jars of wine, well-stoppered so the wine won't slosh out. Then sculpt me a broken vase with a little boy sobbing out his heart over it. And in the middle stick a sundial so that anyone who wants the time of day will have to read my name. And how will this do for the epitaph?

HERE LIES GAIUS POMPEIUS TRIMALCHIO
MAECENATIANUS,
VOTED IN ABSENTIA AN OFFICIAL OF THE
IMPERIAL CULT.
HE COULD HAVE BEEN REGISTERED
IN ANY CATEGORY OF THE CIVIL SERVICE AT ROME
BUT CHOSE OTHERWISE.
PIOUS AND COURAGEOUS,
A LOYAL FRIEND,
HE DIED A MILLIONAIRE,
THOUGH HE STARTED LIFE WITH NOTHING.
LET IT BE SAID TO HIS ETERNAL CREDIT
THAT HE NEVER LISTENED TO PHILOSOPHERS.
PEACE TO HIM
FAREWELL....

At this moment an incident occurred on which our little party almost foundered. Among the incoming slaves there was a remarkably pretty boy. Trimalchio literally launched himself upon him, and to Fortunata's extreme annoyance, began to cover him with rather prolonged kisses. Finally, Fortunata asserted her rights and began to abuse him. "You turd!" she shrieked, "you hunk of filth." At last she used the supreme insult: "Dog!" At this Trimalchio exploded with rage, reached for a wine cup and slammed it into her face. Fortunata let out a piercing scream and covered her face with trembling hands as though she'd just lost an eye. Scintilla, stunned and shocked, tried to comfort her sobbing friend in her arms, while a slave solicitously applied a glass of cold water to her livid cheek. Fortunata herself hunched over the glass heaving and sobbing.

But Trimalchio was still shaking with fury. "Doesn't that slut remember what she used to be? By god, *I* took her off the sale platform and made her an honest woman. But she blows herself up like a bullfrog. She's forgotten how lucky she is. She won't remember the whore she used to be. People in shacks shouldn't dream of palaces, I say. By god, if I don't tame that strutting Cassandra, my name isn't Trimalchio. And to think, sap that I was, that I could have married an heiress worth half a million. And that's no lie. Old Agatho, who sells perfume to the lady next door, slipped me the word: 'Don't let your line die out, old boy,' he said. But not me. Oh no, I was a good little boy, nothing fickle about me. And now I've gone and slammed the axe into my shins good and proper—but someday, slut, you'll come scratching at my grave to get me back! And just so you understand what you've done, I'll remove your statue from my tomb. That's an order, Habinnas. No sir, I don't want any more domestic squabbles in my grave. And what's more, just to show her I can dish it out too, I won't have her kissing me on my deathbed....

"But the hell with her. Friends, make yourselves comfortable. Once I used to be like you, but I rose to the top of my ability. Guts are what make the man; the rest is garbage. I buy well, I sell well. Others have different notions. But I'm like to bust with good luck—you slut, are you still blubbering? By god, I'll give you something to blubber about.

"But like I was saying, friends, it's through my business sense that I shot up. Why, when I came here from Asia, I stood no taller than that candlestick there. In fact, I used to measure myself by it every day; what's more, I used to rub my mouth with lamp oil to make my beard sprout faster. Didn't do a bit of good, though. For fourteen years I was my master's pet. But what's the shame in doing what you're told to do? But all the same, if you know what I mean, I managed to do my mistress a favor or two. But mum's the word: I'm none of your ordinary blowhards.

"Well, then heaven gave me a push and I became master in the house. I was my master's brains. So he made me joint heir with the emperor to everything he had, and I came out of it with a senator's fortune. But we never have enough, and I wanted to try my hand at business. To cut it short, I had five ships built. Then I stocked them with wine—worth its weight in gold at the time—and shipped them off to Rome. I might as well have told them to go sink themselves since that's what they did. Yup, all five of them wrecked. No kidding. In one day old Neptune swallowed down a cool million. Was I licked? Hell, no. That loss just whetted my appetite as though nothing had happened at all. So I built some more ships, bigger and better and a damn sight luckier. No one could say I didn't have guts. But big ships make a man feel big himself. I shipped a cargo of wine, bacon, beans, perfume, and slaves. And then Fortunata came through nicely in the nick of time: sold her gold and the clothes off her back and put a hundred gold coins in the palm of my hand. That was the yeast of my wealth. Besides, when the gods want something done, it gets done in a jiffy. On that one voyage alone, I cleared about five hundred thousand. Right away I bought up all my old master's property. I built a house, I went into slave-trading and cattle-buying. Everything I touched just grew and grew like a honeycomb. Once more I was worth more than all the people in my home town put together, I picked up my winnings and pulled out. I retired from trade and started lending money to ex-slaves. To tell the truth, I was tempted to quit for keeps, but on the advice of an astrologer who'd just come to town, I decided to keep my hand in. He was a Greek, fellow by the name of Serapa, and clever enough to set up as consultant to the gods. Well, he told me things I'd clean forgotten and laid it right on the line from A to Z. Why, that man could have peeked into my tummy and told me everything except what I'd eaten the day before. You'd have thought he'd lived with me all his life.

"Remember what he said, Habinnas? You were there, I think, when he told my fortune. 'You have bought yourself a mistress and a tyrant,' he said, 'out of your own profits. You are unlucky in your friends. No one is as grateful to you as he should be. You own vast estates. You nourish a viper in your bosom.'

There's no reason why I shouldn't tell you, but according to him, I have thirty years, four months, and two days left to live. And soon, he said, I am going to receive an inheritance. Now if I could just add Apulia to the lands I own, I could die content.

"Meanwhile, with Mercury's help, I built this house. As you know, it used to be a shack; now it's a shrine. It has four dining rooms, twenty bedrooms, two marble porticos, an upstairs dining room, the master bedroom where I sleep, the nest of that viper there, a fine porter's lodge, and guestrooms enough for all my guests. In fact, when Scaurus came down here from Rome, he wouldn't put up anywhere else, though his father has lots of friends down on the shore who would have been glad to have him. And there are lots of other things I'll show you in a bit. But take my word for it: money makes the man. No money and you're nobody. But big money, big man. That's how it was with yours truly: from mouse to millionaire."

Philosophy and Religion

73 Marcus Aurelius, *Meditations*

"Either atoms or Providence"

When Marcus Aurelius died in A.D. 180 at Vindobona (Vienna) on the Danube frontier, he had completed thirteen successful years of campaigning against the great wave of Germanic migrations into the Empire. As a Roman emperor, he had fought hard to maintain the security of the state, and as a Roman intellectual, he had written on the values that sustained him in the face of a world beginning to grow turbulent and weary. These thoughts, set down at odd moments late in life under the simple heading of *To Himself*, constitute the last great expression of the classical viewpoint, centered in Stoicism, that human reason is an adequate guide to the good life. His basic view is that there is not to be found "in human life anything better than justice, truth, temperance, fortitude, and, in a word, anything better than your own mind's satisfaction in the things which it enables you to do according to right reason." Yet in the writings of the later Roman Stoics—Seneca, Epictetus, and Marcus Aurelius—it is possible to detect an underlying pessimism about man's ability to save himself by his own resources. When we see Marcus Aurelius

To Himself, based on the translation by George Long; in *The Meditations of Emperor Marcus Aurelius,* translated by George Long (London and New York London Chesterfield Society, 1890).

choosing to rely on "Providence" rather than the "atoms" of the scientific Epicurean outlook, and rejecting the classical "city of Athens" for a spiritual "city of God," we see pagan thought becoming more religious and moving toward the ultimate triumph of Christianity.

II, 1. Begin the morning by saying to yourself, I shall meet with the busybody, the ungrateful, arrogant, deceitful, envious, unsocial. All these things happen to them by reason of their ignorance of what is good and evil. But I who have seen the nature of the good that it is beautiful, and of the bad that it is ugly, and the nature of him who does wrong, that it is akin to me, not only of the same blood or seed, but that it participates in the same intelligence and the same portion of the divinity, I can neither be injured by any of them, for no one can fix on me what is ugly, nor can I be angry with my kinsman, nor hate him. For we are made for cooperation, like feet, like hands, like eyelids, like the rows of the upper and lower teeth. To act against one another then is contrary to nature; and it is acting against one another to be vexed and to turn away.

17. In human life time is only a point, and reality is a flux, the perception dull, the composition of the body subject to putrefaction, the soul a whirl, fortune hard to divine, and fame a thing devoid of judgment. And, to say all in a word, everything which belongs to the body is a stream, and what belongs to the soul is a dream and vapor, and life is a struggle and a stranger's sojourn, and after fame is oblivion. What then is that which is able to conduct a man? One thing and only one, philosophy. But this consists in keeping the spirit within a man free from violence and unharmed, superior to pains and pleasures, doing nothing without a purpose, nor yet falsely and with hypocrisy, not feeling the need of another man's doing or not doing anything; and accepting all that happens, and all that is allotted, as coming from thence, wherever it is, from whence he himself came; and, finally, waiting for death with a cheerful mind, as being nothing else than a dissolution of the elements of which every living being is compounded. But if there is no harm to the elements themselves in each continually changing into another, why should a man have any apprehension about the change and dissolution of all things? For it is according to nature, and nothing is evil which is according to nature.

IV, 23. Everything harmonizes with me, which is harmonious to you, O Universe. Nothing for me is too early nor too late, which is in due time for you. Everything is fruit to me which your seasons bring, O Nature; from you are all things, in you are all things, to you all things return. The poet says, Dear city of Athens; and will you not say, Dear city of God?

41. You are a little soul carrying a corpse, as Epictetus used to say.

48. Think continually how many physicians are dead after often contracting their eyebrows over the sick; and how many astrologers after predicting with great pretensions the deaths of others; and how many philosophers after endless discourses on death or immortality; how many heroes after killing thousands; and how many tyrants who have used their power over men's lives with terrible brutality, as if they were immortal; and how many cities are entirely dead, so to speak, Helice and Pompeii and Herculaneum, and others innumerable. Add to the reckoning all the dead whom you have known, one after another. One man

after burying another has been laid out dead, and another buries him; and all this in a short time. To conclude, always observe how ephemeral and worthless human beings are, and what was yesterday a little mucus, tomorrow will be a mummy or ashes. Pass then through this little space of time comfortably to nature and end your journey in content, just as an olive falls off when it is ripe, blessing nature who produced it, and thanking the tree on which it grew.

V, 27. Live with the gods. And he does live with the gods who constantly shows to them that his own soul is satisfied with that which is assigned to him, and that it does all that the spirit wishes, that portion of himself which Zeus has given to every man for his guardian and guide. And this is every man's understanding and reason.

VI, 7. Take pleasure in one thing and rest in it, in passing from one social act to another social act, thinking of God.

10. Either a confusion of alternate combination and dispersion of atoms, or a unity of order and Providence. If the former, why do I desire to tarry in a random combination of things and such a disorder? And why do I care about anything else than how I shall at last become earth? And why be disturbed, for the dispersion of my atoms will happen whatever I do? But if the latter, then I venerate, and I am content, and I trust in the power that governs.

44. ... My nature is rational and social; and my city and country, so far as I am Antoninus, is Rome, but so far as I am a man, it is the world. The things then which are useful to these cities are alone useful to me.

54. That which is not good for the swarm, neither is it good for the bee.

VII, 18. Is any man afraid of change? Why, what can take place without change? What then is more pleasing or more suitable to universal nature? And can you take a bath unless the wood undergoes a change? And can you be nourished, unless the food undergoes a change? And can anything else that is useful be accomplished without change? Do you not see then that for yourself also to change is just the same, and equally necessary for universal nature?

28. Retire into yourself. The rational principle which rules has this nature, that it is content with itself when it does what is just, and so secures tranquillity.

49. Consider the past, such great changes of political supremacies. You may foresee also the things which will be. For they will certainly be of like form, and it is not possible that they should deviate from the order of the things which take place now; accordingly to have contemplated human life for forty years is the same as to have contemplated it for ten thousand years. For what more will you see?

VIII, 16. Remember that to change your opinion and to follow him who corrects your error is as consistent with freedom as it is to persist in your error. For it is your own, the activity which is exerted according to your own movement and judgment, and indeed according to your own understanding too.

59. Men exist for the sake of one another. Teach them then or bear with them.

IX, 23. As you yourself are a component part of a social system, so let every act of yours be a component part of social life. Whatever act of yours then has no reference either immediately or remotely to a social end, this tears asunder your life and does not allow it to be a unity; it is of the nature of a mutiny, just as when in a popular assembly a man acting by himself stands apart from the general agreement.

X, 10. A spider is proud when it has caught a fly, and a man when he has caught a hare, and another when he has taken a little fish in a net, and another when he has taken wild boars, and another when he has taken bears, and another when he has taken Germans. Are not all these bandits, when you examine their principles?

XI, 3. What an admirable soul that is which is ready, if at any moment it must be separated from the body, and ready for extinction, or dispersal, or survival. This readiness must come from a man's own judgment, not from mere obstinacy, as with the Christians, but with reason and dignity if it is to persuade another, and without tragic show.

4. Have I done something for the general interest? Well then I have had my reward. Let this always be present to your mind, and never stop.

XII, 26. When you are troubled about anything, you have forgotten this, that all things happen according to universal nature; and forgotten this, that a man's wrongful act is nothing to you; and further you have forgotten this, that everything which happens, always happened so and will happen so, and now happens so everywhere; forgotten this too, how close is the kinship between man and the whole human race, for it is a community, not of a little blood or seed, but of intelligence. And you have forgotten this too, that every man's intelligence is divine, and is an emanation of the deity; and forgotten this, that nothing is a man's own, but that his child and his body and his very soul came from the deity; forgotten this, that everything is opinion; and lastly you have forgotten that every man lives the present time only, and loses only this.

32. How small a part of the boundless and unfathomable time is assigned to every man? For it is very soon swallowed up in the eternal. And how small a part of the whole of matter? And how small a part of the universal soul? And on what a small clod of the whole earth you creep? Reflecting on all this consider nothing to be important, except to act as your nature leads you, and to endure that which the common nature brings.

36. Man, you have been a citizen in this great state, the world; what difference does it make to you whether for five years or fifty? For that which is conformable to the laws is just for all. Where is the hardship then, if no tyrant nor yet an unjust judge send you away from the state, but nature who brought you into it, the same as if a praetor who has employed an actor dismisses him from the stage. "But I have not finished the five acts, but only three of them," you say, but in your life the three acts are the whole drama; for what shall be a complete drama is determined by him who was once the cause of its composition, and is now the cause of its dissolution: but you are the cause of neither. Depart then satisfied, for he who releases you is also satisfied.

74 Apuleius, *Golden Ass*

The Cult of Isis and Religious Syncretism

In a famous passage, Gilbert Murray characterized the growing religiosity evident in the Roman Empire as "a failure of nerve":

> It is a rise of asceticism, of mysticism, in a sense, of pessimism; a loss of self-confidence, of hope in this life and of faith in normal human effort; a despair of patient inquiry, a cry for infallible revelation; an indifference to the welfare of the state, a conversion of the soul to God.[1]

This attraction to the certitude and security to be found in religion is well-illustrated in the life of Lucius Apuleius, a second-century-A.D. contemporary of Marcus Aurelius. The son of a wealthy Greek family living in North Africa, he received his higher education first at Carthage and later at Athens. He lived the typical life of the dissolute youth of his day, and he soon squandered his patrimony on drink, women, and disreputable associates. This life was changed by his initiation into the mystery cult of Isis, after which he became a follower of the mystical side of Plato's philosophy (Selection 31B) and spent the rest of his life as a traveling orator and lecturer. Several of his writings have survived, notably *The Golden Ass* (also called *Metamorphoses*), a semi-autobiographical account of a man's rise from a life of dissolute living and misadventures to a new life under the inspiration of religion. The story is based upon an older Greek romance or novel that tells how a man named Lucius, dabbling in magic to further his immoral desires, carelessly used the wrong ointment and was transformed into an ass, the personification of lust and wickedness. He had many adventures, both ribald and sordid, until he regained his human form by means of a magical antidote. Apuleius has changed this ending, his Lucius being transformed through the ministrations of the goddess Isis, whose cult had spread from Egypt throughout the Roman Empire, and the story becomes an allegory of human life moving from the sensual to the spiritual. A similar progression was recorded two centuries later by St. Augustine in his spiritual autobiography, the *Confessions* (Selection 86).

The following selections from *The Golden Ass* describe how Lucius is restored to human form by Isis' providence, becomes a convert to her cult, and visits her temple in the "holy city" of Rome. Also evident is the syncretism—the assimilation and combination of common elements from many religions—that characterized religious practice during the Roman Empire.

---

1. Gilbert Murray, *Five Stages of Greek Religion* (New York: Columbia University Press, 1925), p. 155.

From Apuleius, *Metamorphoses* (or *The Golden Ass*), Book XI, 5–6, 15, 22–26, based on the translation by William Adlington (1566).

Isis Answers Lucius' Prayer for Aid

5. Then the divine shape, breathing out the pleasant spice of fertile Arabia, disdained not with her holy voice to utter these words to me:

"Behold, Lucius, I am come; thy weeping and prayer hath moved me to succor thee. I am she that is the natural mother of all things, mistress and governess of all the elements, the initial progeny of worlds, chief of the powers divine, queen of all that are in hell, the first of them that dwell in heaven, manifested alone and under one form of all the gods and goddesses. At my will the planets of the sky, the wholesome winds of the seas, and the lamentable silences of hell are disposed; my name, my divinity, is adored throughout all the world in divers manners, in variable customs, and by many names. For the Phrygians that are the first of all men call me the Mother of the gods at Pessinus; the Athenians, which are sprung from their own soil, Cecropian Minerva; the Cyprians, which are girt about by the sea, Paphian Venus; the Cretans, which bear arrows, Dictynnian Diana; the Sicilians, which speak three tongues, infernal Prosperpine; the Eleusinians, their ancient goddess Ceres; some call me Juno, others Bellona, others Hecate, others Rhamunsia, and principally both types of Ethiopians which dwell in the Orient and are enlightened by the morning rays of the sun, and the Egyptians, which are excellent in all kind of ancient doctrine and by their own ceremonies accustomed to worship me, do call me by my true name, Queen Isis. Behold I am come to take pity on thy fortune and tribulation; behold I am present to favor and aid thee; leave off thy weeping and lamentation, put away all thy sorrow, for behold the day of salvation which is ordained by my providence...."

6. "... Thou shalt live blessed in this world, thou shalt live glorious by my guide and protection, and when after thine allotted space of life thou descendest to hell, there thou shalt see me in that subterranean firmament shining (as thou seest me now) in the darkness of Acheron, and reigning in the deep profundity of Styx, and thou as a dweller in the Elysian Fields shalt worship me as one that hath been favorable to thee. And if I perceive that thou art obedient to my commandment and devoted to any religion, meriting by thy constant chastity my divine grace, know thou that I alone may prolong thy days beyond the time that the fates have appointed and ordained." ...

Lucius Is Restored to Human Shape

15. The priest, looking upon me with a sweet and benign countenance, began to say in this sort:

"O my friend Lucius, after the endurance of so many labors and the escape of so many tempests of Fortune, thou art now at length come to the port and haven of rest and mercy. Neither did thy noble lineage, thy dignity, neither thy excellent teaching anything avail thee; but because thou didst turn to servile pleasures, by a little folly of thy youthfulness, thou hast had a sinister reward of thy unprosperous curiosity. But howsoever the blindness of Fortune tormented thee in divers dangers, so it is now that by her unthoughtful malice thou art come to the present felicity of religion. Let Fortune go and fume with fury in another place; let her find some other matter to execute her cruelty; for Fortune hath no power against them which have devoted their lives to serve and honor the majesty of our goddess.... Know thou that now thou art safe, and under the protection of that Fortune that is not blind but can see, who by her clear light doth enlighten the other gods: therefore rejoice, and assume a proper bearing in thy white habit, and follow with joyful steps the pomp of this devout and honorable procession. Let the irreligious see, let them see and learn how wrong they are: 'Behold here is Lucius that is delivered from his former so great miseries by the providence of the goddess Isis, and rejoiceth therefore and triumpheth by victory over his Fortune.' And to the end that thou mayest live more safe and sure, make thyself one of this holy order, to which thou wast but a short time ago pledged by oath, dedicate thy mind to the obeying of our religion, and take upon thee a voluntary yoke of ministry: for when thou beginnest to serve and honor the goddess, then shalt thou feel the more the fruit of thy liberty." ...

He Is Initiated into the Cult of Isis

22. ... When I heard these and other divine commandments of the high goddess, I greatly rejoiced, and arose before day to speak with the great priest, whom I fortuned to espy coming out of his chamber. Then I saluted him, and thought with myself to ask and demand with a bold courage that I should be initiated, as a thing now due; but as soon as he perceived me, he began first to say: "O Lucius, now know I well that thou art most happy and blessed, whom the divine goddess doth so greatly accept with mercy. Why dost thou stand idle and delay? Behold the day which thou didst desire with prayer, when thou shalt receive at my hands the order of most secret and holy religion, according to the divine commandment of this goddess of many names." Thereupon the old man took me by the hand and led me courteously to the gate of the great temple, where, after it was ritually opened, he made a solemn celebration, and after the morning sacrifice was ended, he brought out of the secret place of the temple certain books written with unknown [Egyptian] characters, partly painted with figures of beasts declaring briefly every sentence, partly with letters whose tops and tails turned round in fashion of a wheel, joined together above like the tendrils of a vine, whereby they were wholly strange and impossible to read by the uninitiated; thence he interpreted to me such things as were necessary for the use and preparation of my initiation.

23. This done, I diligently gave in charge to certain of my companions to buy liberally whatsoever was needed and appropriate; but part thereof I bought myself. Then he brought me, when he found that the time was at hand, to the baths, accompanied with all the religious sort, and demanding pardon of the gods, washed me and purified my body according to the custom; after this, when two parts of the day were gone, he brought me back again to the temple and presented me before the feet of the goddess, giving me instruction in certain secret things unlawful to be uttered, and commanding me generally before all the rest to fast for the space of ten continual days, without eating of any bread or drinking of any wine; which things I observed with a marvelous care. Then behold the day approached when the sacrifice of dedication would be done, and when the sun declined and evening came, there arrived on every side a great multitude of priests, who according to their ancient order offered me many presents and gifts. Then was all the laity and uninitiated people commanded to

depart, and when they had put on my back a new linen robe, the priest took my hand and brought me to the most secret and sacred place of the temple.

A Psychedelic Assault on the Senses

You would perchance demand, you studious reader, what was said and done there. Truly, I would tell you if it were lawful for me to tell, you would know if it was appropriate for you to hear; but both your ears and my tongue would incur the pain of rash curiosity. However, I will not long torment your mind, which perchance is somewhat religious and given to some devotion; listen therefore, and believe it to be true. You shall understand that I approached near to hell, even to the gates of Prosperpine, and after that I was carried away throughout all the elements. I returned to earth; about midnight I saw the sun brightly shine, I saw likewise the gods celestial and the gods infernal, before whom I presented myself and worshipped them. Behold now have I told you that which, although you have heard, yet it is necessary that you conceal it; this much only will I tell, which I may declare without sin for the understanding of the uninitiated....

To Rome, the "Holy City"

26. ... And so within a short while after, by the exhortation of the goddess I made up my packet and took shipping towards the city of Rome. I voyaged very safely and swiftly with a prosperous wind to the port of Augustus, and thence travelling by chariot, I arrived at that holy city about the twelfth day of December in the evening. And the greater desire which I had there was daily to make any prayers to the sovereign goddess Isis, who, by reason of the place where her temple was built, was called Campensis, and continually is adored by the people of Rome. Her minister and worshipper was I, a stranger to her church, but not unknown to her religion.

SELECTED BACKGROUND READING

Mary T. Boatwright, Daniel J. Gargola, and Richard J. A. Talbert. *The Romans, from Village to Empire* (New York: Oxford University Press, 2004).

Edward N. Luttwak, *The Grand Strategy of the Roman Empire from the First Century* A.D. *to the Third* (Baltimore, Maryland: Johns Hopkins University Press, 1976).

Ramsay MacMullen, *Roman Social Relations, 50* B.C. *to* A.D. *284* (New Haven, Conn.: Yale University Press, 1974).

Fergus Millar, *The Emperor in the Roman World, 31* BC–AD *33* (Ithaca, New York: Cornell University Press, 1977).

David S. Potter, D. *A Companion to the Roman Empire* (Malden, Mass.: Blackwell, 2006).

Roman Civilization. Selected Readings. Vol. II: The Empire, edited by Naphthali Lewis and Meyer Reinhold (New York: Columbia University Press, 1990).

Chester G. Starr, *The Roman Empire 27* B.C.–A.D. *476; A Study in Survival* (Oxford: Oxford University Press, 1982).

Paul Veyne, *The Roman Empire* (Cambridge, Mass.: Harvard University Press, 1997).

CHAPTER VI

Early Christianity
and Late Antiquity

[God] put Peter and Paul in the city of Rome because the capital of the world, being driven insane by her many vices and blinded by darkness, needed the chief doctors.... As the faith grows stronger, error is overcome and will fall away, and with hardly anyone left in the power of evil and death, all Rome acknowledges the name of Christ....

—PRUDENTIUS, *On the Crown of the Martyrs*

A rich set of biblical images found on the sarcophagus, or stone coffin, of a Christianized Roman aristocrat from the late fourth century. From the Sarcophagus of Junius Bassus, now in the Vatican.

A succession of civil wars and barbarian incursions that began in the last decades of the second century A.D., the so-called Third Century Crisis, effectively put an end to Edward Gibbon's "Golden Age of Man." Yet the Roman Empire "buckled" but did not fall, managing to weather the storms while becoming much transformed in the process. The period following the reign of Marcus Aurelius (d. 180), commonly referred to as the Later Roman Empire or Late Antiquity, was a time of dynamic and far-reaching changes. Much of the fundamental recasting of Roman social, economic, and political institutions that occurred during this period was in response to the complex and manifold Crisis of the Third Century. Another source for change was the gradual conversion of the Mediterranean world to Christianity, a process that entailed a significant cultural and religious shift over time.

Gibbon and others who followed in his footsteps attributed what they saw as the decline of Roman civilization to the "triumph of barbarism and religion [Christianity]." According to this view, the Germanic tribes—barbarians to the Romans—succeeded in occupying the western portion of the Roman Empire because the Empire had already been fatally weakened by the adoption of an alien creed, Christianity, itself a barbarian (i.e., Jewish) religion. The Romans thereby lost the aggressiveness and martial virtues with which they had attained world mastery.

Such a view is no longer widely shared among historians. But the task of explaining the roles played by Christianity in transforming Roman society remains. The final chapter of the volume allows readers to assess these transformations by offering selected documents on Christian Origins; Christianity and Its Reception in the Roman World; A New Roman Empire; and New Crises and "Fall of the Roman Empire."

Christian Origins

75 The New Testament

The Beginnings of Christianity

The New Testament (from the Latin word for "covenant"), an anthology consisting of the four Synoptic Gospels (Mark, Matthew, Luke, and John), the Acts of the Apostles, twenty-one Epistles, and the Book of Revelation, is the record of the career and teaching of Jesus of Nazareth and the founding of a new religion by his followers. The growth and spread of Christianity from an obscure Jewish sect in Palestine to the official religion of the Roman Empire is one of the most fascinating dramas in history. The New Testament deals with the first hundred years of this story.

A. THE TEACHINGS OF JESUS

"Turn away from your sins! The Kingdom of heaven is near!"

The life and teachings of Jesus form the central theme of the Christian New Testament. He followed in the tradition of the Hebrew prophets in denouncing the legalism and formalism of the established religion and in emphasizing a renovation of the inner spiritual and ethical content of that religion. His struggle to reform Judaism by breathing new life into old forms led to a conflict with other Jews, including the priests, which in turn led to his tragic death. An integral part of Jesus' teachings consists of the growing apocalyptic and eschatological (from the Greek word for "end" or "final") ideas of his day concerning resurrection of the dead, last judgment, angels, Satan ("the evil one"), hell, and the Messiah (*Christos* in Greek), the "Anointed One" who will usher in the Kingdom of God—also called the Kingdom of Heaven. The following selections from the Gospels (from the Greek word for "good news") illustrate the mingling of ethical and eschatological elements in the teachings of Jesus. They are taken from *Good News for Modern Man,* a completely new translation into "today's English" prepared by the American Bible Society. It "attempts to follow, in [our time], the example set by the authors of the New Testament books who, for the most part, wrote in the standard, or common [*koinē*] form of the Greek language used throughout the Roman Empire."

1. John the Baptist and the Sermon on the Mount

Following his baptism by John the Baptist, a fiery prophet who proclaimed the imminent coming of the Kingdom of God and whose act gave assurance of Jesus' divine appointment as Messiah, Jesus began his ministry, which was to culminate on the cross. One of the great moments in Jesus' messianic ministry was his preaching of the Sermon on the Mount, which has been called the Magna Carta of Christian ethics. It established for Christians a sublime—and largely unattainable—ideal of universal brotherhood and love. An indication of the new and radical nature of Jesus' ethical teaching is the frequent use of the phrase, "You have heard that men were told in the past, ... but now I tell you...." The Sermon on the Mount is reported in the two Gospels of Matthew and Luke, both, along with that of Mark, composed during the last half of the first century A.D.

From Matthew 3:1–17, 4:17–5:48, 6:5 15.

The Preaching of John the Baptist

At that time John the Baptist came and started preaching in the desert of Judea. "Change your ways," he said, "for the Kingdom of heaven is near!" John was the one that the prophet Isaiah was talking about when he said:

> Someone is shouting in the desert:
> "Get the Lord's road ready for him,
> Make a straight path for him to travel!"

John's clothes were made of camel's hair; he wore a leather belt around his waist, and ate locusts and wild honey. People came to him from Jerusalem, from the whole province of Judea, and from all the country around the Jordan river. They confessed their sins and he baptized them in the Jordan.

When John saw many Pharisees and Sadducees coming to him to be baptized, he said to them: "You snakes—who told you that you could escape from God's wrath that is about to come? Do the things that will show that you have changed your ways. And do not think you can excuse yourselves by saying, 'Abraham is our father.' I tell you that God can take these rocks and make children for Abraham! The ax is ready to cut the trees at the roots; every tree that does not bear good fruit will be cut down and thrown in the fire. I baptize you with water to show that you have repented; but the one who will come after me will baptize you with the Holy Spirit and fire. He is much greater than I am; I am not good enough even to carry his sandals. He has his winnowing-shovel with him to thresh out all the grain; he will gather his wheat into his barn, but burn the chaff in a fire that never goes out!"

The Baptism of Jesus

At that time Jesus went from Galilee to the Jordan, and came to John to be baptized by him. But John tried to make him change his mind. "I ought to be baptized by you," John said, "yet you come to me!" But Jesus answered him, "Let it be this way for now. For in this way we shall do all that God requires." So John agreed.

As soon as Jesus was baptized, he came up out of the water. Then heaven was opened to him, and he saw the Spirit of God coming down like a dove and lighting on him. And then a voice said from heaven, "This is my own dear Son, with whom I am well pleased."...

From that time Jesus began to preach his message: "Turn away from your sins! The Kingdom of heaven is near!"

Jesus Calls Four Fishermen

As Jesus walked by Lake Galilee, he saw two brothers who were fishermen, Simon (called Peter) and his brother Andrew, catching fish in the lake with a net. Jesus said to them, "Come with me and I will teach you to catch men." At once they left their nets and went with him.

He went on and saw two other brothers, James and John, the sons of Zebedee. They were in their boat with their father Zebedee, getting their nets ready. Jesus called them; at once they left the boat and their father, and went with Jesus.

The Sermon on the Mount

Jesus went all over Galilee, teaching in their meeting houses, preaching the Good News of the Kingdom, and healing people from every kind of disease and sickness. The news about him spread through the whole country of Syria, so that people brought him all those who were sick with all kinds of diseases, and afflicted with all sorts of troubles: people with demons, and epileptics and paralytics—Jesus healed them all. Great crowds followed him from Galilee and the Ten Towns [Decapolis, a federation of Greek cities in norhern Palestine] from Jerusalem, Judea, and the land on the other side of the Jordan.

Jesus saw the crowds and went up a hill, where he sat down. His disciples gathered around him, and he began to teach them:

> "Happy are those who know they are spiritually poor:
>   the Kingdom of heaven belongs to them!
> "Happy are those who mourn:
>   God will comfort them!
> "Happy are the meek:
>   they will receive what God has promised!
> "Happy are those whose greatest desire is to do what
>   God requires:
>   God will satisfy them fully!
> "Happy are those who show mercy to others:
>   God will show mercy to them!
> "Happy are the pure in heart:
>   they will see God!
> "Happy are those who work for peace among men:
>   God will call them his sons!
> "Happy are those who suffer persecution because they
>   do what God requires:
>   the Kingdom of heaven belongs to them!

"Happy are you when men insult you and mistreat you and tell all kinds of evil lies against you because you are my followers. Rejoice and be glad, because a great reward is kept for you in heaven. This is how men mistreated the prophets who lived before you.

"You are like salt for the earth. If the salt loses its taste, there is no way to make it salty again. It has become worthless, and so it is thrown away where people walk on it.

"You are like the light for the world. A city built on a high hill cannot be hid. Nobody lights a lamp to put it under a bowl; instead he puts it on the lampstand, where it gives light for everyone in the house. In the same way your light must shine before people, so that they will see the good things you do and give praise to your Father in heaven.

"Do not think that I have come to do away with the Law of Moses and the teaching of the prophets. I have not come to do away with them, but to give them real meaning. Remember this! As long as heaven and earth last, the least point or the smallest detail of the Law will not be done away with—not until the end of all things. Therefore, whoever breaks even the smallest of the commandments, and teaches others to do the same, will be least in the Kingdom of heaven. On the other hand, whoever obeys the Law, and teaches others to do the same, will be great in the Kingdom of heaven. I tell you, then, you will be able to enter the Kingdom of heaven only if your standard of life is far above the standard of the teachers of the Law and the Pharisees.

"You have heard that men were told in the past, 'Do not murder; anyone who commits murder will be brought before the judge.' But now I tell you: whoever is angry with his brother will be brought before the judge; whoever calls his brother 'You good-for-nothing!' will be brought before the Council; and whoever calls his brother a worthless fool will be in danger of going to the fire of hell. So if you are about to offer your gift to God at the altar and there you remember that your brother has something against you, leave your gift there in front of the altar and go at once to make peace with your brother; then come back and offer your gift to God....

"You have heard that it was said, 'Do not commit adultery.' But now I tell you: anyone who looks at a woman and wants to possess her is guilty of committing adultery with her in his heart. So if your right eye causes you to sin, take it out and throw it away! It is much better for you to lose a part of your body than to have your whole body thrown into hell. If your right hand causes you to sin, cut it off and throw it away! It is much better for you to lose one of your limbs than to have your whole body go off to hell.

"It was also said, 'Anyone who divorces his wife must give her a written notice of divorce.' But now I tell you: if a man divorces his wife, and she has not been unfaithful, then he is guilty of making her commit adultery if she marries again; and the man who marries her also commits adultery.

"You have also heard that men were told in the past, 'Do not break your promise, but do what you have sworn to do before the Lord.' But now I tell you: do not use any vow when you make a promise; do not swear by heaven, because it is God's throne; nor by earth, because it is the resting place for his feet; nor by Jerusalem, because it is the city of the great King. Do not even swear by your head, because you cannot make a single hair white or black. Just say 'Yes' or 'No'—anything else you have to say comes from the Evil One.

"You have heard that it was said, 'An eye for an eye, and a tooth for a tooth.' But now I tell you: do not take revenge on someone who does you wrong. If anyone slaps you on the right cheek, let him slap your left cheek too. And if someone takes you to court to sue you for your shirt, let him have your coat as well. And if one of the occupation troops forces you to carry his pack one mile, carry it another mile. When someone asks you for something, give it to him; when someone wants to borrow something, lend it to him.

"You have heard that it was said, 'Love your friends, hate your enemies.' But now I tell you: love your enemies, and pray for those who mistreat you, so that you will become the sons of your Father in heaven. For he makes his sun to shine on bad and good people alike, and gives rain to those who do right and those who do wrong. Why should you expect God to reward you, if you love only the people who love you? Even the tax collectors do that! And if you speak only to your friends, have you done anything out of the ordinary? Even the pagans do that! You must be perfect—just as your Father in heaven is perfect....

"And when you pray, do not be like the show-offs! They love to stand up and pray in the meeting houses and on the street corners so that everybody will see them. Remember this! They have already been paid in full. But when you pray, go to your room and close the door, and pray to your Father who is unseen. And your Father, who sees what you do in private, will reward you.

"In your prayers do not use a lot of words, as the pagans do, who think that God will hear them because of their long prayers. Do not be like them; God is your Father and he already knows what you need before you ask him. This is the way you should pray:

> Our Father in heaven:
> May your name be kept holy,
> May your Kingdom come,
> May your will be done on earth as it is in heaven.
> Give us today the food we need;
> Forgive us what we owe you as we forgive what others owe
> us;
> Do not bring us to hard testing, but keep us safe from the
> Evil One.

For if you forgive others the wrongs they have done you, your Father in heaven will forgive you. But if you do not forgive others, then Your Father in heaven will not forgive the wrongs you have done."

2. Parables of the Kingdom

A favorite teaching device used by Jesus is the parable, a humble story of everyday life from which a moral or spiritual truth is drawn. The first three Gospels contain almost fifty parables dealing with such subjects as humility, sympathy, forgiveness, and, above all, the nature of the eschatological concept of the Kingdom of God.

The Parable of the Sower

That same day Jesus left the house and went to the lakeside, where he sat down to teach. The crowd that gathered around him was so large that he got into a boat and sat in it, while the crowd stood on the shore. He used parables to tell them many things.

From Matthew 13:1–30, 36–43, 53–58, 15:21–28; Luke 10:25–37.

"There was a man who went out to sow. As he scattered the seed in the field, some of it fell along the path, and the birds came and ate it up. Some of it fell on the rocky ground, where there was little soil. The seeds soon sprouted, because the soil wasn't deep. When the sun came up it burned the young plants, and because the roots had not grown deep enough the plants soon dried up. Some of the seed fell among thorns, which grew up and choked the plants. But some seeds fell in good soil, and bore grain: some had one hundred grains, others sixty, and others thirty." And Jesus said, "Listen, then, if you have ears!"

The Purpose of the Parables

Then the disciples came to Jesus and asked him, "Why do you use parables when you talk to them?" "The knowledge of the secrets of the Kingdom of heaven has been given to you," Jesus answered, "but the man who has nothing will have taken away from him even the little he has. This is the reason that I use parables to talk to them: it is because they look, but do not see, and they listen, but do not hear or understand. So the prophecy of Isaiah comes true in this case:

> You will listen and listen, but not understand;
> You will look and look, but not see.
> Because this people's mind is dull;
> They have stopped up their ears,
> And they have closed their eyes.
> Otherwise, their eyes might see,
> Their ears might hear,
> Their minds might understand
> And they might turn to me, says God,
> And I would heal them.

As for you, how fortunate you are! Your eyes see and your ears hear. Remember this! Many prophets and many of God's people wanted very much to see what you see, but they could not, and to hear what you hear, but they did not."

Jesus Explains the Parable of the Sower

"Listen, then, and learn what the parable of the sower means. Those who hear the message about the Kingdom but do not understand it are like the seed that fall along the path. The Evil One comes and snatches away what was sown in them. The seed that fell on rocky ground stands for those who receive the message gladly as soon as they hear it. But it does not sink deep in them, and they don't last long. So when trouble or persecution comes because of the message, they give up at once. The seed that fell among thorns stands for those who hear the message, but the worries about this life and the love for riches choke the message, and they don't bear fruit. And the seed sown in the good soil stands for those who hear the message and understand it: they bear fruit, some as much as one hundred, others sixty, and others thirty."...

Jesus Rejected at Nazareth

When Jesus finished telling these parables, he left that place and went back to his home town. He taught in their meeting house, and those who heard him were amazed. "Where did he get such wisdom?" they asked. "And what about his miracles? Isn't he the carpenter's son? Isn't Mary his mother, and aren't James, Joseph, Simon, and Judas his brothers? Aren't all his sisters living here? Where did he get all this?" And so they rejected him. Jesus said to them: "A prophet is respected everywhere except in his home town and by his own family." He did not perform many miracles there because they did not have faith.

The Parable of the Good Samaritan

Then a certain teacher of the Law came up and tried to trap him. "Teacher," he asked, "what must I do to receive eternal life?" Jesus answered him, "What do the Scriptures say? How do you interpret them?" The man answered: "'You must love the Lord your God with all your heart, and with all your soul, and with all your strength, and with all your mind'; and, 'You must love your neighbor as yourself.'" "Your answer is correct," replied Jesus; "do this and you will live."

But the teacher of the Law wanted to put himself in the right, so he asked Jesus, "Who is my neighbor?" Jesus answered: "A certain man was going down from Jerusalem to Jericho, when robbers attacked him, stripped him and beat him up, leaving him half dead. It so happened that a priest was going down that road; when he saw the man he walked on by, on the other side. In the same way a Levite also came there, went over and looked at the man, and then walked on by, on the other side. But a certain Samaritan who was traveling that way came upon him, and when he saw the man his heart was filled with pity. He went over to him, poured oil and wine on his wounds and bandaged them; then he put the man on his own animal and took him to an inn, where he took care of him. The next day he took out two silver coins and gave them to the innkeeper. 'Take care of him.' he told the innkeeper, 'and when I come back this way I will pay you back whatever you spend on him.'" And Jesus concluded, "Which one of these three seems to you to have been a neighbor to the man attacked by the robbers?" The teacher of the Law answered, "The one who was kind to him." Jesus replied, "You go, then, and do the same."

3. Jesus' Instructions to His Disciples

The following passages throw further light on Jesus' own conception of his mission. It is to be preached solely among "the lost sheep of the people of Israel," and he has no illusions concerning the deep cleavage it will produce between those who accept his teachings and those who cling to the established orthodox position. Furthermore, while Jesus appears to accept the belief of his disciples that he is the Messiah, he adds the novel view that he must suffer, die, and be resurrected as a prelude to the troubles of "the end of the age" of evil and the coming of the Kingdom of Heaven.

From Matthew 10:1–42, 16:13–28, 24:3–31, 25:31–46.

The Mission of the Twelve

Jesus called his twelve disciples together and gave them power to drive out the evil spirits and to heal every disease and every sickness. These are the names of the twelve apostles: first, Simon (called Peter) and his brother Andrew; James and his brother John, the sons of Zebedee; Philip and Bartholomew; Thomas and Matthew, the tax collector; James, the son of Alphaeus, and Thaddaeus; Simon, the patriot, and Judas Iscariot, who betrayed Jesus.

Jesus sent these twelve men out with the following instructions: "Do not go to any Gentile territory or any Samaritan towns. Go, instead, to the lost sheep of the people of Israel. Go and preach, 'The Kingdom of heaven is near!' Heal the sick, raise the dead, make the lepers clean, drive out demons. You have received without paying, so give without being paid. Do not carry any gold, silver, or copper money in your pockets; do not carry a beggar's bag for the trip, or an extra shirt, or shoes, or a walking stick. A worker should be given what he needs.

"When you come to a town or village, go in and look for someone who is willing to welcome you, and stay with him until you leave that place. When you go into a house say, 'Peace be with you.' If the people in that house welcome you, let your greeting of peace remain; but if they do not welcome you, then take back your greeting. And if some home or town will not welcome you or listen to you, then leave that place and shake the dust off your feet. Remember this! On the Judgment Day God will show more mercy to the people of Sodom and Gommorrah than to the people of that town!

"Listen! I am sending you just like sheep to a pack of wolves. You must be as cautious as snakes and as gentle as doves. Watch out, for there will be men who will arrest you and take you to court, and they will whip you in their meeting houses. You will be brought to trial before rulers and kings for my sake, to tell the Good News to them and to the Gentiles. When they bring you to trial, do not worry about what you are going to say or how you will say it; when the time comes, you will be given what you will say. For the words you speak will not be yours; they will come from the Spirit of your Father speaking in you.

"Men will hand over their own brothers to be put to death, and fathers will do the same to their children; children will turn against their parents and have them put to death. Everyone will hate you, because of me. But the person who holds out to the end will be saved. And when they persecute you in one town, run away to another one. I tell you, you will not finish your work in all the towns of Israel before the Son of Man comes....

"Do not think that I have come to bring peace to the world; no, I did not come to bring peace, but a sword. I came to set sons against their fathers, daughters against their mothers, daughters-in-law against their mothers-in-law; a man's worst enemies will be the members of his own family.

"Whoever loves his father or mother more than me is not worthy of me; whoever loves his son or daughter more than me is not worthy of me. Whoever does not take up his cross and follow in my steps is not worthy of me. Whoever tries to gain his own life will lose it: whoever loses his life for my sake will gain it.

"Whoever welcomes you, welcomes me; and whoever welcomes me, welcomes the one who sent me. Whoever welcomes God's messenger because he is

Jesus as the Good Shepherd from the catacomb (underground cemetery) of St. Callistus in Rome, about A.D. 250. Jesus is depicted as a young and beardless man with short hair and wearing the ordinary costume of the time.

"So Jesus said: 'I am the good shepherd. The good shepherd is willing to die for the sheep.'"

—John 10:11

God's messenger will share in his reward, and whoever welcomes a truly good man, because he is that, will share in his reward. And remember this! Whoever gives even a drink of cold water to one of the least of these my followers, because he is any follower, will certainly receive his reward."...

Peter's Declaration About Jesus

Jesus went to the territory near the town of Caesarea Philippi, where he asked his disciples, "Who do men say the Son of Man is?" "Some say John the Baptist," they answered. "Others say Elijah, while others say Jeremiah or some other prophet." "What about you?" he asked them. "Who do you say I am?" Simon Peter answered, "You are the Messiah, the Son of the living God." "Simon, son of John, you are happy indeed!" answered Jesus. "For this truth did not come to you from any human being, but it was given to you directly by my Father in heaven. And so I tell you: you are a rock, Peter, and on this rock I will build my church. Not even death will ever be able to overcome it. I will give you the keys of the Kingdom of heaven: what you prohibit on earth will be prohibited in heaven; what you permit on earth will be permitted in heaven." Then Jesus ordered his disciples that they were not to tell anyone that he was the Messiah.

Jesus Speaks About His Suffering and Death

From that time on Jesus began to say plainly to his disciples: "I must go to Jerusalem and suffer much from the elders, the chief priests, and the teachers of the Law. I will be put to death, and on the third day I will be raised to life." Peter took him aside and began to rebuke him. "God forbid it, Lord!" he said. "This must never happen to you!" Jesus turned around and said to Peter: "Get away from me, Satan! You are an obstacle in my way, for these thoughts of yours are men's thoughts, not God's!"

Then Jesus said to his disciples: "If anyone wants to come with me, he must forget himself, carry his cross, and follow me. For the man who wants to save his own life will lose it; but the man who loses his life for my sake will find it. Will a man gain anything if he wins the whole world but loses his life? Of course not! There is nothing a man can give to regain his life. For the Son of Man is about to come in the glory of his Father with his angels, and then he will repay everyone according to his deeds. Remember this! There are some here who will not die until they have seen the Son of Man come as King."...

Troubles and Persecutions: The End of the Age

As Jesus sat on the Mount of Olives, the disciples came to him in private. "Tell us when all this will be," they asked, "and what will happen to show that it is the time for your coming and the end of the age."

Jesus answered: "Watch out, and do not let anyone fool you. Because many men will come in my name, saying, 'I am the Messiah!' and fool many people. You are going to hear the noise of battles close by and the news of battles far away; but, listen, do not be troubled. Such things must happen, but they do not mean that the end has come. One country will fight another country, one king-dom will attack another kingdom. There will be famines and earthquakes every-where. All these things are like the first pains of childbirth.

"Then men will arrest you and hand you over to be punished, and you will be put to death. All mankind will hate you because of me. Many will give up their faith at that time; they will betray each other and hate each other. Then many false prophets will appear and fool many people. Such will be the spread of evil that many people's love will grow cold. But the person who holds out to the end will be saved. And this Good News about the Kingdom will be preached through all the world, for a witness to all mankind—and then will come the end.

"You will see 'The Awful Horror,' of which the prophet Daniel spoke standing in the holy place." (Note to the reader: understand what this means!).[1]...

The Coming of the Son of Man

"Soon after the trouble of those days the sun will grow dark, the moon will no longer shine, the stars will fall from heaven, and the powers in space will be driven from their course. Then the sign of the Son of Man will appear in the sky; then all the tribes of earth will weep, and they will see the Son of Man coming on the clouds of heaven with power and great glory. The great trumpet will sound, and he will send out his angels to the four corners of the earth, and they will gather his chosen people from one end of the world to the other...."

The Last Judgment

"When the Son of Man comes as King, and all the angels with him, he will sit on his royal throne, and all the earth's people will be gathered before him. Then he will divide them into two groups, just as a shepherd separates the sheep from the goats: he will put the sheep at his right and the goats at his left, Then the King will say to the people on his right: 'You who are blessed by my Father: come! Come and receive the kingdom which has been prepared for you ever since the creation of the world. I was hungry and you fed me, thirsty and you gave me drink; I was a stranger and you received me in your homes, naked and you clothed me; I was sick and you took care of me, in prison and you visited me.' The righteous will then answer him: 'When, Lord, did we ever see you hungry and feed you, or thirsty and give you drink? When did we ever see you a stranger and welcome you in our homes, or naked and clothe you? When did we ever see you sick or in prison, and visit you?' The King will answer back, 'I tell you, indeed, whenever you did this for one of these poorest brothers of mine, you did it for me!'

"Then he will say to those on his left: 'Away from me, you who are under God's curse! Away to the eternal fire which has been prepared for the Devil and

---

1. This parenthetical sentence is an addition to a written document and not part of an oral statement.

his angels! I was hungry but you would not feed me, thirsty but you would not give me drink; I was a stranger but you would not welcome me in your homes, naked but you would not clothe me; I was sick and in prison but you would not take care of me.' Then they will answer him: 'When, Lord, did we ever see you hungry, or thirsty, or a stranger, or naked, or sick, or in prison, and we would not help you?' The King will answer them back, 'I tell you, indeed, whenever you refused to help one of these poor ones, you refused to help me.' These, then, will be sent off to eternal punishment; the righteous will go to eternal life."

B. THE WORK OF PAUL

"Jews and Gentiles ... are all one in union with Christ Jesus."

Paul of Tarsus (ca. A.D. 10–ca. 65), a Hellenized Jew of the Diaspora, has been called the second founder of Christianity. He played a crucial role in the initial spreading of Christianity among the Gentiles of the Roman world and in establishing the fundamental Christian doctrines of Jesus as the crucified Christ, the incarnation of God, whose resurrection assured immortality to those who entered into a mystical union with his Spirit. There will always be much debate about the extent to which Pauline Christianity is an elaboration on the teachings of Jesus to meet Gentile needs, but there is complete agreement that Paul was a genius whose work was of epochal significance for the history of Western civilization.

1. Paul's Mission: Failure at Athens, Success at Corinth

Paul's missionary activities took him into the leading cities of Asia Minor, Macedonia, and Greece, seeking converts among both Jews and Gentiles. Our knowledge of this work is derived from the Acts of the Apostles, thought to be the work of Luke, and Paul's own Epistles. Paul's visit to Athens (ca. A.D. 51) is of great interest, even though largely unsuccessful. His failure with one exception to convert the Athenian intellectuals, who are seen still maintaining the famed Greek curiosity about the "latest new thing," is typical of the failure of early Christianity to attract the educated classes; it took the more philosophical approach of the later Apologists to win them over (Selection 76).

Paul's failure at Athens, where he remained only a few days, contrasts sharply with his success at the populous commercial city of Corinth, the capital of the Roman province of Achaia (Greece), where he remained eighteen months and to whose congregation he later wrote two of his most important epistles. While Athens remained a famed intellectual center, Corinth was known for its wealth and gaudy vice. So low was the level of morality in the city that its name became synonymous with degradation. Paul's older contemporary, the Roman geographer Strabo, reports that more than a thousand temple-prostitutes were at one time maintained at Corinth in connection with the orgiastic worship of Astarte, the Phoenician goddess of love and fertility.

From Acts 17:16–34, 18:1–11.

"What Is This Ignorant Show-off Trying to Say?"

While Paul was waiting in Athens for Silas and Timothy, he was greatly upset when he noticed how full of idols the city was. So he argued in the meeting house with the Jews and the Gentiles who worshiped God, and in the public square every day with the people who happened to come by. Certain Epicurean and Stoic teachers also debated with him. Some said, "What is this ignorant show-off trying to say?" Others said, "He seems to be talking about foreign gods." They said this because Paul was preaching about Jesus and the resurrection. So they took Paul, brought him before the meeting of the Areopagus, and said: "We would like to know this new teaching that you are talking about. Some of the things we hear you say sound strange to us, and we would like to know what they mean." (For all the people of Athens and the foreigners who lived there liked to spend all their time telling and hearing the latest new thing.)

Paul stood up in front of the meeting of the Areopagus and said: "Men of Athens! I see that in every way you are very religious. For as I walked through your city and looked at the places where you worship, I found also an altar on which is written, 'To an Unknown God.' That which you worship, then, even though you do not know it, is what I now proclaim to you. God, who made the world and everything in it, is Lord of heaven and earth, and does not live in temples made by men. Nor does he need anything that men can supply by working for him, since it is he himself who gives life and breath and everything else to all men. From the one man he created all races of men, and made them live over the whole earth. He himself fixed beforehand the exact times and the limits of the places where they would live. He did this so that they would look for him, and perhaps find him as they felt around for him. Yet God is actually not far from any one of us; for

> In him we live and move and are.

It is as some of your poets have also said,

> We too are his children.

Since we are his children, we should not suppose that God's nature is anything like an image of gold or silver or stone, shaped by the art and skill of man. God has overlooked the times when men did not know, but now he commands all men everywhere to turn away from their evil ways. For he has fixed a day in which he will judge the whole world with justice, by means of a man he has chosen. He has given proof of this to everyone by raising that man from death!"

When they heard Paul speak about a raising from death, some of them made fun of him, but others said, "We want to hear you speak about this again." And so Paul left the meeting. Some men joined him and believed; among them was Dionysius, a member of the Areopagus, a woman named Damaris, and some others.

"Many People in Corinth Believed and Were Baptized"

After this, Paul left Athens and went on to Corinth. There he met a Jew named Aquila, born in Pontus, who had just come from Italy with his wife

Priscilla—because Emperor Claudius had ordered all the Jews to leave Rome. Paul went to see them, and stayed and worked with them, because he earned his living by making tents, just as they did. He argued in the Jewish meeting house every Sabbath, trying to convince both Jews and Greeks.

When Silas and Timothy arrived from Macedonia, Paul gave his whole time to preaching the message, testifying to the Jews that Jesus is the Messiah. When they opposed him and said evil things about him, he protested by shaking the dust from his clothes and saying to them: "If you are lost, you yourselves must take the blame for it! I am not responsible. From now on I will go to the Gentiles." So he left them and went to live in the house of a Gentile named Titius Justus, who worshiped God; his house was next to the Jewish meeting house. Crispus, the leader of the meeting house, believed in the Lord, he and all his family; and many other people in Corinth heard the message, believed, and were baptized.

One night Paul had a vision, in which the Lord said to him: "Do not be afraid, but keep on speaking and do not give up, for I am with you. No one will be able to harm you, because many in this city are my people." So Paul stayed there for a year and a half, teaching the people the word of God.

2. Paul's Epistles to Christian Communities

"His letters, say they, are weighty and powerful."
II Corinthians 10:10

The New Testament contains fourteen of Paul's letters, undoubtedly only a portion of those he wrote to instruct and encourage the infant Christian communities. As the following passages illustrate, they are a primary source for our knowledge of early Christian theology, and they form a body of devotional literature that has continuously inspired Christian readers.

a. Paul's Answer to Intellectuals

Christ did not send me to baptize. He sent me to tell the Good News, and to tell it without using the language of men's wisdom, for that would rob Christ's death on the cross of all its power.

For the message about Christ's death on the cross is nonsense to those who are being lost; but for us who are being saved, it is God's power. For the scripture says,

> I will destroy the wisdom of the wise,
> I will set aside the understanding of the scholars.

So then, where does that leave the wise men? Or the scholars? Or the skillful debaters of this world? God has shown that this world's wisdom is foolishness!

For God in his wisdom made it impossible for men to know him by means of their own wisdom. Instead, God decided to save those who believe, by means

From I Corinthians 1:17–2:8.

of the "foolish" message we preach. Jews want miracles for proof, and Greeks look for wisdom. As for us, we proclaim Christ on the cross, a message that is offensive to the Jews and nonsense to the Gentiles; but for those whom God has called, both Jews and Gentiles, this message is Christ, who is the power of God and the wisdom of God. For what seems to be God's foolishness is wiser than men's wisdom, and what seems to be God's weakness is stronger than men's strength.

Now remember what you were, brothers, when God called you. Few of you were wise, or powerful, or of high social status, from the human point of view. God purposely chose what the world considers nonsense in order to put wise men to shame, and what the world considers weak in order to put powerful men to shame. He chose what the world looks down on, and despises, and thinks is nothing, in order to destroy what the world thinks is important....

When I came to you, my brothers, to preach God's secret truth to you, I did not use long words and great learning. For I made up my mind to forget everything while I was with you except Jesus Christ, and especially his death on the cross. So when I came to you I was weak and trembled all over with fear, and my speech and message were not delivered with skillful words of human wisdom, but with convincing proof of the power of God's Spirit. Your faith, then, does not rest on man's wisdom, but on God's power....

b. The Resurrection of Christ and the Faithful

And now I want to remind you, brothers, of the Good News which I preached to you, which you received, and on which our faith stands firm. That is the gospel, the message that I preached to you. You are saved by the gospel if you hold firmly to it—unless it was for nothing that you believed.

I passed on to you what I received, which is of the greatest importance: that Christ died for our sins, as written in the Scriptures; that he was buried and raised to life on the third day, as written in the Scriptures; that he appeared to Peter, and then to all twelve apostles. Then he appeared to more than five hundred of his followers at once, most of whom are still alive, although some have died. Then he appeared to James, and then to all the apostles.

Last of all he appeared also to me—even though I am like one who was born in a most unusual way. For I am the least of all the apostles—I do not even deserve to be called an apostle, because I persecuted God's church. But by God's grace I am what I am, and the grace that he gave me was not without effect. On the contrary, I have worked harder than all the other apostles, although it was not really my own doing, but God's grace working with me. So then, whether it came from me or from them, this is what we all preach, this is what you believe.

Now, since our message is that Christ has been raised from death, how can some of you say that the dead will not be raised to life? If that is true, it means that Christ was not raised: and if Christ has not been raised from death, then we have nothing to preach, and you have nothing to believe. More than that, we

From I Corinthians 15:1–55.

are shown to be lying against God, because we said of him that he raised Christ from death—but he did not raise him, if it is true that the dead are not raised to life. For if the dead are not raised, neither has Christ been raised. And if Christ has not been raised, then your faith is a delusion and you are still lost in your sins. It would also mean that the believers in Christ who have died are lost. If our hope in Christ is good for this life only, and no more, then we deserve more pity than anyone else in all the world.

But the truth is that Christ has been raised from death, as the guarantee that those who steep in death will also be raised. For just as death came by means of a man, in the same way the rising from death comes by means of a man. For just as all men die because of their union to Adam, in the same way all will be raised to life because of their union to Christ....

This is what I mean, brothers: what is made of flesh and blood cannot share in God's Kingdom, and what is mortal cannot possess immortality.

Listen to this secret: we shall not all die, but in an instant we shall all be changed, as quickly as the blinking of an eye, when the last trumpet sounds. For when it sounds, the dead will be raised immortal beings, and we shall all be changed. For what is mortal must clothe itself with what is immortal: what will die must clothe itself with what cannot die. So when what is mortal has been clothed with what is immortal, and when what will die has been clothed with what cannot die, then the scripture will come true: "Death is destroyed: victory is complete!"

"Where, O Death, is your victory?
"Where, O Death, is your power to hurt?"

c. Faith and the Law

You must remember this, my brothers: many times I have planned to visit you, but something has always kept me from doing so. I have wanted to win converts among you, too, as I have among other Gentiles. For I have an obligation to all peoples, to the civilized and to the savage, to the educated and to the ignorant. Therefore, I am eager to preach the Good News to you also who live in Rome.

For I have complete confidence in the gospel: it is God's power to save all who believe, first the Jews and also the Gentiles. For the gospel reveals how God puts men right with himself: it is through faith alone, from beginning to end. As the scripture [Habakkuk 2:4] says, "He who is put right with God through faith shall live.".…

But now God's way of putting men right with himself has been revealed and it has nothing to do with law. The Law and the prophets gave their witness to it: God puts men right through their faith in Jesus Christ....

What, then, is there to boast about? Nothing! For what reason? Because a man obeys the Law? No, but because he believes. For we conclude that a man is put right with God only through faith, and not by doing what the Law commands. Or is God only the God of the Jews? Is he not the God of the Gentiles also?

From Romans 1:13–17, 3:21–31; Galatians 3:6–29.

Of course he is. God is one, and he will put the Jews right with himself on the basis of their faith, and the Gentiles right through their faith. Does this mean that we do away with the Law by this faith? No, not at all; instead, we uphold the Law....

It is just as the scripture says about Abraham: "He believed God, and because of his faith God accepted him as righteous." You should realize, then, that the people who have faith are the real descendants of Abraham. The scripture saw ahead of time that God would put the Gentiles right with himself through faith. Therefore the scripture preached the Good News to Abraham ahead of time: "Through you God will bless all the people on earth." Abraham believed and was blessed; so all who believe are blessed as he was.

Those who depend on obeying the Law live under a curse. For the scripture says, "Whoever does not always obey everything that is written in the book of the Law is under the curse!"...

But Christ has set us free from the curse the Law brings by becoming a curse for us. As the scripture says, "Anyone who is hanged on a tree is under the curse." Christ did so in order that the blessing God promised Abraham might be given to the Gentiles by means of Christ Jesus, that we, through faith, might receive the Spirit promised by God.

Brothers, I am going to use an everyday example: when two men agree on a matter and sign a covenant, no one can break that covenant or add anything to it. Now, God made his promises to Abraham and to his descendant. It does not say, "and to his descendants," meaning many people. It says, "and to your descendant," meaning one person only, who is Christ. This is what I mean: God made a covenant and promised to keep it. The Law, which came four hundred and thirty years later [Selection 10C], cannot break that covenant and cancel God's promise. For if what God gives depends on the Law, then it no longer depends on his promise. However, God gave it to Abraham because he had promised it to him.

Why was the Law given, then? It was added in order to show what wrongdoing is, and was meant to last until the coming of Abraham's descendant, to whom the promise was made. The Law was handed down by angels, with a man acting as a go-between. But a go-between is not needed when there is only one person; and God is one.

Does this mean that the Law is against God's promises? No, not at all! For if a law had been given that could give life to men, then man could be put right with God through law. But the scripture has said that the whole world is under the power of sin, so that those who believe might receive the promised gift that is given on the basis of faith in Jesus Christ.

Before the time for faith came, however, the Law kept us all locked up as prisoners, until this coming faith should be revealed. So the Law was in charge of us, to be our instructor until Christ came, so that we might be put right with God through faith. Now that the time of faith is here, the instructor is no longer in charge of us.

For it is through faith that all of you are God's sons in union with Christ Jesus. For all who are baptized into union with Christ have taken upon themselves the qualities of Christ himself. So there is no difference between Jews and Gentiles, between slaves and free men, between men and women: you are all one in union with Christ Jesus. If you belong to Christ, then you are the descendants of Abraham, and will receive what God has promised.

d. Apocalyptic Hope and Predestination

I consider that what we suffer at this present time cannot be compared at all with the glory that is going to be revealed to us. All of creation waits with eager longing for God to reveal his sons. For creation was condemned to become worthless, not of its own will, but because God willed it to be so. Yet there was this hope: that creation itself would one day be set free from its slavery to decay, and share the glorious freedom of the children of God. For we know that up to the present time all of creation groans with pain like the pain of childbirth. But not just creation alone; we who have the Spirit as the first of God's gifts, we also groan within ourselves as we wait for God to make us his sons and set our whole being free. For it was by hope that we were saved, but if we see what we hope for, then it is not really hope. For who hopes for something that he sees? But if we hope for what we do not see, we wait for it with patience....

For we know that in all things God works for good with those who love him, those whom he has called according to his purpose. For those whom God had already chosen he had also set apart to share the likeness of his Son, so that the Son should be the first among many brothers. And so God called those whom he had set apart; not only did he call them, but he also put them right with himself; not only did he put them right with himself, but he also shared his glory with them.

Faced with all this, what can we say? If God is for us, who can be against us?...

e. Love

I may be able to speak the languages of men and even of angels, but if I have not love, my speech is no more than a noisy gong or a clanging bell. I may have the gift of inspired preaching; I may have all knowledge and understand all secrets; I may have all the faith needed to move mountains—but if I have not love, I am nothing. I may give away everything I have, and even give up my body to be burned—but if I have not love, it does me no good.

Love is patient and kind; love is not jealous, or conceited, or proud; love is not ill-mannered, or selfish, or irritable; love does not keep a record of wrongs; love is not happy with evil, but is happy with the truth. Love never gives up: its faith, hope, and patience never fail.

Love is eternal. There are inspired messages, but they are temporary; there are gifts of speaking, but they will cease; there is knowledge, but it will pass. For our gifts of knowledge and of inspired messages are only partial; but when what is perfect comes, then what is partial disappears.

From Romans 8:18–31.

From I Corinthians 13:1–13.

When I was a child, my speech, feelings, and thinking were all those of a child; now that I am a man, I have no more use for childish ways. What we see now is like the dim image in a mirror; then we shall see face to face. What I know now is only partial; then it will be complete, as complete as God's knowledge of me.

Meanwhile these three remain: faith, hope, and love; and the greatest of these is love.

Christianity and Its Reception in the Roman World

76 Christianity and Greco-Roman Thought

"Whatever has been uttered aright by any men in any place belongs to us Christians." *Justin Martyr, Apology*

To the intellectuals of the Greco-Roman world, early Christianity appeared to be just another eastern cult of interest only to the uneducated lower classes; in the words of Tacitus, it was a "pernicious superstition," particularly unattractive because of its "hatred for the whole human race." On the other hand, the earliest Christians were equally hostile to pagan philosophy, and they agreed with St. Paul that God had "made foolish the wisdom of this world." Before Christianity could spread triumphantly through the whole classical world, taking into its fold people on all levels of learning, some solution to this conflict had to be achieved. We have seen that in the early Roman Empire Greek philosophy, notably Stoicism and a revived Platonism, became increasingly imbued with religious values; consequently, when men trained in Greek learning, or *paideia*, began to accept Christianity, an amalgamation of philosophy and Christianity was not difficult to bring about. This process, the work of intellectual Christians known as Apologists and Church Fathers, began in the second century A.D. in the more Christian East and culminated in the work of St. Augustine at the end of the fourth century in the West.

Various methods were used in giving an intellectual tone to Christianity. The personal God of the Jews and Christians was identified with the abstract god of the Greek philosophers—a pure, invisible, incorporeal intelligence.

The literal interpretation of the Old Testament was replaced by an allegorical one in which a deeper symbolical and spiritual meaning was found to lie behind the simple words of the text. Biblical truth, wrote Origen, one of the outstanding third-century Greek Apologists, "is sometimes conveyed in what one might call literal falsehood." Above all, use was made of the Logos doctrine, which explained how God was the source of all truth, both pagan and Christian. "Logos" was a term used in Greek philosophy to signify the powers of reason. It is translated variously as "word," "argument," and "reason." Plato and other Greek thinkers referred to the Logos as eternal and divine, and the Christian Apologists adopted the term for the divine principle regulating all things and bridging the gap between God and humankind. They taught that the Logos (reason) of the Greek philosophers was one means by which God sought to enlighten and save humankind but that, when this attempt failed, He then sent the Logos in the form of his Only-Begotten Son, Jesus. "Thus philosophy was a preparation," wrote Clement, Origen's predecessor as head of the Christian school at Alexandria, "paving the way towards perfection in Christ." (He described the Church as a river emerging from the confluence of Biblical faith with Greek philosophy.) A well-known statement of the Logos doctrine and the incarnation of this divine force in Jesus is found in the Gospel of John: "In the beginning was the Word, and the Word was with God, and the Word was God. ... And the light shineth in darkness; and the darkness comprehended it not. ... And the Word was made flesh and dwelt among us full of grace and truth" (Bk. 1).

A. JUSTIN MARTYR, *APOLOGY*

"Those who lived according to reason are Christians."

The first important Christian Apologist was Justin Martyr, whose *Apology* was addressed to the emperor Antoninus Pius about the middle of second century. Although a Greek, he spent much time in Rome, where he conducted a school and where he ultimately suffered martyrdom. His conversion to Christianity from Stoicism and Platonism illustrates the strong appeal of what he called "the noble precepts of Christ" over the pagan way of life, a view he summarizes in the first excerpt following. The second excerpt is an excellent short statement illustrating the attitude of most of the Church Fathers toward pagan learning.

Christianity and Moral Regeneration

Since our conversion to Christianity, we who formerly delighted in debauchery, now rejoice in purity of life; we who formerly used magical arts, dedicate ourselves to the good and unbegotten God; we who valued above all things the acquisition of wealth and possessions, now bring together all that we have and share it with those who are in need. Formerly, we hated and destroyed one another and, because of differences in nationality and customs, would not allow

From Justin, *Apology*, I, 14, 46; II, 13; based on the translation by Marcus Dods.

strangers to live with us. Now, since the coming of Christ, we live familiarly with them, and pray for our enemies, and endeavor to persuade those who hate us unjustly to live according to the good precepts of Christ, to the end that they may become partakers with us of the same joyful hope of a reward from God the ruler of all....

Christianity and Pagan Learning

Lest some should assert, unreasonably and to turn men from what we teach, that we say that Christ was born one hundred and fifty years ago under Cyrenius, and subsequently, in the time of Pontius Pilate, taught what we say He taught, and then accuse us of saying that all men who were born before Him were irresponsible—let us anticipate and solve this difficulty. We have been taught that Christ is the first-born of God, and we have declared above that He is the Word [reason] of whom every race of men were partakers. Those who lived according to reason are Christians, even though they have been thought atheists—such as, among the Greeks, Socrates and Heraclitus, and men like them; and among barbarians, Abraham, and Ananias....

For each man spoke rightly in proportion to the share he had of the seminal Word, seeing what was related to it. ... Whatever things were rightly said among all men in all places belong to us Christians. For next to God we worship and love the Word who is from the unbegotten and ineffable God, since also He became man for our sakes, that, becoming a partaker of our sufferings, He might also bring us healing. For all the writers were able to see realities darkly through the sowing of the implanted Word that was in them.

B. TATIAN, *ADDRESS TO THE GREEKS*

"Do not resolve your gods and myths into allegories"

As Christianity gradually made inroads into Roman society by converting men and women who had been worshippers of the traditional gods, animosity against it grew. Thus, especially during the second century A.D., a number of Christians took to writing formal defenses of their religion against contemporary prejudices and accusations by hostile critics. The goal of these Apologists—from the Greek term for a formal defense, *apologia*—was to show to Christians and outsiders alike that Christianity was both good and true and also should not be the object of persecution. Born around A.D. 100, Justin, so-called Martyr, was one of the earliest of these Apologists. After his conversion to Christianity in the course of his quest for philosophical truth, turning from the teachings of the Stoa, Aristotle, Pythagoras, Plato, and to that of Christ, Justin rose vigorously to its defense in a series of apologetic works in which he sought to demonstrate that Christianity was the true philosophy. He taught in Rome, where Tatian

From Tatian, *Address to the Greeks* 21–22; in *The Ante-Nicene Fathers: Translations of the Writings of the Fathers down to A.D. 325*, Vol. II, edited by Alexander Roberts and James Donaldson (Grand Rapids, Mich.: Eerdmans, 1989–90), pp. 74–75.

(b. ca. 120), another Greek-educated easterner, became a disciple of his. Tatian was trained previously in Greek rhetoric and philosophy and had embarked on a similar quest for the true philosophy that eventually led him to convert to Christianity. His work *Address to the Greeks* (composed ca. 155–165) belongs to the family of Christian apologetic writings even though it may seem to attack more than it defends. In this work, Tatian criticizes the fundamental bases of the Greeks' notable pride in their own cultural and intellectual achievements. His work thus attacked the premises of *paideia*, the Greek ideal of educated upbringing, in all its forms, as well as Greek beliefs in the gods as depicted in mythological works such those of Homer. For a work that seeks to strip away Greek claims to superiority, it nevertheless shows the clear influence of Tatian's Greek rhetorical education in its use of a highly affected style of prose and known rhetorical tropes and figures. Yet this writing also displays a sheer vehemence that could have only come from deep passion and conviction, aimed against a cultural system and outlook that had formed him and that he must once have loved and maintained to be true.

XXI.—*Doctrines of the Christians and Greeks Respecting God Compared*

We do not act as fools, O Greeks, nor utter idle tales, when we announce that God was born in the form of a man. I call on you who reproach us to compare your mythical accounts with our narrations. Athené, as they say, took the form of Deïphobus [a son of Priam of Troy] for the sake of Hector, and the unshorn Phoebus for the sake of Admetus fed the trailing-footed oxen, and the spouse of Zeus came as an old woman to Semele. But, while you treat seriously such things, how can you deride us? Your Asclepios died, and he who ravished fifty virgins in one night at Thespiae lost his life by delivering himself to the devouring flame. Prometheus, fastened to [Mount] Caucasus, suffered punishment for his good deeds to men. According to you, Zeus is envious, and hides the dream from men, wishing their destruction. Wherefore, looking at your own memorials, vouchsafe us your approval, though it were only as dealing in legends similar to your own. We, however, do not deal in folly, but your legends are only idle tales. If you speak of the origin of the gods, you also declare them to be mortal. For what reason is Hera now never pregnant? Has she grown old? or is there no one to give you information? Believe me now, O Greeks, and do not resolve your myths and gods into allegory. If you attempt to do this, the divine nature as held by you is overthrown by your own selves; for, if the demons with you are such as they are said to be, they are worthless as to character; or, if regarded as symbols of the powers of nature, they are not what they are called. But I cannot be persuaded to pay religious homage to the natural elements, nor can I undertake to persuade my neighbour. And Metrodorus of Lampsacus, in his treatise concerning Homer, has argued very foolishly, turning everything into allegory. For he says that neither Hera, nor Athené, nor Zeus are what those persons suppose who consecrate to them sacred enclosures and groves, but parts of nature and certain arrangements of the elements. Hector also, and Achilles, and Agamemnon, and all the Greeks in general, and the Barbarians with Helen and Paris, being of the same nature, you will of course say are introduced merely for the sake of the machinery of the poem, not one of these personages having really existed. But these things we have put forth only for argument's sake; for it is not allowable even to compare our notion of God with those who are wallowing in matter and mud.

XXII.—*Ridicule of the Solemnities of the Greeks*

And of what sort are your teachings? Who must not treat with contempt your solemn festivals, which, being held in honour of wicked demons, cover men with infamy? I have often seen a man—and have been amazed to see, and the amazement has ended in contempt, to think how he is one thing internally, but outwardly counterfeits what he is not—giving himself excessive airs of daintiness and indulging in all sorts of effeminacy; sometimes darting his eyes about; sometimes throwing his hands hither and thither, and raving with his face smeared with mud; sometimes personating Aphrodité, sometimes Apollo; a solitary accuser of all the gods, an epitome of superstition, a vituperator of heroic deeds, an actor of murders, a chronicler of adultery, a storehouse of madness, a teacher of cynaedi [poems in Ionic meter], an instigator of capital sentences;—and yet such a man is praised by all. But I have rejected all his falsehoods, his impiety, his practices,—in short, the man altogether. But you are led captive by such men, while you revile those who do not take a part in your pursuits. I have no mind to stand agape at a number of singers, nor do I desire to be affected in sympathy with a man when he is winking and gesticulating in an unnatural manner. What wonderful or extraordinary thing is performed among you? They utter ribaldry in affected tones, and go through indecent movements; your daughters and your sons behold them giving lessons in adultery on the stage. Admirable places, forsooth, are your lecture-rooms, where every base action perpetrated by night is proclaimed aloud, and the hearers are regaled with the utterance of infamous discourses! Admirable, too, are your mendacious poets, who by their fictions beguile their hearers from the truth!

C. TERTULLIAN, AGAINST HERETICS

"What is there in common between Athens and Jerusalem?"

Justin had called Heraclitus (late fifth century B.C.) "a Christian before Christ" and this liberal attitude toward pagan philosophers soon became dominant in Eastern Christianity. In the Latin West, however, this point of view did not find great favor until the appearance of St. Augustine in the late fourth century A.D. The outstanding opponent of classical philosophy among the Latin Apologists was Tertullian, who died at Carthage about A.D. 222. He was trained in Roman law, and his view of Christianity was a legalistic one. To him Christianity was essentially a legal and moral code established by God and revealed through Christ. Sin and salvation were based on adherence to the Divine Law as judged by Christ. To Tertullian, the subtleties of Greek philosophy were not only unnecessary but also absurd and dangerous. He preached a "simple

From Tertullian, *Against Heretics*, ch. 7; based on the translation by Peter Holmes.

faith," for "to know nothing against the rule of faith is to know everything." The truest Christian was "the simple and uncultivated soul, whose whole experience has been gleaned on street-corners and cross-roads and in the factory." Such a man, Tertullian boasted, could answer all the questions that had puzzled the minds of the greatest philosophers.

These are "the doctrines" of men and "of demons" produced for itching ears of the spirit of this world's wisdom: this the Lord called "foolishness" and "chose the foolish things of the world" to confound even philosophy itself. For philosophy it is which is the material of the world's wisdom, the rash interpreter of the nature and the dispensation of God. Indeed heresies are themselves instigated by philosophy. From this source came the "Aeons," and I know not what "infinite forms" and the "trinity of man" in the [gnostic] system of Valentinus [an early second century thinker considered heretical by many Christians], who was of Plato's school. From the same source came Marcion's better god, with all his tranquillity; he came of the Stoics. Then, again, the opinion that the soul dies is held by the Epicureans; while the denial of the restoration of the body is taken from the aggregate school of all the philosophers; also, when matter is made equal to God, then you have the teaching of Zeno; and when any doctrine is alleged touching a god of fire, then Heraclitus comes in. The same subject matter is discussed over and over again by the heretics and the philosophers; the same arguments are involved. Whence comes evil? Why is it permitted? What is the origin of man? And in what way does he come? Besides the question which Valentinus has very lately proposed—Whence comes God? Which he settles with the answer: From *enthymesis* and *ectroma*. Unhappy Aristotle! who invented for these men dialectics, the art of building up and pulling down; an art so evasive in its propositions, so far-fetched in its conjectures, so harsh in its arguments, so productive of contentions—embarrassing even to itself, retracting everything, and really treating of nothing!...

What is there in common between Athens and Jerusalem? What concord is there between the Academy and the Church? What between heretics and Christians? ... Away with all attempts to produce a mottled Christianity of Stoic, Platonic, and dialectic composition! We want no curious disputation after possessing Christ Jesus, no inquisition after enjoying the gospel! With our faith, we desire no further belief.

77 Christians and Their Persecutors

"Amid the ruins of a falling age, our spirit remains erect."
Bishop Cyprian of Carthage, third century

Both for its subjects and for later ages the most attractive features of the Roman Empire and the *Pax Romana* were three: a law that stood above the private interests of individuals, a citizenship open to men of all races, and religious toleration. This last assertion appears contradicted by Roman persecution of the Christians; yet hindsight supports the conclusion that the clash could have been avoided, that it was the product of mutual misunderstandings that led to fear, hysteria, intransigence, and the use of force. As the Roman state saw it, the Christians failed to satisfy the terms on which toleration could be granted because they appeared to be subversive of the moral, political, and social order and refused to tolerate other religions. According to Tacitus (*Annals* XV, 44), as early as A.D. 64, when Nero persecuted the Christians in Rome, a general fear and hatred of Christians existed:

> Nero falsely shifted the guilt [for the great fire at Rome] on those people commonly called "Christians" who were hated for their abominations, and inflicted on them the most exquisite tortures. Christus, from whom the name had its origin, suffered the extreme penalty during the reign of Tiberius at the hands of one of our procurators, Pontius Pilate, and a most mischievous superstition, thus checked for the moment, again broke out not only in Judea, the first source of the evil, but even in Rome, where all things hideous and shameful from every part of the world find their center and become popular. Accordingly, an arrest was made of all who pleaded guilty; then, upon their information, an immense multitude was convicted, not so much of the crime of firing the city, as of being haters of the human race.

Such hostility embittered the Christians and turned them away from the position announced by Jesus ("Render unto Caesar the things which are Caesar's") and Paul ("The powers that be are ordained by God"). But by keeping themselves aloof from pagan society the Christians contributed to the suspicion of subversion and treason.

A. PLINY, LETTERS ON CHRISTIANS:
TRAJAN'S ENLIGHTENED POLICY

There is no evidence of an official state pronouncement regarding Christianity before the early second century A.D. Persecutions were sporadic and local, being the product of popular hostility and action. They were handled by provincial governors (with the exception of Nero's persecution at Rome), who based their action on the laws against secret societies and the refusal of the Christians to demonstrate their loyalty to the state by the purely political gesture of sacrificing to the emperor. This is referred to in the famous letter written about A.D. 112 by Pliny the Younger, governor of Bithynia in Asia Minor, to the emperor Trajan. Pliny asked for more definite instructions with regard to the Christians, and Trajan's reply established an official policy based upon precedents set by earlier governors. This policy, which placed the label of traitor upon convicted Christians but also protected them against both sporadic

From Pliny, *Letter* X, 96, 97; adapted from *Translations and Reprints from the Original Sources of European History*, vol. IV, no. 1, edited by Dana C. Munro and Edith Bramhall (Philadelphia: University of Pennsylvania Department of History, 1898).

and systematic persecution, continued until the empire began to disintegrate in the last half of the third century. Measures to wipe out Christianity as a danger to the unity and security of a troubled state culminated in the Great Persecution (A.D. 303–311) under Diocletian. When this failed, Constantine's proclamation of toleration in 313 became the established policy.

Pliny to Trajan

It is my custom, my lord, to refer to you all things concerning which I am in doubt. For who can better guide my indecision or enlighten my ignorance?

I have never taken part in the trials of Christians; hence I do not know for what crime or to what extent it is customary to punish or investigate. I have been in no little doubt as to whether any consideration should be given to age, or should the treatment of the young differ from that of the old; whether pardon is granted in case of repentance, or should a man who was once a Christian gain nothing by having ceased to be one; whether the name itself without the proof of crimes, or only the crimes associated with the name, are to be punished.

Meanwhile I have followed this procedure in the case of those who have been brought before me as Christians. I asked them whether they were Christians; those who confessed I questioned a second and a third time, threatening them with punishment; those who persisted I ordered executed. For I did not doubt that, whatever it was that they had confessed, their stubbornness and inflexible obstinacy ought to be punished. There were others of similar madness; but because they were Roman citizens, I signed an order sending them to Rome.

Soon, the crime spreading, as is usual when attention is called to it, more cases arose. An anonymous accusation, containing many names, was presented. Those who denied that they were or had been Christians, ought, I thought, to be dismissed since they repeated after me a prayer to the gods and made supplication with incense and wine to your image, which I had ordered to be brought for the purpose together with the statues of the gods, and since besides they cursed Christ, not one of which things they say those who are really Christians can be compelled to do. Others, accused by the informer, said that they were Christians and afterwards denied it; in fact, they had been but had ceased to be, some many years ago, some even twenty years before. They all worshipped your image and the statues of the gods, and cursed Christ. They maintained that the substance of their fault or error had been that on a fixed day they were accustomed to come together before daylight and sing by turns a hymn to Christ as though he were a god, and to bind themselves by oath, not for some crime, but not to commit robbery, theft, or adultery, nor to betray a trust or deny a deposit when called upon. After this it was customary to disperse and to come together again to partake of food of an ordinary and harmless kind. Even this they ceased to do after the publication of my edict in which, according to your orders, I had forbidden associations. Hence I believed it the more necessary to examine two female slaves, who were called deaconesses, in order to find out what was true, and to do it by torture. I found nothing but a vicious, extravagant superstition.

Consequently I postponed the examination and hastened to consult you. For it seemed to me that the subject would justify consultation, especially on account of the number of those involved. For many of all ages, of every rank, and even of both sexes are and will be endangered. The infection of this superstition has not only spread to the cities but also to the villages and country districts. But it seems possible to check it and cure it. It is plain enough that the temples, which had been almost deserted, have begun to be frequented again, that the sacred rites, which had been neglected for a long time, have begun to be restored, and that food for sacrifices, for which until now there was scarcely a purchaser, is sold. From this it is easy to imagine what a multitude of people can be reclaimed if repentance is permitted.

Trajan to Pliny

You have followed the correct procedure, my dear Pliny, in conducting the cases of those who were accused before you as Christians, for no general rule can be laid down as a set form. They are not to be sought out; if they are brought before you and convicted, they ought to be punished, with the proviso that whoever denies that he is a Christian and proves it by worshipping our gods, even though he may have been under suspicion in the past, shall obtain pardon on repentance. In no case should attention be paid to anonymous charges, for they afford a bad precedent and are not worthy of our age.

B. THE *MARTYRDOM OF POLYCARP OF SMYRNA*: EARLY PERSECUTIONS AGAINST CHRISTIANS

"I am a Christian."

Polycarp, the bishop of the Greek-speaking city of Smyrna (modern Izmir, Turkey), was a prominent Christian leader in Roman Asia Minor. Eighty-six years old at the time of his death, Polycarp had a long career before he was arrested and put on trial by the Roman authorities in the middle of the second century A.D. We do not know all the circumstances for this particular, probably quite local, persecution of Christians. Some Jewish inhabitants of Smyrna are said to have stirred up enmity against the Christians, with the result that Polycarp and a few other Christians were brought before the local Roman magistrate on charges. Refusing to renounce the Christian name, he and others were sentenced to die in the amphitheater of Smyrna by burning, a form of Roman execution for lowly criminals.

    The following account of Polycarp's death, purportedly written by a Christian named Marcion, is one of the earliest surviving accounts of Christian martyrdom, which means testimony for Christ. It comes in the form of a letter that the Christian community of Smyrna sent to the neighboring city of Philomelium. The ideology of martyrdom inspired a form of heroic Christianity that became, for Christians, a source of immense inspiration. For many pagans, such behavior was irrational and foolhardy, proof that Christianity served to mislead the unwary.

The church of God dwelling in Smyrna to the church of God of Philomelium and to all the communities of the holy Catholic Church everywhere: *may the mercy, peace, and love* of God the Father and Jesus Christ our Lord *be multiplied*.

1. We are writing to you, dear brothers, the story of the martyrs and of blessed Polycarp who put a stop to the persecution by his own martyrdom as though he were putting a seal upon it. For practically everything that had gone before took place that the Lord might show us from heaven a witness in accordance with the Gospel. Just as the Lord did, he too waited that he might be delivered up, that we might become his imitators, *not thinking of ourselves alone, but of our neighbours as well*. For it is a mark of true and solid love to desire not only one's own salvation but also that of all the brothers.

2. Blessed indeed and noble are all the martyrdoms that took place in accordance with God's will. For we must devoutly assign to God a providence over them all. Who indeed would not admire the martyrs' nobility, their courage, their love of the Master? For even when they were torn by whips until the very structure of their bodies was laid bare down to the inner veins and arteries, they endured it, making even the bystanders weep for pity. Some indeed attained to such courage that they would utter not a sound or a cry, showing to all of us that in the hour of their torment these noblest of Christ's witnesses were not present in the flesh, or rather that the Lord was there present holding converse with them. Fixing their eyes on the favour of Christ, they despised the tortures of this world, in one hour buying themselves an exemption from the eternal fire. The fire applied by their inhuman torturers was cooled: for they kept before their eyes the knowledge that they were escaping that eternal fire never to be extinguished; and with the eyes of the soul they looked up to those good things that are saved up for those who have persevered, which *neither the ear has heard nor the eye seen, nor has it entered into the heart of man*: but to them the Lord revealed it seeing they were no longer men but angels.

Similarly did those who were condemned to the beasts endure terrifying torments, being laid out upon trumpet-shells, and bruised by other different kinds of tortures. The purpose was that, if possible, the tyrant might persuade them to deny the faith by constant torment. 3. For many were the stratagems the Devil used against them. But thanks be to God, he did not prevail over all of them. The most noble Germanicus gave them encouragement by the perseverance he showed; he even fought manfully with the beasts. The governor tried to persuade him, telling him to spare his young manhood; but he with a show of force dragged the beast on top of him, intending to be freed all the more quickly from this unjust and lawless life. At this then all the mob was astonished at the courage of this pious and devoted race of Christians, and they shouted out: 'Away with these atheists! Go and get Polycarp!'

4. There was a Phrygian named Quintus who had only recently come from Phrygia, and when he saw the wild animals he turned cowardly. Now he was the one who had given himself up and had forced some others to give

themselves up voluntarily. With him the governor used many arguments and persuaded him to swear by the gods and offer sacrifice. This is the reason, brothers, that we do not approve of those who come forward of themselves: this is not the teaching of the Gospel.

5. Now at first when the most admirable Polycarp heard of this, he was not disturbed and even decided to stay in Smyrna; but most people advised him to slip out quietly. And so he left secretly for a small estate on the outskirts, staying there with a few friends. Day and night he did little else but pray for everyone and for all the churches scattered throughout the world, as he was indeed accustomed to do.

Three days before he was captured he fell into a trance while at prayer: he saw his pillow being consumed by fire. He turned and said to his companions: 'I am to be burnt alive.'

6. The pursuivants persisted on his trail, and so he moved to a different estate. Shortly thereafter they arrived. Not finding Polycarp they seized two slaves, and one of them told everything under torture....

7. With the slave then, the police and cavalry set out on Friday at the dinner hour with the usual arms *as though against a brigand*. It was late in the evening when they closed in: they found him reclining in a small room upstairs. He could have left and gone elsewhere but he refused, saying: *'May the will of God be done.'* And so, hearing that they had arrived he went downstairs to talk with them, while all those present were surprised at his composure and his old age, and why there should have been such concern to capture so elderly a man.

At any rate Polycarp immediately ordered food and drink to be set before them, as much as they wished, even at this hour, and only requested that they might grant him an hour to pray undisturbed. When they consented, he stood up and began to pray facing the east, and so full was he of God's grace that he was unable to stop for two hours, to the amazement of those who heard him, and many were sorry that they had come out to arrest such a godlike old man.

8. Finally he finished his prayer, after calling to mind all those who had ever come into contact with him, both important and insignificant, famous and obscure, and the entire Catholic Church scattered throughout the world. It was now time to go, and so they put him on a donkey and thus conducted him into the city....

The police captain Herod with his father Nicetes came up to meet Polycarp; they shifted him into their own carriage, and after sitting down beside him they tried to persuade him, saying: 'Now what harm is there for you to say "Caesar is lord," to perform the sacrifices and so forth, and thus save your life?'

At first Polycarp would not answer them; but when they persisted, he said: 'I do not intend to do what you advise.'

They then gave up their attempt to move him and spoke threateningly to him, and took him down from the carriage so hastily that he scraped his shin. But taking no notice, as though nothing had happened, he walked on eagerly and quickly; and as he was brought into the amphitheatre there was such an uproar there that no one could even be heard.

9. As Polycarp entered the amphitheatre, a voice from heaven said: *'Be strong, Polycarp, and have courage.'* No one saw who was speaking, but those of our people who were present heard the voice.

Then, as he was brought in, a great shout arose when the people heard that it was Polycarp who had been arrested. As he was brought before him, the governor asked him: 'Are you Polycarp?' And when he admitted he was, the governor tried to persuade him to recant, saying: 'Have respect for your age (and another similar things that they are accustomed to say); 'swear by the Genius of the emperor. Recant. Say, "Away with the atheists!"'

Polycarp, with a sober countenance, looked at all the mob of lawless pagans who were in the arena, and shaking his fist at them, groaned, looked up to heaven, and said: 'Away with the atheists!'

The governor persisted and said: 'Swear and I will let you go. Curse Christ!'

But Polycarp answered: 'For eighty-six years I have been his servant and he has done me no wrong. How can I blaspheme against my king and saviour?'

10. But the other insisted once again, saying: 'Swear by the emperor's Genius!'

He answered: 'If you delude yourself into thinking that I will swear by the emperor's Genius, as you say, and if you pretend not to know who I am, listen and I will tell you plainly: I am a Christian. And if you would like to learn the doctrine of Christianity, set aside a day and listen.'

The governor said: 'Try to move the people.'

And Polycarp said: 'I should have thought you worthy of such a discussion. For we have been taught to pay respect to the authorities and powers that God has assigned us (for this does not harm our cause). But as for the mob, I do not think they deserve to listen to a speech of defence from me.'

11. The governor said: 'I have wild animals, and I shall expose you to them if you do not change your mind.'

And he answered: 'Go and call for them! Repentance from a better state to one that is worse is impossible for us. But it is good to change from what is wicked to righteousness.'

And he said again to him: 'Since you are not afraid of the animals, then I shall have you consumed by fire—unless you change your mind.'

But Polycarp answered: 'The fire you threaten me with burns merely for a time and is soon extinguished. It is clear you are ignorant of the fire of everlasting punishment and of the judgement that is to come, which awaits the impious. Why then do you hesitate? Come, do what you will.'

12. As he said these and many other words he was filled with a joyful courage; his countenance was filled with grace, and not only did he not collapse in terror at what was said to him, but rather it was the governor that was amazed. He sent his herald into the centre of the arena to announce three times: 'Polycarp has confessed that he is a Christian.'

After the herald had spoken, the entire mob of pagans and Jews from Smyrna shouted out aloud in uncontrollable rage: 'Here is the schoolmaster of Asia—the father of the Christians—the destroyer of our gods—the one that teaches the multitude not to sacrifice or do reverence!'

And while they were saying all this they shouted and asked Philip the Asiarch to have a lion loosed on Polycarp. But he said that he was not allowed to do this since the days of the animal games were past. Next they decided to shout out all together that Polycarp should be burnt alive. For the vision he had seen regarding his pillow had to be fulfilled, when he saw it burning while he was at prayer and turned and said to his faithful companions. 'I am to be burnt alive.'

13. All of this happened with great speed, more quickly than it takes to tell the story: the mob swiftly collected logs and brushwood from workshops and baths, and the Jews (as is their custom) zealously helped them with this. When the fire was prepared, Polycarp took off all his clothing, loosed his belt and even tried to take off his own sandals, although he had never had to do this before: for all the Christians were always eager to be the first to touch his flesh. Even before his martyrdom he had been adorned in every way by reason of the goodness of his life. Straightway then he was attached to the equipment that had been prepared for the fire. When they were on the point of nailing him to it, he said: 'Leave me thus. For he who has given me the strength to endure the flames will grant me to remain without flinching in the fire even without the firmness you will give me by using nails.'

14. They did not nail him down then, but simply bound him; and as he put his hands behind his back, he was bound like a noble ram chosen for an oblation from a great flock, a holocaust prepared and made acceptable to God. Looking up to heaven, he said: 'O Lord, *omnipotent God* and Father of your beloved and blessed child Christ Jesus, through whom we have received our knowledge of you, the God of the angels, the powers, and of all creation, and of all the family of the good who live in your sight: I bless you because you have thought me worthy of this day and this hour, to have a share among the number of the martyrs in the cup of your Christ, *for the resurrection unto* eternal *life* of both the soul and the body in the immortality of the Holy Spirit. May I be received this day among them before your face as a rich and acceptable sacrifice, as you, the God of truth who cannot deceive, have prepared, revealed, and fulfilled beforehand. Hence I praise you, I bless you, and I glorify you above all things, through that eternal and celestial high priest, Jesus Christ, your beloved child, through whom is glory to you with him and the Holy Spirit now and for all ages to come. Amen.'

15. He had uttered his Amen and finished his prayer, and the men in charge of the fire started to light it. A great flame blazed up and those of us to whom it was given to see beheld a miracle. And we have been preserved to recount the story to others. For the flames, bellying out like a ship's sail in the wind, formed into the shape of a vault and thus surrounded the martyr's body as with a wall. And he was within it not as burning flesh but rather as bread being baked, or like gold and silver being purified in a smelting-furnace. And from it we perceived such a delightful fragrance as though it were smoking incense or some other costly perfume.

16. At last when these vicious men realized that his body could not be consumed by the fire they ordered a *confector* to go up and plunge a dagger into the

body. When he did this there came out such a quantity of blood that the flames were extinguished, and even the crowd marvelled that there should be such a difference between the unbelievers and the elect. And one of the elect indeed was the most venerable martyr Polycarp, who was in our day a teacher in the apostolic and prophetic tradition and a bishop of the Catholic Church in Smyrna. Every word that he uttered from his mouth was indeed fulfilled and shall be fulfilled....

19. This then was the story of the blessed Polycarp, who, counting those from Philadelphia, was the twelfth to be martyred in Smyrna; yet he alone is especially remembered by everyone and is everywhere mentioned even by the pagans. He was not only a great teacher but also a conspicuous martyr, whose testimony, following the Gospel of Christ, everyone desires to imitate. By his perseverance he overcame the unjust governor and so won the crown of immortality; and rejoicing with the apostles and all the blessed he gives glory to God the almighty Father and praise to our Lord Jesus Christ, the saviour of our souls, the pilot of out bodies, and the shepherd of the Catholic Church throughout the world....

C. TERTULLIAN, *APOLOGY*: A CHRISTIAN VIEW OF THE PERSECUTIONS

Tertullian, Latin Christianity's first great writer and its outstanding opponent of pagan classical thought, wrote an *Apology* (A.D. 197) for Christianity that is an eloquent defense against attacks by both the hostile provincial governments and the ill-informed populace. Mixing passion with irony, he attacks the illegality of judicial procedures in which Christians are involved, castigates the unreasoning hatred shown them, and refutes the numerous charges, from treason to drunkenness, leveled at them. Indeed, "the *Apology* is one of those works which survive the circumstances which gave them birth and which enter into the common treasury of civilized nations. Nowhere shall we listen to more fervid demands for justice, tolerance, or the rights of an accused man; to more vivid protestations against the tyranny of unjust laws assumed to be irrevocable; lastly, to a more eloquent defense of Christianity [and] of its moral nobility...."[2]

"Let the Truth Reach Your Ears"

1. Magistrates of the Roman Empire, seated as you are before the eyes of all, in almost the highest position in the state to pronounce judgment: if you are not to conduct an open and public examination and inquiry as to what the real truth is with regard to the Christians; if, in this case alone your authority fears or

---

2. P. De Labriolle, *History and Literature of Christianity* (New York: Alfred A. Knopf, 1924), p. 70.

From Emily Joseph Daly, *Tertullian: Apologetical Works, and Minucius Felix Octavius, The Fathers of the Church, Vol. X* (New York: The Catholic University of America Press, 1950). Reprinted by permission of The Catholic University of America Press.

blushes to conduct a public investigation with the diligence demanded by justice; if, in fine—as happened lately in the private courts—hatred of this group has been aroused to the extent that it actually blocks their defense, then let the truth reach your ears by the private and quiet avenue of literature.

Truth makes no appeal on her own behalf, because she does not wonder at her present condition. She knows that she plays the role of an alien on earth, that among strangers she readily discovers enemies, but she has her origin, abode, hope, recompense, and honor in heaven. Meanwhile, there is one thing for which she strives: that she be not condemned without a hearing....

This, then, is the first grievance we lodge against you, the injustice of the hatred you have for the name of Christian. The motive which appears to excuse this injustice is precisely that which both aggravates and convicts it; namely, ignorance. For, what is more unjust than that men should hate what they do not know, even though the matter itself deserves hatred? Only when one knows whether a thing deserves hatred does it deserve it. ... We counterbalance each attitude by its opposite: men remain in ignorance as long as they hate, and they hate unjustly as long as they remain in ignorance.

The proof of their ignorance, which condemns while it excuses their injustice, is this: In the case of all who formerly indulged in hatred (of Christianity) because of their ignorance of the nature of what they hated, their hatred comes to an end as soon as their ignorance ceases. ... Christians are really as numerous as you allege us to be. Men cry that the city is filled with Christians; they are in the country, in the villages, on the islands; men and women, of every age, of every state and rank of life, are transferring to this group, and this they lament as if it were some personal injury....

2. If, then, it is decided that we are the most wicked of men, why do you treat us so differently from those who are on a par with us, that is, from all other criminals? The same treatment ought to be meted out for the same crime. When others are charged with the same crimes as well, they use their own lips and the hired eloquence of others to prove their innocence. There is full liberty given to answer the charge and to cross-question, since it is unlawful for men to be condemned without defense or without a hearing. Christians alone are permitted to say nothing that would clear their name, vindicate the truth, and aid the judge to come to a fair decision. One thing only is what they wait for; this is the only thing necessary to arouse public hatred: the confession of the name of Christian, not an investigation of the charge. Yet, suppose you are trying any other criminal. If he confesses to the crime of murder, sacrilege, incest, or treason—to particularize the indictments hurled against us—you are not satisfied to pass sentence immediately; you weigh the attendant circumstances, the character of the deed, the number of times it was committed, the time, the place, the witnesses, and the partners-in-crime. In our case there is nothing of this sort. No matter what false charge is made against us, we must be made to confess it; for example, how many murdered babies one has devoured, how many deeds of incest one has committed under cover of darkness, what cooks and what dogs were on hand. Oh, what glory for that governor who should have discovered someone who had already consumed a hundred infants!

Trajan's Letter: "How ... Ambiguous Was That Decision!"

On the other hand, we find that it has been forbidden to search us out. For when Pliny the Younger was in charge of his province and had condemned certain Christians and had driven others from their established position, he was so disturbed because of the numbers involved that he consulted Trajan, emperor at the time, as to what he should do thereafter. He explained that, except for their obstinate refusal to offer sacrifice, he had learned nothing else about their religious rites except that they met before daybreak to sing to Christ and to God and to bind themselves by oath to a way of life which forbade murder, adultery, dishonesty, treachery, and all other crimes. Trajan wrote back that men of this kind should not be sought out, but, when brought to court, they should be punished.

Oh, how unavoidably ambiguous was that decision! He says that they should not be sought—as though they were innocent; then prescribes that they should be punished—as though they were guilty! He spares them, yet vents his anger upon them; he pretends to close his eyes, yet directs attention toward them! Judgment, why do you thus ensnare yourself? If you condemn them, why not also search for them? If you do not search for them, why not also acquit them? Throughout the provinces troops of soldiers are assigned to track down robbers. Against traitors and public enemies each individual constitutes a soldier: the search is extended even to comrades and accomplices. Only the Christian may not be sought out— but he may be brought to court. As though a search were intended to bring about something else than his appearance in court! So, you condemn a man when he is brought into court, although no one wanted him to be sought out. He has earned punishment, I suppose, not on the ground that he is guilty, but because he was discovered for whom no search had to be made....

"Such Hatred of the Name"

3. What should one say of the fact that many shut their eyes and force themselves to such hatred of the name that, even when they speak favorably of someone, they insert some hateful remark about this name? "Caius Seius is a good man, except that he is a Christian." Similarly, someone else says: "I am surprised that Lucius Titius, otherwise a man of sense, has suddenly become a Christian!" No one stops to think whether Caius is good and Lucius sensible because he is a Christian, or is a Christian because he is sensible and good! Men praise what they know and find fault with what they do not know. They contaminate their knowledge with their ignorance, although it would be more correct to form a preconceived idea with regard to what is unknown from what is known than to condemn beforehand what is known because of what is unknown.

Others censure those whom they knew in the past, before they acquired this name, as vagrant, good-for-nothing scoundrels, and they censure them in the very act of praising them. In the blindness of their hatred they stumble into favorable criticism. "That woman! How dissolute and frivolous she was! And that young man, how much more prodigal and debauched he used to be! They have become Christians," Thus, the name which was responsible for their reformation is set down as a charge against them. Some, even, at the expense of their own advantage, bargain with their hatred, satisfied to suffer a personal loss, provided that their home be freed from the object of their hatred. A wife who has become chaste is cast out by her husband now that he is relieved of his jealous suspicions of her. A son, now docile, is disowned by a father who was patient with him in the past. A servant, now trustworthy, is banished from the sight of a master who was formerly indulgent. To the degree that one is reformed under the influence of the name he gives offense. The Christians' goodness is outweighed by the hatred borne them....

"Rumor Alone ... Is the Witness You Bring Forth Against Us"

4. Now that I have set down these remarks as a preface, as it were, to stigmatize the injustice of the public hatred against us, I shall take the stand to defend our innocence. ... [I] shall reply to each charge individually: to those which we are said to commit in secret, and to those which we are found to be committing before the eyes of all—charges on the basis of which we are held to be criminals, deceivers, reprobates, and objects of ridicule....

7. We are spoken of as utter reprobates and are accused of having sworn to murder babies and to eat them and of committing adulterous acts after the repast. Dogs, you say, are our pimps in the dark who overturn candles and procure license for our impious lusts. We are always spoken of in this way, yet you take no pains to bring into the light the charges which for so long a time have been made against us. Now, either bring them into the light, if you believe them, or stop believing them, inasmuch as you have not brought them to light!...

The origin of this religion ... dates from the time of Tiberius. Truth and hatred came into existence simultaneously. As soon as the former appeared, the latter began its enmity. It has as many foes as there are outsiders, particularly among Jews because of their jealousy, among soldiers because of their blackmailing, and even among the very members of our own household because of corrupt human nature. Day by day we are besieged; day by day we are betrayed; oftentimes, in the very midst of our meetings and gatherings, we are surprised by an assault. Who has ever come upon a baby wailing, as the accusation has it? Who has ever kept for the judge's inspection the jaws of Cyclopes and Sirens, bloodstained as he had found them? Who has ever found any traces of impurity upon [Christian] wives? Who has discovered such crimes, yet concealed them or been bribed to keep them secret when dragging these men off to court? If we always keep under cover, whence the betrayal of our crimes?

Rather, who could have been the traitors? Certainly not the accused themselves, since the obligation of pledged silence is binding upon all mysteries by their very nature. The mysteries of Samothrace and of Eleusis are shrouded in silence; how much more such rites as these which, if they were made public, would provoke at once the hatred of all mankind—while God's wrath is reserved for the future? If, then, Christians themselves are not the betrayers, it follows that outsiders are. Whence do outsiders get their knowledge, since even holy initiation rites always ban the uninitiated and are wary of witnesses?...

Rumor, a word designating uncertainty, has no place where there is certainty. But does anyone except the unthinking believe rumor? One who is wise surely does not heed uncertainty. Everyone can reflect that however great the zeal with which the tale has been spread, however strong the assertion with which it was fabricated, it necessarily started at some time or other from one source. Thence it creeps gradually along the grapevine of tongues and ears, and a defect in the tiny seedlings so overshadows the other details of the rumor that no one reflects whether the first mouth sowed the seed of falsehood, as often happens, from a spirit of envy or a suspicious thought or from the pleasure some derive from lying—a pleasure not new-born, but inborn.

It is well that time brings all things to light, as even your own proverbs and sayings testify, in accordance with the design of nature which has so ordained things that nothing remains a secret for long, even though rumor has not spread it abroad. Rightly, then, is rumor alone for so long a time aware of the crimes of Christians; this is the witness you bring forth against us. What it has sometime or other spread abroad and over such an interval of time hardened into a matter of opinion, it has not yet been able to prove, so that I call upon the steadfastness of nature itself against those who assume that such accusations are credible....

"The Chief Accusation Against Us"

10. "You do not worship the gods," you say, "and you do not offer sacrifice for the emperors." It follows that we do not offer sacrifices for others for the same reason that we do not do it even for ourselves—it follows immediately from our not worshipping the gods. Consequently, we are considered guilty of sacrilege and treason. This is the chief accusation against us—in fact, it is the whole case—and it certainly deserves investigation, unless presumption and injustice dictate the decision, the one despairing of the truth, the other refusing it.

We cease worshipping your gods when we find out that they are nonexistent. This, then, is what you ought to demand, that we prove that those gods are nonexistent and for that reason should not be worshipped, because they ought to be worshipped only if they were actually gods. Then, too, the Christians ought to be punished if the fact were established that those gods do exist whom they will not worship because they consider them nonexistent. "But, for us," you say, "the gods do exist." We object and appeal from you to your conscience. Let this pass judgment on us, let this condemn us, if it can deny that all those gods of yours have been mere men. But, if it should deny this, it will be refuted by its own documents of ancient times from which it has learned of the gods. Testimony is furnished to this very day by the cities in which they were born, and the regions in which they left traces of something they had done and in which it is pointed out that they were buried....

"We Pray for the Welfare of the Emperors"

28. ... We have come, then, to the second charge alleged against us, that of offending a more august majesty. You pay your obeisance to Caesar with greater fear and craftier timidity than to Olympian Jupiter himself. And rightly so, if you

but knew it! For, what living man—whoever he may be—is not more powerful than any of your dead ones? But you do this, not for any logical reason, but out of regard for his manifest and perceptible power. In this point, too, it will be seen that you are lacking in religious feeling towards your gods, since you show more fear to a human lord. Finally, one is more ready among you to take a false oath by all the gods together than by the lone genius of Caesar....

30. ... We pray for the welfare of the emperors to the eternal God, the true God, the living God, whom even the emperors themselves prefer to have propitious to them before all other gods. They know who has given them power; they know—for they are men—who has given them life; they feel that He is the only God in whose power alone they are, commencing with whom they are second, after whom they stand first, who is before all and above all gods. ... Looking up to Him, we Christians—with hands extended, because they are harmless, with head bare because we are not ashamed, without a prayer leader because we pray from the heart—constantly beseech Him on behalf of an emperors. We ask for them long life, undisturbed power, security at home, brave armies, a faithful Senate, an upright people, a peaceful world, and everything for which a man or a Caesar prays....

31. Well, now, we have been flattering the emperor and have lied about the prayers we said just to escape rough treatment! That ingenious idea of yours is certainly of advantage to us, for you permit us to prove whatever we allege in our defense. If you think that we have no interest in the emperor's welfare, look into our literature, the Word of God. We ourselves do not keep it concealed; in fact, many a chance hands it over to outsiders. Learn from this literature that it has been enjoined upon us, that our charity may more and more abound, to pray to God even for our enemies, and to beg for blessings for our persecutors. Now, who are any greater enemies and persecutors of Christians than those on whose account we are charged with the crime of treason? But it is clearly and expressly said: "Pray for kings, for princes and for rulers, that all may be peaceful for you!" For, when the Empire is shaken, and its other members are shaken, we, too, although we are considered outsiders by the crowd, are naturally involved in some part of the disaster.

32. There is also another, even greater, obligation for us to pray for the emperors; yes, even for the continuance of the Empire in general and for Roman interests. We realize that the tremendous force which is hanging over the whole world, and the very end of the world with its threat of dreadful afflictions, is arrested for a time by the continued existence of the Roman Empire. This event we have no desire to experience, and, in praying that it may be deferred, we favor the continuance of Rome....

Politics and Public Shows

38. Accordingly, ought not this religion to be regarded with somewhat milder judgment among those societies which cannot legally exist? Its members commit no such crimes as are regularly feared from illegal associations. For, unless I am mistaken, the motive for prohibiting associations rests on the prudent care of public order, lest the state be split into parties, a situation which would easily disturb voting assemblies, council meetings, the Senate, mass meetings, and

even public entertainments by the clash of rival interests, since by now men have even begun to make a business of their violence, offering it for sale at a price. But, for us who are indifferent to all burning desire for fame and honor, there is not need of banding together. There is nothing more unfamiliar to us than politics. There is only one state for all which we acknowledge—the universe.

Likewise, we renounce your public shows just as we do their origins which we know were begotten of superstition, while we are completely aloof from those matters with which they are concerned. Our tongues, our eyes, our ears have nothing to do with the madness of the circus, the shamelessness of the theater, the brutality of the arena, the vanity of the gymnasium. How, then, do we offend you? If we prefer different pleasures, if, in fine, we do not want to be amused, that is our loss—if loss there be—not yours....

"The Practices of the Christian Church"

39. Now I myself will explain the practices of the Christian Church, that is, after having refuted the charges that they are evil, I myself will also point out that they are good. We form one body because of our religious convictions, and because of the divine origin of our way of life and the bond of common hope. We come together for a meeting and a congregation, in order to besiege God with prayers, like an army in battle formation. Such violence is pleasing to God. We pray, also, for the emperors, for their ministers and those in power, that their reign may continue, that the state may be in peace, and that the end of the world may be postponed. We assemble for the consideration of the Holy Scriptures, [to see] if the circumstances of the present times demand that we look ahead or reflect. Certainly, we nourish our faith with holy conversation, we uplift our hope, we strengthen our trust, intensifying our discipline at the same time by the inculcation of moral precepts. At the same occasion, there are words of encouragement, of correction, and holy censure. Then, too, judgment is passed which is very impressive, as it is before men who are certain of the presence of God, and it is a deeply affecting foretaste of the future judgment, if anyone has so sinned that he is dismissed from sharing a common prayer, assembly, and all holy intercourse. Certain approved elders preside, men who have obtained this honor not by money, but by the evidence of good character. For, nothing that pertains to God is to be had for money.

Even if there is some kind of treasury, it is not accumulated from a high initiation fee as if the religion were something bought and paid for. Each man deposits a small amount on a certain day of the month or whenever he wishes, and only on condition that he is willing and able to do so. No one is forced; each makes his contribution voluntarily. These are, so to speak, the deposits of piety. The money therefrom is spent not for banquets or drinking parties or good-for-nothing eating houses, but for the support and burial of the poor, for children who are without their parents and means of subsistence, for aged men who are confined to the house; likewise, for shipwrecked sailors, and for any in the mines, on islands or in prisons. Provided only it be for the sake of fellowship with God, they become entitled to loving and protective care for their confession. The practice of such a special love brands us in the eyes of some. "See," they say, "how they love one another" (for they hate one another), "and how ready they are to die for each other." (They themselves would be more ready to kill each other.)

Over the fact that we call ourselves brothers, they fall into a rage—for no other reason, I suppose, than because among them every term of kinship is only a hypocritical pretense of affection. But, we are your brothers, too, according to the law of nature, our common mother, although you are hardly men since you are evil brothers. But, with how much more right are they called brothers and considered such who have acknowledged one father, God, who have drunk one spirit of holiness, who in fear and wonder have come forth from the one womb of their common ignorance to the one light of truth! Perhaps this is why we are considered less legitimate brothers, because no tragic drama has our brotherhood as its theme, or because we are brothers who use the same family substance which, among you, as a rule, destroys brotherhood.

So, we who are united in mind and soul have no hesitation about sharing what we have. Everything is in common among us—except our wives....

Why wonder, then, if such dear friends take their meals together? You attack our modest repasts—apart from saying that they are disgraced by crimes—as being extravagant....

Our repast, by its very name, indicates its purpose. It is called by a name which to the Greeks means "love." Whatever it costs, it is gain to incur expense in the name of piety, since by this refreshment we comfort the needy, not as, among you, parasites contend for the glory of reducing their liberty to slavery for the price of filling their belly. ... No one sits down to table without first partaking of a prayer to God. They eat as much as those who are hungry take; they drink as much as temperate people need. They satisfy themselves as men who remember that they must worship God even throughout the night; they converse as men who know that the Lord is listening. After this, the hands are washed and lamps are lit, and each one, according to his ability to do so, reads the Holy Scriptures or is invited into the center to sing a hymn to God. This is the test of how much he has drunk. Similarly, prayer puts an end to the meal. From here they depart, not to unite in bands for murder, or to run around in gangs, or for stealthy attacks of lewdness, but to observe the same regard for modesty and chastity as people do who have partaken not only of a repast but of a rule of life.

Such is the gathering of Christians. There is no question about it—it deserves to be called illegal, provided it is like those which are illegal; it deserves to be condemned, if any complaint is lodged against it on the same ground that complaints are made about other secret societies. But, for whose destruction have we held a meeting? We are the same when assembled as when separate; we are collectively the same as we are individually, doing no one any injury, causing no one any harm. When men who are upright and good assemble, when the pious and virtuous gather together, the meeting should be called not a secret society but a senate.

40. On the other hand, those men deserve the name of a secret society who band together in hatred of good and virtuous men, who cry out for the blood of the innocent, at the same time offering as a justification of their hatred the idle plea that they consider that the Christians are the cause of every public calamity and every misfortune of the people. If the Tiber rises as high as the city walls, if the Nile does not rise to the fields, if the weather will not change, if there is an

earthquake, a famine, a plague—straightway the cry is heard: "Toss the Christians to the lion!" So many of them for just one beast?

A New Roman Empire

78 The Reforms of Diocletian

"… by whose virtue and foreseeing care all is being reshaped
for the better."

As we have seen (introduction to Selection 64), Augustus hoped that his settlement of Roman affairs would be permanent. It lasted for some two hundred years before collapsing in the third century and was perhaps as permanent as purely human institutions can ever hope to be. In A.D. 284 Diocletian was thus faced by the necessity of again reconstructing the Roman state. His reforms—the embodiment of tendencies already evident—were more extreme than those of Augustus, no doubt because the decline had been far greater, and he substituted a regime of authoritarian despotism for the constitutional monarchy of Augustus. This late Roman Empire was relatively as totalitarian as some modern dictatorships; the state imposed a pattern of regimentation on all aspects of life, including religion—hence Diocletian's ruthless persecution of Christianity. The verdict of Aurelius Victor (late fourth century A.D.) indicates, however, that although Diocletian's rule was strong, it was not altogether harsh: "Diocletian's faults were counterbalanced by good qualities; for even if he took the title of lord (*dominus*), he did act [toward the Romans] as a father." His system of bureaucratic controls, completed by Constantine, remained characteristic of the succeeding thousand-year history of the East Roman (or Byzantine) Empire and was undoubtedly a major factor in the latter's longevity.

A. ADMINISTRATIVE REORGANIZATION

"This man … overturned the Roman Empire."

The essence of Diocletian's cure for the chronic ills of the third-century Roman world can be simply put—more government. Because the problems of empire had proved too great for one man, the empire was divided into four parts,

---

From Lactantius, *On the Deaths of the Persecutors*, ch. 7, based on the translation by William Fletcher.

each under an emperor (the Tetrarchy). The provinces were reduced in size and more than doubled in number. The 120 provincial governors were supervised by twelve vicars, whose unit of administration was called a diocese. The vicars in turn were controlled by four prefects who served directly under the four emperors. Civil and military functions were separated, and a different hierarchy of officials exercised military authority within these numerous administrative units. Secret agents, called "agents for public affairs," kept watch over the efficiency of the entire administration. To support this enormous bureaucratic machine, citizens were burdened with new and higher taxes and strict economic controls.

Did Diocletian's reforms stabilize the empire or contribute further to its decline? The latter view was held by Diocletian's contemporary, the Christian polemicist Lactantius, whose account of the reforms is given below. It is taken from *On the Deaths of the Persecutors,* which Lactantius wrote so "that all who are afar off, and all who shall arise hereafter, may learn how the Almighty manifested His power and sovereign greatness in rooting out and utterly destroying the enemies of His name."

While Diocletian, that author of ill and deviser of misery was ruining all things, he could not withhold his insults even against God. This man, by avarice partly, and partly by timid counsels, overturned the Roman Empire: for he chose three persons to share the government with him; and thus, the Empire having been quartered, armies were multiplied, and each of the four rulers strove to maintain a much more considerable military force than any sole emperor had done in times past. There began to be fewer men who paid taxes than there were who received wages [from the state]; so that the means of farmers were being exhausted by enormous assessments, farms were abandoned, cultivated grounds became wilderness, and universal dismay prevailed. In addition, the provinces were divided into minute portions, and many governors and a multitude of inferior officers lay heavy on each territory, and almost on each city. There were also many procurators of different degrees, and deputies of prefects. Very few civil cases came before them: but there were condemnations daily, and forfeitures frequently inflicted; taxes on numberless commodities, and those not only often repeated, but perpetual, and, in exacting them, intolerable wrongs.

Whatever was laid on for the maintenance of the soldiery might have been endured; but Diocletian, through his insatiable avarice, would never allow the sums of money in his treasury to be diminished; he was constantly heaping together extraordinary taxes and free gifts so that his original hoards might remain untouched and inviolable. He also, when by various extortions he had made all things exceedingly dear, attempted by an ordinance to limit their prices [see part B of this selection, below]. Then much blood was shed for the veriest trifles; men were afraid to expose anything for sale, and the scarcity became more excessive and grievous than ever, until, in the end, the ordinance, after having proved destructive to multitudes, was from mere necessity abrogated. To this there were added a certain endless passion for building, and, on that account, endless exactions from the provinces for furnishing wages to laborers and artisans, and supplying carriages and whatever else was required for the works that he projected. Here public halls, there a circus, here a mint, and there a shop for making implements of war; in one place a palace for his empress, and in another for his daughter. Presently a great part of the city [Nicomedia, Diocletian's capital] was emptied, and all men removed with their wives and children, as from a town taken by enemies; and when those buildings were completed to the destruction of whole provinces, he said, "They are not right, let them be done on another plan." Then they were pulled down, or altered, to undergo perhaps a future demolition. By such folly was he continually endeavoring to equal Nicomedia with the city of Rome in magnificence.

I omit mentioning how many perished on account of their possessions or wealth; for such evils were exceedingly frequent, and through their frequency appeared almost lawful. But this was peculiar to him, that whenever he saw a field remarkably well cultivated, or a house of uncommon elegance, a false accusation and capital punishment were straightway prepared against the proprietor; so that it seemed as if Diocletian could not be guilty of rapine without also shedding blood.

B. EDICT OF MAXIMUM PRICES: FIGHTING INFLATION IN THE LATER ROMAN EMPIRE

The collapse of the Roman economy in the third century called for drastic action. In A.D. 301 Diocletian issued an edict of prices that sought to end runaway inflation and stabilize the economy by fixing a scale of maximum prices and salaries ranging from "peas, split" and "not split" to haircuts. In all, well over a thousand items were listed. Despite the death penalty for violators, the edict apparently proved unworkable and was rescinded, a fact sometimes cited by those today who are opposed to state-imposed price controls.

In the following preamble to his edict, Diocletian describes the evils he sought to remedy and the social philosophy that inspired his actions. It serves well to illustrate the paternalistic character of the late Roman Empire, and it helps us to understand why a contemporary North African inscription should honor Diocletian as one "by whose virtue and foreseeing care all is being reshaped for the better."

"Unrestrained Madness"

That the fortune of our state—to which, after the immortal gods, as we recall the wars which we have successfully fought, we must be grateful for a world that is tranquil and reclining in the embrace of the most profound calm, and for the blessings of a peace that was won with great effort—be faithfully disposed and suitably adorned, is the demand of public opinion and the dignity and majesty of Rome. Therefore, we, who by the gracious favor of the gods have repressed the former tide of ravages of barbarian nations by destroying them, must guard by the due defences of justice a peace which was established for eternity.

Reprinted by permission of the publishers from the translation by E. R. Graser in Tenney Frank ed., *An Economic Survey of Ancient Rome*, 6 vols. (Baltimore, Md.: 1940), V, pp. 311–17. Copyright 1940, The Johns Hopkins Press.

If, indeed, any self-restraint might check the excesses with which limitless and furious avarice rages—avarice which with no thought for mankind hastens to its own gain and increase, not by years or months or days but by hours and even minutes—or, if the general welfare could endure undisturbed the riotous license by which it, in its unfortunate state, is from day to day most grievously injured, there would perhaps be left some room for dissembling and silence, since human forbearance might alleviate the detestable cruelty of a pitiable situation. Since, however, it is the sole desire of unrestrained madness to have no thought for the common need; and since among the unscrupulous and immoderate it is considered almost the creed of avarice, swelling and rising with fiery passions, to desist from ravaging the wealth of all only when necessity compels them; and since those whom extremes of need have brought an appreciation of their most unfortunate situation can no longer close their eyes to it, we—the protectors of the human race—viewing the situation, have agreed that justice should intervene as arbiter, so that the long-hoped-for solution which mankind itself could not supply might, by the remedies of our foresight, be applied to the general betterment of all....

"The Remedies Long Demanded by the Situation"

We, therefore, hasten to apply the remedies long demanded by the situation, satisfied that there can be no complaints that the intervention of our remedy may be untimely or unnecessary, or thought to be trivial or unimportant by the unscrupulous who, in spite of perceiving in our silence of so many years a lesson in restraint, have been unwilling to copy it. For who is so insensitive and so devoid of human feeling that he cannot know, or rather, has not perceived, that in the commerce carried on in the markets or involved in the daily life of cities, immoderate prices are so widespread that the uncurbed passion for gain is lessened neither by abundant supplies nor by fruitful years. ... Who does not know that wherever the public safety demands that our armies directed, not in villages or towns only, but on every road, the profiteers insolently and covertly attack the public welfare? They extort prices for merchandise, not fourfold or eightfold, but such that human speech is incapable of describing either the price or the act; indeed, sometimes in a single purchase a soldier is deprived of his bonus and salary. The contributions of the whole world to support the armies fall as abominable profits to thieves, and our soldiers seem with their own hands to offer the rewards of their military service and their bonuses to the profiteers. The result is that the pillagers of the state constantly seize more than they know how to hold.

Aroused justly and rightfully by all the facts detailed above, and with mankind itself now appearing to be praying for release, we have decreed that there be established, not the prices of articles for sales—for such an act would be unjust when many provinces occasionally rejoice in the good fortune of wished-for low prices and, so to speak, the privilege of prosperity—but a maximum, so that when the violence of high prices appears anywhere—may the gods avert such a calamity!—avarice ... might be checked by the fixed limits of our statute and by the boundaries of a regulatory law. It is our pleasure, therefore, that the prices listed in the subjoined schedule be observed in the whole of our empire in such fashion that every man may know that while permission to exceed them has been forbidden him, the blessing of low prices has in no case been restricted in those places where supplies are seen to abound....

Since it is agreed that even in the time of our ancestors it was customary in passing laws to restrain insolence by attaching a prescribed penalty—since it is indeed rare for a situation tending to the good of humanity to be embraced spontaneously, and since fear is always found the most influential guide and regulator in the performance of duty—it is our pleasure that anyone who shall have resisted the provisions of this statute shall for his daring be subject to a capital penalty. And let no one consider the penalty harsh since there is at hand a means of avoiding the danger by the observance of moderation. To the same penalty, moreover, is he subject who in the desire to buy shall have conspired against the statute with the greed of the seller. Nor is he exempt from the same penalty who, although possessing necessities of life and business, believes that subsequent to this regulation he must withdraw them from the market, since a penalty should be even more severe for him who introduces poverty than for him who operates against the law. We, therefore, urge the loyalty of all our people, so that a law instituted for the public good may be observed with willing obedience and due care; especially since in such a statute provision has been made, not for single cities and peoples and provinces, but for the whole world, to whose rain a few are known to have raged excessively, and whose avarice neither the fullness of time nor the riches for which they strive could lessen or satisfy.

C. DIOCLETIAN'S EDICT OF PERSECUTION
AGAINST CHRISTIANS

"There are profane persons here...."

In Roman eyes, political loyalty to the state and religious piety toward the gods were intricately connected. The worship of the gods guaranteed the safety and prosperity of the empire; the state therefore had a vested interested in seeing that the gods received their proper due. As a result of the "Crises of the Third Century," many Romans wondered whether the gods had been made angry by those who refused to worship them in the traditional manner. These atheists had to be made to conform for the good of all.

Emperor Diocletian's first act of religious persecution was directed against Manichaeans in the Roman Empire. Later, on February 23, 303, he issued the first persecution edict against Christians from the eastern imperial capital of Nicomedia (Asia Minor). This persecution was one of the most comprehensive campaigns against Christianity undertaken by the Roman emperors; most of the previous persecutions had been much more local in scope.

The persecution of Christians should be seen as part of Diocletian's larger reform program. He had sought to restore the traditional worship of the gods because he and others thought that the neglect of divine worship had been the cause of the Romans' recent sufferings. The restoration of divine worship involved not only the rebuilding of temples; it also required the emperor to move against those who refused to worship the gods and who sometimes even denied their existence. The Christians were deemed atheists whose non-participation in the religious cult of the gods made the gods angry and caused them to punish all Romans.

Christianity had gained momentum in the Roman world by converting polytheists. These converts no longer worshipped the gods of their ancestors. In response, Diocletian used coercion to put an end to or at least seriously retard the growth of Christianity. He targeted mainly the most prominent elements of the Christian religion: its physical churches, its priests, and its sacred books. Christian clergy were compelled to sacrifice to the gods, and those who refused faced the penalty of death. The following selection comes from Lactantius' *On the Death of the Persecutors* (see Selection 79) and represents a Christian appraisal of the circumstances surrounding Diocletian's persecution. In this account, the emperor is generally presented in a negative light, and his decision to persecute Christians is attributed to trivial reasons.

... 10. Diocletian, as being of a timorous disposition, was a searcher into futurity, and during his abode in the East he began to slay victims, that from their livers he might obtain a prognostic of events; and while he sacrificed, some attendants of his, who were Christians, stood by, and they put the *immortal sign* on their foreheads. At this the demons were chased away, and the holy rites interrupted. The soothsayers trembled, unable to investigate the wonted marks on the entrails of the victims. They frequently repeated the sacrifices, as if the former had been unpropitious; but the victims, slain from time to time, afforded no tokens for divination. At length Tages, the chief of the soothsayers either from guess or from his own observation, said, "There are profane persons here, who obstruct the rites." Then Diocletian in furious passion, ordered not only all who were assisting at the holy ceremonies, but also all who resided within the palace, to sacrifice, and, in case of their refusal, to be scourged. And further, by letters to the commanding officer, he enjoined that all soldiers should be forced to the like impiety, under pain of being dismissed the service. Thus far his rage proceeded; but at that season he did nothing more against the law and religion of God. After an interval of some time he went to winter in Bithynia; and presently Galerius Caesar came thither, inflamed with furious resentment, and purposing to excite the inconsiderate old man to carry on that persecution which he had begun against the Christians. I have learned that the cause of his fury was as follows.

11. The mother of Galerius, a woman exceedingly superstitious, was a votary of the gods of the mountains. Being of such a character, she made sacrifices almost every day, and she feasted her servants on the meat offered to idols: but the Christians of her family would not partake of those entertainments; and while she feasted with the Gentiles, they continued in fasting and prayer. On this

account she conceived ill-will against the Christians, and by woman-like complaints instigated her son, no less superstitious than herself, to destroy them. So, during the whole winter, Diocletian and Galerius held councils together, at which no one else assisted; and it was the universal opinion that their conferences respected the most momentous affairs of the empire. The old man long opposed the fury of Galerius, and showed how pernicious it would be to raise disturbances throughout the world and to shed so much blood; that the Christians were wont with eagerness to meet death; and that it would be enough for him to exclude persons of that religion from the court and the army. Yet he could not restrain the madness of that obstinate man. He resolved, therefore, to take the opinion of his friends. Now this was a circumstance in the bad disposition of Diocletian, that whenever he determined to do good he did it without advice, that the praise might be all his own; but whenever he determined to do ill, which he was sensible would be blamed, he called in many advisers, that his own fault might be imputed to other men: and therefore a few civil magistrates, and a few military commanders, were admitted to give their counsel; and the question was put to them according to priority of rank. Some, through personal ill-will towards the Christians, were of opinion that they ought to be cut off, as enemies of the gods and adversaries of the established religious ceremonies. Others thought differently, but, having understood the will of Galerius, they, either from dread of displeasing or from a desire of gratifying him, concurred in the opinion given against the Christians. Yet not even then could the emperor be prevailed upon to yield his assent. He determined above all to consult his gods; and to that end he despatched a soothsayer to inquire of Apollo at Miletus, whose answer was such as might be expected from an enemy of the divine religion. So Diocletian was drawn over from his purpose. But although he could struggle no longer against his friends, and against Caesar and Apollo, yet still he attempted to observe such moderation as to command the business to be carried through without bloodshed; whereas Galerius would have had all persons burnt alive who refused to sacrifice.

12. A fit and auspicious day was sought out for the accomplishment of this undertaking; and the festival of the god Terminus, celebrated on the seventh of the kalends of March, was chosen, in preference to all others, to terminate, as it were, the Christian religion.

> "That day, the harbinger of death, arose,
> First cause of ill, an long enduring woes;"

of woes which befell not only the Christians but the whole earth. When that day dawned, in the eighth consulship of Diocletian and seventh of Maximian, suddenly, while it was yet hardly light, the prefect, together with chief commanders, tribunes, and officers of the treasury, came to the church in Nicomedia, and the gates having been forced open, they searched everywhere for an image of the Divinity. The books of the Holy Scriptures were found, and they were committed to the flames; the utensils and furniture of the church were abandoned to pillage: all was rapine, confusion, tumult. That church, situated on rising ground, was within view of the palace; and Diocletian and Galerius stood, as if on a watch-tower, disputing long whether it ought to be set on fire. The sentiment of Diocletian prevailed, who dreaded lest, so great a fire being once kindled, some part of the city might be burnt; for there were many and large buildings that surrounded the church. Then the Pretorian Guards came in battle array, with axes and other iron instruments, and having been let loose everywhere, they in a few hours levelled that very lofty edifice with the ground.

13. Next day an edict was published, depriving the Christians of all honours and dignities; ordaining also that, without any distinction of rank or degree, they should be subjected to tortures, and that every suit at law should be received against them; while, on the other hand, they were debarred from being plaintiffs in questions of wrong, adultery, or theft; and, finally, that they should neither be capable of freedom, nor have the right of suffrage. A certain person tore down this edict, and cut it in pieces, improperly indeed, but with high spirit, saying in scorn, "These are the triumphs of Goths and Sarmatians." Having been instantly seized and brought to judgment, he was not only tortured, but burnt alive, in the forms of law; and having displayed admirable patience under sufferings, he was consumed to ashes....

79 Lactantius, *On the Deaths of the Persecutors*

"This man ... overturned the Roman Empire"

A Christian and a professor of Latin rhetoric in Nicomedia (Asia Minor) under Diocletian, Lactantius was dismissed from his post when the emperor's Edict of Persecution was promulgated in A.D. 303. Reduced to penury, he moved westward and eventually befriended Constantine, who entrusted the tutorship of his son Crispus to him. Lactantius wrote a work called the *Divine Institutes* between 303 and 311 when he was still suffering from the consequences of unemployment and disfavor. The work presents itself in the tradition of Christian apologetic literature and seeks to defend the religion against critics. In another work, *On the Death of the Persecutors*, he used his historical knowledge and rhetorical/stylistic training to pen a stinging attack on the Roman emperors who persecuted Christians, giving painstaking attention especially to the manner in which divine retribution was visited upon them. The list included earlier emperors such as Nero, Domitian, and Decius as well as late third- to early fourth-century contemporaries such as Diocletian and Galerius.

From Lactantius, *On the Death of the Persecutors* 1–5, 8–17, 30, 64, 72, 91–94; in *The Ante-Nicene Fathers: Translations of the Writings of the Fathers Down to A.D. 325*, Vol. VII, edited by Alexander Roberts and James Donaldson (Grand Rapids, Mich.: Eerdmans, 1982), pp. 302–3, 305–6, 314–15.

Chap. IV

This long peace, however, was afterwards interrupted. Decius appeared in the world, an accursed wild beast, to afflict the Church,—and *who* but a bad man would persecute religion? It seems as if he had been raised to sovereign eminence, at once to rage against God, and at once to fall; for, having undertaken an expedition against the Carpi, who had then possessed themselves of Dacia and Moesia, he was suddenly surrounded by the barbarians, and slain, together with great part of his army; nor could he be honoured with the rites of sepulture, but, stripped and naked, he lay to be devoured by wild beasts and birds,—a fit end for the enemy of God.

Chap. V

And presently Valerian [r. 253-260] also, in a mood alike frantic, lifted up his impious hands to assault God, and, although his time was short, shed much righteous blood. But God punished him in a new and extraordinary manner, that it might be a lesson to future ages that the adversaries of Heaven always receive the just recompense of their iniquities. He, having been made prisoner by the Persians, lost not only that power which he had exercised without moderation, but also the liberty of which he had deprived others; and he wasted the remainder of his days in the vilest condition of slavery: for Sapores [Shapur I], the king of the Persians, who had made him prisoner, whenever he chose to get into his carriage or to mount on horseback, commanded the Roman to stoop and present his back; then, setting his foot on the shoulders of Valerian, he said, with a smile of reproach, "*This* is true, and not what the Romans delineate on board or plaster." Valerian lived for a considerable time under the well-merited insults of his conqueror; so that the Roman name remained long the scoff and derision of the barbarians: and this also was added to the severity of his punishment, that although he had an emperor for his son, he found no one to revenge his captivity and most abject and servile state; neither indeed was he ever demanded back. Afterward, when he had finished this shameful life under so great dishonour, he was flayed, and his skin, stripped from the flesh, was dyed with vermilion, and placed in the temple of the gods of the barbarians, that the remembrance of a triumph so signal might be perpetuated, and that this spectacle might always be exhibited to our ambassadors, as an admonition to the Romans, that, beholding the spoils of their captived emperor in a Persian temple, they should not place too great confidence in their own strength.

Now since God so punished the sacrilegious, is it not strange that any one should afterward have dared to do, or even to devise, aught against the majesty of the one God, who governs and supports all things?...

Chap. VII

While Diocletian [r. 284-305], that author of ill, and deviser of misery, was ruining all things, he could not withhold his insults, not even against God. This man, by avarice partly, and partly by timid counsels, overturned the Roman empire. For he made choice of three persons to share the government with him; and thus, the empire having been quartered, armies were multiplied, and each of the four princes strove to maintain a much more considerable military force than any sole emperor had done in times past. There began to be fewer men who paid taxes than there were who received wages; so that the means of the husbandmen being exhausted by enormous impositions, the farms were abandoned, cultivated grounds became woodland, and universal dismay prevailed. Besides, the provinces were divided into minute portions, and many presidents and a multitude of inferior officers lay heavy on each territory, and almost on each city. There were also many stewards of different degrees, and deputies of presidents. Very few civil causes came before them: but there were condemnations daily, and forfeitures frequently inflicted; taxes on numberless commodities, and those not only often repeated, but perpetual, and, in exacting them, intolerable wrongs.

Whatever was laid on for the maintenance of the soldiery might have been endured; but Diocletian, through his insatiable avarice, would never allow the sums of money in his treasury to be diminished: he was constantly heaping together extraordinary aids and free gifts, that his original hoards might remain untouched and inviolable. He also, when by various extortions he had made all things exceedingly dear, attempted by an ordinance to limit their prices. Then much blood was shed for the veriest trifles; men were afraid to expose aught to sale, and the scarcity became more excessive and grievous than ever, until, in the end, the ordinance, after having proved destructive to multitudes, was from mere necessity abrogated. To this there were added a certain endless passion for building, and on that account, endless exactions from the provinces for furnishing wages to labourers and artificers, and supplying carriages and whatever else was requisite to the works which he projected. *Here* public halls, *there* a circus, *here* a mint, and *there* a workhouse for making implements of war; in one place a habitation for his empress, and in another for his daughter. Presently great part of the city was quitted, and all men removed with their wives and children, as from a town taken by enemies; and when those buildings were completed, to the destruction of whole provinces, he said, "They are not right, let them be done on another plan." Then they were to be pulled down, or altered, to undergo perhaps a future demolition. By such folly was he continually endeavouring to equal Nicomedia with the city Rome in magnificence....

Chap. XI

The mother of Galerius [emperor 305-311], a woman exceedingly superstitious, was a votary of the gods of the mountains. Being of such a character, she made sacrifices almost every day, and she feasted her servants on the meat offered to idols: but the Christians of her family would not partake of those entertainments; and while she feasted with the Gentiles, they continued in fasting and prayer. On this account she conceived ill-will against the Christians, and by woman-like complaints instigated her son, no less superstitious than herself, to destroy them. So, during the whole winter, Diocletian and Galerius held councils together, at which no one else assisted; and it was the universal opinion that their conferences respected the most momentous affairs of the empire. The old man long opposed the fury of Galerius, and showed how pernicious it would be to raise disturbances throughout the world and to shed so much blood; that the Christians were wont with eagerness to meet death; and that it would be enough for him to exclude persons of that religion from the court and the army. Yet he could not restrain the madness of that obstinate man. He resolved, therefore, to take the opinion of his friends. Now this was a circumstance in the bad disposition of Diocletian, that whenever he determined to do good, he did it without advice, that the praise might be all his own; but whenever he determined to do ill, which he was sensible would be blamed, he called in many advisers, that his own fault might be imputed to other men: and therefore a few civil magistrates, and a few military commanders, were admitted to give their counsel; and the question was put to them according to priority of rank. Some, through personal ill-will towards the Christians, were of opinion that they ought to be cut off, as enemies of the gods and adversaries of the established religious ceremonies. Others thought differently, but, having understood the will of Galerius, they, either from dread of displeasing or from a desire of gratifying him, concurred in the opinion given against the Christians. Yet not even then could the emperor be prevailed upon to yield his assent He determined above all to consult his gods; and to that end he despatched a soothsayer to inquire of Apollo at Miletus, whose answer was such as might be expected from an enemy of the divine religion. So Diocletian was drawn over from his purpose. But although he could struggle no longer against his friends, and against Caesar and Apollo, yet still he attempted to observe such moderation as to command the business to be carried through without bloodshed; whereas Galerius would have had all persons burnt alive who refused to sacrifice.

Chap. XII

A fit and auspicious day was sought out for the accomplishment of this undertaking; and the festival of the god Terminus, celebrated on the seventh of the kalends of March, was chosen, in preference to all others, to terminate, as it were, the Christian religion.

> "That day, the harbinger of death, arose,
> First cause of ill, and long enduring woes;"

of woes which befell not only the Christians, but the whole earth. When that day dawned, in the eighth consulship of Diocletian and seventh of Maximian, suddenly, while it was yet hardly light, the prefect, together with chief commanders, tribunes, and officers of the treasury, came to the church in Nicomedia, and the gates having been forced open, they searched everywhere for an image of the Divinity. The books of the Holy Scriptures were found, and they were committed to the flames; the utensils and furniture of the church were abandoned to pillage: all was rapine, confusion, tumult. That church, situated on rising ground, was within view of the palace; and Diocletian and Galerius stood, as if on a watch-tower, disputing long whether it ought to be set on fire. The sentiment of Diocletian prevailed, who dreaded lest, so great a fire being once kindled, some part of the city might be burnt; for there were many and large buildings that surrounded the church. Then the Pretorian Guards came in battle array, with axes and other iron instruments, and having been let loose everywhere, they in a few hours levelled that very lofty edifice with the ground.

Chap. XIII

Next day an edict was published, depriving the Christians of all honours and dignities; ordaining also that, without any distinction of rank or degree, they should be subjected to tortures, and that every suit at law should be received against them; while, on the other hand, they were debarred from being plaintiffs in questions of wrong, adultery, or theft; and, finally, that they should neither be capable of freedom, nor have right of suffrage. A certain person tore down this edict, and cut it in pieces, improperly indeed, but with high spirit, saying in scorn, "These are the triumphs of Goths and Sarmatians." Having been instantly seized and brought to judgment, he was not only tortured, but burnt alive, in the forms of law; and having displayed admirable patience under sufferings, he was consumed to ashes.

Chap. XIV

But Galerius, not satisfied with the tenor of the edict, sought in another way to gain on the emperor. That he might urge him to excess of cruelty in persecution, he employed private emissaries to set the palace on fire; and some part of it having been burnt, the blame was laid on the Christians as public enemies; and the very appellation of *Christian* grew odious on account of that fire. It was said that the Christians, in concert with the eunuchs, had plotted to destroy the princes; and that both of the princes had well-nigh been burnt alive in their own palace. Diocletian, shrewd and intelligent as he always chose to appear, suspected nothing of the contrivance, but, inflamed with anger, immediately commanded that all his own domestics should be tortured to force a confession of the plot. He sat on his tribunal, and saw innocent men tormented by fire to make discovery. All magistrates, and all who had superintendency in the imperial palace, obtained special commissions to administer the torture; and they strove with each other *who* should be first in bringing to light the conspiracy. No circumstances, however, of the fact were detected anywhere; for no one applied the torture to any domestics of Galerius. He himself was ever with Diocletian, constantly urging him, and never allowing the passions of the inconsiderate old man to cool. Then, after an interval of fifteen days, he attempted a second fire; but that was perceived quickly, and extinguished. Still, however, its author remained unknown. On that very day, Galerius, who in the middle of winter had prepared for his departure, suddenly hurried out of the city, protesting that he fled to escape being burnt alive.

Chap. XV

And now Diocletian raged, not only against his own domestics, but indiscriminately against all; and he began by forcing his daughter Valeria and his wife

Prisca to be polluted by sacrificing. Eunuchs, once the most powerful, and who had chief authority at court and with the emperor, were slain. Presbyters and other officers of the Church were seized, without evidence by witnesses or confession, condemned, and together with their families led to execution. In burning alive, no distinction of sex or age was regarded; and because of their great multitude, they were not burnt one after another, but a herd of them were encircled with the same fire; and servants, having millstones tied about their necks, were cast into the sea. Nor was the persecution less grievous on the rest of the people of God; for the judges, dispersed through all the temples, sought to compel every one to sacrifice. The prisons were crowded; tortures, hitherto unheard of, were invented; and lest justice should be inadvertently administered to a Christian, altars were placed in the courts of justice, hard by the tribunal, that every litigant might offer incense before his cause could be heard. Thus judges were no otherwise approached than divinities....

Chap. XXXIII

And now, when Galerius was in the eighteenth year of his reign [A.D. 311], God struck him with an incurable plague. A malignant ulcer formed itself low down in his secret parts, and spread by degrees. The physicians attempted to eradicate it, and healed up the place affected. But the sore, after having been skinned over, broke out again; a vein burst, and the blood flowed in such quantity as to endanger his life. The blood, however, was stopped, although with difficulty. The physicians had to undertake their operations anew, and at length they cicatrized the wound. In consequence of some slight motion of his body, Galerius received a hurt, and the blood streamed more abundantly than before. He grew emaciated, pallid, and feeble, and the bleeding then stanched. The ulcer began to be insensible to the remedies applied, and a gangrene seized all the neighbouring parts. It diffused, itself the wider the more the corrupted flesh was cut away, and everything employed as the means of cure served but to aggravate the disease.

"The masters of the healing art withdrew."

Then famous physicians were brought in from all quarters; but no human means had any success. Apollo and Aesculapius were besought importunately for remedies: Apollo did prescribe, and the distemper augmented.... The stench was so foul as to pervade not only the palace, but even the whole city; and no wonder, for by that tune the passages from his bladder and bowels, having been devoured by the worms, became indiscriminate, and his body, with intolerable anguish, was dissolved into one mass of corruption.

"Stung to the soul, he bellowed with the pain,
So roars the wounded bull."—PITT.

They applied warm flesh of animals to the chief seat of the disease, that the warmth might draw out those minute worms; and accordingly, when the dressings were removed, there issued forth an innumerable swarm: nevertheless the prolific disease had hatched swarms much more abundant to prey upon and consume his intestines. Already, through a complication of distempers, the different parts of his body had lost their natural form: the superior part was dry, meagre, and haggard, and his ghastly-looking skin, had settled itself deep amongst his bones; while the inferior, distended like bladders, retained no appearance of joints. These things happened in the course of a complete year; and at length, overcome by calamities, he was obliged to acknowledge God, and he cried aloud, in the intervals of raging pain, that he would re-edify the Church which he had demolished, and make atonement for his misdeeds; and when he was near his end, he published an edict of the tenor following:

Chap. XXXIV

"Amongst our other regulations for the permanent advantage of the commonweal, we have hitherto studied to reduce all things to a conformity with the ancient laws and public discipline of the Romans.

"It has been our aim in an especial manner, that the Christians also, who had abandoned the religion of their forefathers, should return to right opinions. For such wilfulness and folly had, we know not how, taken possession of them, that instead of observing those ancient institutions, which possibly their own forefathers had established, they, through caprice, made laws to themselves, and drew together into different societies many men of widely different persuasions.

"After the publication of our edict, ordaining the Christians to betake themselves to, the observance of the ancient institutions, many of them were subdued through the fear of danger, and moreover many of them were exposed to jeopardy; nevertheless, because great numbers still persist in their opinions, and because we have perceived that at present they neither pay reverence and due adoration to the gods, nor yet worship their own God; therefore we, from our wonted clemency, in bestowing, pardon on all, have judged it fit to extend our indulgence to those men, and to permit them: again to be Christians, and to establish the places of their religious assemblies; yet so as that they offend not against good order.

"By another mandate we purpose to signify unto magistrates how they ought herein to demean themselves.

"Wherefore it will be the duty of the Christians, in consequence of this our toleration, to pray to their God for our welfare, and for that of the public, and for their own; that the commonweal may continue safe in every quarter, and that they themselves may live securely in their habitations."

Chap. XXXV

This edict was promulgated at Nicomedia on the day preceding the kalends of May, in the eighth consulship of Galerius, and the second of Maximin Daia. Then the prison-gates having been thrown open, you, my best beloved Donatus, together with the other confessors for the faith, were set at liberty from a jail; which had been your residence for six years. Galerius, however, did not, by publication of this edict, obtain the divine forgiveness. In a few days after he was consumed by the horrible disease that had brought on an universal putrefaction.

Dying, he recommended his wife and son to Licinius, and delivered them over into his hands: This event was known at Nicomedia before the end of the month.

80 Eusebius of Caesarea

Life of the Emperor Constantine

"Serving God … with his every action"

Constantine came to power at a time of uncertainty and crisis in the Roman Empire. The college of four co-emperors, a system called the Tetrarchy and instituted by Emperor Diocletian a generation ago, was not working smoothly and imperial colleagues fought each other. Proclaimed emperor by the Roman army stationed in York (in modern northern England), Constantine marched to Rome, where he defeated his colleague and rival, Maxentius, in the famous Battle of the Milvian Bridge in 312. According to somewhat later sources, Constantine saw a vision involving the figure of Christ prior to the battle, and this experience radically altered his outlook.

Historians still hotly debate how significant a watershed in ancient history is the year A.D. 312. In that year, Emperor Constantine the Great embraced Christianity, setting into motion the process whereby a polytheistic Mediterranean society would become transformed into a Christian one. While this process had barely begun at the time when Constantine himself died in A.D. 337, his role in this transformation has generally been acknowledged as pivotal by both ancient and modern authors.

Constantine was the first Roman emperor who was also Christian. He took an active role in establishing the right of Christians to worship without fear of persecution. Furthermore, as a rich and powerful patron of the Christian churches, he presided over their transition from persecuted communities to major public institutions throughout the empire. Helped by his generous donations and grants of land and income, churches, especially the church of the city of Rome, became wealthy and respectable. Constantine's reign established the pattern for the growing cooperation between the Roman state and the churches. Subsequent Christian authors regarded him as the paradigmatic Christian ruler.

The selection below is a particularly glowing assessment of the emperor's contributions. According to Eusebius, the Christian God granted Constantine and Rome itself worldly success so that the cause of the Christian faith might be advanced. In this view, Constantine, a Roman emperor, was an agent of God's divine will.

From Averil Cameron and Stuart Hall, *Eusebius: Life of Constantine. Introduction, Translation, and Commentary* (Oxford: Oxford University Press, 1999). © Averil Cameron and Stuart Hall 1999. Reprinted by permission of Oxford University Press.

Among the many actions undertaken by Constantine on behalf of Christianity was his mediation in Christian theological disagreements. One such disagreement in the Greek east was called the Arian Controversy, after Arius of Alexandria, who was accused of expounding heretical ideas. Christian communities were fragmented over questions surrounding the divinity of Christ to the point where the emperor felt obliged to intervene. Constantine called together the first universal Christian council ever to take place at the city of Nicaea (Asia Minor) in A.D. 325 to encourage greater unity among his Christian subjects. The active participation of Christian emperors in church affairs became a common feature in later Byzantine history, and the unique combination of secular political authority and religious power embodied in the emperor has at times been described by historians as a form of "Caesaro-papism."

The Tyranny of Maxentius

33 (1) Indeed, the one who had thus previously seized the imperial city [i.e., Maxentius] was busily engaged in abominable and sacrilegious activities, so that he left no outrage undone in his foul and filthy behaviour. He parted lawful wives from husbands, and after misusing them quite disgracefully returned them to their husbands. He did this not to obscure or insignificant persons, but insolently to those who held highest positions in the Roman Senate. So he misused disgracefully innumerable free-born women, yet found no way to satisfy his unrestrained and insatiable appetite. (2) But when he turned his hand also to Christian women, he was no longer able to devise convenient means for his adulteries. They would sooner yield their life to him for execution than their body for immoral use....

35 (1) Before the one who committed such outrages all men cowered, peoples and princes, high and low, and were worn down by savage tyranny. ... On one occasion on a slight pretext he gave the people over to slaughter by his escorting guards, and there were killed countless multitudes of the people of Rome right in the middle of the city, by the weapons and arms, not of Goths or barbarians, but of their own countrymen. (2) The number of senators whose murder was encompassed as a means to acquire each one's property it would not be possible to calculate, since thousands were put to death, sometimes on one fictitious charge, sometimes on another. 36 (1) At their peak the tyrant's crimes extended to witchcraft, as for magical purposes he split open pregnant women, sometimes searched the entrails of new-born babies, slaughtered lions, and composed secret spells to conjure demons and to ward off hostilities. By these means he hoped he would gain the victory. (2) Ruling by these dictatorial methods in Rome he imposed on his subjects unspeakable oppression, so that he brought them finally to the utmost scarcity and want of necessary food, such as our generation never remembers happening in Rome at any other time.

Battle of the Milvian Bridge, 312

37 (1) Constantine meanwhile was moved to pity by all these things, and began making every armed preparation against the tyranny. So taking as his patron God who is over all, and invoking his Christ as saviour and succour,

and having set the victorious trophy, the truly salutary sign, at the head of his escorting soldiers and guards, he led them in full force, claiming for the Romans their ancestral liberties. (2) Maxentius put his confidence more in the devices of sorcery than in the loyalty of his subjects, and did not even dare to go beyond the gates of the city, but fortified every place and territory and city which was under his dominion with an immense number of soldiers and countless military units. But the Emperor who relied upon the support of God attacked the first, second, and third formations of the tyrant, overcame them all quite easily at the very first onslaught, and advanced to occupy most of the land of Italy.

38 (1) He was now very near to Rome itself. Then, so that he should not be forced because of the tyrant to fight against the people of Rome, God himself drew the tyrant out, as if with chains, far away from the gates; and those ancient words against the wicked, widely disbelieved as mere legend, though in sacred books believably recorded for believers, by his divine actions he proved to be true for every single eye which saw his marvels, believing and unbelieving alike. (2) Accordingly, just as once in the time of Moses and the devout Hebrew tribe 'Pharaoh's chariots and his force he cast into the sea, and picked rider-captains he overwhelmed in the Red Sea' (Exodus 15:4), in the very same way Maxentius and the armed men and guards about him 'sank to the bottom like a stone' (Exodus 15:5), when, fleeing before the force which came from God with Constantine, he went to cross the river lying in his path [with a pontoon bridge made from linked boats]. ... [B]y God's will the mechanism in the link and the device concealed in it gave way at a time which was not intended, the crossing parted, and the boats sank at once to the bottom with all their men, the coward himself first of all, and then the infantry and guards about him, just as the divine oracles had previously proclaimed: 'They sank like lead in much water' (Exodus 15:10)....

Triumph of Constantine

... (2) Immediately all the members of the Senate and the other persons there of fame and distinction, as if released from a cage, and all the people of Rome, gave him a bright-eyed welcome with spontaneous acclamations and unbounded joy. Men with their wives and children and countless numbers of slaves with unrestrained cheers pronounced him their redeemer, saviour and benefactor. (3) He, however, being possessed of inward fear of God, was not inflated by their cries nor over-exuberant at their praises, but was conscious of the help of God; so he immediately offered up a prayer of thanksgiving to the Giver of his victory. 40 (1) He announced to all people in large lettering and inscriptions the sign of the Saviour, setting this up in the middle of the imperial city as a great trophy of victory over his enemies, explicitly inscribing this in indelible letters as the salvific sign of the authority of Rome and the protection of the whole empire. (2) He therefore immediately ordered a tall pole to be erected in the shape of a cross in the hand of a statue made to represent himself, and this text to be inscribed upon it word for word in Latin: 'By this salutary sign, the true proof of valour, I liberated your city, saved from the tyrant's yoke; moreover the Senate and People of Rome I liberated and restored to their ancient splendour and brilliance.'

41 (1) The Godbeloved Emperor, proudly confessing in this way the victory-bringing cross, was entirely open in making the Son of God known to the Romans. (2) All the city's population together, including the Senate and all the people, as they recovered from bitter tyrannical repression, seemed to be enjoying beams of purer light and to be participating in rebirth to a fresh new life. All the nations which bordered on the Ocean where the sun sets, set free from the evils which formerly oppressed them, kept rejoicing in happy gatherings as they hymned the mighty Victor, the Godfearing, the general Benefactor, and with one single voice they all acknowledged the common good of mankind which by God's grace had dawned in Constantine.

Constantine and Christians

(3) An imperial letter was also published everywhere, granting the enjoyment of their goods to those whose property had been confiscated, and recalling to their own homes those who had suffered unjust exile. It also released from imprisonment and every kind of liability or threat at law those subjected to them by the tyrant's savagery.

42 (1) The Emperor personally called together the ministers of God, regarding them honourably and cherishing them with highest consideration, since he favoured those men by deed and word as consecrated to his God. ... Indeed he also supplied rich help from his own resources to the churches of God, enlarging and elevating the places of worship, while beautifying the grander ecclesiastical sacred buildings with many dedications.

43 (1) He made all sorts of distributions to the poor, and apart from them showed himself compassionate and beneficent to those outside who approached him. For some poor desperate wretches who publicly solicited alms he would provide not only money or necessary food, but decent clothing for the body. For those who were originally of higher birth but had run on hard times he made more generous provision, with imperial magnanimity providing munificent benefactions to such persons: to some he made grants of land, others he promoted to various offices. (2) Those unfortunate enough to be orphaned he cared for in the father's stead, and repaired the vulnerability of widowhood for women by personal concern, so far as to find them husbands from his acquaintance, and rich men for orphaned girls deprived of parents. He managed this by supplementing the dowry needed for the brides to bring to those who were receiving them in the bond of marriage....

44 (1) ... But to the Church of God he paid particular personal attention. When some were at variance with each other in various places, like a universal bishop appointed by God he convoked councils of the ministers of God. (2) He did not disdain to be present and attend during their proceedings, and he participated in the subjects reviewed, by arbitration promoting the peace of God among all; and he took his seat among them as if he were one voice among many, dismissing his praetorians and soldiers and bodyguards of every kind, clad only in the fear of God and surrounded by the most loyal of his faithful companions. (3) Then such as he saw able to be prevailed upon by argument and adopting a calm and

The *Liberalitas* of Constantine. The emperor distributes largesse to his people. From the Arch of Constantine, early fourth century A.D., Rome.

conciliatory attitude, he commended most warmly, showing how he favoured general unanimity, but the obstinate he rejected. 45 (1) There were even some who spoke harshly against him, and he tolerated them without resentment, with a gentle voice bidding them to behave reasonably and not be contentious. Some of them respected his rebukes and desisted, while those who were past curing and could not be brought to a sound mind he left in the hands of God, being unwilling himself to devise anything whatever to any person's hurt....

46   Thus then the Emperor, serving God the overseer of all with his every action, took untiring care of his churches. God repaid him by putting all the barbarian nations beneath his feet, so that always and everywhere he raised trophies over his foes, and by proclaiming him Victor among them all, and making him a terror to foes and enemies, though he was not naturally such, but the gentlest, mildest, and kindest man there ever was....

Constantine Promotes Christianity

44   From this the Emperor went on to take practical steps. He first sent governors to the peoples in their various provinces, for the most part men consecrated to the saving faith; those who preferred paganism he forbade to sacrifice. The same applied also to the ranks above provincial government, the highest of all, who held office as prefects. If they were Christians, he permitted them to make public use of the name; if otherwise disposed, he instructed them not to worship idols. 45 (1) Next, two laws were simultaneously issued. One

restricted the pollutions of idolatry which had for a long time been practised in every city and country district, so that no one should presume to set up cult-objects, or practise divination or other occult arts, or even to sacrifice at all. The other dealt with erecting buildings as places of worship and extending in breadth and length the churches of God, as if almost everybody would in future belong to God, once the obstacle of polytheistic madness had been removed....

(2) That the Emperor both held such views and was writing then to the authorities in each place was indicated by his sacred decree about God, and the law provided that no financial cost should be spared, but the expenses actually furnished from the imperial funds....

47 (1) Carrying yet further his piety towards God, the Emperor sent to the provincials in every national area an instructive decree refuting the idolatrous error of his predecessors in power; he urged that it was more rational for his subjects to acknowledge the God over all and expressly to adopt his Christ as Saviour....

The Arian Controversy and The Council of Nicaea

4   These things then were done as he desired. But the effects of the resentment of Envy dreadfully agitating the churches of God in Alexandria, and the evil schism in the Thebaid and Egypt, disturbed him considerably. The bishop of one city was attacking the bishop of another, populations were rising up against one another, and were all but coming to physical blows with each other, so that desperate men, out of their minds, were committing sacrilegious acts, even daring to insult the images of the Emperor. But this did not so much rouse him to anger as to mental anguish, as he grieved at the senseless conduct of the deranged....

(3) Once he received news of what has been described, and perceived that the letter which he had sent to those in Alexandria had failed, he applied his own mind to the matter, and said that this was another war which he must struggle to win against the invisible enemy disturbing the Church. 6 (1) Then, as if to march against him, he marshalled a legion of God, a world-wide Council, with respectful letters summoning the bishops to hasten from every place. It was not a simple command, but the Emperor's will reinforced it also with practical action; to some it offered the right to use the public post, to others a generous supply of pack-animals. A city was also designated which was appropriate for the Council, one bearing the name of victory, Nicaea in the province of Bithynia....

7 (1) From all the churches which filled all Europe, Libya, and Asia the choicest of the servants of God were brought together; and one place of worship, as if extended by God, took them in all together: Syrians with Cilicians; Phoenicians and Arabians and Palestinians; besides these, Egyptians, Thebans, Libyans, and those who came from between the rivers. Even a Persian bishop was present at the council, nor was a Scythian lacking from the assembly. Pontus and Galatia, Cappadocia and Asia, Phrygia and Pamphylia provided their chosen men. Thracians too and Macedonians, Achaeans and Epirotes, and among them those who lived far up-country, were present; and even of the Spaniards the very famous one was among those joining the assembly with all the rest. (2) The one in charge of the imperial city [Rome] was absent because of his old age, but his presbyters were present and deputized for him. Alone in all of history one

emperor, Constantine, wove such a crown for Christ with the bond of peace, and to his Saviour dedicated a thank-offering fit for God for his victory over enemies and foemen, gathering among us this replica of the apostolic assembly....

The Proceedings of the Council

10 (1) On the day appointed for the Council, on which it was to reach a resolution of the issues in dispute, every one was present to do this, in the very innermost hall of the palace, which appeared to exceed the rest in size. Many tiers of seating had been set along either side of the hall. Those invited arrived within, and all took their appointed seats. (2) When the whole council had with proper ceremony taken their seats, silence fell upon them all, as they awaited the Emperor's arrival. One of the Emperor's company came in, then a second, then a third. Yet others led the way, not some of the usual soldiers and guards, but only of his faithful friends. (3) All rose at a signal, which announced the Emperor's entrance; and he finally walked along between them, like some heavenly angel of God, his bright mantle shedding lustre like beams of light, shining with the fiery radiance of a purple robe, and decorated with the dazzling brilliance of gold and precious stones. (4) Such was his physical appearance. As for his soul, he was clearly adorned with fear and reverence for God: this was shown by his eyes, which were cast down, the blush on his face, his gait, and the rest of his appearance, his height, which surpassed all those around him ... by dignified maturity, by the magnificence of his physical condition, and by the vigour of his matchless strength. All these, blended with the elegance of his manners and the gentleness of imperial condescension, demonstrated the superiority of his mind surpassing all description. (5) When he reached the upper end of the rows of seats and stood in the middle, a small chair made of gold having been set out, only when the bishops assented did he sit down. They all did the same after the Emperor.

11   The bishop who was first in the row on the right then stood up and delivered a rhythmical speech, addressing the Emperor, and offering a hymn of gratitude for him to God the ruler of all. When he too had sat down, silence fell on all as they gazed intently at the Emperor. He with shining eyes looked kindly on them all, and then, collecting his thoughts, in a soft and gentle voice he gave a speech somewhat like this:

12 (1) 'It was the object of my prayers, my friends, to share in your company, and now that I have received this, I know I must express my gratitude to the King of all, because in addition to everything else he has allowed me to see this, which is better than any other good thing; I mean, to receive you all gathered together and to observe one unanimous opinion shared by all. (2) Let no jealous enemy ruin our prosperity; now that the war of the tyrants against God has been swept away by the power of God the Saviour, let not the malignant demon encompass the divine law with blasphemies by other means. For to me internal division in the Church of God is graver than any war or fierce battle, and these things appear to cause more pain than secular affairs. (3) When therefore I won victories over enemies through the favour and support of the Supreme, I considered that nothing remained but to give thanks to God, and to rejoice also with those who had been liberated by him through our agency.

When contrary to all expectation I learnt of your division, I did not defer attention to the report, but, praying that this too might be healed through my ministration, I immediately sent for you all. (4) I rejoice to see your gathering, and I consider that I shall be acting most in accordance with my prayers, when I see you all with your souls in communion, and one common, peaceful harmony prevailing among you all, which you, as persons consecrated to God, ought yourselves to be announcing to others. (5) So do not delay, my friends, ministers of God, and good servants of the common Lord and Saviour of us all, to begin now to bring the causes of the division between you into the open, and to loosen all shackles of dispute by the laws of peace. Thus you will both achieve what is pleasing to the God of all, and you will give extreme gratification to me, your fellow servant.'

13 (1) When he had spoken these words in Latin, with someone interpreting, he made way for the leaders of the Council to speak. Some then began to accuse their neighbours, while the others defended themselves and made countercharges. A great many proposals were made by each side, and there was at first much controversy. The Emperor listened to all, without resentment, and received the proposals with patient flexibility; he took up what was said by each side in turn, and gently brought together those whose attitudes conflicted. (2) He addressed each person gently, and by speaking Greek—for he was not ignorant of that language either—he made himself pleasant and agreeable, persuading some and shaming others with his words, praising those who were speaking well, urging all towards agreement, until he had brought them to be of one mind and one belief on all the matters in dispute. 14 Thus the Faith prevailed in a unanimous form, and the same timing for the Festival of the Saviour was agreed on all sides. The general decisions were also ratified in writing through the individual signatures. When these things were finished, the Emperor said that this was the second victory he had won over the enemy of the Church, and held a victory-feast to God....

81 Athanasius, *Life of Anthony*

Ascetic as Holy Man and Celebrity

"... they saw that even demons feared Antony"

The rise of asceticism was a signal development in the history of early Christianity. In Syria and Egypt, men and women carried out forms of spiritual discipline or exercise (*askesis* in Greek) to suppress their earthly passions in the

From Athanasius, *Life of Anthony* 15, 14, 49, 51–52, 56, 64, 72–73, 91–94; in *Nicene and Post-Nicene Fathers of the Christian Church*, series II, Vol. IV, edited by Philip Schaff and Henry Wace (Grand Rapids, Mich.: Eerdmans, 1980–83), pp. 195–97, 200, 209–11, 213, 215, 220–21.

name of spiritual progress. One such ascetic named Anthony became a famous iconic figure who inspired others to pursue a similar path. Anthony of Egypt (ca. A.D. 251–356), forsaking his future as head of a prosperous family in Lower Egypt, took to following the dictates of Jesus and sold his possessions and distributed the money to the poor and to neighbors. He himself sought the path of a solitary hermit and repaired to the desert of Nitria outside Alexandria where he perfected his spiritual life for some thirteen years. During this time, he subjected himself to privations and torments of temptation. While the illiterate Anthony sought solicitude, his story was publicized by Athanasius, a powerful and controversial bishop of Alexandria, whose *Life of Anthony* in Greek became wildly popular and was translated into Latin and thereby influenced the development of asceticism in the Latin west.

The life and conversation of our holy Father, Antony: written and sent to the monks in foreign parts by our Father among the Saints, Athanasius, Bishop of Alexandria.

Athanasius the bishop to the brethren in foreign parts.

You have entered upon a noble rivalry with the monks of Egypt by your determination either to equal or surpass them in your training in the way of virtue. For by this time there are monasteries among you, and the name of monk receives public recognition. With reason, therefore, all men will approve this determination, and in answer to your prayers God will give its fulfilment. Now since you asked me to give you an account of the blessed Antony's way of life, and are wishful to learn how he began the discipline, who and what manner of man he was previous to this, how he closed his life, and whether the things told of him are true, that you also may bring yourselves to imitate him, I very readily accepted your behest, for to me also the bare recollection of Antony is a great accession of help. And I know that you, when you have heard, apart from your admiration of the man, will be wishful to emulate his determination; seeing that for monks the life of Antony is a sufficient pattern of discipline....

Antony's Background and Call to Asceticism

1. Antony you must know was by descent an Egyptian: his parents were of good family and possessed considerable wealth, and as they were Christians he also was reared in the same Faith. In infancy he was brought up with his parents, knowing nought else but them and his home. But when he was grown and arrived at boyhood, and was advancing in years, he could not endure to learn letters, not caring to associate with other boys; but all his desire was, as it is written of Jacob, to live a plain man at home. With his parents he used to attend the Lord's House, and neither as a child was he idle nor when older did he despise them; but was both obedient to his father and mother and attentive to what was read, keeping in his heart what was profitable in what he heard. And though as a child brought up in moderate affluence, he did not trouble his parents for varied or luxurious fare, nor was this a source of pleasure to him; but was content simply with what he found nor sought anything further.

2. After the death of his father and mother he was left alone with one little sister: his age was about eighteen or twenty, and on him the care both of home

and sister rested. Now it was not six months after the death of his parents, and going according to custom into the Lord's House, he communed with himself and reflected as he walked how the Apostles left all and followed the Saviour; and how they in the Acts sold their possessions and brought and laid them at the Apostles' feet for distribution to the needy, and what and how great a hope was laid up for them in heaven. Pondering over these things he entered the church, and it happened the Gospel was being read, and he heard the Lord saying to the rich man, "If thou wouldest be perfect, go and sell that thou hast and give to the poor; and come follow Me and thou shalt have treasure in heaven." Antony, as though God had put him in mind of the Saints, and the passage had been read on his account, went out immediately from the church, and gave the possessions of his forefathers to the villagers they were three hundred acres, productive and very fair—that they should be no more a clog upon himself and his sister. And all the rest that was movable he sold, and having got together much money he gave it to the poor, reserving a little however for his sister's sake.

3. And again as he went into the church, hearing the Lord say in the Gospel, "be not anxious for the morrow," he could stay no longer, but went out and gave those things also to the poor. Having committed his sister to known and faithful virgins, and put her into a convent to be brought up, he henceforth devoted himself outside his house to discipline, taking heed to himself and training himself with patience. For there were not yet so many monasteries in Egypt, and no monk at all knew of the distant desert; but all who wished to give heed to themselves practised the discipline in solitude near their own village. Now there was then in the next village an old man who had lived the life of a hermit from his youth up. Antony, after he had seen this man, imitated him in piety....

4. Thus conducting himself, Antony was beloved by all. He subjected himself in sincerity to the good men whom he visited, and learned thoroughly where each surpassed him in zeal and discipline. He observed the graciousness of one; the unceasing prayer of another; he took knowledge of another's freedom from anger and another's loving-kindness; he gave heed to one as he watched, to another as he studied; one he admired for his endurance, another for his fasting and sleeping on the ground; the meekness of one and the long-suffering of another he watched with care, while he took note of the piety towards Christ and the mutual love which animated all. Thus filled, he returned to his own place of discipline, and henceforth would strive to unite the qualities of each, and was eager to show in himself the virtues of all....

Antony's Spiritual Trials and Triumphs

5. But the devil, who hates and envies what is good, could not endure to see such a resolution in a youth, but endeavoured to carry out against him what he had been wont to effect against others. First of all he tried to lead him away from the discipline, whispering to him the remembrance of his wealth, care for his sister, claims of kindred, love of money, love of glory, the various pleasures of the table and the other relaxations of life, and at last the difficulty of virtue and

the labour of it; he suggested also the infirmity of the body and the length of the time. In a word he raised in his mind a great dust of debate, wishing to debar him from his settled purpose. But when the enemy saw himself to be too weak for Antony's determination, and that he rather was conquered by the other's firmness, overthrown by his great faith and falling through his constant prayers, then at length putting his trust in the weapons which are "in the navel of his belly" and boasting in them—for they are his first snare for the young—he attacked the young man, disturbing him by night and harassing him by day, so that even the onlookers saw the struggle which was going on between them. The one would suggest foul thoughts and the other counter them with prayers: the one fire him with lust, the other, as one who seemed to blush, fortify his body with faith, prayers, and fasting. And the devil, unhappy wight, one night even took upon him the shape of a woman and imitated all her acts simply to beguile Antony. But he, his mind filled with Christ and the nobility inspired by Him, and considering the spirituality of the soul, quenched the coal of the other's deceit.…

Antony the Holy Man

14. And so for nearly twenty years he continued training himself in solitude, never going forth, and but seldom seen by any. After this, when many were eager and wishful to imitate his discipline, and his acquaintances came and began to cast down and wrench off the door by force, Antony, as from a shrine, came forth initiated in the mysteries and filled with the Spirit of God. Then for the first time he was seen outside the fort by those who came to see him. And they, when they saw him, wondered at the sight, for he had the same habit of body as before, and was neither fat, like a man without exercise, nor lean from fasting and striving with the demons, but he was just the same as they had known him before his retirement. And again his soul was free from blemish, for it was neither contracted as if by grief, nor relaxed by pleasure, nor possessed by laughter or dejection, for he was not troubled when he beheld the crowd, nor overjoyed at being saluted by so many. But he was altogether even as being guided by reason, and abiding in a natural state. Through him the Lord healed the bodily ailments of many present, and cleansed others from evil spirits. And He gave grace to Antony in speaking, so that he consoled many that were sorrowful, and set those at variance at one, exhorting all to prefer the love of Christ before all that is in the world. And while he exhorted and advised them to remember the good things to come, and the loving-kindness of God towards us, "Who spared not His own Son, but delivered Him up for us all," he persuaded many to embrace the solitary life. And thus it happened in the end that cells arose even in the mountains, and the desert was colonised by monks, who came forth from their own people, and enrolled themselves for the citizenship in the heavens.…

49. But when he saw himself beset by many, and not suffered to withdraw himself according to his intent as he wished, fearing because of the signs which the Lord wrought by him, that either he should be puffed up, or that some other

should think of him above what he ought to think, he considered and set off to go into the upper Thebaid, among those to whom he was unknown.

But the voice said unto him, 'Even though you should go into the Thebaid, or even though, as you have in mind, you should go down to the Bucolia', you will have to endure more, aye, double the amount of toil. But if you wish really to be in quiet, depart now into the inner desert' And when Antony said, 'Who will show me the way for I know it not?' immediately the voice pointed out to him Saracens about to go that way. So Antony approached, and drew near them, and asked that he might go with them into the desert. And they, as though they had been commanded by Providence, received him willingly. And having journeyed with them three days and three nights, he came to a very lofty mountain, and at the foot of the mountain ran a clear spring, whose waters were sweet and very cold; outside there was a plain and a few uncared-for palm trees.

51. So he was alone in the inner mountain, spending his time in prayer and discipline. And the brethren who served him asked that they might come every month and bring him olives, pulse and oil, for by now he was an old man. There then he passed his life, and endured such great wrestlings, 'Not against flesh and blood,' as it is written, but against opposing demons, as we learned from chose who visited him. For there they heard tumults, many voices, and, as it were, the clash of arms. At night they saw the mountain become full of wild beasts, and him also fighting as though against visible beings, and praying against them. And those who came to him he encouraged, while kneeling he contended and prayed to the Lord. Surely it was a marvellous thing that a man, alone in such a desert, feared neither the demons who rose up against him, nor the fierceness of the four-footed beasts and creeping things, for all they were so many. But in truth, as it is written, 'He trusted in the Lord as Mount Sion,' with a mind unshaken and undisturbed; so that the demons rather fled from him, and the wild beasts, as it is written, 'kept peace with him.'

52. The devil, therefore, as David says in the Psalms', observed Antony and gnashed his teeth against him. But Antony was consoled by the Saviour and continued unhurt by his wiles and varied devices. As he was watching in the night the devil sent wild beasts against him. And almost all the hyenas in that desert came forth from their dens and surrounded him; and he was in the midst, while each one threatened to bite. Seeing that it was a trick of the enemy he said to them all: 'If ye have received power against me I am ready to be devoured by you; but if ye were sent against me by demons, stay not, but depart, for I am a servant of Christ.' When Antony said this they fled, driven by that word as with a whip.

55. And henceforth many resorted to him, and others who were suffering ventured to go in. To all the monks therefore who came to him, he continually gave this precept: 'Believe on the Lord and love Him; keep yourselves from filthy thoughts and fleshly pleasures, and as it is written in the Proverbs, be not deceived "by the fulness of the belly." Pray continually; avoid vain-glory; sing psalms before sleep and on awaking; hold in your heart the commandments of Scripture; be mindful of the works of the saints that your souls being put in remembrance of the commandments may be brought into harmony with the zeal of the saints.'

56. This was the advice he gave to those who came to him. And with those who suffered he sympathised and prayed. And oft-times the Lord heard him on behalf of many: yet he boasted not because he was heard, nor did he murmur if he were not. But always he gave the Lord thanks and besought the sufferer to be patient, and to know that healing belonged neither to him nor to man at all, but only to the Lord, who doeth good when and to whom He will. The sufferers therefore used to receive the words of the old man as though they were a cure, learning not to be downhearted but rather to be long-suffering. And those who were healed were taught not to give thanks to Antony but to God alone.

64. And another, a person of rank, came to him, possessed by a demon; and the demon was so terrible that the man possessed did not know that he was coming to Antony. But he even ate the excreta from his body. So those who brought him besought Antony to pray for him. And Antony pitying the young man prayed and kept watch with him all the night. And about dawn the young man suddenly attacked Antony and gave him a push. But when those who came with him were angry, Antony said, "Be not angry with the young man, for it is not he, but the demon which is in him. And being rebuked and commanded to go into dry places, the demon became raging mad, and he has done this. Wherefore give thanks to the Lord, for his attack on me thus is a sign of the departure of the evil spirit." When Antony had said this, straightway the young man had become whole, and having come at last to his right mind, knew where he was, and saluted the old man and gave thanks to God....

72. And Antony also was exceeding prudent, and the wonder was that although he had not learned letters, he was a ready-witted and sagacious man. At all events two Greek philosophers once came, thinking they could try their skill on Antony; and he was in the outer mountain, and having recognised who they were from their appearance, he came to them and said to them by means of an interpreter, "Why, philosophers, did ye trouble yourselves so much to come to a foolish man?" And when they said that he was not a foolish man, but exceedingly prudent, he said to them, "If you came to a foolish man, your labour is superfluous; but if you think me prudent become as I am, for we ought to imitate what is good. And if I had come to you I should have imitated you; but if you to me, become as I am, for I am a Christian." But they departed with wonder, for they saw that even demons feared Antony.

73. And again others such as these met him in the outer mountain and thought to mock him because he had not learned letters. And Antony said to them, "What say ye, which is first? mind or letters? And which is the cause of which—mind of letters or letters of mind?" And when they answered mind is first and the inventor of letters, Antony said, "Whoever, therefore, hath a sound mind hath not need of letters." This answer amazed both the bystanders and the philosophers, and they departed marvelling that they had seen so much understanding in an ignorant man. For his manners were not rough as though he had been reared in the mountains and there grown old, but graceful and polite, and his speech was seasoned with the divine salt, so that no one was envious, but rather all rejoiced over him who visited him....

End of Antony's Earthly Life

91. ... Having summoned those who were there—they were two in number who had remained in the mountain fifteen years, practising the discipline and attending on Antony on account of his age—he said to them, "I, as it is written, go the way of the fathers, for I perceive that I am called by the Lord. And do you be watchful and destroy not your long discipline, but as though now making a beginning, zealously preserve your determination. For ye know the treachery of the demons, how fierce they are, but how little power they have. Wherefore fear them not, but rather ever breathe Christ, and trust Him. Live as though dying daily...."

92. Having said this, when they had kissed him, he lifted up his feet, and as though he saw friends coming to him and was glad because of them—for as he lay his countenance appeared joyful—he died and was gathered to the fathers. And they afterward, according to his commandment, wrapped him up and buried him, hiding his body underground. And no one knows to this day where it was buried, save those two only. But each of those who received the sheepskin of the blessed Antony and the garment worn by him guards it as a precious treasure. For even to look on them is as it were to behold Antony; and he who is clothed in them seems with joy to bear his admonitions.

93. This is the end of Antony's life in the body and the above was the beginning of the discipline. Even if this account is small compared with his merit, still from this reflect how great Antony, the man of God, was. Who from his youth to so great an age preserved a uniform zeal for the discipline, and neither through old age was subdued by the desire of costly food, nor through the infirmity of his body changed the fashion of his clothing, nor washed even his feet with water, and yet remained entirely free from harm. For his eyes were undimmed and quite sound and he saw clearly; of his teeth he had not lost one, but they had become worn to the gums through the great age of the old man. He remained strong both in hands and feet; and while all men were using various foods, and washings and divers garments, he appeared more cheerful and of greater strength. And the fact that his fame has been blazoned everywhere; that all regard him with wonder, and that those who have never seen him long for him, is clear proof of his virtue and God's love of his soul. For not from writings, nor from worldly wisdom, nor through any art, was Antony renowned, but solely from his piety towards God. That this was the gift of God no one will deny. For from whence into Spain and into Gaul, how into Rome and Africa, was the man heard of who abode hidden in a mountain, unless it was God who maketh His own known everywhere, who also promised this to Antony at the beginning? For even if they work secretly, even if they wish to remain in obscurity, yet the Lord shows them as lamps to lighten all, that those who hear may thus know that the precepts of God are able to make men prosper and thus be zealous in the path of virtue.

94. Read these words, therefore, to the rest of the brethren that they may learn what the life of monks ought to be; and may believe that our Lord and Saviour Jesus Christ glorifies those who glorify Him: and leads those who serve Him unto the end, not only to the kingdom of heaven, but here also—even

though they hide themselves and are desirous of withdrawing from the world—
makes them illustrious and well known everywhere on account of their virtue
and the help they render others. And if need be, read this among the heathen,
that even in this way they may learn that our Lord Jesus Christ is not only God
and the Son of God, but also that the Christians who truly serve Him and reli-
giously believe on Him, prove, not only that the demons, whom the Greeks
themselves think to be gods, are no gods, but also tread them under foot and
put them to flight, as deceivers and corrupters of mankind, through Jesus Christ
our Lord, to whom be glory for ever and ever. Amen.

82 John Chrysostom, *On the Priesthood*

Ascetic as Bishop

"… the exceeding sanctity of this office…"

This most famous of early Christian preachers was nicknamed the Golden
Mouth (*chrysostomos*) on account of the power of his sermons. Originally a
Christian ascetic, John Chrysostom was appointed to the priesthood in Antioch in Syria where he preached and exercised pastoral care. Later, and much
against his own personal will, he was elevated to the see of Constantinople in
A.D. 398. During his time in Antioch as a priest, he wrote *On the Priesthood*, a
treatise on the challenges and responsibilities that Christians faced when they
were called to the priesthood. He used this to text to highlight the wear and
tear that the demands of the office—as both spiritual advisor and church
administrator, among other roles—imposed on its holder. Always open to
accusations and to temptations stemming from vainglory and the wealth that
comes under his control, a Christian priest must exercise self-control in order
to navigate the straight and narrow path of virtue. John would come to experience the pressures of holding high ecclesiastical office most acutely during
his tenure as archbishop. In Constantinople, he became embroiled in high-
level imperial and ecclesiastical intrigue, was condemned by a council convened by his rival Bishop Theophilus of Alexandria in 403, and died while en
route to his place of exile.

Christian Priesthood as a Holy Office

III, 4. For the priestly office is indeed discharged on earth, but it ranks
amongst heavenly ordinances; and very naturally so: for neither man, nor angel,
nor archangel, nor any other created power, but the Paraclete [Holy Spirit]

From John Chrysostom, *On the Priesthood* 3.4–6, 10–17; in *Nicene and Post-Nicene Fathers of the Christian Church*, series I, Vol. IX, edited by Philip Schaff (Grand Rapids, Mich.: Eerdmans, 1980–83), pp. 46–59.

Himself, instituted this vocation, and persuaded men while still abiding in the flesh to represent the ministry of angels. Wherefore the consecrated priest ought to be as pure as if he were standing in the heavens themselves in the midst of those powers. Fearful, indeed, and of most awful import, were the things which were used before the dispensation of grace, as the bells, the pomegranates, the stones on the breastplate and on the ephod, the girdle, the mitre, the long robe, the plate of gold, the holy of holies, the deep silence within. But if any one should examine the things which belong to the dispensation of grace, he will find that, small as they are, yet are they fearful and full of awe, and that what was spoken concerning the law is true in this case also, that "what has been made glorious hath no glory in this respect by reason of the glory which excelleth." For when thou seest the Lord sacrificed, and laid upon the altar, and the priest standing and praying over the victim, and all the worshippers empurpled with that precious blood, canst thou then think that thou art still amongst men, and standing upon the earth? Art thou not, on the contrary, straightway translated to Heaven, and casting out every carnal thought from the soul, dost thou not with disembodied spirit and pure reason contemplate the things which are in Heaven? Oh! what a marvel! what love of God to man! He who sitteth on high with the Father is at that hour held in the hands of all, and gives Himself to those who are willing to embrace and grasp Him. And this all do through the eyes of faith! Do these things seem to you fit to be despised, or such as to make it possible for any one to be uplifted against them?

Would you also learn from another miracle the exceeding sanctity of this office? Picture Elijah and the vast multitude standing around him, and the sacrifice laid upon the altar of stones, and all the rest of the people hushed into a deep silence while the prophet alone offers up prayer: then the sudden rush of fire from Heaven upon the sacrifice:—these are marvellous things, charged with terror. Now then pass from this scene to the rites which are celebrated in the present day; they are not only marvellous to behold, but transcendent in terror. There stands the priest, not bringing down fire from Heaven, but the Holy Spirit: and he makes prolonged supplication, not that some flame sent down from on high may consume the offerings, but that grace descending on the sacrifice may thereby enlighten the souls of all, and render them more refulgent than silver purified by fire. Who can despise this most awful mystery, unless he is stark mad and senseless? Or do you not know that no human soul could have endured that fire in the sacrifice, but all would have been utterly consumed, had not the assistance of God's grace been great.

Priests and Christian Sacraments

5. For if any one will consider how great a thing it is for one, being a man, and compassed with flesh and blood, to be enabled to draw nigh to that blessed and pure nature, he will then clearly see what great honor the grace of the Spirit has vouchsafed to priests; since by their agency these rites are celebrated, and others nowise inferior to these both in respect of our dignity and our salvation. For they who inhabit the earth and make their abode there are entrusted with

the administration of things which are in Heaven, and have received an authority which God has not given to angels or archangels. For it has not been said to them, "Whatsoever ye shall bind on earth shall be bound in Heaven, and what-soever ye shall loose on earth shall be loosed in Heaven." They who rule on earth have indeed authority to bind, but only the body: whereas this binding lays hold of the soul and penetrates the heavens; and what priests do here below God ratifies above, and the Master confirms the sentence of his servants. For indeed what is it but all manner of heavenly authority which He has given them when He says, "Whose sins ye remit they are remitted, and whose sins ye retain they are retained?" What authority could be greater than this? "The Father hath committed all judgment to the Son?" But I see it all put into the hands of these men by the Son. For they have been conducted to this dignity as if they were already translated to Heaven, and had transcended human nature, and were released from the passions to which we are liable. Moreover, if a king should bestow this honor upon any of his subjects, authorizing him to cast into prison whom he pleased and to release them again, he becomes an object of envy and respect to all men; but he who has received from God an authority as much greater as heaven is more precious than earth, and souls more precious than bodies, seems to some to have received so small an honor that they are actually able to imagine that one of those who have been entrusted with these things will despise the gift. Away with such madness! For transparent madness it is to despise so great a dignity, without which it is not possible to obtain either our own salvation, or the good things which have been promised to us. For if no one can enter into the kingdom of Heaven except he be regenerate through water and the Spirit, and he who does not eat the flesh of the Lord and drink His blood is excluded from eternal life, and if all these things are accomplished only by means of those holy hands, I mean the hands of the priest, how will any one, without these, be able to escape the fire of hell, or to win those crowns which are reserved for the victorious?

6. These verily are they who are entrusted with the pangs of spiritual travail and the birth which comes through baptism: by their means we put on Christ, and are buried with the Son of God, and become members of that blessed Head. Wherefore they might not only be more justly feared by us than rulers and kings, but also be more honored than parents; since these begat us of blood and the will of the flesh, but the others are the authors of our birth from God, even that blessed regeneration which is the true freedom and the sonship accord-ing to grace. The Jewish priests had authority to release the body from leprosy, or, rather, not to release it but only to examine those who were already released, and you know how much the office of priest was contended for at that time. But our priests have received authority to deal, not with bodily leprosy, but spiritual uncleanness—not to pronounce it removed after examination, but actually and absolutely to take it away....

Temptations and Challenges Facing Christian Priests

10. And let not any one suppose that I subject all to the aforesaid charges: for there are some, yea many, who are superior to these entanglements, and

exceed in number those who have been caught by them. Nor would I indeed make the priesthood responsible for these evils: far be such madness from me. For men of understanding do not say that the sword is to blame for murder, nor wine for drunkenness, nor strength for outrage, nor courage for foolhardiness, but they lay the blame on those who make an improper use of the gifts which have been bestowed upon them by God, and punish them accordingly. Certainly, at least, the priesthood may justly accuse us if we do not rightly handle it. For it is not itself a cause of the evils already mentioned, but we, who as far as lies in our power have defiled it with so many pollutions, by entrusting it to commonplace men who readily accept what is offered them, without having first acquired a knowledge of their own souls, or considered the gravity of the office, and when they have entered on the work, being blinded by inexperience, overwhelm with innumerable evils the people who have been committed to their care. This is the very thing which was very nearly happening in my case, had not God speedily delivered me from those dangers, mercifully sparing his Church and my own soul. For, tell me, whence do you think such great troubles are generated in the Churches? I, for my part, believe the only source of them to be the inconsiderate and random way in which prelates [bishops] are chosen and appointed. For the head ought to be the strongest part, that it may be able to regulate and control the evil exhalations which arise from the rest of the body below; but when it happens to be weak in itself, and unable to repel those pestiferous attacks, it becomes feebler itself than it really is, and ruins the rest of the body as well. And to prevent this now coming to pass, God kept me in the position of the feet, which was the rank originally assigned to me. For there are very many other qualities, Basil, besides those already mentioned, which the priest ought to have, but which I do not possess; and, above all, this one:—his soul ought to be thoroughly purged from any lust after the office: for if he happens to have a natural inclination for this dignity, as soon as he attains it a stronger flame is kindled, and the man being taken completely captive will endure innumerable evils in order to keep a secure hold upon it, even to the extent of using flattery, or submitting to something base and ignoble, or expending large sums of money. For I will not now speak of the murders with which some have filled the Churches, or the desolation which they have brought upon cities in contending for the dignity, lest some persons should think what I say incredible. But I am of opinion one ought to exercise so much caution in the matter, as to shun the burden of the office, and when one has entered upon it, not to wait for the judgment of others should any fault be committed which warrants deposition, but to anticipate it by ejecting oneself from the dignity; for thus one might probably win mercy for himself from God: but to cling to it in defiance of propriety is to deprive oneself of all forgiveness, or rather to kindle the wrath of God, by adding a second error more offensive than the first.

11. But no one will always endure the strain; for fearful, truly fearful is the eager desire after this honor. And in saying this I am not in opposition to the blessed Paul, but in complete harmony with his words. For what says he? "If any man desireth the office of a bishop, he desireth a good work." Now I have not said that it is a terrible thing to desire the *work*, but only the authority and

power. And this desire I think one ought to expel from the soul with all possible earnestness, not permitting it at the outset to be possessed by such a feeling, so that one may be able to do everything with freedom. For he who does not desire to be exhibited in possession of this authority, does not fear to be deposed from it, and not fearing this will be able to do everything with the freedom which becomes Christian men: whereas they who fear and tremble lest they should be deposed undergo a bitter servitude, filled with all kinds of evils, and are often compelled to offend against both God and man. Now the soul ought not to be affected in this way; but as in warfare we see those soldiers who are noble spirited fight willingly and fall bravely, so they who have attained to this stewardship should be contented to be consecrated to the dignity or removed from it, as becomes Christian men, knowing that deposition of this kind brings its reward no less than the discharge of the office. For when any one suffers anything of this kind, in order to avoid submitting to something which is unbecoming or unworthy of this dignity, he procures punishment for those who wrongfully depose him, and a greater reward for himself. "Blessed," says our Lord, "are ye when men shall revile you and persecute you, and shall say all manner of evil against you falsely for my sake; rejoice and be exceeding glad, for great is your reward in Heaven." And this, indeed, is the case when any one is expelled by those of his own rank either on account of envy, with a view to the favor of others, or through hatred, or from any other wrong motive: but when it is the lot of any one to experience this treatment at the hand of opponents, I do not think a word is needed to prove what great gain they confer upon him by their wickedness.

It behoves us, then, to be on the watch on all sides, and to make a careful search lest any spark of this desire should be secretly smouldering somewhere. For it is much to be wished that those who are originally free from this passion, should also be able to avoid it when they have lighted upon this office. But if any one, before he obtains the honor, cherishes in himself this terrible and savage monster, it is impossible to say into what a furnace he will fling himself after he has attained it. Now I possessed this desire in a high degree (and do not suppose that I would ever tell you what was untrue in self-disparagement): and this, combined with other reasons, alarmed me not a little, and induced me to take flight. For just as lovers of the human person, as long as they are permitted to be near the objects of their affection, suffer more severe torment from their passion, but when they remove as far as possible from these objects of desire, they drive away the frenzy: even so when those who desire this dignity are near it, the evil becomes intolerable: but when they cease to hope for it, the desire is extinguished together with the expectation.

12. This single motive then is no slight one: and even taken by itself it would have sufficed to deter me from this dignity: but, as it is, another must be added not less than the former. And what is this? A priest ought to be sober minded, and penetrating in discernment, and possessed of innumerable eyes in every direction, as one who lives not for himself alone but for so great a multitude. But that I am sluggish and slack, and scarcely able to bring about my own salvation, even you yourself would admit, who out of love to me art especially

eager to conceal my faults. Talk not to me in this connexion of fasting, and watching, or sleeping on the ground, and other hard discipline of the body: for you know how defective I am in these matters: and even if they had been carefully practised by me they could not with my present sluggishness have been of any service to me with a view to this post of authority. Such things might be of great service to a man who was shut up in a cell, and caring only for his own concerns: but when a man is divided among so great a multitude, and enters separately into the private cares of those who are under his direction, what appreciable help can be given to their improvement unless he possesses a robust and exceedingly vigorous character?

Qualifications for Christian Priesthood

13. And do not be surprised if, in connexion with such endurance, I seek another test of fortitude in the soul. For to be indifferent to food and drink and a soft bed, we see is to many no hard task, especially at least to such as are of a rough habit of life and have been brought up in this way from early youth, and to many others also; bodily discipline and custom softening the severity of these laborious practices: but insult, and abuse, and coarse language, and gibes from inferiors, whether wantonly or justly uttered, and rebukes vainly and idly spoken both by rulers and the ruled—this is what few can bear, in fact only one or two here and there; and one may see men, who are strong in the former exercises, so completely upset by these things, as to become more furious than the most savage beasts. Now such men especially we should exclude from the precincts of the priesthood. For if a prelate did not loathe food, or go barefoot, no harm would be done to the common interests of the Church; but a furious temper causes great disasters both to him who possesses it, and to his neighbours. And there is no divine threat against those who fail to do the things referred to, but hell and hell-fire are threatened against those who are angry without a cause. As then the lover of vainglory, when he takes upon him the government of numbers, supplies additional fuel to the fire, so he who by himself, or in the company of a few, is unable to control his anger, but readily carried away by it, should he be entrusted with the direction of a whole multitude, like some wild beast goaded on all sides by countless tormentors, would never be able to live in tranquillity himself, and would cause incalculable mischief to those who have been committed to his charge....

The souls therefore of men elected to the priesthood ought to be endued with such power as the grace of God bestowed on the bodies of those saints who were cast into the Babylonian furnace. Faggot and pitch and tow are not the fuel of this fire, but things far more dreadful: for it is no material fire to which they are subjected, but the all-devouring flame of envy encompasses them, rising up on every side, and assailing them, and putting their life to a more searching test than the fire then was to the bodies of those young men. When then it finds a little trace of stubble, it speedily fastens upon it; and this unsound part it entirely consumes, but all the rest of the fabric, even if it be brighter than the sunbeams, is scorched and blackened by the smoke. For as long as the life of the priest is well regulated in every direction, it is invulnerable to plots; but if he happens to overlook some trifle, as is natural in a human being, traversing the treacherous ocean of this life, none of his other good deeds are of any avail in enabling him to escape the mouths of his accusers; but that little blunder overshadows all the rest. And all men are ready to pass judgment on the priest as if he was not a being clothed with flesh, or one who inherited a human nature, but like an angel, and emancipated from every species of infirmity. And just as all men fear and flatter a tyrant as long as he is strong, because they cannot put him down, but when they see his affairs going adversely, those who were his friends a short time before abandon their hypocritical respect, and suddenly become his enemies and antagonists, and having discovered all his weak points, make an attack upon him, and depose him from the government; so is it also in the case of priests. Those who honored him and paid court to him a short time before, while he was strong, as soon as they have found some little handle eagerly prepare to depose him, not as a tyrant only, but something far more dreadful than that. And as the tyrant fears his body guards, so also does the priest dread most of all his neighbours and fellow-ministers. For no others covet his dignity so much, or know his affairs so well as these; and if anything occurs, being near at hand, they perceive it before others, and even if they slander him, can easily command belief, and, by magnifying trifles, take their victim captive. For the apostolic saying is reversed, "whether one member suffer, all the members suffer with it; or one member be honored, all the members rejoice with it;" unless indeed a man should be able by his great discretion to stand his ground against everything....

Priests and Charitable Works

Now in the first place, to start from that subject which seems to be simpler than the others, the charge of widows appears to cause anxiety to those who take care of them only so far as the expenditure of money is concerned; but the case is otherwise, and here also a careful scrutiny is needed, when they have to be enrolled, for infinite mischief has been caused by putting them on the list without due discrimination. For they have ruined households, and severed marriages, and have often been detected in thieving and pilfering and unseemly deeds of that kind.... [S]trict and accurate scrutiny ought to be made so as to prevent the supply of the indigent being wasted, not only by the women already mentioned, but also by those who are able to provide for themselves. And this scrutiny is succeeded by no small anxiety of another kind, to ensure an abundant and unfailing stream of supply as from a fountain; for compulsory poverty is an insatiable kind of evil, querulous and ungrateful....

But the superintendent of these persons ought not only to be gentle and forbearing, but also skillful in the management of property; for if this qualification is wanting, the affairs of the poor are again involved in the same distress. One who was entrusted not long ago with this ministry, and got together a large hoard of money, neither consumed it himself, nor expended it with a few exceptions upon those who needed it, but kept the greater part of it buried in the earth until a season of distress occurred, when it was all surrendered into the hands of the enemy. Much forethought, therefore, is needed, that the resources of the Church should be neither over abundant, nor deficient, but that all the supplies which are provided should be quickly distributed among those who require them, and the treasures of the Church stored up in the hearts of those who are under her rule.

Moreover, in the reception of strangers, and the care of the sick, consider how great an expenditure of money is needed, and how much exactness and discernment on the part of those who preside over these matters. For it is often necessary that this expenditure should be even larger than that of which I spoke just now, and that he who presides over it should combine prudence and wisdom with skill in the art of supply, so as to dispose the affluent to be emulous and ungrudging in their gifts, lest while providing for the relief of the sick, he should vex the souls of those who supply their wants. But earnestness and zeal need to be displayed here in a far higher degree; for the sick are difficult creatures to please, and prone to languor; and unless great accuracy and care are used, even a slight oversight is enough to do the patient great mischief.

17. But in the care of virgins, the fear is greater in proportion as the possession is more precious, and this flock is of a nobler character than the others. Already, indeed, even into the band of these holy ones, an infinite number of women have rushed full of innumerable bad qualities; and in this case our grief is greater than in the other; for there is just the same difference between a virgin and a widow going astray, as between a free-born damsel and her handmaid. With widows, indeed, it has become a common practice to trifle, and to rail at one another, to flatter or to be impudent, to appear everywhere in public, and to perambulate the marketplace. But the virgin has striven for nobler aims, and eagerly sought the highest kind of philosophy, and professes to exhibit upon earth the life which angels lead, and while yet in the flesh proposes to do deeds which belong to the incorporeal powers. Moreover, she ought not to make numerous or unnecessary journeys, neither is it permissible for her to utter idle and random words; and as for abuse and flattery, she should not even know them by name. On this account she needs the most careful guardianship, and the greater assistance. For the enemy of holiness is always surprising and lying in wait for these persons, ready to devour any one of them if she should slip and fall; many men also there are who lay snares for them; and besides all these things there is the passionateness of their own human nature, so that, speaking generally, the virgin has to equip herself for a twofold war, one which attacks her from without, and the other which presses upon her from within....

Bishops as Judges

Again, the judicial department of the bishop's office involves innumerable vexations, great consumption of time, and difficulties exceeding those experienced by men who sit to judge secular affairs; for it is a labor to discover exact justice, and when it is found, it is difficult to avoid destroying it. And not only loss of time and difficulty are incurred, but also no small danger. For ere now, some of the weaker brethren having plunged into business, because they have not obtained patronage have made shipwreck concerning the faith. For many of those who have suffered wrong, no less than those who have inflicted wrong, hate those who do not assist them, and they will not take into account either the intricacy of the matters in question, or the difficulty of the times, or the limits of sacerdotal authority, or anything of that kind; but they are merciless judges, recognizing only one kind of defence—release from the evils which oppress them. And he who is unable to furnish this, although he may allege innumerable excuses, will never escape their condemnation....

And how can one speak of the distress which bishops undergo, whenever it is necessary to cut some one off from the full communion of the Church? Would indeed that the evil went no further than distress! but in fact the mischief is not trifling. For there is a fear lest the man, if he has been punished beyond what he deserves, should experience that which was spoken of by the blessed Paul and "be swallowed up by overmuch sorrow." The nicest accuracy, therefore, is required in this matter also, lest what is intended to be profitable should become to him an occasion of greater damage. For whatever sins he may commit after such a method of treatment, the wrath caused by each of them must be shared by the physician who so unskillfully applied his knife to the wound. What severe punishment, then, must be expected by one who has not only to render an account of the offences which he himself has separately committed, but also incurs extreme danger on account of the sins committed by others? For if we shudder at undergoing judgment for our own misdeeds, believing that we shall not be able to escape the fire of the other world, what must one expect to suffer who has to answer for so many others? To prove the truth of this, listen to the blessed Paul, or rather not to him, but to Christ speaking in him, when he says: "Obey them that have the rule over you, and submit, for they watch for your souls as they that shall give account."

83 The *Theodosian Code*

Legislating a Christian Roman Empire

"Superstition shall cease...."

The transformation of an ancient polytheistic society to a Christian one was bound to be a long and arduous process. Following Constantine's conversion to Christianity in A.D. 312, all but one of the succeeding emperors were

Clyde Pharr, *The Theodosian Code and Novels and the Sirmondian Constitution* (Princeton, New Jersey: Princeton University Press, 1952). Copyright © 1952 by Princeton University Press. Reprinted by permission of Princeton University Press.

Christian. Large segments of the population also began to convert. These individual conversions took place alongside a slow remolding of the institutions of the Roman state. By the end of the fourth century A.D., the alliance between the church and the state had been consolidated to such an extent that one may begin to speak of a Christian Roman Empire. While few ancient societies, if any, observed the principle of the separation of church and state, this Christian empire featured the rare cooperation between the state and the institutions of a monotheistic religion, which by definition saw all other religions as erroneous. In this empire, non-Christians were prodded to convert to Christianity and those who persisted in their errors were subject to legal penalties. In addition, the state sought to distinguish between the "right" sort of Christians (the "orthodox") and the "wrong" sort of Christians and practiced a policy of discrimination, or one might even say persecution, against the latter. The rise of the Christian empire thereby heralded a decisive change in the nature of classical political society: religious affiliation was becoming just as important as citizenship for determining one's status.

Like Rome itself, this Christian empire was not made in a day. The public stance adopted by the state evolved over many decades and in response to specific contingencies. Over the years, the emperors were asked to rule in religious matters, their right to do so being widely recognized by all Christians since the time of Constantine. Several of these laws have been preserved in subsequent law codes. In A.D. 429, Emperor Theodosius II commissioned a panel to collect the laws from the preceding century and a half and put them in an authoritative collection that was later published as the *Theodosian Code*. The following laws, which regulate religious life in the Roman Empire, have been culled from this collection.

Book XVI

Title 1: The Catholic Faith

2. Emperors Gratian, Valentinian, and Theodosius Augustuses: An Edict to the People of the City of Constantinople.

February 28, 380.

It is Our will that all the peoples who are ruled by the administration of Our Clemency shall practice that religion which the divine Peter the Apostle transmitted to the Romans, as the religion which he introduced makes clear even unto this day. It is evident that this is the religion that is followed by the Pontiff Damasus and by Peter, Bishop of Alexandria, a man of apostolic sanctity; that is, according to the apostolic discipline and the evangelic doctrine, we shall believe in the single Deity of the Father, the Son, and the Holy Spirit, under the concept of equal majesty and of the Holy Trinity.

1. We command that those persons who follow this rule shall embrace the name of Catholic Christians. The rest, however, whom We adjudge demented and insane, shall sustain the infamy of heretical dogmas, their meeting places shall not receive the name of churches, and they shall be smitten first by divine vengeance and secondly by the retribution of Our own initiative, which We shall assume in accordance with the divine judgment.

3. The same Augustuses to Auxonius, Proconsul of Asia.

July 30, 381.

We command that all churches shall immediately be surrendered to those bishops who confess that the Father, the Son, and the Holy Spirit are of one majesty and virtue, of the same glory, and of one splendor; to those bishops who produce no dissonance by unholy distinction, but who affirm the concept of the Trinity by the assertion of three Persons and the unity of the Divinity; to those bishops who appear to have been associated in the communion of Nectarius, Bishop of the Church of Constantinople, and of Timotheus, Bishop of the City of Alexandria in Egypt; to those bishops also who, in the regions of the Orient, appear to be communicants with Pelagius, Bishop of Laodicea, and with Diodorus, Bishop of Tarsus; also, in the Proconsular Province of Asia and in the Diocese of Asia, with Amphilochius, Bishop of Iconium, and with Optimus, Bishop of Antioch; in the Diocese of Pontus, with Helladius, Bishop of Caesarea, and with Otreius of Melitene, and with Gregorius, Bishop of Nyssa; with Terennius, Bishop of Scythia, and with Marmarius, Bishop of Martianopolis. Those bishops who are of the communion and fellowship of such acceptable priests must be permitted to obtain the Catholic churches. All, however, who dissent from the communion of the faith of those who have been expressly mentioned in this special enumeration shall be expelled from their churches as manifest heretics and hereafter shall be altogether denied the right and power to obtain churches, in order that the priesthood of the true Nicene faith my remain pure, and after the clear regulations of Our law, there shall be no opportunity for malicious subtlety....

Title 2: [The Privileges of the Clergy]

2. [Emperor Constantine] Augustus to Octavianus, Governor of Lucania and of Bruttium.

October 21, 319.

Those persons who devote the services of religion to divine worship, that is, those who are called clerics, shall be exempt from all compulsory public services whatever, lest, through the sacrilegious malice of certain persons, they should be called away from divine services....

INTERPRETATION: This law by special ordinance directs that no person whatsoever by sacrilegious ordinance shall presume to make tax collectors or tax gatherers of clerics. The law commands that such clerics shall be free from every compulsory public service, that is, from every duty and servitude, and shall zealously serve the Church....

4. The same Augustus to the People [of Rome].

July 3, 321.

Every person shall have the liberty to leave at his death any property that he wishes to the most holy and venerable of the Catholic Church. Wills shall not become void. There is nothing which is more due to men than that the expression of their last will, after which they can no longer will anything, shall be free and the power of choice, which does not return again, shall be unhampered....

12. Emperors Constantius and Constans Augustuses to their dear friend Severus, Greetings.

October 7, 355.

By a law of Our Clemency We prohibit bishops to be accused in the courts, lest there should be an unrestrained opportunity for fanatical spirits to accuse them, while the accusers assume that they will obtain impunity by the kindness of the bishops. Therefore, if any person should lodge any complaint, such complaint must unquestionably be examined before other bishops, in order that an opportune and suitable hearing may be arranged for the investigation of all concerned.

INTERPRETATION: It is specifically prohibited that any person should dare to accuse a bishop before secular judges, but he shall not delay to submit to the hearing of bishops whatever he supposes may be due him according to the nature of the case, so that the assertions which he makes against the bishop may be decided in a court of other bishops....

14. The same Augustus and Julian Caesar to Bishop Felix.

December 28, 357(?)

Clerics shall be protected from every injustice of an undue suit and from every wrong of an unjust exaction, and they shall not be summoned to compulsory public services of a menial nature. Moreover, when tradesmen are summoned to some legally prescribed tax payment, all clerics shall cease to be affected by such a disturbance; for if they have accumulated anything by thrift, foresight, or trading, but still in accordance with honesty, this must be administered for the use of the poor and needy, and whatever they have been able to acquire and collect from their workshops and stalls they shall regard as having been collected for the profit of religion.

1. Moreover, with respect to their men who are employed in trade, the statutes of the sainted Emperor, that is, of Our father, provided with manifold regulations that the aforesaid clerics should abound in numerous privileges. 2. Therefore, with respect to the aforesaid clerics, the requirement of extraordinary services and all molestation shall cease. 3. Moreover, they and their resources and substance shall not be summoned to furnish supplementary postwagons.

4. All clerics shall be assisted by the prerogative of this nature, namely, that wives of clerics and also their children and attendants, males and females equally, and their children, shall continue to be exempt forever from tax payments and free from such compulsory public services....

Title 5: [On] Heretics

1. Emperor Constantine Augustus to Dracilianus.

September 1, 326.

The privileges that have been granted in consideration of religion must benefit only the adherents of the Catholic faith. It is Our will, moreover, that heretics and schismatics shall not only be alien from these privileges but shall also be bound and subjected to various compulsory public services....

4. Emperors Valens, Gratian, and Valentinian Augustuses to Hesperius, Practorian Prefect.

April 22, 376(?)

Previously, in behalf of the religion of Catholic sanctity, in order that the illicit practice of heretical assembly should cease, We commanded that all places should be confiscated in which their altars were located under the false guise of religion, whether such assemblies were held in towns or in the country outside the churches where Our peace prevails. If such forbidden practice should occur, either through the connivance of the judges or through the dishonesty of the profane, the same destruction shall ensue in either case....

5. Emperors Gratian, Valentinian, and Theodosius Augustuses to Hesperius, Praetorian Prefect.

August 20, 379.

All heresies are forbidden by both divine and imperial laws and shall forever cease. If my profane man by his punishable teachings should weaken the concept of God, he shall have the right to know such noxious doctrines only for himself but shall not reveal them to others to their hurt. If any person by a renewed death should corrupt bodies that have been redeemed by the venerable baptismal font, by taking away the effect of that ceremony which he repeats, he shall know such doctrines for himself alone, and he shall not ruin others by his nefarious teaching. All teachers and ministers alike of this perverse superstition shall abstain from the gathering places of a doctrine already condemned, whether they defame the name of bishop by the assumption of such priestly office, or, that which is almost the same, they belie religion with the appellation of priests, or also if they call themselves deacons, though they may not even be considered Christians....

6. The same Augustuses to Eutropius, Praetorian Prefect.

January 10, 381.

No place for celebrating their mysteries, no opportunity for exercising the madness of their excessively obstinate minds shall be available to the heretics. All men shall know also that even if some concession has been impetrated by that kind of men through any special rescript whatever, if it has been fraudulently elicited, it shall not be valid.

1. Crowds shall be kept away from the unlawful congregations of all the heretics. The name of the One and Supreme God shall be celebrated everywhere; the observance, destined to remain forever, of the Nicene faith, as transmitted long ago by Our ancestors and confirmed by the declaration and testimony of divine religion, shall be maintained. The contamination of the Photinian pestilence, the poison of the Arian sacrilege, the crime of the Eunomian perfidy, and the sectarian monstrosities, abominable because of the ill-omened names of their authors, shall be abolished even from the hearing of men.

2. On the other hand, that man shall be accepted as a defender of the Nicene faith and as a true adherent of the Catholic religion who confesses that Almighty God and Christ the Son of God are One in name, God of God, Light of Light, who does not violate by denial the Holy Spirit which we hope for and receive

from the Supreme Author of things; that man who esteems, with the perception of inviolate faith, the undivided substance of the incorrupt Trinity, that substance which those of the orthodox faith call, employing a Greek word, *ousia*. The latter beliefs are surely more acceptable to Us and must be venerated.

3. Those persons, however, who are not devoted to the aforesaid doctrines shall cease to assume, with studied deceit, the alien name of true religion, and they shall be branded upon the disclosure of their crimes. They shall be removed and completely barred from the threshold of all churches, since We forbid all heretics to hold unlawful assemblies within the towns. If factions should attempt to do anything, We order that their madness shall be banished and that they shall be driven away from the very walls of the cities, in order that Catholic churches throughout the whole world may be restored to all orthodox bishops who hold the Nicene faith....

Title 10: [On] Pagans, Sacrifices, and Temples

.... 2. Emperor Constantius Augustus to Madalianus, Vice praetorian Prefect.

341

Superstition shall cease; the madness of sacrifices shall be abolished. For if any man in violation of the law of the sainted Emperor, Our father, and in violation of this command of Our Clemency, should dare to perform sacrifices, he shall suffer the infliction of a suitable punishment and the effect of an immediate sentence....

3. The same Augustuses to Catullinus, Prefect of the City.

November 1, 346.

Although all superstitions must be completely eradicated, nevertheless, it is Our will that the buildings of the temples situated outside the walls shall remain untouched and uninjured. For since certain plays or spectacles of the circus or contests derive their origin from some of these temples, such structures shall not be torn down, since from them is provided the regular performance of long established amusements for the Roman people....

4. The same Augustuses to Taurus, Praetorian Prefect.

December 1, 346.

It is Our pleasure that the temples shall be immediately closed in all places and in all cities, and access to them forbidden, so as to deny to all abandoned men the opportunity to commit sin. It is also Our will that all men shall abstain from sacrifices. But if perchance any man should perpetrate any such criminality, he shall be struck down with the avenging sword. We also decree that the property of a man thus executed shall be vindicated to the fisc. The governors of the provinces shall be similarly punished if they should neglect to avenge such crimes....

11. The same Augustuses to Evagrius, Augustal Prefect, and Romanus, Count of Egypt.

June 16, 391.

No person shall be granted the right to perform sacrifices; no person shall go around the temples; no person shall revere the shrines. All persons shall recognize that they are excluded from profane entrance into temples by the opposition of Our law, so that if any person should attempt to do anything with reference to the gods or the sacred rites, contrary to Our prohibition, he shall learn that he will not be exempted from punishment by any special grants of imperial favor. If any judge also, during the time of his administration, should rely on the privilege of his power, and as a sacrilegious violator of the law, should enter polluted places, he shall be forced to pay into Our treasury fifteen pounds of gold, and his office staff a like sum, unless they opposed him with their combined strength....

12. Emperors Theodosius, Arcadius, and Honorius Augustuses to Rufinus, Praetorian Prefect.

November 8, 392.

No person at all, of any class or order whatsoever of men or of dignities, whether he occupies a position of power or has completed such honors, whether he is powerful by the lot of birth or is humble in lineage, legal status and fortune, shall sacrifice an innocent victim to senseless images in any place at all or in any city. He shall not by more secret wickedness, venerate his lar with fire, his genius with wine, his penates with fragrant odors; he shall not burn lights to them, place incense before them, or suspend wreaths for them.

1. But if any man should dare to immolate a victim for the purpose of sacrifice, or to consult the quivering entrails, according to the example of a person guilty of high treason he shall be reported by an accusation which is permitted to all persons, and he shall receive the appropriate sentence, even though he has inquired nothing contrary to, or with reference to, the welfare of the Emperors. For it is sufficient to constitute an enormous crime that any person should wish to break down the very laws of nature, to investigate forbidden matters, to disclose hidden secrets, to attempt interdicted practices, to seek to know the end of another's life, to promise the hope of another person's death.

2. But if any person should venerate, by placing incense before them, images made by the work of mortals and destined to suffer the ravages of time, and if, in a ridiculous manner, he should suddenly fear the effigies which he himself has formed, or should bind a tree with fillets, or should erect an altar of turf that he has dug up, or should attempt to honor vain images with the offering of a gift, which even though it is humble, still is a complete outrage against religion, such person, as one guilty of the violation of religion, shall be punished by the forfeiture of that house or landholding in which it is proved that he served a pagan superstition. For We decree that all places shall be annexed to Our fisc, if it is proved that they have reeked with the vapor of incense, provided, however, that such places are proved to have belonged to such incense burners.

3. But if any person should attempt to perform any such kind of sacrifice in public temples or shrines, or in the buildings or fields of others, and if it is proved that such places were usurped without the knowledge of the owner, the offender shall be compelled to pay twenty-five pounds of gold as a fine. If any person should connive at such a crime, he shall be held subject to the same penalty as that of the person who performed the sacrifice.

4. It is Our will that this regulation shall be so enforced by the judges, as well as by the defenders and decurions of the several cities, that the information

learned by the defenders and decurions shall be immediately reported to the courts, and the crimes so reported shall be punished by the judges. Moreover, if the defenders and decurions should suppose that any such crime should be concealed through favoritism or overlooked through carelessness, they shall be subjected to judicial indignation. If the judges should be advised of such crimes and should defer punishment through connivance, they shall be fined thirty pounds of gold; their office staffs also shall be subjected to an equal penalty....

14. Emperors Arcadius and Honorius Augustuses to Caesarius, Praetorian Prefect.
December 7, 396.

   If any privileges have been granted by ancient law to civil priests, ministers, prefects, or hierophants of the sacred mysteries, whether known by these names or called by any other, such privileges shall be completely abolished. Such persons shall not congratulate themselves that they are protected by any privilege, since their profession is known to be condemned by law....

New Crises and "Fall of the Roman Empire"

84 Jerome, *Letter*: Lament on Rome

"The world sinks into ruin ... "

Jerome (ca. A.D. 347–420), a key figure in the Latin-speaking church, translated the Bible from Greek into Latin in the form of the Vulgate. He was an assiduous scholar and a writer of biblical commentaries and lives of Christian ascetics. He also penned a large number of letters that address the moral questions and ascetic pursuits of his mainly elite correspondents. Jerome was particularly prominent in the city of Rome as the spiritual adviser to aristocratic Christian women who, despite their patrician lineage and superlative wealth, wanted to emulate St. Antony's life in the desert and sought to dispose of their belongings so as to live as ascetics. Amidst jealous accusations by the Roman clergy that he was having an improper sexual relationship with the widow Paula, Jerome accompanied Paula and her daughter Eustochium in their pilgrimage to the Holy Land. There, after an extensive tour of the

From Jerome, *Letter* 128.4; in *Nicene and Post-Nicene Father of the Christian Church*, series 1, Vol. VI, edited by Philip Schaff and Henry Wace (Grand Rapids, Mich.: Eerdmans, 1980–83, revised edition 1983), p. 260.

places sacred to Christians at the time, Jerome retired in 388 to Bethlehem in the company of the two female noblewomen turned ascetics and lived in that town until his death in 420. In 410, after the Goths under Alaric managed to sack Rome for ten days, news of this event reached distant Bethlehem and ruptured the peace of his solitude. Jerome inserted a description of his shocked response in a letter he was composing at the time. To him, a devout Christian, Rome still represented nothing short of the *caput mundi*, and the evil tidings were greeted as that of the end of the world itself.

The world sinks into ruin: yes! but shameful to say our sins still live and flourish. The renowned city, the capital of the Roman Empire, is swallowed up in one tremendous fire; and there is no part of the earth where Romans are not in exile. Churches once held sacred are now but heaps of dust and ashes; and yet we have our minds set on the desire of gain. We live as though we are going to die tomorrow; yet we build as though we are going to live always in this world. Our walls shine with gold, our ceilings also and the capitals of our pillars; yet Christ dies before our doors naked and hungry in the persons of His poor. The pontiff Aaron, we read, faced the raging flames, and by putting fire in his censer checked the wrath of God. The High Priest stood between the dead and the living, and the fire dared not pass his feet. On another occasion God said to Moses, "Let me alone ... that I may consume this people," shewing by the words "let me alone" that he can be withheld from doing what he threatens. The prayers of His servant hindered His power. Who, think you, is there now under heaven able to stay God's wrath, to face the flame of His judgment, and to say with the apostle, "I could wish that I myself were accursed for my brethren"? Flocks and shepherds perish together, because as it is with the people, so is it with the priest. Of old it was not so. Then Moses spoke in a passion of pity, "yet now if thou wilt forgive their sin—; and if not, blot me, I pray thee, out of thy book." He is not satisfied to secure his own salvation, he desires to perish with those that perish. And he is right, for "in the multitude of people is the king's honour."

85 Augustine, *City of God*

The Unimportance of the Earthly City

"The fire which makes gold shine makes chaff smoke...."

The decisive shift toward a Christian empire in the later fourth century coincided with several humiliating reverses that the Romans suffered in their dealings with barbarian tribes. In 378, at the battle of Adrianople, Emperor Valens

From *St. Augustine, Concerning the City of God Against the Pagans*, translated by Henry Bettenson, pp. 6–7, 14–20. Copyright © 1972 by Penguin Books. Reproduced by permission of Penguin Books, Ltd.

and his eastern army were destroyed by the Goths. In 410, Alaric led the Goths in the infamous sack of Rome, in which the Eternal City was plundered and partly destroyed. The psychological trauma that the fall of Rome occasioned exceeded even the damage in terms of property and lives lost. Romans, including Roman Christians, had long believed that Rome was the embodiment of the empire, which would fall when the city fell. That the city should fall to barbarians created a severe crisis in confidence that was felt as far away as Palestine in the east.

At the time, pagans began to accuse the Christians for the disaster because, they argued, it was only after the Roman state had taken up the side of the Christians that these misfortunes began. Clearly the gods had been angered by the failure of the Romans to perform their customary sacrifices and were therefore punishing them accordingly. These pagans stressed the idea that Rome had risen to its destined greatness during a time when it honored its gods, when it was pagan. Now that it was no longer pagan, it was running the risk of losing both its greatness and its empire. Even some Christians were swayed by these arguments or at least found them difficult to rebut. As a result, certain Christian writers attempted to make systematic replies to these charges, in part to silence the pagan critics and in part to reassure wavering Christians.

Into this debate stepped Augustine of Hippo, the famous bishop, writer, and theologian from Roman North Africa. Augustine had long been concerned with the role of God's providence in human history and with important theological questions about why evil has often been allowed to triumph in the world. "Why does God allow just men to suffer?" "Why do bad things happen to good and bad people alike?" These were critical questions to which he and others sought answers, especially in the aftermath of the events of 410. Augustine made a significant attempt to address these issues in his *magnum opus,* a monumental treatise of twenty-two books entitled the *City of God.* This work uses copious examples from Roman history and argues that Christianity was neither bad for Rome nor antithetical to its history and destiny. Instead, Christianity fulfilled the true purpose of the Roman Empire, which had been ordained by God to bring order to the world. Yet this empire must now, under its Christian emperors, worship God and use its power to advance the cause of Christianity. Even so, the Christian Roman Empire, Augustine argued, is not the City of God that the scriptures promised. That city will never become truly identified with any earthly human community. Instead, Rome represented the City of Man, in which one expected to find a mixture of good and evil. Both good and bad things happened and will continue to happen in this earthly city. When bad things happen, it is because God wanted to use the events to chastise the people for their own good. Good, spiritual Christians should remain more or less indifferent to their own varying fortunes and to those of others, and even to the fate of the empire itself.

Some critics, both ancient and modern, have viewed this attitude as one that contributed to the erosion of Roman patriotism, a process that they claimed finally resulted in the empire's loss of its western half to Germanic barbarians. But in Augustine's ideas, we also find an influential new formulation of the relationship among the divine, human beings, and the state, one that leaves in place much of the classical heritage behind it.

Pagan and Christian Recriminations

From this world's city there arise enemies against whom the City of God has to be defended, though many of these correct their godless errors and become useful citizens of that City. But many are inflamed with hate against it and feel no gratitude for the benefits offered by its Redeemer. The benefits are unmistakable; those enemies would not today be able to utter a word against the City if, when fleeing from the sword of their enemy, they had not found, in the City's holy places, the safety on which they now congratulate themselves. The barbarians spared them for Christ's sake; and now these Romans assail Christ's name. The sacred places of the martyrs and the basilicas of the apostles bear witness to this, for in the sack of Rome they afforded shelter to fugitives, both Christian and pagan. The bloodthirsty enemy raged thus far, but here the frenzy of butchery was checked; to these refuges the merciful among the enemy conveyed those whom they had spared outside, to save them from encountering foes who had no such pity. Even men who elsewhere raged with all the savagery an enemy can show, arrived at places where practices generally allowed by laws of war were forbidden and their monstrous passion for violence was brought to a sudden halt; their lust for taking captives was subdued.

In this way many escaped who now complain of this Christian era, and hold Christ responsible for the disasters which their city endured. But they do not make Christ responsible for the benefits they received out of respect for Christ, to which they owed their lives. They attribute their deliverance to their own destiny; whereas if they had any right judgement they ought rather to attribute the harsh cruelty they suffered at the hands of their enemies to the providence of God. For God's providence constantly uses war to correct and chasten the corrupt morals of mankind, as it also uses such afflictions to train men in a righteous and laudable way of life, removing to a better state those whose life is approved, or else keeping them in this world for further service.

Moreover, they should give credit to this Christian era for the fact that these savage barbarians showed mercy beyond the custom of war—whether they so acted in general in honour of the name of Christ, or in places specially dedicated to Christ's name, buildings of such size and capacity as to give mercy a wider range. For this clemency our detractors ought rather to give thanks to God; they should have recourse to his name in all sincerity, so as to escape the penalty of everlasting fire, seeing that so many of them assumed his name dishonestly, to escape the penalty of immediate destruction. Among those whom you see insulting Christ's servants with such wanton insolence there are very many who came unscathed through that terrible time of massacre only by passing themselves off as Christ's servants. And now with ungrateful pride and impious madness they oppose his name in the perversity of their hearts, so that they may incur the punishment of eternal darkness; but then they took refuge in that name, though with deceitful lips, so that they might continue to enjoy this transitory light....

Reasons why the good and the wicked are equally afflicted

... [W]hen the good and the wicked suffer alike, the identity of their sufferings does not mean that there is no difference between them. Though the sufferings are the same, the sufferers remain different. Virtue and vice are not the same, even if they undergo the same torment. The fire which makes gold shine makes chaff smoke; the same flail breaks up the straw, and clears the grain; and oil is not mistaken for lees because both are forced out by the same press. In the same way, the violence which assails good men to test them, to cleanse and purify them, effects in the wicked their condemnation, ruin, and annihilation. Thus the wicked, under pressure of affliction, execrate God and blaspheme; the good, in the same affliction, offer up prayers and praises. This shows that what matters is the nature of the sufferer, not the nature of the sufferings. Stir a cesspit, and a foul stench arises; stir a perfume, and a delightful fragrance ascends. But the movement is identical.

9. Thus, in this universal catastrophe, the sufferings of Christians have tended to their moral improvement because they viewed them with the eyes of faith.

First, they consider in humility the sins which have moved God's indignation so that he has filled the world with dire calamities. And although they are free from criminal and godless wickedness, still they do not regard themselves as so far removed from such wrongdoing as not to deserve to suffer the temporal ills which are the recompense of sin. Everyone of them, however commendable his life, gives way at times to physical desires, and, while avoiding monstrous crimes, the sink of iniquity and the abomination of godlessness, is yet guilty of some sins, infrequent sins, perhaps, or more frequent because more trivial. Apart from this, it is not easy to find anyone who, when confronted with those whose fearful arrogance, lust, and greed, whose detestable wickedness and impiety, have caused God to give effect to his threats and warnings by bringing destruction on the earth—it is not, I say, easy to find anyone who regards such men they should be regarded—who, when he meets them, treats them as they should be treated.

We tend culpably to evade our responsibility when we ought to instruct and admonish them, sometimes even with sharp reproof and censure, either because the task is irksome, or because we are afraid of giving offence; or it may be that we shrink from incurring their enmity, for fear that they may hinder and harm us in worldly matters, in respect either of what we eagerly seek to attain, or of what we weakly dread to lose. And so, although the good dislike the way of life of the wicked, and therefore do not fall into the condemnation which is in store for the wicked after this life, nevertheless, because they are tender towards damnable sins of the wicked, and thus fall into sin through fear of such people (pardonable and comparatively trivial though those sins may be), they are justly chastised with afflictions in this world, although they are spared eternal punishment; and they rightly feel this life to be bitter when they are associated with the wicked in the afflictions sent by God. But it was through love of this world's sweetness that they refused to be bitter to those sinners.

If anyone refrains from reproof and correction of ill-doers because he looks for a more suitable occasion, or because he fears that this will make them worse, or fears that they will hinder the instruction of others, who are weak, in a good and godly way of life, and that they will oppress them, and turn them away from the faith, in such a case the action seems to be prompted not by self-interest but counsels of charity. What is culpable is when those whose life is different and who abhor the deeds of the wicked are nevertheless indulgent to the sins of others, which they ought to reprehend and reprove, because they are concerned to avoid giving offence to them, in case they should harm themselves in respect of things which may be rightly and innocently enjoyed by good men, but which they desire more than is right for those who are strangers in this world and who fix their hope on a heavenly country.

There are the weaker brothers, in the married state, who have children or look to have them, who are masters of houses and households; the Apostle addresses them in the churches, teaching them and warning them how they ought to live, wives with husbands and husbands with wives, children with parents and parents with children, servants with masters and masters with servants. Such men are eager to acquire many of this world's temporal goods, and grieve to lose them, and for that reason they have not the heart to offend men whose lives of shame and crime they detest. But they are not alone.

Even those who have a higher standard of life, who are not entangled in the bonds of marriage, who are content with little food and scanty clothing, are often fearful of attacks by the wicked upon their reputation and their safety, and so refrain from reproaches. They are not so afraid of the wicked as to yield to their villainous threats to the extent of committing crimes like theirs; but though they do not commit them they too often fail to reprehend them, for although they might perhaps convert some by such rebuke they fear that, if the attempt failed, their safety and reputation might be endangered or destroyed. And this is not due to prudence, nor is it because they see their reputation and safety as essential means whereby mankind may receive the benefit of instruction; it is rather due to weakness—because they delight in flattery and popularity and because they dread the judgement of the mob, and the torture or death of the body. In fact, they are constrained by self-interest, not by the obligations of charity.

So this seems to me a major reason why the good are chastized along with the evil, when God decides to punish moral corruption with temporal calamities. Good and bad are chastised together, not because both alike live evil lives, but because both alike, though not in the same degree, love this temporal life. But the good ought to have despised it, so that the others might be reformed and corrected and might aim at life eternal; or, if they refused to be partners in this enterprise, so that they might be borne with, and loved as Christians should love their enemies, since in this life it is always uncertain whether or not they are likely to experience a change of heart.

In this matter a uniquely heavy responsibility rests on those to whom this message is given by the prophet: 'He indeed will die in his sin, but I will require his blood at the hand of the watchman.' For 'watchmen', that is, leaders of the people, have been appointed in the churches for this purpose, that they should be unsparing in their condemnation of sin. This does not mean that a man is entirely free from blame in this regard if, without being a 'watchman', he recognizes but ignores, opportunities of warning and admonishing those with whom the exigencies of this life force him to associate—if he evades this duty for fear of offending them, because he is concerned for those worldly advantages, which are not in themselves discreditable, but to which he is unduly attached. There is a further reason for the infliction of temporal suffering on the good, as is seen in the case of Job—that the spirit of man may be tested, that he may learn for himself what is the degree of disinterested devotion that he offers to God.

The Saints Lose Nothing by Being Deprived of Temporal Goods

10. After giving proper attention and consideration to these points, observe whether any disaster has happened to the faithful and religious which did not turn out for their good; unless we are to suppose that there is no meaning in the Apostle's statement, 'We know that God makes all things co-operate for good for those who love him.' They lost all they had. Did they lose faith? Or devotion? Or the possessions of the inner man. Who is 'rich in the sight of God'? These are the riches of Christians, and the Apostle, who was endowed with this wealth, said,

> Devotion combined with self-sufficiency yields great profit. For we brought nothing into this world, and we cannot take anything away with us. So, if we have food and clothes, we are content with that. For those who wish to become rich fall into temptation and into a snare, and into many foolish and harmful desires, which plunge men into death and destruction. For acquisitiveness is the root of all evils; and those who have this as their aim have strayed away from the faith and have entangled themselves in many sorrows.

If those who lost their earthly riches in that disaster had possessed them in the spirit thus described to them by one who was outwardly poor but inwardly rich; that is, if they had 'used the world as though not using it', then they would have been able to say, with that man who was so sorely tired and yet was never overcome: 'I issued from my mother's womb in nakedness, and in nakedness I shall return to the earth. The Lord has given, the Lord has taken away. It has happened as God decided. May the Lord's name be blessed.' Thus a good servant would regard the will of God as his great resource, and he would be enriched in his mind by close attendance on God's will; nor would he grieve if deprived in life of those possessions which he would soon have to leave behind at his death.

The weaker characters, who clung to their worldly goods with some degree of avarice, even if they did not prefer them to Christ, discovered, in losing them, how much they sinned in loving them. They 'entangled themselves in sorrows', as I have already quoted from the Apostle, and they suffered in proportion. They refused for so long to be taught by words, and they had to have the added teaching of experience. For when the Apostle said, 'Those who wish to become rich fall into temptation ...' what he condemns in riches is the desire for them, not the opportunities they offer. This is clear from his injunction in another passage:

> I enjoin the rich of this world not to feel proud, and not to fix their eyes on the uncertainty of riches, but on the living God, who supplies us liberally with all things for our enjoyment. Let them do good; let them be rich in good works; let them be ready to give; let them share their wealth; let them store up a good foundation for the future; let them get hold of true life.

Those who have done this with their riches have had great gains to compensate them for light losses, and their joy at what they assured for themselves more securely by readiness to give outweighed their sadness at the surrender of possessions they more easily lost because they clung to them fearfully. Reluctance to remove their goods from this world exposed them to the risk of loss. There were those who accepted the Lord's advice: 'Do not store your treasures on earth, where moth and rust destroy, and where thieves break in and steal. Pile up treasure in heaven, where no thief comes near and no moth destroys. For where your treasure is, your heart will be also; and such people proved in the time of tribulation how wise they were in not despising the finest of advisers and the most faithful and unconquerable guardian of treasure. For if many rejoiced at having their riches in a place which fortunately escaped the enemy's approach, with how much greater certainty and confidence could those rejoice who at the warning of their God removed themselves to a place to which the enemy could never come. Hence our friend Paulinus, bishop of Nola, deliberately reduced himself from great wealth to extreme poverty and the great riches of holiness; and when the barbarians devastated Nola, and he was in their hands, he prayed in his heart, as I learnt from him afterwards, 'Lord, let me not be tortured on account of gold and silver; for you know where all my riches are.' For he kept all his possessions in the place where he had been told to store and preserve them by him who foretold those troubles which were to come upon the world. In this way, those who obeyed their Lord's advice about where and how they ought to amass treasure, did not lose even their worldly riches in the barbarian invasions. But those who had to repent of their disobedience learnt what they should have done in this matter; if they failed to learn by wisdom before the event, at least they learned by experience after it.

It will be objected that some Christians, and good Christians, were tortured to make them hand over their goods to the enemy. But they could not hand over, nor lose, that good which was the ground of their own goodness; and if they preferred to be tortured rather than surrender 'the Mammon of unrighteousness', then they were not good. Those who suffered so much for the sake of gold should have been warned how much they should endure for the sake of Christ, so that they might learn, instead of loving gold and silver, to love him who would enrich with eternal felicity those who suffered for his sake. To suffer for the sake of wealth was pitiable, whether the wealth was concealed by telling lies, or surrendered by telling the truth. For under torture no one lost Christ by confessing him, no one preserved his gold except by denying it. In this respect we might say that torture conveyed the lesson that what is to be loved is the incorruptible good; and so torture was more useful than those possessions which tormented their owners, through the love they aroused, without bringing them any useful profit.

But there were some who were tortured even though they possessed nothing to surrender. They were tortured because they were not believed. Perhaps they desired possessions, and were not voluntarily poor through holiness. They had to be shown that the mere desire for wealth, even without the enjoyment of it, deserved such torments. As for those who had no gold and silver stored away because they had set their hearts on a better life, I am not sure that any of such people were so unfortunate as to be tortured because of their supposed wealth. But even if this did happen, those who confessed holy poverty when tortured were confessing Christ; and so anyone who confessed holy poverty, even if he did not win credence from the enemy, could not be tortured without winning a heavenly reward.

'But', they say, 'many Christians have been destroyed by prolonged starvation.' Well, the loyal and faithful turned this also to their own advantage by enduring it in fidelity to God. For when starvation killed any, it snatched them away from the evils of this life, as disease rescues men from the sufferings of the body, and if it spared their lives, it taught them to live more frugally and to fast more extensively.

The End of This Present Life Must Come, Whether Sooner or Later

11. 'But', they will say, 'many Christians also have been killed, and many carried off by hideous diseases of all kinds.' If one must grieve at this, it is certainly the common lot of all who have been brought into this life. I am certain of this, that no one has died who was not going to die at some time, and the end of life reduces the longest life to the same condition as the shortest. When something has once ceased to exist, there is no more question of better or worse, longer or shorter. What does it matter by what kind of death life is brought to an end? When man's life is ended he does not have to die again. Among the daily chances of this life every man on earth is threatened in the same way by innumerable deaths, and it is uncertain which of them will come to him. And so the question is whether it is better to suffer one in dying or to fear them all in living. I am well aware that a man would sooner choose to live under threat of all those deaths than by one death to be thereafter free of the fear of them. But there is a wide difference between the body's instinctive shrinking, in weakness and fear, and the mind's rational conviction, when deliberately set free from the body's influence. Death is not to be regarded as a disaster, when it follows on a good life, for the only thing that makes death an evil is what comes after death. Those who must inevitably die ought not to worry overmuch about what accident will cause their death, but about their destination after dying. Christians know that the death of a poor religious man, licked by the tongues of dogs, is far better than the death of a godless rich man, dressed in purple and linen. Why then should those who have lived well be dismayed by terrors of death in any form?...

86 Augustine, *Confessions*

"How did I burn to fly from earthly things to You."

Frequently when reading the works of the Church Fathers, one comes across the statement, "Christians are not born but made." This cogently expresses the fact that Christianity came to these Greco-Roman intellectuals as a final and satisfying answer to their long search for truth and meaning. The classical

From St. Augustine, *Confessions*, I, 9, 13, 14; II, 1, 3, 4, 6, 9; III, 1–7; IV, 3; V, 10, 13, 14; VII, 9, 20; VIII, 3, 4, 6, 8, 11, 12; based on the translation by E. B. Pusey.

emphasis on rationalistic humanism was no longer satisfying, and people turned from it to the spiritual truths of Christianity. This story is best told in the intellectual and spiritual autobiography of St. Augustine (A.D. 354–430), bishop of Hippo in North Africa. We see the picture of a man akin to ourselves in his gropings after truth in an age grown weary from disorder and anxiety.

As a boy, Augustine tells us, he thought of God in childish terms, as one who could hear such petitions as would help him escape punishment in school. As he grew older and attended the university at Carthage, he discarded such simple beliefs and, plunging into a life of romantic excitements, "walked the streets of Babylon and wallowed in the mire thereof." But university life also marked an important advance toward maturity because it turned him from the pursuit of sensual pleasures to a love of wisdom, a transformation he attributed to the writings of Cicero. Yet this new love was barren of permanently satisfying results, and a similar discouragement resulted when he turned to religion. The Christian Scriptures repelled him; he could not accept the immoralities and anthropomorphism of the Old Testament and he saw only a deficiency of style and charm in the New Testament. The Manichaean religion interested him for several years before it was revealed to be a tissue of "empty falsehoods." Then he "despaired of finding the truth" and found congenial the dictum of the Skeptic philosophers that "no truth can be comprehended by man." The major barriers to his conversion to Christianity were removed by Ambrose, who gave him the allegorical method of interpreting the Scriptures, and by Neoplatonism, which taught him the immateriality of God. He felt that the affinities between Christianity and Platonism were so close that, as he stated later in his essay *Of True Religion,* all that was needed to convert Platonists was the modification of a few words and formulae. Like Platonism, too, which Plato said could be accepted only by "some few who are able ... to find it out for themselves," Augustine's Christianity is a way of life that cannot be taught by one person to another. The real significance of Christianity can be grasped only by one who has experienced much, suffered much, and thought much; and such is the final message of the *Confessions:* "You, O God, are the Good, which is in need of no other good.... What man shall teach another to understand this? Or what angel another angel? Or what angel man? This must be *asked* of you, *sought* in you, *knocked* for at you: thus only shall it be received, thus shall it be found, thus shall it be opened to us. Amen" (XIII, 38).

The final step for Augustine is a wrenching free from a confused rationalism by a deliberate act inspired by the example of the unlearned, of reaching up to "take heaven by force." Once more, in this final mystical step, we find an echo of Plato's words: "suddenly a light, as it were, is kindled in one soul by a flame that leaps to it from another, and thereafter sustains itself."

Schooldays

O God, my God, what miseries and mockeries did I now experience, when obedience to my teachers was proposed to me as proper in a boy in order that in this world I might prosper and excel in rhetorical learning, which would obtain for me the praise of men and deceitful riches. Then I was put to school to get learning, in which I (poor child) knew not what use there was; and yet, if idle in learning, I was beaten. For this was considered right by our forefathers; and many, passing the same way before us, had built for us a weary path along which we were compelled to go, multiplying toil and grief upon the sons of Adam.

Yet we noticed, Lord, that men prayed to You, and we learned from them to think of You (according to our capacities) as some great One, who, though hidden from our senses, could hear and help us. So as a boy I began to call upon You, my Aid and Refuge; though small, yet with no small earnestness, I broke the fetters of my tongue to call on You, praying to You that I might not be beaten at school. And when You did not hear me (not thereby encouraging my folly), my elders, yes, even my parents, who yet wished me no harm, laughed at my stripes, which were a great and grievous ill to me....

It was not that we lacked, O Lord, memory or capacity; You gave us enough of these for our age. But our sole delight was play, and for this we were punished by those who were themselves doing the same thing. But older folks' idleness is called "business"; the idling of boys, though really the same, is punished by these older folks, and no one is sorry for either boys or men. For will anyone of sound discretion approve of my being beaten as a boy because, by playing ball, I made less progress in studies which, by learning, I might as a man play some more unbecoming game?...

Why I so much hated Greek, which I had to study as a boy, I do not fully understand. For I loved Latin; not the elementary grammar, but the literature. As for the rudiments—reading, writing, and arithmetic—I found them as hard and hateful as Greek....

Why then did I hate Greek literature? ... The difficulty of learning a foreign language sprinkled bitterness over all the sweetness of the Greek stories. For not one word of it did I understand, and to make me understand I was urged vehemently with cruel threats and punishments. There was a time also (as an infant) when I knew no Latin; but I learned it without fear or suffering, by mere observation, amid the caresses of my nurses and the jests of friends, whose smiles and laughter encouraged me. I learned it without any pressure or punishment to urge me on, for my heart urged me to give birth to thoughts which I could only do by learning words not from instructors but from those who talked with me and for whom I was able to express what I was feeling. There is no doubt, then, that free curiosity has more value in learning languages than harsh enforcement....

"To Whom Am I Telling This? ... And to What Purpose?"

I will now call to mind my past foulness and the carnal corruptions of my soul, not because I love them but that I may love You, O my God. For love of Your love I do it, reviewing my most wicked ways in the very bitterness of my remembrance, that You may grow sweet to me (O sweetness never failing, blissful and assured sweetness). And I gather myself together out of that dissipated state, in which I was torn to pieces while turned from You, the One Good, while losing myself among a multiplicity of things.

Having arrived at adolescence, I was on fire to take my fill of hell. I became like an animal, pursuing various and shady lusts: *my beauty consumed away* and I stank in Your sight; pleasing myself and desirous to please in the sight of men....

To whom am I telling this? Not to You, my God, but in Your presence to my own kind, to that small portion of mankind as may come upon these writings of mine. And to what purpose? Simply that I and whoever reads this may think *out of what depths we are to cry unto Thee*. For what is nearer to Your ears than a confessing heart and a life of faith?...

An Act of Vandalism: "Seeking Only to Be Wicked"

Theft is punished by Your law, O Lord, and the law written in the hearts of men.... Yet I wanted to steal, and did steal, compelled not by hunger or poverty but because I lacked a sense of justice and was filled with iniquity. For I stole that of which I had plenty, and of much better quality. Nor cared I to enjoy what I stole; I enjoyed the theft itself, and the sin.

There was a pear tree near our vineyard, laden with fruit but tempting neither in color or taste. To shake it and rob it, I and some lewd young fellows went late one night (having according to our depraved custom prolonged our sports in the street till then) and took huge loads, not for eating—we barely tasted them—but to fling to the hogs. Our real pleasure in doing this was that it was forbidden. Such was my heart, O God, such was my heart which You had pity on when it was at the bottom of the bottomless abyss. Now let my heart tell You what it sought there, when I was evil for no purpose, having no reason for wrongdoing except wrongdoing itself. It was foul, and I loved it; I loved destroying myself, I loved my sin, not the thing for which I had sinned but the sin itself. Foul soul, falling from Your firmament to utter destruction; not seeking profit from wickedness, but seeking only to be wicked!...

Did I find pleasure in appearing to break Your law, doing so by stealth since I had no real power to do so? Was I, like a prisoner, making a small show of liberty by doing unpunished what I was not allowed to do and so getting a false sense of omnipotence? Behold Your servant, fleeing from his Lord and pursuing a shadow! What rottenness! What monstrosity of life and abyss of death! Could I enjoy what was forbidden only because it was forbidden?...

See, my God, this vivid memory of my soul. Yet I could not have committed that theft alone.... When someone cries "Come on, let's do it," we are ashamed to be ashamed....

"Loving a Vagrant Liberty"

I came to Carthage, where there sang all around me in my ears a cauldron of unholy loves. I was not yet in love, yet I loved the idea of love, and out of a deep-seated want I hated myself for not wanting more. I sought for something to love, being in love with loving, and I hated security and a life without snares. For within me was a famine of that spiritual food, Yourself, my God.... To love then, and to be loved, was sweet to me; but more so when I obtained the enjoyment of the body of the person I loved. Thus I defiled the spring of friendship with the filth of physical desire and beclouded its brightness with the hell of lust....

Stage plays also carried me away, full of images of my miseries and of fuel for my fire. Why is it that man desires to be made sad, beholding miserable and tragic things which he himself would by no means wish to suffer? Yet he desires as a spectator to feel sorrow, and this sorrow is his pleasure....

O my God, my exceeding great mercy, my refuge from those terrible destroyers, among whom I wandered in my arrogance, withdrawing further from You, loving my own ways and not Yours, loving a vagrant liberty.

"Aroused ... to ... Seek ... Wisdom ... Whatever It Might Be"

These studies of mine also, which were considered commendable, were designed to fit me to excel in the law courts—the more crafty I was, the more famous I should become. Such is men's blindness, that blindness itself should become a source of pride! And by now I was a leader in the school of rhetoric, which I proudly enjoyed, swelling with arrogance, though (Lord, You know) I was far quieter and entirely removed from the subvertings of those "Subverters" (for this cruel and devilish name was their badge of sophistication) among whom I lived, with a shameless shame that I was not like them. With them I went about and sometimes I enjoyed their friendship, although I always hated their actions—that is, their "subvertings," when they wantonly persecuted the modesty of freshmen whom they disturbed by mocking and jeering for no reason whatever, feeding thereby their own malicious mirth. Nothing can be more like the behavior of devils than this. They were rightly called "subverters," being themselves subverted and perverted by the same deceiving spirits which secretly derided and seduced them when they amused themselves by jeering and deceiving others.

Among such companions, in that unsettled age of mine, I studied books of eloquence, wherein I desired to be eminent for a damnable and vainglorious end—joy in human vanity. In the normal course of study I fell upon a certain book by Cicero, whose style almost all admire, though not his heart. This book of his contains an exhortation to philosophy, and is called *Hortensius* [now lost]. But this book altered my mind; it turned my prayers to You, O Lord, and gave me other purposes and desires. Every vain hope suddenly became worthless to me; I longed with an incredibly burning desire for an immortality of wisdom, and I began now to rise, so that I might return to You. For not to sharpen my tongue (which was the goal of the education I was purchasing with my mother's allowances, in my nineteenth year, my father having died two years before), not to sharpen my tongue did I use that book; what moved me was not its style, but its content.

How did I burn then, my God, how did I burn to fly from earthly things to You. But I did not know what You would do with me; for with You is wisdom. But the love of wisdom is in Greek called "philosophy," and it was with wisdom that that book inflamed me.... And since at that time (You, O light of my heart, know this) Apostolic Scripture was not known to me, the one thing that delighted me in Cicero's exhortation was that I was greatly aroused, kindled, and inflamed to love, seek, obtain, hold, and embrace not this sect but wisdom itself, whatever it might be. And this alone checked my ardent desire, that the name of Christ was not there. For this name, O Lord, this name of my Savior, Your Son, had my tender heart, even with my mother's milk, devoutly drunk in and deeply treasured; and whatsoever was without that name, however learned, polished, or true, could not hold me entirely.

"The Holy Scriptures ... Seemed to Me Unworthy"

I resolved then to direct my attention to the Holy Scriptures, that I might see what they were like. And what I saw was something not understood by the proud nor laid open to children; and I was not one who could enter into it, or stoop my neck to follow its path. For not as I now write did I feel when I first turned to those Scriptures; they seemed to me unworthy to be compared to the stateliness of Cicero. My swelling pride shunned their style, nor could my sharp wit pierce their depths. Yet they were such as would grow up with a little child; but I disdained to be a little child, and, swollen with pride, took myself to be grown-up.

The Manichaeans: "Foolish Deceivers"

Therefore I fell among men who were proudly raving, exceedingly carnal and wordy, in whose mouths were the snares of the Devil, smeared with a mixture of the syllables of Your name and of our Lord Jesus Christ and of the Holy Ghost, the Paraclete, our Comforter. These names were always in their mouths, but only as sounds and the noise of the tongue, for their hearts were void of truth. Yet they cried out "Truth, Truth" and spoke much thereof to me, yet the truth was not in them.... Yet because I thought them to be You, I fed upon them; not eagerly, for you did not in them taste to me as You are; for You are not these empty falsehoods, nor was I nourished by them, but exhausted rather....

   For that which really is, I knew not; and I was through my sharpness of wit persuaded to assent to foolish deceivers when they asked me, "What is the origin of evil?" "Is God bounded by a bodily shape and has he hair and nails?" "Are those [patriarchs of the Old Testament] to be esteemed righteous who had many wives at the same time and killed men and sacrificed living creatures?" At which I, in my ignorance, was much troubled and, while departing from the truth, seemed to myself to be drawing towards it. This was because as yet I did not know that evil is nothing but an absence of good.... I did not even know that God is a spirit, having no parts extended in length and breadth....

"Those Imposters Called Astrologers"

Thus I did not hesitate to consult those imposters called astrologers, because they offered no sacrifices and prayed to no spirit to assist their divinations. Yet true Christian piety necessarily rejects and condemns their art. For *it is a good thing to confess unto Thee,* and to say, *Have mercy upon me, heal my soul, for I have sinned against Thee,* and not to misuse Your mercy as a license, but to remember the Lord's words, *Behold, thou art made whole, sin no more, lest a worse thing happen to thee.* All this wholesome truth the astrologers strive to destroy, saying: "The cause of your sin is inevitably determined in the heavens" and "This did Venus do, or Saturn or Mars." As though man, who is flesh and blood and proud corruption, should be blameless, while the Creator and Ruler of heaven and the stars is to bear the blame. And who is He but our God?...

The governor of the province in those days was a wise man, skillful and renowned in medicine.... When I told him that I was much given to reading the books of the horoscope-casters, he kindly and in a fatherly way advised me to throw them away and not to waste on such nonsense care and attention that could be put to better use.... When I asked him why it was that many things were foretold by astrology, he reasoned that it was due to the force of chance, which is diffused throughout the whole order of things. Thus while haphazardly paging through a book of poetry, one often comes upon a line which is wondrously appropriate to some matter on one's mind, though the poet was singing and thinking of something quite different. So, he said, it is not to be wondered at if a man's mind should unconsciously by some instinct, and by chance rather than by art, produce an answer that would seem to correspond with the affairs and actions of the inquirer....

Skepticism: *"Men Ought to Doubt Everything"*

At Rome I again associated with those false and deceiving "holy ones" [Manichaeans], not only with the "hearers" (one of whom was the man in whose house I had fallen sick and recovered), but also with those whom they call "the elect." For I still held the belief that it is not we who sin but some other nature sinning in us; it gratified my pride to think myself free of blame when I had done anything evil.... However, I now despaired of finding any profit in that false doctrine, and I began to hold laxly and carelessly even those ideas with which I had decided to rest content if I could find nothing better.

The thought occurred to me that those philosophers whom they call Academics were wiser than the rest because they held that men ought to doubt everything and had concluded that no truth can be comprehended by man [Selection 59]. For so I was clearly convinced that they thought (as is commonly believed), though I did not yet understand their real meaning. And I did openly discourage my host from that overconfidence which I perceived him to have in those fables of which the books of Mani are full. Yet I lived on more friendly terms with them than with others who were not of this heresy. I no longer defended it with my former eagerness; still my friendship with that sect (Rome secretly harboring many of them) made me slower to seek any other belief, especially since I despaired of finding the truth in Your Church, O Lord of heaven and earth, Creator of all things visible and invisible. For they had tamed me against it, and it seemed to me degrading to believe that You had the shape of human flesh and were bounded by the bodily outlines of our limbs....

Ambrose

To Milan I came, to Ambrose the bishop, known to the whole world as among the best of men, Your devout servant whose eloquence did then plentifully dispense to *Thy people the fatness of Thy wheat, the gladness of Thy oil and the sober intoxication of Thy wine*. To him was I unknowingly led by You, that I might knowingly be led to You by him. That man of God received me as a father, and as bishop welcomed my coming. I began to love him, at first indeed not as a teacher of the truth (which I utterly despaired of finding in Your Church), but as a person who was kind to me. I listened diligently to him preaching to the people, not with the right intent but, as it were, judging his eloquence, whether it was equal to his fame or flowed higher or lower than was reported. So I hung intently on his words, but of what he said I was a careless and scornful onlooker. I was delighted with the charm of his discourse; it was more learned, yet less winning and harmonious than that of Faustus. Of the actual matter, however, there was no comparison; Faustus was merely wandering amid Manichaean delusions, while Ambrose was soundly teaching salvation. But salvation is far from sinners such as I then was. Yet I was drawing nearer little by little, though unconsciously.

For though I took no pains to learn what he said but only to hear how he said it, ... yet together with the words which I liked came also into my mind the subject matter to which I was indifferent, for I could not separate them. And while I opened my heart to admit how eloquently he spoke, it also occurred to me gradually how truly he spoke. The things he said now began to appear to me capable of being defended. The Catholic faith, for which I had thought nothing could be said against the Manichaean objections, I now thought might be maintained on sound grounds—especially after I had heard one or two passages of the Old Testament explained figuratively, which, when I had taken them literally, I was slain spiritually. Many passages then of those books having been explained in a spiritual sense, I now blamed my conceit for having believed that no answer could be given to those who hated and scoffed at the Law and the Prophets. Yet I did not then feel that the Catholic way was to be followed merely because it also could find learned maintainers who could at length and with some show of reason answer objections, nor that the faith which I held was to be condemned because both faiths could be defended. Thus the Catholic cause seemed to me not vanquished, nor not as yet victorious.

Then I earnestly bent my mind to see if in any way I could by any certain proof convict the Manichaeans of falsehood. Could I only have been able to conceive of a spiritual substance, all their strongholds would have collapsed and been cast out of my mind. But I could not. However, concerning the body of this world and the whole of nature which our senses can reach to, as I more and more considered and compared things, I judged the views of most of the philosophers to be much more probable. So then after the supposed manner of the Academics, doubting everything and wavering between all, I decided that I must leave the Manichaeans. I judged that, while in a state of doubt, I could not continue in that sect to which I now preferred some of the philosophers. These philosophers, however, because they were without the saving name of Christ, I utterly refused to commit the cure of my sick soul. I determined therefore to be a catechumen in the Catholic Church, which my parents had encouraged me to join, until something certain should dawn upon me by which I might steer my course....

"Some Books of the Platonists"

By means of a man puffed up with the most exaggerated pride, You brought to my attention some books of the Platonists translated from Greek into Latin. And therein I read, not of course in the same words but to the very same effect and supported by many sorts of reasons, that *In the beginning was the Word, and the Word was with God, and the Word was God: the same was in the beginning with God. All things were made by Him, and without Him was nothing made: that which was made by Him is life, and the life was the light of men, and the light shineth in the darkness, and the darkness comprehended it not.* And that the soul of man, though it *bears witness to the light,* yet itself *is not that light;* but the Word of God, being God, *is that true light that lighteth every man that cometh into the world.* Also that *He was in the world, and the world was made by Him, and the world knew Him not.* But I did not read there that *He came unto His own, and His own received Him not, but as many as received Him, to them gave He power to become the sons of God, as many as believed in His name.*

I also read there that *God the Word was born not of flesh, nor of blood, nor of the will of man, nor of the will of the flesh, but of God.* But I did not find there that *the Word was made flesh, and dwelt among us....*

And You have called the Gentiles into Your inheritance. I myself had come to You from the Gentiles, and I set my mind upon the gold which You willed Your people to take from Egypt, since it was Yours, wherever it was. And to the Athenians You said by Your Apostle [Paul], that in You we live, move, and have our being, as of their own poets had said. And certainly these books came from Athens....

Having then read those books of the Platonists, which taught me to search for incorporeal truth, I came to see Your *invisible things, understood by those things which are made.* And though I fell back from this point, I still perceived what that was which, through the darkness of my mind, I was unable to contemplate; I was certain that You are and that You are infinite, yet not being diffused in space whether finite or infinite: that You truly are and are ever the same, in no part or motion varying; and that all other things are from You, as is proved by the sure fact that they exist.... I believe it was Your will that I should come upon these books before I studied Your Scriptures, that it might be imprinted on my memory how I was affected by them; and that afterwards when my spirits were tamed through Your books, and my wounds dressed by Your healing fingers, I might be able to distinguish between presumption and confession, between those who see the goal but not the way—the way that leads us not only to see but to dwell in the country of blessedness....

Christians Are Made, Not Born

Good God! what takes place in man that he should more rejoice at the salvation of a soul despaired of or freed from a great peril, than if there had always been hope or the peril had been less?...

What is it in the soul, then, which makes it more delighted at finding or recovering the things it loves than if it had always had them? Indeed, other creatures bear the same witness; everywhere all things cry out, "So it is." The conquering general has his triumph; yet he would not have conquered if he had not fought; and the more peril there was in the battle, the more joy there is in the triumph. The storm tosses the sailors and threatens shipwreck; all are pale at the approach of death; then the sky and sea are calmed, and they are as exceedingly joyful as they had been fearful. A friend is sick and his pulse threatens danger; all who long for his recovery are sick in mind with him. He recovers, though as yet he walks not with his former strength; yet there is more joy than there was before when he walked sound and strong. Even the ordinary pleasures of human life men acquire through pain, not only those pains which fall upon us unlooked for and against our will, but also self-chosen and pleasure-seeking pain. Eating and drinking give no pleasure unless they are preceded by the pains of hunger and thirst. Drunkards eat certain salty things to procure an uncomfortable dryness which drink alleviates, thus causing pleasure. It is also customary that the engaged girl should not at once give herself, lest the husband later should hold her cheap whom, as betrothed, he no longer sighed after....

Do not many, out of a deeper hell of blindness ... , come back to You and are enlightened by that light which *they who receive, receive power from Thee to become Thy sons?*...

Antony the Egyptian Monk

One day there came to see Alypius and me a certain Ponticianus, our countryman, an African holding high office in the emperor's court. What he wanted of us I did not know, but we sat down to converse. It chanced that he noticed a book on a gaming table beside us. He took it, opened it, and contrary to his expectation—he thought it would be one of those books which I was wearying myself in teaching—found that it was the Apostle Paul. Smiling and looking at me, he expressed his joy and wonder that he had come suddenly upon this book, and only this book, beside me. For he was a Christian, and baptized. He often bowed himself before You, our God, in Church, in long and frequent prayers. When I then told him that I gave great attention to these works of Scripture, a conversation began, suggested by him, about Antony the Egyptian monk, whose name was very well known among Your servants, though up to that hour unknown to Alypius and me. When he discovered this he talked all the more about him, informing us and wondering at our ignorance of one so eminent. And we were amazed to hear of Your wonderful works so fully attested in times so recent—almost in our own time—and done in the true Faith and catholic Church. All three of us were filled with wonders; we because the deeds were so great, and he because they had not reached as.

He spoke next of the flocks of men in the monasteries, of their holy ways full of the sweet fragrance of You, and of the fruitful deserts in the wilderness, about which we knew nothing. There was actually a monastery at Milan outside the walls, full of good brothers under the care of Ambrose, and we knew nothing of it. He went on speaking, and we listened in intense silence.

Ponticianus' Story: "The Burden of the World"

He told us how one afternoon at Triers, when the emperor was at the chariot races in the Circus, he and three companions went for a walk in the gardens near the city walls. They happened to walk in pairs, one of the three going with him and the other two wandering off by themselves. As the latter two strolled along, they came upon a cottage inhabited by some of Your servants, *poor in spirit, of whom is the kingdom of heaven,* and there they found a little book containing the life of Antony. This one of them began to read. He became full of wonder and excitement, and as he read on he began to think of taking up such a life, giving up his secular service to serve You. For these two men were state officials called "agents for public affairs." Then, suddenly filled with a holy love and a sober shame, in anger with himself he turned to his friend and said: "Tell me now, what do we expect to attain by all these labors of ours? What do we aim at? Why do we serve the state? Can our hopes at court rise higher than to be the emperor's favorites? And is that not a difficult position to hold, and full of dangers? And how many dangers must we survive before we reach a position that is even more dangerous? And how long before we arrive there? But a friend of God, if I wish it, I can become now at once." So he spoke. And in pain with the birth of a new life, he turned his eyes again upon the book. He read on and was changed inwardly, where You alone could see; and his mind, it soon appeared, threw off the burden of the world. For as he read and the waves of his heart rolled up and down, he stormed at himself awhile, then saw the better course and chose it for his own. Being now Yours, he said to his friend, "Now I have broken loose from those hopes we had and have decided to serve God; and I begin this service at this moment, in this place. If you do not wish to imitate me, at least do not oppose me." The other answered that he would stay with him and be his comrade in so glorious a service and for so glorious a reward.... This was the story Ponticianus told us....

"Sick at Heart and Tormented"

Then in this great tumult of my inner dwelling, which I had stirred up against my soul in the chamber of my heart, troubled in mind and countenance, I turned toward Alypius. "What ails us?" I exclaimed. "What is this that you have just heard? The unlearned rise up and take heaven by force, and we with all our learning wallow in flesh and blood! Are we ashamed to follow because others have gone before us? And do we feel no shame at not following?" Some such words I uttered, and then my feverish mind tore me away from him while he stared silently at me in astonishment. For it was not my usual voice; my forehead, cheeks, eyes, color, and tone of voice spoke my mind more than the words I uttered.

There was a garden next to our lodging, and we used it as well as the whole house; for the owner of the house, our landlord, did not live there. The tumult in my breast drove me into this garden, for there no one could intervene in this ardent suit I had brought against myself until it should end as You knew, but I did not. But there I was, going mad in order to become sane, dying in order to have life, knowing how evil I was, not knowing how good I was soon to become. I retired then into the garden, Alypius following my steps....

Thus was I sick at heart and tormented, accusing myself much more bitterly than ever, rolling and turning in my chain till I could break free. I was held only slightly, but I was still held.... I kept saying within myself, "Let it be done now, let it be done now!" and as I spoke the words I began to do it. I almost made it, but not quite....

Those toys and trifles and vanities of vanities, my old mistresses, held me back. They pulled at my garment of flesh and whispered softly. "Are you casting us off?" and "From this moment shall we be no more with you forever?" and "From this moment shall you not be allowed to do this or that forever?" ... What defilements did they suggest! What shame! And now I only half heard them; they no longer openly showed themselves to contradict me, but they were muttering behind my back and stealthily puffing on me, as I departed, to make me look back at them. Yet they did retard me, so that I hesitated to tear myself free from them and leap in the direction I was called; and the strong force of habit kept saying to me, "Do you think you can live without them?"...

"All the Darkness of Doubt Vanished Away"

But when my searching thought had from the secret depths of my soul drawn up all my misery and heaped it in the sight of my heart, a mighty storm rose up within me, bringing a mighty shower of tears. I stood up and left Alypius so that I might weep and cry to my heart's content, solitude seeming more suited for the business of weeping. I moved away far enough so that his presence would not embarrass me.... Somehow I flung myself down under a fig tree and gave way to my tears.... And in my misery I kept crying, "How long shall I go on saying 'tomorrow, tomorrow'? Why not now? Why not make an end of my ugly sins at this moment?"

Such things I said, weeping all the while with the most bitter sorrow in my heart. Suddenly I heard the sing-song voice of a child in a nearby house. Whether it was the voice of a boy or a girl I cannot say, but again and again it repeated the refrain, "Take it and read, take it and read." Instantly I looked up, thinking hard whether there was any kind of game in which children chanted such words, but I could not remember ever hearing anything like it before. I checked my tears and stood up, telling myself that this could only be a command from God to open my book of Scripture and read the first passage I should find. For I had heard the story of Antony, and I remembered how he had entered a church during the reading of the Gospel and had taken it as an admonition addressed to him when he heard the words: *Go, sell all that thou hast, and give to the poor, and thou shalt have treasure in heaven, and come and follow me.* And by such an oracle he had been immediately converted to You. Eagerly then I returned to the place where Alypius was sitting, for there I had put down the volume of the Apostle Paul when I arose. I snatched it up, opened it, and in silence read the first passage on which my eyes fell: *Not in rioting and drunkenness, not in chambering and wantonness, not in strife and envying, but put ye on the Lord Jesus Christ, and make not provision for the flesh, to fulfill the lusts thereof.* I had no wish to read more and no need to do so. For instantly, as I came to the end of that sentence, it was as though the light of confidence streamed into my heart, and all the darkness of doubt vanished away.

87 Salvian of Marseille

On the Governance of God

"Where or in whom are evils so great,
except among the Romans?"

In the early Roman Empire, Tacitus had praised the Germans for their noble simplicity and virtue, using them as a foil to criticize what he regarded as the vices of his own contemporary Romans. The idea of the "noble savage" was often used in the construction of a social critique. But Tacitus' Germans were eventually mastered by the Romans, who introduced to them their own civilization. In the fifth century, the political realities were different. The Germanic peoples managed to establish their political and military hold over parts of the western Roman Empire and the Romans were powerless to stop them. For many Romans, this barbarian domination was a disaster that demanded an explanation, especially since many of the Romans in the west had become Christians. Why did God allow all this to happen?

Augustine had already made one response to this question. Another Christian, Salvian (ca. A.D. 400–480), a Roman notable who became a priest at Marseilles (in southern France), developed some of the ideas already expressed by Augustine. But he also resorted to a penetrating social critique of contemporary Roman society to explain the current successes of the barbarians. His words remind us that the high ideals of classical civilization, propounded by the likes of Aelius Aristides, were not necessarily embraced by all segments of the Roman Empire. After all, the empire remained a hierarchical place, with marked winners and losers. While the "winners" lived well and enjoyed full lives, the "losers" had to endure heavy taxation and other evils. At some point, Salvian suggested, the latter would prefer to be ruled by barbarians rather than Romans, an idea that must have shocked many Romans. While the attitude described by Salvian cannot be ascribed wholly to a new set of Christian attitudes, the fact that he could so easily look past the powerful Roman–barbarian divide may be explained by the fact that cultural-political identities were no longer as critical as they used to be now that religious status increasingly defined one's place in a Christian society.

From *The Writings of Salvian, the Presbyter,* translated by Jeremiah F. O'Sullivan (Washington, D.C.: The Catholic University of American Press, 1962), pp. 132–41. Copyright © 1962 by The Catholic University of America Press. Reprinted by permission.

... [H]eretics, of whom there is a huge multitude[,] ... are worse than the Romans through their lack of faith and more base than the barbarians in the foulness of their lives. This not only does not help us, but, even beyond that, it grieves us that we are hurt by our own people, because those whom I say are like this are Romans. Hence, we can understand what the whole Roman state deserves when one group of the Romans offend God by their way of living, another by their lack of faith as well as their way of living....

(4) Furthermore, insofar as it pertains to the way of life among the Vandals and Goths, in what way are we better than they, or can even be compared with them? First, let me speak of their love and charity which the Lord teaches is the chief of virtues and which He not only commends throughout Sacred Scriptures but even in His own words: 'by this shall it be known that you are my disciples, that you love one another.' Almost all barbarians, at least those who are of one tribe under one king, love one another; almost all Romans persecute each other.

Who is there who does not envy his fellow citizen? Who gives complete love to his neighbor? Indeed, all are distant in affection from each other, although they are not distant in location; although they are proximate in living, they are remote in mind. Although this is really a great evil, would that it were true only of citizens and neighbors! More serious is the fact that relatives do not respect the bonds of relationship. Who behaves toward those nearest to him as he should? Who gives what he knows he owes to charity or to his name? Who, in his heart, lives up to his name? Who feels as closely related in his heart as he is by blood? Who is he in whom the yellow jealousy of ill-will does not burn? Who is he whose senses have not been invaded by spite, whom another's good fortune is not his own ill-fortune, who does not believe that the good of another is his own evil, to whom his own happiness so suffices that he also wishes another to be happy? There is now a new and immeasurable evil among most men: it is not enough for anyone to be happy himself, unless another is unhappy.

What kind of situation is this; how cruel, how deep-rooted in wickedness, how foreign to barbarians but how familiar to Romans that they proscribe one another with exactions? Indeed, not each other, for this would be almost more tolerable if each would endure what he inflicts on others. It is a more serious situation that the many are proscribed by the few, to whom public requisitions are their private booty, who make the bills of the fiscal debt into private gain. And not only the highest officials, but often the least officials do this; not only judges, but even the underlings of the judges.

What towns, as well as what municipalities and villages are there in which there are not as many tyrants as *curiales* [town councilors]. Perhaps they glory in this name of tyrant because it seems to be considered powerful and honored. For, almost all robbers rejoice and boast, if they are said to be more fierce than they really are. What place is there, as I have said, where the bowels of widows and orphans are not devoured by the leading men of the cities, and with them those of almost all holy men? For, they consider the latter as widows and orphans because they are either unwilling to protect themselves in their zeal for their profession, or they cannot protect themselves because of their simplicity and humility. Not one of them, therefore, is safe. In a manner, except for the very powerful, neither is anyone safe from the devastation of general brigandage, unless they are like the robbers themselves. To this state of affairs, indeed, to this crime has the world come that, unless one is bad, he cannot be safe.

(5) Since there are so many who despoil the good, perhaps there are some who bring aid in this despoliation, who, as it is written, snatch the needy and poor from the hand of the sinner. 'There is none who does good, there is almost not even one.' The prophet said 'almost not even one' because, such is the rarity of good men, there seems to be scarcely one of them. Who gives help to the distressed and those that labor, when even the Lord's priests do not resist the violence of wicked men?

Either most of them are silent or, even though they speak, they are like those who are silent, and many do this not from lack of resolution, but, as they think, with considered discretion. They are unwilling to mention the manifest truth because the ears of wicked men cannot bear it. They not only flee from the truth, but they hate and curse it and in no way revere or fear it. When they hear it, they also condemn it in the hostility of their prideful stubbornness. Therefore, even they who can speak are silent while, in the meantime, they spare those very evil men. Nor do they wish to publish openly the force of truth to them, lest they make them worse by truth repeated more pointedly.

All the while, the poor are despoiled, the widows groan, the orphans are tread underfoot, so much so that many of them, and they are not of obscure birth and have received a liberal education, flee to the enemy lest they die from the pain of public persecution. They seek among the barbarians the dignity of the Roman because they cannot bear barbarous indignity among the Romans. Although these Romans differ in religion and language from the barbarians to whom they flee, and differ from them in respect to filthiness of body and clothing, nevertheless, as I have said, they prefer to bear among the barbarians a worship unlike their own rather than rampant injustice among the Romans.

Thus, far and wide, they migrate either to the Goths or to the Bagaudae, or to other barbarians everywhere in power; yet they do not repent having migrated. They prefer to live as freemen under an outward form of captivity than as captives under an appearance of liberty. Therefore, the name of Roman citizens, at one time not only greatly valued but dearly bought, is now repudiated and fled from, and it is almost considered not only base but even deserving of abhorrence.

And what can be a greater testimony of Roman wickedness than that many men, upright and noble and to whom the position of being a Roman citizen should be considered as of the highest splendor and dignity, have been driven by the cruelty of Roman wickedness to such a state of mind that they do not wish to be Romans? Hence, even those who do not flee to the barbarians are forced to be barbarians. Such is a great portion of the Spaniards and not the least portion of the Gauls, and, finally, all those throughout the whole Roman world whom Roman wickedness has compelled not to be Romans....

(7) ... [T]he lower classes ... are driven by one cause to two very different choices. The highest force demands that they wish to aspire to liberty, but the same force does not permit them to be able to do what it compels them to wish

to do. Perhaps it can be charged against them that they wish to be men who desire nothing more than not to be forced to wish for liberty. Their greatest misfortune is what they wish for. For, it would be much better for them if they were not compelled to wish for it.

But what else can these wretched people wish for, they who suffer the incessant and even continuous destruction of public tax levies. To them there is always imminent a heavy and relentless proscription. They desert their homes, lest they be tortured in their very homes. They seek exile, lest they suffer torture. The enemy is more lenient to them than the tax collectors. This is proved by this very fact, that they flee to the enemy in order to avoid the full force of the heavy tax levy. This very tax levying, although hard and inhuman, would nevertheless be less heavy and harsh if all would bear it equally and in common. Taxation is made more shameful and burdensome because all do not bear the burden of all. They extort tribute from the poor man for the taxes of the rich, and the weaker carry the load for the stronger. There is no other reason that they cannot bear all the taxation except that the burden imposed on the wretched is greater than their resources.

They suffer from envy and want, which are misfortunes most diverse and unlike. Envy is bound up with payment of the tax; need, with the ability to pay. If you look at what they pay, you will think them abundant in riches, but if you look at what they actually possess, you will find them poverty stricken. Who can judge an affair of this wretchedness? They bear the payment of the rich and endure the poverty of beggars. Much more serious is the following: the rich themselves occasionally make tributary levies which the poor pay.

But, you say, when the assessment due from the rich is very heavy and the taxes due from them are very heavy, how does it happen that they wish to increase their own debt? I do not say that they increase the taxes for themselves. They increase them because they do not increase them for themselves. I will tell you how this is done. Commonly, new envoys, new bearers of letters, come from the imperial offices and those men are recommended to a few well-known men for the mischief of many. For them new gifts are decreed, new taxes are decreed. The powerful levy what the poor are to pay, the courtesy of the rich decrees what the multitude of the wretched are to lose. They themselves in no way feel what they levy.

You say they who were sent by our superiors cannot be honored and generously entertained otherwise. Therefore, you rich men, you who are the first to levy, be the first to give. Be the first in generosity of goods, you who are the first in profusion of words. You who give of mine, give of thine. Most justly, whoever you are, you who alone wish to receive favor, you alone should bear the expense. But to your will, O rich men, we the poor accede. What you, the few, order, we all pay. What is so just, so humane? Your decrees burden us with new debts; at least make your debt common to us all. What is more wicked and more unworthy than that you alone are free from debt, you who make us all debtors?

Indeed, the most wretched poor thus pay all that I have mentioned, but for what cause or for what reason they pay, they are completely ignorant. For, to whom is it lawful to discuss why they pay; to whom is permitted to find out what is owed? Then it is given out most publicly when the rich get angry with each other, when some of them get indignant because some levies are made without their advice and handling.

Then you may hear it said by some of them, 'What an unworthy crime! Two or three decree what kills many; what is paid by many wretched men is decreed by a few powerful men.' Each rich man maintains his honor by being unwilling that anything is decreed in his absence, yet he does not maintain justice by being unwilling that evil things be done when he is present. Lastly, what these very men consider base in others they themselves later legalize, either in punishment of a past contempt or in proof of their power. Therefore, the most unfortunate poor are, as it were, in the midst of the sea, between conflicting, violent winds. They are swamped by the waves rolling now from one side, now from the other.

(8) But, surely, those who are wicked in one way are found moderate and just in another, and compensate for their baseness in one thing by goodness in another. For, just as they weigh down the poor with the burden of new tax levies, so they sustain them by the assistance of new tax reliefs; just as the lower classes are oppressed by new taxes, so they are equally relieved by tax mitigations. Indeed, the injustice is equal in taxes and reliefs, for, as the poor are the first to be burdened, so they are the last to be relieved.

For when, as has happened lately, the highest powers thought it would be advisable that taxation should be lessened somewhat for the cities which were in arrears in their payments, the rich alone instantly divided among themselves the remedy given for all. Who, then, remembers the poor? Who calls the poor and needy to share in the common benefit? Who permits him who is first in bearing the burden even to stand in the last place for receiving redress? What more is there to say? In no way are the poor regarded as taxpayers, unless when the mass of taxes is imposed upon them; they are not reckoned among the number of taxpayers when the tax-reliefs are portioned.

Do we think we are unworthy of the punishment of divine severity when we thus constantly punish the poor? Do we think, when we are constantly wicked, that God should not exercise His justice against all of us? Where or in whom are evils so great, except among the Romans? Whose injustice so great except our own? The Franks are ignorant of this crime of injustice. The Huns are immune to these crimes. There are no wrongs among the Vandals and none among the Goths. So far are the barbarians from tolerating these injustices among the Goths, that not even the Romans who live among them suffer them.

Therefore, in the districts taken over by the barbarians, there is one desire among all the Romans, that they should never again find it necessary to pass under Roman jurisdiction. In those regions, it is the one and general prayer of the Roman people that they be allowed to carry on the life they lead with the barbarians. And we wonder why the Goths are not conquered by our portion of the population, when the Romans prefer to live among them rather than with us....

SELECTED BACKGROUND READING

Glen W. Bowersock, Peter Brown, and Oleg Grabar, *Late Antiquity: A Guide to the Postclassical World* (Cambridge, Mass. Belknap Press at Harvard University Press, 1999).

Peter R. L. Brown, *The World of Late Antiquity, A.D. 150–750* (New York: W.W. Norton, 1989).

Averil Cameron, *The Later Roman Empire, AD 284–430* (Cambridge, Mass. Harvard University Press, 1993).

Averil Cameron, *The Mediterranean World in Late Antiquity, A.D. 395–600* (London: Routledge, 1993).

Robin Lane Fox, *Pagans and Christians* (New York: Alfred A. Knopf, 1987).

Charles Freeman, *A New History of Early Christianity* (New Haven, Conn.: Yale University Press, 2009).

Keith Hopkins, *A World Full of Gods: Pagans, Jews and Christians in the Roman Empire* (London: Weidenfeld & Nicholson, 2000).

Howard C. Kee and Franklin W. Young, *Understanding the New Testament*, 4th ed. (Englewood Cliffs, New Jersey: Prentice-Hall, 1983).

Philip Rousseau and Jutta Raithel, *A Companion to Late Antiquity* (Chichester, U.K.: Wiley-Blackwell, 2009).

Robert L. Wilken, *The Christians as the Romans Saw Them* (New Haven, Conn.: Yale University Press, 1984).